Berit Liland

The Norwegian Coastal Voyage
HURTIGRUTEN

Detailed 11-day voyage guide

nature - culture - history - legends

Forlaget 67N

Author: Berit Liland
Editor: Rolf Liland
Graphic design and layout: Anne Cathrine Jansen, Anca grafisk design AS
Cover design: Anne Cathrine Jansen
Translators: Andrew Lomax, Noricom, Øivind Martinsen.

Photography: Special thanks are extended to the many photographers that contributed images to the book. Without their quality and vitality, the book would have been quite different. Pictures are credited individually.

Maps, municipal and county coats-of-arms: Ugland IT

Illustrations: Kristij Krüger

Printing and binding: SNP Leefung Printers Limited, China

Statistical data updated 1. January 2007
Text updated 1. March 2008

ISNB 978-82-997206-4-9

Forlaget 67N
May 2008

Berit Liland

The Norwegian Coastal Voyage
HURTIGRUTEN
Detailed 11-day voyage guide
nature - culture - history - legends

Forlaget 67N

CONTENTS

FROM THE AUTHOR

Many of the world's leading travel writers claim that the voyage on board the Norwegian"Hurtigruten" may be justly called "The World's Most Spectacular Coastal Journey". The eleven-day round voyage starts from and ends at Bryggen, in Bergen. The voyage includes the spectacular Geiranger Fjord (summer season only), the Jugend town of Ålesund and Trondheim with its rich history from the Middle Ages, Lofoten and its many islands, Raftsundet with the magical Trollfjorden, the narrow Risøyrenna, the idyllic Gisundet, the polar cities of Tromsø and Hammerfest, the barren, Arctic coastline of Finnmark with Nordkapplatået (the North Cape Plateau), and Kirkenes close to the border with Russia. In addition to these fascinating destinations, the company offers many and varied excursions that may be taken whilst at the ports of call.

The aim of this book is to provide the traveller with a little background material about the innumerable places and sights that are experienced along the voyage. If you travel in the summertime, the days are long and there is of course the opportunity to see the midnight sun. Should you prefer to make the trip during the winter months, you may see the spectacular display created by the Northern Lights (aurora borealis). Whatever the season, the impressions are equally overwhelming and fascinating!

The author's main aim has been to try and impart some of the culture, history and detailed information about the places and landscapes that we sail by on our voyage along the coast. A small fjord may today be empty and abandoned – however it may have archaeological traces of a busy Viking village or earlier settlements. A hundred years ago, a now-tranquil bay may have had a bustling harbour where fishing fleets would gather, waiting for the right weather to sail out to look for "the ocean's silver"- the herring. The Norwegian coast is long and its history complex and intriguing.

The author has sailed in the Norwegian Merchant Navy as a Radio Officer for several years, crossed the seven seas and sailed along many coastlines but has always missed having information at hand about the countries and the history of their people and places. Today's modern technology and GPS (Global Positioning Systems) has made this possible. The entire voyage is recorded electronically and all places along the route have their own registered GPS position. To have a GPS would be useful in order to maximise the information given by the book. But, of course not everybody carries such equipment. So, to compensate for this, the passing times of places is also given, with as much accuracy as possible - regardless if the ship is on schedule or not. The author's aim is to provide the traveller with the best experience and visual impressions possible.

I wish you all an enjoyable voyage on "The World's Most Spectacular Coastal Journey".

Berit Liland

© HANS SEJRUP

Bergen municipality

Municipal coat of arms, signification: From approx. 13th century. The mountains below the castle show the contours of seven mountains.
Meaning of name: Norse; *Bergvin* or *Bjorgvin*, from *berg* or *bjorg*, and *vin*, 'pasture'.

Municipal seat: Bergen. **Position:** 60°23'N 5°18'E.
Area: 465 km². **Population:** 244 620.
Pop. density: 526.1/km².
Area distribution: Farming 8 %, forestry 22 %, fresh water 5 %, other area 65 %.
Commerce: Shipping: several large companies, maritime equipment industries, several service industries and institutions for further education. NIS: Ships register. Mechanical industries and some active shipyards. Petroleum related activities. Food processing, textiles, graphic design industries and publishing houses. Bank, finance and insurance companies.
Places to return to: In addition to those included in our wander around town: St. Jørgens Hospital (Leprosy Museum) in Bergen, Damsgård homestead, Gamlehaugen, Lysøen, Barony in Rosendal.
Activities to return to: Flåmsbanen. Bergensbanen. Cruise with the training ship "Statsraad Lehmkuhl".
Bergen municipality's home page:
www.bergen.kommune.no

Bergen was originally a small village by the shoreline, which was granted a town charter by King Olav Kyrre (1050-1093) in 1070. The location of the town had many advantages, largely due to the bay, Vågen, which at that time was deeper and wider than it is today. It carved its way inland from the inshore sailing channel along the west coast. **Nordnes Peninsula** and **Askøy** on the outer side protected Vågen from the Atlantic storms. The mountains surrounding the town provided shelter against winds from the east and the south. Most importantly, Vågen was sheltered from the strong northerly gales that often occurred in the area. Ships frequently called at the town and due to the amount of rainfall in the area, the supplies of fresh water were always plentiful. Most of the shoreline was flat and wide, providing opportunities for the town to expand. Bergen was surrounded by rich arable land, which was perfect for farming. In the mountains and forests hunting and trapping was also excellent and the islands in the west supported an expanding fishing community. The catch was originally brought by boat. Later, however, much of the trade goods were eventually transported overland on paths and roads that were kept open all year round.

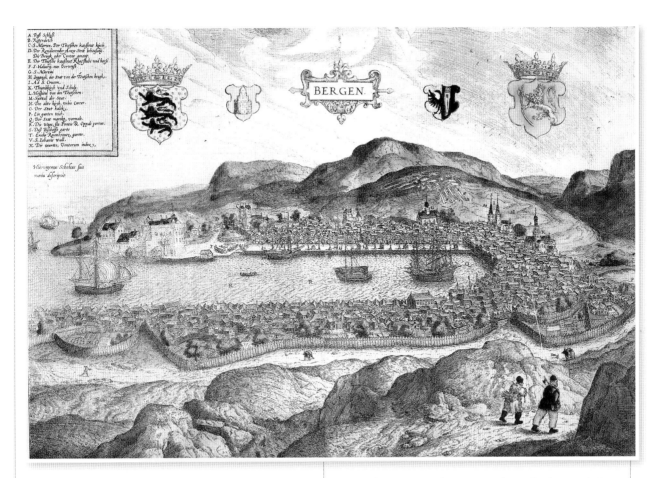

Bergen was strategically placed between the rich fishing grounds in **Lofoten** and **Vesterålen** and the large ports in **Northern Europe**, and it was centrally located for trade with the islands in the west, **Iceland**, the **Faeroe Islands**, **Shetland** and **England**. Because of the great sailing distance from northern Norway to the European harbours, Vågen became a natural transit port.

The royal estate, **Alrekstad** was situated approx. two km from Vågen. Relics have been found on the estate in graves dating from approx. 400 A.D. and in burial mounds from the Viking period (p 83). Alrekstad became the site of many and varied commercial activities which led to the development and expansion of Vågen into a trading centre for goods coming both from inland regions and from abroad. The King's residence was later relocated to Holmen (today called Bergenhus). A royal chapel and a large hall, which was the biggest and most famous timber building in Norway were built here. Several impressive buildings were erected on Holmen at a later date, one being Håkonshallen and the other being the Rosenkrantz Tower, both of which have been restored and remain standing today.

King Olav Kyrre and successive kings had several churches built in Bergen in the 12th century. The largest was the Bishop's Church, Kristkirken, built next to the King's residence on Holmen. The Bishop's residence was also located on Holmen. The Episcopal residence for the diocese of West Norway was moved from **Selje,** south of **Stad** (p 34) to Bergen in 1163, and some time later the shrine containing the relics of St. Sunniva (p 34), was moved to the town. As Bergen now became a cathedral town, considerable expansion took place. The clergy purchased their goods from the surrounding districts and craftsmen came to build, repair and maintain houses and churches. It became necessary to increase trade with foreign countries on order to satisfy the growing demands of private citizens and the clergy. Three monasteries and at least 11 churches were built, mostly in the populated areas on the east side of Vågen. Little remains of Kristkirken, which was demolished in 1531. Today there are only a few stones remaining.

On the other side of Vågen, King Øystein (I) Magnusson (1088-1123) built one of the first monasteries in Norway, St. Mikal's Monastery (Munkeliv cloister), belonging to the Benedictine Order. The King also built a church and

a harbour at **Agdenes** at the entrance to Trondheimsfjorden (p 338), a church in **Vågan** in Lofoten (p 157) and at **Trondenes** near Harstad (p 273). Exports of dried fish from northern Norway shipped via Bergen probably began around this period. (Fishermen in Lofoten had to pay duties of five fishes to the King.) Other communities delivering fish to Bergen were **Borgund** in Sunnmøre (p 70), **Veøy** near Molde (p 360) and **Vågan** in Lofoten (p 156).

After its foundation in 1070, Bergen's importance in Norway gradually increased and the town was on its way to becoming the country's capital city. The royal family and prominent politicians took up residence with their associated royal and local administrations. During this period, Bergen and Vågen were scenes of many disputes and battles between various pretenders to the throne. Vågen has also been the scene of many international disputes and even piracy.

As Catholics were not allowed to eat meat during Lent, dried fish from Norway became very popular in other catholic countries, even more so than cod liver oil and herring. With its excellent harbour facilities and central location, Bergen developed into an international trading centre. Traders came from the north, west (Orkney, Faeroe Islands and Iceland), south west (England) and south (Baltic Sea, Germany, Holland and Belgium). Goods exported from the regions north and west of Bergen were brought to the town during the summer months and stored in warehouses. Ships from Europe collecting these goods brought corn and other types of food that was not available in Norway - and sometimes decorative and useful articles. When the dried fish was offloaded in Bergen, the empty boats transported these goods back up north. Bergen became thereby a very important transit port for goods coming into and out of Norway. In addition to becoming an important commercial centre, the town received many new impulses in architecture, arts and crafts, painting and literature.

The town continued to grow and develop, and for a time Bergen was probably the largest town in the north. Many new buildings rose up along the shoreline between Holmen and Vågen as a consequence of several town fires. Eventually the harbour expanded and buildings and wharfs were built. The port area was very hectic; as soon as a ship had finished loading operations it had to leave the wharf and make room for the next ship.

As a royal, episcopal and political centre in the 12th century, influential men were attracted to Bergen. Magnus

Erlingsson (1156-84) was crowned King of Norway here in September 1163, only seven years old. This was the first coronation in the north and an important event in the development of the state of Norway. Bergen was the first capital of Norway and held this status until 1299 when Oslo became the country's capital city.

Towards the end of the Middle Ages (p 83) the town displayed its importance by having five monasteries, at least 20-23 churches and chapels and two hospitals - more than any other town in the north at that time. Through its judicial system with special laws and privileges the foreign merchants had limitations imposed on their trading practices both inside and outside the town's borders. They were also restricted in taking their goods north of Bergen. Most merchants were from Germany and England. From 1250 onwards, the German merchants were allowed to remain in the town for longer periods. However, increasing numbers of mariners and merchants taking lodgings with the townspeople and remaining there throughout the winter resulted in increased civil disturbance, drunkenness and prostitution.

During late summer 1349, a ship from England arrived in Bergen and along with it, the plague, the Black Death. It is thought that the disease originated from the Mediterranean area and spread through Europe via England to Bergen, which was very badly affected. The Black Death spread throughout Norway and over two-thirds of the population perished. Farms and fisheries were left derelict and trade was severely reduced. The population only recovered some 100 years later, however commercial trade recovered more rapidly and soon returned to previous levels.

Bergen lost its status as a royal city shortly after the Black Death. This led to the gradual decline of the town's status as an ecclesiastical and cultural centre. As a trading centre however, Bergen developed significantly. Buildings were constructed along the east side of Vågen and the inner part of the bay was filled in to create more building sites. The west side of Vågen was also developed. The milieu became more cosmopolitan since Bergen was visited by a great deal of foreign ships that brought many exotic goods from abroad when they came to collect their cargoes of fish and other export products from the north and the western islands.

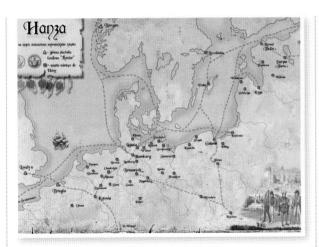

German traders were very active in Bergen already in the 13th century along with the English. Strict rules regulating trade in and around the town were enforced by royal decree in order to protect the local merchants, and this prevented the Germans from trading freely. The Hanseatic League began to influence areas around the German Baltic Sea, including merchants from several towns, but mostly from Lübeck. The League's objective was to promote its member's interests and to protect their civilian welfare and financial activities in foreign towns. In the most important ports such as **Novgorod** (in Russia), **Brügge**, **London** and **Bergen** they established so-called "Offices" that were appointed to look after the League's interests. The trade in Bergen was, however, minor in comparison with other "office-towns". For a time the League had as many as 70 members, and in some countries they held special privileges.

In the aftermath of the Black Death (1349-50), financial activity in Bergen and the surrounding areas was partly paralysed. The League saw the opportunity to fill the gap created by the ravages of the plague and during the next 150 to 200 years, they consolidated their position in the town; however, this was not without problems both amongst the members of the "Offices", and the townspeople. The trading patterns were also changing, in that traders from the north brought their own goods to Bergen, in competition with the local merchants and they also sold goods at the markets in Vågan in Lofoten (p 156) and Borgund in Sunnmøre (p 70).

A census, taken in the period 1400-1500, shows that of a population of approx. 7 000, almost 2 000 were Germans permanently resident in Bergen. During the summer season this could increase to as many as 3 000. Most of these were unmarried men. Nearly 200 German craftsmen worked in town; the largest group of workers were cobblers who held a monopoly on the manufacture of footwear. Those Germans living in Bergen permanently

were not allowed to marry Norwegian women, so many of them had 'common law' relationships. However, they took responsibility for their partners and their children.

The Hanseatic League started to lose its power in the 16th century and the German merchants and craftsmen became gradually integrated into the local community. Although the Hanseatic "Office" still existed, its influence gradually diminished and the people of Bergen began to take over more and more of the trade in town and in the north. In 1766, the last German residence was sold to a Norwegian citizen.

Throughout the ages, Bergen has been ravaged by fires but it was rebuilt each time. Vågen was filled in even more to create building sites and the urban area grew in size. However, it was not before 1830 that Oslo became larger in terms of population than Bergen. The town experienced periods of both prosperity and decline but established itself as an important cultural, commercial and shipping town. In the latter half of the 19th century, sailing ships were replaced by steamers and several steamship companies became established in Bergen. These eventually took over both the coastal and international traffic. Fish exports were still important but the timber trade had also grown into a major industry over several hundreds of years (p 333). Many people began to move in to town from the surrounding districts. The growing industries concentrated mainly on shipbuilding, textiles and clothing factories and food processing industries. In 1909, the 485 km long railway line between Bergen and Oslo was opened. In 1916 a large area southwest of Vågen was destroyed by fire - the subsequent rebuilding of Bergen gave the town a more modern centre which we can still see today; wide streets, open parks and large, monumental buildings.

After the First World War and the worldwide economic slump that followed, Bergen was greatly affected. Recovery started again in the mid-thirties.

After having received information that German warships had been observed steaming northward off the coast of Denmark on 8th April 1940, the fortifications around Bergen were put on alert. As Norway was historically a neutral country, the number of men stationed at the forts was reduced for this reason. The coastal forts along the approaches to Bergen offered some resistance, but could not stop the German convoys with their invasion forces and approx. 1 900 men headed for Bergen on the night of 9th April. One of the ships, the cruiser "Königsberg", was hit and immobilised but the remaining vessels arrived in Bergen undamaged. When the citizens of Bergen woke up the next morning the German flag was seen flying from the mast at Bergenhus Fort and heavily armed

German soldiers were standing guard at several public buildings in town.

This was the start of the German occupation that lasted for five years. Compared to some other towns and counties Bergen and the surrounding areas did not experience severe war damage. The crippled cruiser "Königsberg" was bombed by British RAF aircraft and sank at the quayside on 10th April. Several more Allied attacks followed. On 15th June, ships moored in the harbour were bombed and 113 houses in Nordnes on the west side of Vågen burnt down.

In May 1941, the German battleship, the "Bismarck", at that time the world's largest and fastest of its type, was anchored in Grimstadfjorden, one of the smaller fjords on the Bergen peninsula. When the ship was spotted by a British reconnaissance plane, she left for open waters without taking extra fuel onboard. A week later the battleship was finally sunk by British torpedo planes operating from an aircraft carrier in the Atlantic Ocean with the loss of a thousand of lives.

In April 1944, the Dutch ship "Voorbode", carrying 124 tons of explosives, blew up near Bergenhus Fort (p 13).

In 1941, the Germans began to construct U-boat bunkers in Bergen and Trondheim (p 99). The Allied forces were reluctant to bomb the bunker "Bruno" in Laksevåg in Bergen, as it was situated in a populated area and the town had not been evacuated. However, in spite of this the bunker was bombed several times. Eventually the bunker "Bruno" had the capacity to house 12 U-boats and became a serious threat to the Allied convoys sailing to England and Murmansk (p 220). On the 4th October 1944, 140 Allied planes attacked the bunker; however, most of the bombs fell on residential areas. The primary school at Holen, which stood close to where "Bruno" was located, was hit with the loss of 61 children, teachers and other civilian personnel. A total of 193 civilians were killed during the raid and many houses were destroyed. On the night of 29th October the bunker was bombed again, this time with limited damage. The bombs were dropped over Laksevåg and Engen, the area close to where the Hurtigrute Terminal is located today. On 12th January 1945, 31 Lancaster bombers from the Royal Air Force repeated the attack and this time the damage was considerably greater.

On 7th May 1945, The Second World War ended.

Bergen has experienced considerable development since the Second World War. Boundaries have been moved many times and the town, once a separate county, is now part of Hordaland county (p 26).

In addition to trade, shipping, mechanical industries and public administration, oil and gas-related activities have also become an important part of the town's commercial life. The town has several thriving universities and research institutions.

Source: Bergen Bys Historie I –IV. Knut Hjelle.,
Anders Bjaarne Fossen

A WANDER AROUND THE CENTRE OF BERGEN

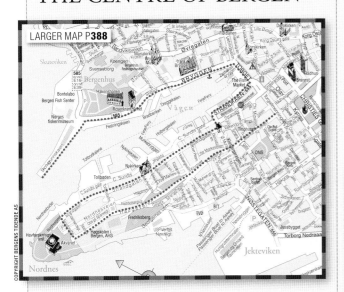

LARGER MAP P**388**

the port is frequented by supply ships and other vessels working for the oil companies in the North Sea.

Close to the quay, we can see **Bergenhus**, the previous royal court Holmen, with **Håkonshallen** and **Rosenkrantz Tower** (p 9). The banqueting hall, Håkonshallen, was originally built by King Håkon IV Håkonsson (1204-63) for his son's (Magnus V Lagabøte) wedding in 1261. The hall has been extended several times and during major restoration work that began in 1873 new gables, walls, roof beams and a stairwell in front of the entrance were built and exclusive decorations were added to the interior.

On 20th April 1944 the Dutch ship, "Voorbode" exploded at the quayside near Bergenhus. The ship was on her way from Oslo to Kirkenes with a cargo of 124 tons of dynamite, percussion caps and fuses; however, the ship had to call at Bergen for engine repairs. The ship was not actually allowed to call in at any major Norwegian port, but due to lack of proper controls, she was eventually permitted to dock near Bergenhus Fort with her cargo of dynamite on board.

We can start on north-easterly side of Vågen, close to Bergenhus, formerly known as Holmen (p 9). The quayside area is called **Skolten**, and is a terminal for the passenger traffic sailing between Bergen and Newcastle in England. This route was started in 1852 by the former "Det Bergenske Dampskipsselskap", Norway's oldest passenger shipping line. Today the route is operated by the Danish company DFDS with several weekly sailings to Newcastle via Haugesund and Stavanger. The company also operates ferries between Bergen and Hanstholm in Denmark. Smyril Line has sailings between Bergen and the Faeroes, Iceland and Scotland. Bergen is Norway's and one of Northern Europe's busiest cruise harbours. In the summer season, most of the cruise ships sailing in Norway will call at the port and for the rest of the year

In the morning of the fourth day the ship was docked, the ship's chief engineer and two Norwegian workers observed smoke coming up from the cargo hold in the "Voorbode". They managed to escape from the ship and at 08.39, the cargo exploded. A water column several hundred meters high rose up from the bay followed by sand, mud, stones, iron plates, timber and steel structures from the ship. Parts of the anchor were blown all the way up to the top of Sandviksfjellet, behind Bergenhus Fort. The pressure wave from the explosion swept along both sides of Vågen and crushed everything in its path. Houses were reduced to splinters, large brick buildings were damaged, and win-

© BERGEN TOURIST BOARD/PER NYBØ

dows were broken more than two kilometres away. The tidal wave that followed cast several boats on land, flooded cellars in cabins and warehouses, and dragged both people and animals into the bay. Both sides of Vågen were ablaze and Bergen was soon declared a disaster area. More than half of the town's buildings were affected in some way - in total 4 536 buildings were destroyed or damaged. 131 were totally destroyed and another 117 so badly damaged that they were beyond repair. Bergenhus Fort, Håkonshallen and Rosenkrantz Tower were left in ruins as were several churches and much of the town's character was lost.

160 persons were killed by the explosion and more than 5 000 were injured. Medical personnel from around the whole of the country came to Bergen to help. 5 000 people were left homeless and 4 260 children were evacuated to other areas of the country to prevent sickness and epidemics. Great deals of valuable things were lost, both material and cultural. The explosion was the worst disaster of its kind in Norway during the Second World War and by far the greatest catastrophe in Bergen's history over 900 years.

The newly restored Håkonshallen was destroyed. However, in 1961 after approx. ten years of archaeological excavations, Håkonshallen was once again rebuilt and today it functions as a concert hall and is Bergen's guild hall.

Rosenkrantz Tower is situated next to Håkonshallen. It was built mid-13th century in connection with Håkon IV Håkonsson's royal mansion. In the basement is the infamous dungeon used from the end of the 15th century to mid 19th century. The tower was ravaged by fire in 1513 and repaired in 1523. In 1530, the gunpowder room exploded and 20 years later it was partly repaired. In 1562 Sheriff Erik Rosenkrantz decided to build a completely new tower. The family crest was included on the façade and two older establishments were incorporated into the tower. In 1848 yet another restoration was started. The Rosenkrantz Tower was also badly damaged in the 1944 explosion. The tower is regarded as Norway's most important monument from the Renaissance period and was later restored in cooperation with the Directorate of Cultural Heritage.

With luck, we may see the training vessel, "**Statsraad Lehmkuhl**" in the harbour. The ship was built as a training ship for the German merchant navy in Bremerhaven in 1914 and was taken as war compensation by the British after the First World War. The ship was later brought to Bergen by cabinet minister K. Lehmkuhl in 1921. From 1923 until 1968 she was used as a training ship, except for during the war 1940-45. "Statsraad Lehmkuhl" is now owned by a foundation and is leased for certain periods to the Navy for training purposes.

As we wander along the quayside we pass **Mariakirken** and **Bryggen Museum**, both of these are in pedestrian areas. Mariakirken, built between 1130 and 1170, is the oldest parish church in Bergen and the oldest preserved building. The church has burned down twice; first in 1198 and in 1248. The church is a typical basilica-style church with a high nave, two lower side-naves and a special roof. The two towers at the western portal are original, but were added after the church was finished. From 1408 until 1766 the church was used by the Hansa merchants and church services were held in German up to 1906. Today it is a regular Norwegian church with services in Norwegian.

The church is richly decorated. The church's oldest artefact, the gilded altar cabinet, most probably originates from Lübeck at the end of the 15th century. It is decorated with carved wooden figures and is divided into three sections; a wide mid-section and two opening side sections. In 1634, Mariakirken received a gift of 15 full-size apostle statues, mounted on carved plinths. The unique pulpit was received as a gift in 1676. It is partly made of tortoise hide and is richly decorated. The globe is also unusual in that one half is embedded into the

panelled ceiling as a dome whilst the other half forms the sun's lower part. In addition to the altar board and the pulpit, the paintings are also of interest. In the course of the 17th and 18th century, the church's walls were covered with paintings in memory of influential citizens connected to the church. The majority of these paintings were removed during the restoration works in 1860, but some are still hung on the walls. The church's bible, printed in Nürnberg in 1692 is not in daily use.

❧

Next to Mariakirken is the Bryggen Museum, opened in 1976. In the summer of 1955, parts of Bryggen burnt down and a minor fire also occurred in 1958. Between 1955-1974, large-scale archaeological

excavations were carried out on parts of the burnt-out ruins. The finds that were made show how people lived in Bergen in the Middle Ages, and by studying these objects, we get an insight into their way of life, commerce and trade, shipping and arts and crafts from that period. The oldest buildings date from the 12th century and some of the objects uncovered have been left by the archaeologists in their original positions, as they were found.

❧

Next to Bryggen Museum is the hotel, **Radisson SAS Royal Hotel** that was opened in 1982. The architecture was adapted to the historical surroundings and maintains the characteristic frontage of Bryggen.

❧

Bryggen is one of Bergen's most unique and oldest areas and here we can see remains of the old harbour faci-

lities and buildings. The oldest parts of Bryggen we see today go back to the years after the great fire of 1702, when approx. 80 % of Bergen was burnt to ashes. Bryggen was rebuilt as it was around 1350 when it was the main seat of the Hansa merchants' activities in Bergen (p 10). In its golden age Bryggen was comprised of 11 double houses; i.e. a long row of houses on either side of a common courtyard, four single houses and a merchant's house in the middle. At the rear, we can see some stone cellars that date back to the 15th–16th century. Today, there are only three and a half double houses and three single houses left in the northern part of Bryggen, and a half double house in the south. The northern part, where Bryggen Museum and SAS Radissons Royal Hotel are located was destroyed by fire in the summer of 1955, but has been rebuilt using the same style of gables. Through archaeological excavations carried out over a period of 24 years, a huge amount of material from Bergen's older history was uncovered. It was discovered that the quay was originally situated some 140 m away from the present location and dates back to about the year 1200. It has been excavated to a length of 55 m.

Remains of several hundred houses have been found, mostly warehouses, however some dwellings and community houses have been found at the rear. Remains of a church, referred to in documents from 1206, have also been excavated. Other finds uncovered are domestic utensils, pottery and glass, objects of wood, bone and stone, shoes, textiles, foodstuffs, tools, parts of ships and many rune-sticks (runic inscriptions carved onto wooden sticks) that contained a message or a short note to someone - these provide a valuable insight to everyday life and trading habits. Most of the finds can be viewed at Bryggen Museum

Bryggen in Bergen was included on UNESCO's World Heritage list in 1979 and is conscientiously looked after and maintained. Bryggen ranks as the second most popular attraction in Norway, and received 583 510 visitors in the period 1st May-31st August 2006.

At the beginning of the 20th century the southern half of Bryggen's dwellings were demolished and replaced with brick houses modelled on the typical quayside housing found in Lübeck.

Hanseatic Museum is located farthest south on Bryggen. The building is called Finnegården. This was constructed after the fire of 1702 and is one of the oldest and best-preserved buildings in Bergen. As the museum

expanded an adjacent building, "Murtasken" was taken in use. The museum shows how the German merchants belonging to the Hansa League lived and established their trade here in the period from 1360 to 1754. The museum was founded in 1872 and was privately owned and operated until 1916 when it was taken over by Bergen municipality.

Kjøttbasaren (meat market) was opened in 1877. For the first 18 years it was known as "Byens Bazaar". Previously, most food products were sold at the town's market place close by, but the vendors had a poor reputation in regard to cleanliness. A new health law was introduced in Norway in 1860 whereby the authorities could regulate and control the market, which resulted in the establishment of Kjøttbasaren. The customers had 44 stalls to choose from and there were also 27 cellar rooms. The town's first library was also located here. In 1965, the building had become so dilapidated that the decision was made to pull it down. This decision was later rescinded and the building eventually became listed in 1982. In the 1990's it was refurbished and modernised.

At the end of **Vetrlidsallmenningen,** south-east of Kjøttbasaren, is a small white building marking the entrance to the well-known "**Fløibane**", the only rail/cable funicular in Scandinavia. The idea for the Fløibane was already on the drawing board in 1895 but lack of funding delayed the start of construction until 1914. The following year, 150 men were working on the

installation and it finally opened in 1918. It is an electrically driven system, running on a one-metre gauge track, which is 850 m long, rising up to 302 m above the town with a gradient that varies between 15° and 26°. The trip to the top takes approx. five–six minutes. Fløibanen is a famous tourist attraction, receiving approx. one million visitors per year. Convenient access to the recreational areas around the upper terminal makes it easy to take a trip around the forests and mountains before returning to the town. At the top, there is a restaurant and a kiosk.

Fløyen (399 m above sea level) is the mountain that rises behind Bryggen and is the most well-known and visited of the seven mountains that surround Bergen, mostly due to its close proximity to the town centre and easy access. It was not until the late 19th century that the town's people began using Fløyen - access became easier after the Fjellveien road and Fløysvingene were constructed in 1891. These are described in many romantic folk songs from Bergen written around that time.

Next to Fløibanen's lower terminal is the school, **Christi Krybbe** dating from 1738. It was built on the foundations of St. Martin's church that burned down in 1702. The school was built to provide an education for poor and orphaned children. It was rebuilt and extended in 1874 with a new wing next to the old school and became a regular primary school. In 1999, it was once more refurbished and rebuilt.

Behind Fløibanen's terminal building are **Skansesvingene** that wind their way up towards the part of the city called **Skansen**. Here we see the typical small, old wooden houses, steep and narrow streets; called "smau" (p 19). From Skansen there is a fine view over central Bergen and Vågen. The fine white wooden building is Skansen Fire Station, which was built following the great fire in 1901 and finally opened in 1903. The station had rooms for the fire tenders, stables and workshops. From the observation tower the guard maintained contact with the main fire station using a field telephone. The first motorised tender was taken into use in 1936. Skansen Fire Station finally closed down in 1969. **Skansedammen** -

the pond (66 m above sea level) next to the station was used as a water supply for the fire tenders.

If we continue straight ahead, we pass two of Bergen's oldest churches. The nearest of them is **Korskirken,** which is mentioned in documents before 1181. This church has burned down and been rebuilt several times. Today's church is very different from the original Romantic-style stone church with a timber tower. The wings, typical of a cruciform church were built in the years 1615-32, and the west tower was added in 1596.

Bergen Cathedral is situated approx. 150 m southeast of Korskirken, on the same site of the former Olav's Church in Vågsbotn, dedicated to St. Olav (p 88), built approx. 1150-80. A small part of the small stone church with a west tower, rectangular nave and narrow chancel that burnt down in 1248 and 1270 is incorporated into the northern wall of the Cathedral. The old church became the Franciscan cloister church in 1248. It was rebuilt in Gothic style after the fire in 1270. After the Reformation in 1537, Bergen Cathedral was extended and enhanced. In 1665, a battle was fought on Vågen between the English and the Dutch. During the battle, a cannonball struck the cathedral tower. It is still embedded in the wall of the tower and is a reminder that times have not always been as peaceful in Bergen!

North-west of the cathedral is the old building that once housed **Bergen Katedralskole (cathedral school),** the town's oldest school, which was founded around 1153. The school was originally located at Holmen close to Håkonshallen, but was moved in 1537.

Vågsbunnen has been a trading centre in Bergen since the town was founded in 1070. Today, **Fisketorget** in Bergen is situated here. Through the ages, this part of Vågen has been gradually filled in to

create land for building and archaeological excavations have uncovered the various activities that took place here. Amongst other things, evidence has been found that sho-

emaking and tannery activity took place here during the Hansa period.

Century-old paintings and old photographs show life around Torget (market) to be very different from what we see today. Sailing ships unloading and loading were assisted by small tenders, sailing vessels and rowboats moored side by side in Vågen. Farmers from near and far arrived in their boats carrying fruit, farm produce and timber. From the north, the boats brought dried fish, barrels of cod liver oil and other goods. Local fishermen brought live fish in wooden crates towed behind their rowing boats and the traders met at Torget where the local gentry and commoners bought their fish. Hygiene and quality control was somewhat doubtful; the milk could be watered down and flour was sometimes mixed with sawdust, but it was here most of the town's trading took place .

Especially during the summer season, Torget has many stalls selling fish, flowers, vegetables and other products. Although the town's supermarkets have taken over a good deal of the fresh food trade, Torget and Fisketorget are still popular places to congregate for local people and tourists.

As we wander on a little bit further, we approach **Torgallmenningen,** the town's 'grand plaza'. In 1916 when the last big town fire occurred, central parts of the town on the west side of Vågen were destroyed. As in the case of so many other towns in Norway that were damaged or destroyed by fire, the new town houses were required to be constructed from bricks and mortar, and the streets were built wide with open areas. These regulations were designed to prevent the spread of fire to adjacent buildings. The wide, open 'grand plaza' with the monumental buildings on either side was constructed after the 1916 fire. In the eastern part of the plaza, we see the Sjøfartsmonumentet (Seamen's monument), which honours the Norwegian mariner and maritime history, from Viking times up to the oil boom of the 1970s and 80s.

Johanneskirken, a brick construction, can be seen southwest on the plaza on top of a hill. The church has a Neo-Gothic style and seating for 1 250 and was built in 1894. The church tower is 61 m tall, the tallest in Bergen.

In the spring of 1986 Bergen was the host for the final of the Eurovision Song Contest. The town arranged all types of festivities, and a ski jump was built on the hill leading up to Johanneskirken. Snow from Hardangervidda (a mountain plateau between Oslo and Bergen), was transported into town by rail and placed on the hill. Huge crowds gathered to see some of the country's most famous ski jumpers compete for the longest jump.

At the south-western end of Torgallmenningen we see **Musikkpaviljongen** (the Music pavilion) built in 1888, restored in 1991, and **Lille Lungegårdsvannet** with the Norwegian State Railways grey brick buildings and Bergen public library located on the south side of the lake. On the west side there are several art museums .

In the background we can see **Ulriken** (643 m above sea level), the highest of the seven mountains surrounding Bergen. Behind the steep mountain, there is a highland plateau, which is a very popular recreational area. Here it is possible to wander almost 10 km in practically level terrain at an elevation of approx. 600 m. The Bergen song, "Jeg tok min nystemte Cithar i Hænde", "I carried my newly tuned zither" – written by Bishop Johan Nordal Brun (1745-1816) is a song tribute to the town in which he describes the view from "Ulriken's peak".

Ulriksbanen is an 1 120 m long cableway with two gondolas, built in 1961 with the top terminal at 607 m above sea level. The terminal has a restaurant and a coffee bar.

In 1959 a telecommunications mast was erected on Ulriken in spite of considerable protests from the local people. The mast is 40 m high with a further 38 m steel extension on top.

Located to the north-west end of Torgallmenningen is the theatre, **Den Nationale Scene,** which opened in 1909. Den Nationale Scene was actually founded in 1850, as Norway's first theatre, wholly financed by the internationally famous violinist, Ole Bull. The theatre director was the then unknown playwright Henrik Ibsen.

Back at Vågsbunnen and Torget we see the building that is the head office of Norway's largest bank, at the south-westerly corner of Torget. The old **Børsbygningen** (Stock Exchange Building) was opened in 1862 and extended in 1893. Within this building we find **Frescohallen**. The fresco paintings on the walls are regarded as one of Norway's national treasures. Painted by the artist Axel Revold (1887-1962) during the period 1921 to 1923 they are divided into three themes:

- **Nordlandsveggen** – Nordland's Wall, with three scenes depicting the fishing for cod in Lofoten, preparation of the fish onshore and the voyage to Bergen to sell the produce.
- **Bergensveggen** – Bergen's Wall, with four scenes depicting the "northerners'" arrival in town, the fish's further transport out into the world, trade in goods from abroad and shipbuilding.
- **Verdendsveggen** – the World's Wall, depicts the transportation and mariners' work onboard a ship, the many phases of farming and a motif from a primeval forest showing the harvesting of nature's plenty.

The Tourist Information Centre in Bergen is located in Frescohallen.

As we wander on along the west side of Vågen we come to the busy **Strandkaien**. Many coastal passenger ferries and express boats serving the districts around Bergen dock here. At the inner part of the quay area

there is a vegetable and flower market during the summer months. The impressive brick buildings constructed here after the fires of 1901 and 1916 house offices, hotels, cafés, shops and several warehouses. 150 years ago and earlier we would have seen sailing ships of all sizes from many countries, unloading or loading their goods along the quays from Vågen to Tollboden (the Customs House). The ships would be docked in rows, three or four abreast with bows pointing outward.

At the end of the quay and to the west we can see **Muren**, or **Murhvelvingen**. Muren was built in 1562 as a private residence for Sheriff Erik Rosenkrantz, who built the Rosenkrantz Tower (p 13). The building has been damaged by fire and rebuilt many times and is one of the few preserved buildings in Bergen dating from the 16th century. The ground floor has been used by traders since the 17th century. In the beginning there was a well located under the arch but this was sealed in the 1880s. Muren became a listed building in 1927, and was one of the few buildings left undamaged by the "Voorbode" explosion in 1944 (p 13). Today, the building is the home of the Buekorpsmuseet (Boy's Brigade Museum) (p 23).

Above Muren our walk takes us through the pedestrian area, **Småstrandgaten**. Between this street and **Kloster-haugen,** where we find the remains of Munkeliv monastery (p 9) and the old and typical town area with "smitt and smau", old, small wooden houses and narrow, often winding steep streets - "smau". These were mostly paved with paving stones with a special pattern in the midd-

© BERGEN TOURIST BOARD/ODDLEIV APNESETH

le that prevented the horses from slipping on the stones when pulling heavy loads up the hill. These "smau" were constructed in the 17ᵗʰ century to transport goods from Vågen to other parts of the town.

Further ahead we see newer buildings, which were erected after the Second World War. This area was badly damaged by the explosion near Bergenhus in 1944 (p 13) and by bombs that missed their targets.

Nykirken, or Den Nye Kirke, (the New Church) was built in 1621, as the people in this area thought it was too far to walk to the Cathedral (p 17). Nykirken was built on top of the remains of the old archbishop's rectory dating back to the 13ᵗʰ century. The conditions stipulated that the 'relics and remains of the old rectory were to be preserved and kept in good order'. Today, this area has been properly excavated and over a 500 m² site we can see how large and grand this rectory actually was. From 1637 to 1856 parts of the old foundations were used as a mortuary and later extended to incorporate a burial place for the town's poorer citizens.

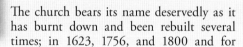

The church bears its name deservedly as it has burnt down and been rebuilt several times; in 1623, 1756, and 1800 and for the final time in 1944 after the "Voorbode" explosion near Bergenhus. The current church was consecrated in 1956.

The wide **Tollbodalmenningen** is located farther out on **Nordneshalvøya**, on Vågen's west side. On the seaside we see **Tollboden i Bergen** (Bergen Customs House). The old Tollboden, the biggest timber building from that period, was located here from 1651 onwards. The first brick building on this site was planned in 1761, when the reconstruction of the town after the great fire in 1756 began. The current building is regarded as one of Bergen's finest. It was completed in 1954 and is a replica of the old Tollboden, which was damaged in the 1944 explosion (p 13).

Further on and towards the tip of Nordnes Peninsula and **Nordnesparken**, we pass the modern, turquoise and white pointed gable-building belonging to **Fiskeridirektoratet i Bergen** (Directorate of Fisheries). The building has received an award for its design and incorporation to the neighbouring maritime milieu.

In Nordnesparken up ahead is **Bergen Aquarium**. The aquarium was opened in 1960 and is Norway's oldest

and largest and one of the most advanced in Europe. It has more than 60 small and large aquaria where visitors can study sea life typical of Norwegian waters, coastal species, life under the quaysides, on the sandy seabed and in the ocean depths. There is an outdoor penguin pool, a pond for carp and a pool for seals. More than three million litres of water is pumped up into the saltwater basins daily from a depth of 130 m out in Byfjorden. This water is then circulated through the aquarium. A newly constructed building contains a natural cliff for nesting birds, a large landscaped aquarium, a reptile section and a small cinema that shows informative films both from the aquarium in Bergen and from the local coast. Next to the aquarium is **Havforskningsinstituttet i Bergen.** (Oceanic Research Centre in Bergen).

Nordnesparken is located furthest out on the peninsula that divides Vågen and **Puddefjorden**. In the Middle Ages this area belonged to Munkeliv monastery (p 9). From 1600-1700 the current park was part of the ramparts surrounding Fredriksberg Fort, which we will pass later (p 10). The area has something of a dark past as the site of many executions that took place in Bergen, from the Middle Ages (p 83), up to 1876. For several hundred years the site was used for burning witches at the stake and for beheading prisoners. Nordnesparken was established in 1888-98. A "Witches Stone" has been erected as a reminder of all the witch burnings that took place here.

In Nordnesparken there is also a "totem pole" that was given as a gift to Bergen town from its twin city, Seattle, on USA's west coast.

On the northwest side of the park is Nordnes Sjøbad, with a fenced in seawater pool and an outdoor heated seawater swimming pool kept at a constant temerature of 25°C

On the west side of the park is the majestic building that previously housed **Bergen Sjømannsskole** (Bergen Maritime College). In many Norwegian towns the prevalence of maritime colleges shows how important shipping and maritime industries have been in Norway. Most colleges were placed on exclusive, fine sites with magnificent views. Bergen Sjømannsskole opened in 1904. The college was extended in the 1950's and 1960's. From 1991 the building has been used by the Health and Social Studies Department of Bergen College.

Nordnes School is situated behind Bergen Sjømannsskole. It was built in 1903 for 1 800 pupils divided into 54 classes. Lessons had to be held in two shifts - in the mornings and the afternoons - as the school could not house all the students at once. Nordnes was at this time quite densely populated, a fact sometimes expressed as "denser than in Hong Kong"! Later the population diminished somewhat. The school is still used as a primary school.

Fredriksberg Fort, which was built in 1666-67 and extended in the 1690s, is now closed down. In August 1665 a sea battle was fought between the English and the Dutch at Vågen and many ships were sunk. From the various fortifications in Bergen more than 1 000 cannonballs of various calibres were fired. This battle highlighted how necessary it was to reinforce the fortifications around Bergen. Bergenhus Fort was upgraded and Fredriksberg Fort was constructed. In the beginning the fort was mostly surrounded by mounds of earth. Around 1690, ramparts were constructed from stone; these were completed in 1706. It never participated in an actual conflict, but was very useful for fire prevention as it served as a permanent lookout post for the fire brigade. From Fredriksberg it was possible to look out over most of the town. Whenever a fire was discovered, a signal of three shots was fired from the fort. A fire station was built in 1905 in the fort but this was closed down in 1926.

On our way back to town centre we pass several "smitt and smau", the old wooden houses so characteristic of Bergen, located in narrow and steep winding streets (p 19). The area, **Verftet,** has ties to the former shipyard, **Georgnes Verft** which began operations before 1850, however this no longer exists. The buildings were mainly houses for the shipyard workers. One of the roads here is called **Galgebakken (Gallows Hill)**, previously an execution site where a gallows once stood. The west side of Nordneshalvøya faces Puddefjorden and on the other side of the fjord we can see the part of town called, **Laksevåg** under **Løvstakkfjellet**.

The open area known as **Klosteret** takes its name from Munkeliv Kloster (monastery), built by King Øystein (I) Magnusson (1088-1123) (p 9). No evidence remains of this monastery, which was built free-standing on a hill with walls and towers with a good view out over Vågen. The monastery was the wealthiest in Bergen; it had large farms that provided more than adequate income. For long periods Munkeliv had a peaceful monastery life with prayers and good work. However, Munkeliv monastery was also on many occasions involved in political unrest. The monastery was burnt down in 1198, and attacked by pirates in 1393. In 1455 a large, armed, Hanseatic mob burnt down the monastery and killed a tax collector that had been pirating the German ships. Along with the tax collector, they also killed the bishop. The monastery burnt down several times and was always rebuilt, but after the final fire in 1536, some years after the Reformation, it was not restored. The remains of Munkeliv monastery are supposed to be under the large site called Klosteret.

Our wandering ends here at the town's 'grand plaza', Torgallmenningen (p 17).

Bergen has many sights outside the town centre that are worth visiting. Two of the most popular are **Trollhaugen** and **Gamle Bergen** (Old Bergen).

Trollhaugen is the former home of Edvard Grieg (1843-1907), the internationally famous Norwegian composer. The idyllic estate, next to the lake Nordåsvannet south of Bergen is preserved just as when he lived there and is used today as a museum and for smaller concerts.

The town museum, **"Gamle Bergen"** is located in an idyllic area by the sea in the northern part of town. Approximately 50 listed and protected 'Bergen houses' from 18th-, 19th- and 20th century Bergen have been moved from their original sites to be rebuilt in "Gamle Bergen". The houses have retained their original styles and interior details and show how private homes were during these periods. Several workshops, stores and exhibitions can be seen.

The people of Bergen have many reasons for believing that their 'town between the mountains' is special:

Bergensværet (Bergen weather) is in a class of its own! It is famous far beyond the town's borders. The simple statement is: **I Bergen regner det!!** (**In Bergen it rains!!**)

© BERGEN TOURIST BOARD/ODDLEIV APNESETH

The town lies on the northwest coast of the world's largest continuous land mass that, apart from the Baltic Sea between Sweden and Finland, stretches southwards towards the Pacific Ocean on Russia's east coast. A maritime climate is predominant, but the winter chill coming in from the Russian plains can result in very cold winters and high-pressure patterns from Southern and Eastern Europe can result in dry and warm summers.

When Cardinal Vilhelm of Sabina came to town for the coronation of King Håkon Håkonsson in 1247 it rained "day and night". He gave the farmers permission to salvage their hay, corn and vegetables on the Sabbath and holy days if it was impossible due to bad weather on ordinary working days. He had himself experienced how bad it could be. From mid-June to the end of August it could

sometimes rain so much here that it was impossible to plough or sow corn properly.

Even today, rainy periods can be very lengthy. During the winter 2006/2007 it rained continuously for 84 days.

The traditional '**buekorpsene' (Boy's Brigades)** in Bergen are special boy's organisations dating back to the 1850's. They have their roots in the civil defences of that period - the town's merchants and inhabitants had a duty to defend their town along with the armed forces on Bergenhus Fort and therefore had to have the necessary weapons at the ready. The boys imitated the adults' weapons with homemade wooden ones, wore uniforms and formed platoons, companies and brigades (corps). This of course was just for play but as a result, each part of town had its own "buekorps". In addition to drills and marching the 'corps' also promoted various sporting activities. The boys were between the ages of 9-10 up to 20.

© BERGEN TOURIST BOARD/ODDLEIV APNESETH

In the "buekorps" season, that normally runs from March until June it can become quite noisy in the streets of Bergen. They march through the streets to the beat of energetic drumming. Until 1991 the "buekorps" were restricted to boys only, however more recently, girls have formed their own corps.

Festspillene i Bergen (the Bergen Music Festival) was founded in 1951. The first festival was also held in 1951 and has since become a very popular annual event that takes place over two weeks in May/June. 'Festspillene' is a musical, theatre and arts festival with the objective of promoting Norwegian art and culture and to present foreign artists for a Norwegian audience. The programme consists of concerts, plays, ballet, opera and folklore performances, also art exhibitions and events for children. The most important concert halls are Grieghallen, Håkonshallen, Trollhaugen and local churches. Edvard Grieg's music has always held a central place in the festival's programme.

Bergen residents are known for being individualists and fiercely proud of their town. A well-known expression is "eg e ikkje fra Norge, eg e fra Bergen" ("I am not from Norway, I am from Bergen!").

THE VIEW FROM THE SHIP
BEFORE DEPARTURE FROM BERGEN

From the ship, there is a 360° view of Bergen and Askøy.

On the port side, we can see three of the famous seven mountains around Bergen. The outermost is **Lyderhorn**, then **Damsgårdsfjellet** (350 m above sea level) and **Løvstakken** (477 m above sea level), a favourite area for hiking.

Lyderhorn is well-known in Norway as a "witch mountain". Legend has it that when the witches of the mountain **Domen** near **Vardø** (p 231) set off on their broomsticks at a terrible speed, they were then on their way to Lyderhorn near Bergen or to other witch gatherings in the country.

Just beyond Damsgårdsfjellet is a large floating dock. The dock was constructed as part of a plan to help the high unemployment rate in 1932-33, when many shipyard workers were idle.

During the war, the floating dock was the scene of many dramatic events, as it lay close to the German submarine bunker known as "Bruno" (p 12) and a German shipyard that repaired warships and submarines. The bunker "Bruno" and the floating dock near **Laksevåg** were the targets of British bombers and were attacked several times (p 12). The floating dock was also attacked a number of times by battery-driven mini-submarines that had been towed from Scotland. The mini-sub "X.24" was shaped like a huge cigar and had a crew of four. It failed to cause any damage on its first attack in April 1944. On the second attempt on the 11th September the same year, the "X.24" managed to place four explosive devices under the floating dock. When these exploded, the dock was so badly damaged that it sank rapidly and 17 Norwegian workers were killed. The floating dock was raised some years later.

On the port side aft rises the mountain of **Sydnesfjellet,** later known as **Dragefjellet**. During the middle 1600s, the town suburbs had reached **Nøstet** and **Sydnes**, and eventually the fell sides were also built upon. From 1641, one of the town's execution sites was located on Dragefjellet and a fort was built in the middle 1600s. The last execution on Dragefjellet took place in 1803; a man was beheaded because he refused to do his military service.

The immense brick building outermost on the fell, Dragefjellet School, was built in 1891. It was an elementary school until 1946, after which it became a college until the buildings were taken over by Bergen University. The buildings have been modernised and an extension was built in 1995. The Faculty of Law at Bergen University and the faculty library are now located here.

The high stone wall of Johanneskirken (p 18) can be seen southeast of the school buildings.

The bay **Jekteviken** and the Hurtigrute terminal reflect both historical and modern times in the area. The areas of Nordnes (to starboard), Nøstet (aft) and Sydnes (to port) are all mentioned in the town's historical documents as early as the 1400s. Smaller houses for those less well-off were built here, among them fishermen, seamen, manual workers and tradesmen. At the end of the 1600s, a soap factory was opened, also a herring oil factory, salt mill and oil plants in the Sydnes area. The area grew during the next hundred years, but without an organised town plan – hence the many "smau" that are typical of these parts, especially of the area around the harbour. Primitive sanitary conditions and the lack of space between houses led to poor health and high mortality rates among people living in the Sydnes area, compared to other areas of Bergen. The old wooden jetties were replaced with new quaysides during the 1880s.

Activity at the two quaysides **Nøstekaien** and **Sukkerhusbryggen** was considerable, small craft rowed passengers to and from Laksevåg and Askøy. Cargo ships from far and wide came to the quayside and packing warehouses. As an increasing number of tourists began to visit the beautiful Norwegian fjords and Northern Norway, passenger ships began to anchor out in the fjord and tourists were brought ashore in smaller craft to Nøstekaien.

The areas of Nøstet and **Engen** aft of the ship have both new and older styled buildings. A fire in 1930

and several bombing raids during the war in 1944 destroyed parts of the old wooden buildings at Nøstet and Engen just beyond. Newer and more practical buildings, offices and public buildings have been erected on the former sites. Sentralbadet, the town's first modern public baths and swimming pool, was constructed in 1960 and the cinema complex, Engen Kino, was opened in 1961.

Behind Nøstet and Engen is **Ulriken** (643 m above sea level), the highest of the seven mountains of Bergen, with its telecommunications mast on the peak (p 18).

Norway's second largest TV station, TV2, has its head office over to starboard (aft). It can be easily spotted with its giant satellite dishes. The TV station is based in Bergen, but also has a large news department in Oslo. TV2 is privately owned and financed by advertising. It was founded in Bergen in 1992.

Behind the TV2-building, we can see the top of a green church spire. This is the spire of Nykirken on the eastern side of Nordnes peninsula (p 20).

In the background is the mountain **Fløyen**, with the Fløyen restaurant, the top Fløibane station and Fløibanen itself (p 16). **Sandviksfjellet** (417 m above sea level) stands north-west of Fløyen. In the background, between the two mountains is **Rundemanen** (586 m above sea level), with the radio masts of the former coastal radio station Bergen Radio that was decommissioned in 1960.

The cultural centre USF Verftet is on the starboard side towards **Nordnespynten**. The 1 200 m² site, is comprised of two buildings joined together (one in white and the other in red brick). The buildings have a tall factory chimney. The buildings formerly housed a sardine factory, USF, which is now no longer in operation. USF Verftet has stages for music, theatre, dance and film, also 80 studios for artists and sculptors. There are a total of 180 different art and cultural enterprises here.

On the hill behind the culture centre we can see the west side of Fredriksberg fort (p 21) and the former Bergen Maritime College (p 21).

The new houses at **Georgenes Verft** (verft = shipyard) are built on the site of the old shipyards of Georgenes Verft that began operations in 1784. The shipyard built only a few sailing ships during its first few years – its main business was then repairing and maintaining ships. Later a great number of sailing vessels were constructed at the shipyards, the last of these in 1883. A few wooden steamships were also built here. After 1890, the enterprise was reduced considerably and it finally closed in 1912.

The old buildings at Georgenes Verft, small houses and "smau", have escaped most of the large fires in Bergen and some remain as they were built in the 1600s. Most of the residents here were workers at the shipyard.

Near **Nordnespynten** are the bath-houses of Nordnes Sjøbad, with heated saltwater pools on shore and an enclosed sea pool (p 20).

In front is **Askøy** (100 km²). After departure we pass the island on our way northwards. The regular sailing route is on the south side of the island. This will be described in more detail in Day 12 (p 384).

Hordaland county

Origin of name: First segment; horthar, from old *haruthóz*, probably a Celtic name meaning 'warrior, hero', last segment; 'landscape'.
Area: 15 460 km². **Population:** 456 711.
Population density: 29.5/km².
Municipal seat: Bergen (pop.: 244 620).
Municipalities, in the order we pass them on our voyage north: Bergen, Askøy, Fjell, Øygarden, Meland, Radøy, Fedje, Austrheim.
Topography: The fjords and valleys around Bergen are dominated by the so-called Bergensbuene, two concentric arches of Cambric-Silurian rock with blocks of Pre-Cambric rock formations in between. The arches open towards the west and give the landscape its characteristic features. Two of Norway's biggest glaciers, Folgefonna and Hardangerjøkul are located in this county, as are some of Norway's highest mountains and most famous waterfalls.
Climate: The county has the heaviest rainfall in all of Norway, especially along the coast due to the winds bringing moist air from the west and southwest. The mountains along the coast provide shelter from the rains to the areas behind. Wind conditions in the lowlands are dependent upon the terrain. In the winter, the winds come mainly from south and east. January and February are the coldest months with an average temperature of 2 °C on the coast and -5 °C inland. The average temperature in July is 14-16 °C. Most rain falls in October and the driest month is May.
Population: Hordaland is one of Norway's most densely populated counties. Approx. 66 % of the population lives in the Bergen area, 53 % in Bergen town itself.

TRADE, INDUSTRY:

Farming and forestry: Mainly farming, especially cattle and sheep. 97 % of arable land is used as pasture. The county has one-third of Norway's fruit producing areas but relatively little forestry.
Fishing: A reduction in traditional fishing activities over the last decade has been compensated by the increase in fish farming. The most important areas for traditional fishing are Bergen, Askøy and Austevoll. The county is an important area for fish farming, 75 % of this is salmon.
Industry: Hordaland is also Norway's second most im-portant county in regard to oil-related industries. Mechanical industries, shipbuilding and textile and clothing industries were all important at one time, however the shipbuilding industry has declined in recent years. Today, mechanical industries are the most important followed by shipbuilding and transport services. In 2002, Bergen was home to 46 % of the entire county's industry. Several of the industrial counties have one or two cornerstone industries.
Energy: Hordaland is Norway's most energy-rich county with approx. 13 % of the country's power production capacity.
Merchant shipping: Several of the country's larger shipping companies have their main offices here in Bergen. There has been something of a decline, however, in recent years.
Tourism: Hordaland is a county that offers a wide variety of sights and activities for the visitor. Coastal areas, fjords, mountains, glaciers and a wonderful city - Bergen itself, the most important tourist attraction. We also have Hardanger with the hiker's and fell walker's paradise of Hardangervidda. Cultural and historical sights such as the Middle Age churches in Bergen and the rest of the county, Håkonshallen and Rosenkrantz Tower in Bergen, Finneloftet in Voss, one of the country's oldest, timber buildings. Ruins of monasteries. Rosendal Barony in Kvinnherad with a preserved farm from the 17th century. There are a number of art, culture and natural history museums in Bergen. In addition, we have Fløybanen, the Aquarium and Bryggen in Bergen.
Communications: Railway, i.e. Bergensbanen from Bergen to Oslo. Four main roads take us over the mountains to the eastern part of the country, of which three are open all year round. The large fjords could present a communications problem, but ferries, several bridges and tunnels tie the county together, especially between Bergen and the islands to the west. There is also a very good bus service in and out of Bergen and many car ferries and passenger boats. Bergen is the starting point for Hurtigruten and several other boat services.

The airport at Flesland south of Bergen is the main airport for this region and has the second largest number of annual passengers in Norway. Stord (Sunnhordaland) has its own airport with regular service.

Source: Store norske Leksikon

The Norwegian coast – the historical highway

Norway is a country with high mountain ranges that divide the regions. It has a coast approx. 83 000 km in length (mainland 25 148 km and islands 58 133 km) and long, deep fjords. The first people to settle along the coast, approx. 10 000 years ago, came by boat.

Throughout history, until approx. the 1930s, the sea route has been the main 'highway', connecting the various regions together. The oldest evidence of the use of boats is contained in cave paintings and remains of primitive vessels and hollowed tree trunks have been found in marshes – the oldest of these to be discovered, dates from 170 B.C. Other types of boats were constructed from animal skins stretched over a wooden frame, and logs bound together in the form of a raft. The boats were rowed using oars. One of the oldest finds is the 'Kvalsundbåtene' (Kvalsund boats) in Herøy municipality (p 42) which date from approx. 600-700. Archaeological finds from the Viking period reveal boats constructed some 1 000-1 200 years ago. These used sails in addition to oars. Archaeological excavations carried out on the site of the fires in Bergen (p 15) reveal evidence of shipbuilding in Norway in the Middle Ages, a period dominated by the Hanseatic League and their 'kogger' (high-sided, wide vessels) and 'holker' (de-rigged ships used for storage).

The shipping routes between Northern Norway and the regions in the south developed in line with the expansion of tra-

de in fish between the northern parts of the country and Bergen. Boat designs developed over time, however the typical Nordland boats with sails, had clear similarities to the ancient Viking ships. The 1700s and 1800s were the golden era of the sailing ship and the Norwegian fleet expanded considerably. The paddle steamer "Prinds Gustav" (124 ft) sailed between Trondheim and Hammerfest in 1838, and in 1851 "Prinds Carl", also a paddle steamer, began plying the route between Bergen and Hammerfest. In 1893 the first scheduled sailings of the Hurtigruten began with m/s "Vesteraalen" (168 ft, 200 passengers), with sailings to Vadsø during the summer and to Hammerfest during the winter. The first ships to operate the route left from Trondheim and from 1898 from Bergen.

Sailing along the long, rugged Norwegian coast was often a treacherous affair and the Sagas tell of bonfires that were lit along the coast to show the way for mariners. The first sea charts were produced during the 1700s, made by the Dutch. These were largely for use in the south and east of Norway and were not especially accurate. The very first lighthouse to be constructed was built in the south (Lindesnes), in 1655. Up to 1814 a total of ten lighthouses were built; five coastal lighthouses and five beacons. In 1841, the number had increased to 27. The first lighthouses used open fires that burned coal, peat and wood in a large iron 'pot'. Gradually, navigating at night became safer. Up to 1932, 212 manned lighthouses were constructed along the coast, in addition to approx. 4 000 beacons, lanterns and light buoys.

When the coast began to be marked by lighthouses and beacons, ships could sail safely at night. The first few years after the Hurtigrute began its regular services in 1893, the ships sailed only during daylight. A marine

pilot was necessary along the entire route and navigational aids such as watches, compasses and careful calculation were used to determine the ship's position. Today, all lighthouses along the coast are automated and equipped with electrically driven beacons and advanced lens technology that can be monitored and controlled from stations on shore.

Coastal traffic and navigation methods have seen rapid developments. Today's ships are specially constructed according to the freight they carry. In addition to oil tankers – from supertankers to more modest coastal tank ships, dry bulk carriers of varying sizes, container ships and heavy cargo ships, there are also different types of gas and chemical transport ships. The oil industry in the North Sea has specially-built supply ships, often fitted with an on-board helicopter landing pad. The fishing fleets also have a number of specialist vessels, from factory ships and trawlers to the traditional coastal smack. Passenger ships of many sizes visit well-known tourist spots and sail along the coast, and small car ferries provide transport connections between small communities and their fjords and islands.

Navigation technology has also developed at a furious pace - from the sextant that was once used to measure the angle of the sun on the horizon to today's satellite navigation systems based on global positioning and computerised marine charts. Despite the abundance of modern technology, radar, traditional charts and visual navigation based on lighthouses and beacons are still used.

Much of the passenger and goods traffic that formerly sailed along the 'ocean highway' has now moved inland, to fast roadway networks or air routes. However, in this long and largely narrow country, the coast is still very much in use.

DAY 2

Florø, Måløy, Torvik, Ålesund, Geiranger, Ålesund and Molde

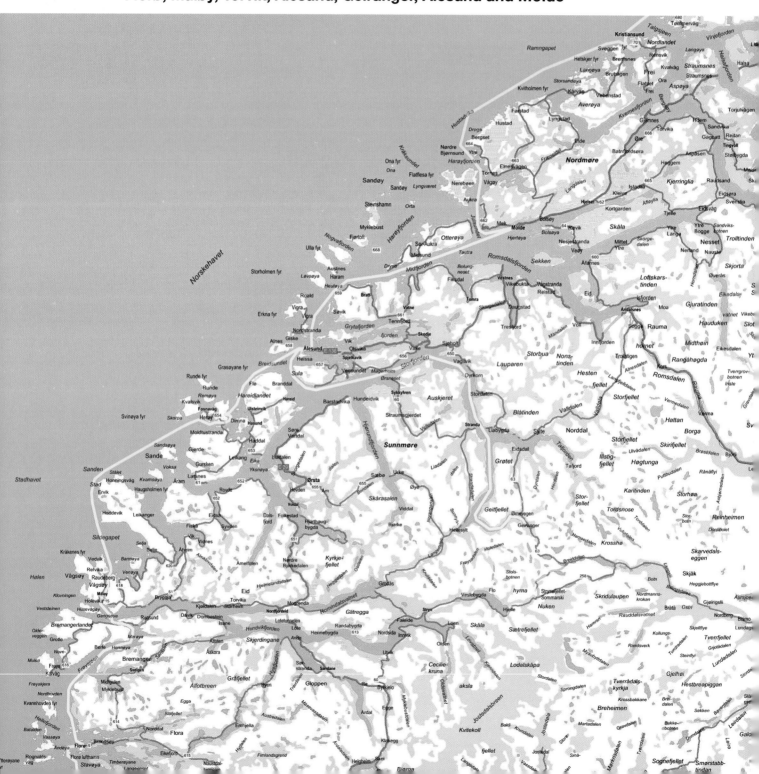

After departure from Bergen the ship has passed the municipalities of Askøy, Meland, Radøy, Fedje and Austrheim in Hordaland county, Gulen, Solund, Hyllestad, Askvoll, Flora with the first port of call **Florø** (61°36'N 5°01'34"E, Time: 0150-0215) and Bremanger in Sogn and Fjordane county. We are in the northern part of Skatestraumen, with Rugsundøya on our starboard side and Fåfjorden on our port side.

Approx. 61°53'N 5°10'12"E

We cross the municipal boundary between Bremanger (p 365) and Vågsøy municipalities

Vågsøy municipality

Municipal coat of arms, significance: Control.
Meaning of name: The main island, våg = 'bay'.
Municipal seat: Måløy (pop. 3 003).
Position: 61°56'31"N 5°07'35"E.
Area: 176 km². **Population:** 6 064.
Pop. density: 34.5 /km².
Area distribution: Farming 4 %, forestry 14 %, fresh water 3 %, other 79 %.
Trade and industry: Fishing, fishing industry (processing, fish oils and animal feed and export of fish products. Industry is closely linked to the fishing fleet. Farming (cattle and sheep), often combined with fishing.
Places to return to: Kråkenes lighthouse. Refviksanden. Vågsberget old trading post.
Vågsøy municipality's home page: www.vagsoy.kommune.no

The municipality includes the island of Vågsøy, parts of the mainland east of Ulvesundet, and the islands of Husevågøy, Gangsøy and Silda north of Ulvesundet. Most of Vågsøy's population lives along Ulvesundet.

61°53'N 5°10'E

To starboard, we have the entrance to **Nordfjord** (106 km long). The fjord is located north of **Rugsundøya**, has several 'branches' and is Norway's fourth longest. **Eidsfjorden** (13 km long) with **Nordfjordeid** village (pop. 2 645), **Hundvikfjorden/Utfjorden/Nordfjord** with the village of **Stryn** (pop. 2 140), **Loen** and **Olden** (pop. 473), **Gloppenfjorden** (12 km long) with the village of **Sandane** (pop. 2 079), **Hyenfjorden** (14 km long) with the village of **Hyen,** the short **Ålfotenfjorden** and the village of **Ålfoten**.

On our starboard side, we have the village of **Allmenningen**, where among other industries, there is an active timber industry producing windows and doors.

On our port side we can see **Husevågøy** (9.3 km² including Gangsøya). Stone carvings from the Bronze Age (p 83) have been found on this island. These show 15 ships and are thought to be part of a religious

© RAGNAR MYRE / WWW.VIVEST.NO

offering ritual intended to protect the fields and harvest. Close by are signs of a soapstone quarry. Because of its heat-retaining qualities, the stone was formerly used for making cooking utensils and heating stones.

On our starboard side is the village of **Angelshaug.** During the Second World War, a German torpedo battery was located on the southeast headland of Husevågøy. The battery, originally intended to be temporary, had two 45 cm Norwegian launchers. The torpedo battery had been placed there to control the entrance to Nordfjord. It was small, well camouflaged, located in a small bay and was constructed like a boathouse so as not to be too conspicuous. The battery was commissioned in December 1940 and from August 1944, a German command post was also located in the village.

61°55'N 5°07'E

On our port side, we can see **Vågsfjorden** between the islands of Husevågøy in the south and Vågsøy in the north.

Vågsøya (59.1 km², 604 m above sea level), is separated from the mainland by the narrow **Ulvesundet**. The houses are concentrated mostly along the shore of Ulvesundet. The villages of Måløy and **Raudeberg** have the largest populations.

To starboard is the bay **Skavøypollen,** with the village of **Tennebø,** that has a school and a sports centre, a shipyard and a timber yard. References to the farm, also known as Tennebø, have been found in documents dating from 1563.

We enter Ulvesundet and dock in Måløy. On our port side is Vågsøya, and to starboard is the mainland.

© RAGNAR MYRE / WWW.VIVEST.NO

Måløy Bridge (1 224 m) was Norway's longest bridge when it opened in 1974. It has a total of 34 bridge spans. The two mid-spans are 125 m long and 42 m above mean sea level. The bridge connects Vågsøya to the mainland, and was built to withstand wind forces up to 75 m/s. The prevailing wind speed is displayed at each end of the bridge, and if the wind exceeds a preset force, the bridge is closed. The bridge 'sings' a clear 'C' note when the wind blows from a certain direction.

The church of Sør-Vågsøy in Måløy is located on the west side of the bridge. This fine church was built in 1907 and has seating for 500. Near to the church is the restored outdoor staircase with 250 steps, leading up to a former cannon position and a lookout point on the mountain above Måløy Sound.

On our starboard side is the village of **Deknepollen** (pop. approx. 500) situated behind the headland, **Naustneset**. Before the Måløy Bridge was built, the ferry landing was located here. Today, Deknepollen has a fishing industry and a shipyard.

The small island of **Moldøen** is situated in the middle of Ulvesundet. Snorre Sturlason's King's Sagas tells the story of King Magnus the Good (1024-47), that he landed on the small island, Moldøen, in Ulvesundet and called for an assembly, a 'ting'. He requested the support of the influential people of the Nordfjorden region in order to succeed his father, King Olav the Holy (p 88), as the next king. Moldøen is strategically placed in Ulvesundet, and all shipping had to pass through the area. Thus the place has developed over the centuries to become an important trading centre. Amongst others, King Fredrik IV of Denmark-Norway stayed here during his trip to Norway in 1704. Large warehouses were built on the island, but towards the end of the 19th century Moldøen lost its importance. Some activities were moved over to the mainland but most went to Måløy on Vågsøya. During the Second World War, many of the old buildings were demolished to make room for the German gun emplacements and the rest were destroyed during the Måløy raid (p 31). A causeway was built in 1951 between the islands of Moldøen and Måløy on Vågsøya, so now all shipping in Ulvesundet pass outside of the island. In recent times, a good deal of new industry has been established on Moldøen.

The ship docks at the quayside in Måløy

The village of **Måløy** received its town charter in 1997 and takes its name from Moldøen. The original settlement comprised of five estates that today only exist as geographical areas. A town plan was agreed in 1920 to house 10 000 residents. The streets run almost parallel up the sloping terrain. They are not named but numbered - Gate 1 to Gate 8. Gate 1, (Sjøgaten), was to have an electric tram and a railway station. The bridge connection to the mainland came some 50 years later.

The fishing industry has always been important for Måløy's development and in the late 19th century, Måløy became the main fishing centre in Sogn and Fjordane. The large seasonal cod and herring catches in the area around and north of Vågsøya were mainly landed at Måløy together with other species, mainly halibut, from the banks lying north of Stad. In 1899 there were 1 620 men and 323 boats taking part in the winter cod catches in the area of Selje (p 34) -Vågsøya. On the west side of Vågsøya from 1890 until approx. 1920, there were incredible catches of cod. Many of the sheds built here to process the catches are still standing today.

The fishing fleet grew and eventually became motorised. A newspaper article in 1905 stated that 'in Moldøen they are fishing using 4-5 steam ships and 40 sailing boats. It was a busy time for everyone, with activity almost round the clock everywhere'. Måløy became the natural centre of the modernised fishing fleet. From 1858 Måløy was a port of call for the regional boat services in Sogn and Fjordane, and other traffic along the coast.

It is reported that "Sjøgutten", a ship from Stavanger, ran aground in Måløy Sound in February 1905 on its route northbound through the sound. The ship's cargo, destined for Ålesund, was 700 tons of bricks. Heavy snow was falling and she grounded at about 9 a.m. At noon, she sank in 30 feet of water, breaking five steel cables. (The ship was resting on telegraph cables recently laid across the sound to Vaagsøen). The cable to Nordfjord was already cut. The crew was unharmed. The sunken ship lay such that she could be a hindrance to shipping passing through the sound, and so the assistance of divers was requested from Bergen. The cargo was eventually salvaged the following spring and the sale of bricks in Måløy was a success. When the ship was raised from the sea the engine still functioned in spite of being submerged all winter. In early June, the ship left Måløy under her own steam with two tugs as escorts. ...The farewell was a tremendous sight, with signals sounding from the steamers and waving of handkerchiefs and flags...

From the year 1900 to 1920 the population in Måløy increased from 400 to 1 200 and large sheds and freezer stores made from concrete were built along the sea front. This development took place from 1910 until 1920 - but when the financial crash occurred, many of the fish exporters were bankrupted. However, herring fishing picked up again in 1928 and with catches of piked dogfish and porbeagle for export, the area was once again revitalised.

Måløyraidet (Operation Archery) took place on 27th December 1941. At 9 a.m., 576 Allied commandos, amongst them 43 Norwegians from the Linge Company, landed on the south side of Vågsøya. Their mission was to attack the estimated 300 German troops and to sink any German warships in the area. The German forts were bombed and shelled from aircraft and ships. The attack lasted some six hours. 17 Allied soldiers were killed, one of them the Norwegian Captain Martin Linge, and another 58 were wounded. The Germans suffered 150 fatalities and another 98 were taken prisoner. No civilians in Måløy were killed, but many cabins, houses

and two factories were destroyed. German coastal artillery was later reinforced in the Måløy area. The strategic purpose of the Måløy-raid and a similar raid in Lofoten (p 159), was to deceive the German army into believing that an Allied invasion of Norway was planned. This was successful in that the Germans retained a large force in Norway for the rest of the Second World War despite military activity being rather moderate compared with the rest of Europe. A memorial to Captain Martin Linge was unveiled by King Olav V in 1965 close to Måløy Bridge where he fell in 1941.

A further large-scale air attack took place on 22nd April 1945 in which 49 Allied aircraft took part. Twenty-six Beaufighters arrived first, attacking three ships in the Vågsøy/Måløy area They had been discovered during a reconnaissance flight earlier that day. Close support was provided by 24 Mustang fighters. One of the aircraft went missing on the way over and another was shot down during the attack.

Måløy's existence has always been - and still is - dependent on fishing and as we have seen this industry has had seen some hard times. A new period of huge herring catches started in 1947 where, during the best seasons, more than 100 boats and 10 000 men were employed fishing for herring and thousands were employed in the processing industries on shore. 1956 was the peak year, however in 1960 the herring shoals almost disappeared and the boom period was over once more.

Thereafter the fishing industry in Måløy was based upon fish catches, which had very large seasonal variations up to the 1980s. The factories were therefore not fully utilised so the local industry had to base production on supplies of fish brought from fishermen further away and from fish farms. The remaining factories are now capable of utilising the whole fish, i.e. filleting, cod liver oil and animal feed, and Måløy remains one of Norway's most important fishing ports and exports fish products all over the world. It is also an important commercial and maritime centre.

The wreck of SS "Klaus Fritzen" is situated at a depth of 40–55 m in Ulvesundet, between Måløy and Deknepollen. The ship, built in 1922, was attacked and bombed in May 1942 by British RAF aircraft from 608 squadron. She was anchored in Måløy harbour and sank quickly. 19 of her crew were lost. Apart from the damage sustained during the attack the ship is still in remarkably good condition.

The German vessel "Anhalt", built in 1921, was also hit during this attack. She had been damaged several times before; once by a British mine close to the Swedish coast in 1940 and she was later bombed on the Dutch coast in 1941 with the loss of many lives. During the raid on Måløy this ship was located within the target area and was severely damaged, but remained afloat until a further air raid in May 1942. Today the 'Anhalt' is located in shallow waters close to Vågsøy.

To starboard we can see the mountain called **Hanekammen** (652 m above sea level) on the mainland and on our port side we pass **Veten** (604 m above sea level) which is often used as a landmark for shipping. It is assumed that the name comes from the Norwegian word "vetesystemet" which was the name of an alarm system used along the coast until up to about 200 years ago (p 82).

| The ship continues to Torvik | + 0 hrs 00 min |

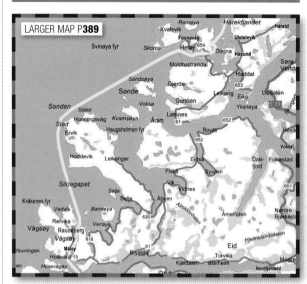

LARGER MAP P**389**

After leaving Måløy, we continue through **Ulvesundet**. The sound has an important place in Norwegian history. On many occasions, the sound has provided shelter to

mariners sailing northwards, that did not dare to negotiate the notorious waters off the coast of Stad during stormy weather. In Snorre Sturlason's King's Sagas we can read about the sons of King Eirik Blodøks (Bloodaxe) (895-954), who were sailing northward with a large army around the year 955. They were on their way to Nordmøre for a surprise attack on King Håkon the Good, but ran into rough seas at Stad and were weather-bound for seven days. King Håkon's supporters were thus given time to send a message overland to warn the King who managed to assemble his own army in time to meet them and win the battle.

To our starboard side is the industrial village of **Trollebø** where factories produce herring oil and other fish products. The village is developing into an industrial area. Thereafter follow the villages of **Saltkjelen** and **Hagevik,** which are mentioned in documents dating back to 1563.

| 61°58'16"N 5°09'E | + 0 hrs 20 min ① |

Kapellneset is on our port side. A belfry was raised there in 1944 to commemorate the first church that was built on the site in 1580, and remained in use until 1854. In 1949, the remains of a Viking ship were found, just below the church cemetery. The ship had most likely run aground in this area approx. 1000 years ago. More recently, a considerable amount of industry has been established at Kapellneset.

On our port side is the village of **Raudeberg** (pop. 671) the second largest village in Vågsøy municipality.

Raudeberg is also mentioned in documents dating back to 1563. The name is probably derived from the typically reddish rocks found in the village. Commerce is based on the fishing industry (rock-dried and split cod) and shipyards (repair and refitting of fishing vessels).

Nord-Vågsøy church is located on the next headland after Raudeberg. It was consecrated in 1960 and has seating for 492. The old wooden church that once stood on the site burned down when it was struck by lightning in 1945.

After Raudeberg and on our starboard side we can see Ulvesund lighthouse, which is situated on **Hjarteneset** near Osmundsvåg. It is built in 1870, automated and de-manned in 1985 and eventually restored in 2003. The lighthouse is now privately owned. There is a café here and the facilities can be rented for art and cultural exhibitions.

In the village of **Osmundsvåg** and on our starboard side by the north-easterly exit from Ulvesundet, a Stone Age settlement (p 83) was found along with many artefacts such as tools and weapons.

In 1707 the owners of the trading post in Osmundsvåg were granted a licence (from the King) to trade and provide accommodation for travellers. There was also a cannery opened around the year 1875 producing crab and fish products. The factory was the first of its kind in Sogn and Fjordane county (p 386), and the products received a great deal of acclaim at an exhibition held in Philadelphia, USA, and received awards from exhibitions in Europe. The factory was closed down in the 1880s. From the beginning of the 20th century, activity in Osmundsvåg slowly dwindled and in 1956 the houses burnt down.

From November 1942 until August 1944, a German fort was located in the area to guard Sildegapet to the north and the northerly approaches to Ulvesundet. The fort had, amongst other armaments, four Belgian 155 mm field cannon with a range of 13 km, five smaller cannon for close quarter protection, a powerful searchlight and the fort was surrounded by 1 650 mines. Another German fort was located at Halsør to our port side and farther north on Vågsøya. The cannon used on these coastal forts were a mixture of guns and ammunition taken from captured ships and newly reconditioned arms.

On our port side, we can see the mountain **Ramnereiret** (407 m above sea level) north of Raudeberg, and at the foot of the mountain, we find the villages of **Halsør** and **Langenes**. A German command bunker was positioned in the mountain behind Halsør to cover the same area as the fort at Osmundsvåg.

62°00'31"N 5°09'E	+ 0 hrs 24 min

On our starboard side is the island of **Silda** (1.1 km²), which is situated on a very exposed location out toward Sildegapet and the sea at Stad. Silda is one of the oldest fishing ports in Vågsøy municipality, mentioned in documents from 1340. A small chapel stood on the island from 1320 until 1580, but this was closed down when a new church was built on Nord-Vågsøy. Today there is a memorial where the old church once stood. Silda provided shelter for ships waiting for fair weather in order to sail beyond Stad and was a base for the marine pilots serving at the pilot station. In common with the areas around Stad this island has also a rich history.

In Snorre Sturlason's King's Sagas and in the saga of King Håkon Håkonsson (1204-63) it is said that, on the 20th anniversary of his reign, the King and Sture Jarl planned to travel to Trondheim on April 24th 1237. When they arrived at Stad the weather broke and they were forced to seek shelter at Silda. The Saga also tells us that King Magnus Lagabøte (1238-80) visited Silda in November 1264. King Magnus intended to travel north to Trondheim in the autumn, but was delayed starting his voyage, and by the time of All Saints Mass he was still in Leirgulen, he then travelled onward to Selje and so to Silda and thereafter to Eidet (Dragseidet, p 36), to avoid sailing around Stad.

In July 1810, during the Napoleonic Wars (p 85), when Norway was still in union with Denmark, Silda was attacked by two British frigates, the "Nemesis" and the

"Belvedere". The frigates fired at the two gunboats that were stationed there, then confiscated the boats and took the Norwegian crews prisoner. They then pursued the Norwegian soldiers on shore into the mountains by Osmundsvåg on the mainland.

An extension of the harbour on the island with two breakwaters started in the 1860s. Many fishing boats had Silda as their home port at that time and many dramatic events took place here. The last marine pilot working from this island was drowned when he went down with the schooner "Marie" from Drammen in December 1862.

> On January 22nd 1925, SS "Aladdin" ran aground near Silda. The ship had been anchored in Måløy Sound during a severe storm. The moorings broke and the ship went adrift, but with help from another ship and heroic assistance from the people on the island no lives were lost. Ever since then the date has been known as "Aladdin-natten" (Aladdin night).

During the Second World War the inhabitants on Silda were very much involved in the smuggling of Norwegian refugees over to Shetland and to England, and some took part in other illegal resistance activities.

Today, only approx. 30 people live on the island. However, during the summer season many more arrive to visit and stay on Silda, it is now a popular holiday resort with daily ferry connections to Måløy.

The mountainous island of **Barmøya** (9 km²) is situated between Silda and the mainland in Selje municipality (p 36). On the edge of the sea on the east side of the island is a stone monument, 1.55 m high, 50-70 cm wide and 15 cm thick. This is thought to be from the early Iron Age (p 83) and is located in an area containing many burial mounds and stone monuments.

The area ahead of us where we pass the Stad peninsula is infamous as one of Norway's most dangerous waters. This has prompted many discussions about building the "Stad-tunnel", to ease the passage of ships. In September 1874 the concept was presented in a newspaper article and since then the project has been considered many times. However, the lack of political support means that the final decision concerning the construction of the Stad Shipping Tunnel has not yet been taken.

The tunnel will be approx. 1 700 m in length, 49 m from bottom to tunnel roof and approx. 36 m wide. The tunnel is large enough for ships with a height of 29.5 m, a draught of 8 m and a width of 21.5 m. If the decision is taken to go ahead with the construction of the tunnel, it is estimated that the actual building period will be five years. The shipping tunnel will start at the inner part of Moldefjord, behind Silda and Barmøya, to Kjødepollen in the innermost part of Vanylvsfjorden behind Stadlandet, where the peninsula is narrowest approx. 1 900 m). The mountain that the tunnel will cut through is approx. 400 m in height.

In addition to greatly increasing the safety of shipping the "Stad Shipping Tunnel" would also be very important for tourism in the area. It would be the world's only tunnel designed for ships. The Corinth Canal in Greece, constructed 100 years ago, may be comparable, but it was constructed as more of a channel, in porous rock without a roof and the sides are only 70 m high.

Sildegapet is the name given to the fjord between Kråkenes lighthouse, Vågsøya and Furenes on Stadlandet. This exposed opening out to the Stad Sea, between these two geographical points is approx. 10 km wide and the fjord is approx. 33 km long.

62°01'28"N 5°08'38"E   + 0 hrs 32 min ②

On our starboard side we can see the small island **Selja** (1.6 km²). On the island are the ruins of an old monastery, Selje Monastery, probably the oldest church on our west coast.

The Sagas tell the story of a Christian Irish princess who, in company with her followers, fled from a pagan suitor in the 10th century onboard three ships. The ships drifted without oars and sails towards the Norwegian coast and stranded at Selja. The small party sought shelter in the caves now known as "Sunniva-Helleren". When the pagan Norsemen under Håkon Jarl wanted to drive them off the island, the Irish refugees prayed to God for help. An avalanche buried them all in the cave. A mysterious light beam later appeared above Selja and King Olav Tryggvason (968-1000) (p 88) ordered the bones of these martyrs to be gathered. Sunniva's body was found intact and undamaged, and was placed in a casket (Norwegian: skrin) called 'Sunniva-skrinet' and she became the local martyr of the west coast.

In 996 the King built the first Sunniva-church, a timber structure, just outside the cave where the bodies of Sunniva and her followers were found. In the year 1070, at about the same location, one of the first stone churches in Norway was built in finely sculptured olivine stone and this was also called the Sunniva Church.

Inside the cave are traces of the Hall, or Michael's Church, which is though to be one of the first churches on the island. It was dedicated to the archangel Michael. The remains constitute a brick wall and an inverted stone in the bottom of the cave, which, most probably has functioned as an altar-stone.

Shortly after the year 1100, Benedictine monks built a monastery near the shore at Selja to honour the English Saint Alban, who was believed to be Sunniva's brother and had accompanied her to Norway. A separate part of the monastery was located in the mountain under the "Sunniva-cave". The monastery, probably the oldest Christian sanctuary in Norway, is dominated by a massive square 14 m high tower and is situated on the plains near the sea on the west side of the island. The monastery is believed to have been completed in the 14th century. It was restored in 1913 and in the years from 1935 to 1940.

Around this time, in the early 12th century, and on the plains beneath the mountain, an Albanus church was built, which also belonged to the monastery at Selje. The exterior and interior of the church were decorated with finely sculptured olivine stones, showing clear markings from the masons chisel. The church was later extended, probably after a fire in 1305.

From 1068 to 1170 Selja was the first episcopal seat for all of the west coast. When the episcopal seat was moved to Bergen in 1170 the Benedictine monks took over the Albanus church. The "Sunniva-skrinet" (casket) was also relocated and placed on the Cathedral's altar. It is assumed that the casket was destroyed when Munkeliv monastery in Bergen was demolished during the Reformation in 1537.

62°02'N   5°09'E

Skongenes lighthouse is on the port side, at Vågsøy's northernmost point. The lighthouse was built in 1870,

has a light range of 13.9 nautical miles and serves as a channel marker. A foghorn or nautophone was installed in 1963. The lighthouse was automated in 1985. The station has four buildings arranged around a courtyard and is a popular tourist attraction.

Skongeneshellaren is a cave close to the lighthouse, approx. 100 m from the beach and 20 m above sea level. The cave is 40-50 m deep, 30–35 m in height, and relics from the Early Iron Age, some 2 400 years ago, have been found there.

62°03'N   5°07'40"E   + 0 hrs 40 min ②

Kråkenes lighthouse is located further to our port side on Vågsøy's north-westerly point. It was constructed in 1906, stands 45 m above sea level, and has a range of 17.5 nautical miles. It is one of the main lighthouses in the shipping channel.

During the Second World War, German artillery troops were stationed on **Kråkenes** and in 1942 one of the first radar stations in Norway was installed here. In 1944 another radar station was built on the mountain, at Kjerringa on Stad (p 38). Kråkenes lighthouse burnt down

in 1945, after being hit by Allied bombs. A provisional beacon was erected the year after and a new lighthouse was built and opened in 1950. In 1961 Kråkenes lighthouse was electrified, automated in 1986 and de-manned in 1991. A weather station is still in use on the site.

Kråkenes is one of the most exposed locations in Norway. Waves as high as 26 m have been measured. In 1994 the station was sold into private hands and was restored. It has a café and lodgings.

Refvika bay and **Refviksanden** are located between the lighthouses on Kråkenes and Skongenes. It is said that Refviksanden has one of the finest sandy beaches in Norway. During the war 7 100 landmines were placed on and around Vågsøy, 4 000 of these were buried on Refviksanden.

> Just south of Kråkenes lies the wreck of the German steamer, "Gilhausen" (built 1921) which ran aground at Palleneset on the 26th September 1941. The wreck lies at a depth of 36 to 50 m and is still in reasonably good condition.

Approx. 62°03'N   5°07'37"E
We cross the municipal boundary between Vågsøy and Selje municipalities

Selje municipality

Municipal coat of arms, significance: St. Sunniva.
Meaning of name: Originally the name of an island. Possibly from seal, 'seterbu', after sal, referring to Sunnivahulen on the island.
Municipal seat: Selja (pop. 685).
Position: 62°03'N 5°20'43"E.
Area: 226 km². **Population:** 2 911.
Pop. density: 19.9 /km².
Area distribution: Farming 6 %, forestry 7 %, fresh water 3 %, other 85 %.
Trade and Industry: Agriculture, including cattle and sheep. Fur farms. Fishing and fish farming. Shipyards, food processing, textile and clothing industries. Tourism.
Places to return to: Selje monastery (guided tours in summer). The Vestkapp (West Cape) plateau and Vestkapp house.
Activities to return to: Hoddevika with surfing. Mountain trips across Stad peninsula. Historical outdoor play "På Sverdeggja" near Dragseidet during Whitsun holiday every second year.
Selje municipality's home page: www.selje.kommune.no

Selje municipality on our starboard side encompasses the peninsula, **Stadlandet,** an area to the south and the islands of Barmen and Selja. The population is spread along the coast with the biggest concentration in the village of Selje on the mainland's west side, behind the island of Barmen.

The outermost part of Stadlandet has practically no reefs or skerries and is therefore very exposed to the weather. The name is derived from 'stadr', meaning 'to stop', because in former times mariners had to stop here and wait for fair weather in order to continue their voyage.

© STIG SILDEN

62°04'24"N   5°06'44"E   + 0 hrs 46 min

On our starboard side we can see the village of **Dragseidet**, where we find the lowest mountain pass over the peninsula, Stadlandet. The alternative to waiting for fair weather in order to sail around Stad, was to transport the boats over land and the point at Dragseidet was best suited for the purpose. The boats were pulled over rolling timber logs. It is assumed that this method was often used in Viking times when it was important to get to the desired place quickly. We do not know for certain where this route actually was, but it is assumed that the boats on the west side of Stadlandet were taken ashore near **Drage**, and on the north-east side of the peninsula the boats were taken ashore at **Leikanger**. The route today is an old postal road approx. 5 km long. The highest point is **Kongshaugen**, approx. 240 m above sea level.

History tells us that in the year 997, King Olav Tryggvason (p 88), who had converted to Christianity, christened many people from the four counties of Sogn, Nordfjord, Sunnmøre and Romsdal here at Kongshaugen. Just north of Kongshaugen is a monument, Olavskrossen, (Olav's Cross) which was erected in 1913 as a tribute to this event. The monument is located at the spot where the people were said to have been christened.

Snorre Sturlason's King's Sagas from the year 1220 tells us a somewhat different story of the christening at Dragseidet. King Olav summoned the four regional councils and met them with many of his followers and an army from Rogaland and Hordaland. The King told all those assembled there were two options available; either convert to the Christian faith and be christened, or he would wage war against them. When the assembled farmers realised that it would be useless to fight the King they chose instead to be christened.

At the shore at Drage and the neighbouring village of **Austmyr** is a cemetery containing 16 graves, dating mainly from the early and late Iron Age. The contents of the graves were meagre but one grave contained remains of pottery dating back to the Migration period (p 83).

| **62°06'N   5°05'42"E** | **+ 0 hrs 53 min** |

On our starboard side we can see the mountain, **Signalen** (441 m above sea level), also known as **Revjehornet**. This mountain was part of the military signalling system that used markers (veter) in Selje and Nordfjord (p 82).

The next headland, **Gamla,** is the most south-westerly point on the mountain of Signalen, with the village of **Indre Fure** and the now deserted village of **Ytre Fure** on the east side of the mountain.

| **62°07'22"N   5°05'E** | **+ 0 hrs 59 min** |

Furestaven, a cone-shaped low mountain top can be seen on the outermost north-westerly point on Signalen. Here we find an outcrop of soapstone approx. 50 m above sea level. Soapstone was much sought after in the south of Europe for artwork and pottery. In the rock face near Furestaven, there are traces of around 50 excavations, which are believed to be from the Viking period or possibly earlier (p 83).

In the bay of **Hoddevika** between the mountains Signalen and **Måsekleivhornet** (540 m above sea level) we find the village of **Hoddevik**. It is a farming community and is well known for its beautiful beaches and is a popular place for surfers.

The mountain **Hovden** juts out into the sea between the two bays, Hoddevika and Ervika. A Norwegian air-raid warning station was located on Hovden in 1932. In 1942-43 a German coastal fort was built here, which was finally ready in the summer of 1944. It was still in German hands a month after Germany had surrendered in 1945. The fort had four 105 mm cannon, three 40 mm and two 20 mm anti-aircraft cannon, and two 60 cm searchlights. A 94 m long tunnel was blasted through the mountain, which was fitted with tracks to operate a cable car system used to transport ammunition to the cannon. A second tunnel, 104 m long, led to one of the cannon positions situated on top of the mountain. A command post, communications room, and ammunition depots were located inside the mountain in bunkers. There was also a German observation post and navigational equipment installed on the mountain. The fort was demobilised after the war.

In this area there were no safe havens for ships or convoys, where they could seek shelter in order to avoid being attacked by aircraft. The strategically important sea area around Stad was exceptionally well fortified. From Vågsøy in the south to Åram, northeast of Stad there were in total 19 large cannon and 14 anti-aircraft cannon.

At the end of the war, in the summer of 1945, large caches of German equipment were destroyed by the British forces, that could have been utilised both in civilian and military projects that were rebuilding the country after the Second World War. German planes and vehicles were also destroyed soon after the war. The coastal fortifications, however, were left intact – possibly because they were situated far from populated areas and were protected by minefields, which were difficult to clear.

The village of **Ervika,** the outermost village on the west coast is situated in the bay between the mountains Hovden and Kjerringa/Vestkapp. An infamous and brutal prisoner of war camp holding 120 prisoners was situated in the village. The East European and Russian prisoners were used as forced labour to build the fortifications at Stad. Remains of the camp can still be seen.

Located between the point of Gamla and Ervika are approx. 58 shipwrecks, mostly unidentified, and stories of shipwrecks in this area abound. In 1594 15 ships went down in a storm and some 20-40 lives were lost on each ship. In 1692 16 ships, on their way to Bergen, were lost and most of their crews were drowned. In 1763 14 ships and 15-20 sailors lost their lives. In 1920 30 fishing boats with approx. 60 men on board were fishing out from Ervika, when a sudden, violent storm overturned their boats - however most of the men were saved. In 1956 the fishing vessel "Brenning" capsized. The rescue crews heard knocking from inside the hull but were not able to tow the boat to safety before it sank. 19 men lost their lives. These are just some of the many stories of shipwrecks in the Stad area.

Near Buholmen just outside of Ervika are the broken remains of the wreck of the steamer "Sanct Svithun". The ship was on its way from Ålesund to Måløy on 30th September 1943 when it was attacked by six British aircraft - despite showing clear markings indicating that she was a Norwegian unarmed civilian ship. "Sanct Svithun" caught fire and many of those on board were killed by the flames, others jumped from the ship and were drowned, but against

heavy odds people from Ervika managed to save 76 lives. The ship ran aground at Kobbeholmen, between Buholmen and the mainland, where she later sank. It was later estimated that 50 people lost their lives in this incident. The circumstances surrounding this dramatic event were for a long time kept from the public. It was assumed that the reason for the attack was that reports had been received that there were 50 German soldiers on board. They had in fact left the ship at Ålesund but the Allies had not been informed of this fact.

In memory of the heroic rescue of the survivors a small chapel was later built on the beach at Ervika. The salvaged ship's clock from "Sanct Svithun" was presented as a gift of thanks to the people of Ervika and it now hangs in the chapel's belfry.

Many artefacts dating from different periods have been found in the sands on Ervika beach. Most originate from wrecks from the early Iron Age up to the 18th century. A few metres from the beach is 'Kjempehaugen', a man-made mound probably dating from the later Iron Age (p 83). It is approx. 10 m in diameter and approx. 1 m high. Next to the chapel at Ervika are three smaller burial mounds from the same era, however no artefacts have been found in the graves.

62°11'32"N 5°05'E	+ 1 hr 16 min ③

The plateau, **Kjerringa** (497 m above sea level) is also known as **Vestkapp** (West Cape). It plunges vertically down into the sea below. There are reefs and skerries in the area, which make it a very dangerous area for shipping.

In 1944, a huge radar station was built on the mountain, which comprised of two "Würsburg-Riese" units, one "Wassermann" and one "Freya" unit. The operational range was 350 km, and they were intended to be used for surveillance and guidance for fighter planes. A 52 m high radio mast and navigational aid equipment with a range of 300 km were also installed. The installations escaped undamaged throughout the war and was, for a short time, used by the Norwegian Armed Forces before they were finally dismantled and removed.

At Stad the **North Sea** and the **Norwegian Sea** meet. Stadlandet is often called "the clenched fist against the sea" and a look at the atlas confirms this popular description.

"FULL STORM AT STAD" is a warning often issued by meteorologists in Norway. It is said that 51 sailors have lost their lives at Stad after the Second World War and in the previous century more than 100 have lost their lives in these waters.

The village of **Honningsvåg** is located in the bay behind Kjerringa, thereafter we can see the mountain, Stålet (397 m above sea level) that faces both the Norwegian Sea and Vanylvsgapet, the open stretch of sea, which is the entrance to Vanylvsfjorden.

The village of **Eltvik** is located outermost in **Vanylvsgapet**, behind the mountain called **Stålet**. South of the village and on a headland the Germans built a huge fort to guard the opening into Vanylvsgapet between Stålet/Stad and Kvamsøya, and to block the entrance to Vanylvsfjorden. The fort was constructed in 1942. The whole installation was protected by 2 256 mines, all of which were later defused and removed. The fort was manned by approx. 100 soldiers and 26 officers and NCOs.

Vanylvsfjorden is on our starboard side. Its total length is approx. 30 km. The fjord divides into **Syltefjorden** and **Kjødepollen**.

Approx. 62°14'N   5°12'E

We cross the county boundary between Sogn og Fjordane (p 386) and Møre og Romsdal counties (p 81)

We cross the municipal boundary between Selje and Sande municipalities

Sande municipality

Municipal coat of arms, significance: Fishing.
Meaning of name: Name of farm, Norse sandr, 'sand'.
Municipal seat: Larsnes (pop. 490).
Position: 62°12'N 5°34'E.
Area: 93 km². **Population:** 2 526.
Pop. density: 27.2 /km².
Area distribution: Farming 9 %, forestry 3 %, fresh water 6 %, other 83 %.
Trade and industry: Shipyards. Food processing. Timber, textile and plastics industries. Farming.
Places to return to: Svinøy lighthouse. Dollstein cave.
Activities to return to: King Arthur plays.
Sande municipality's home page:
www.sande-mr.kommune.no

Haugsholmen lighthouse is situated in the middle of Vanylvsgapet, at the entrance to Vanylvsfjorden. It was built in 1876, automated in 1979 and in the summer of 2006 it was sold to private business interests.

62°15'40"N   5°16'20"E   + 1 hr 42 min

On our starboard side we can see the island of **Kvamsøya** (7.5 km², 272 m above sea level) on the northeast side of Sildegapet. Some of Norway's largest burial mounds are found on this island, which also has some fine beaches. Several plastics factories are established here and there is a car ferry service to the mainland.

On our starboard side we can see the small island of **Riste** to the north of Kvamsøya.

On our port side is the Svinøya lighthouse located on the small island with the same name. It is a coastal lighthouse, built of stone in 1905. The light itself is 46.2 m above sea level and has a range of 18.5 nautical miles. In 1938 a fog-horn and a diaphone were installed, these were dismantled in 1982 and the station was automated in 2005.

In 1856 a stone cairn was erected on **Svinøy** to assist mariners in determining their position. It was so difficult to land on the island, even in fair weather conditions, that it was many years before a lighthouse was built here. In 1901 it was proposed to build a lighthouse on the island and a year later the island was purchased. Three lighthouse keepers were necessary but the difficult landing conditions made it practically impossible to allow families

to live there. For this reason the keepers only worked for short periods on the island and in 1952 the lighthouse was converted into a rota-based station with one master lighthouse keeper and three assistants with a system of regulated leave. As the use of helicopters became more common along the coast, the crew was reduced in 1970 to two keepers on duty with two others on leave ashore.

Svinøy radio beacon was built in 1946. The transmitter's frequency is 293 MHz, with a range of 100/70 nautical miles. Since 1993 the beacon has transmitted calibration signals to the satellite based navigation system, Navstar GPS.

During the Second World War, Svinøy was occupied by German troops and bullet marks are still visible from the many attacks carried out by Allied planes. Today the station has a guesthouse with a conference centre and helicopter transport is available from the mainland.

> In the summer of 2004 a wreck was found in open waters north of Kjerringa and the remains were found to be from the Norwegian ship, "Joarnes" that sank there in 1929. She was on her way from Sande in Møre and Romsdal to Sarpsborg in Østfold with a cargo of soapstone when she ran aground and disappeared. The wreck is located just outside of Svinøya in 50 m of water.

62°17'N   5°23'E   + 1 hr 54 min ④

On our starboard side are the island of **Sandsøya** (12 km², 369 m above sea level) and the mountain known as **Rinden** (369 m above sea level). The name of the municipality, Sande, comes from the farm and the church located on the south side of the island. A church has existed on the farm Sande since the 13ᵗʰ century. Historical sources indicate there was a stave church there already in 1329. The present day church is a longhouse-style timber church built in 1880, with a unique altarpiece.

On Sandsøya there is a bird sanctuary where as many as 90 species have been registered (p 218). On the northeast side of the island we can find one of Norway's largest Sea Eagle colonies (p 161). A bridge and car ferry connect the island to the mainland.

Dollsteinshulen (cave) is located on the south side of the steep mountain of **Dollsteinen** (227 m above sea level) on the northwest side of Sandsøya. The mouth of the cave is 60 m above sea level and it is considered to be one of the largest - and most remarkable - caves in Norway. It is approx. 185 m long with five grottoes in a line, separated by long and narrow passages. Some parts have high ceilings

© SANDE MUNICIPALITY

and create the impression of a church. The cave was formed by the sea at the time the land was lower than at present. There is evidence that the cave has been inhabited by hunters in prehistoric times and the cave is mentioned in several ancient legends and texts. Dollsteinshulen is also mentioned in an old edition of Encyclopaedia Britannica, published before 1800. The article claims that the cave goes under the sea, all the way to Scotland – however this is of course merely a legend. Another legend has it that a dog disappeared inside Dollsteinshulen but later came out in Scotland, hairless and starving!

A third legend claims that in the 6th century, King Arthur of England buried precious treasures in Dollsteinshulen. To date, no-one has found any valuable relics in the grottoes, but the Sagas tell us that Ragnvald Kole Kolson, Earl of the Orkneys, visited the cave in 1127 to look for the treasure said to be hidden in the cave. However, he was unable to find anything at all, as his torch flare would not remain lit, according to the Orkney saga. The Earl later told tales of a dragon lurking in the dark, dank rocks where he had searched for valuable rings.

Each year, on the second weekend in August, the people of Sande perform an open-air play, "Kong Arthur-spelet" (The King Arthur play). The play is based on some of the Arthurian and Knights Of The Round Table legends that, according to certain myths, King Arthur came to Sandsøya (Dollsøy) to look for the "Ring-treasure" and the Holy Grail. The treasure, some historical researchers say, was buried in Dollsteinshulen by Olav Ring (Arthur's father) and folklore has it that the treasure is guarded by the troll, Bruse. In writings originating from the times when King Arthur reigned over vast areas of land, one of these areas was called Havlandet, and many believe that this corresponds to our present day Møre. Arthur became the warrior king of Britannia after pulling the sword, "Excalibur" out of the stone in which it was embedded. King Arthur's closest adviser, the sorcerer Merlin, accompanied the King on his journeys and it is said that he ended his days on the island where the treasure is buried.

The following is taken from the introduction to the play:

" King Arthur" is a fabled and legendary figure in British, French and Nordic literature. According to one of the many varied legend of Arthur, he was crowned King in Wales aged 15 and his royal seat was known as Camelot. In the latter part of his reign he was also King of Havlandet (Norway) – he was a descendant of Fridulev Hvate (known as Volse), a Norwegian king, a member of the Ringhuset clan that had conquered England in 383.

After leading an illustrious life he was seriously wounded at The Battle of Camlann in Cornwall in 542. After being wounded he sailed to Havet, to Marr or Mer – the name used at that time for Norway/Møre. He took his royal seat at Kongsvollen near Earnaness (Ørneneset – 'Eagle Point') near Arihaugane (Ørnehaugene – 'Eagle Fell') on the island of Dol (Celtic 'table') that is now known as Sandøy. According to the fable, Excalibur, King Arthur's legendary sword, was given to him by the Lady of the Lake.

In the version of the legend as depicted in the play, King Arthur was the son of Olav Ring, of Norwegian lineage. He inherited the Ring Treasure and Havet (Norway/Møre). Legend has it that the Ring Treasure also contained the Holy Grail, which was hidden in Dolsteinhola (Scandinavia's largest mountain cave) under the mountain Rinden on the island of Dol (Sandsøy). In the battle for possession of the treasure King Arthur was killed by Wiglaf, a kinsman of Beowulf, King of Geatland (the lands lying south of the Oslo fjord).

Beowulf's days ended in a battle with The Dragon at Havet, in Mer. In the Arthurian legends, Arthur is the Norwegian King and the Dragon, searching for the golden Grail that someone had 'stolen' from him. His search finally led him to Havet. The same story is repeated in the epic poem Beowulf, about the Dragon at Havet, who was known as Én, or High King of Norway – who was also searching for the Grail. Since Arthur and the Dragon are said to have lived at the same time – there can be no doubt as to their identities.

Beowulf also had a cunning plan to seize the Dragon's precious Ring Treasure. Beowulf brought along with him the man who had stolen the Holy Grail. The man knew the way to the secret place where the treasures were hidden. It is said that the man knew of 'a fell and all its hollows and grottoes at the shore, an underground cave.'

Dolshelleren is Norway's largest cave. The Earl Ragnvald Kole Kolson tried to locate the treasure; however, he was unable to do so, because his torch would not remain lit, according to the Orkney Saga. The Earl later wrote about the Dragon in Dol's murky caves, where he had sought the highly prized, fabulous treasure.

There is hardly any doubt that the Beowulf epic poem tells the story of the battle between the Dragon and Beowulf, and that this took place at Dol. As the story goes, the Dragon lived there in the underground caves on the shore overlooking the sea, most likely at the place now known as Sandshamn, on the eastern side of the island, where there is a harbour.

One day Beowulf found himself alone with the Dragon, at the place where the treasure was said to have been hidden. Beowulf tried to kill Arthur. However, Beowulf had greatly underestimated the Dragon and Beowulf was mortally wounded. However, Beowulf's loyal warrior kinsman Wiglaf had remained close by. Wiglaf tried to rescue Beowulf and in doing so, slew the Dragon.

It seems clear from Beowulf's epic poem that this took place in Møre in Norway, near a place called Earnaness.

The fact that Arthur had chosen to establish his Norwegian seat at Dol, has an interesting aspect. His mother tongue was Celtic, and Dol in that language means 'a table'. His standard, according to the Arthur legend was 'The Round Table", in his language, dol.

'Bruse', The Troll of Saudøy.
The tale of Orm Storolvsson and the troll Bruse is an ancient myth. According to Orm Storolvsson's saga, the following events occurred at the end of Håkon Jarl's reign, in the first half of the decade circa 990:

In the north, just off the coast of Møre, are two islands that are together known as Saudøy. On the outermost island there lived a troll, known as Bruse. His mother, who was said to be "a jet-black cat as big as the largest ox", lived on the innermost island.

Orm's friend, Åsmund, despite being warned of the dangers, went ashore on Ytre (Outer) Saudøy and was brutally killed by Bruse. When Orm found out about what had happened, he set off for the troll's cave to avenge his friend. On his way he met the troll's sister, Menglød, who took Orm aside and gave him some advice before the fight. After a fearsome battle, both the troll and his mother were killed.

In Sunnmøre, the legend is told somewhat differently. The event is said to have taken place on Sandsøy in Sande. This is, as in the case of so many other myths, a supposition – as the geographical descriptions are notoriously unreliable. A certain degree of confirmation is found, however in the similarity of the placenames and also that Dollsteinshola was said to have been the place where Bruse lived.

Dollstein juts out from the west side of Sandøya. In the dark area in the centre of the mountain, approx. 70 m above sea level, is the entrance to Dollsteinshola. It is the largest cave in Sunnmøre and goes approx. 150 m into the mountain.

The cave has been formed by faults in the rocks and the mass of stone and rocks transported by the movement of ice during the last ice age. These were deposited in a moraine in the fault. The moraine mass closed off a part of the cave, so that today the cave is actually formed between the mountain rock and the moraine mass. Innermost in the cave there are huge stone blocks that have fallen from the 'roof' of the cave due to the effect of freeze/thaw cycles. Both Dollsteinen and the cave are impressive. It is no wonder that these features inspire legends of the troll Bruse and his family. It is also understandable that Kali Olsson was curious as to what lay in the cave – but he had obviously not dared to go all the way inside. The 'water' that he swam across in the cave was probably a mud pool, as conditions in the cave at that time are believed to have been similar to what they are today.

Three km south of Dol is Kvamsøy. On Kvamsøy, some of the largest burial mounds have been discovered. The evidence indicates that at one time there has been a chieftain seat in the region.

In the background we can see the famous Sunnmøre Alps.

We cross the municipal boundary between Sande and Herøy municipalities

Herøy municipality

Municipal coat of arms, significance: Reflects the Kvalsund ships from the 7th century.
Meaning of name: First part, Norse "herr", probably meaning 'harbour'.
Municipal seat: Fosnavåg (pop. 3 518).
Position: 62°20'N 5°36'E.
Area: 121 km². **Population:** 8 321.
Pop. density: 69.3 /km².
Area distribution: Farming 9 %, forestry 4 %, fresh water 1 %, other 86 %.
Trade and industry: Fishing and food- and fish processing industry. Fish farming. Shipyard and manufacture of fibreglass boats. Mechanical, textile, timber and clothing industries. Some agriculture.
Places to return to: Runde. Runde lighthouse. Herøy Coastal Museum.
Activities to return to: Herøy plays.
Herøy municipality's home page: www.heroy.kommune.no

Our voyage continues in to **Herøyfjorden**.

62°18'17"N   5°31'E   + 2 hrs 10 min ⑤

© WENCHE MOLTU

We pass on our port side the island of **Skorpa** (2.8 km², 431 m above sea level) in Herøy municipality. It is no longer inhabited and it is used mostly as a recreational area and as pasture for wild goats. The island played an important role during the Second World War in connection with the evacuation of resistance fighters to the Shetlands. The underground activities on Skorpa were not discovered by the Germans, unlike so many other places along the coast of Norway, and they operated successfully until the war ended in 1945. Many fishing boats left the west coast for Shetland with Norwegians onboard that wished to join the allied forces, or for various reasons, had to flee the country. Some were arrested, some were lost at sea in storms or killed by German planes, whilst others arrived safely and even made the trip several times. From many of the islands Norwegian agents radioed information back to the Allied intelligence services in London about shipping activities along the coast. The Germans needed to transport material and troops from Norway to Germany to reinforce both the eastern and western battle fronts in the period 1944-45.

It became vital for the Allies to stop these transports, and to prevent supplies from Germany reaching the important U-boat bases in Norway (p 24, p 99).

Gurskøya (137 km², 621 m above sea level) on the starboard side is divided between Herøy and Sande municipalities. On the island's north west side is the mountain **Veten** (556 m above sea level) (p 75). On the island's western side in Sande municipality is the community of **Gursken**, home of Myklebust Shipyard (approx. 130 employees), which is part of Kleven Maritime in Ulsteinvik (p 46). Gurskøya has a bridge to the island of Hareidlandet, and a car ferry over to the mainland.

The community of **Moltustranda** (pop. 356) is over on the starboard side. Most of the population lives along the coastline and most commercial activities are associated with fishing and the fish processing industry.

On our port side and northeast of Skorpa is the island of **Nerlandsøya** (15 km²) and the mountain **Varden** (highest point 430 m above sea level). On our port side we can see the fishing village of **Kvalsund** (pop. 531) and the port of **Kvalsvik** (pop. 265), situated on the northeast side of the island. Several bridges stretching over a number of islands connect the community to the mainland.

In 1920 two boats, apparently built around the year 600 were found in a marsh on the farm, Kvalsund. They are believed to be a so-called "marsh-offering" and were broken up before they were buried. The largest boat, known as 'Kvalsundskipet', was a rowing boat with ten pairs of oars, it was 18 m long, 3.2 m wide and had a draught of 0.78 m. It is assumed that the boat was used inshore for shorter journeys, possibly used in connection with rituals/ceremonies or to signify the owner's status, possibly a local chieftain. The smallest boat, 'Kvalsund-færingen', had three pair of oars, it was 9.5 m long and 1.5 m wide. The construction materials were oak and fir and the design itself was much like a Viking longship.

The group of islands, known as **Flåværøyene** to our starboard side is comprised of the smaller islands **Flåvær**,

© WENCHE MOLTU

Husholmen, **Torvholmen** and **Varholmen**. The islands are no longer inhabited, but Flåvær was formerly the main island with a fishing port and a general store. During the herring season as many as 1 500 persons were gathered here. A post office operated here from 1873 until 1976 and a school up to 1984. Today you can take a holiday here or even hold conferences on Flåværøyene.

On our port side we can see Flåvær lighthouse. It was built in 1870 and has a range of 13 nautical miles. It was reinforced in 1952, then automated, and finally de-manned in 1979.

62°19'24"N 5°35'45"E	+ 2 hrs 19 min

The island of **Bergsøya** (7.6 km²) on our port side is the most populated island in Sunnmøre. Located on the north side of the island is the municipal centre of Fosnavåg, which was granted a town charter in 2002. North of Bergsøya are the two islands of Remøya and Runde that are connected by a bridge.

Fosnavåg has the largest natural harbour in Norway and is, therefore a popular port for boats in the area. The town is the main trading centre for Herøy, and for industrial activities connected with fishing and other maritime industries.

© WENCHE MOLTU

The "Bourbon Dolphin" was an anchor handling tug supply vessel (AHTS), one of the fleet belonging to Bourbon Offshore Norway, based in Fosnavåg. On April 12th 2007, the ship capsized north-west of Shetland, sinking three days later while preparations were being made to tow it to shore. The ship lies at a depth of 1 100 feet. Eight lives were lost in the shipwreck.

The industrial estate of **Eggesbønes** on the port side passes on the south side of the island. Eggesbønes is a base for various companies within the plastics and cement, fish farming and fish processing industries.

62°19'N 5°40'43"E	+ 2 hrs 30 min

On our starboard side we can see the island of **Nautøya** (0.7 km²). A bridge connection between Leinøya and Gurskøya crosses this island.

The island, **Herøya** (0.2 km²) is northwest of Nautøya and is one of the smaller islands in Herøyfjorden and has lent its name to the municipality, Herøy. The island is mentioned in the Sagas and history through the ages as a trading centre and a location of the governing assembly for the district.

In accordance with the Sagas, the Joms Vikings moored their ships at Herøya on their way to the fjord of Hjørungavåg in Hareid municipality in 986 en route to fight the famous battle against Earl Håkon (935-995) (p 52). The Joms Vikings came from the Danish Viking Castle, Jomsborg, believed to be situated in Wollin, a town at the mouth of the River Oder in Germany.

One of the first churches in Sunnmøre county was built on Herøya. It was a stone church dating back to the 11th-12th century. It was demolished in 1859 and replaced by a larger and more soundly constructed church built of timber. This new church was demolished in 1916 and parts of it were moved to Fosnavåg.

A legend tells us how this little island, which is not exactly an ideal place to build a church for such a large congregation, was chosen. Three sisters were shipwrecked out at sea and one of them prayed to God to save them. In her prayer, she promised to build a church if they were safely brought ashore. They drifted onto Herøya, she kept her promise and built a stone church on the island.

The old shipping channel passed between Leinøya, on our port side, and Gurskøya, on our starboard side. Herøya was situated in the middle of this channel and was an excellent port north of Stad. There is evidence that the port functioned as a trading and meeting place as early as the Viking period and therefore Herøy should have a church. However, the priests of the time did not want to live there. When a burial took place, earth had to be transported from elsewhere, as there was very little on the island itself. The original stone Catholic church was 22.3 m long, 8.6 m wide and 11.3 m high and built in the same style as churches in Ireland and England of that period.

After the Reformation in 1537, every object, artefact and connection to Catholicism was removed, and thereafter the church on Herøya became Lutheran. No seats were provided, as standing kept the congregation awake! Later the church was extended to seat 260. The foundation from the old church was used when the bigger and more modern timber church was built in 1859. It was a large church and could seat 483; however, it was demolished in 1916 when a new church was built on Bergsøya.

In the old cemetery on Herøya, there is an old iron cross with the inscription, "Anna and the Child". The legend is that a young woman, Anna, lived there in the middle of the 19th century. Anna died just before she was due to

give birth. She was buried, but due to scarcity of earth on the island, her coffin was not properly covered. A guard passing the cemetery during the night heard the cries of a child. He went for help and the coffin was opened the next morning. In the coffin were Anna and a newborn baby, they were both dead. Anna had actually been buried alive, she gave birth to her child during the night and they both died buried in the coffin.

During the 18th century, Herøya was one of the most important commercial centres in the region - a position it later lost to Fosnavåg on Bergsøya, especially after the larger islands in the municipality became interconnected by bridges. Herøya is still a busy cultural centre. It has a Coastal Museum that opened in 1981 and an amphitheatre seating approx. 1 500. Historical plays are performed annually.

On our port side is the island of **Leinøya** (14.4 km², 363 m above sea level) which is the third largest island in Herøy municipality. On the west side is the island's largest village, **Leinstrand.**

The ship passes under Herøy Bridge. When the bridge was completed in 1976, it was the world's longest with main spans of 85, 170 and 90 m. It is a pre-stressed, box-girder bridge built using the cantilever method. Total length is 544 m.

Further ahead and to starboard we can see the industrial centre of Ulsteinvik.

Before passing the bridge and on our starboard side, is the village of **Røyra**, southwest of the mountain called **Staven**. The village northeast of the mountain is **Frøystad.**

The island to starboard is called **Dimna** (9 km²) located in Ulstein municipality. The island got its name from appearing "dull" when seen by mariners approaching land. There are some farms and a few boatyards on the island, which has a bridge connection to the mainland.

The village of **Hasund** (pop. 1 100) is located on Hareidlandet, behind Dimna. Most of the population is employed in the shipyards.

Before Torvik and on our starboard side are the small islands called **Torvikholmane**.

In the winter of 1987 the fishing boat "Pastan" (113 gross tons) ran aground here. She was built in 1956 in Ulsteinvik. "Pastan" sank for the first time in 1966 after running aground near Sula in Fosna, due to a navigational error. She was later salvaged by employing a flotation technique using expandable foam. The boat was towed to Ålesund where she was repaired and lengthened. The boat was sold and sailed again for some years but ran aground for the second time in 1987 in 58 m of water near Torvikholmane.

The ship docks at the quayside in Torvik

In addition to the coastal traffic of cargo ships, the Hurtigruten calls in at the port of **Torvik**. The freight terminal, Herøyterminalen, located in Torvik harbour distributes all cargo to and from industries in Herøy municipality. A fishing gear factory is located in Torvik. From Torvik and on our starboard side we can see Ulsteinvik on the island of Hareidlandet.

North of Torvik we can see the steep mountain known as **Kattulhammareren**. On our port side and north of Torvik, we can see the village of **Bø**, where factories manufacture equipment for fishing boats and fish farming.

The mountainous island of **Hareidlandet** (165 km²) on our starboard side is the largest island in Sunnmøre. The island's west side is in the municipality of Ulstein and the east side is in Hareid. The mountain **Blåtind** (697 m above sea level) is located in the southeast, the mountain **Botnen** (654 m above sea level) stands southeast of the island of Dimna, then **Melshornet** (668 m above sea level) is on the island's east side and the mountains known as **Sneldelida** (633 m above sea level) and **Signalhornet** (627 m above sea level) are to the north.

The ship continues to Ålesund **+ 0 hrs 00 min**

LARGER MAP P**389**

Alnes · Giske 658 · Ålesund E 136 · Sp · Heissa 657 · Ve · Breidsundet · Grasøyane fyr · Sula · Flø · Branddal · Hareidlandet · Hareid · Barstadvik · 654 · Ulsteinvik · Dimna · Hasund · Ida · Søre Vartdal

Approx. 62°21'N 5°45'E

We cross the municipal boundary between Herøy and Ulstein municipalities

Ulstein municipality

Municipal coat of arms, significance: Illustrates the municipality's name.
Meaning of name: Norse ulfsteinn, name of mountain. First part may originate from a river or ulv, 'wolf'.
Municipal seat: Ulsteinvik (pop. 5 094).
Position: 62°20'N 5°50'E. **Area:** 97 km².
Population: 6 841. **Pop. density:** 70.5 /km².
Area distribution: Farming 6 %, forestry 13 %, fresh water 2 %, other 79 %.
Trade and industry: Shipyards and mechanical industries. Some fishing and farming.
Places to return to: Village of Flø.
Ulstein municipality's home page: www.ulstein.kommune.no

Ulsteinvik received official town status in the year 2000.

Outside Ulsteinvik and to our starboard side we can see the low, narrow island of **Hatløya** (Borgarøya) where the so called "borgere" (citizens) lived. In the 17th century, they were granted "borgerbrev" – a "trading permit" – with which they had license to travel and trade along the coast, hence the name, **Borgarøya**. Merchants from Bergen had warehouses here from where they bartered for imported goods from the Hansa towns in Germany, mainly fish and farm produce. At its peak, there were 17 different buildings here and trading continued until the 1880s. As the road systems improved, most of the trade moved to Ulsteinvik.

The administrative centre of **Ulsteinvik** with the familiar tower crane skyline can be seen behind Hatløya. Ulsteinvik is the centre of shipbuilding in Sunnmøre, and is Norway's largest and most active shipbuilding region. Shipping companies from all over the world come to Sunnmøre to negotiate orders for ships, even from such industrial giants as Korea and Shanghai who have some of the world's largest shipyards on their own doorstep.

This industrial phenomenon in Ulsteinvik began in 1917 when Martin Ulstein and Andreas Flø, both technically minded men, started "Ulstein mechanical workshops - for repairs of all types of engines, winches, gears and machines". The workshop area was 50 m² in size and had two slipways. The Hatlø Brothers' shipyard was also located in this area.

Around 1880, changes occurred within the fishing industry; the boats became larger and more advanced and farmers/fishermen had to concentrate increasingly on fishing in order to justify their investments. At the beginning of the 20th century a large part of the fishing fleet was motorised and Ulstein Mek. Verksted had to expand in order to follow developments. Difficult times followed when the depression set in between the 1920-1932. Many of the boat owners had financial problems, which in turn affected the shipyards in Sunnmøre. In spite of these difficulties, the yard survived and in the latter part of the 1930s, a completely new shipyard was equipped and ready to carry out maritime repairs and maintenance work.

Ulstein Mek. Verksted was very seldom involved in mandatory Second World War production, but was very much involved in refurbishing the dilapidated fishing fleet after the war. This resulted in yet another period of growth and extra workers had to be employed. From 1917 until 1957, the actual production area increased from 50 m² to 1 870 m². In 1963, the peak year, the order book was so full that work had to be sub-contracted out to other yards, sister companies or partners. In 1974, Ulstein merged with Hatlø Verft, and became Ulstein Hatlø AS, a fusion that more than doubled the company's capacity.

At this time, the North Sea oil industry was expanding and Ulstein Hatlø AS began to concentrate more on offshore support and supply vessels for the oil industry. The enterprise grew such that once again some projects had to be sub-contracted to other yards. The Ulstein Group also manufactured equipment of its own design and production, such that the ship-owners could have their ships custom built. In the 1970s, Ulstein Hatlø established marketing and sales divisions in four different countries and eventually the Group became a truly international concern with sales offices and yards in Europe, Asia and the USA. Ulstein International was established in 1988 as a part of Ulstein Holding AS. The company's objective was to make Ulstein internationally recognised as a reliable supplier of products and services to maritime industries worldwide.

In 1999, the Ulstein Group (except for the shipyard) was bought up by the British company Vickers plc that shortly after became a part of Rolls-Royce. The concern is today managed by Rolls-Royce Marine AS, with approx. 3 500 employees in 24 countries. The Rolls-Royce Marine AS department Ship Technology Ulstein develops and markets concepts and integrated marine systems and offers engineering consultancy services. They develop new concepts for specialised vessels for use in the oil industry, and other types of specialised ships for other purposes. These ships are built in yards all over the world. Rolls-Royce Commercial Marine's main office is in Ulsteinvik and here approx. 100 persons are employed. In addition, Rolls-Royce Marine Propulsion is also located in Ulsteinvik. This company develops and produces propeller systems for main propulsion and thruster units for

ships and offshore mobile drilling rigs for the international market and employs approx. 400 including the work force at Volda.

The shipyards in the earlier Ulstein Group are now gathered under Ulstein Mekaniske Verksted Holding ASA, which comprises Ulstein Verft AS, Ulstein Elektro AS, a shipping company and a local property company. The company has approx. 400 employees.

Kleven Maritime AS is also an important company in Ulsteinvik. It was started by M. Kleven in 1939, offering repairs and maintenance services to the ever-expanding motorised and technically advanced local fishing fleet. The company has since then grown into one of Europe's

leading suppliers of highly specialised ships to the offshore oil industry, freighters for chemical products, fruit-juice and other specialised tankers. They also deliver fish factory ships, seismic vessels and coast guard ships. Three of the new types of Hurtigruten ships were built here at Kleven.

A business phenomenon known as "The Maritime Cluster" on Sunnmøre is well known. It comprises of the two key companies mentioned above and several other companies who mostly supply products and services to the shipping industry. In addition, there are many smaller and medium sized companies and sub-contractors that compete against each other in a tough and competitive local environment, but also co-operate to supply national and international clients.

On the headland of **Osnes** near Ulsteinvik, lies Oshaugen, where there is one of Norway's largest burial mounds, approx. 45 m in diameter and 5–6 m high. Along the outer shipping channel on Sunnmøre, there are 5–6 similar, large burial mounds measuring more than 30 m in diameter, probably dating from 300-400 A.D. Many other burial mounds have been found close to the village of Ulsteinvik. Archaeological digs at Osnes have revealed that people lived here as long as 5 000 years ago.

To starboard, we can see the village of **Ulstein**. Along the river, Ulsteinelven, which runs through the village, are signs of settlements dating back to the Iron Age (p 83). The first church at Ulstein was probably built at the end of the 12th century, where it remained until 1878 when it was moved to Ulsteinvik. It is said that when a burial took place it experienced the same problem as many other churches; namely, that the dead had to be buried in consecrated soil but it could take weeks before a priest could come to the grave. To solve the problem, a vertical pipe was placed on the coffin before the grave was filled in. Therefore, when the priest finally came he simply poured consecrated soil down the pipe onto the coffin and thereafter the pipe was pulled up.

62°21'23"N   5°46'E   + 0 hrs 09 min ①

On our port side is the island of **Remøya** (3.6 km²), behind and northwest of Leinøya. Commerce on the island is mostly related to coastal and polar fishing. There is a bridge connecting the islands of Runde and Leinøya.

On our port side is the island of **Runde** (6.2 km²), north of Remøya. Runde is one of the country's best-known islands, both nationally and internationally. Especially famous is **Rundebranden** (294 m above sea level), on the islands west side. It is the country's most southerly bird cliff. It plunges almost vertically down into the sea

TORVIK - ÅLESUND | **DAY 2**

and is home to many species of rare birds. Rundebranden is the home of about 500 000 individuals, amongst them Puffins, Shags and Kittiwakes (p 218). About 240

different species can be observed here and approx. 80 of these actually nest on the island. Rundebranden is said to be the most 'complete' bird sanctuary in Norway. Four bird sanctuary areas were established on Runde in 1981 where all visits, landings or tourism is prohibited during the birds' nesting season from 15th March until 31st August. Of indigenous species, only the Cormorant and the Little Auk are not found here. The cliffs offer nesting places for the country's largest colonies of Fulmars, Gannets and Skuas.

At the foot of Rundebranden, there are several caves. The largest, Storhulen, is 120 m deep and a smaller one penetrates 64 m into the cliff. In fair weather, these caves can be reached by boat. Runde is also known for its special geological formations - deep holes and pillars of stone on the beach rising straight up from the sea.

The highest point on Runde is the mountain called **Varden** (332 m above sea level) in the southeast. The village of **Goksøyr** is on the northeast and the farm, also known as Runde, is on the southeast of the island. Runde Bridge connects the island to the rest of Herøy (opened 1982). Before the bridge was opened, the only access to the island was by boat.

Runde's main income is derived from fishing, farming, market gardening and tourism.

Runde has a long history of shipwrecks and dramatic events of which some are legendary. A ship from the Spanish Armada was wrecked here in the late 16th century. One of the most dramatic incidents was in March 1880 when eight persons, most of them from the island itself, lost their lives here.

There are many shipwrecks lying on the reefs and skerries surrounding the island. One of them is the Dutch East India trader, the "Akarendam" that sailed off course en route from the Netherlands to Java and sank here on 8th March 1725. The ship was 145 feet long, had a crew of 200 and a cargo of 230 000 Dutch florins. Five of the 19 chests containing the coins were salvaged and brought back to the Netherlands. In the summer of 1972 three

sports divers found approx. 6 000 gold and some 39 000 silver coins. The coins were of Dutch, Spanish-Dutch and Spanish-American origin. The treasure was eventually divided between the finders (67.6 %), the Norwegian State (25.4 %) and the Netherlands (7 %).

On March 12th 1992 the 75 361 tonne Panama-registered ship, "Arisan", ran aground just west of Runde. Approx. 150 tonnes of heavy fuel oil and diesel leaked out resulting in a 32.5 km stretch of contaminated shoreline. 570 tonnes of the fuel oil was pumped out of the wreck but several thousand birds were killed due to the spillage.

Runde, a coastal lighthouse southwest of the island is one of the oldest in Norway, built in 1767 as a private lighthouse. It used coal and peat fuel that was fired in an iron pot. The flame was visible to the seafarers, but the peat gave poor light. In 1807, the lighthouse was taken over by the state but was closed down the same year so as not to aid the English enemy fleets during the Napoleonic Wars (p 85). In 1826, the lighthouse was upgraded from the iron pot system to a closed, coal-fired light in a square tower. In 1858, a 27 m tall oil-fired cast iron tower was lit outermost on Kvalvågneset, and in 1935, the lighthouse was replaced by a concrete tower further up the hill. It was finally automated in 2002. The light is 49.5 m over the sea level at high tide and has a range of 19 nautical miles. Today, the station is comprised of six buildings; the lighthouse, the forge, living quarters, combined cowshed and barn and an oil and wood store. For many years the lighthouse keepers and their families, assistants, teachers, servants and farm animals all lived around the small courtyard.

62°22'N   5°47'23"E   + 0 hrs 12 min

Close to our port side, we pass the small island of **Vattøya**, which has a fine harbour. The island has played a minor role as a trading centre for fish, especially herring. There is a burial mound here dating back 2–3000 years. The main income came from farming, herring and lobster fishing. The last permanent residents left the island in 1973.

On our port side is the parish of Bølandet on Leinøya.

62°24'N   5°49'E   + 0 hrs 21 min ②

Grasøyane is a group of islands that lie outermost in Rundefjorden, located between the islands of **Runde** and **Godøy,** in Giske municipality. These islands and the area surrounding them are, like Runde, restricted areas during the sea birds' nesting period from 15th April to 15th August. Here we also find colonies of two types of seals.

In an old description of this island from 1766 it states; "Græs-øen, (Grass Island) is a round, flat grassy island that close to its beaches along the cliffs has a few large caves that may serve as a sanctuary for the traveller in inclement weather. Here they may venture outside all year round, in winter as in summer. For this it may be used and at times it will even yield some hay as well". This is possibly the origin of the island's name.

Grasøyane, a beacon lighthouse, was listed as a cultural heritage site in 1999. The station was built in 1886. 100 years later, it was automated and de-manned in 1986. The station has two towers made of timber; however, the corner tower was destroyed during an aerial attack in 1945. The second tower is a 16 m high cast iron tower built in 1950, in typical colours - red with a white belt, the last of its kind built in Norway. The light itself is 29 m above sea level and has a range of 7–9 nautical miles. Thirty-six solar panels provide electricity for the station. There is a machine room, some outhouses, a boathouse and a jetty.

The ship is sailing along Hareidlandet that can be seen on our starboard side with its steep mountainsides and small communities along the coast.

On our starboard is the village of **Flø** situated at the foot of the mountain called **Sneldelida** (623 m above sea level), that has no shelter from the Norwegian Sea beyond. Farming is the main source of income for the parish but the fine sandy and pebble stone beaches and beautiful nature have led to an increasing number of tourists.

Between the islands of Runde on our port side and Godøya up ahead is **Breidsundet**, a, 270 m deep subsea trench.

The municipality of **Hareid** is located on the east side of the island, Hareidlandet (p 44).

Behind **Hareidlandet** lies the fjord **Vartdalsfjorden**. A road tunnel, 7 765 m in length and 287 m at its deepest point, has been constructed under the fjord. The tunnel, part of the Eikesund communication system, is currently world's deepest road tunnel. It was opened in February 2008 and provides a mainland connection for the island municipalities of Hareid, Herøy, Sande and Ulstein.

Sulafjorden stretches in a north-easterly direction north of Hareidlandet, between the peninsula Sula and Hareidlandet.

Sulafjorden and Vartdalsfjorden come together in Storfjorden. Storfjorden has many branches and one of these is the famous Geirangerfjorden.

Approx. 62°26'N 5°57'E

We cross the municipal boundary between Ulstein and Giske municipalities on the port side

We cross the municipal boundary between Ulstein and Sula municipalities on the starboard side

Giske municipality

Municipal coat of arms, significance: Reference to the Giske family.
Meaning of name: Norse gizki, possibly meaning 'textile'.
Municipal seat: Valderhaug. (Pop. -).
Position: 62°30'N 6°08'29"E.
Area: 40 km². **Population:** 6 647.
Pop. density: 166.2 /km².
Area distribution: Farming 28 %, forestry 2 %, fresh water 3 %, other 67 %.
Trade and industry: Fishing and fish food processing. Shipyards. Furniture factories. Some farming. About 25 % of the population works in Ålesund.
Places to return to: Alnes lighthouse, Eilivsrøysa, Skjonghellaren, Giske church.
Giske municipality's home page: www.giske.kommune.no

In 1943, the German forces seized the Italian ship "Fidelitas" in Bordeaux, France and used the ship in commercial service. On 27th November 1944, she was in a convoy with another ship and four German escort vessels sailing towards Ålesund. In Sulafjorden, the convoy was attacked by ten Australian Beaufighters from the RAF squadrons 404 and 489 using machine guns and torpedoes. "Fidelitas" and two other ships were badly damaged. "Fidelitas" eventually sank and 35 of her crew were killed. In 1988, the wreck was found by divers in 107 m of water.

62°26'46"N 6°00'E   + 0 hrs 31 min ③

The headland to starboard is **Eltraneset,** on the northwest side of the island of Sula in Sula municipality (p 51). Next is **Heissafjorden**, with the villages of Langevåg (p 51) and Spjelkavik lying innermost in the fjord.

Godøya (10.87 km²) in Giske is on our port side. The mountainous island of Godøya is one of the four largest islands in the municipality with **Storehornet** (497 m above sea level) located in the centre. **Alnesvatnet**, approx. 1 km² on top of Storehornet, is used as a reservoir, providing drinking water for the islands in the municipality. The most important sources of income are fishing, fish trading and fish food processing. A subsea

tunnel, opened in 1989, 3 844 m long and 153 m below sea level on the northeast side of Godøya, provides a road connection with the neighbouring island of Giske to the northeast.

On the southeast point of Godøya, close to where Hurtigruten sails is the lighthouse at Hogsteinen. It was built in 1857, outermost on a stone breakwater. It was closed down in 1905. The tower, 11 m high, was originally built by Nes Jernverk, but was later replaced with a cast iron tower. The lighthouse is now a listed building and the white tower is still an important landmark.

Eilifrøysa, located on Hogsteinen is one of the biggest burial mounds found in Norway. The mound measures approx. 40 m in diameter, approx. 5 m high and dates back to A.D. 300-400. The mound was found to contain amongst other things, a "vestlandskjel" (cooking vessel typical of the area) in bronze, two silver beakers, a 311 gram gold ring, a medallion of gold and ashes from a cremation. It was once wrongly assumed that Earl Eilif was buried here, hence the name, however he lived much later.

Godøya's name has a mythological origin. It comes from the name Gudøy (God island). It is thought that the outer part of the island near the mountain, **Lesten**, was used as a site for sacrifices or punishment in pagan times. Sacrifices were thrown off the steep cliff at the moment the sun rose above the horizon. The pagan place of worship, dedicated to the Norse god Odin (p 163), could have been located on the farm, Godøgården on the island's south side. Godøgården was the biggest farm on the island and in 1864 had a courtyard containing 128 buildings. In 1945, approx. 90 of these buildings were demolished or moved. Later excavations on the farm revealed a sacrificial stone with runic inscriptions. In the superstitious era of the Middle Ages, Lesten in Sunnmøre was thought to be the home of sorcerers, witches, demons and trolls (p 231).

Northwest on Godøya is the small village of **Alnes** where the houses are tightly spaced and little has changed since 1905. Alnes was once the biggest fishing village in Sunnmøre.

On Alnes, we find one of the island's two lighthouses. The first was only a small light beacon, built in a small timber hut with an oil lamp to guide local cod fishermen and funded by local donations in 1853. In 1869, the lighthouse was taken over by the authorities and a new timber building was built in 1878 to improve the living conditions for the lighthouse keeper, with further improvements made in 1892. Before 1928 gas and paraffin was used as fuel for the light, later it was electrified. The present steel structure tower was built in 1937 and is 18 m high. The station was automated and de-manned in 1982 and became a listed building in 2000. The light is 36 m above sea level with a range of 16.4 nautical miles.

Located on the north-easterly point on the small island of **Furkenholmen**, was probably Sunnmøre's largest fishing village in the 1880s. In the season February-March, on average 500-600 men could be staying on the island at any one time working on 90 to 100 boats out from Furkenholmen. In 1884, there were probably 1 000 men on the island, living in large cabins with as many as 120 men in each. The last of these cabins were demolished in the 1960s.

Godøya has many ancient relics and remains from Stone Age settlements. Approx. 130 burial mounds are found here, 60 of these have been dated to A.D. 500-600.

Northeast of Giske is the small island of **Havstein**.

Giske (2.5 km²) and Valderøya (6.5 km²) on our port side, are the two other islands in Giske municipality – Giske lies furthest to the west (p 73).

62°27'N 6°00'E   + 0 hrs 35 min

Our ship is in **Breidsundet**. Hareidlandet is behind and to our starboard. Sulafjorden is on our starboard side, thereafter the peninsula of Sula and the fjord Heissafjorden. Ahead and to our starboard is the island of Heissa with the characteristic peak known as **Sukkertoppen** ('Sugar Mountain').

Godøya is on our port side.

Approx. 62°27'33"N   6°03'47"E

We cross the municipal boundary between Sula and Ålesund municipalities on starboard side

Ålesund municipality

Municipal coat of arms, significance: Depicts fishing.
Meaning of name: Probably from the name ål = eel, but could also come from áll = "strip, narrow trench".
Municipal seat: Ålesund (pop. 41 478).
Position: 62°28'N 6°09'E.
Area: 98 km². **Population:** 41 478.
Pop. density: 462.2 /km².
Area distribution: Farming 2 %, forestry 12 %, fresh water 6 %, other 80 %.
Trade and industry: Fish food processing. Shipyards. Mechanical, graphic, plastics, textile and clothing industries.
Places to return to: (p 72). More information at: www.virtualalesund.com
Ålesund municipality's home page: www.alesund.kommune.no

The town of **Ålesund** is built on several inter-connected islands and has some of the features of a typical "canal town". The island of Heissa (4 km²) on our starboard is the most westerly of the islands. The well-known and characteristic mountaintop called Sukkertoppen (Sugar Mountain) (316 m above sea level) often reminds past and present mariners of her so-called "sister" peak in Rio de Janeiro, Brazil.

The ship docks at the quayside in Ålesund

Ålesund will be described after the return from Geirangerfjorden in the summer season. For those travelling in the winter season, the information continues on p 68.

The ship continues to Geiranger with return to Ålesund   + 0 hrs 00 min

LARGER MAP P**390**

The ship leaves Ålesund, heading for the famous Geirangerfjord. Ahead is the island of Godøya (p 49), and on our starboard side Giske and Valderøya (p 72). On our port side, Sukkertoppen on the island of Heissa.

Approx. 62°27'N 6°03'E ①

We cross the municipal boundary between Ålesund and Sula municipalities

Sula municipality

Municipal coat of arms, significance: Reflects upon the name, Sula.
Meaning of name: Norse Súla, 'cleft', between mountains or coastline, possibly 'pillar, column or strut'.
Municipal seat: Langevåg (pop. -).
Position: 62°27'N 6°13'E.
Area: 59 km². **Population:** 7 538.
Pop. density: 127.8 /km².
Area distribution: Farming 3 %, forestry 19 %, fresh water 2 %, other 75 %.
Trade and industry: Fishing. Shipyards. Textile and furniture industries. 48 % of the working population work outside the municipality.
Sula municipality's home page: www.sula.kommune.no

On our port side is Heissafjorden, the boundary between Ålesund and Sula is in the middle of the fjord. At the head of the fjord is the village of Spjelkavik, today regarded as a suburb of Ålesund. In Spjelkavik, there are furniture, timber, textile and plastics industries.

In **Langevåg** on Sulaøya's north side, there are textile and clothing factories, food processing industries, timber production and mechanical workshops. O. A. Devolds Sønner A/S, bespoke clothing manufacturer, is located in Langevåg. The company was founded in 1850 and had as many as 800 to 900 employees at one time. Their factory chimney is an unusual cultural landmark in Langevåg. The D/S "Thorolf", Scandinavia's oldest steam-powered wooden vessel, built in 1911, belonged to this factory. She ferried salesmen, raw materials and finished products along the entire coast.

In the village of **Fiskarstranda**, on the island's north side and inside the fjord we find Fiskarstranda Slip & Motorverksted, founded in 1909. The yard builds and repairs ferries and fishing boats.

Between Eltraneset and Langevåg, inside the fjord and on the north side of Sula, is a large cultural landscape containing ancient relics. Several ancient dwelling sites are found along the seashore, the oldest dates from the Iron Age (A.D. 0-200), and farms from Roman times (p 83) up to the 18th century.

About 6 km inside Heissafjorden lies the wreck of M/S "Øygar" (1908). The boat was used as a passenger ferry and as a coast guard vessel, patrolling Icelandic and Norwegian waters. The Germans renamed it 'Bisam NB07' and used her as a coast guard vessel, and later renamed her 'V-5507'. She escaped damage in the war and was later re-instated as a passenger vessel used along the coast. After long and faithful service, she was finally scuttled in November 1983 and is now resting in 23 m of water.

On our port side is Eltraneset. We are entering Sulafjorden - ahead is the village of Brandal.

62°27'17"N 6°03'30"E

We cross the municipal boundary of Hareid municipality on starboard side

Hareid municipality

Municipal coat of arms, significance: Depicts the battle at Hjørungavåg/Liavågen in Hareid.
Meaning of name: First part the island name hod, 'spray', last part eid, 'neck of land'.
Municipal seat: Hareid (pop. 3 647).
Position: 62°22'N 6°02'E
Area: 82 km². **Population:** 4 675.
Pop. density: 57.0 /km².
Area distribution: Farming 8 %, forestry 18 %, fresh water 6 %, other 68 %.
Trade and industry: Mechanical industry. Furniture, food processing and textile industries. Coastal and foreign fishing. Some scattered farming in combination with fishing.
Places to return to: Brandal Arctic Museum. Hjørungavåg.
Activities to return to: Hjørungavåg plays.
Hareid municipality's home page: www.hareid.kommune.no

Kvitneset is a headland at the foot of the mountain called Signalhornet (627 m above sea level). The mountain is in Hareid municipality on the island of Hareidlandet, (on our starboard side), opposite Eltraneset, on the other side of Sulafjorden. On Kvitneset are the remains of a German coastal fort, used from 1941-1945. At the most, there were as many as 500 German troops stationed at Kvitneset. Located close by was a prisoner of war camp housing more than 100 prisoners, mostly from Russia and some from Yugoslavia. The prisoners were used as labourers on the fort.

To starboard on Hareidlandet, we can see the parish of **Brandal** (pop. 313). Formerly, Brandal was an important harbour for Arctic fishing and seal hunting. People living here started seal hunting in the Arctic Sea, on Greenland and Newfoundland in 1898. Brandal was the home port for 47 of these vessels from the very beginning until the last hunting trip made in 1998. Factories ashore processed the seal products when the boats returned with their catches. Oil was extracted from the seal blubber and the pelts were processed. Polar bears and musk oxen were also caught and sold to zoos in Europe. While waiting to be sold the musk oxen were sent to pastures in the mountains, the polar bears were kept in cages in the sheds and the walruses swam around under the floorboards of the sheds.

The Arctic Museum in Brandal is a monument to the strong ties Brandal once had to Norwegian seal hunting. The museum exhibits the preserved polar vessel, the "Aarvak", built in 1912, now in dry dock, and houses approx. 2 000 exhibition items. This Arctic Museum is the only polar museum in Norway south of Tromsø.

62°24'N   6°05'E   + 0 hrs 30 min ②

On our starboard side, in between the mountains, **Ska-fjellet** (573 m above sea level) and **Melshornet** (668

m above sea level) we can see **Hareid** (pop. 3 647), the administrative and industrial centre in Hareid municipality. Here we find electronics, technology, plastics/GRP and production industries. One of the major industries here manufactures plastic vacuum toilets for ships and offshore platforms.

A previous church in Hareid burned down after being hit by lightning in 1806. A new church was built the following year. The current church was built in 1877, a long-house-style church made of timber with floral decorations inside. The church seats 500. The altarpiece is from 1660. It was bought at an auction in Stavanger in 1915 and moved to Hareid. It was refurbished for the church's centenary celebrations in 1977 and craftsmen spent almost 1 000 working hours on restoring the altarpiece.

From Hareid there is a fast boat service to Ålesund, Valderøya and Vigra airport and a car ferry connection to Sulasundet on Sula.

The village of **Hjørungavåg** (pop. 940) is located near Hareidlandet's most easterly point, southeast of Hareid, by the foot of Melshornet (668 m above sea level). The place is famous for the battle between Håkon Jarl's conscripted army and the feared Joms Viking army in 986. The battle at Hjørungavåg is described in Snorre Sturlason's King's Sagas and is the first battle fought in the attempt to achieve supremacy over Norway.

Håkon Jarl (Earl) (approx. 935-995) was the King of the Danes, Harald Blåtann's Earl in Norway. Harald Blåtann (died 985) and his son, Svend Tveskæg, ruled over large areas of Sweden and Norway, but was displeased with Håkon Jarl because he refrained from collecting taxes on their behalf, and he led a heathen and dissolute lifestyle. Therefore, Svend Tveskæg summoned the Joms Vikings, got them drunk and had two of their chieftains, Sigvalde Jarl and Bue Digre, promise that within three days they would kill Håkon Jarl or have him driven out of Norway. (The Joms Vikings were a group of Vikings that lived in Joms Castle on the coast of Germany or Poland, possibly by the town of Wollin, near Stettin in Germany. They existed in the 10th and 11th centuries but in 1043, King Magnus den Gode (the Good) attacked Joms Castle, destroyed it, and killed them all.)

The winter when the two Joms Viking's chieftains had made their promises, a large Joms force went north along the Norwegian coast. They plundered and killed all they came across. Word of their deeds reached Håkon Jarl who conscripted an army from all of Trøndelag, Nordmøre, Sunnmøre and Romsdal, Namdalen and Hålogaland.

The Joms Vikings came up from the south, sailed beyond Stad and landed first at Herøya (p 43), thereafter on the outside of Hareidlandet. They were not aware of the large army gathered in the north. They were told, however that Håkon Jarl had sailed into Hjørundfjorden with three ships or less and that he was not aware of the Joms Viking's army. They hurriedly boarded their ships and sailed into Hjørundfjorden. Håkon Jarl and his son, Eirik Jarl had in fact 180 ships assembled in the fjord, some of them quite small. When the two were told that Sigvalde Jarl and the Joms Vikings were moored outside Hareidlandet, they rowed their boats west to find them and the two armies met in battle at Hjørungavågen.

The battle was fought furiously with great losses on both sides - mostly Norwegians as the Joms Vikings were more capable warriors. However, when the battle eventually was fought at close quarters, the Norwegians gained the advantage. During a hailstorm with unusually large hailstones, Sigvalde Jarl with his Viking army fled the scene on board 70 ships. Bue Digre remained with his 25 ships and continued the battle, but he was eventually outnumbered and had to admit defeat. After being wounded, Bue Digre grabbed two chests of gold, one under each arm and shouted at top of his voice: "Overboard, all of Bue's men!", and dived overboard. Many of his men followed, others were killed on board the ships. The survivors, fewer than 30 men, were taken prisoner and brought ashore. Twelve were killed but the remaining 18 or so were pardoned and eventually released.

In 1986, a monument was raised to commemorate the battle in Hjørungavåg 1000 years ago. It shows the bows of three longships rising towards each other. Several other monuments are found in the area and each summer the Hjørungavåg-spelet (play) is performed to commemorate the events that happened before and after the battle.

One of the largest companies in Hjørungavåg today is an expanding oil-related technology company with more than 250 employees and sister companies in USA and Canada. Another cornerstone industry is a fish food processing plant with a capacity of 250 tonnes of fish per day.

Legends of sea serpents and monsters are common around the world. This also includes the waters around Sula. In the 13th century, as the story goes, a sea serpent blocked the entrance to the narrow Hjørungavågen. The serpent was large and said to have had 12 humps but the bishop of the time managed to drive the serpent away with prayers and holy water.

In March 1999, two fishermen claim that they saw, in clear, calm waters, for several minutes, a large animal that could have been a sea serpent in Sulafjorden, southwest of Sula. In June that same year, also in calm and clear weather conditions a serpent-like animal, 25-30 metres long and 1.5 m around the body, was observed for almost an hour, and was filmed whilst it was swimming close to the shore eating from a dead whale's body floating in the fjord. Several people saw the sea monster at the same time.

62°23'N 6°10'41"E   + 0 hrs 40 min

On our starboard side is **Sulasundet** with car ferry connection to Hareide on Hareidlandet and behind we can see **Tverrfjellet** (776 m above sea level).

We are sailing into **Storfjorden** (86 km long), Norway's ninth longest fjord, on our way towards Geiranger. Here Sulafjorden and **Vartdalsfjorden** on the port side become one and the depth is approx. 440 m. Vartdalsfjorden continues on our port side and to the rear of Hareidlandet.

We can see the northern part of Ørsta municipality on starboard side

Ørsta municipality

Municipal coat of arms, significance: Mountains mirrored in the fjord.
Meaning of name: Norse ørstr, name of fjord.
Municipal seat: Ørsta (pop. 6 382).
Position: 62°12'N 6°09'E.
Area: 805 km². **Population:** 10 162.
Pop. density: 12.6 /km².
Area distribution: Farming 5 %, forestry 16 %, fresh water 2 %, other 76 %.
Trade and industry: Furniture, metal, food processing and electronics industries. Farming and animal husbandry.
Places to return to: Hotel Union, Øye.
Activities to return to: Hiking in the Sunnmøre Alps.
Ørsta municipality's home page: www.orsta.kommune.no

62°23'36"N 6°15'E	+ 0 hrs 49 min ③

On our starboard side, we can see the villages of **Barstadvika** and **Romestrand** with the mighty Sunnmøre Alps in the background. Barstadvika is situated between the high peaks of **Klovekinn** (920 m above sea level) in the southwest, **Middagshornet** (1091 m above sea level) behind the parish, **Jønshornet** (1419 m above sea level) in the east and Festøykollen in the northeast.

On our port side is the village of **Eikrem,** located on Sula.

62°24'N 6°19'19"E	+ 0 hrs 51 min ④

Also on Sula and to our port side are **Solevåg**, **Sunde** and **Leirvåg.** A car ferry connection operates from Sunde to **Festøya** in Ørsta.

On our starboard side and at the foot of **Festøykollen** (911 m above sea level) we can see **Festøya**, just west of the entrance to Hjørundfjorden. From Festøya to **Sunde** in Sula and to **Hundeidvik** there is a car ferry service.

Hjørundfjorden (35 km long) on our starboard side is a branch of Storfjorden and it cuts its way through the near vertical **Sunnmøre Alps** - the common name given to the mountain range either side Hjørundfjorden. The fjord splits further in into **Norangsfjorden** and the short **Storfjorden**. Innermost in Norangsfjorden we find the popular tourist community of **Øye** with the famous and distinctive hotel, Union Hotell,

© SVEIN LUNDE

© UNION HOTELL ØYE

which opened in 1891. For a long time the hotel was a favourite meeting place of Europe's aristocracy and elite. Amongst prominent guests were Kaiser Wilhelm II of Germany, Queen Wilhelmina of the Netherlands, King Oscar II of Sweden, King Haakon VII and Queen Maud of Norway, the "Sherlock Holmes" author Sir Arthur Conan Doyle, the polar explorers Roald Amundsen and Fridtjof Nansen and the Danish author, Karen Blixen.

In the 1800s and the first half of the 1900s the area attracted mountain climbers and other nature lovers from abroad. The farmers in the district started a transport service for tourists. With their numbered horse-drawn carriages, they brought tourists from where they had gone ashore from the cruise ships at Øye, up through the beautiful, wild valleys of Norangsdalen and Nibbedalen that connect Øye and the community of Hellesylt near Geirangerfjorden, where they were taken on board the ship once again. The journey took them past Øyebakken, a stop along the way where the passengers and horses could take a well-earned rest.

The mountains surrounding Hjørundfjorden are: on the west side **Festøykollen** (911 m above sea level) and Jønshornet, on the east side is **Sunnavindsnipa** (1 367 m above sea level), **Skopphornet** (1 226 m above sea level) and **Blåbretinden** (1 476 m above sea level).

Approx. 62°24'N 6°22'E

We cross the municipal boundary between Ørsta and Sykkylven municipalities on starboard side

Sykkylven municipality

Municipal coat of arms, significance: Resembles Sykkylvfjorden.
Meaning of name: From Norse sikifkir, from sik, "small bay, pond" and iflir, "low wetland".
Municipal seat: Sykkylven (Aure) (pop. 3 996).
Position: 62°24'N 6°35'E. **Area:** 338 km².
Population: 7 467. **Pop. density:** 22.1 /km².
Distribution: Farming 5 %, forestry 22 %, fresh water 3 %, other 71 %.
Trade and industry: Furniture and interior decoration production. Mechanical industry. Farming and animal husbandry. Fish farming.
Activities to return to: Hiking in the Sunnmøre Alps.
Sykkylven municipality's home page: www.sykkylven.kommune.no

On our starboard is the parish of **Hundeidvik** at the east side of the entrance to Hjørundfjorden, located next to Sunnavindsnipa in the west and Skopphornet to the east.

Approx. 62°24'N 6°22'E

We cross the municipal boundary between Sula and Ålesund (p 50) municipalities on port side

On our port side is the industrial community of **Vegsund** in Ålesund municipality, which is located in a bay behind the headland of **Flisneset**. It is part of the village of Spjelkavik (p 67), which has a variety of industry - textiles, plastics, furniture, timber production and mechanical workshops. After Vegsund are the villages of **Emblem** and **Aksla**.

On our starboard side and at the foot of Skopphornet are the small settlements of **Kurset**, **Litlevik** and **Tusvika**.

Ahead and to starboard, we see the municipal centre of Sykkylven/Aure.

62°25'28"N 6°29'32"E   + 1 hr 16 min ⑤

Sykkylvsfjorden (8 km in length) to starboard is situated between Skopphornet and Blåbretinden in the west and Sandvikshornet, **Langfjella** and **Dravlausnyken** (1 056 m above sea level) in the east. The majority of the municipality's population live along the fjord and at the head of the fjord is the village of **Straumsgjerdet** (pop. 479). Most of the working population is employed in furniture manufacture.

From **Ørsneset,** located at the east side of the fjord there is a car ferry connection to **Magerholm,** seen on our port side. This is the busiest ferry crossing in Møre and Romsdal county. Out on the headland are six well-preserved burial mounds dating from the Iron Age. It is assumed that these mounds were built as boundary demarcations for the large properties located at Aure in the Iron Age (p 83).

Close to the entrance to the fjord, we can see the two industrial areas of Ikornnes on the western side and Sykkylven/Aure on the eastern side of the fjord. Sykkylvsbroen, an 890 m long concrete box-girder bridge (completed in 2000) connects these two places.

Ikornnes (pop. 826) is best known for its furniture industry. Ekornes ASA (approx. 1 500 employees) was founded in 1934 and is Norway's largest manufacturer of mattresses, chairs, sofas, other home and office furniture and foam rubber. Their 'Stressless' lounge chair is one of the world's best known brands of furniture. The company's products are sold in over 20 countries worldwide.

The municipal centre, **Sykkylven/Aure** inside Ørsneset has furniture and timber-related industries and mechanical workshops.

Aure is known as an old church site. Burial mounds have also been found nearby and relics originating from people and farms have been discovered dating back to 800 B.C. Here we can find evidence of dwellings, structures, hearths, and several pits, that were probably used in preparing food on fires or embers. Some of the support structures for these houses could be 1–2 m in diameter, 70–90 cm deep and are some of the largest found in Scandinavia. It is believed that the buildings these structures supported must have been 40 - 60 m long and could have been ceremonial halls where chieftains and dignitaries would meet for ritual or festive occasions. This hall was in use from approx. A.D. 100 until A.D. 500-600. In the same area are remains of 10 to 15 other houses were also found, somewhat smaller than the hall, some 8 m and 15 m long with smaller supports. These houses date back to the Bronze and Iron Ages (p 83).

The current church in Sykkylven was built in 1990 in concrete and is a so-called 'working church'.

62°26'30"N 6°37'E	+ 1 hr 32 min

We are continuing into Storfjorden and the mountain called **Sandvikshornet** (876 m above sea level) is on our starboard side. The depth of the fjord is approx. 590 m. We pass the farm named **Sandvika.**

Approx. 62°27'N   6°41'E

We cross the municipal boundary between Ålesund and Skodje municipalities on port side

Skodje municipality

Municipal coat of arms, significance: Skodje Bridge over Skodjestraumen.
Meaning of name: Norse Skodin, 'skad' (uncertain), vin, 'pasture'.
Municipal seat: Skodje (pop. 1 673).
Position: 62°30'N 6°41'E.
Area: 120 km². **Population:** 3 668.
Pop. density: 30.6 /km².
Area distribution: Farming 5 %, forestry 48 %, fresh water 8 %, other 40 %.
Trade and industry: Wood- and furniture industry. Mechanical industry. Some farming. 60% of the working population works outside the municipality.
Skodje municipality's home page:
www.skodje.kommune.no

© PER EIDE/DESTINATION ÅLESUND & SUNNMØRE

62°27'N 6°38'E	+ 1 hr 34 min

On our port side we are passing **Heggebakk** near **Meraftafjellet** (576 m above sea level), thereafter **Nesvika**, at the entrance to **Honningdalsvågen** with the village of **Glomset.** Thereafter, we have **Ytrevika** and Solnørvika.

The large farm, **Solnør,** innermost in **Solnørvika** has been active since the end of the 17th century and was then part of the Giske – Bjarkøy Estate (p 73). The existing main building was built in 1825 and was listed and protected in 1939. The farm has one of the country's largest private libraries with a collection of approx. 10 000 books.

Approx. 62°26'N   6°54'E

We cross the municipal boundary between Skodje and Ørskog municipalities on port side

Ørskog municipality

Municipal coat of arms, significance: Symbolises fur trade and forests.
Meaning of name: Norse øyr, 'gravel ridge', skog, 'forest'.
Municipal seat: Sjøholt (pop. 1 167).
Position: 62°29'N 6°48'42"E.
Area: 129 km². **Population:** 2 088.
Pop. density: 16.2 /km².
Area distribution: Farming 4 %, forestry 26 %, fresh water 3 %, other 67 %.
Trade and industry: Farming with dairy produce, market gardening and fruit production, fur- and fish farming and some plastic-, wood- and mechanical industries and some winter tourism.
Ørskog municipality's home page:
www.orskog.kommune.no

Remains of early settlements have been discovered on most of the farms near Storfjorden in Ørskog. Conditions were favourable in this area and it is assumed that the earliest settlements in Sunnmøre were established here.

The island of **Langskipsøya** at the mouth of Solnørvika was a busy port in the 17th century, exporting timber from Ørskog to Europe, especially to the Netherlands and Scotland (p 333). In the years 1603-1623, 113 shiploads of timber were exported to 30 different European destinations.

62°27'37"N 6°42'44"E	+ 1 hr 42 min ⑥

On our port side, we are passing **Håeim** and **Tyssegardene**. In the bay between them and the headland of **Gausneset** ahead and to our port side is **Sjøholt**. The main enterprises here are furniture, wood and plastics industries and some tourism.

Sjøholt's first hotel was a timber building, erected in 1887. It burned down in 1900, was rebuilt in 1901 and after many refurbishments, it is still in use today. As the fjords of Sunnmøre were 'discovered' by tourists at the end of the 19th century the number of visitors to Sjøholt increased. Sjøholt has also been a strategic military centre and is recorded as such on old maps.

The church at **Ørskog** is situated in Sjøholt. The existing church was consecrated in 1873. It is a longhouse style church with seating for 650. The old church became too small and was sold and later moved to Herøy municipality (p 42), where it is still in use today.

Historically, Ørskog was one of the most traditional centres of religious worship in the region and it was probably here that one of the first Christian churches was officially established. The first church in Ørskog was built during the period 1103-1123 during the reign of King Øystein Magnusson. According to ancient documents, a stave church could have been situated here as early as 1280.

We are passing **Røneset** to starboard, vis-à-vis Gausneset on our port side. Water depth here is 666 m.

The parish of **Dyrkorn** is ahead.

62°27'N   6°46'E   + 1 hr 50 min

In the bay to starboard, we can see the parishes of **Søvika** and **Ramstad**. Surrounding the bay are the mountains, **Rømerhornet** (866 m above sea level), **Auskjeret** (1 202 m above sea level) and **Ramstadvarden** (962 m above sea level).

On out port side we pass the smaller villages of **Åmdåm**, **Vestre** and **Vagsvik**.

Approx. 62°25'N   6°53'E

We cross the municipal boundaries between Ørskog on port side, Sykkylven on starboard side and Stordal municipalities.

Stordal municipality

Municipal coat of arms, significance: Symbolises furniture production.
Meaning of name: Norsk Stóladal, from the mountain 'Stolen'.
Municipal seat: Stordal (pop. 611).
Position: 62°23'N 6°59'E.
Area: 247 km². **Population:** 984.
Pop. density: 4.0 /km².
Area distribution: Farming 2 %, forestry 15 %, fresh water 1 %, other 82 %.
Trade and industry: Farming and animal husbandry. Furniture industry.
Places to return to: Mountain farm at Ytste Skotet. Stordal old church.
Activities to return to: Salmon fishing. Winter tourism.
Stordal municipality's home page: www.stordal.kommune.no

62°25'13"N   6°54'28"E   + 2 hrs 06 min ⑦

The mountain farm called **Ytste Skotet** (from 'ytterste', 'outermost') is on our starboard side before we pass the headland of **Skotshalsen**. The farm is located on a ridge 225 m above sea level, and was inhabited from the Viking period until 1954. It was renowned as a productive corn farm. It had 8–9 buildings and an area of approx. 3 000 hectares. Fishing was also part of the farm's livelihood. There is still quite a lot of activity here during the summer months, with haymaking and general work being carried out at the well-preserved farm.

Snorre Sturlason's King's Sagas tell the legend of King Olav the Holy (995-1030) (p 88), when sailing into Storfjorden in 1028–29, shot an arrow up into the mountainside with such force that a section of the mountain fell away and created Skotet. People have lived here since the time of King Håkon den Gode (920-960) – more than 1 000 years ago.

We are passing the headland of **Skotet** on our starboard side. On our port side, we have the village of **Dyrkorn**, which has a fish equipment factory. Between Dyrkorn and Skotet, Storfjorden is 682 meters deep.

62°23'N   6°55'26"E   + 2 hrs 14 min ⑧

On our port side, the village of **Stordal** lies at the entrance to the valley with the same name and the famous and protected salmon river, **Stordalselva**. The mountain known as **Varden** is located between **Dyrkorn** and Stordal. The Dyrkorn tunnel through the mountain provides a road connection between the two villages. For many years, Stordal has been one of Norway's largest furniture manufacturing communities and still has a sizeable production. There are also good conditions for farming.

The first church in Stordal was built around the year 1200. It stood on the same site as the present day

ROSEKIRKEN © KRISTIAN ALMÅS

Stordal gamle kirke (old church). It was a stave church with a tower at one end and is mentioned in documents from 1432.

Stordal old church was built in 1789 by the local farmers and remained in use until 1907. The octagonal-shaped church is also known as "Rosekirken", the Rose Church, because of the unique interior rose-painting decorations. The inside walls, ceiling, and beams are decorated with figures, ornaments and vines on a white background. The decorations are in Baroque and Renaissance styles both in motif and expression and is therefore one of Norway's most finely decorated churches. In 1884, this privately owned church was taken over by Stordal municipality. Since 1908 the church has been under the auspices of the "Foreningen til Norske Fortidsminnesmerkers Bevaring", the Association for the Preservation of Norwegian Cultural Heritage.

Stordal church is a longhouse-style timber church built in 1907, which seats 270. Some of the materials and furnishings from the first stave church have been re-used in the new church. Adjacent to the church is the Prestestova, which serves as a heated waiting room for children at christenings and for the congregation.

Stordalsholmen, the headland that appears just after Stordal, is the site where the last 'witch' in Norway is said to have been burnt at the stake, at the end of the 1700s.

Some episodes of the BBC TV-series, "Mälstrøm" (whirlpool) were filmed here some years ago. The series was shown on many TV stations throughout the world.

© SVEIN LUNDE

We are sailing alongside the mountain called **Jolgrøhornet** (1 253 m above sea level) on our port side and into Stranda municipality.

Stranda municipality

Municipal coat of arms, significance: Fjords and mountains.
Meaning of name: Strand, 'beach'.
Municipal seat: Stranda (pop. 2 483).
Position: 62°18'N 6°57'E.
Area: 866 km². **Population:** 4 500.
Pop. density: 5.2 /km².
Distribution: Farming 2 %, forestry 11 %, fresh water 2 %, other 85 %.
Trade and industry: Food processing-/furniture industry. Some metal/plastics and clothing industries. Farming and dairy products. Sheep and goats. Fruit growing. Tourism, especially in Geiranger.
Places to return to: Geirangerfjorden and Geiranger. Hellesylt.
Activities to return to: Winter sports at Stranda. Trips to the mountain farms at Geirangerfjorden.
Stranda municipality's home page: www.stranda.kommune.no

On our starboard side we are passing the parish of **Fausa**, and the mountain, **Roaldshornet** (1 230 m above sea level).

Further ahead, between Fausa and Stranda, we can see the farm called **Espehjelle** approx. 200 m up on the mountainside. The farm was cleared in 1560 and the oldest building there today dates from the 18th century. Along the dangerously steep track, seven schoolchildren walked 4 km – each way – to their school in Stranda in all sorts of weather up to the time the farm was abandoned in 1961.

Across the fjord from Espehjelle and up the mountainside is the farm called **Djupdalen**. As the forest around this farm had such a rich supply of timber, the farm also made rowing boats. The finished boats were lowered down the steep mountainside using ropes and steel wires.

62°19'42"N 6°57'09"E   + 2 hrs 32 min ⑨

The headland of **Uraneset** on our port side is located between Stordal and Gravaneset. On the small ochre coloured farm by the fjord across from Stranda, lived the Uranes family, between 1892 and 1929, with their ten children. They lived by keeping animals, cutting timber and fishing. In order to obtain more pastures for growing

hay they stretched a cable, some 1 500 m long, from the house by the fjord and up the mountainside behind where they built a hayloft. To attend school, the local children rowed across the fjord to Stranda.

On our starboard we can see **Stranda** which has the highest population density in the municipality. It is well known for its furniture industry, which started in 1907. Several of the furniture manufactures in Sunnmøre have a branch in Stranda and the furniture industry accounts for more than a third of employment in the area. The food producer Stabburet, Norway's biggest producer of deep-frozen pizzas, including the famous Grandiosa, are also here, and for that reason the place was given the nickname "Grandiosa-bygden" (Grandiosa village).

In an opinion poll, Stranda was named the best place to live in Norway. It has many recreational activities to offer and the winter sports centre situated in the unique nature of Strandafjellet is first class.

The first church at Stranda is presumed to have been built around the year 1000. A second church was built in the 15th century but this was destroyed by a giant wave caused by a landslide in 1731, when a huge rock fall plunged into the fjord on the other side (Skafjell catastrophe).

The present church at Stranda was built in 1838. The octagonal-shaped church was built of timber and could seat approx. 400. The valuable altar cabinet was probably made in Lübeck by a North German craftsman living in Bergen at the end of the 15th century and it was extended in the first half of the 17th century. Recessed in the altar-table is a white marble slab, which has probably been used in the church in Stranda for more than 800 years. The pulpit is from 1648. The church was refurbished in 1927.

Car ferry between Stranda and **Gravaneset** by Liabygda on our port side.

Liabygda (pop. 260) on our port side and on the other side of Storfjorden, at the entrance to **Norddalsfjorden**. Furniture industry.

Liabygda Church is a longhouse-style timber church built in 1917 and seats 165.

The mountain farm called **Ovrå** is situated east of Liabygda, at the start of Norddalsfjorden.

Sandvika and **Uksvik** on our starboard side, near **Uksneset**, before the ship steers into the narrow **Synnulvsfjorden**.

Approx. 62°17'N   7°01'E

We cross the municipal boundary between Stranda and Norddal municipalities

---

Norddal municipality

Municipal coat of arms, significance: Depicts strawberry farming.
Meaning of name: (-).
Administrative centre: Sylte (pop. 401).
Position: 62°17'50"N 7°15'37"E.
Area: 944 km². **Population:** 1 817.
Pop. density: 1.9 /km².
Area distribution: Farming 1 %, forestry 11 %, fresh water 5 %, other 83 %.
Trade and industry: Market gardening, fruit farming and furniture production. Farming and animal husbandry.
Activities to return to: Nature experiences.
Stordal municipality's home page: www.stordal.kommune.no

Up ahead is **Norddalsfjorden** which continues into the approx. 12 km long **Tafjorden**. In April 1934, approx. 2 million m³ of rock plunged into the fjord from a height of approx. 700–750 m above sea level. The wave created was 62 m high near the area where it occurred, 4 m high 7 km further out in the fjord and 15.6 m high at the head of the fjord approx. 7 km from the disaster area. This is believed to be one of Norway's worst natural catastrophes in the 20th century. Fourty lives were lost and many buildings, jetties and farms were swept away into the fjord.

The ship is now on a southerly heading and is entering the narrow Sunnylvfjorden with its steep mountainsides. The high mountain **Grøtet** (1 519 m above sea level) is on our port side and to our starboard, **Heimste** (1 336 m above sea level).

62°15'N   7°01'13"E   + 2 hrs 50 min ⑩

To our port side we pass **Røbbervika** where olivine (chrysolite) rock is mined. 500 000 tonnes of this rock is shipped annually to various steelworks, mostly in Europe and the USA.

Olivine, green in colour, is a heavy and hard mineral, which melts at approx. 1 800 °C. For this reason, crushed olivine is used in the manufacture of heat-resistant materials, as slag in the steel production process and as a mould liner in foundries as it does not present a health risk. Olivine is also used as ballast in oil platforms.

62°14'20"N   7°01'17"E   + 2 hrs 54 min ⑪

The abandoned farms of **Ytste** (ytterste, 'outermost') **Smoge**, **Vonheim** and **Smogeli** are on the port side, approx. 300 metres up the mountainside between the mountains of **Grøtet** (1 519 m above sea level) and **Smogehornet** (1 446 m above sea level). At one time the farms had their own post office and in 1938, a telephone line was installed. The farmers transported the telephone poles by horse-drawn sleds across the mountain and installed the lines themselves. An aerial cableway between the farms provided a means of transporting food and materials up the mountainside. The farms were abandoned in the 1950s but are still maintained and used as holiday homes.

Remains of a Viking grave have been found at Smoge, containing many ancient artefacts.

Approx. 62°13'41"N   7°01'18"E

We cross the municipal boundary between Norddal and Stranda municipalities on our port side

---

62°10'08"N   7°01'17"E   + 3 hrs 10 min ⑫

The steep mountainside at **Åknes** on the starboard side is known as a very dangerous avalanche area. The mountain has a 600 metre long cleft that expands several centimetres per year, located some 1000 (practically vertical) metres above sea level. Extensive geological surveys of this unstable mountain are continually carried out in order to determine the extent of expansion. Radar technology devices, laser reflectors and global positioning points are placed on the rock face and by using satellite technology images are taken at regular intervals. By analysing these images, it is possible to determine the stability of the mountain. Instruments are placed along the cleft and long chains with computer-assisted measuring devices are lowered into boreholes in order to monitor all movements, temperature changes and water pore pressure in the danger zone. Measurements are taken 140 metres inside the mountain. Daily reports are sent via the internet to the staff at the control station at Stranda, and by e-mail or mobile phone, if necessary. Åkneset is considered to be the point of the biggest potential cata-strophe in Norway. In a worst-case scenario, several tens of millions of cubic metres of rock could fall into Geir-angerfjorden and Sunnylvsfjorden, creating a 40-metre high flood wave.

Experience and knowledge of rock avalanches along with the technology installed could warn of an event 24 hours in advance.

After a small change of heading at **Åknes** on the star-board side, we can see the abandoned mountain farms, **Me-Åknes** and **Inste Åknes,** approx. 100 m up on the mountainside. Behind these are **Overvollshornet** (1 502 m above sea level) and **Flosteinnibba** (1 501 m above sea level).

The farm called **Me-Åknes** has five buildings connected such that the residents there could carry out their chores without going outside and they are situated close to a ste-ep overhanging ridge such that the roofs are flush with the terrain. This was to protect them against landslides and avalanches.

The abandoned village of **Oaldsbygda** can be seen on our port side. At one time, there were several farms lo-cated here and in the 1900s, the village had the largest number of children attending the school in this area.

Further ahead and on our port side we can see the farm, **Furnes** approx. 450 m above sea level up on the mountain, **Geitfjellet** (1 615 m above sea level). The now abandoned farm is located on a flat protruding ridge. It is said that on a fine day it was possible to shout across the fjord to the farm at Timbjørgane.

Timbjørgane, on the starboard side, has been farmed since the 1750s. At one time, the largest group of bears in Sunnmøre lived in this area. The hungry bears were always trying to raid the houses and stables. The farmer who lived here in the beginning of the 19th century died only 48 years old. He was completely worn out from carrying the family's supplies up the steep climb from the fjord to the farm. His widow continued to live there with her six children for many more years – always managing to keep the bears at distance. One Christmas Eve, a large bear tried to break down the front door. After a while, all went quiet and the mother and her children thought the bear had disappeared until they suddenly saw his head peering down the chimney! The smell of good Christmas cooking had lured him up onto the roof. The farm is now abandoned.

Ahead we can see the village of **Hellesylt** (pop. 235). Finds of Stone Age artefacts indicate that people have

lived here as long ago as the end of the last Ice Age. Hellesylt began to develop commercial tourism in 1875 when the first tourist ships came into Geirangerfjorden and the first hotel was built. The parish has had a post office and transport companies for more than 100 years. Today, Hellesylt is visited by more than 100 cruise liners and 200 000 tourists annually. In the centre of the village is the well-known and impressive waterfall, Hellesyltfossen.

The first church at Hellesylt was destroyed by an ava-lanche in 1727. The following church, built in 1730, was demolished in 1858. The new church was consecra-ted in 1859. Norway's world famous author, Henrik Ib-sen (1823–1906), stayed here for a short period in 1862, during which time he was inspired to write the play "Brand".

In Hellesylt, we find timber, plastics and food processing industries. The place has a considerable and impressive amount of through traffic considering its size.

62°06'33"N 6°58'E   + 3 hrs 29 min ⑬

Near **Lundanes** under the mountain **Geitfjellet** (1 615 m above sea level) on the port side our heading turns approx. 90°. On the starboard side is the mountain called **Nokkenibba** (1 380 m above sea level) and Geiranger-fjorden (16 km long) begins here.

Lundaneset, on the port side, at the foot of **Lundanes-egga**, is one of the few places in the area where archaeological finds have been made. Tools and arrowheads made of flint from the late Stone Age (2-3000 B.C.) have been found here (p 83).

On the mountainside on our port side are the farms of **Øvre** and **Nedre Ljøen** and parts of Rv. 60 – the road from Hellesylt to Ålesund that has several tunnels along the route, two of which we can see above the Ljøen farms: Hamregjølet tunnel, 590 m long with its southern entrance at 370 m above sea level, and Ljønibba tunnel, 2 531 m long, with its highest point 440 m above sea level.

In 2003, 151 cruise ships carrying approx. 378 000 passengers sailed into the fjord. In addition to this amazing number of tourists, many also arrived by road. As many as 500-600 000 visitors came here in 2002.

Near Lundaneset, the ship turns 90° and heads into **Geirangerfjorden.** Geiranger is one of the most popular tourist spots in Norway. An area of 498 km² around and north of the fjord is designated as a cultural heritage landscape including 46 km² of fjord areas. On 14th July 2005, Geirangerfjorden, Nærøyfjorden and the surrounding areas in Sogn and Fjordane county (p 386), were included in the prestigious UNESCO's World Heritage List, which lists the world's most important cultural and natural monuments and places. The grounds for inclusion were given as: …"Geirangerfjorden and Nærøyfjorden are considered to be some of the most beautiful fjord landscapes in the world. Their unique natural beauty, with narrow valleys and steep crystalline rock faces stretches from 500 metres below sea level to 1 400 metres above the Norwegian Sea. Countless waterfalls cascade down the near-vertical rock faces whilst numerous rivers flow from jagged mountains, glaciers and lakes, through forests and down into the fjord below. An abundance of natural phenomena, on land and in water with amongst other subterranean moraines and sea mammals reinforces the experience. Remains of old, now abandoned farms and mountain pastures increase the natural landscape's cultural dimension dramatically, which complements and magnifies the area's collective value"…

In 2006, the 'West Fjords' area received the top rating of the 830 World Heritage Destinations surveyed by the National Geographic Society and the area was said to be (quote) 'authentic, unspoiled, and likely to remain so'.

The abandoned farm, **Matvika** is on our port side. The place is so named because the soil here was very fertile

(mat=food). At one time 100 kg apricots were grown here, something of a record!

62°05'26"N   7°01'53"E   + 3 hrs 36 min ⑭

On our starboard side is the farm called **Blomberg**, where the fjord makes a turn toward the northeast. The winding, steep path up to the farmhouse has 28 turns, rising up to 452 m above sea level to the houses above. The farm was noted in documents in 1650. The farmer first leased and later bought the property in 1875 and subsequently raised 10 children there. The babies were carried down to the rowboat moored at the farm, **Syltevika,** 452 metres below Blomberg when they were to be christened. They then rowed the 11.5 kilometres to the church at Maråk (Geiranger) where the christening ceremony took place. They then rowed back the same distance along the fjord. The child was again carried up the 450 metres along the path with 28 turns to the farm above. Below, in Syltevika, near the boathouse, was a small cabin with a stove where they could change into their finer clothes, if necessary, and back into their regular daily clothes on their return and before starting the ascent to their farm. If the weather was bad and the journey up the steep path became too dangerous, they would spend the night in the cabin. The housewife of the farm died in 1942, aged 100 years! The farm was abandoned in 1948. It is now listed and protected property and has been restored.

62°05'28"N   7°02'48"E   + 3 hrs 38 min ⑭

The famous waterfall known as Brudesløret ('bridal veil') is on our port side. The waterfall, some 300 m high, is not regulated like many of the waterfalls in Geirangerfjorden. The amount of water coming over the falls is dependent on rainfall and melting snow in the area. In dry periods, the waterfall may dry up completely.

As we pass Brudesløret, we can see the farm **Horvadraget** on the mountainside. Access to the farm is very difficult and, as stated in a document from 1866:

> …"If the people living at Horvadraget wanted to go to church in the winter after heavy snowfall, two men had to go down early in the morning in order to make the path passable. Snow and ice had collected in crevices, which needed to be removed; steps had to be cut in the ice. Whilst one was working, the other had to watch out for possible avalanches and ice falling down the hill. If this occurred, they sought shelter under a slab of rock.
>
> …When the path was very icy, women and children were lowered down using ropes.
>
> …One did not stay too long by the boathouse either; rock slides could also occur and on 28th May 1879 a rock fall destroyed farmer Ingebrigt Horvedrag's boathouse and boat"…

> Source for Geirangerfjorden: "Fjellet, fjorden og folket"
> by Arild Flydal.

To get to the church in Geiranger it was necessary to row 8 km there and back.

The farm at Horvadraget was abandoned in 1899, as it had become just too dangerous to live there. The year before, a rockslide demolished half the house. Six frightened people huddled together in the remains, which were protected by a protruding slab of rock. In 1994, an almost 100 m wide landslide occurred near Horvadragsgården and the results can be clearly seen on the mountainside.

62°06'08"N   7°05'47"E   + 3 hrs 44 min ⑮

On our port side, we can see the famous 300 m high falls, "De Syv Søstre" (The Seven Sisters). Like Brudesløret, which we have just passed, these falls also vary in flow. Under average weather conditions, there is water in the falls, but in dry periods and limited snow melting this can be reduced quite dramatically.

On the starboard side of "De syv søstre" we can see the waterfall known as "Friaren" (the Suitor), 440 m high. Legend has it that "Friaren" proposed to the "De syv søstre" on the other side of the fjord, but being stubborn and haughty waterfalls, they never gave him an answer. Frustrated by this, "Friaren" found solace in the bottle, which can be seen in the middle of the waterfall, where the water is divided.

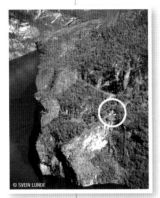

The abandoned farm of **Knivsflå** with two courtyards is situated 250 m above sea level northeast of "De syv søstre" (Knivsflåfossene). Knivsflå is mentioned in documents dating from 1603. The farm was abandoned in 1899. Although the farm was quite fertile it became too dangerous for people to live there due to frequent snow and rock slides. A slab of rock right above the farm might also have slid out with possible loss of lives. At the time the farms were abandoned 13 children were living there, the youngest girl only was two years old. She later married the founder of the Ulstein Group in Ulsteinvik (p 45). The farm pastures were used for many years for growing hay. The hay was sent by an aerial cableway down to the fjord and rowed in to Geiranger.

Gomsdalen is located further in Geirangerfjorden, on a plateau up on the mountain. A stretch of terrain from Gomsdalen to Skageflå has been given the name "Jordmorruten"- "the midwife's route". The name stems from the route taken by a 77 year-old neighbour, Kristianne, during mid-winter on Christmas Eve 1892. She struggled in darkness against the elements from Gomsdalen to Knivsflå to assist with a delivery. When she finally arrived at Knivsflå, she heard a baby cry and found the baby and mother doing well. The next day she returned to Gomsdalen. The route is so dangerous and steep that visitors are recommended to use ropes.

Soon after passing "Friaren" (Skageflåfossen) on our starboard side, we can see the abandoned, well-known farm called **Skageflå** located 270 metres up on the steep mountainside. In certain parts, the path is so steep that ladders had to be used to reach the farm. It is said that when the tax collector came the farmer would pull the ladders up to avoid paying tax! Children and animals had to be tethered to prevent them falling down the mountainside. At one time, there were 118 sheep, cows, an ox and a horse on the farm. One theory is that the horse must have been carried up as a foal; it was the only way that it could get there. The farm was eventually abandoned in 1916.

When King Harald and Queen Sonja celebrated their silver jubilee in 1993, they invited over 30 prominent guests from the various European monarchies for lunch at Skageflå. The guests were offered helicopter transport; however none of them accepted the offer and they all climbed up on foot. The four houses on Skageflå were renovated in honour of the visit.

Approx. 300 metres above Skageflå we can see the cliff known as '**Prekestolen**' (Preacher's Pulpit or Pulpit Rock).

62°07'N   7°08'E   **+ 3 hrs 47 min** ⑯

Gomsdalen, a 'hanging valley', located 600 m above sea level, can be seen on our port side. People have lived here since the Stone Age (p 83). It was here the midwife lived that we read about earlier. The steep path to the farm ran along the river, **Bringe**. The farms there were inhabited until 1907. There were a number of children living here and the journey to the school in Geiranger was difficult; 600 metres down to the boat, then rowing to and from Geiranger and the 600 metre clime back up to the farms - in all kinds of weather conditions. When they eventually moved away from the farms, one of the families took parts of their home with them. They carried the materials down the steep path, loaded them onto a boat, rowed to Geiranger, and rebuilt the house there.

On our port side, we pass the steep and notoriously windy Ørneveien. The National Route, Rv 63 connects Geiranger to Åndalsnes, near Molde (p 360). This road is the only road open to Geiranger all year round. It has 11 turns up the 8.6 km mountainside and each turn has a radius of approx. 13 m. The steepest gradient is 1:10.

At the foot of Ørneveien are Geiranger Holiday Centre and the Grande Hotel.

The ship sails into Geiranger   ⑰

The community of **Geiranger** (pop. 240) was formerly an isolated village innermost in Geirangerfjord. The trip to other villages by rowing boat was arduous and the track over the mountain was long and winding, and difficult to negotiate. The weekly scheduled boat connections that started up in 1858 provided better communications with the neighbouring villages and with Ålesund.

In 1869, the first 'låna' (small store and 'guest house'), which later became Meroks Hotel, was built. However, the guesthouse and store did not provide enough income, so the owner also farmed cattle, sheep and pigs. Around the same time, the preparations for the construction of the new Geiranger road began. When the road was finally opened in 1889, it brought new groups of tourists and visitors to the village, which in turn provided a basis for an expansion of the hotel capacity. Hotel Geiranger was built in 1885, Hotel Union in 1891, Hotel Utsikten in 1893 and Djupvasshytta in 1892.

In 1906, 112 tourist ships called at Geiranger and approx. 11 000 passengers went ashore. Statistics from 1910, of tourists that arrived on various cruise ships show that of these, there were 4 914 Germans, 4 793 Englishmen, 3 562 Norwegians and 532 tourists from other countries. During the summer of 1926, 50 larger ships and a total of 19 000 passengers visited Geiranger. This large influx of tourists provided the local people with a welcome extra income. Some local boat owners provided 'shuttle' services to and from the ships and others took passengers up the steep paths in horse-drawn carriages. In 2006, a total of 156 cruise ships sailed into the fjord, in addition to the Hurtigruten ships.

The present Geiranger church was built in 1842. It is an octagonal timber construction, with seating for 200. The first church in Geiranger is believed to have been built in 1450. It was not a 'pure' stave church; the additions of a chancel and porch were of log timber. This church was demolished in 1742. A new cruciform church was built two years later, with a rose-painted interior. The church was totally destroyed by a fire, said to have been arson, in 1841. The present church is thus the third to be built on the same site.

The natural surroundings in the innermost part of Geirangerfjord and in the village of Geiranger are magnificent and majestic, framed in the background by the mountains of **Grindalsnibba** (1 636 m above sea level) to the north, **Vinsåshornet** (1 343 m above sea level) in the centre and **Dalsnibba** (1 476 m above sea level) to the south. They offer a fantastic view of the fjords and mountains and the winding road that descends the mountain. The viewpoint of **Flydalsjuvet** is just by the road that runs between the village and Dalsnibba. This is known for its exceptional view and is one of Norway's most photographed tourist motifs. Close to Flydalsjuvet is the road

known as **Knuten**, which is a still-driveable part of the original Geirangerveien. It was opened in 1889 and is an example of outstanding engineering expertise.

Geiranger is the starting point for car, bus and boat trips around the impressive landscape. There are four hotels, several guesthouses and cafes. In the centre of Geiranger is **Storseterfossen**, a waterfall that it is possible to actually walk underneath.

The ship departs from Geiranger   + 0 hrs 00 min

On the mountainside, just after the ship sails out of the fjord, we can see the waterfall "**Geirangerelva**" on the port side.

62°07'N   7°09'E   + 0 hrs 08 min ⑯

On the mountainside, 600 m above sea level we can see the hanging valley of **Gomsdalen** (p 64).

On our port side lies the farm called **Skageflå** and the waterfall **Friaren** (p 64).

On our starboard side is the farm **Knivsflå** and the seven falls, "De syv søstre" (p 63).

62°05'50"N   7°04'55"E   + 0 hrs 23 min ⑭

On the starboard side is the waterfall "**Brudesløret**" (p 62).

Ahead, and on our port side is the farm **Blomberg** (p 62).

62°06'27"N   6°58'20"E   + 0 hrs 31 min ⑬

The farm of **Matvika** is on our starboard side (p 62).

On the mountainside ahead we can see the farms **Øvre** and **Nedre Ljøen** (p 62).

We pass **Lundaneset** as we sail northwards (p 61).

We have left Geirangerfjorden and are on our way into Sunnylvsfjorden. On our port side we can see the village of **Hellesylt** (p 61).

62°09'N   6°59'E   + 0 hrs 47 min ⑫

On our starboard side is the farm at **Furnes** (p 61).

On our port side we can see the farm **Timbjørgane** (p 61).

On our port side are the farms **Inste Åknes** and **Me-Åknes** (p 61).

On our starboard side we pass the olivine quarries at **Røbbervika** (p 60).

We pass **Uksneset** on our port side and exit **Sunnylvsfjorden**.

In front and on the north side of Storfjorden is the village of **Liabygda** (p 60).

Norddalsfjorden is on our starboard side (p 60).

Our heading is now north-westerly and we continue into **Storfjorden**.

We pass the village of **Stranda** on our port side (p 59).

On our starboard side is **Uraneset** and the farm at **Djupedal** (p 59).

62°19'38"N 6°57'E	+ 1 hr 29 min ⑧

We are sailing along the mountain known as Roaldshornet. On our port side is the farm of **Espehjelle.**

The parish of **Fausa** is on our port side (p 59).

Stordalsholmen is over on our starboard side (p 58).

We are passing the village of **Stordal** on our starboard side (p 57).

62°24'37"N 6°55'23"E	+ 1 hr 51 min ⑦

We pass the headland of **Skotet** and the farm **Ytste Skotet** on our port side (p 57).

On our starboard side is the village of **Dyrkorn** (p 57).

62°26'18"N 6°52'08"E	+ 1 hr 59 min ⑦

On our port side, we pass the three small villages of **Vagsvik**, **Vestre** and **Åmdåm** in Ørskog municipality (p 57).

62°27'N 6°46'27"E	+ 2 hrs 12 min ⑥

The headland, **Gausneset** lies in the bay before the village of **Sjøholt** (p 56).

On our starboard side are the parishes of **Ramstad** and **Søvika,** just before the headland at **Røneset**.

Ahead and to our starboard side we can see **Solør**, and in the distance we can see **Skodje** (p 56).

Behind these farms is the notoriously dangerous mountainside, **Åkneset** (p 60).

62°13'20"N 7°01'E	+ 1 hr 03 min ⑪

To our starboard side are the farms called **Smogeli**, **Vonheim** and **Smoge** (p 60).

In the bay on our starboard side is **Glomset**.

62°25'49"N   6°32'32"E   + 2 hrs 39 min ⑤

We are heading towards **Ørsneset** and the villages of **Sykkulven/Aure** and **Ikornnes**, with **Sykkulvsfjorden** on our port side and **Magerholm** on our starboard side (p 55).

We have passed **Flisneset**, **Vegsund**, **Leirvåg**, **Solevåg** and **Eikreim** on our starboard side (p 55).

62°24'24'''N   6°23'E   + 2 hrs 57 min ④

On the starboard side are **Hjørundfjorden** and the parish of **Hundeidvik** and the ferry landing at **Festøya** (p 54).

On the starboard side is the parish of **Solevåg** and the ferry quay (p 54).

62°24'N   6°17'E   + 3 hrs 09 min ③

On the starboard side is the parish of **Eikrem**, and on the port side the parish of **Barstadvika** (p 54).

62°23'N   6°12'E   + 3 hrs 19 min ②

We are sailing along the east coast of **Sula** (p 54) (to starboard) with **Vartdalsfjorden** (p 53) on our port side. The fjord stretches in a south-easterly direction, behind the island called Hareidlandet (p 44). In front is Hareid municipality with the centre, Hareid (p 52).

Our voyage continues into **Sulasundet**. We have passed the ferry terminal on the starboard side, which connects to Hareid over on the port side.

North of Hareid, in front and on our starboard side is the parish of Brandal, famous for its close association with polar and arctic seal hunting (p 52).

62°24'N   6°05'E   + 3 hrs 33 min ②

Just ahead is Godøya (island of Gods) that has an ancient history of human sacrifices, on the mountain, Lesten, on the western part of the island. It is said that witches also congregated on this mountain in the Middle Ages. There are many other relics from ancient times on the island (p 49).

Breidsundet, southwest of Godøya has a 270 m deep channel which continues into Storfjorden and Hjørundfjorden (now behind us), where the channel deepens to 450 m.

We are passing **Eltraneset** on our starboard side, which is the most westerly point on the island of Sula. The north side of the island faces Heissafjorden (p 51).

A few kilometres east of Eltraneset, in Heissafjorden, is a large cultural landscape with many relics from ancient times. Several dwelling sites have been discovered along the shore, the oldest dates from the Iron Age (A.D. 0 – 200), and remains of homesteads that existed in Roman times and up to the 18th century have also been found in this area (p 83).

The village of **Spjelkavik**, an important communication centre, is situated at the head of Heissafjorden. The village is now regarded as part of the town of Ålesund, and has various industries including furniture, timber, textile, clothing and plastics factories.

The ship docks at the quayside in Ålesund

THE HISTORY OF THE TOWN OF ÅLESUND

In 1968, **Ålesund** and **Borgund** were joined as one municipality, Ålesund. In Borgund we find the old and well-known Borgund kaupang (trading centre, town), situated on the east side of Ålesund, facing Borgundfjorden and Heissafjorden.

Borgund was an important trading centre in the Middle Ages and was closely connected with the Giske family on the island of Giske (p 72). The trading centre functioned as a gathering and distribution centre for products from the districts that would be sent on to Bergen and then sold on to the Hansa traders for export to Europe (p 9). Exchange goods, such as ceramics from Germany and textiles from England were brought back from Bergen. Within a relatively small area, archaeological digs have revealed an earlier township, which existed here in the 11th century. It consisted of 40-50 dwellings, warehouses and stables, wharfs, roads and wells. In addition, Borgund had three or four churches in the 13th century, but gradually its importance was reduced in the 14th and 15th century until around 1450 Borgund lost its privileges as a trading centre.

The town of Ålesund is actually spread over several islands. Outermost to the west is **Heissa** (4 km²), then **Aspøya** (0.5 km²), **Nørvøya** (7 km²), half of **Oksenøya** (58 km²) in the east. The long and narrow **Ellingsøya** (28 km²) in the north is separated from the other islands by **Ellingsøyfjorden**. The islands are interconnected by bridges and subsea tunnels. Traces of settlements have been found dating from the Stone Age (p 83). In addition there are many smaller, uninhabited islands.

Ålesund's town centre was built around the narrow sound, Ålesundet, between the islands, Aspøya in the west and Nørvøya. The first settlers came from Bergen; these lived and traded there part of the year. They exchanged fish for corn and other provisions. Along the banks of Ålesundet, now named **Brosundet**, and at the foot of the mountain, Aksla, the town prospered and grew in the 19th century.

The excellent harbour is the main reason for Ålesund's location today. The town had long since taken over the role Borgund Kaupang had previously held. From 1824 it was granted town status (but without full trading rights, which were not fully granted until 1848). The town's further development was closely linked to the fishing industry along the coast of Sunnmøre during the latter part of the 19th century. Ålesund provided a good harbour for the expanding fishing fleet of sailing ships, motor boats and steamships and became an important town for trade and the export of fish products at that time.

Due to its Jugend-style architecture, Ålesund has become known as Jugendbyen (Jugend town). Until the 23rd January 1904 the buildings in the town were mostly old, somewhat randomly built timber buildings. On that date, during a storm from the south-west a fire spread rapidly through the town and left large areas, including the town centre, in ruins. It is thought that approx. 800 buildings burned down and 10 000 people were made homeless. Amazingly, only one person was killed, an elderly woman who in fact was the nearest neighbour to the fire station - because she re-entered her burning home to rescue some of her belongings. In one area just one house remained. The owner refused to leave his home so his family and neighbours carried his furniture and belongings out in order to rescue them from the fire. After the fire, the house stood alone amongst several burnt out neighbouring houses, but his furniture and belonging had been lost to the flames!

The homeless in Ålesund received help from home and abroad. One particularly grand gesture was the donation made by the German Kaiser Wilhelm II (1859-1941). The Kaiser frequently spent his holidays on board his yacht, "Hohenzollern" along the Norwegian coast and in the fjords in western Norway. He immediately sent five support ships fully laden with food, medicines, construction materials, blankets and other aid to the town. As a mark of gratitude, the main street in Ålesund was named after him. Help was received from all over the world.

The architecture of the rebuilt town stood in great contrast to the somewhat disorganised timber houses that

existed before the fire. The approx. 50 architects that participated in the rebuilding were young Norwegians who had studied abroad and were strongly influenced by the Jugendstilen (French: Art Nouveau, English: New Style), which flourished in the middle of the 1890s until approx. 1910, and also prevailing national impulses in construction design.

By 1906, a major portion of the town had been rebuilt, in accordance with a street plan and strict building specifications that forbade timber buildings from being built in the centre. The town centre was dominated by beautiful structures in brick and mortar with towers, spires and ornamental frontage. The rapid rebuilding was possible because there were many tradesmen without work at that time so it was relatively easy to hire well-qualified construction workers. Ålesund today has a town centre that is unique in Europe and is one of the few towns to have such a well-preserved style.

The town's architecture also bears signs of its fishing and maritime heritage with its preserved fishermen's cabins and warehouses that today have been refurbished as hotels, restaurants and apartments. The harbour has been at the centre of activity throughout generations; the Dutch timber trade (p 333), the war with England (1808-14) (p 85), the herring fishing boom, development of the fishing fleet and export of fish products, especially rock dried cod (bacalao), which started already in 1823, right up to today's busy trade and exports. The harbour and town with all its activities have developed in unison.

Ålesund is today the regional centre for all of Sunnmøre, and the centre of Norway's largest and most modern ocean-going fishing fleets that fish in national as well as in-ternational waters. Large catches of fish are landed in Ålesund, which in turn provides work for the fish and food processing industries in the area. Rock-dried cod is still the main export article from Ålesund – "Bacalao de Noruega" is world-famous.

In Ålesund, there are also other industries such as shipyards and mechanical workshops. In addition, there are many textile, furniture, plastics and graphic design industries in the Ålesund area.

Sunnmøre folk from Ålesund and the coastal districts have influenced fishing industries all over the world. They were instrumental in establishing the factory ship fleet in Seattle on USA's northwest coast and fish farming in both USA and Canada. They have helped to develop the deep-sea fishing industry in New Zealand, Argentina and Chile and along the coast of Africa. Recently, Sunnmøre fishing technology and competence has contributed in the development and modernisation of the Russian fishing fleet.

Attractions in Ålesund

The mountain **Aksla** (189 m above sea level), just behind the town centre offers a splendid view of the town below and the surrounding islands and the Sunnmøre Alps in the background. 418 steps take you up to the top of the mountain from the town centre. In a park at the foot of the mountain there is a statue of the Viking 'Gange-Rolv', or 'Rollon', as he was named by the French. He came from Vigra, north-west of Ålesund. He was declared an outlaw and had to flee from Norway. In the year 911, he founded the Duchy of Normandy in France. The statue was a gift from the town of Rouen in Normandy, donated in 1911, to celebrate the millennium of the founding of Normandy (p 74).

Close to the top of Aksla is a modern sports centre and at the top there is a restaurant. You can also reach the top by road.

As we sail into Ålesund, we pass **Atlanterhavsparken** (Ålesund Aquarium), just west of Sukkertoppen. It is one of Europe's largest saltwater aquariums and has many fascinating exhibitions showing life under water. The aquarium is built into the surrounding landscape and exhibits marine life from the whole Atlantic, with special emphasis on sea life along the west coast. Here one can study the marine life near the ferry terminal, in the ocean currents, between reefs and skerries and out in the depths of Storfjorden (p 53). The park was opened in 1998 and is approx. five minutes drive from Ålesund centre.

Ålesund's **Art Nouveau Senter** was opened in 2003 and exhibits the architectural style that dominate Ålesund's town centre. The centre's international importance is reinforced by a close co-operation with other European cities that have similar architecture, such as Glasgow in Scotland, Nancy in France, Vienna in Austria, Barcelona in Spain, Brussels in Belgium and Riga in Latvia.

Ålesund Museum, in the centre of town.

Sunnmøre Museum, Borgund

Town walks in Ålesund, either organised or on an individual basis.

The ship continues to Molde   + 0 hrs 00 min

LARGER MAP P**390**

Shortly after leaving Ålesund we cross the boundary into the municipality of Giske. Godøya in Giske is behind and to our port side (p 49).

62°29'N 6°09'E   + 0 hrs 06 min

Ellingsøyfjorden is on our starboard side. Thereafter we can see the long and narrow 16 km long **Ellingsøya** (28 km²). The place called **Hovland** is located on the tip of Ellingsøya. The Ellingsøy tunnel, (3 250 m long, 140 m below sea level), is a subsea road tunnel that connects Ålesund and Ellingsøya. Another subsea tunnel that runs under Valderhaugfjorden connects the town to Valderhaugstranda, seen on our port side.

The two islands of Giske (2.5 km²) and Valderøya (6.5 km²) in Giske municipality are on our port side. Giske, the most westerly of the two, as well as being the smallest in the municipality is also quite flat, its highest point being only 23 m above sea level. Fishing and fish farming are the two most important activities and there is a subsea tunnel connection with Godøya in the south. The tunnel was opened in 1989. It is 3 844 m long and 153 m below sea level. Giskebrua, a 552 m long concrete bridge, connects the island to Valderøya in the east.

Giske is historically important. The island has been the main family seat of the Giske family and Arnunge family, which were at one time Norway's most powerful noble families. One of the oldest manors in Norway is located on Giske, which was their ancestral home through the centuries. Kalv Arneson came from the Arnunge family. He was one of the chieftains of the army that met King Olav Haraldsson (Olav den hellige (Olav the Holy)) 995-1030) at the battle of Stiklestad 29th July 1030, where the King was killed (p 88). The family lived here from the 10th century until 1582. (The Sagas tell the story that the family's ancestor, Finnvid Funnen, was found in an eagle's nest swaddled in silk.) Members of the family married into other influential families. King Harald Hardråde's queen, Tora, came from this family and was the ancestor of a number of Norwegian kings.

© TERJE RAKKE/NORDIC LIFE/ DESTINATION ÅLESUND & SUNNMØRE

Giske church is located on the south side of the island and is the most notable monument from the Giske/Arnunge family's most influential period. The church, which is Sunnmøre's oldest, was built in the 12th century as a chapel for the Giske family. It is built in marble in the Roman style. The church and the interior were restored in 1756 and new beautifully carved alter board and pulpit were installed. The altar cloth is from 1688 and the font dates from 1707. More recent restorations were carried out in 1860 and 1930.

Mjeltehaugen is an archaeologically famous area where burial mounds were found in a natural sand bank on the southeast side of Giske. The mound was originally 30 m in cross-section and approx. 2 m high. During excavations in 1847, 1867 and 1878 two graves from differing historical eras were found in the mound. One dated back to the Bronze Age (1500-500 B.C.), a coffin with eight decorative stones; the other was a woman's grave with rare, western Norwegian silver-plated bron-ze buckles from approx. A.D. 200 and many charred human bones. Mjeltehaugen is considered unique and is now preserved as a cultural heritage site (p 83).

62°30'N   6°08'46"E   + 0 hrs 12 min ①

We are passing **Valderøya** on our port side, the most populated island in Giske. The population is mostly concentrated on the island's southern and eastern sides. The centre, **Valderhaug,** faces the shipping lane. The island is hilly and the mountain **Signalen** (231 m above sea level) is the island's highest point. The main industries are fishing, fish-food processing and mechanical industries. A subsea road tunnel, Valderøytunnelen, runs from the island's southern point and connects it to Ellingsøy (to starboard). The tunnel was opened in 1987 and is 4 222 m long and runs 137 m below sea level.

On the south of the island lies Valderøy Church. It is a long concrete church built in 1961 and seats 530.

Close to Valderøy's town hall is Kongshaugen, a burial mound that is 42 m in cross section and 3 m high. It is located in a marsh and was made from beach stones covered with peat. According to the Sagas, King Valder was buried here and gave his name to the island. It is thought that Kongshaugen dates from A.D. 350-400. During the archaeological digs of 1824-27, boat remains, estimated to be 3 000 years old were discovered. These are some of the oldest ever found in Europe. The boat planks were stitched together using pleated sinews and between the boards, wool was used as packing material. Many other relics were also found. The mound was quite large and it is assumed that several graves were added later. However, a complete excavation was not performed and a building now stands on top of the mound preventing any further excavation.

The cave at Skjonghelleren is situated on the northwest side of Valderøya. The entrance to the cave is 57 m above sea level. It was formed at the time the sea was at this level. The opening to the cave is approx. 38 m high and it is 111 m deep. In 1875, 1878 and 1983 excavations were made in the cave and find from these confirmed

© IDA DYRKORN HEIERLAND

that people had lived there during the Iron Ages, (approx. 500 B.C.). Hunting and household equipment were found along with remains of fish, birds and mammals that existed during the last Ice Age (approx. 30 000 years ago). Some species have been identified from these remains.

62°31'N 6°09'E   + 0 hrs 15 min

We are sailing along the east side of Valderøya and can see the connected settlements of **Skjong** in the south, **Valderhaugsstranda**, **Nordstranda** and **Uksneset** in the north.

On our starboard side we can see the small island of **Kjeholmen,** northeast of the larger island, **Kalvøya**, with **Oksebåsen** lighthouse on the southern point.

62°31'42"N 6°09'27"E   + 0 hrs 18 min ②

On our port side is **Vigra** (18.9 km²), which is the largest island in Giske municipality, located north of Valderøya with a bridge connection. The island is flat with large marshy areas and the highest point is **Molnesfjellet**, 128 m above sea level in the north. There are many small bays with fine sandy beaches, especially on the island's west side. The main industries are fishing, fish processing and farming.

Vigra, Ålesund's airport is located on the island's east side. The airport was opened in 1958 and a new terminal building was built in 1986. The runway is 2 314 m long. North European Aviation Resources AS (NEAR- training centre) is located at Vigra. The training centre is run in cooperation with the North American Institute of Aviation (NAIA), and the students come from many different European countries. The airport has direct flights to Oslo, Bergen and Trondheim and charter operations to many southern European destinations.

Vigra broadcasting station on **Synes** is located in the southwest. The original station had two 106 m high masts. Broadcasting began in November 1935 with a 10 kW RCA transmitter. A 100 kW transmitter was installed in 1939.

When the German forces invaded Norway in April 1940, the station was attacked during a transmission and this event was actually reported "live". The original transmitter (complete with bullet holes) is preserved and displayed as curiosity. In 1952, the station was equipped with a cylindrical 242 m high antenna, at the time Norway's tallest. The mast is a steel pipe construction with a diameter of over 2 m. The mast has a ladder running up the centre all the way to the top. The record for climbing to the top currently stands at 17 minutes. The mast was later reduced down to 180 m to comply with air traffic regulations.

Synes lighthouse, built in 1867 is also located here.

Blindheim farm, located on the west side of the island was the ancestral home of the well-known Blindheim family (1120-1228) that is mentioned in Snorre's Saga of Kings. Two sons married King Harald Gille's (1103-36) (p 97) daughters. The family played an important role in the rebellion against King Sverre (1184-1202). The island has several burial mounds; two of these are located at Blindheim. Stølshaugen was found in 1874. The mound had a diameter of 30 metres, and was 3-4 m high. It is assumed that an important, influential person was buried here during the Migration period around A.D. 400. The bodies had been cremated and the remains placed in a bronze receptacle together with other relics and a bronze plate was used as a lid. The other grave at Blindheim is 'Blimshaugen'. It has a diameter of 36 m, is 5 m high and assumed to date back to A.D. 300-350. Excavations of the mound were made in 1901 and 1942. Four graves were found in the mound; those of a man, a girl and two women and the mounds are now listed and protected.

Historians believe that Ragnvald Mørejarl, who lived at the end of the 9th century, lived on one of the islands in Giske. One of his sons, Gange-Rolv or Rollon, grew up on Vigra. He was declared an outlaw in Norway and had to flee the country. After many adventures, he finally settled down in France where he founded the Duchy of Normandy, in the year 911. Gange-Rolv is the ancestor of William the Conqueror and therefore a distant relative of the English monarchy.

Gange-Rolv or Rollon (as he is known by the French), got his name because he was so big and heavy that no horse could carry him and was for this reason forced to walk rather than ride (gange=walk).

© JEFF GILBERT, SUNNMØRSPOSTEN

ROLLON
© MICHAEL SHEA

The village of **Roald** (pop. 690) is located on the north of the island.

Between Vigra and the island, Løvsøya in the north is **Vigrafjorden**.

We cross the municipal boundary between Giske and Haram municipalities

Haram municipality

Municipal coat of arms, significance: The sea as a workplace and method of communications.
Meaning: Norse Harhamarr - har 'steep', hamarr, 'cliff'.
Municipal seat: Brattvåg (pop. 2 128).
Position: 62°36'N 6°27'E.
Area: 257 km². **Population:** 8 606.
Pop. density: 33.5 /km².
Area distribution: Farming 9 %, forestry 25 %, fresh water 3 %, other 63 %.
Trade and industry: Shipyards and maritime industries, food processing, textile, and furniture industries. Farming and animal husbandry combined with some fishing.
Places to return to: Hamnsundhellaren. Petter Dyrkorn local museum at Fjørtoft.
Haram municipality's home page: www.haram.kommune.no

Behind the islands, on our starboard side, **Grytafjorden** stretches towards the east. The boundary between Ålesund and Haram divides the fjord. The village of **Tennfjord** is at the head of Grytafjorden and we can see the parish of **Engeset** on the southwest side of the peninsula.

At the south-westerly point of Haram peninsula we can see the parish of **Hamnsund.** At Hamnsund is the cave known as Hamnsundhellaren, which was excavated for the first time in 1877. The cave is believed to have been formed approx. 24 500 years ago, during a period when the land was covered in ice. Finds from the early Iron Age, Stone Age and Bronze Age were discovered, as were the bones of humans from around approx. 50 B.C. (p 83).

Hamnsund church is a longhouse-style timber church, built in 1875 and seats 350. The church was refurbished in 1899 and 1956/57.

Just outside of Hamnsund, on the starboard side, is the low-lying island of **Kalvøya.**

On the mainland to our starboard side we can see the village of **Søvik** (pop. 604). Søvik has some mechanical industry, among others Søviknes Verft, which is an Aker Brattvåg company (p 77).

Northwest of Søvik we can see two islands. **Bjørnøya** is the outermost, also **Terøya.** The coastal fort at Bjørnøya built in 1942 had four 10.5 cm guns.

On our port side we have **Vigrafjorden,** north of Vigra.

To our port side we can see, in a row, the four islands of Lepsøya/Løvøya, Haramsøya, Flemsøya (Skuløya) and Fjørtofta.

Lepsøya/Løvøya (12.1 km²), with the mountain of **Goaldet** (490 m above sea level). The island is densely populated along its shore and has a ferry connection to the mainland and its neighbour, Haramsøya. The village of **Lausund** is on the island's south side.

© HARAM MUNICIPALITY

In Rønstadhelleren, a cave on the mountainside on the island's west side, evidence of human habitation was discovered. The remains in the cave could have told us much about the early life in the area but unfortunately, they were removed and sold to a guano factory! Beneath the cave in **Columbine Bay** is a memorial plate of a shipwreck from 1886.

Haramsøya (13.3 km²) is north of Lepsøya/Løvøya with the mountain **Mannen**, (347 m above sea level). On the southeast side is the island's largest village of **Austnes** (pop. 375).

One of the richest archaeological finds ever made in Norway was made here on Haramsøya in 1968. It dated from the Roman Iron Age period (p 83). Parts of a large Roman bronze plate were uncovered in a stone coffin, which also contained remains that showed indications of a funeral pyre ceremony. In addition to charred human bones, there were three gold rings, a large golden bracelet and gold medallions. In total approx. 623 grams of gold were discovered, which makes this the most valuable early Iron Age grave in Northern Europe. The medallions had a Roman Emperor's image on them and inscriptions that proved that they originated from the reign of Emperor Constantine II (A.D. 337-361).

Haramsøy church, on the south-easterly tip of the island is a hexagonal-shaped timber church built in 1838. The church's altar table is from 1660 and the interior decorations are from 1911.

Haramsøya has a bridge connection with Skuløya/Flemsøya and a ferry connection with Lepsøya/Løvsøya and the mainland.

On Haramsøya and neighbouring, Flemsøya/Skuløya an application has been made for a licence to build and operate a windmill park.

Skuløya/Flemsøy (14.3 km²) is the third of the four islands on our port side. The mountain, **Skulen**, (492 m above sea level) is the highest point. Many tree roots have been discovered in local marshes, an indication that a large forest once grew here.

On the island's southwest side is the village of **Longva** where Rolls Royce Marine AS provides the community with more than 100 jobs. The company produces panels and consoles, starters and dynamic positioning equipment for marine use. The company is part of Rolls Royce Marine in Ulsteinvik (p 46).

At Longva, archaeological finds indicate that there were settlements in the area more than 9 000 years ago.

The island of **Fjørtoft** (9.2 km²) is situated north of Skuløya/Flemsøya. In contrast to the three previous islands, Fjørtoft is low and marshy. The highest point is **Fjørtofta** (113 m above sea level).

In the autumn of 1940, two boats, known as the Fjørtoftbåtene (Fjørtoft-boats), were found in a marsh on the island. One of them was 10 m long, constructed from oak and with boards joined with iron rivets. The second boat was smaller. The boats were filled with stones, sunk into the marsh and later overgrown. There is no evidence that boats were used as graves. It is likely that they were used in some sacrificial ceremony. It has been difficult to determine the exact age of the boats but it is assumed that they date from the year A.D. 860 or earlier. In the spring of 1973, a flooded Stone Age settlement was found intact on the island. The place was inhabited more than 8 000 years ago but was later claimed by the sea and covered with gravel and stones.

Remains of a woman's grave were found in 1965 on Oterlei that are believed to be approx. 1 100 years old. The wo-

man was buried in a boat, along with a long necklace with hundreds of pearls of coloured glass and some large ceramic pots, most probably originating from the Middle East.

It is said that Fjørtoft is famous amongst geologists because of the micro-diamonds in the species of rocks found here in 1993.

The mountain **Gamlemsveten** (790 m above sea level) (p 82) is on our starboard side, on Haramshalvøya. On top of the mountain is a communications mast for radio and TV broadcasts that covers most of the Sunnmøre and Romsdal region. It is part of NRK's telecommunications services.

62°35'32"N 6°15'26"E   + 0 hrs 38 min ④

Lepsøyrev lighthouse on our starboard side is Norway's first floating, permanently anchored lighthouse ship, "Enigheten", which was positioned there in 1856. In the spring of the following year, the ship was lost. After several unsuccessful trials using other ships, a permanent 11.5-metre high stone tower was built in 1879. The station was manned until 1956 when it was automated.

Between **Lepsøya** on the port side and its neighbour to the north, **Haramsøya**, is **Haramsfjorden**. Northeast of Lepsøya on the port side, we pass a group of smaller islands, the largest of which is **Hestøya**.

The island of **Skuløya** is in the north west and north of Haramsøya.

Our voyage takes us along the low, populated and cultivated, Haramslandet on the starboard side. We pass the village of **Skjelten,** which has car ferry services to the islands to the northwest.

Ahead we can see the mountains on **Otterøya,** just before we reach Molde.

62°37'N 6°20'E   + 0 hrs 48 min ④

The parish of **Hildre** to the starboard side is located in the northwest point on Haram peninsula.

Hildre chapel on **Hildrestranda** on the starboard side is a longhouse-style church constructed of timber in 1934, with seating for 385.

The village of **Alvestad** on the starboard side is situated at the foot of the long and narrow mountain called **Hildrehesten**. The ship is sailing in towards **Midfjorden**, on course for Molde. On the port side our view is out to **Harøyfjorden.**

62°37'28"N 6°25'15"E   + 0 hrs 58 min ⑤

At the mouth of the 5 km long **Samfjorden**, we can see the industrial centre of **Brattvåg** on our starboard side. Brattvåg was founded on 11.11.1911, when some visionaries from the parishes of Skjelten and Hildre, (which we have just passed) leased the rights to the river **Synnalands-elven,** and built a power station down by the mouth of the river. The flywheel from this first power plant is located in the power station building, complete with the inscription: Kring dette hjulet vaks Brattvåg fram. ("Around this wheel, Brattvåg grew") Brattvåg is today one of the biggest industrial centres in Sunnmøre.

Aker Brattvaag is the cornerstone industry in Brattvåg (founded in 1936 as Brattvaag Shipyards). The yard was bought by Aker Yards in 1993. Aker Brattvaag is part of the Aker Yards Group, one of the world's five largest shipbuilders and one of the biggest in Europe with its head office in Oslo. Aker Yards Group is known for building some of the world's largest and most luxurious cruise ships, at their shipyards in Finland and Germany. Royal Caribbean and Carnival Cruises are two of the major companies included on their list of clients.

Under the "Aker Brattvaag" umbrella are Brattvaag Offshore, Søviknes Verft (purchased in 1995) (p 75), Aker Tulcea, Romania (purchased in 2000) and Aker Estaleiro Promar, Brazil (acquired in 2001). A number of smaller, technology-oriented companies in the county are also part of the Aker Brattvaag concern. In total, approx. 3 650 people are employed by Aker Brattvaag. At Brattvåg shipyard alone, there are approx. 150 employees.

Because of its diversified structure, through the many group companies Aker Brattvåg offers various services in the fields of electro-technology and electric installations, pipe production and installation, deck machinery and cranes, design and engineering services, pressure vessel design and project management in Norway, Romania and Brazil. Aker Brattvaag supplies many purpose-built ships, including offshore supply ships and fishing vessels for customers from all over the world. They offer "turn-key" projects and the Group carries out large refurbishing and maintenance contracts.

Rolls Royce Deck Machinery division in Brattvåg is the second largest employer in Brattvåg. It is part of Rolls Royce Marine in Ulsteinvik (p 46), which is a world leader in ship design, marine equipment and complete system solutions for most type of ships. It employs approx. 6 500 people worldwide. The company is the world's largest marine winch manufacturer. It markets and supplies specialised winches to merchant ships, rigs and anchor handling vessels and is a major supplier of bulk handling equipment.

There are also textile and fish food processing industries in Brattvåg.

Immediately after passing Brattvåg and Samfjorden we can see a long white building. This is where H-windows, common in all types of buildings in Norway, are produced.

The ship continues into **Midfjorden**, north side of Haram peninsula on the starboard side.

62°37'50"N 6°31'E   + 1 hr 08 min

On the starboard side is the village of **Skor** shortly before the headland of **Baraldsneset** at the foot of **Storfjellet** (950 m above sea level).

Approx. 62°37'40"N   6°28'48"E

We cross the municipal boundary between Haram and Midsund municipalities on the starboard side

Midsund municipality

Municipal coat of arms symbolises: Two silver triangles, the lower is inverted on a blue background, indicating the two largest islands in the sound.
Meaning: Name of farm, Norse; Midja, 'Midtøya' with reference to the sound between the largest islands.
Municipal seat: Midsund (pop. 473).
Position: 62°39'N 6°33'40"E.
Area: 94 km². **Population:** 1 910.
Pop. density: 20.3 /km².
Area distribution: Farming 7 %, forestry 6 %, fresh water 1 %, other 86 %.
Trade and industry: Fishing from relatively large, modern boats, fish farming, fishing industry, farming and animal husbandry and some small mechanical industries.
Midsund municipality's home page: www.midsund.no

62°38'N   6°30'E   + 1 hr 09 min ⑥

On the port side is the small island of **Dryna,** with a bridge connection to Midøya in the east and ferry connection to Brattvåg and the larger islands to the northwest.

About 4-500 metres from the ferry landing on Dryna and on the island's south side is Franskhellaren, a cave that goes approx. 55 m into the mountain. The cave got its name from an incident involving four young French prisoners of war that escaped from the prison camp on Otterøya in November 1944. They were picked up by friendly locals during the night, transported by rowing boat to Dryna, and hidden in the cave. A small cabin was built inside the cave to provide shelter from the cold and damp. The locals brought food to the French soldiers at pre-arranged times and the four escapees lived in the cave until the war was over in May 1945. They were brought back to France as heroes and the cave has been called "Franskhellaren" ever since.

On the starboard side, we pass **Baraldsneset**, on the port side **Drynasundet**, between the islands of **Dryna** and **Midøya**.

The concrete bridge between Dryna and Midøya was built in 1969, but the islands have actually been connected via a bridge since 1904. One of the farmers on Dryna wanted his children to get to school safely. Alone, with just his own two hands, he built a bridge, 'Varnesbrua' across the sound in just two years. The bridge is preserved as a memorial to his efforts.

62°38'N   6°35'E   + 1 hr 17 min ⑦

Vatnefjorden (approx. 7 km. long) on the starboard side, with the industrial (mostly furniture manufacture) village of **Vatne** (pop. 1 586) at the head of the fjord, with the island of **Tennøya** in the middle of the mouth of the fjord.

On the port side we can see **Midøya** (13.9 km²). The mountain called **Bløkallen** (521 m above sea level) is the highest point on the island. Several settlements have been found on the island. On **Bjørnarem**, on the north side of Midøya, there are three caves quite close to each other, **Sauhellaren** (21 m long, 3 m wide and 10 m high), **Geithellaren** (20 m wide, 15 m high and 10 m long), **Lillehellaren** (8-9 m long and 3-4 m high). The three caves were partly excavated in 1912. It is believed that the first settlers in Romsdal lived here. Tools made of bones and stone were found in the caves, which are assumed to stem from the time of the European migration period. Skeleton remains of 29 species of birds and 20 species of mammals were found.

Norway was in union with Denmark from 1380 until 1814. Denmark/Norway was at war with Sweden in the middle of the 17th century and, after being defeated, had to relinquish large land areas to the Swedes. Denmark/Norway attempted to regain these areas by launching an attack on the Swedes in 1657, but was again defeated. At the conclusion of the hostilities on 28th February 1657 Denmark/Norway was forced to give up more land areas to the Swedes, including Bohuslen and Trondhjemslen. Norway was in essence split in two. The new national boundary in the west between Sweden and Denmark/Norway ran across Midøya, following the course of a huge stone wall, a former local boundary. A new war between the two countries lasted from August 1658 until May 1660 and this time, after peace was declared, Trondhjemslen was returned to Denmark/Norway. The stone fence is still used as a boundary marker between the local communities on the island.

Midøya has a bridge connection to its neighbour, Otterøya.

After **Ørsnes,** on the starboard side, east of **Vatnefjorden,** we can see the short **Vestrefjorden**, thereafter the parishes of **Birkeland**, **Rekdal** and **Dragneset** at the foot of the mountain **Rekdalshesten** (775 m above sea level). The mountain known as **Blåskjerdingen** (1 062 m above sea level) is in the background.

62°39'N   6°41'E   + 1 hr 29 min ⑦

Otterøya (76 km²) on the port side, is the largest island in Midsund municipality. The administrative centre of **Midsund** is located on the southwest side at the foot of mount **Klausethornet** (660 m above sea level).

We are sailing past the villages of **Klavset**, **Sør-Heggdal**, **Oppstad** and **Nord-Heggdal**.

© ODD FREMSTEDAL

Behind **Oppstad**, in the centre of the island, we can see the steep mountain called **Oppstadhornet** (737 m above sea level). Geologists have discovered minor movements in the mountainside and fear that a massive rock formation some 20 million m³ in size may fall into the fjord below. The actual probability of this happening is small, but a landslide of this magnitude would create a flood wave that could reach a height of 20 metres, which would devastate the whole area. Measuring devices and sensors, linked to the global positioning system are placed at strategic points in the 700 x 700 m endangered area.

After we have passed Oppstadhornet, we can then see the small island of **Tautra** on the starboard side. The island has many historically valuable old burial mounds and stone monuments.

Before Tautra, and on our starboard side, **Tomrefjorden** (approx. 9 km.) opens up. At the head of the fjord is the village of **Tomra** (pop. 1 152) with shipyards and clothing industries.

Approx. 62°42'N   6°58'E

We cross the municipal boundary between Midsund and Molde municipalities on the port side

Molde municipality

Municipal coat of arms symbolises:
A black whale pushing a yellow barrel on a blue background; depicts the herring fisheries, the former livelihood of the area.
Meaning: Norse word for farm; Moldar, plural of mold, 'earth'.
Municipal seat: Molde (pop. 18 631).
Position: 62°44'N 7°09'15"E.
Area: 363 km². **Population:** 24 254.
Pop. density: 66.8 /km².
Area distribution: Farming 4 %, forestry 47 %, fresh water 2 %, other 47 %.
Trade and industry: Fishing is relatively important with large, modern boats, fish farming and fish food processing, farming and animal husbandry, some mechanical industries.
Molde municipality's home page:
www.molde.kommune.no

The ship continues in Moldefjorden towards Molde. The 15 km long **Julsundet** (on the port side) separates Otterøya from the mainland. Then we have **Julneset,** with the mountain **Julaksla** (476 m above sea level).

A long most of our coast there are legends of sea serpents. One such legend tells of a serpent observed by the crew of a ship near Julneset in August 1746. The captain shot at the beast with his flintlock rifle. The serpent's head was more than 60 cm above the water. It had the shape of a horse's head, was greyish in colour with a black muzzle, very large eyes and a long white mane from the neck, which hung down into the sea. The body was very thick and 7-8 coils of the body were visible. The story was told and registered in documents from a magistrate's court in Bergen in 1751.

62°40'N   7°13'E   + 2 hrs 15 min ⑧

The island of **Sekken** (18.37 km²) can be seen ahead and to our starboard side with the mountain **Tranhaugen** (304 m above sea level). This island is mentioned in Snorre Sturlason's King's Sagas under Håkon Herdebrei's reign (1147-1162). He was the illegitimate son of King Sigurd Munn. Håkon Herdebrei reigned from 1157 and was killed by Erling Skakke in a sea battle offshore of the island in 1162.

Between Otterøya and Sekken, **Moldefjorden** splits into Moldefjorden and Romsdalsfjorden. Moldefjorden continues along the mainland and beyond the town of Molde and then becomes Fannefjord, which is approx. 30 km long.

Romsdalsfjorden lies southeast of Sekken. It splits into Langfjorden that branches off to the north, and Romsdalsfjorden (55 km long) that continues to the east. After the village of Åndalsnes (pop. 2 067), Romsdalsfjorden continues as **Isfjorden**. The village of **Isfjorden** (pop. 1 240) has a clothing industry with a museum.

East of Sekken is the 35 km long **Langfjorden** and near its head is the side branch, **Eresfjorden** that runs in a north-south direction.

On 22nd February 1756, innermost in Langfjorden, near the village of Tjelle a large landslide occurred. It is probably the largest recorded landslide in Norwegian history. 15 million m³ (40 million tons) of earth and rocks fell from Tjellfjellet, creating a flood wave 40-50 m high inside this narrow fjord. 32 people were killed, 168 houses, buildings and boathouses were destroyed and 198 boats were crushed. A memorial monument was raised in 2006 near the disaster area, 250 years after the disaster.

The small islands of Hjertøya, Seterøya, Fårøya and Bolsøya are on the starboard side and ahead as we approach Molde.

On **Hjertøya** on our starboard side, we can see the Department of Fisheries Museum in Molde. The museum, with 15-20 buildings, has scenes from fishing activities and exhibitions of approx. 20 open rowing and sailing boats and thousands of implements and fishing gear used by the local fishing communities. Since it opened in 1948, buildings from the whole region have been dismantled, moved and re-erected in these maritime and idyllic surroundings. Like many other islands around Molde, Hjertøya was owned by Moldegaard on the mainland (p 362). The island was permanently inhabited from the 18th century up to 1950. Hjertøya and the other islands are today nature reserves and recreational areas.

The German avant-garde artist, Kurt Schwitters, who by many was considered to be one of the fathers of modern art, was so fond of Hjertøya that he spent many summers in the 1930s renting a stone cottage from a tenant farmer on the island.

The long and narrow island of **Fårøya** (69 m above sea level) east of Hjertøya joins with the low, tree-clad island of **Bolsøya** (5.15 km²) in the northeast. The island is a popular residential area as it has a bridge (555 m) and a subsea road tunnel (2 743 m) connection to the mainland.

Archaeological finds show evidence of boat building activities from long ago. From the end of the 19th century up to 1905 there was a shipyard at Bolsøya where ocean-going sailing ships and vessels used by seal hunters were constructed.

A short distance from the old churchyard on Bolsøya is one of our largest stone monuments; however, no one knows who actually raised it. A legend tells us, however, the following;

> **"** King Olav the Holy travelled by Bolsøya just after the introduction of Christianity to Romsdal. The King pointed at Bolsøya and said that the island was a good place to build a church. Trollkjerringa (the witch) on Skåla (the highest mountain on the mainland behind the island, 1 128 m above sea level) did not like the idea of having a church close by, so she took her bow, aimed her witch's arrow and shot it at the church. The arrow did not reach its target and landed where it is today. The witch got into such a mad rage that she exploded, creating the lake, Skaalvatnet. The truth is however that the type of rock that the arrow was made of was not indigenous to Bolsøya, but was abundant on Skåra".

For centuries, Bolsøya has been a centre for the region and this is where the main church was located. The church was demolished in 1907 when there were no more funds available for its upkeep. Some of the church's inventory is to be found in other churches in Molde municipality.

Bolsøya is very interesting from a geologist's point of view. Here we can find mica-slates and many other different types of slate: limestone slates, many types of gneiss and amphibolites. Large amounts of stones have been quarried and used for buildings, roads and kerbstones and at its peak, as many as 60 masons worked in the quarry. In 1940 a stone crushing mill was constructed here, but this has since been demolished and removed.

Archaeologically, Bolsøya is also of interest. Excavations show that it was here the town of Molde actually originated. On one of the headlands, (Tingneset) there is evidence of permanent settlements from more than 800 years ago. Finds from Stone Age settlements and the oldest remains of blacksmith's activity registered in Norway are also found here together with tools and artefacts made from flint.

The main employer on the island has a workforce of approx. 30 persons producing fittings and furniture for ships.

The ship docks at the quayside in Molde (p 360)

Møre and Romsdal county

Coat of arms: Symbolises the shipping channel.
Origins: Norse: mærr, 'land', and Norse: marr, 'ocean', i.e. 'land by the sea' or 'marshland'. Romsdal takes its name from the river, Rauma, possibly from, straumr, 'stream'.
Area: 15 121 km². **Population:** 244 689.
County seat: Molde.
On our way northwards we pass several municipalities: Sande, Herøy, Ulstein, Giske, Ålesund, Sula, (Hareid, Ørsta, Sykkulven, Skodje, Ørskog, Stordal, Stranda, Norddal), Haram, Midsund and Molde. Municipalities in brackets are visited in the summer season only when we sail into Geirangerfjorden.
Topography: During the Caledonian orogeny the bedrock was pressed together by pressure from the north west, forming fissures running southwest-northeast. Crevices were created across the longitudinal axis. Erosion forces have widened the crevices, creating a system of deep valleys and fjords between high mountains, with large and small islands offshore. The mountains reach up to over 1 900 m above sea level. Approx. 55 % of the area lies above the climatic tree line (220 m in outer regions to approx. 600 m in inner regions). Flatter areas are found in the valley floors. The shorelines along the outer areas towards the coast form larger continuous lowlands. Much of this is marshy.
Climate: The climate is influenced by the ocean in the north west and the high mountains that provide shelter towards the east and south. In the winter, the wind blows most often from the southeast and the southwest. In the fjords, the wind direction is often influenced by the terrain. In the summer the wind often blows from the north east on the coast. Low-pressure systems create gales, sometimes storms, most often from the south west and north west. February is normally the coldest month along the coast, with a mean temperature of approx. 2 °C. In the fjord areas, the temperature is under 0 °C and in inner valley areas approx. - 5 °C. August is the warmest month with temperatures along the coast of average 14 °C.
Annual precipitation is 1 000-2 000 mm. Only a narrow zone along the coast has an annual precipitation level of 750–1 000 mm. Most precipitation falls in the autumn.
Settlement: Greater population density in the lowlands along the coast and along some of the fjords. Also in lower areas in inland valleys. A large proportion of the population lives on islands. The three largest towns are located at the mouth of their respective fjord systems.

COMMERCE:
Agriculture and forestry: Varying conditions for agriculture. Especially in the south, there are smaller farms, in the central and inner areas there are good agricultural areas and farms are somewhat larger. Many of the old labour-intensive farms have been abandoned and a good deal of new cultivation is taking place. There are large reserves of arable land in the north and inner areas. 95 % of the agricultural areas are used for the production of hay and as grazing land. Cattle rearing is the most important, alongside sheep and goat farming. Some vegetable, fruit and berry cultivation. 19 % of the county's area is productive forest; however, it has a slow rate of growth. This type of activity is more important in the northern part of the county.
Fishing: Møre and Romsdal is the most important fishing county alongside Nordland, relative to the number of fisheries and the value of landed catches. The most important fish species are mackerel, cod, herring and coalfish (seithe). There are a number of salmon processing plants. The county's fishermen have always been pioneers and are well known for their adaptability, due to the changing conditions for fishing and the arrival of new technology. They have started fishing activities in new waters such as the Polar seas and were the first to use new concepts such as factory trawlers. They fish along the Norwegian coast, in the North Sea and in distant waters.
Industry: Oil and gas land terminals. Shipbuilding industry. Furniture manufacture. Fisheries industries (herring oil, canneries and fish processing), boatyards, motor factories and fishing gear factories. Timber trading. Production of electricity. Textile industry is now somewhat reduced.
Merchant fleet: Not significant in terms of tonnage, however extremely important in terms of employees.
Tourism: Fjord and mountain areas in Sunnmøre (Geirangerfjorden, Hjørundfjorden) and the Sunnmøre Alps, p 54. Romsdalen (Romsdal Alps with Trolltindan) and Nordmøre (Sunndal mountains, Trollheimen). Spectacular roads (Trollstigen, Dalsnibbevegen). Mardalsfossene waterfalls. Bird sanctuary on Runde p 46. The now uninhabited fishing village on Grip p 347. Molde Jazz festival p 361. Atlantic Road, p 353, alpine skiing.
Communications: Extremely rugged landscape makes communications difficult. Relatively well developed road network, especially in the outlying areas, connected by numerous ferries. Recent, large bridge and ferry projects. The three largest towns have airports: Ålesund airport at Vigra, Molde airport at Arø and Kristiansund airport at Kvernberget. Ørsta-Volda has a short take-off and landing airport.

Source: Store Norske Leksikon.

TROLLVEGGEN

© MICHAEL.HJORTH@BIGWALL.DK

© EILIV LEREN

Communication along the coast in former times

Many of the mountains we pass on our journey have names associated with communications. Two such examples are the names **Veten** and **Signalen**.

Using 'veter' as warning signals goes back approx. 1 500 years, to A.D. 500-600 and they were in common use well into the 18th century. King Håkon the Good (approx. 920-960) introduced the 'vete' signalling system as part of coastal defences. 'Vetene' (beacons or bonfires made of wood) were used to signal an impending threat, for example by invaders. They were often erected on elevated sites and strategically placed in relation to each other. For the most important coastal 'veter', they had to be placed such that there was a clear view of 30-40 km between each one. A similar system was also in place in the fjords and valleys. The King ordered this system of 'veter' to be used from the Swedish border all the way up to Finnmark.

The expressions: **varder**, **bauner and veter** are used alternately.
- A 'Varde' was built using rocks and stones and was primarily used to mark a path in the mountains, as a marker along the coast or a boundary marker.

- 'Baune' were lit to warn of enemy activity. They were seldom placed more than 150 metres above sea level. Baune were more of a local system used for signalling or as markers for sailors.

- A 'Vete' was a wooden beacon erected within a low stone wall where logs, timber and sticks were raised to form a pyramid shape. Inflammable materials were placed under the pile of wood. Where whalebone was available then this was preferred as it burned well even when wet.

Small watch houses or cabins could also be erected next to the beacons so that the lookouts could see in all directions. If the cabin was situated on a mountain-top, it had an opening in each direction. The local people were responsible for the maintenance and manning of the beacons, especially if there was a threat of war or unrest in the area. Beacon duty was delegated by the local assembly. The teams were split into three 24-hour shifts. The men had to be young and healthy, Norwegian, free men (not a slave or a prisoner), of adult age and capable of carrying weapons, have good eyesight, hearing and good legs. Sending false signals, not turning up for duty or falling asleep on duty was punishable. The fine was determined in accordance with the actual offence and serious offences could be punished by being declared an outlaw.

The most important function of the system was to signal danger and threats of war. If the guards saw a fleet of 3-5 men-of-war ships or more the beacon had to be lit. The signal could be transmitted from one end of the country to the other in a matter of days, at the most, seven.

It is presumed that there were 800-1 000 beacons in Norway and we have information on approx. 770 of these along the coast today. This system functioned until the beginning of the 19th century.

The kingdom of Denmark-Norway took part in the Napoleonic Wars (1807–1814), on the side of the French and was therefore at war with England and Sweden. Many ships were captured along the coast and a coastal defence system was established.

In addition to the beacon system a network of much faster and effective optical telegraphs were built on centrally located high ground, with a good view out to

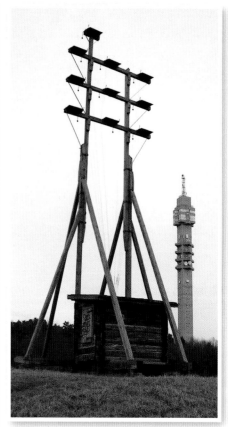

sea. These covered parts of the coast from Sweden to North-Trøndelag. In total, this system of telegraphs stretched some 1 300 km and included 175 stations. One such station was built on the mountain, **Signalen** on Stad.

On top of the signal masts, wooden paddles ('lem') were installed that could be turned around on a horizontal axis. In this way, the masts could show different layouts depending on the combination of an open 'lem' or a closed 'lem'. Some advanced signal systems could indicate numbers from 1 to 42221. The system used in Norway involved 229 signals. Each station had a codebook that deciphered each number code. The masts were placed at approx. 6–8 km intervals with a clear line of sight between each station. In this way, the signals were transmitted from station to station. Some were only relay stations whilst others were main stations.

These optical telegraph stations were expensive to maintain and were closed down after the Napoleonic Wars.

Norway from the Stone Age to the Middle Ages

On our voyage along the Norwegian coast, we pass many places where remains of ancient settlements have been found. The following chapter explains how people lived and traded along the coast through the ages - from the Stone Age to the Middle Ages.

EARLY STONE AGE (approx. 9000 B.C. to 4000 B.C.). The oldest archaeological finds from this period have been made in Finnmark and in the south. The climate was then somewhat milder and the people lived from hunting, trapping, fishing and gathering. They had effective clothing made from hides and an adequate food supply. They were very mobile and used kayaks or canoes or wandered on foot. The kayaks could be made from wood and skins and the canoes from hollowed tree trunks. These people lived in small family groups that led a nomadic lifestyle. Their dwellings were usually tents or small huts. They also lived in caves and caverns, where it was dry and they could keep warm.

Tools and weapons from this period were made from flint or another suitable material as long as it was strong and sharp. The arrowheads were fastened to long wooden sticks with animal sinews, hide, bark or grass. Among other types of tools and weapons made of flint were axes, spears and knives. Sharp-edged flint tools were used to scrape and clean animal hides of blood and fat to preserve the hides and to soften them to make them suitable for clothing or tents. Small fishing weights made of soapstone have also been found. Fishing lines were often made from animal intestines and the hooks were made from bone or horn. Towards the end of this period, people began to settle and build more permanent dwellings and remain longer in each place. Remains of these settlements have been excavated.

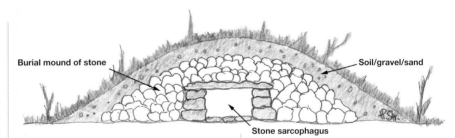

Burial mound of stone

Soil/gravel/sand

Stone sarcophagus

LATER STONE AGE (approx. 4000 B.C. to 1800 B.C.). People began to cultivate the soil and keep farm animals. Settlements became gradually more permanent. They still lived close to the coast where they could catch fish or in the mountains where they could hunt reindeer. They lived in tents and small huts, or 'long-houses' made from animal hides and skins, peat, stone, branches and other materials. They also domesticated animals such as cows, pigs, sheep and goats. The meat, horns and hides from the animals was all used, and of course the wool and milk. The oxen were used as draught animals. Barley and wheat were the first types of cereals grown in Norway and were used to make porridge and bread and also to brew beer.

Archaeological finds indicate that the Stone Age people were slighter and shorter then we are today. They knew how to spin, weave and make clothes. They were also skilled at making garments from skins.

BRONZE AGE (approx. 1800 B.C. to 300 B.C.).
Early Bronze Age (approx. 1800 B.C. to 1100 B.C.).
Later Bronze Age (approx.1100 B.C. to 300 B.C.).
In the Bronze Age, people still used flint and other hard rock materials for tools and weapons. The newly discovered metal, bronze, was very expensive and therefore little used. Farming was established as an important way of life in many parts of the country.

People started to make large and elaborate graves. On the west coast, there are many graves from this period. The burial mounds are situated on headlands and can be clearly seen from the sea. Sometimes there were many valuable items

in the graves, but many that have been excavated by modern archaeologists have been almost empty. These mounds may have been plundered, or placed there primarily as a marker, to show those sailing by that the land was owned and lived on and therefore unavailable or inaccessible for others. Some of the graves from the Bronze Age could be up to 30 m in diameter and up to 6 m in height.

THE IRON AGE (approx. 300 B.C. to A.D. 1030)
Pre-Roman Period (approx. 500 B.C. to year 0). The process of making iron had been discovered. Arts and culture made great advances in central Europe.

There are few finds in Norway that date from the Pre-Roman period. Burial rituals had changed and large burial mounds were no longer common. The dead were often cremated and their ashes were buried in "fire-graves" in the fields. The deceased took little or no property or gifts with them into the grave and the graves were made in large groups in a field or on a piece of flat land. In the Pre-Roman period of the Iron Age the tradition of stone carving (common in the Stone and Bronze Ages) declined.

Roman Iron Age (approx. Year 0 to A.D. 400). Roman items made from bronze, such as pots, pans and bowls have been found in Norway. They were often used as burial urns. Also, Roman spoons, strainers, vases and glass of different colours have been excavated. These goods came to Norway via traders and merchants. The Romans were in Gaul and England and they had trade centres near the Danube and Rhine but were seldom seen as far north as Norway.

Burial customs had changed once more. Wealthy people were often given an elaborate burial and valuable gifts were buried with them in their graves. The deceased was often buried without being cremated and their grave could be covered and marked with stones. An ordinary person would be buried much more humbly.

The Migration Period (approx. A.D. 400 to A.D. 550). The Roman Empire was in decline and the trade routes were changed. Norway's west coast, which had been an intermediary centre for trade from the north, lost its position. Village fortifications became defence posts and the coastal forests on the west coast were severely exploited.

The Merovinger Period (approx. A.D. 550 to A.D. 800) introduces the Early Iron Age. People in Trøndelag and Nordland, after a long period of trading directly with Denmark and France, were seeing an increasing trade from the North and from Russia in the east. Styles and fashions changed and it became modern to display animal ornaments and weapons. The increased amount of ships at sea both with oars and sails (Kvalsundbåten p 84, Viking ship p 123) led to new types of boats and a change in construction techniques. From this period, fewer burial mounds have been discovered, but those that have been excavated show that the deceased had farming implements with them in their grave, which tells us that farming was an important part of the communal economy.

The Viking Period (approx. A.D. 800 to A.D. 1066). The Vikings went out on their notorious raids and waged many

wars in this period. However, they also conducted peaceful trading missions and colonisation. They populated the Orkneys, the Shetlands, the Isle of Man, and The Hebrides in northern Scotland and Ireland. Dublin was founded by the Vikings in the 840s and remained a Norse kingdom until 1171. They also settled on Iceland and Greenland.

The Arabs now controlled the Mediterranean Sea area, and new trading routes were therefore opened towards Scandinavia. One of them went via Finnmark, to the White Sea and Bjarmeland. From the Baltic Sea, traders sailed up the huge Russian rivers into the Black Sea. Trading routes went across the sea to the islands in the west and the British Isles. The Norse-

men traded mostly in animal products and hides, but also bartered goods for products made from soapstone and iron. As payment, they received coins, precious metals, fine clothes, glass, jewellery and other valuable goods.

The Christianisation of Norway occurred around 1030 and with new burial rituals, the rich adornment of graves ended once more. The Viking Period ended with the battle at Stamford Bridge in York, England, where the Norwegian Viking King Harald Hardråde was defeated and killed.

THE MIDDLE AGES (approx. A.D. 1066 to A.D. 1536). Norway was now ruled by one king. There was one law for the whole country and it became more and more common to trade with foreign countries. Bergen became a major commercial centre from 1200 and onwards. Dried fish products were traded for goods such as corn, textiles, canvas, linen, wine, silver, pots, honey and salt. Nearly all goods were transported by sea. Therefore, it became necessary to establish good harbours close to the larger commercial centres.

The Black Death came to Bergen in 1349, probably on one of the ships that called at the port. It wiped out more than half of Norway's population. In 1380, Norway entered into a Union with Denmark, which lasted until 1814. The Hanseatic period, with Bergen emerging as Norway's most important town started around 1350, when German merchants, mostly from Lübeck, opened their own shops and offices here

After the Reformation, which began in 1537, Norway became Protestant when the Catholic and the Protestant churches became divided.

Source: www.uib.no/gamlenaboar

The Gulf Stream

The **Gulf Stream** is one of the important ocean currents. It transport large volumes of water over great distances and is tied into a complex system where individual currents influence each other. The effects of the Gulf Stream (together with its northern extension towards Europe, the North Atlantic Drift) mean that Norway has a considerably higher mean temperature compared to other countries at the same latitude (for example, Baffin Island in Canada, the inland ice areas on Greenland and the tundra regions of Siberia). These places have quite different climatic conditions. The Gulf Stream brings huge masses of temperate water to our coast and has therefore a remarkable influence on our climate. The westerly winds over Europe are heated largely by the current. It is assumed that this phenomenon developed about 10-20 million years ago.

The powerful Gulf Stream is a surface current that originates in the Strait of Florida and the Gulf of Mexico and along the eastern continental shelf of the USA. It flows with a speed of approx. 1.0-1.5 m/s near Florida and 0.5 -1.0 m/s at a depth of approx. 500 m. It has a volume of approx. 30 million m^3 per second before it meets the cold, south-flowing Labrador Current that diverts it out into the Atlantic Ocean towards Europe, between 35-40°N (between Cape Hatteras, North Carolina and Philadelphia). Initially the water temperature is 25 - 27°C with high salinity. As the current moves northwards, the warm surface water mixes with surrounding cooler water. The water temperature falls, the salinity is reduced, the seawater's density increases, and it sinks. This process creates an enormous 'pump effect' which draws warm surface water from the south towards the north.

West of Ireland the current splits into two. One part goes north-northeast between Scotland and Iceland (the North Atlantic Drift) and part of that current flows into the Norwegian Sea between Shetland and the Faeroe Islands and follows the continental shelf along the coast of Norway (The Norwegian Atlantic Current). Again it branches off – one into the Barents Sea (the North Cape Current), while the other continues towards Svalbard in the north (the West Spitsbergen Current). Although the water's temperature is greatly reduced on its way northwards, it is still several degrees above zero as it passes the Arctic Circle.

The current passes Greenland before it joins the cold south flowing Labrador Current that again meets the Gulf Stream farther south.

The Napoleonic Wars

Norway was in Union with Denmark from 1380 till 1814. This period is often referred to as "dansketiden" – the Danish period. The Norwegian State Council, however, existed until 1536. The actual Danish period is therefore regarded as starting around this time.

Because Denmark-Norway was allied with France and Emperor Napoleon Bonaparte during the Napoleonic Wars, that lasted from 1807 to 1814, the major powers of England, Russia, Austria and Prussia instigated a naval blockade of Norway. The country was isolated from Denmark and its markets in Europe. The timber trade and shipping activity was halted, resulting in famine throughout the country. In several places along Hurtigruten's voyage, there are stories of English Navy ships attacking and raiding Norwegian coastal villages.

Sweden was offered Norway as war reparations if they would assist in conquering France. France and Denmark-Norway

were eventually defeated and as a result Norway was handed over to the Swedes in 1814.

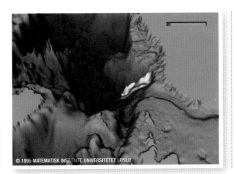

© 1995 MATEMATISK INSTITUTT, UNIVERSITETET I OSLO

The Storegga Slide

About 70 km from the coast is **Storegga** ('the Great Edge'), the continental shelf that falls steeply from a depth of 100 to 200 m to about 900 m. Storegga is about 100 km long and stretches from Stad to the island of Smøla (p 344).

Approximately 8 200 years ago, an enormous sub-sea landslide occurred at Storegga. About 3 000 km^3 of the continental shelf (about the same size as Denmark) slid away, leaving behind an edge about 300 km long. The mass shifted 800 km out into the North Sea. The Storegga Slide was one of the world's largest sub-sea landslides and it created a huge tsunami on Iceland, Shetland, the Faeroes and Scotland. Along the northwest the tsunami was 5 to 10 m high. Inside the fjords it could reach a height of 40 to 50 m.

URBS NORRIGIÆ CELEBERRIMA NIDROSIA ÆRI INCISA HIC EXHIBETUR A° J 674

Trondheim municipality

Municipal coat of arms, significance: One half is dominated by a figure in a bishop's mitre, holding a staff (symbols of dignity), standing in a church. The other half shows a king with a crown and scales, surrounded by a building that may be a castle. The scales symbolise justice.

Meaning of name: The first syllable is the folk name 'trændr', which most likely means 'strong, fertile'. The second syllable is heimr 'dwelling'.

Municipal seat: Trondheim (pop. 158 513).

Position: 63°26'N 10°24'E.

Area: 342 km². **Population:** 158 513.

Pop. density: 456.6 /km².

Area distribution: Farming 21 %, forestry 34 %, fresh water 6 %, other 39 %.

Trade and industry: Commerce closely connected with Trondheim city, the commercial centre of the region. Most types of industry are represented here with many large companies. Considerable activity in connection with the research institutions SINTEF and NTNU (Norwegian University of Science and Technology). Breweries, chocolate and confectionery factories, canneries, mechanical workshops, timber industry and agriculture.

Places to return to: Trondheim city, Nidarosdomen, Munkholmen, Ringve Museum (Norway's National museum of music and musical instruments), the Archbishop's Palace.

Activities to return to: City walks.

Trondheim municipality's home page: www.trondheim.kommune.no

After departing from Molde, we have passed the municipalities of Aukra, Fræna, Eide, Averøy and Kristiansund with the port of **Kristiansund** (60° 07'N 7°44'E) followed by the municipalities of Aure and Smøla in Møre and Romsdal county

We are now in the city of Trondheim.

Trondheim is Norway's third largest city and one of the oldest in Scandinavia. The town was founded by the Viking King Olav Tryggvason in 997 and was the country's first capital. However, evidence has been found of settlements close to the mouth of the river Nidelv that existed

Peter Nicolai Arbo: The arrival of Olav Tryggvason in Norway.

well before this time. Snorre Sturlason wrote in his sagas: "No King in Norway could rule successfully without
the cooperation of the Trøndelag people". In olden times,
kings were paid homage to at **Øretinget** in Trondheim,
the assembly site near the mouth of the river, Nidelv.
Harald Hårfagre (Harald Fairhair) (865-933), who united Norway as one kingdom, was crowned king here.

Peter Nicolai
Arbo: The battle
in Stiklestad

Olav Tryggvason (968-1000) was the great-grand-
child of King Harald Hårfagre. He spent his childhood
in Gardarike (Russia), and took part in Viking raids
around the Baltic regions and in England, and converted
to Christianity in 995. His main aim became to
resist and Christianise the pagans and to win the crown
of Norway. Olav Tryggvason was received with great
enthusiasm when he arrived in Trøndelag and was
crowned at Øretinget. He is said to have founded the
town of Nidaros (Trondheim), that already had quite a
large population, and he built his royal residence there.
King Olav began his task of Christianising the country;
however, he was killed at the battle of Svolder in the year
1000, before he could fully achieve his life's work. In
the sea battle, the King and his men fought against the
Swedish and Danish kings near the island of Rügen, just
off the coast of Germany, or in Øresund. There is some
uncertainty as to the exact location of Svolder.

The succeeding King, **Olav Haraldsson** (Olav the Holy)
(995-1030) was also a descendant of Harald Hårfagre. He
joined Viking raids when he was only 12 years old and
he was part of the Danish army that attacked London in
1009. Olav Haraldsson returned to Norway in 1015 and
established himself as the country's King with a royal seat
in Trondheim after securing his status as King in southern Norway. He built the wooden church of **St. Clemens**
near the royal residence in 1016. During the next ten

years he travelled around the country, formalised the
judicial system according to Christian principles, and
built up the church's power among the people. However,
this Christianization process led to conflict with the
established clan chiefs in the area, and he was forced
to flee to Gardarike (Russia) in 1028. He returned the
following year, but was killed in the battle of Stiklestad in
the summer of 1030. Several inexplicable incidents after
his death led to his sanctification. Christianity became
established in Norway and the resistance from the pagan
clan chiefs dwindled. Pilgrims from home and abroad
travelled to St. Clemens church, close to the King's
estate, where his casket had been placed on the high alter
in 1031. A wooden chapel was built over St. Olav's burial
site the same year.

In 1070, the foundation stone of a new church,
Kristkirken, was laid, at the same site as the chapel. The
high altar with St. Olav's casket was placed where the
King's grave once stood. In 1080, Trondheim became
an Episcopal seat and the number of pilgrims increased
further. In 1150, a new nave was built in the church and
in 1152, a new Norwegian Episcopal seat was established at Nidaros (Trondheim). Eystein Erlandsson, from
Trøndelag was the archbishop from 1161 until 1188.
He was responsible for the further extension of the
church and the construction of a special and rare type of
octagonal chancel in the east. He also ordered a large
church nave to be built, the largest room in existence
in Norway until the end of the 1800s. The church was
completed in 1320.

The construction of the **Archbishop's Palace** (in stone)
began at roughly the same time as the Episcopal seat was
established. It became a spiritual and political centre in

the Norwegian church pro-
vince, which not only in-
cluded Norway, but also
The Faeroe Islands, Shet-
land, Isle of Man, Iceland
and Greenland.

Archbishop Eystein was declared Most Holy in 1229
and was finally canonised
by the Vatican in 2001, as
one of only four Norwegi-
an saints.

Despite the fact that Norway was now united as one
kingdom, there was still a good deal of conflict surrounding the claim to be the rightful king. There were
many pretenders to the throne and many who fought to
achieve power. The famous battle at **Kalvskinnet,** was
fought between the then King Sverre Sigurdsson (1150-

1202) and Erling Jarl (Skakke) in 1179. King Sverre won the battle and gained control of large areas of Norway, more than any King before him. Norway's first stone castle, **Zion**, was built in 1182-83 in connection with these battles. The castle is a central part of the folk museum at the castle of **Sverresborg**. Kalvskinnet is now an area in the southwest part of Trondheim centre.

From 1130, Trondheim was Norway's capital; however, the town lost its status and trade rights to Bergen in 1217, when King Håkon Håkonsson (1204-63) took his seat in Bergen. Trondheim went into a period of stagnation and the increase in population experienced before 1200 waned. The population did not begin to rise again until approx. 1500.

Trondheim has been ravaged by many fires. In 1295, much of the town and the Episcopal Palace were destroyed. In 1328 there was another fierce town fire, in which Kristkirken (also known as **Nidarosdomen**), that had been completed in approx. 1300, burned down for the first time. The church was richly decorated and was regarded as Norway's finest and most magnificent holy place. The fire destroyed the wooden construction, the roof and the interior and inventory. A complete renovation had to be carried out. A new fire in 1432 caused considerable damage, however the repairs required were less serious. In 1531, the town and the church were once more destroyed by fire. The rebuilding process was however somewhat limited as the church's income, immediately prior to the Reformation, had been greatly reduced. Parts of the church were left without a roof and stood as ruins for almost 400 years.

When Archbishop Olav Engelbrektsson, the last Catholic bishop, fled from Trondheim in 1537, just before the Reformation in 1537, this coincided with the end of Trondheim's glory days.

Norway was in union with Denmark from 1380 until 1814. Denmark/Norway and Sweden were involved in several conflicts during these years. One of them was the 7-Year War between 1563 and 1570. In 1564, the Swedish army entered Trondheim and laid siege to the town for two months. The army was later driven out of the country. After a new war between Sweden and Denmark/Norway in the years 1657/58, that was won by Sweden, Trøndelag was ceded to the Swedes in February 1658 by deed of the so-called 'Treaty of Roskilde'. In December of the same year, Trondheim 'len' was returned to Norway after the Swedes were expelled by Norwegian forces.

After a serious town fire in 1681 the General Johan Caspar de Cicignon (1625-1696), from Luxembourg, was called to Trondheim to draw up a rebuilding plan for the town, a plan designed with fire prevention in mind. The centre of the town, Midtbyen, was built with large, wide, open streets and a quadratic layout as a result of the new plan, which is regarded as the finest example of a Baroque town plan in Norway. Incorporated in the plan was a military/strategic aspect and thus **Kristiansten fort** was built.

NIDAROSDOMEN 1857 WIKIPEDIA

Yet again, in 1708, the town was ravaged by fire. Nidarosdomen was destroyed, only the stone walls remained. The restoration was only just completed when the church burned down again after being struck by lightning in 1719. The church was then rebuilt over time in the simplest way possible, among other things a simple pyramid-formed roof was constructed over the old tower. The octagonal chancel was crowned by a dome in the Baroque style and the old chapel from the Middle Ages was rebuilt as a mausoleum for the wealthier citizens of the town.

Several more town fires occurred between 1788 and 1842. Due to all the damage caused by these fires, the street plan had been changed after each rebuilding phase. The requirement that new buildings had to be built of stone to prevent further fires was introduced in 1845. This requirement was, however, not followed and there was a general agreement that Trondheim should continue as a "timber town". Several of the large commercial businesses in town had interests in the timber trade. It was not before still another fire destroyed parts of the town in 1899 that the 'brick law' was enforced. Some elements of the strict law were altered in 1906, something that is evident in the town's villas from that period.

© AXEL LINDAHL (1814-1906)

Only a few areas of wooden buildings have been left untouched by fire since the beginning of the 1700s, however regular worker's houses and several magnificent wooden buildings were constructed between 1760 and 1811; some of these remain standing today. The most interesting of these is **Stiftsgården,** one of Scandinavia's largest wooden buildings and the town's official royal residence from 1906. The estate was inaugurated in 1778. It has two high storeys and a floor plan measuring almost

4 000 m² and has 140 rooms. Two other preserved buildings in Trondheim are **Hornemannsgården** (1780) and **Svaneapoteket/Sommergården** (1770s).

Trondheim has long traditions as a trading city. Timber (p 333), mining and fishing have been important industries in connection with the development of the town. A brick factory was in operation as early as the 1200s and a ropeworks, shipyards and mills were built later. The first 'modern' industry, 'Fabriken' was established near the Nidelv river in 1843. The factory had a mechanical workshop and a casting foundry. Between 1842 and 1870 there was considerable economic development in Trondheim; several businesses that were formerly based on manual piece work became industrialised. The town's commercial and industrial enterprises followed the international trends, with considerable development around the time of the First World War and the depression between the wars. After the Second World War there was a sustained period of growth and prosperity, that lasted until 1975 – during this time many new enterprises were established. Some other industries were closed or greatly reduced, such as the clothing industry in the 1960s and the building materials industry along with several brick factories that closed in the 1980s. The same effect was experienced by the mechanical industries, which included the former major employers in the town, the metal foundries, the chemical companies and furniture manufacturers.

Trondheim is Norway's second largest university city and is known as the "Technology Capital". In 1760 the college known as "Det Kgl. Norske Videnskabers Selskab" – the Royal Scientific Society, was founded. **NTH**, Norwegian Technical College opened in 1910. Some time later, other institutions and colleges were established in Trondheim, such as the College of Arts and Sciences, the Faculty of Medicine and the Science Museum. In 1996, these were brought together as **NTNU**, the Norwegian University of Science and Technology. NTNU has a professional basis in education and research in social sciences, humanistic sciences, scientific subjects, medicine, architecture and art. There are approx. 19 700 students and approx. 2 500 professional employees (2006).

© ALEX BRASETVIK

The research institution **SINTEF** is associated with NTNU. SINTEF's objective is to promote technological and other industrial research at NTNU and to develop the cooperation with commercial enterprises and other research institutions and academic milieu. SINTEF is the country's largest independent organisation for research assignments within private and public sectors related to technology, natural science, medicine and social sciences in Scandinavia and has approx. 1 400 employees in Trondheim. SINTEF was established in 1950.

King Harald V

Trondheim has always been the 'city of Kings'. Several of the Kings that reigned during the Middle Ages have been buried in St. Olav's city. Despite their death in other parts of Norway or even abroad, they were brought to Trondheim to be buried here. During the union with Sweden (1814-1905), Carl Johan XIV was crowned here in 1818, Carl XV and Queen Louise in 1860, Oscar II and Queen Sophie in 1873. During the last century, King Haakon VII (1872-1957) and Queen Maud (1869-1938), the first independent Norwegian royalty, were crowned in Nidarosdomen in 1906. King Olav V (1903-91) and his son King Harald V (1937-) and Queen Sonja (1937-) were blessed in Nidarosdomen in 1958 and 1991 respectively.

A WALK AROUND TRONDHEIM

LARGER MAP P**392**

The ship remains at the quayside in Trondheim for a few hours. There are several opportunities to make the most of the time available. It is possible to take a walk around the town's central areas.

The ship docks at Pier 1. After leaving the ship, we can see the new, modern school, shopping and office complex known as **Pirsenteret**, and the Emigrant Monument, a statue of Leiv Eriksson (p 123) that was given as a gift to the city in connection with the millennium celebrations in 1997. The statue is dedicated to the many thousands of emigrants that left for America. The statue is an exact copy of the original that stands in Seattle in the USA. After Pirsenteret, we pass a roundabout and the walk continues to the right, in a southwesterly direction along Brattørkaia. Just before the small cross-canal, use the underground walkway to reach Fosenkaia and turn left along the inner canal dock in an easterly direction. At Fosenkaia, cross the canal bridge to Fjordgata and head to the right. At the end of Fjordgata is Trondheim's popular and bustling 'fisketorg' (fish market) with many stalls selling fresh fish and seafood. Between the street and the canal are the quays (jetties) that were built in the 1700s. Today, these are apartments, offices and restaurants.

Fish and seafood have been traded in the square at **Ravnkloa,** since olden times. The name is mentioned in historical documents dated as early as 1619. During the 1800s, there was a market square and in 1896, the fish market was established. The area and market were improved in the middle 1990s and in 2000, the new fish market hall was opened. A copy of the old Ravnklo clock stands on the site, also the sculpture "The Last Viking", a work by Nils Aas. During the summer, it is possible to take a boat over to Munkholmen (p 97).

From Ravnkloa, we continue up **Munkegaten**, Trondheim's tree-lined parade street. Munkegaten stretches from Nidarosdomen to Ravnkloa. In a theoretical straight line northwards along the street is Munkholmen. The street is a typical example of the quadratic town plan of 1681, drawn up

by Johan Caspar de Cicignon (p 89). The street, that was formerly lined with low, timber houses, now has a more mixed style of architecture, with buildings from many periods, due to the many fires throughout the years.

Olav Tryggvason's gate is the first and furthest north of the wide streets that cross Munkegaten. This was also constructed according to the town plan of 1681. The corner building, Thaulowgården (no. 42) on the west side of Munkegaten is a timber mansion built in the Empire style in 1807.

Dronningens gate is the next street to cross Munkegaten. **Stiftsgården** lies on the southeastern corner of Munkegaten and Dronningens gate, with the address Munkegaten 23. As we have previously mentioned, it is Trondheim's royal residence and is the largest timber mansion in Scandinavia. The building, that has a façade of 58 m towards Munkegaten, has 140 rooms and a total area of some 4 000 m² and was built for a rich widow, Privy Counsellor Cecilie Christine Schøller. The

building was sold to the State in 1800 and it became the residence of the County Governor. Stiftsgården was used as the starting point of the coronation processions to Nidarosdomen several times in the 19th and 20th centuries – for the first time in connection with King Karl Johan's coronation of 1818 and later for Norwegian-Swedish regents. In 1906, the Norwegian King Haakon VII was crowned and Stiftsgården became the royal residence.

Stiftsgården is built in the Baroque-Classic style; however, there are elements of Rococo and Neo-Classic design. The exterior has not been altered to a great degree, in contrast to the interior. The form of the building, its décor and details create a genuine palace, made of timber. The drawing rooms stretch along the entire first and second floors. The Throne Room, also known as the Ballroom, is on the ground floor. The Queen's salon is on the first floor. On either side of these are a number of rooms combined with smaller anterooms. The décor is artistic with elegant ornamental elements, wall paintings and original wall hangings with painted Chinese motifs. Restoration and maintenance work has been carried out almost continually during recent years. The main objective is to restore the building to its former style. (During the summer season, there are hourly guided tours.)

At the junction of Munkegaten/Kongens gate is Trondheim's town square. This square was also designed by Johan Caspar de Cicignon after the fire of 1681. Before the square was built, there were several other smaller squares in the town. However, the market was brought here in 1797 and regulated by decree the following year.

In the middle of the square is a statue of the town's founder, Olav Tryggvason (968-1000) (p 88) A statue of the King was planned as early as 1860, however the statue was not unveiled before 1921 by King Haakon VII. The bronze statue is 3.5 m in height and stands on a 14.5 m high granite pedestal. In the King's left hand is a communion chalice and in his right is a sword. At the feet of the King is the beheaded god Tor, which symbolises the King's 'victory' over the pagans. The whole statue functions as a horizontal sundial with a vertical pointer, in which the statue is the pointer and the hours are indicated on the cobblestones below.

There are several fine buildings located around the square. In the north west corner (Munkegaten 26) is **Hotell Residence,** built in a Baroque style in 1914. The hotel was formerly known as Phoenix Hotell and you can see the sculpture of the Phoenix rising from the ashes.

The Middle Ages church, **Vår Frue kirke** is at Kongens gate 5. The stone-built church has been damaged by fire several times, and has been rebuilt each time. The chancel and the eastern half of the church were the 'Mariakirke' - the Middle Ages name that was used until the 1400s. After the reformation in 1537, the church was extended to the west and is now the third largest preserved Middle Age church in Norway. In 2004, the church was included in the Directorate of Cultural Heritage's list of 12 large churches of national significance. The church has been renovated considerably during the last few years.

The age of the church and its history are somewhat uncertain. King Harald Hardråde (1015-66) is said to have built a church close to the present site of Nidarosdomen, in 1060. The church was known as 'the older Maria church' and was demolished at the end of the 1100s. It is likely that the construction of the present church, 'the new Maria church' started shortly afterwards. The shape of the church is traditional, with a rectangular nave of 25 x 18 and a square chancel 11.5 x 11.5 m. It was one of the country's largest churches (apart from the cathedrals). One theory is that the church was first built as a stave church and was ruined by fire in 1206, and it was later rebuilt in stone. However, the materials used in the church imply that it is somewhat older than this, probably from around the latter part of the 1100s. The church was destroyed by the great fire of 1531, as was the Nidarosdomen and much of the town, however unlike Nidarosdomen, Vår Frue kirke was completely restored. The church is the only remaining parish church from the Middle Ages that has survived in Trondheim. The church did burn down in 1599 but was rebuilt. In the 1640s, a spire was built with room for bells and a tower clock. The church burned down once more in 1651 and several more times after that, the final time in 1708. In 1662, a new, robustly-constructed tower was built in solid stone, which was brought from Rein monastery in Trondheimsfjorden (p 102).

At Kongens gate 7 is the large wooden mansion, **Hornemansgården,** that covers an entire block. The oldest part of the building is on one floor that was built around 1720. In 1765, the mansion was taken over by the Horneman family that also owned Rein monastery (p 102). At the end of the 1770s, the mansion was rebuilt and parts of the house received an extra storey. In 1840, the façade was altered with new windows and portals in the classic style. Hornemansgården was purchased by Trondheim municipality in 1870 and was used as a police station – a function it served for approx. 100 years. The mansion, that was granted listed status in 1984, is currently a home for senior citizens.

At the southeast corner of the square is **Matzowgården** (Munkegaten 19) which houses Trondheim Tourist Information centre.

On the other side of the street is **Trondheim Tinghus** (courthouse). The foundation stone was laid before the Second World War by the cabinet minister Trygve Lie (later UN General Secretary). At the outbreak of war in 1940, the building was almost completed. Most of the building could be used in 1949; however, it was not before 1951 that the work was finally completed.

South of Trondheim Tinghus (Munkegaten 10) is the **Fylkeshuset** (County Hall).

Munkegaten 8 is the **Harsdorff-building,** the oldest part of **Trondheim Cathedral School**. The school was founded as 'Scholae Cathedralis Nidrosiensis' in 1152

and is Norway's oldest school. It was located in at least five different locations in the town before finally moving into the present building, which was designed by one of the period's most famous Danish architects. The building was completed in 1786. The Harsdorff-building was granted listed status in 1983. During the 1920s the school was extended, and again in 1960. The latest extension faces the side street, Erling Skakkes gate.

Nordenfjeldske Kunstindustrimuseum (The National Museum of Decorative Arts) is located at Munkegaten 5, previously the site of the two-storey wooden Hegdahlsgården from the 1770s. It was demolished to make way for the museum, which opened in 1968.

Nordenfjeldske Kunstindustrimuseum was established in 1893. The museum's collections exhibit decorative artwork, textiles, glass, silverwork, costumes, furniture and ceramics from the 1500s to today. The permanent exhibitions display decorative art from the whole of Europe, especially from the 1900s. An interior from 1907 has been specially designed for the museum. It reflects the Art Nouveau period. Another specially designed room is the office interior from 1952. The Museum has a permanent theme exhibit "Three women, three artists" that shows tapestries created by two of the country's most prominen décorative artists and glass created by a well-known glass artist. The museum stages approx. 25 changing exhibitions per year.

The three buildings closest to Nidarosdomen, Munkegaten 6, 4 and 2 all belong to the military administration.
- **Nr. 6** is known as the **"Non-Commissioned Officers Academy"**. It was built in 1812-14 for the Engineer Corps as a depot, but it was also used as a training college for Non-commissioned officers, hence the name. From 1930 the college became the Officers Academy.
- **No. 4, Exercise house,** was built in 1806 as a physical training centre for soldiers in Trondheim. It has a gym hall approx. 350 m².
- **No. 2** is the military **Bakery,** built in 1808-1810. Up to 1870, the building housed the bakery for the military institutions in Trondheim. For a time it was then a cobbler's and tailor's workshop and it has at one time been used as a Commandant's office.

From 1945, all three buildings were used by the **Trøndelag Regional Military Command.**

Munkegaten 1 is **Trondheim Town Hall.** The Neo Renaissance style building was originally built as Trondhjem Tekniske Læreanstalt (Trondheim Technical College) in

1895-96. From 1912 the building was used by Trondheim Engineering College. The building was rebuilt in 1929-30 and became the town hall. In addition to the regular functions of the town's administration, the town hall also houses an art collection and a gallery of portraits of most of the town's mayors.

*

The street crossing Munkegaten is **Bispegata**, which marks the southern end of the street.

*

Nidarosdomen is east of Bispegata. This monumental cathedral has a history dating back almost to the very origin of the town in 977 (p 87). The history and description of the building is so comprehensive that it is impossible to describe here in just a few lines. Hurtigruten arrange guided tours that include Nidarosdomen. If you would like to see the town 'under your own steam' – we recommend one of the professional, multi-language guided tours.

*

Just east of Nidarosdomen is the Archbishop's Episcopal Palace. Also here, a short description would not do justice to this particular attraction. A guided tour is highly recommended.

The oldest part of the **Archbishop's Episcopal Palace,** the East house, dates back to approx. 1152 when the Episcopal seat was founded. Archaeological excavations of a foundation wall from the 1200s have revealed that the original Episcopal Palace was probably larger than the current one. The foundation wall and the remains of a stone hall are built into the museum and show some of the oldest parts of the estate's history, dated to the period 1150-1500.

Closest to Nidarosdomen are the stone buildings that house the archbishop's private halls and residence, built in 1500-1550. Along the foundation wall to the east and south were workshops. The wall, weapons smithy and coin foundry can be seen in the museum. The estate was plundered and burned by the King's men in 1532.

After the Reformation, the Archbishop's Palace was confiscated by the King and was renamed **Kongsgården.** The feudal overlords were based here and new buildings were added. The former Archbishop's Palace acquired the character of a manor house, with a residential wing and a tower above the entrance that faced Nidarosdomen. From the end of the 1600s, Kongsgården was used as a military depot with an arsenal and textile store for the northern troops. The old buildings near Nidarosdomen were rebuilt to provide greater capacity. The quartermaster lived in a separate house near the southern end of the foundation wall.

The Archbishop's Palace has been plundered and burned several times, however it has always been rebuilt. The last fire was in the 1990s; two store buildings were destroyed and later replaced by a new building at an angle.

The Archbishop's Palace is now a large museum centre that exhibits important aspects of Trondheim's and Norway's history.

Museet Erkebispegården (The Archbishop's Palace museum) was opened in 1997 and is found at

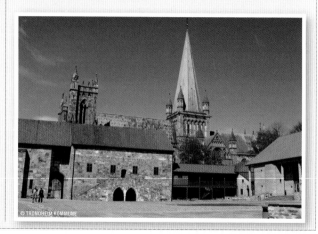

the south end of the site. The museum, that was given the award "Museum of the Year" in 1998, was built on the site of the old storage houses that were destroyed by fire in 1983. Before the new building was constructed, 120 archaeologists from 12 different countries carried out excavations of the site, from 1991 to 1995. Approx. 150 000 artefacts were found that were archived and conserved at the NTNU Science Museum. Approx. 500 of these artefacts are on display at the museum. The old defence walls were uncovered and these are now an integral part of the museum. The Archbishop's coin foundry from the 1400s was also uncovered and remains just as it was discovered by the archaeology teams. The museum also contains original sculptures from Nidarosdomen. These are unique in Scandinavia.

In the north wing that dates from the 1160s, it is possible to view the large hall that the Archbishop used when receiving guests and where he lived. Rustkammeret/Hjemmefrontmuseet (Home Front Museum) shows exhibits connected with the defence of Norway through the ages up to 1945.

In the Archbishop's Palace west wing, 'The Crown Regalia', a new, permanent exhibition opened in 2006 in the vaults in the basement. The collection includes three royal crowns, two sceptres, two orbs, two state swords, state standard and anointing horn and other coronation items.

In addition there is a **Rustkammer** (Armoury chamber) that shows exhibitions of knives, swords axes (white arms), armour and hand guns, and **Hjemmefrontmuseum**, (Resistance Museum) that shows the working conditions of the Norwegians that were part of the Home Defence Forces during the Second World War.

Just outside of the Archbishop's Palace in the southern corner, is the old saddlemaker's and gunsmith's workshop. These were built in the 1700s. The Archbishop's Palace was then known as Kongsgården and was used as a military store for the troops in the north. Naturally, buildings that housed open-flame activities were located away from the military stores that stored, among other things, gunpowder. The restaurant 'Grenaderen' is now located in the former workshop.

The walk around town may either continue along **Kongsgårdsgata,** past Nidarosdomen to **Bispegata**, then to the right on Bispegata towards the Nidelv river. You can also follow the footpath along the river from the Archbishop's Palace. Both of these alternatives end up at Kjøpmannsgata, which runs parallel to the river.

Gamle Bybro (old town bridge) stands at the eastern end of Kjøpmannsgata. It goes from Midtbyen to Bakklandet east of the Nidelv river. The first bridge on this site was built in 1685. The location

had a military/historical origin; it led to Fredriksten fort. The bridge had a tollbooth and a guard at each end and the guardhouse at the west side was manned by a 12-man troop up to 1816. The guardhouse remains today. In the middle of the bridge, at one time, was an iron grate. The bridge in its current form was built in 1861. The bridge is also known as the 'gate to happiness/luck' and is one of Trondheim's characteristic landmarks.

From Gamle Bybro we can see the quaysides along the Nidelv river, which was packed with cabins, warehouses and jetties in olden times. Extensive trading took place here. In the time of King Sverre (1177-1202) the quays were also used as defence barriers. Towards the river, fences and walkways were built where attackers could be warded off with stones.

The river **Nidelv** runs through Trondheim. It is the northern part of the 153 km long Nea watercourse that has its source in Nesjön in Sweden (950 m above sea level). Hydro-electric plants along the river provide electricity to Trondheim and the surrounding areas. The river has been used for industrial purposes since the Middle Ages; at many of the waterfalls along the watercourse, mills were built to grind the farmers' corn and the river itself was used to float timber. The Nidelv river is still regarded as one of Norway's finest salmon rivers.

At Gamle Bybro it is possible to continue the walk around town along **Kjøpmannsgaten** on the west side of Nidelva or cross the bridge and visit Bakklandet on the river's east side.

The bicycle lift, **'Trampe'** is on the east side of Gamle Bybro. It is currently the only bicycle lift in the world, installed in 1993. The lift has a length of 130 m, a height difference of 24 m and a gradient that varies from 1:11 to 1:5. The speed is 2 m per second and the lift has a capacity of 288 cyclists per hour, with a maximum of five cyclists simultaneously.

Bakklandet is one of Trondheim's old town areas. It grew up around 1600-1700 and the old wooden houses were used by seamen, fishermen and manual workers. The area had been in decline for a number of years and

it was anticipated that it would be condemned and demolished; however, in 1983 a decision was made to preserve the historical buildings. Today, Bakklandet has well cared-for houses and distinctive cafes. By following the street Nedre Bakklandet you can stroll through the area and take in the picturesque and charming atmosphere. At the roundabout after Verftstomta, we pass Bakke bridge and we are back in the northern part of Kjøpmannsgata.

ↂ

Bakke bridge was opened in 1887 as a wooden drawbridge and for many years was known as Nybrua (the new bridge). It was rebuilt as a steel bridge in 1928.

ↂ

Following **Kjøpmannsgata** on the west side of the river Nidelv, you are still in Midtbyen. Kjøpmannsgata was built as part of the town plan in 1681. Up to the end of the 1800s, the west side of the street was dominated by the merchants' houses. The street is on two levels, with a wide sloping dividing section, on which the trees function as 'spark catchers' in the event of a fire. During several town fires, but not all, the trees have prevented the quayside buildings from catching fire. Up to the 1700s the quaysides along Nidelv were the town's only shipping port. Today, only a few remain. In the 1930s, a suggestion was made that the quaysides along Kjøpmannsgata should be demolished and replaced by functionalist slatted blocks.

ↂ

On the corner of Kjøpmannsgata (no. 12) and Erling Skakkes gate is **Håndverkerforeningens hus** (Trondheim Trade Association offices). After a fire in 1898 that destroyed the whole block, remains of a church from the Middle Ages were discovered beneath the ruins. The current building dates from 1898 and was a prestige project for Trondheim Trade Association. It has exquisite stonemason and carpentry work.

ↂ

The neighbouring building is **Huitfeldtgården**, Kjøpmannsgata 14, it was built in 1900. The building is regarded as the town's last mansion and is constructed from stone in contrast to the earlier mansions. The style is a French-inspired neo renaissance.

ↂ

Lorckgården near the corner of Kjøpmannsgata and Kongens gate was formerly Trondheim's old town hall and is now the home of the town library. The ground floor is probably from 1708 and the first floor is from 1790. After a fire in 1957, the north end of the building was demolished. The remaining section of the building was granted listed status in 1984. A visit to the library is recommended. During archaeological excavations carried out on the site of the fire, a church from the Middle Ages was discovered. Parts of the ruins and preserved skeletons from the cemetery have been discovered at the rear, between the old and the new library buildings.

ↂ

The current site of Kjøpmannsgata 34 was formerly **Gram-gården** that was demolished in 1951. In 2001, it was reconstructed and now stands at Trøndelag Folk Museum at Sverresborg. The Gram-gården was built in 1745 for the mayor, and was one of the town's few private houses constructed from stone. The walls were 90 cm in thickness. It is said that the owner, during the town fire of 1841 "went to his office, closed the iron grates in front of the windows and remained there whilst the fire raged on all sides".

ↂ

Olavskvartalet (Olav's quarter) lies northeast of Bakke bridge. The foundation stone for the building site was laid by King Olav V in 1988. Olavskvartalet is comprised of private and public sections. The public section is comprised of **Olavshallen's** concert halls, Trondheim Symphony Orchestra, NTNU, Music Institute and Trondheim municipal music and culture academy. The commercial section has a hotel, shops and service offices. Olavshallen was opened in September 1989.

ↂ

After we have passed Olavskvartalet, the walk continues over **Brattørbrua** bridge, built in the early 1880s. It was rebuilt in 1938-39, adding rolling ridge spans. The bridge has three spans and a total length of 32 m. Brattørbrua is included in the national plan for the preservation of bridges.

ↂ

Our walk around Trondheim is concluded when we stroll along **Havnegata** back to the ship, which is docked at **Pier 1**.

| The ship continues to Rørvik | + 0 hrs 00 min |
| Map section 1: Trondheim – Bjugn | |

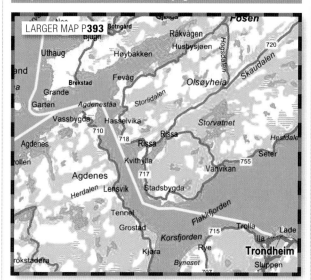

LARGER MAP P**393**

S oon after leaving Trondheim, on our starboard side we pass the small island of **Munkholmen** (0.013 km²). For a long time the island was known as Holmen or Nidarholmen. It was most likely renamed Munkholmen in 1573.

Munkholmen is quite prominent, in both history and mythology. The island was used as a site of executions before the monastery was built. Snorre Sturlason's King's Saga tells us that Håkon Jarl (935-995), who was the victor in the battle against the Joms Vikings in Hjørungavågen in 986 (p 52) and his slave Kark were both beheaded here in 995. Their heads were put on stakes on the island by order of King Olav Tryggvason (p 88).

It is somewhat unclear when the monastery was built. It was most likely between 1000 and 1100, and it probably was the first to be built in Norway. The monastery was dedicated to St. Benedict and the martyr St. Laurentius. The Benedictine Order had strict rules in regard to life in the monastery and how the monks had to divide their time between prayer and work. The Order was characterised as a 'bearer of culture'. Through testamentary gifts the monastery at Munkholmen became the owner of more than 200 estates in the Trondheimsfjord area. The monks were also engaged in milling and ship-

ping and created commercial ties with England. The monastery was the last Catholic bastion in Norway when the archbishop was forced to flee the country in the year 1537.

King Magnus Sigurdsson (Magnus the Blind) (1115-1139)) was a monk at Munkholmen. He was the illegitimate son of Sigurd Jorsalfare (1090-1130). He ruled alongside his uncle, Harald Gille (1103-1136) who was better favoured as king amongst the powerful clan leaders. Magnus eventually came into conflict with Harald Gille, and Magnus was captured by Harald's men and castrated, blinded, mutilated and imprisoned at Munkholmen in 1135. When Harald Gille was killed in 1136, Magnus was brought from the monastery. He was killed in battle in the year 1139.

After the Reformation, the buildings deteriorated and were in ruins by 1600s. The area was used by the town bailiff of Trondheim as farmland. Archaeological digs have revealed many important aspects of the ancient monastery.

The most well-known prisoner held at Munkholmen was the Danish Count Peder Schumacher Griffenfeld (1635-1699), who was imprisoned on the island from 1680 until 1698. He was born in Germany and came from a middle-class family. Due to his evident ability, he rapidly made a career in the Danish state administration. In 1668, aged 33, he became a chancery advisor, and in 1673 a state chancellor. The same year he became a Count in the province of Tønsberg with the title of Count Griffenfeld. Through his work for King Christian V (1646-1649, Griffenfeld was instrumental in limiting the power of the Danish nobility and thus became unpopular with this particular group. He also worked to avoid war between Sweden and Denmark. Sweden would then have France on their side. Ultimately, he failed in this task and the war, which broke out against Sweden in 1675 led to his downfall. He maintained contact with the French, unknown to the Danish King and for this, he was tried and sentenced to death for high treason in 1676. However, his sentence was commuted to life imprisonment and he was sent to Munkholmen in 1680. Griffenfeld remained there until 1698, he was released one year before his death. During the last year of his life, he lived in Trondheim where he enjoyed a certain degree of freedom.

Munkholmen before 1537.

Munkholmen from 1537 to 1814.

Chamberman Ahlefeldt was another well-known Danish prisoner on Munkholmen. His crime was the seduction of Princess Louise, King Fredrik V's (1723-1766) sister. After five years incarceration in the fort Kastellet in Copenhagen, he was moved to Munkholmen in 1752. He was released in 1755 and became the Commander of the fortifications in Helgoland.

Munkholmen also played a role when the Swedish king Karl XII (1682-1718) ordered General Armfelt to advance into Trøndelag with an army of 7 000 - 10 000 soldiers. The Norwegian army Commander, Major-General Vincent Budde had his forces, which numbered approx. 1 000 soldiers, encamped at Kristiansten fort and at Munkholmen. When King Karl XII was shot at Fredriksten fort near Halden, the siege of Trondheim ceased. A large number of Armfelt's men froze to death during the retreat to Sweden in December 1718.

At the end of the Napoleonic Wars in Europe from 1807-1814, in which Denmark/Norway participated on the French side against England, Munkholmen was re-mobilized for warfare. The old fort had become outdated due to the introduction of newer and more powerful weaponry. The fortress was upgraded to be able to withstand the new methods of warfare. Apart from Munkholmen, all other defences in Trøndelag were demobilized in 1816.

Munkholmen was rebuilt between 1825 and 1850, when the fortress gained the form we see today. It was built with low granite walls and 8-10 m thick ramparts. The central tower was rebuilt and a new gunpowder store was built. The prison cells in the tower were removed and less than half of the foundations remained. Despite the fact that Munkholmen had become one of Norway's strongest fortresses, it was never actually involved in any battles.

Munkholmen was a state prison from 1680 until 1850.

Munkholmen was closed down as a fortress in 1893 and became thereafter a favourite recreational area for the people of Trondheim.

During the Second World War, Munkholmen was used as a fort by the German occupying forces. The Germans installed six anti-aircraft batteries on the island to defend Dora, the German U-boat base (p 99). The top of the stone tower was removed and guns and an observation post were mounted on the flat roof. 180 German troops were stationed on the island.

Munkholmen has also had a lighthouse installation, and the island was part of the town's fire warning system. The island also functioned as a customs clearing post for goods brought by shipping into Trondheim harbour.

We leave Trondheim behind us as we sail out of **Trondheimsfjord** (130 km long and Norway's third longest). Trondheimsfjord has several 'branches'.

Steinkjer municipality (1 564 km², pop. 20 624), with **Steinkjer** town (pop. 11 338) is situated innermost in **Beitstadfjord**, the northernmost branch of Trondheimsfjord. Steinkjer was a commercial centre during the Viking period. Today, Steinkjer's economy is mostly based on agriculture and timber supply industries.

Verdal municipality (1 548 km², pop. 13 962) is a typical farming area with the municipal centre of Verdalsøra (pop. 7 474), situated at the innermost part of the main branch of Trondheimsfjord.

Verdalsøra is a modern port with various industries. Among them are: Manufacture of prefabricated concrete elements, metal works, saw mills, cement plant, a mill, corn silos and a large dairy with a cheese production. From 1973-1982 the Aker Kværner shipyards built their semi-submersible drilling rigs at Verdal. The yards are acknowledged specialists in the construction of large steel structures for the offshore oil industry.

The historic site of **Stiklestad** is also situated in Verdal. One of Norway's most famous battles was fought here on 29th July 1030. King Olav Haraldsson (993-1030) met a peasant army led by Kalv Arneson from Giske (p 73), Hårek from Tjøtta, (p 319) and Tore Hund from Bjarkøy (p 166). King Olav Haraldsson was killed in the battle and was later canonised as Saint Olav. Thus he came to be known as a martyr for Christians in Norway. Olsok, as this day is commonly known as, has been celebrated by the church since the Middle Ages and has been an official flag day (29th July) since 1930. The current church, built in the 10th century, stands where the King fell. Stiklestad was a place of pilgrimage in the Middle Ages.

In 1954, the first open air performance of the historical play 'The Saint Olav Drama' was held at Stiklestad.

From 1960, this has become an annual event in which local people play supporting roles. The event has developed into a festival over several days, known as 'The Saint Olav Festival'.

Levanger municipality (656 km^2, pop. 18 173) with the administrative centre of **Levanger** (pop. 8 681) is located southwest of Verdal. Levanger has some of the finest agricultural areas in Trøndelag. Norway's largest newspaper production plant is located in Levanger.

Stjørdal municipality (938 km^2, pop. 20 273) and the administrative centre, **Stjørdalshalsen** (pop. 10 494), lie to the east of Levanger in the short but wide 'arm of Trondheimsfjord, **Stjørdalsfjord**. Stjørdal is also a significant agriculture and forestry community. Trondheim's airport, Værnes, is located in Stjørdal. The small village of **Hell** has become internationally famous because of its name and its meaning in English in relation to Norwegian. At the railway station, next to the station's name is a sign that says – 'Gods expedition' (Gods in Norwegian means goods!).

Malvik municipality (172 km^2, pop. 12 322) and the administrative centre, **Hommelvik** (pop. 4 259) lie to the south of Trondheim. Malvik is a typical suburban area of Trondheim. Industries include paper factories, production of wooden articles and farming. Hommelvik was once the seaplane base for the district and was used by the German Luftwaffe in the Second World War. It continued as a seaplane base until Værnes airport opened in the 1950s.

Frosta municipality (76 km^2, pop. 2 461), with the administrative centre of Frosta, is a peninsula that juts out into the middle of Trondheimsfjorden. Frosta municipality's industry is dominated by agriculture. Many finds from ancient settlements and several burial mounds have been discovered in this area. On the estate known as Logtun in the south, the "Frostatinget" was held (Frosta + 'ting' – an assembly). The church is from the 1100s. A document is kept at the church, dating from the 1200s that contains the ancient 'Frostating law'.

Between Munkholmen and the mainland, east of the island Ladehammeren, lies the wreck of the tug MS "Herkules" (140 gross tons), built in 1914, which sank in September 1957. The tug was towing another ship, and the tow cable came across the tug and pulled her over on her port side. Water flooded the vessel and shortly afterwards the tug sank in 35 metres of water. There were no fatalities. The tug has not been salvaged. "Herkules" came to Norway in August 1957 in connection with the post-Second World War Marshall-program to serve as a combined tug and salvage vessel.

63°27'N   10°21'E   + 0 hrs 12 min

We sail out of Trondheimsfjord and pass between Munkholmen (0.013 km^2, on our starboard side) and the mainland. On our port side, we can see the headland of **Høvringen**. Here, approx. two-thirds of Trondheim's effluent water is treated. The water treatment plant is built inside the mountain.

In the bay near **Ila**, just before Høvringen, are the wrecks of three seaplanes, Heinkel 115 twin-engined torpedo bombers built in Germany before and during the Second World War. It is assumed that these planes were shot down during an Allied air raid on Dora in 1943. It is rumoured that 13 more aircraft were also shot down, but these have not yet been located. The submarine bunker Dora was built by the German occupying forces. It was intended to be the largest marine base in Northern Europe and was set to dominate the North Sea and the North Atlantic from Trondheim. Dora had room for 16 submarines and could be completely closed off and sealed in the event of an attack.

63°27'22"N   10°19'34"E   + 0 hrs 14 min ①

We pass Trolla Brug on our port side, which can be recognised by the four-storey building on the quayside. Trolla Brug was founded in 1650 and was at one time the main employer in the local community. The well known Trolla cast iron ovens and fireplaces were made here. Trolla Brug was finally closed down in 1987.

Up ahead is Leksvik, situated on the north side of the fjord

Leksvik municipality

Municipal coat of arms, significance: Reflects growth and vitality.
Meaning of name: First part: ancient name of river, second part: uncertain.
Municipal seat: Leksvik (pop. 1 078).
Position: 63°40'N 10°38'E.
Area: 431 km². **Population:** 3 484.
Pop. density: 8.08 / km².
Area distribution: Farming 5 %, productive forest 36 %, fresh water 7 %, other 52 %.
Employment: High-tech industry. Chemical industry. Plastics and rubber. Agriculture and dairy farming. Forestry.
Places to return to: Leksvik Village Museum, Grande trading post & museum, Leksvik church from 1668, Borgåsen fort, Amborneset.
Leksvik municipality's home page: www.leksvik.kommune.no

We can see the small community of **Vanvikan** (pop. 748) on our port side on the north side of the fjord. Vanvikan has a factory manufacturing plastic pipes, and electro-mechanical and oil related industries. Stranda church is a longhouse-style church built in 1897. There is a ferry service between Vanvikan and Trondheim.

We are approaching the municipality of Rissa on our starboard side

Rissa municipality

Municipal coat of arms, significance: Duke Skule Bårdssons (owner of Reinskloster monastery) crown.
Meaning of name: Possibly name of a fjord, from Norse ris 'rock ridge' or the verb risa, 'climb'.
Municipal seat: Årnset (pop. 1 003).
Position: 63°35'N 9°58'E.
Area: 621 km². **Population:** 6 366.
Pop. density: 10.25 / km².
Area distribution: Farming 10 %, forestry 29 %, fresh water 6 %, other 55 %.
Trade and industry: Fosen Mek. AS. Workshops. Foodstuffs production. Timber industry. Agriculture with cattle farming and corn production, vegetable and fruit growing. Salmon fishing.
Places to return to: Reinskloster and the ruins of the church. Rissa Village Museum. Coastal Heritage Museum. Rødberg bell tower. Quaysides in Råkvåg.
Rissa municipality's home page: www.rissa.kommune.no

After Vanvikan on our starboard side, we see the village **Vikan** and **Rørvika** ferry landing. From Rørvika there is a car ferry to **Flakk** (port side). This is one of the busiest ferry crossings in Norway. Rørvika is the main entry port to Fosen peninsula. The fjord between Rørvika and Flakk is called **Flakkfjord**.

63°28'N   10°07'E   + 0 hrs 36 min ②

We sail on and out of Flakkfjord. Ahead and to port, we see the communities of **Trongan** and Rein.

To the south of the Flakk ferry landing on the port side, we can see **Korsfjord**. The boundary between Trondheim and Orkla/Agdenes municipalities runs approx. in the middle of the fjord. Korsfjord splits into two branches, **Gaulosen** to the southeast with the settlement of **Buvika/Ilhaugen** (pop. 1 805), and **Orkdalsfjord** to the south-west and the Orkanger/Fannreim industrial area (pop. 6 754).

On the western side of Korsfjord is the municipality of **Orkdal** (594 km², pop. 10 812). Orkdal's main commercial activities are industry, agriculture and forestry.

63°28'N   10°03'E   + 0 hrs 42 min ③

The settlement of **Rein** on our starboard side is located just before the headland of **Raudberg** that we see up ahead.

At the headland, **Raudberg**, we now turn 90° towards the north-north-west. Outermost on the headland we can see an old white, square bell tower that was used to guide shipping in and out of the approach to Trondheim under foggy conditions. The tower is owned and maintained by the Norwegian Coastal Administration.

The village of **Stadsbygda** is located just inside of Raudberg. The ancient name of Stadsbygda was 'Stadr' which means 'stop'. Here at the headland at Raudberg, shipping had to change course and in the era of sailing ships, seafarers very often had to 'stop' here and wait for favourable winds.

Stadsbygda (pop. approx. 1 500) is historically an agricultural community. Stone carvings of five elk figures, said to be 5 500 years old, were found here, carved on a 10 m vertical rock face.

From 1806 and until the 1900s, many men from Stadsbygda went north to take part in the lucrative fishing season in Lofoten. The village and neighbouring **Reins-grenda** are thought to represent the home villages of the characters that feature in Johan Bojer's book, 'The Last Viking', which describes this special fishing activity at the turn of the century. 'The Coastal Heritage Museum', located on the shoreline, shows traditions and scenes described in the book and each year a play, based on events written of in the book is staged in an amphitheatre close by the museum.

The main commercial activity in Stadsbygda is a timber factory, which employs approximately 100 persons.

Stadsbygd church, completed in 1842, was built in timber using traditional methods. It is 34 metres long and 12.5 metres wide and can seat 140. Nearby is the site of the old church that burned down in 1837. The outline of the original church wall is marked by stones.

Up ahead and to our port side we can see the municipality of Agdenes

Agdenes municipality

Municipal coat of arms, significance: Ermine is traditionally the symbol of royalty; in this case, it represents the fur industry in the municipality.
Meaning of name: First part is of the same origin as Aga and Agder, from Norse, 'sharp', i.e. land that juts into the sea.
Municipal seat: Selbekken (pop. 394).
Position: 63°30'N 9°48'E.
Area: 318 km². **Population:** 1 775.
Pop. density: 5.58/km².
Area distribution: Farming 5 %, forestry 26 %, fresh water 7 %, other 62 %.
Employment: Agriculture. Strawberry growing. Fur farms. Forestry. Salmon fishing. Small boat builder's yard.
Places to return to: Agdenes lighthouse. King Øystein's harbour. Museum.
Agdenes municipality's home page: www.agdenes.kommune.no

63°29'39"N 9°56'E   + 0 hrs 57 min ④

The small village of **Ingdalen** in Agdenes community can be seen ahead on our port side and on the west side of Trondheimsfjord. We also see Ingdalen chapel, which was built in 1960, and seats 140.

On our port side we pass the community of **Brøskift** (Brødreskift – literally 'brother exchange'), located in the municipality of Rissa, directly across from

Ingdal. The name comes from an old legend from the 11th century.

> ❞ Two brothers inherited a farm; however, they disagreed on the how the farm was to be divided between them, something that created ill feeling between the families. The younger brother wanted more land than his parents had given to him. Eventually the authorities had to intervene, but on the night before they were to meet and settle the matter a tremendous storm swept in with thunder and heavy rain, with the result that a large rock broke loose from the mountain above. It made its way down and across the farm fields and left a huge furrow filled with water all the way down to the shoreline. The next morning when they awoke and saw what had happened, the brothers believed that the division of land between them in this way was the will of the Almighty. People came from far and wide to gaze with awe of what had taken place and named the place and the farms 'Brødreskifte' ".
>
> During an archaeological dig in 1928, a large 9-ton rock was found buried on the beach.

On our port side, we see **Lensvik** and the municipal centre of **Selbekken** (pop. 376). The port of Lensvik has long been known as the most sheltered and safest port in Trondheimsfjord. Especially in the era of sailing ships, the port was much used as a safe refuge in periods of bad weather. One story is that Håkon Håkonsson, some time in 1236, sought refuge in the port Lensvik with 40 ships.

Modern-day Lensvik is well known for its excellent strawberries and has even been given the nickname of the 'strawberry community'.

The church in Lensvik was built using cogged-joint timber in 1863. It is a longhouse-style church seating 230.

Lensvik's most famous son is the tunnel pioneer Ole Singstad, born here in 1882. He left for America in 1905 where he found work as a draughtsman and assistant engineer. In 1913, plans were drawn up to build a tunnel under the Hudson River, connecting New Jersey and Manhattan. Many contemporary engineers, including the highly regarded Thomas Edison, said this was impossible. Ole Singstad from Lensvik managed it!

Behind Lensvik, we see the two mountains, **Hestegrovheia** (656 m above sea level) and **Langrøheia** (631 m above sea level). In the hillside north-west of Lensvik, we can easily see a long, grey, flat area with a large building.

This is a fur farm where the municipality's fur breeders have gathered their activities on one site. Approx. 20 % of the world's supply of silver fox fur comes from Agdenes.

On our starboard side, we see the small community of **Reinsgrenda** in Rissa municipality. Like Stadsbygda, mentioned earlier, this community's history is also closely associated with the fishing activities in Lofoten (p 144) from 1806 until the 1900s, as described in Johan Bojer's book 'The Last Viking'. Rein church was a gift to the people of Reinsbygda from the author in 1932 and is a copy of a previous church that had been demolished.

On a hill that runs down to the shore of Lake **Botnen** (5.6 km², 2 m above sea level), unfortunately, not visible from the ship, lies the historical estate of **Reinskloster**. It is located in a natural park with many fine pathways. This was a royal seat during the Viking period and many of Norway's kings and queens have ancestors originating from Rein. It is said the family of Duke Skule Bårdsson (1189-1240) head of the influential Rein dynasty, received the estate as a gift from King Olav Kyrre (1050-1093) (p 9). The estate remained in the family until 1226 when the owner, on his sickbed, promised to build a monastery at Rein. He had a stone church and a convent built and gave land to the monastery. Reinskloster was an important religious and cultural centre for 300 years. In 1532, Fru Inger til Austrått (p 106) was chosen as leader of the monastery and took up the position in 1541. By then, 202 large farms were managed by the monastery. Some of the farms were returned to previous owners at the time of the Reformation in the 14th century. For many years, the monastery was poorly maintained, as it was managed by various owners that did not have a personal attachment to Reinskloster, and in 1675, it lay virtually in ruins. Masonry was removed and taken to other building sites, such as Vår Frue church in Trondheim in the 1600s (p 92). In 1675, Rein monastery was sold to private owners and today's owners bought the estate in 1704. Most of the lands are now sold. The main residential building from 1866 was built on the site of the old monastery. Rissa's municipal museum now stands on this site.

The industrial site known as **Kvithylla** is seen on our starboard side, then Reinskloster, and thereafter **Sundsbukta**. Lake Botnen (5.2 km², 2 m above sea level) is located just in from Kvithylla.

In 1978 the Rissa landslide occurred. Approx. 6 million m³ of 'quick clay' (a unique form of highly sensitive marine clay) from an area of 330 decares slid into Lake **Botnen** in the small village of **Rissa**. The slide left a scar in the landscape 1.5 km long. We cannot see this from the ship as it is situated further inland and by Lake Botnen. Two dwellings, 15 farms, 1 cabin and the parish civic centre vanished in the mudslide. One person was killed in the incident, which is Norway's biggest quick clay slide in the 20th century. A 3 m high flood wave caused immense damage along the shores of Lake Botnen.

At Kvithylla, just before Sundsbukta, we see Fosen Shipyard (FMV). The story of Fosen is a modern day fairytale. The founder of the shipyard, Jens Peter Bye, came from a poor background, from a family with many children. He earned his first penny as a seven-year-old, as a shepherd.

As a fourteen-year-old, he went to sea as a galley boy and cook. He learned more and more about commerce and trade and made many useful contacts in maritime and shipping circles. As a 17-year-old, he joined a ship as an engineer and sailed as a crewmember until 1940. At the age of 21, he gained his Master's Certificate and bought his first ship. Later, he bought several more ships and sailed trade routes along the coast of Norway during the Second World War, but had to flee to Sweden in 1944 because of illegal wartime activities. After the war, he resumed his shipping activities with the four ships he now owned.

For family reasons, he decided to 'go ashore'. He sold some of his ships and managed in 1961 to get a loan to buy a small shipyard with 12-14 employees in Frengen in the north west of Rissa municipality. The yard built and repaired wooden boats, but he soon realized that the future lay in ships built of steel. He therefore bought an old steel ship and rebuilt it, and retrained his workforce to become welders and plateworkers. Due to the lack of shipbuilding expertise, Bye had great problems in acquiring his first construction contract. Finally, he was awarded a contract to build a ship for a large shipping company in Oslo. His first delivery was a complete success. The ship was launched in November 1966 and he received wide media attention. The second ship from the yard, also received much attention when it was launched in 1967. The yard expanded and built larger and larger ships.

The shipyard in Frengen eventually became too small and the business was relocated to Kvithylla. Further expansion saw the establishment of Fosen Shipyards. The yard continued to grow, building bigger, more modern and technically advanced ships. Orders kept coming in. Some difficult years were encountered in the mideighties but Fosen managed to secure more work and the yard was once again doing well. Several cruise ships and ferries have been constructed for Swedish, Greek and Turkish shipping companies.

The exclusive apartment/cruise ship, "The World", with 110 apartments and 88 luxury suites was built at Fosen. The ship's 200-metre long hull was built at the Landskrona yard in southern Sweden, which is owned by the Fosen concern. The ship is the first of its kind with apartments ranging from 100 m² up to 300 m². The suites are available for lease. "The World" was launched in 2002.

Two of the newest and largest Hurtigruten ships – MS 'Trollfjord' (2002) and MS 'Midnattsol' (2003) were built at Fosen as were several newer passenger ferries designed for routes in the Mediterranean.

In June of 2007, Fosen Mek. Verksted acquired new owners.

After passing the Fosen Yard we have **Sundsbukten** on our starboard side. North of the bay, we see the mountain of **Blåheia** (392 m above sea level) and inside the bay, we can see the village of **Uddu**.

63°37'23"N   9°47'E   + 1 hr 30 min ⑥

To our port side and just south of Selvnes, we can see **Hambåra** fort. It was part of the Agdenes fortifications that included the forts at Hysnes and Brettingen that can be seen on our starboard side. Hambåra fort originally dates back to 1897. The fort had two 210 mm Armstrong cannon. In 1942/43 it was reinforced by additional cannon from Brettingen fort. The Hambåra cannon were sent out of Norway by the German forces in 1944 and it is believed that they were used during the failed German attempt to invade the islands of Åland and Suursaari/Gogland in the Gulf of Finland. In March 1945 they were replaced by three 120 mm Armstrong cannon. There was also a German torpedo battery located at Hambåra, mounted on the deck of a barge. Later it was taken onshore and camouflaged inside a wooden shed.

Next, we see the headland at **Selvnes** and the community of **Selva** in the bay. Both of these places are significant in Norway's history. In the middle of the 9th century, there was a chieftain's seat at Selva. Håkon Grjotgardsson lived at Selva, he controlled the strategically important sailing channels into Trondheim, and became one of King Harald Hårfagre's (865-933) most trusted men. His daughter, Åsa, married the King and thus became unified Norway's first Queen. One of their children, Halvdan Svarte, spent his childhood at Selva along with his two brothers. One winter, on a visit to Selva, it is said that he set fire to the house in which his half-brother Eirik Blodøks was staying, in an attempt to kill him. It is claimed by some that the red spot in the municipality's shield signifies the arson attempt.

Agdenes is the outermost headland that we see on our port side.

Next, we pass **Hysnes** fort on our starboard side, which was once a part of the naval fortifications on the approach to Trondheim, built in 1897. The cannon were used to lay a barrage of crossfire across the fjord since it was too deep to lay mines. During the period from 1880 to the 1890s, there was tension between Norway and Sweden, and Norway had introduced parliamentary system. The 'Swedish-Norwegian' Crown Prince threatened to send a 'military promenade' to Christiania (Oslo). This led to an extensive reinforcement of the fortifications around the largest Norwegian towns. Barracks were built at Hasselvika and a naval training academy was established at Hysnes fort. Hysnes fort is no longer used as a defence position and is now used as a rehabilitation centre.

We pass **Hasselvika** in the municipality of Rissa. Thereafter, we see the headland of Hysneset and the bay, Hasselvika. The longhouse-style church was consecrated in 1951 and seats 200. The altarpiece is unique in that the decorative image portrays the parishioners.

On the headland at Bretting, north of Hasselvika, is the former Bretting fort, built in 1898. The fort is now protected as a cultural heritage site.

© MICHAEL W. POCOCK

Hysnes and Brettingen forts were formerly a part of the former Agdenes fortifications.

During a rapid development in the war, the German forces invaded Norway on 8th–9th April 1940. The Agdenes fortifications were only manned by a quarter of the operative force. German marine forces went ashore at night and captured the forts after a short exchange of fire.

"In 1940 the sea approach to Trondheim was guarded by three forts that were located here to prevent an enemy reaching all the way into Trondheim city. These three forts were Brettingen, Hysnes and Hambåra. In April 1940, Brettingen, (with five cannon) and Hysnes, (four cannon) were manned by a skeleton company. Hambåra was completely unmanned, however the fort commander was ordered to mobilise the necessary troops and the forts were made ready for action. The information received in Trondheim of events taking place in the south was inaccurate and the local forces were unaware of the large German naval force that was on its way into the fjord. Therefore, it was assumed, wrongly, that a German attack was not imminent and no orders were given to increase the level of readiness.

During the night of 9th April, the troops at the three forts were told that some forts in the Oslo area were engaged in battle and the order was issued to bring up more ammunition to the cannon. Just before 3 a.m. a large vessel was observed on its way into the fjord. It was the heavy cruiser "Admiral Hipper" leading the flotilla 'Kampfgruppe 2', on its way in towards Trondheim at a speed of approx. 25 knots. "Admiral Hipper" informed the guard boat "Fossen", in plain English, that no aggression was intended, as they had been instructed by the government to enter into the port of Trondheim. "Fossen" trained its light on the cruiser, that responded by aiming two powerful spotlights at "Fossen", which blinded the crew. In order to alert the forts, the crew of "Fossen" sent up two red signal flares. The same action was repeated by the second guard boat, "Stenkjær", located further down the fjord. The alarm was raised at both Hysnes and Brettingen forts. It took 12 to 13 minutes from the alarm was given until the cannon positions at Brettingen opened fire. As most of the troops were occupied with transporting ammunition, the "Admiral Hipper" was well past the fort before the troops could man the cannon and open fire. Their fire was therefore directed toward the destroyers following the cruiser; however, they did not hit their targets. The cruiser's spotlights blinded the crews on Brettingen fort and one of the cruiser's grenades struck the fort's power cable, plunging the forts into darkness. Brettingen fort was therefore incapacitated.

A similar situation was played out at Hysnes fort. When the troops and cannon were eventually ready to fire the German flotilla was abreast of the fort, however the fort lost its power for the same reason as at Brettingen. At the same time, the German ships laid a dense smoke screen. With the smoke obscuring the ships on the fjord, the forts were prevented from shooting at the enemy ships and when the smoke eventually cleared the German flotilla had sailed away down the fjord".

Source: www.daria.no

The fortifications were rebuilt and extended during the Second World War by the German forces and further extended and modernised some time later, mostly in the late 1960s. The term 'Agdenes Fort' is no longer in use and both Brettingen and Hysnes forts are closed down.

63°38'26"N   9°46'28"E   + 1 hr 34 min

Near **Djupvika**, in the municipality of Agdenes on our port side, we can see Tjalvehellaren a short distance up the slope from the fjord. Hellaren has its own place in Norway's history. Håkon Jarl, who had won the battle against the Joms Vikings at Hjørungavågen in 986 (p 52), managed in 995 to lure his rival to the throne, Olav Tryggvason (p 88), who at the time lived in Dublin, to Norway in order to have him murdered. Olav Tryggvason and his men anchored their longships overnight, in Djupvika near Tjalvehellaren. After having been warned

© TERJE OTTO RØSTAD

by people from Selva what Håkon Jarl had in mind for him, Olav Tryggvason sailed his ships further into the Trondheimsfjord. There he discovered that one of Håkon Jarl's slaves, Kark, had killed the Jarl and for this Kark had been beheaded. Both heads were placed on stakes at Nidarholmen (p 97).

Agdenes lighthouse, first lit in 1804, is on our port side and located at the mouth of the fjord into Trondheim. It was moved and rebuilt in 1828. It was build using notched timber, measuring 7.5 x 7.5 m, and contained in addition to the fire-room, a kitchen, living room, bedrooms and entrance hall. In 1956 a 14 m high square concrete tower was built and in 1984, the old lighthouse was closed down and replaced by a fully automated lighthouse 600 m east of the original lighthouse. A burial mound, most likely from the Middle Ages, has been found close to the lighthouse.

According to historical documents from around 1540, a valuable treasure, 'the Olav treasure' lies in the deep ocean off the coast of Agdenes lighthouse. In 1540, the Danish-Norwegian King Christian III (1503-59) sent two ships to Nidaros (Trondheim) to bring the church's treasures to Copenhagen to have them melted down. All of St Olav's relics and objects from his shrine were collected and taken on board the ships that set sail for Denmark. One of these ships ran aground and sank at Agdenes. The cargo on board the ship is said to have been a large

silver crucifix from 1052, bells from Nidaros cathedral and other churches and an assortment of smaller treasures. For many years, divers, amateurs and professionals alike, alone and in groups have made many attempts to locate the treasure in this vast, deep area with strong undercurrents, – so far without success.

63°39'N 9°43'E	+ 1 hr 42 min ⑦

Our heading now changes westwards, and on our port side is Agdenes and the sound called **Trondheimsleia**.

'King Øystein's harbour' lies in an inlet to the west of Agdenes and southwest of Agdenes lighthouse. It is believed that the harbour was built by king Øystein (I) Magnusson (1088–1123), whilst his brother and co-ruler, Sigurd Jordsalfare was travelling abroad. Remains of a harbour construction were found, by chance, at a depth of 7-8 m, centrally located in the harbour area by divers in 1991. The constructions were made of notched timber frames filled with stones. These are the only known remains of a harbour found in Norway that date from the Viking period and the middle Ages. An ongoing marine archaeological exploration in the area is being conducted by the Scientific Museum.

On the starboard side, just ahead is Ørland municipality

Ørland municipality

Municipal coat of arms, significance:
Motif from the Rømer family.
Meaning of name: From Norse Yrjar,
from aurr, 'gravel'.
Municipal seat: Brekstad (pop. 1 828).
Position: 63°40'N 9°35'E.
Area: 74 km². **Population:** 5 091.
Pop. density: 68.8 / km².
Area distribution: Farming 53 %, forestry - %,
fresh water - %, other 45 %.
Trade and industry: Ørland main Air Station. Ørland
dairy. Fish processing. Textile industry. Prefabricated
concrete production. Agriculture with large farms.
Corn production and cattle farming.
Places to return to: Austrått mansion. Austrått Fort.
Ørland church. Remains of town fort at Borgklinten.
Ørland municipality's home page:
www.orland.kommune.no

Ahead and to our starboard side, we have the municipality of Ørland and the municipal centre of Brekstad. **Stjørnfjord** is on our starboard side and innermost in the fjord we find **Råkvåg** (pop. 255) with the largest number of herring landing stages outside of any town in Norway. Many of these were built in the 19th century. From 1920-30, when herring fishing was at its peak, Råkvåg was a bustling port for the fishing industry. The boats could be moored side by side, such that you could walk across the whole harbour from boat to boat without getting wet.

☙

In Stjørnfjord on our starboard side and east of Brekstad we see Austrått manor and Austrått fort. The manor's tower can be seen through the trees and to the left of the main outhouse building.

☙

63°39'N 9°45'25"E	+ 1 hr 44 min

Austrått manor is one of the oldest and most well known stately homes and cultural heritage sites in Norway from the Middle Ages and early modern times. A feudal lord,

Finn Arneson from the Arnunge family in Giske outside Ålesund (p 73) is thought to have been the first resident at Austrått at around year 1000. He was closely involved in the conflict and intrigues surrounding King Harald Hardråde (1015-66), but fled the country and went to serve the Danish king. It is believed that Austrått then became a royal estate. The estate has been owned by various noble families, some closely associated with the Rein monastery in Trondheimfjord (p 102). From 1500-1552, Privy Council and Major Domus Niels Henriksøn Gyldenløve and his wife Inger Ottersdatter Rømer (Fru Inger) were the owners of Austrått mansion. Fru Inger was a very prominent person during the Reformation period (she became the role figure in Henrik Ibsen's play of 1854, 'Fru Inger til Østeraad'). For the last 32 years of her life she was a widow, managing the estate on her own and during that time she acquired many more farms and land. Shortly before her death in a shipwreck in 1555, aged 85, she transferred the estate to her daughter, who had married into the Bjelke family. In the 17th century, the estate comprised of more than 100 farms, among them the manor at Storfosna (p 108). Austrått estate was owned by the Bjelke family until 1719. In 1935, the estate was purchased by Ørland municipality. In 1947, it was sold to the county of Sør-Trøndelag, but repurchased by Ørland municipality in 1985.

The original buildings from the Middle Ages (apart from the church) were constructed in timber. The church, a private chapel, was built of stone in the middle of the 13th century. It had a huge, strong tower, erected to defend the manor and the surrounding grounds.

The castle at Austrått was built during 1654-56 by the owner at that time, Ove Bjelke. It was a rectangular structure surrounding upper and lower courtyards. The rebuilt church and part of the main building were connected by stone walls to two lower adjacent buildings. The magnificent main portal was framed by the coat-of-arms engraved in soapstone (steatite). Fittings and ornaments were of the finest quality. According to historical documents, the castle was built because Ove Bjelke's wife had claimed that 'her father's cow shed was of higher standard than the parlours at Austrått'!

OVE BJELKE

During the Second World War, the German for-

ces built massive fortifications at Austrått fort. The fortifications, located at the approach to Trondheim, are the only kind to be found in the world. The main section is the five-storey cannon tower with three barrels. The cannon tower goes five storeys down into the mountain below and weighs over 800 tons. The cannon were originally part of the battleship "Gneisenau's" armour. The ship was destroyed by British bombers whilst in dry dock in Kiel in 1942. The three cannon became thereafter part of the fortifications at Austrått. The cannon have a range of 42.6 km and all three can be fired simultaneously. 117 men were required to operate them; however, they were never used in battle. Parts of the installation needed ball races to be mobile, and these alone weighed more than 600 tons. Austrått fort has barracks blasted into the mountain that provided quarters for several hundred soldiers.

The fort was closed down in 1968, but maintained until 1977. After this time, the Norwegian Air Force was responsible for the maintenance of the cannon. After a large-scale refurbishing operation paid for by the Defence Department the responsibility for the cannon was handed back to the municipality of Ørland and the installation became a tourist attraction.

At the municipal seat of **Brekstad** in front, we find Norway's oldest dairy, which has remained in continuous production since 1878. It has been extended and refurbished many times, most recently in 2000. The dairy has specialized in the production of 'Norvegia' cheese. Brekstad is a communication centre for the local region, with a fast ferry service to Trondheim and a car ferry service to Valset (p 338) south of Agdenes lighthouse. Three windmills are located at Brekstad.

The German tugboat, DS "Seeadler" (191 gross tons) sank near Kvitsandskjæret just outside of Brekstad in November 1942. The tug was built in Copenhagen in 1867 and refitted in Germany in 1923. It was snowing and visibility was poor when the boat ran aground late at night. The tug was badly damaged and sank in 3-10 m of water. There were no fatalities.

From historical sources, we know that the church at Ørland dates back to 1342. The present stone church has walls built in the Middle Ages (p 83). The timber structure was rebuilt in 1855 after a fire the previous year. None of the original inventory survived the fire, however it is Fosen's oldest preserved parish church.

Hovde is located at the headland south of Brekstad. Here, there are traces of the remains of six long-houses, which were part of a farm that was built in two phases. In the first phase, three houses were built in a u-shaped arrangement and occupied in the period about 300 B.C. till about A.D. 50. The second phase, also three houses, was occupied from about A.D. 500. A prison camp for Serbian prisoners of war was located at Hovde during the Second World War.

There is a local legend that a sea serpent frequently appeared in the waters between Hovde and Brestad and for that reason, none dared to go to sea to fish. The local blacksmith, Bjørn Hovde, knew what to do. He found a sturdy log, drove iron spikes into it and sailed out to meet the beast. When the serpent came close, he threw the log at it and impaled the serpent, killing it.

The settlements of Grande and Beian pass on our starboard side.

63°38'34"N   9°35'E   + 1 hr 56 min ⑧

Beian had been granted 'licence' or status as a guesthouse and coaching inn as early as 1799, due to its central location in relation to the transport network. Beian was part of the Storfosen estate and the licence was granted to the owner of the estate. A new owner took over in 1828 and three years later he was given permission to operate as a trader, in addition to innkeeper. In 1840, Beian became a regular port of call for steamships.

In 1859, a post office was opened in Beian and a short time later a telegraph office. In connection with an application to improve the harbour in 1876 it was stated that 3 100 passengers had passed through Beian and that more than 4 000 boats and 1 028 steam ships had called in the port. Various owners later managed the trading activities, however the business became less and less profitable and the trading post finally closed in 1938.

The four islands we see ahead are **Garten** (1.5 km²) on starboard side, behind we see **Storfosna** (11 km²) and even farther beyond is **Hitra** (571.5 km²) (with windmills), and ahead on our port side is the fourth island, **Sørleksa**.

We are heading towards Garten on our starboard side. The island has a breakwater and bridge connection to the mainland.

After passing Garten we sail through the channel that separates the islands of **Fosenheia** and Storfona on our port side and Garten to our starboard side. These waters have an abundance of fish due to the strong tidal currents that run between the islands.

The island, **Storfosna** (158 m above sea level) is hilly and cultivated. There is a car ferry connection to the mainland.

The oldest archaeological finds on Storfosna estate date back to the 7th century. Some of the early owners are mentioned in the Snorre Sturlason's King's Sagas. The estate was a royal seat during the reign of Håkon Håkonsson (1204-63). The Sagas tell of the following bloody incident at the manor: In 1239, Duke Skule rebelled and pronounced himself King. King Håkon sent two soldiers of the Royal Guard, carrying letters from the King. The Duke received them graciously, arranged a feast in their honour, and gave them valuable gifts. However, on their way home they were attacked by the Duke's men from Storfosna. One of the royal guards was killed within the courtyard of the manor, whilst the other managed to escape half-naked up on the church roof where he spent the night. At daylight he was discovered and stabbed to death – it is said that his blood ran down the church wall.

For many years Storfosna estate was part of the Austrått estate, which was run by the wilful owner Fru Inger (p 106). For the next few hundred years, many other well-known families from Trøndelag were among the owners. Storfosna estate became Crown property until 1574 and had an influential position in the area together with the Austrått estate up to the 19th century, when Storfosna lost its aristocratic rights. The estate has had the same owners from 1969 until the present.

Today Storfosna estate has a number of various activities. Dairy farming is the most important, with an annual production of more than 900 000 litres of milk. A herd of 400 cattle supplies gourmet beef to the Trondheim area and the estate also has a land-based halibut farm. The water is pumped up into basins from a depth of 50 m, 150 m offshore from the island. The large flock of fallow deer on the island is also an attraction for hunters.

Outside Storfosna on our starboard side we see the northernmost tip of **Fjellværsøya** in the municipality of Hitra (p 340).

After rounding Garten we head northward once again and on our starboard side we pass the west side of Beian village.

63°40'N   9°29'E   + 2 hrs 17 min ⑨

To our starboard side we have the shallow, wide sound of **Grandfjæra**, which has been reclaimed from the sea by constructing a dyke using ca 2.5 km² of earth. The area is now used as agricultural land.

Ørland Main Air Station, over to starboard is the largest employer in the region. It is also the main base for the Norwegian Air Force in Trøndelag and one of the few remaining fully equipped fighter aircraft and helicopter units. The airfield was built by the German forces during The Second World War. It has since been extended several times. The concrete landing strip is 2 700 m long.

330 Squadron was established in 1973 and is equipped with Sea King rescue helicopters (SAR-search and rescue). The squadron has approx. 340 missions annually, mostly air ambulance and SAR tasks and is part of Norway's flying ambulance service. They cover large areas of the coastline, along with units in Rygge in Østfold, Sola near Stavanger, Bodø and Banak, near Lakselv in Finnmark. From 2007 a system will be in place that will allow helicopter rescue teams, with a doctor onboard, to respond in less than 15 minutes.

Up ahead we can see the easily recognisable Steinsvikfjellet (324 m above sea level) and the village of Djupfest. The mountain lies north of Bjugnfjord.

63°43'30"N   9°32'E   + 2 hrs 33 min ⑩

At the entrance to **Bjugnfjord** we pass Kjeungskjæret lighthouse. This distinct and well-known lighthouse rises 20.6 m above sea level and the light itself is 17.5 m above high tide. It has a range of 13.1 nautical miles. The light-

Map section 2: Bjugn – Rørvik

LARGER MAP P**395**

house stands on a concrete base located on a rock that is flooded at high tide. It is the only octagonal lighthouse in Norway. It was built in 1880 and was manned by keepers and their families until 1947. Thereafter it became a 'roster' lighthouse, which meant that the lighthouse keepers lived on land and manned the lighthouse in shifts. In 1956, a power cable was laid out to the lighthouse and for the first time the installation had electricity. In 1987, Kjeungskjæret became fully automated and unmanned. It became a protected lighthouse in the year 2000.

The lighthouse started out being a 'family' installation, i.e. the keeper lived at the lighthouse with his wife and children (along with their own teacher). The lighthouse required attention around the clock and therefore the keeper's wife had to help out when necessary. If the weather was good they could row to the mainland to purchase supplies, but in stormy periods they were completely isolated. The lighthouse did not have a telephone and so those at the lighthouse had to send messages to the mainland using Morse code. One of the teachers living there in 1938 described the living conditions at the lighthouse: 'We used to put a rag in the sink to prevent salt water spraying all over the floor. If the weather was really bad, the rag would fly out of the sink nearly hitting the ceiling.' The children living there had to be tethered to a pole out on the rock when they were outside playing and had to be brought inside before the tide came in. Today it is possible to visit the lighthouse and even stay overnight. The longest continuous period for one keeper at Kjeungskjær lighthouse was 26 years, from 1926 until 1952.

The boundary between the municipalities of Ørland and Bjugn bisects Bjugnfjord

Bjugn municipality

Municipal coat of arms, significance: The importance of fishing and shipping for the area.
Meaning of name: Norse bjugr, 'curved', uncertain origin, poss. name of fjord, estate or river.
Municipal seat: Botngård (pop. 1 126).
Position: 63°46'N 9°48'E. **Area:** 382 km².
Population: 4 561. **Pop. density:** 11.9 /km².
Area distribution: Farming 10 %, forestry 26 %, fresh water 7 %, other 57 %.
Trade and industry: Offshore-related companies. Foodstuffs. Timber industries. Fish and mollusc farming. Animal feed production. Agriculture with cattle farming and corn production. Tourism.
Places to return to: Kjeungskjæret lighthouse. Vallersund trading post, with old houses. Uthaug estate. Mølnargården with exhibitions and open-air theatre. Bjugn church. Sjøgata at Uthaug. Nes church.
Activities to return to: Coastal culture festival in Lysøysund.
Bjugn municipality's home page:
www.bjugn.kommune.no

The wide opening into **Bjugnfjord** can be seen on our starboard side. The fjord cuts 14 km into Fosen peninsula. **Botngard** located at the head of the fjord, is the municipal centre. Bjugnfjord was formerly an excellent herring fishing area.

The small community of **Uthaug** (approx. pop. 411) is on our starboard side, close to Kjeungskjæret lighthouse at the entrance to the fjord. Uthaug has a good harbour and has been an active fishing port since the 17th century. The old and listed area around Sjøgata along the seafront in the old harbour area has charming single-

© ANDREAS HVIOSTEN

NORSK KULTURARV / NORWEGIAN HERITAGE

storey wooden houses built by the local fishermen in the 19th century. Norway's first fishermen's association was founded here in 1896.

Uthaug manor was built by the Austrått estate (p 106) around the year 1740. The manor has 40 rooms, all retain the original fittings and inventory and there is a Renaissance-inspired garden. The barn has three floors, all the farm equipment has been kept intact. The manor has important cultural and historical value.

Bjugn church is situated approx. 8 km inside the fjord. There has been a church on this site since 1637 - the original church was struck by lighting and burned down in 1952. A new church was built and consecrated in 1956.

The group of islands known as **Tarva** (12.8 km²) can be seen on our port side approx. 10 km from the mainland. (Tarva has as many islands as there are days in a year). The highest point is only 23 m above sea level. **Husøya** is the largest island (7.8 km²). Southwest of Tarva is Karlsøya where archaeological surveys have uncovered old settlements. There is also a military shooting range on this island. Tarva came under the Austrått estate until 1858 when it was separated from Austrått and became an estate in its own right with 10–15 tenant farmers. In the northeast is **Været**, which has burial mounds from the Viking period and a nature reserve.

Fishing and the associated trades were very important for Tarva in the 19th century, resulting in a large increase in the population on the islands. The islanders' way of life was based on fishing combined with farming and hunting. The population began to dwindle around 1960.

As early as 1878, some of the islands were granted protected status as egg and down resources (p 333). The island of Været and some smaller islets are now nature reserves and have been a protected landscape since 1982. 206 different plant species have been recorded and over 100 different species of birds have been observed. The islands have the largest preserved areas of coastal heather in mid-Norway, and for this reason, they are kept as a national cultural landscape. The islands are now a recreational area and a popular destination for summer tourists.

There was a great deal of activity around the Tarva islands during the Second World War when the German forces were building coastal fortifications. At the peak of the construction period, there were as many as 2 000 soldiers on the islands. Prisoners of war from many na-

tions were used as manual labourers. The German Luftwaffe erected a Mammut radar installation on Tarva. The bunker

on which it stood was 24 x 25 metres square and 2 500 m³ of concrete was used in the construction. The large radar toppled over in an autumn storm in 1944. The bunker was camouflaged with stonework and from a distance, it looked like an enormous burial mound.

63°45'N   9°32'E   + 2 hrs 39 min ⑪

On the shoreline under **Steinsvikfjellet** (324 m above sea level), we see the villages of **Berg**, **Nes** and **Djupfest**. The latter has a car ferry connection to Tarva. Djupfest is partly hidden behind a stone breakwater. Evidence of ancient settlements has been found in this area, such as burial mounds and several objects of archaeological interest.

DS "Irma" sank outside Djupfest 14th March 1944 in 10-46 m of water. The ship (3 757 gross tons) was built in Sunderland in 1906 but was registered in Hamburg. The ship was sailing from Narvik to Hamburg, carrying a cargo of iron ore. The ship ran aground and broke in two. There were no fatalities. The fore section of the vessel came to rest on land and the valuable cargo was recovered. One of the ship's anchors was recovered in 2001 and is now located outside 330 squadron's HQ at the SAR station at Ørland airfield as a symbol of the security the rescue helicopters provide.

Nes church, on the starboard side, just northwest of Djupfest, was built in the early part of the 16th century. The church burnt down after being struck by lightning in 1770. A new church, seating 250, was built and consecrated in 1774. It had an impressive spire that became a familiar navigational aid for sailors. This church eventually became too small and was sold and moved to Sunnmøre. The new church was built using cogged-joint timber and has seating for 500. It was consecrated in 1879 and has been extensively refurbished several times. It is hidden from sight at this point of our journey; however, it can be seen from Bjugnfjord and as we approach Valsfjord.

In the background, we can see **Kopparen** (483 m above sea level). On top of the mountain, there is a telecommunications mast that is used by the state-owned broadcasting company.

63°48'N 9°35'E   + 3 hrs 02 min ⑫

Valsfjord, on our starboard side, runs northwest in the direction before **Vallersund** peninsula. At the head of this short fjord lies **Valseidet**, a narrow neck of land that connects the mainland with the peninsula and separates Valsfjord from the 7.1 km long and 1.5 km wide inland fjord, **Koetfjord**. At Valseidet, several burial mounds da-

ting from the Iron Age (p 83) have been discovered. These were probably made for wealthy people, as some of the mounds excavated contained articles of gold and silver, bracelets and decorative bronze plates.

On our starboard side, we pass Valsneset and **Vallersund** peninsula with power generator windmills on the headland.

63°51'25"N 9°40'E   + 3 hrs 08 min ⑬

We pass the village of **Haldorhamn** on our starboard side.

By **Vasøya** close to Haldorhamn lies **Torra**, 'Norway's mid-point'. Measured along the coast from north to south this is the exact halfway point.

The small island groups of **Tristeinen** and **Gjæsingen** are ahead to our port side.

Our voyage takes us past innumerable small islets, rocks and skerries. The ship sails in amongst these islands during the summer season, but mostly outside during the winter season.

63°51'N 9°41'37"E   + 3 hrs 09 min

We pass **Valsøya** on our starboard side, it is connected to the mainland by a bridge built in 1977. On the east side of the island is an old trading post, **Vallersund**, dating from the late 18th century. Well into the 19th century, it had a very active trade in fish from Lofoten. The fish (mainly cod) was dried on the rocks. Dried fish

is the main ingredient of the dish known as bacalao, which is very popular in southern Europe. This trade continued up to the beginning of the 20th century. Today Vallersund has a fish processing industry.

63°52'33"N 9°46'E   + 3 hrs 10 min

Jøssund, with its church, is on our starboard side, further north-eastwards on the island. The present church is a longhouse-style church, seating 450 and built in 1886 using notched timber with inside and outside panelling. The church was refurbished in 1951-53. It replaced the old church, which was taken down and sold.

We sail on into the narrow channels between islands and skerries. After passing Jøssund on our starboard side, we pass between the islands of **Skjørøya** on port side and first **Madsøya** on our starboard side, then **Lysøya** with the village of **Lysøysund** (pop. 299) on the mainland. Lysøysund has various industries, such as food processing, offshore industry and fish farming.

On our port side, we can see the island of **Asen**, and Asen-Vågsøy lighthouse, which was completed in 1921. The lighthouse was built in order to assist sailors during the herring season as most boats sailed into Lysøysund and Stokksund. It was automated in 1975.

Approx. 63°54'40"N 9°52'E

We pass the municipal boundary between Bjugn and Åfjord municipalities

Åfjord municipality

Municipal coat of arms, significance: Symbolises Åfjord-boat.
Meaning of name: From estate of Å, from Norse á, å – 'river'.
Municipal seat: Årnes/Å (pop. 1 126).
Position: 63°57'N 10°13'E.
Area: 955 km². **Population:** 3 258.
Pop. density: 3.4 /km².
Area distribution: Farming 3 %, forestry 17 %, fresh water 6 %, other 74 %.
Trade and industry: Smaller industries, foodstuffs and timber supply. Prefabricated concrete production. Construction industry. Åfjord-boat. Agriculture and cattle farming. Fishing along the coast. Forestry in inland areas.
Places to return to: Harbak cave. Burial sites from Viking period at Å. Stone monuments at Dragseid.
Åfjord municipality's home page: www.afjord.kommune.no.

63°54'40"N 9°52'E   + 3 hrs 26 min ⑭

Lauvøyfjord begins between **Lysøya** and **Lauvøya** on our starboard side. It continues into **Åfjorden**, which cuts 15 km into the mainland in a north-easterly direction. At the head of the fjord is **Å/Årnes** with timber and concrete industries and a flour mill.

Skråfjord runs parallel and north of Åfjord.

Selnes, on our starboard side, is located outermost on the narrow peninsula between Åfjord and Skråfjord. 6 km on the inside of Selnes and between these two fjords lies **Dragseid**. The name clearly indicates that it was on this narrow neck of land that boats were dragged overland, between the two fjords. At Dragseid is Norway's largest collection of stone monuments and various burial mounds, some round, some long and one star-shaped. All these finds indicate that there was considerable activity in this area, particularly during the migratory period (A.D. 400-600) (p 83).

63°55'N   9°53'E   + 3 hrs 28 min ⑮

The lush island of **Lauvøya** is on our starboard side, situated at the entrance to Skråfjorden. Approx. 80 persons live on the island, which has a bridge connection to the mainland.

The entrance to Skråfjord is on our starboard side and in the background, we can see **Kvenndalsfjellet** and **Bjørnbakk**-klumpen (444 m above sea level).

63°56'15"N   9°48'E   + 3 hrs 33 min

On our port side, we have passed the island of Asen and Asen-Vågøy lighthouse. Ahead and on our port side is the island of **Linesøya** (17 km²) with **Linesfjellet** (230 m above sea level). The island's inhabitants live mostly along the eastern and northern shores. A bridge, to be constructed in 2007/2008, will join this island and its neighbour, **Stokkøya**. Until the bridge project is completed, a ferry connection is in operation.

On our starboard side, we see **Tårnes** to the north of Skråfjorden and thereafter the villages of **Tørhogg**, **Ratvika** and **Grøttingen**.

64°00'27"N   9°58'E   + 3 hrs 58 min

We continue our journey into **Linesfjorden** and see Stokkøya ahead and to our port side. On our starboard side, we pass the small villages of **Herfjorden**, **Lauvik** and **Lauvstranda**.

Near Maltsekken on the island of Stokkøya, lies the wreck of the MS "Moi", 490 gross tons, built in 1952. The ship, loaded with stone, on its journey south in January 1975 ran aground in bad weather and sank in 25 m of water.

For a brief period, sea urchins were farmed at Stokkøya, mostly for export to Japan. The project proved not to be economically viable and production was eventually halted.

We are now approaching **Stokksundet**, which is one of Hurtigruten's most famous passages on the stretch between Trondheim and Rørvik, as it negotiates the narrow sound between Stokkøya (16.7 km²) on  our port side and the mainland. At its narrowest point, the sound is only 45 m wide.

As we sail into Stokksundet, we see **Harsvika** on our port side.

We are passing under Stokkøy Bridge, opened in December 2000, which is the longest, at 525 m, in the co-

unty of Sør-Trøndelag. It has six spans, the longest is 206 m in length and the bridge has 30 m clearance at mean sea level. Near the starboard side pier, we see a ship wrecker's yard.

Just after passing the bridge, we see **Kuringvågen** Marina on our starboard side where there is an example of the Åfjord boat. This type of boat was developed in Åfjord over many hundreds of years and used for fishing and for carrying cargo until steam-powered and motorised vessels took over. The boats were built on the farms, which had their own timber. At the peak of production, approx. 1 000 of these boats were built annually.

© TOR SKJEVDAL

The red Stokksund church can now be seen at **Revsnes** to our starboard side. The wooden cruciform church was built in 1825 and seated 300. It has been restored twice, once in 1885 and later, in 1955.

Before heading 90° northwest in the middle of **Stokken** sound we pass **Langholmen** and **Høgholmen** on our starboard side.

West of Langholmen lies the wreck of DS "Lita", 318 gross tons, at a depth of 27-50 m. She ran aground on January 30th 1944, on her way south carrying ballast from Brønnøysund to Trondheim. The ship was built in Germany in 1890 and sold to Norwegian owners in 1936. "Lita" was used by the German navy along the coast during the Second World War.

Approx. 60 m from the wreck are the remains of the German patrol boat "V-5706/Ostmark", 204 gross tons. The ship was originally built as a whaling boat in 1925, but was used as a patrol boat by the Norwegian Navy. After the invasion of Norway in April 1940, the ship was fitted with a 76 mm cannon and sailed under the German flag. She ran aground in June 1941 near Stokksundet and now lies in 35-45 m of water. The wreck is in surprisingly good condition. The hazardous cargo was eventually removed in the middle of the 1990s.

It is said that before the First World War the German Keiser Wilhelm II was on one of his many sea voyages along the Norwegian coast. He failed to see the entrance to **Stokksundet** and scolded the pilot as it appeared his royal yacht was heading straight for the rocks.

We are now sailing through the narrow sound of **Stokken**. On our starboard side is Harbakfjellet and on our port side is **Nyphoggfjellet** (225 m above sea level).

In 1948, the postal ship "Uranus", built in 1925, 935 gross tons, ran aground on Svartskjær in Stokksundet in thick fog on its passage from Bergen to Tromsø. The ship had often come under fire from Allied aircraft during the Second World War but has escaped serious damage. After running aground several ships came to her assistance and some of her cargo was saved. Twenty minutes after a salvage vessel arrived, "Uranus" slid off the rocks and vanished into the depths. The wreck is still in good condition and lies in 70-90 m of water.

To our starboard side is **Harbakstranda**, which is located on a green neck of land out towards Stokken sound with the impressive **Harbakfjellet** (363 m above sea level) in the background.

The village of **Harbak** is situated behind the headland that we pass after leaving Stokksundet. Harbak was actually a part of the Rein monastery on Rissa (p 102), but was bought by two brothers in 1754. There are approx. 30 people living and farming here today. The well-known and magnificent **Harbakhula** (cave) is located approx. 50 m up the mountainside above Harbak village. The cave was formed by a fissure in the rock, during a period when the land level was lower. The sea has eroded the rocks and hollowed out the cave. It is 140 m deep and approx. 30-40 m high, it reaches 160 m into the mountain. The acoustics inside the cave are excellent and several concerts and art exhibitions have been held there. No evidence has been found that indicates the cave has been inhabited for any length of time, however there are traces of a stone wall spanning across the cave. This may indicate that the cave has been used as a refuge by the early settlers. The cave is one of the most magnificent natural formations in South-Trøndelag and we can best see it when we head north again.

According to an old story, some time in the Middle Ages, a Portuguese ship ran aground just off the coast of Harbak:
…"The survivors managed to find shelter in Harbak-hula (the cave). From here, way up on the hillside, they eventually found their way down to civilisation where they were offered passage back to Portugal. According to the story, one of the sailors preferred to stay behind – he had fallen in love with a girl from Stokksund. They married, cleared some land and became farmers; however, some time later they moved to Harbak. They had four sons who divided the farm between themselves when their Portuguese father died. The story goes on to tell us the descendants of Harbak had special features and these have been passed down through the generations. A true Harbaker is short of stature, has jet-black hair and dark, sparkling eyes. He is modest, thrifty and seldom loses his temper. His dialect differs very much from that normally spoken in the village. They are also known for being generous and welcoming…"

As we leave Stokksundet we see a number of islands up ahead and to our port side. These include **Hosnaøyan**, **Flesa** and **Gjæsingen**. On our starboard side, we pass **Pålsodden** on Harbak peninsula.

To our starboard side we pass the sound of **Skjørin**.

64°06'42"N   10°02'34"E   + 4 hrs 36 min ⑯

We pass the municipal boundary between Åfjord and Roan municipalities

Roan municipality

Municipal coat of arms, significance: Symbol of the coast and the bird life.
Meaning of name: Norse (*róða* 'staff', in reference to mountain peaks.
Municipal seat: Roan (pop. -).
Position: 64°10'N 10°13'43"E.
Area: 373 km². **Population:** 1 030.
Pop. density: 2.8 /km².
Area distribution: Farming 3 %, forestry 9 %, fresh water 5 %, other 83 %.
Trade and industry: Fish farms. Building and construction firms. Agriculture, cattle farming. Fishing.
Places to return to: Bessaker. Roan church.
Activities to return to: Fishing Festival at Bessaker.
Roan municipality's home page: www.roan.kommune.no

64°07'43"N   10°05'E   + 4 hrs 41 min ⑰

The parish of **Kiran** is over to our starboard side, with **Kiranfjellet** (308 m above sea level) in the background, followed by **Hongsand**, the tiny island of **Sørkråkøya** and the larger, inhabited **Brandsøya**, which has a bridge across to the mainland.

On our port side, we have a series of smaller islands: **Almenningen** (1.7 km²), where marble for the Nidaros cathedral was quarried, then **Farmannøya**, **Kjeøya** and **Værøya**.

64°11'N   10°09'42"E   + 4 hrs 58 min ⑱

Berfjorden, on our starboard side, runs behind Brandsøya. **Utro** Bygdetun (village green), located on the northern side of the entrance to the fjord, has a collection of old buildings dating back some 300 years that depict the traditional way of life on the coast at Roan.

Roan church, also known as 'Fosen cathedral' is located further down along Berfjorden. The church was built in 1702, and the altarpiece, pulpit, epitaph and chalice are from even earlier period, with the oldest objects dating back to 1639. The church is regarded as one of the finest in the region.

© JOAR HAUKNES

64°12'32"N   10°12'E   + 5 hrs 10 min ⑲

© JOAR HAUKNES

On the island of **Kaura** to our port side is Kaura lighthouse. Built in 1931, it is a 22 m high cast iron tower, painted with a white belt, and stands on a foundation of stone 30 m above sea level. It was the penultimate manned cast iron lighthouse to be built in Norway. The lighthouse was automated and de-manned in 1959. The light has a range of 12.2 nautical miles. It was converted to a solar power supply in 1984. Kaura lighthouse has been preserved because of its historical value.

At the entrance to **Brandsfjorden** we see the island **Terningen** to our starboard side. The island was de-populated in the 1970s. In Brandsfjorden, we find the villages of **Hofstad** and **Straum**.

© JOAR HAUKNES

64°14'N 10°15'45"E	+ 5 hrs 15 min ⑳

We are now passing between the islands of **Sandøya** and **Børøya** on our port side and the mainland, where we see the villages of **Storvika** and **Bessaker**. There is an annual fishing festival held at Bessaker. Further along, we can see the parish of **Vik**, under the mountain of **Skjelden** (360 m above sea level).

Approx. 64°18'N   10°21'E
We pass the municipal boundary between Roan and Osen municipalities

Osen municipality

Municipal coat of arms, significance: Symbolises fishing.
Meaning of name: Probably named after a farm near the mouth of Steinsdalselva. The innermost part of the fjord that lies beyond is also named Osen.
Municipal seat: Steinsdalen (pop. -).
Position: 63°35'N 9°58'E. **Area:** 387 km².
Population: 1 051. **Pop. density:** 2.7 /km².
Area distribution: Farming 10 %, forestry 5 %, fresh water 83 %, other 18 %.
Trade and industry: Gravel quarry. Plastic piping manufacture. Agriculture with cattle farming. Fishing. Some fish farms.
Places to return to: Vingsand village green. Cave paintings at Sand. Halvik cave.
Osen municipality's home page: www.osen.kommune.no

As we head towards **Sandviksberget** up ahead we pass the two islands, **Skjervøyan** on our port side and up ahead we can see **Hepsøya**.

64°18'43"N 10°24'E	+ 5 hrs 44 min ㉑

Osen bay is now on our starboard side, along with **Osen** community that has also lent its name to the municipality. Osen church is from 1878. Near the church there is a stone monument erected in the memory of the fishermen who lost their lives in the 'Storuværsdagen' ('the day of the great storm') in 1859, and the victims of the Second World War. Thereafter we pass **Sundet** and the bridge across the mouth into the bay.

64°19'23"N 10°25'47"E	+ 5 hrs 48 min ㉒

The ship sails between Ramsøya and the mainland. To our starboard side we see first the village of **Strand**, then **Sandviksberget** at the foot of **Hopaheia** (311 m above sea level), where eight figures carved in stone have been found, dating back to the Stone Age. One of them is almost 3 m long and depicts what is thought to be a pilot whale. A burial site dating back to the Bronze Age has also been found here (p 83). Due to expanding industry, more houses are being built to cater for a growing population. Strand harbour has been modernised to be able to handle all types of coastal vessels.

The bay **Høvika** is on our starboard side and north of Sandviksberget we have Ramsøya and Stokkeløyan on our port side. Then we have the short fjord **Hopen** to our starboard side and the fishing harbour **Vingsand**.

64°22'N 10°27'E	+ 6 hrs 03 min ㉓

The two islands, **Raudøyan** on our port side and **Fårøya** on our starboard side are located at the mouth of the narrow **Vingen** fjord. We now see a peninsula with **Langstrandheia** (344 m above sea level), then the small bay, **Helvika** before passing **Svesfjorden** on our starboard side and to the southeast.

We are heading towards Buholmråsa lighthouse and on the headland up ahead and to our starboard side is the village of **Sætervika**, at the south point of **Oksbåsheia** (268 m above sea level). Sætervika was previously a typical fishing village that now, like many other similar villages along the coast, caters for an increasing number of tourists.

64°23'N 10°26'46"E	+ 6 hrs 07 min ㉔

Buholmråsa lighthouse, on our starboard side, is located on the small island of **Sønnaholmen**, just off the main-

land. The lighthouse was built in 1917 and functioned as a navigational aid in the main coastal shipping channel. The 23.5 m high structure is made from cast iron and is painted with a typical white band. The light, situated 36 m above sea level, has a range of 17 nautical miles. Radar beacon was installed in 1992 and the lighthouse was automated. It was de-manned in 1994 and became a protected property in 2000. Dwellings and outhouses belonging to the lighthouse are arranged in a 'courtyard' and paved pathways connect the jetty, boathouse and lighthouse. The lighthouse was bombed and damaged during the Second World War but was repaired and today has appreciable historical value.

After passing Buholmråsa lighthouse, we enter the infamous sea passage called Folda.

> **DS** "Pollux", 1 676 gross tons, built in Helsingør, Denmark in 1921, sank outside Buholmråsa in November 1900, on a voyage from England to Tromsø with a cargo of coal. The ship finally sank in 34 m of water, after salvage operations lasting for almost a week failed to save the ship. The wreck is still today practically intact.

Kya lighthouse is situated on a small, exposed islet some way out to sea northwest of Buholmråsa lighthouse. The structure is a 22.5 m high cylindrical cast iron tower placed on a robust, meticulously carved stone foundation. The light itself is 29 m above sea level and has a range of 12.3 nautical miles. The lighthouse is automated and battery powered. It has a simple cabin lodging with four berths. The boathouse is purpose-built to be able to withstand the harsh climate. The islet is considered to be one of Norway's most exposed locations and landing at the lighthouse is difficult even in fine weather. Kya has considerable historical value.

We are now sailing along the side of **Oksbåsheia** on our starboard side, into the municipality of Flatanger.

Approx. 64°26'N   10°27'E

We pass the county boundary between Sør-Trøndelag and Nord-Trøndelag (p 332) counties

We pass the municipal boundary between Osen and Flatanger municipalities

Flatanger municipality

Municipal coat of arms, significance: Symbolises boat bows seen from the front. **Meaning of name:** Likely origin is flat, meaning 'shallow', and angr, 'fjord or inlet'. **Municipal seat:** Lauvsnes (pop. 439). **Position:** 64°30'N 10°54'E.
Area: 458 km². **Population:** 1 168.
Pop. density: 2.6 /km².
Area distribution: Farming 2 %, forestry 16 %, fresh water 5 %, other 77 %.
Trade and industry: Metal working industry. Fish farms/processing. Relatively small farms, agriculture combined with fishing. Cod fishing most important.
Places to return to: Utvorda coastal fortifications.
Flatanger municipality's home page: www.flatanger.kommune.no

Folda is now ahead of us. This open stretch of sea begins at Buholmråsa lighthouse and continues until we reach the islands of Gjæslingane and Grinna lighthouse in the north, a distance of 30 nautical miles. The ship requires two hours to negotiate this exposed and notorious stretch of sea, which quite rightly, is nicknamed 'the sailors' cemetery'.

> It is said about Folda: "One moment she is generous and friendly and offers us the most delightful experience; whilst in the next moment she can turn and flare up in an angry fury like an inferno. Surrounded as she is in the north by thousands of islets and many treacherous skerries and reefs she will always keep you on your toes."

64°30'N   10°34'E   + 6 hrs 41 min

We pass on our starboard side the four islands, Aspøya, Halmøya (173 m above sea level), Værsøy and Villa (106 m above sea level).

64°31'22"N   10°35'35"E   + 6 hrs 45 min ㉕

Halmøya has been a central meeting place for the people living in this area from the times of the Sagas and up to the late 19th century. Here we find remains of an early church. No one knows when the first church was actually built, but records show that one existed here in 1468.

The church was struck by lightning in 1724 and badly damaged but was later repaired and extended. The same occurred again in 1773 and the church was once more repaired and in use by 1779. Lightning struck a third time in 1873, this time the church remains were demolished. The cemetery with its large stone monument (can be seen from the fjord) was in use until 1887. Services are held on the old church site on special occasions.

On Halmøya is the cave known as Håkkahallar'n. The cave is 32 m deep, 12 m wide and 6 m high. Due to its very good acoustics, concerts are sometimes held inside the cave.

64°32'48"N   10°37'30"E   + 6 hrs 53 min ㉖

© LARS FORSETH

The very special and robust Villa lighthouse can be seen on our starboard side. The construction, located on a hill, is hexagonal and made from hewn granite. The lighthouse is only 14.7 m high but the light is 39.2 m above sea level and the beam has a range of 18 nautical miles.

Villa lighthouse was built in 1838 and was the first to be commissioned north of Trondheim. Most probably, it was also the last of the 'coal-flame' type to be built in the world, as coal-flame lights were already obsolete compared with oil-fired lights, which had become the favoured method by then. However, it was argued that the supply of coal was easier to maintain at remote locations than oil. In addition to the lighthouse itself, dwellings were built to house the keeper, also outhouses and a forge, two coal bunkers, a boathouse and a loading jetty. During the peak of construction activity, 70 men were on the site. More than 59 700 stone blocks were used and some 1 600 roof tiles. The lighthouse used nearly 500 barrels of coal per year that was brought from Scotland and the Channel Isles. Villa was converted to an oil-flame lighthouse in 1859. It was de-commissioned in 1890 and is now a protected site. The lighthouse equipment was moved over to Nordøyan (p 119), but the stone structure still stands on **Villa**.

On Villa and on the neighbouring island of Halmøya there are traces of ancient settlements that indicate that the islands were used as fishing ports as early as the Viking period and in the Middle Ages.

64°36'49"N   10°42'29"E   + 7 hrs 15 min

Utvorda Fort (which cannot be seen from the ship) lies behind several islands to our starboard side. This coastal fort was the largest of 11 forts built along the coast of **Namdal** and **Namsenfjord** between 1941 and 1945. Construction work was carried out by several hundred German soldiers, 'Organisation Todt' workers, Norwegian workers and Russian prisoners of war. When completed in 1945, the site had more than 100 buildings, of which 14 were concrete bunkers. The fort had 10 large fixed cannon, moveable cannon, mortars, anti-aircraft guns, flame-throwers, spotlights and radar. Chambers and tunnels connecting ammunition depots and trenches were constructed inside **Utvordfjellet** (277 m above sea level). Nine minefields containing approx. 5 000 landmines were laid and 4 km of barbed wire fencing was installed to protect the fort. Mines were also laid offshore. When fully mobilised, 1 200 to 1 400 German soldiers were stationed at the fort. A radar station was built at Utvorda and a similar fort was constructed at Rørvik. These two forts had therefore complete control over all shipping sailing on Folda.

After the war, the German forces cleared the minefields and the Norwegian engineers destroyed the bunker entrances and trenches. The barracks and prisons were demolished. The scope of the remains of the German installations show just how enormous the forts actually were.

We pass the municipality of Namsos on our starboard side

Namsos municipality

Municipal coat of arms, significance: Represents the moose, common in the area (Namdalen).
Meaning of name: From the name of the river, Namsen and os, 'river mouth'.
Municipal seat: Namsos (pop. 9 230).
Position: 64°28'N 11°30'E.
Area: 775 km². **Population:** 12 573.
Pop. density: 16.2 /km².
Area distribution: Farming 3 %, forestry 40 %, fresh water 3 %, other 54 %.
Trade and industry: Timber and sawmills. Foodstuffs manufacture. Graphic design and printing. Workshops, steel fabrication and electronics. Considerable agriculture with cattle farming and forestry.
Places to return to: Namsos town. Fosnes. Overhalla.
Namsos municipality's home page: www.namsos.kommune.no

When Norway was invaded by the German army in April 1940, the town of **Namsos** became strategically important. The rail connection northward was a vital supply route for the German troops. However, it was just as important for the Allied forces; they needed the railway to be able to travel southward towards Stjørdal and Trondheim. Thus it became essential for the Germans to prevent a counter-invasion by the Allies. On April 14th 1940, a large Allied force, mainly British and French troops, landed at Namsos with a mission to recapture the airfield at Værnes and the city of Trondheim. The Germans began bombing Namsos on the 20th, forcing the Allied forces to retreat. On May 3rd the Allied forces, totalling some 6 000 soldiers, were evacuated back to Britain. Only a few buildings remained in Namsos. To prevent a renewed attack on Namsos, this time from the sea, Utvorda Fort and several minor forts were built.

64°37'N   10°42'E

The islands in Vikna municipality: Yttre-Vikna, Mellom-Vikna and Inner-Vikna can be seen on our port side.

Approx. 64°38'N   10°45'E

Vikna municipality

Municipal coat of arms, significance: Symbolises fishing and fish farming (salmon). **Meaning of name:** Norse vikn, 'inlet' – an ancient island name, very suitable for the topography of the islands.
Municipal seat: Rørvik (pop. 2 640).
Position: 64°51'37"N 11°14'23"E.
Area: 310 km². **Population:** 4 019.
Pop. density: 13.0 /km².
Area distribution: Farming 5 %, forestry 6 %, fresh water 2 %, other 87 %.
Trade and industry: Fish farms. Large landing stages for fish catches. Foodstuffs manufacture. Timber supplies. Workshops. Agriculture with cattle farming.
Places to return to: Norveg Coastal Museum. Sør-Gjæslingane fishing village.
Activities to return to: Sea fishing. Recreational cabins by the shore.
Vikna municipality's home page: www.vikna.kommune.no

Vikna is famous for having Norway's longest coastline with 5 712 islands, islets, reefs and many skerries. This is the reason why we see so many markers and lighthouses along our route.

Fosnes municipality is on our starboard side (546 km², pop. 712), with the highest mountain, **Grønkleppen** (765 m above sea level) and the largest island, **Jøa** (55 km²). It is a typical coastal farming community with limited traditional fishing activity. Jøa is the birthplace of the Norwegian poet, Olav Duun. A lot of his work is inspired by life on Jøa.

64°42'N   10°52'E   **+ 7 hrs 45 min ㉗**

Among the scores of islands to our port side is **Sør-Gjæslingan**, an old fishing port situated on a group of small islands. This port was once one of the most important fishing communities south of Lofoten. As the fishing boats in the early 20th century became gradually motorized these communities expanded in activity and grew in size. During the spring cod season there could be as many as 1 300 boats and 4 000 men working here at any one time. It is claimed that it was possible to walk across the bay from boat to boat without getting your feet wet! The village had a clinic and a telegraph station, a home for pensioned fishermen, community centre and many shops. Eventually the industry dwindled to almost nothing and in 1975, the inhabitants were given grants to assist them in moving off the island. The Nord-Trøndelag Coastal Museum now owns and maintains the old buildings.

An account of the 1906 Gjæsling tragedy describes the following drama, in which 1 500 men fought desperately for their lives in the rough Folda sea. Most managed to struggle through the waves and onto the shore, but over 30 men lost their lives:

"Earlier that week the weather had been poor and the nets had been out for a long time. The spring cod was plentiful this year so lines and nets were surely full of fish. The weather became fair after days of rough seas. Some of the veterans had been out looking westward since the early hours. Some felt that there was a strange atmosphere, but the departure signal was given at the usual time.

The spring cod shoals were far out at sea that year and the voyage out took a long time. It was so calm that most boats had taken their sails down. To make rowing easier, many threw their ballast overboard. The ballast was used to improve the sailing qualiti-

de-manned in 1987. The interior was damaged in a storm, but a room was refurbished and shows how high the standard of living on the station had actually been. A proposal has been made to make the area, together with Sør-Gjæslingan, a cultural heritage listed site. The station architecture displays different uses of building materials, from two distinct historical periods. The lighthouse station has considerable historical value.

es of the boats in strong winds. In the course of the day's fishing, the ballast would be replaced by the catch anyway.

However, it was not to be. A storm blew up from the north west before the fishing had even started. The winds came suddenly and with tremendous force. The seas were whipped up and it started to snow. It was impossible to see from one end of the boat to the other. There is an old saying: 'The Sea takes what the Sea wants'. The sea did indeed take what it wanted on the fatal day of the hurricane at Folda, 2nd March 1906.

Source: Unknown

The **Nordøyan** islands, located far out to our port side, are probably Norway's oldest fishing ports as they are situated in a very good fishing area. There is documented evidence of settlement as far back as 1521. The fishing community has always remained operative during the winter fishing season.

Nordøyan lighthouse station is situated on an islet by the old fishing port north of Folda. The large wooden lighthouse building is located on top of a low cast iron tower on a stone foundation reaching up to the gables. The lighthouse equipment was moved from Villa station (p 117) in 1890, when Nordøyan lighthouse was built. The large French-made lens has special optical qualities and is therefore still in use. The light rotating equipment is partly preserved. The living quarters have been modernised, but still have many of the original fittings. Today's station houses stand on the foundation of a previous station building, and the sheds and oil tanks are arranged as a courtyard. The boathouse and landing stage is located north on the island and have good facilities. The station is located in a rich cultural area with traces of farming activity. Together, the preserved fishing port on Nordøyan and the lighthouse are of appreciable historical value.

Gjeslingene lighthouse is located on a small islet in the main shipping channel north of Sør-Gjæslingane. The lighthouse station was built in 1877. It is a 24.3 m high cast iron tower on a stone foundation and a four-storey reinforced concrete block built in 1938, which contains a boathouse, technical equipment and living quarters. The station has PRB-searchlights installed. It has a concrete bridge and landing stage and was automated and

Due to a navigational error, the Hurtigruten ship, 'Sanct Svithun', ran aground nearby Nordøyan in October 1962. The ship should have followed the main route from Buholmråsa across Folda to Rørvik, but instead took the wrong course northwestwards towards Nordøyan lighthouse. The ship, with 89 people onboard, should have docked at Rørvik at approx. 2130 but did not arrive. 30 minutes later, a distress signal was picked up. The hull of the 'Sanct Svithun' had been torn open and the ship had sunk. As the ship's heading had been incorrect the search for survivors was conducted in the wrong area. Both the ship's crew and the search party believed the ship had grounded close to Grinna lighthouse (p 120). Late that night, some survivors drifted ashore at Nordøyan and were able to inform the rescuers where the ship had actually grounded. Forty-one lives were lost that night at Folda. The pilot, the mate and helmsman, all those on the bridge at the time, lost their lives. A stone monument was raised in 2002 to commemorate the tragedy.

Foldafjord is now on our starboard side. The entrance is 4-7 km wide and goes in between the islands Jøa and Abelvær and far into Nærøy municipality.

Approx. 64°43'N   10°55'E
Nærøy municipality is on our starboard side

Nærøy municipality north of Rørvik is described during day 10 (p 330).

64°44'25"N   11°00'E   + 8 hrs 00 min ㉘
Grinna lighthouse on our port side was commissioned August 1st 1904. Today it is automated and de-manned. Folda Coastal Association manages and maintains the site.

64°46'37"N   11°03'42"E   + 8 hrs 13 min ㉙
On our starboard side we see the village of **Abelvær**, located on the island **Store Kalvøy** (0.48 km²). Abelvær was formerly a fishing port, with a general store and a tavern, a canning factory, a slipway and a mechanical workshop.

On **Ramstad** island (120 m above sea level), next to Abelvær, lived an important chieftain in the Viking period. One of the largest burial mounds in this region is Kjetilhaugen on Ramstad. The grave is shaped like a boat.

Ahead we see the two Abelvær islands, **Jernøy** and **Storøya** (127 m above sea level).

The three large islands (in Vikna municipality) on our port side are separated by narrow sounds.

Yttre-Vikna (85 km²) is the outermost island and thereafter to our port side are **Mellom-Vikna** (50 km²) and then the flat, barren and marshy **Inner-Vikna** (99 km²). On **Borgan** island north-west of Yttre-Vikna, artefacts and traces of Stone Age settlements have been discovered. Many burial mounds have been found here in Vikna. The largest of these was discovered in 1991 at **Ryum** on

Inner-Vikna. The size and scope of the mounds indicates that Ryum was also an important centre in the Viking period. Due to agriculture, most of the burial mounds are gone, but many artefacts have been preserved. In addition, sacrificial sites, Stone Age sites and stone monuments have all been found on Vikna (p 83).

We continue into **Nærøysundet** and our next stop, Rørvik, now up ahead. Arnøyan is over to our starboard side, and then we pass the two small islands, **Nordøyan** and **Treholmen**.

64°48'N   11°07'E   + 8 hrs 23 min ㉚
Close to the shipping lane and to our starboard side we see **Nærøya** (149 m above sea level.). This island was a cultural, economic and religious power centre for the Outer Namdal region for more than a thousand years. The old St. Maura church at Nærøy, built in the 12th century, is one of Norway's oldest stone churches. The church has been destroyed by fires several times, but has always been restored. The church is now in ruins, but it is nonetheless maintained as a historic site. The rectory was in charge of farming on the island. The protected main building is also restored and the old foundations are visible, but the rest of the farmhouses are now in some disrepair.

The Norwegian priest and poet Petter Dass (p 318) spent some of his childhood here on Nærøya.

Rørvik airport, (with its tall mast, on our port side) was opened in 1986. The landing strip is 800 m long. The airport has connections to Trondheim's airport, Værnes and some other smaller airports in Helgeland.

64°50'N   11°12'E   + 8 hrs 34 min
Marøya lies north of Nærøya. **Martnadssundet** is the sound between the two islands and from approx. 1600 until 1877, this was a central and very busy trading place on this coast. It has been a trading post for a long time and during archaeological excavations carried out on the sea bed nearby, articles from the 14th century were discovered. The main livelihood on the island has been farming and fishing. Today there are a few active fishermen on the island, but no longer any farming.

We pass underneath Nærøysund Bridge, which was opened in 1981. The suspension bridge is 701 m long and has 17 spans. The main span is 325 m long and has a mast clearance of 41 m. Nærøysund Bridge connects the islands Inner-Vikna and Marøya. Marøysund Bridge on our starboard side connects Marøya with the mainland in Nærøy municipality.

The ship docks at the quayside in Rørvik (p 331)

The fishermen had their own rules about what to do (and not to do) in a boat:

© KYSTMUSEET

1. When you rowed or sailed out in the morning, it was a good sign if a Cormorant followed you. It was safe to go out to sea that day. If the Cormorant flew ahead of you, crossed your bow or flew towards you, it meant danger and you should turn about and head for home.

2. Another bad sign was if a grey seal surfaced ahead of the boat when rowing out. If the seal came up behind you, it was a good sign.

3. It would not be a good herring catch if the crew did not have lice. The more lice the better the catch. Dreaming about lice meant there would be plenty of herring.

4. An old skipper once said that when a certain person in his crew sang and was in good spirits in the morning before leaving, the boat could expect trouble - probably with the engine or the fishing gear.

5. People or animals that experienced a difficult birth only actually delivered their young when the tide came in.

6. Herring and other fish are easiest caught when there is a new moon and full moon.

7. If it was calm, one way of getting fair winds was to scratch the mast or drive a coin into the mast.

8. Fair winds could also be called up by biting off a splinter along the mast.

9. Certain women should not cross over gear that had been made ready. This could bring trouble and lead to a poor catch.

10. Never talk about cowsheds and farm animals when fishing. Do not mention horses and goats - that could bring bad luck. Do not mention otters and foxes.

11. Never, never, board a boat with cow dung on your shoes or hay seeds on your clothes. This is certain to bring bad luck.

12. Do not talk about anything that has to do with farming when fishing. This was also certain to bring bad luck.

13. Our forefathers did not have compasses. If they got lost, they would lay a louse on the deck and the louse would always crawl towards the north.

14. Fishcakes prepared during a rising tide were always more porous and tastier than those made during an ebb tide.

15. When going to sea you should always turn your boat in the direction of the sun's path across the sky. If you turn it the other way it could mean trouble and a poor catch.

16. If the fish raised its fin after being caught and thrown into the holding tank, that could mean a good catch, usually up to where the fish had raised its fin – it was measuring the amount, so they said.

17. If you spat on the bait and say "fish for the cat" before casting the line, it guaranteed a good catch.

18. Never thank anyone for herring bait. To be thankful for bait might lead to bad luck.

19. When someone had drowned and a search party was sent out to look for them, it was best to take a full-grown cockerel along. When the boat sailed over where the body lay, the cockerel would crow.

20. Never start a voyage on a Friday or on the 13th of any month. The number 13 is unlucky.

21. If a fisherman on his way out to sea saw a woman throw out her dishwater, this could mean bad luck.

Sør-Trøndelag county

Coat of arms: Reflects archbishop's coat of arms 1475-1510.
Origins of name: From Norse thrændr, and og, 'law, area, local jurisdiction.
Area: 18 848 km². **Population:** 278 836.
County seat: Trondheim
We pass the following municipalities on our way northwards (in order): Hitra, Hemne, Snillfjord, Agdenes, Orkdal, Trondheim, Rissa, Ørland, Bjugn, Åfjord, Roan, and Osen municipalities.
Topography: Border areas in the south and east are high mountain ridges. In the southwest are Trollheimen and Dovrefjell with peaks over 1 600-1 700 m above sea level. In the southeastern region is Røros plain, here the mountains are somewhat lower, less than 1 200 m above sea level. Along the Swedish border, the mountains reach up to 1 762 m above sea level. Out towards the fjords and the coast the landscape is lower. In the large valleys, there is rich moraine soil and the tree line here is approx. 800 m above sea level. The lowlands of Trondheimsfjorden and outermost areas in the valleys are covered with marine clay and sand and several clay slides have occurred. Along the coast, there is a good deal of bare rock and few forests. Approx. 46 % of the county is over 600 m above sea level, 26 % between 300 m and 600 m. 28 % lies less than 300 m above sea level.
Climate: Maritime climate in the north west, continental in the southeast. High mountains shelter towards the south and east. The most common wind direction in the winter is from east to south. Trondheimsfjorden functions as the channel for the cold air coming from inland areas. During the summer, the wind is most often from northwest-northeast. The mean temperature in January is normally around 0 °C along the coast, -2 to -5 °C in the interior lowlands and approx. -10 °C in inner valley areas. The mean temperature in the warmest month (July or August) is approx. 14 °C in the coastal areas and slightly higher, approx. 10-15 °C inland. Annual precipitation is approx. 1 200 mm along the coast, 1 500-2 000 mm on coastal mountains. Other areas approx. 800-1 000 mm. Most precipitation occurs in autumn and winter.
Settlement: Mostly around the lowlands around Trondheimsfjorden, along the coast and the larger valleys. Trondheim is the largest community. There are also several other large communities spread along Trondheimsfjorden. Of the 14 larger communities (apart from Trondheim) that have a population of over 1 000, seven of these are less than 45 km from Trondheim and many residents of these areas commute into Trondheim.

COMMERCE:
Agriculture and forestry: Large agricultural areas with good soil. Larger farms along Trondheimsfjord and the low-lying valleys. Most farms are larger than the national average. Good agricultural areas in the valleys and in the mountain villages, although somewhat smaller in size. 4.1 % of the area is used for agriculture. 22 % of the agricultural areas in the lowlands are used for growing cereals, mostly barley. In the coastal areas, valleys and mountain villages, animal husbandry and milk production is the most important commercial activity, some sheep farming in valleys and mountain areas. Approx. 20 % of the area within the county is productive forest.
Fishing: Fishing is an important industry on the larger islands of Hitra and Frøya and in the coastal municipalities north of Trondheimsfjorden. The most important fish species are herring, cod and shellfish. Considerable amounts of salmon and sea trout are fished in the sea and in rivers. The county has several well-known salmon rivers. Fish farming is an important commercial activity and Sør Trøndelag is the fourth largest fish farming county in Norway.
Mining and industry: Mining was formerly of great importance; however, the mines are now closed. Most industry is concentrated around Trondheim. Large foodstuffs industry and processing plants for agricultural products. Chocolate factory and breweries. Timber manufacture, cellulose sulphate and paper factories, graphic design industry. Ferrosilisium plant. Shipbuilding industry in Rissa.
Service industry: Service industries have experienced considerable growth, especially in Trondheim, which is the centre of higher education and research. Trading, banks and services of considerable size.
Tourism: Tourism in towns and tourism/recreation in the coastal areas during the summer season, a large number of winter tourists in mountain areas. In Trondheim, the most visited places are Nidarosdomen, Munkholmen and Ringve Museum. In Røros, the old mines and the traditional houses have been included on the list of UNESCO's World Heritage sites since 1980. Cruise journeys along the coast, Rein monastery (p 102), Austrått fort (p 107) and mansion (p 106) are the mountain areas that attract most tourists and the ski centre in Oppdal is the most popular winter ski resort.
Communications: Trondheim is the central hub for all communications in the county. There is an extensive road network, fast boat services to several places along the coast and a railway connection to Bodø in the north, Oslo in the south and Østersund and Stockholm in Sweden. Trondheim airport Værnes, Røros airport and Ørlandet military airport with civil flights provide air routes to most of Norway.

Source: Store Norske Leksikon

The Vikings

The Viking period lasted from approx. 800 to about 1066. One of the first references to the Vikings was made in 793 by the Northumbrian scholar, Alcuin of York. "Hordes of heathens came and destroyed the Abbey church on Lindisfarne, a centre of learning famous across the continent. Monks were killed in the abbey itself, thrown into the sea to drown or carried away as slaves along with the church treasures. Never before has such an atrocity been seen". Lindisfarne (5 km²) is an island off the coast of Northumberland in England.

During this time, the population in Scandinavia was increasing. Along the west coast, arable land was becoming scarce, and so alleviate the problem, the Vikings began to journey to foreign lands. The Vikings that came from the area where Sweden is today, sailed up the Russian rivers. From what is now Demark they sailed south towards England and France. Those from Norway ventured westward to the Faeroes, Iceland and Greenland and as far away as Newfoundland on the coast of Canada.

The Vikings were skilled shipbuilders and competent mariners. The large, magnificent Viking longboats were especially seaworthy and spacious, with a riveted construction and propelled by sails and oars. The longboats could be 25 m long. Along the gunwales, holes were cut out for the oars and the mast was secured mid-ships. They were mostly built using timber and planks of oak and were adorned with intricate carvings in the bow and stern. The oars were made of pinewood. The ships were relatively flat-bottomed with a draught of only around 1 m when fully laden. The Vikings could sail long distances relatively quickly. They sailed as far south as Istanbul, northwards to the White Sea, westwards to Vinland (Newfoundland) and eastwards to Novgorod in Russia. Two Viking ships have been restored and are exhibited in the Viking Museum in Oslo.

The Vikings, or "Norsemen", as they were also called, plundered riches and property, burnt villages and took slaves. They also colonised captured areas and founded towns and villages in Ireland (Dublin) and England (York). Conflicts in Europe at that time made this colonising easier. The Vikings were said to be brutal, but they were also admired for their daring and their roving, adventurous lifestyle. Some served in armies as bodyguards for foreign kings, princes and emperors.

The Arabian influence in the Mediterranean opened new trade routes to the east and south towards the Middle East, the Mediterranean areas in the east, via the Black Sea to the Russian rivers and to a lesser degree northward via Finnmark to the White Sea. The Vikings traded extensively, acquiring much sought-after Norwegian goods such as furs, walrus tusks, iron and steatite (soapstone), a mineral used for making decorative articles and pottery. The barter trade between the Vikings and other nationalities was important for the 'economy' of the time.

Some of the most well known Norwegian Viking Chieftains were Tore Hund from Bjarkøy (p 166), Hårek from Tjøtta (p 319), Asbjørn Selsbane from Trondarnes (p 273), Tore Hjort from Lofoten and Raud the Ramme from Salten (p 138).

During the Viking period, Denmark, Sweden and Norway became independent countries and Norway was united by King Harald Hårfagre around the year A.D. 880. Several of the Norwegian Viking Kings became Christianized after encountering missionaries during their visits to foreign countries. Some even tried to convert the Norwegians on their return. Olav Haraldsson (Olav the Holy) (p 88) was the Christian king who led the conversion of Norway to Christianity. Olav Haraldsson was killed at the battle of Stiklestad in 1030.

Historically, the Viking era ended in 1066 when King Harald Hardråde was killed in the battle at Stamford Bridge near York in England.

Ottar Viking

When King Alfred the Great (848-900) was rewriting the historical work by the late Roman author Orosius, the King told the story of the Norse Viking, Ottar, who had visited the English court around A.D. 890. Ottar had said that he "lived farther north than any other Norseman" – probably between Gibostad and Tromsø. At the end of the 9th century he had sailed northwards, then eastwards past the North Cape, along the Kola Peninsula, into the White Sea and on to Bjarmeland (in the Sagas, Bjarmeland was the name used for the lands in northwest Russia) which he said was a prosperous region. He had not come across any settlements between his home and Bjarmeland. Ottar had only seen desolate lands on his way east, meeting only a few fishermen and hunters.

Ottar described himself as a rich man and said that his fortune came from trade and from taxes levied on the Sámi people. He traded in many types of hides, eider down and in ships' ropes made from whale and seal skins.

Ottar's stories are believed to be the oldest eye-witness reports of the conditions and times in the then unknown Northern Norway.

DAY 4

Brønnøysund, Sandnessjøen, Nesna, Ørnes, Bodø, Stamsund and Svolvær

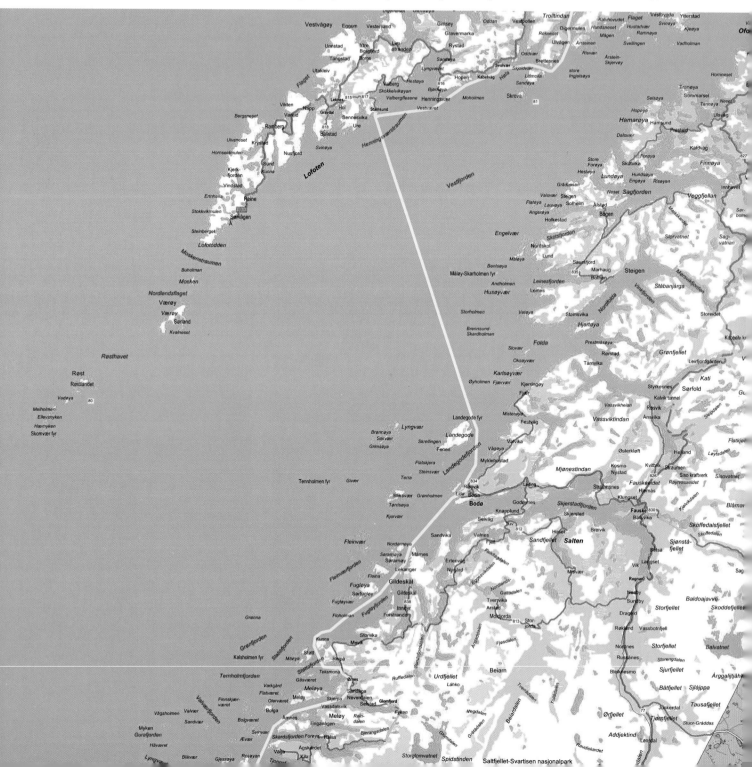

During the night we have sailed past the municipalities of Nærøy and Leka in Nord-Trøndelag county, and crossed the county boundary into Nordland. Thereafter, we passed the municipalities of Sømna and Brønnøy with the port of **Brønnøysund** (0030 - 0100), then Vevelstad and Alstahaug with the port of **Sandnessjøen** (0315-0415). Further on we have sailed past Dønna and Nesna municipalities, with a brief stop at the port of **Nesna** (0525-0530). Finally we have sailed beyond Lurøy and Rødøy. We are now in Meløy municipality, on our way to our next port of call, Ørnes.

Meløy municipality

Municipal coat of arms, significance: The 'black ice' poppy grows here.
Meaning of name: Most likely Norse mjol, 'flour', possibly fine sand.
Municipal seat: Ørnes (pop. 1 565).
Position: 66°52'N 13°42'E.
Area: 871 km². **Population:** 6 663.
Pop. density: 7.6 /km².
Area distribution: Farming 2 %, forestry 11 %, fresh water 6 %, other 81 %.
Trade and industry: Chemical industry, mechanical and foodstuffs industries. Fishing, both coastal and deep sea. Fish farming. Agriculture, dairy farming and meat and egg production. Electric power generation.
Places to return to: Engabreen/Svartisen, Meløy Folk Museum, Ørnes. Bolga. Svinvær.
Meløy municipality's home page: www.meloy.kommune.no

66°41'32"N   13°09'16"E

We are in **Rødøyfjorden**. On our starboard side is the village of **Værnes** near the magnificent mountain range, with **Værnestinden** (688 m above sea level) and **Blokkstinden** (1 032 m above sea level). Thereafter we see Tjongsfjorden. Norway's second largest glacier, Svartisen can be seen on our starboard side. The well-known landmark and legendary mountain, **Rødøyløva** (p 305) with Rødøy Church is on our port side. Rødøyløva

appears to be lying on its back with its head raised, looking for **Hestmannen**, a mountain located farther south (p 306).

On the north side of Tjongsfjorden and to our starboard side, we see the relatively low mountains beyond the village **Sleipnes**, between Tjongsfjorden and Skardsfjorden.

66°44'N   13°12'E

We are in **Bolgfjorden** on our way to the next port of call, Ørnes. Ahead and to our port side, we see the island Bolga, shaped like a pyramid, and the group of islands known as **Bolgværet** with a multitude of skerries and reefs.

On our starboard side, we see **Skardsfjorden** on the south side of Åmnøya (p 126). Skardsfjorden divides east of Åmnøya into Holandsfjorden, the barren and narrow Bjærangfjorden and the valley, **Bjærangsdalen**. In a side arm of Holandsfjorden is the narrow, steep **Nordfjorden** and Svartisen power station located at **Kilvik** at the head of the fjord. At the head of Holandsfjorden, it is possible to walk on the glacier, Engabreen, which is a side arm of Svartisen.

Behind the two small islands of **Forøya** and **Esøya** in Skardsfjorden on the west side of the headland between **Holandsfjorden** and **Bjærangfjorden,** we find the village of **Halsa.** Burial mounds have been found on Forøya dating back to the Stone Age (p 83). Halsa has some of Norway's largest fish farm installations and fish feed factories, established in 1989.

On our port side, we pass the island groups of Svinvær and Bolgværet. Svinvær has about 60 islands of varying size and many have rich, fertile soil that has supported several farms. Sea birds nest here and provide the farms with extra income from eggs and down (p 333).

Svinvær is one of the oldest trading places along the coast of Helgeland. Archaeological excavations show that there were settlements here dating back to the Stone Age (p 83). From 1620 a general store, licensed to sell liquor, was owned and managed here by the same family through several generations. Svinvær was also the site of the assembly of the local council for the area. The trading post was sold at an auction in 1850. It eventually lost out to competition from other locally established and better-placed trading centres. The old building burnt down in 1958, but was later rebuilt.

On our port side is **Bolgværet** with its characteristic pyramid-shaped island, Bolga farther north. It is surrounded by many smaller islands, in total 365 - one for every day of the year, as the saying goes.

On our starboard side we pass the island, **Åmnøya** (23.4 km²) with the fishing village of **Åmnøyhamn** on the southwest point. The mountains, **Harfjelltinden** (488 m above sea level), **Snødalstinden** (640 m above sea level) and **Skardstinden** (648 m above sea level) dominate the island's topography. In the background and on the mainland, once again we can see the glacier Svartisen. On the island's northerly point, we have the settlement of **Åmnes**. Rock carvings dating back some 4–5 000 years have been found here. The carvings are special in that they have been honed, not chiselled, onto the rock face and show full size animal figures. Their site above sea level, the technique and style indicate that the carvings are from the Stone Age (p 83).

66°46'N   13°13'E   ②

The island, **Bolga** (2.4 km²) is now on our port side. The mountain, Bolgtinden/Bolgbørra (338 m above sea level), like the more famous, Torghatten farther south on the coast of Helgeland, has a hole running through it. Ruggesteinen (lit. 'rocking stone') is another attraction on the island. This colossal stone weighs more than 60 tons but is so finely balanced that it can be moved about 10 cm by just pushing it with one hand.

The fishing village, **Bolga** faces the shipping channel and with its population of approx. 141 is the outermost permanent settlement in Meløy municipality. Here is also one of Norway's largest fish farming sites, a mechanical workshop and a slipway. Bolga hosts many festivals and is a popular location for aerial sports such as hang-gliding and paragliding.

We continue our voyage into **Meløyfjorden**. In the sound between the islands Bolga and Meløya are two groups of islands, **Oterværet** and **Flatværet,** which are comprised of a myriad of small islets, skerries and reefs.

© BRITA KJERPESETH OMNES

Ahead, and on our port side is the island of **Meløya** (21.8 km²). Meløya has an interesting history that goes back over 10 000 years. For centuries, boats were the commonest form of transportation along the coast. The island is close to the sailing channel and so Meløy Church, or Meløy Cathedral and Meløygården in the village became natural places to congregate. The mountain **Meløytinden** (582 m above sea level) is the highest point on the island.

Today's Meløy Church was consecrated in 1867 and is one of Norway's largest longhouse-style timber churches. It could originally seat 800 and has been rebuilt and refurbished many times. There was a church here on Meløy already in the 14th century; however, the first church blew down in a storm in the autumn of 1655. The next burnt down in 1703; most likely, it was struck by lightning. The next was sold at an auction and pulled down in 1868 as a new church was already under construction. When the church was demolished, 70 coffins were found under the floorboards. The oldest was from 1741. It was very expensive to be buried under the church floor and was the privilege of the wealthy.

It is assumed that Meløygården was the residence of one of the wealthy aristocratic families in Nordland county, the Benkestok-family. The family got its name, so the story goes, after one of the family's ancestors hid the King who was fleeing from his enemies in a chest/bed (sengebenk) or under a log (stokk). The story has not been verified in recognised historical documents.

At its peak, the estate comprised of 13 buildings. Today, there are only seven buildings left standing - each with its special history. Meløy municipality's administration offices were based in these buildings from 1884 until the 1950s when they were moved to Ørnes.

In 1910, the 90 m long meticulously hewn granite breakwater at **Meløysjøen** by Meløygården was completed. The breakwater was designed to protect the approach to the harbour and jetty from the winds from southwest.

The western part of the island is flat farmland whilst the eastern part is more hilly.

✌

We pass the village **Åmnes** on our starboard side on Åmnøya's northern point.

✌

66°48'N   13°26'E

We have almost passed the low, forested island, **Grønøya** (2.6 km²) on our starboard side, northeast of Åmnøya. The village **Jektvika,** on the northeast point on Grønøya was an important trading centre on the coast of Helgeland in the 18th century. Between 1914 and 1933, the Hurtigruten ships called at Jektvika six times a week. Thereafter and until 1957, four of the weekly stops were transferred to Ørnes and in 1957 Jektvika was omitted altogether and Ørnes became the main port of call.

It should be mentioned as something of a curiosity, that Norway's most familiar coastal fir tree - the same that is depicted on Nittedal's matchboxes is taken from a painting with a motif from Grønøya, a work of the Norwegian painter, T. Holmboe.

✌

We have already seen the glacier, Svartisen along our voyage. We will see the glacier several more times along our route, on our starboard side.

✌

66°47'N   13°21'E   ③

The ship stops at Jektvika in the summer season allow passengers to disembark to take a trip to Svartisen. They are transferred to a smaller craft, which takes them into Holandsfjorden, a branch from Skardsfjorden, south of Åmnøya.

✌

Svartisen (375 km²) is Norway's second largest glacier after Jostedalsbreen (415 km²) in Sogn and Fjordane county (p 386). **Snøtind** (1 594 m above sea level), is Svartisen's highest point which juts up just above the level of the ice.

Svartisen 1950

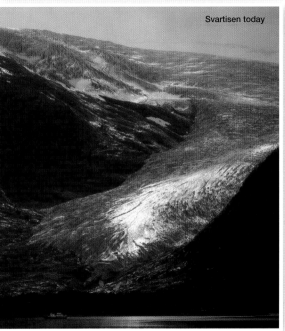
Svartisen today

The glacier is divided into two arms, **Vestisen** (221 km²) and **Østisen** (148 km²) near the narrow **Vesterdalen** valley that runs in a northeast/southwest direction. The name 'Svartisen' ('black ice') comes from the contrast in the colour of the blue ice base and the white snow. The ice can sometimes appear dark or even black by comparison. We can see Vestisen from the ship.

Svartisen is a so-called 'blanket' glacier and covers a mountain range with an elevation between 1 100 and 1 500 m above sea level, from where the ice flows in all directions. The glacier has approx. 60 branches. The best known is **Østerdalsisen** in the southeast. **Fonndalsbreen** and **Engabreen** are two arms that run westward. Some 100-200 years ago, Engabreen's face reached almost down to Holandsfjorden. Today it has receded a few kilometres back from the fjord and is now only approx. 5 m above sea level. It is therefore the lowest situated glacier on the European continent. Climate changes have influenced the thickness of the glacier and the receding or advancing of the glacier arms. At its thickest, the ice is 450 m.

Saltfjellet-Svartisen National Park (1 840 km²) is the second largest in Norway. The area is very varied and is mostly mountains with some lush valleys with birch forests. The flora is rich and interesting. The municipalities of Rødøy and Meløy and Svartisen are included in the Park.

It was suggested that the Park should have been established already in 1936, but due to conflicting interests over the utilisation of the area, it was not until 1989 that the area became a protected National Park.

℅

The legend how Svartisen came into existence has at least three versions.

℅

In "Nordlands Amt" (1908) the well-known geologist from Bergen, Amund Helland quotes Ivar Aasen as a source.

He tells of a woman who wanted to send a gift to her sister who lived on Meløya. A man (of Finnish origin) was hired to travel over the mountain with the package. When the Finn reached a point from where he could see the sea he became curious and wanted to see what was in the box. But as he removed the lid a spark fell out. When the spark hit the ground, it spread out until it covered the adjacent mountains. "From this came the large Fonn (snowdrift/glaciers) that still cover these mountains. Some have tried to melt parts of it, but have not succeeded" writes Aasen.

℅

In the Sagas we find the following version of how Svartisen came to be - as described in Ryvarden and Wold: "Norges isbreer" (Norway's glaciers) (Oslo 1991).

❞❞ On Rødø in the olden days there lived a Finn that was driven out either for his magical powers or for other misdeeds. Exasperated, he went up to the mountains near the Swedish border where he met a Lapp (Sámi) sorcerer and was given a pair of flies, (Gandfluer – magic flies). With these he immediately returned to destroy all of Rødøen; but he became curious and thought he would take at

look at the flies. However, as soon as he opened the box where they were kept they flew away, and the snowdrift that was to bury Rødøen, fell where the Fongfjord glacier is located; and as the flies flew huge deposits of snow followed. They then flew towards the sea and for that reason the glacier stretched all the way down to the sea and it was 7 Milde (70 km) from where he let the flies out to where they reached the snow."

℅

The third version can be found in O.T. Olsen's: "Norske folkeeventyr og sagn" (Norwegian folk tales and legends) Kristiania 1908.

❞❞ When St. Olav was on his way to Helgeland to christen the people living there, the King of Finns at Misvær, who was a great sorcerer and pagan, wanted to block his passage by creating an ice wall across the waters between the mainland and Rødøy. If successful, Saltdalen and Misvær would be spared St. Olav's visit. The King filled a large box full of magic flies (Gandfluer) and chanted his most powerful magical spells over them. Then he got a Finn to carry the box on his back and go up Misværmarka to Rippevagga where he was to let the flies out of the box. At Rippevagga the Finn let the flies out. As the flies flew, snow fell so thick that it filled the valleys all the way to the mountaintops for miles around. After a while, the snow became hard ice. When St. Olav reached Bliksvær and saw all the snow, he realised immediately that great magical powers lay behind such a deed. He took his sword, made the sign of the cross and cursed the evil powers in the name of Christ. At that moment the swarm of flies fell into the sea and the snow only reached as far as the coast. Had the flies managed to reach Rødøyløva the seaway would have been blocked by ice and the King of Finns would have prevailed. The ice lay now only as far down as the flies had flown; from Rippevagga to the coast at Rødøy, where we find it today and its name is Svartisen."

℅

66°48'31"N   13°28'E   ④

On our starboard side on the headland is **Dyrneset,** just before the village of **Valla** on the mainland. Eight burial mounds have been discovered here, that date back to the Iron Age. The mounds are 4-10 m across. Two stone monuments, arrowheads of slate and a stone axe dating back to the Stone Age (p 83) were also uncovered at the same site.

After passing Valla on the mainland and the small island, **Oksholmen** on our starboard side, we continue our voyage to the next port of call, Ørnes.

At the entrance to the wide U-valley on our starboard side we can see the village of **Vassdalsvik** located between the mountains, **Stordalstinden** (573 m above sea level), **Oldratinden** (802 m above sea level) and **Hesten** (822 m above sea level). At Vassdalsvik is a car ferry connection with Ørnes and Meløy/Bolga.

On our port side we have the narrow sound, **Meløysund** between the islands Meløya and the smaller neighbour, **Skjerpa** (275 m above sea level), opposite Vassdalsvik.

The island, **Messøya** (8 km², 364 m above sea level) is now ahead and to our port side.

66°49'30"N   13°38'20"E   ⑤

The entrance to **Glomfjorden** is on our starboard side. It is 21 km long and 1-3 km wide with steep sides that plunge straight down into the fjord. At the head of the fjord, in Fykendalen is an area with 8000-year-old rock carvings.

The village and industrial centre of **Glomfjord** (pop. 1 178) is located nearby at the head of the fjord. Most of Meløy's industrial sites are located here. Glomfjord was offered cheap electrical power from Glomfjord Power Station when it was built as Norway's first large-scale power station. Water is transported in pipes from approx. 468 m above. The construction started in 1912, initiated by private interests, however it was taken over by the state authorities in 1918. The first phase was completed in 1920 and two years later, the station was extended. The electricity supplied power to a zinc processing plant at one time. British and German concerns began aluminium production in 1927. This plant was taken over by new owners in 1932.

Norsk Hydro in Glomfjord.

A number of dramatic events occurred in Glomfjord during the Second World War. The following is an extract from "Krigens dagbok" (War Journal), by Otto Ruge (1946):

"At midnight on the 20th September 1942, 12 uniformed Allied commando troops (two from Company Linge, p 31) attacked the heavily guarded power station in Glomfjord, which supplied electricity to the aluminium smelting plant at Haugvik. The operation was codenamed "Musket". The commandos split into smaller groups. One three-man group placed dynamite on the pipelines that ran down from the steep mountainside into the generator plant. Seven other men entered the station itself whilst two men were stationed outside as guards. The commandos placed explosives on the generators and turbines while the German guard sat sleeping on a crate outside the generator hall. Five German guards were innside the hall, elsewhere in the building.

The saboteurs alerted the Norwegians working there and others who lived in the upper storeys. At half-past midnight most of the charges exploded. The explosion was huge and shook the whole of Glomfjord. Windows were shattered as far away as 3 km from the Site. The sound of the explosion was also heard by the saboteurs at the pipelines way up on the mountainside. This told them it was time for them to detonate their charges. Enormous amounts of water cascaded down towards the plant, entered the generator hall and destroyed the entire installation. No more aluminium could be manufactured in Glomfjord during the rest of the war.

The saboteurs' next objective was to try to make their escape across the border to Sweden. On their arrival on the 16th September, they had gone ashore from the French U-boat, the "Juno" in Bjærangfjorden and found their way up an arm of the Svartisen glacier and down to Glomfjord where the German forces had posted a 100-man guard. These forces, along with search planes were sent out to catch the saboteurs. The German troops captured seven of the men. They were imprisoned and later executed in Germany. An eighth man was fatally wounded and died later at Bodø Hospital. The remaining four, after enduring incredible hardships, finally managed to cross the border into Sweden."

Glomfjord Power Station was extended after the war when Norsk Hydro started operations in 1947 and continued production of ammonia here until 1993.

From 1955, the plant produced fertilizers and saltpetre. Glomfjord Power Station was the only supplier of electricity to this type of production from 1993. After 1993, Svartisen Power Plant in Kilvik in Nordfjorden started to deliver electricity to Glomfjord (p 125).

Glomfjord is today an industrial centre with varied industry and many types of enterprises. Glomfjord Industrial Park includes the following companies:

• Yara Norge AS Glomfjord is a subsidiary of Yara International ASA (formerly Norsk Hydro agricultural division), the world's leading supplier of mineral fertilizer. The company is the largest in Glomfjord, with approx. 170 employees. Yara Norge has an annual production of approx. 740 000 tonnes of fertilizer and calcium nitrate.

• REC ScanWafer AS is one of the world's largest manufacturers of crystalline silicon wafers, used in solar cell construction. The company was founded in 1994 and has its Norwegian production facilities in Glomfjord and Porsgrunn. The company had approx. 180 employees in 2007.

• REC SiTech AS manufactures monocrystalline silicon rods, which are a part of the process in the production of monocrystalline wafers. These form the basis for the manufacture of high-effect solar cells. The company, which was established in 2004, is now in a process of considerable expansion with a projected staff of 180 in 2010.

• Marine Harvest Norway AS, Glomfjord Smolt farm is involved in the farming of salmon and trout parr/smolt. The farm has a licence to produce up to 5 million smolt p.a. The company has 16 employees (2007).

The harbour in Glomfjord is amongst the busiest in Northern Norway where ships anchor waiting for available berths.

On the mountain behind Glomfjord village is the glacier, **Glombreen** (approx. 8 km²). The highest point is **Istind** (1 194 m above sea level) on the northwest side of the glacier. The glacier is uniform, without branches.

Glomfjord has a road connection south through the tunnel, **Svartistunnelen** (7 615 m long). The tunnel goes under one of Svartisen's branches and when it was opened in 1987 it was one of Northern Europe's longest road tunnels.

In **Neverdal** in the outer reaches of Glomfjorden a monument has been raised in memory of Russian prisoners of war.

We are sailing into **Eidet**, the sound between the peninsula, **Glomneset** on our starboard side and the island, **Mesøya** (8 km², 242 m above sea level) on our port side.

On our starboard side, the steep profile of the mountain **Spildrehesten** with settlements of **Våtvika**, **Nedre** and **Øvre Spildra** along the shoreline. Behind the mountain we can see Glombreen once more.

The village of **Spildra** is on our starboard side under the mountain known as Spildrehesten.

In front we have Ørnes, our port of call, situated between the mountains **Spilderhesten** (815 m above sea level) with its characteristic profile and Blåtinden. In the background, we see the peak **Ruffedalstinden** (939 m above sea level) and right behind Ørnes, is **Raudhaugen**. The approach to Ørnes is considered to be one of the most spectacular on the Hurtigruten tour.

The ship docks at the quayside in Ørnes

© EILIV LEREN

Ørnes is the administrative centre for the area and is mentioned in documents dating from 1610 when a tenant farmer lived here. In 1794, a member of the noble Benkestok- family from Meløya (p 126) leased the farm and was permitted to open a trading post on Ørnes. He lived at Meløya but when he died in 1802, his widow moved to Ørnes and continued trading. The business changed owners within the Benkestok family, but was continued by others when the old family died out. These would typically combine trading with shipping.

The settlement at Ørnes was ravaged by fire several times, but some of the original buildings from approx. 1800 remain intact; several dwellings, fishermen's cabins, boathouses, barns and a forge are kept in good condition and several are listed and protected.

The administrative centre of Ørnes is a central hub of bus, boat and ferry traffic. Festivals are arranged during the summer - "Summer Days", a whole week of cultural events, and "Revue Festival" (every second year), with theatre and revue performed by actors from the region.

The ship continues to Bodø   + 0 hrs 00 min

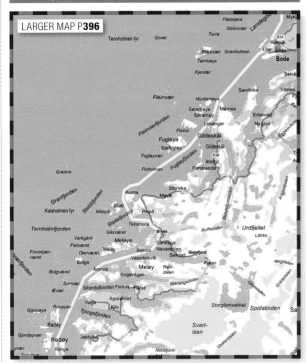

LARGER MAP P**396**

After leaving Meløy we sail past **Blåtinden** (716 m above sea level) on our starboard side.

Ahead and to our port side, we see the islands, Mesøya and Teksmona. Ahead and on the mainland, the parish of Reipå is located at the foot of the mountain Skjeggen.

66°53'15"N   13°37'E   + 0 hrs 09 min ⑥

We are passing **Teksmona** (5.2 km²) with the mountain **Nattmålstuva** (227 m above sea level) on our port side. Part of the island was listed as a nature reserve in December 1992 because of its ancient and untouched fir forest, in some places very dense. The objective was to protect a small coniferous forest, typical for this area growing on the edge of the sea in virtually marine conditions. Teksmona is one of the few islands on the coast of Nordland that has a coniferous forest.

On our starboard side we can see **Reipå** (pop. 310) located between the mountains, Blåtinden, **Breitinden** (727 m above sea level) and Skjeggen (904 m above sea level). On the point of the headland is **Skroven** (463 m above sea level). Reipå with Meløy Folk Museum is the northernmost settlement in the municipality.

West of Reipå is the village of **Fore** and Fore Church. The original prayer-house was refurbished and consecrated as a chapel in 1909. It was a timber church built in New-Gothic style, seating 500. The church was restored in 1932.

In an area near Fore, remains of a settlement and a burial mound with a 3.6 m high rock monument, 'Pila' have been excavated. These date from the Viking period approx. A.D. 800 (p 83).

The ship continues between the northern side of Teksmona on our port side and the mainland and **Fore** on our starboard side. Ahead and to our port side, we see the small group of islands, **Gåsværet. Støttafjorden** lies between the group of islands, Gåsværet and Støttvær. The largest islands in **Støttvær,** the group of low, small islets ahead are: **Innerstøtt** with the fishing village of **Støtt** (2.7 km²), **Svenningen** (1.6 km²) and **Helløya** (1.4 km²). On Svenningen (highest point 76 m above sea level), are several bunkers and remains of the four 10.5 cm cannon foundations built here by the German forces in February 1943.

Støtt was formerly a trading centre and has always been important for shipping.

West of Støttvær, in clear weather it is possible to see the lighthouse, **Kalsholmen** on the small island of **Ternholmen**. Kalsholmen was built in 1916 and had a light beam with a range of 16 nautical miles. It was automated and de-manned in 1993.

66°55'N   13°30'E   + 0 hrs 24 min ⑦

The island of Innerstøtt is on our port side.

After passing Skroven on our starboard side we can see ahead and to our starboard side the peninsula, **Kunna** and mountain **Kunna** (599 m above sea level). Before the narrow neck of land that connects the peninsula to the mainland, we see the communities of **Nerstranda, Øysund** and **Øra**.

At Nerstranda, we can see the upper section of the antenna mast that also functions as a marker when approaching Bodø Airport from the south.

An influential chieftain resided in the area around Øysund and Kunna in the Iron Age. More than 30 graves, 11 boathouses, a courtyard with farmhouses tell their story. The oldest layers may be from the Viking period; the upper layers date from the Middle Ages. Amongst the relics found in the graves dating from the Iron Age are the remains of a man buried in his boat. His dog was buried at his feet. The man had a sword, shield, spear, a sharpening tool and fine jewellery. The houses in this courtyard are from the Viking period. In contrast to other courtyards that usually were arranged in a circle around an open area, the houses in Øysund were arranged in a long row with their long sides adjacent to each other. The outer walls were covered in peat (p 83).

In the Iron Age when the land level was somewhat lower, ships could sail across **Kunnavalen**, which lies between Kunna and the mainland. The waters outside Kunna were known to be treacherous but farming conditions in the area were good. Additionally, Kunna was well placed in relation to the sailing channel, therefore the Øysund - Kunna area was a good location to establish a chieftain's seat.

Øysund is first mentioned in documents dating from the 1430s, Kunna in 1530.

66°57'26"N   13°28'53"E

We sail by the peninsula of Kunna. On our starboard side we pass the short **Kunna Sound**, with the narrow isthmus, Kunnavalen, between Kunna and the mainland.

On the border between Meløy and Gildeskål municipalities is the memorial for the submarine, "KNM Uredd". The submarine is located southwest of the island, Fugløya. The submarine sailed into an unmarked German minefield in Fugløyfjorden in 1943, struck a mine and sank with 42 persons onboard. It was on a top-secret mission during which British and Norwegian agents were to be brought on land in occupied Norway. These agents were saboteurs attacking the German war machine and reporting shipping activities along the Norwegian coast. "KNM Uredd" was found by a mini-submarine in 1983 at a depth of 105 metres. In 1986 the wreck was declared a war grave.

Fugløya can be seen ahead and to our port side.

On our port side, in clear weather we can see the outermost islands in Lofoten, with Røst, Værøy and the mountains on Moskenesøya.

Approx. 66°58'N   13°34'E

We cross the municipal boundary between Meløy and Gildeskål municipalities

Gildeskål municipality

Municipal coat of arms, significance: Secular feasts and ecclesiastical ceremonies. **Meaning:** From Norse; gildaskáli, 'ceremonial feast'.
Municipal seat: Inndyr (pop. 658).
Position: 67°02'N 14°01'E.
Area: 664 km². **Population:** 2 081.
Pop. density: 3.1 /km².
Distribution: Farming 2 %, forestry 13 %, fresh water 6 %, other 79 %.
Trade and industry: Coastal fishing. Farming, dairy, beef cattle and sheep. Fish farming. Salmon processing. Fish food industry. Shipyard with slipway. Quartz mining. Power generation.
Places to return to: Gildeskål kirke, Rødgården på Inndyr, Blixgården på Våg, Fugløya.
Gildeskål municipality's home page: www.gildeskal.kommune.no

66°58'22"N   13°34'E   + 0 hrs 46 min ⑧

We have passed the steep side of Skjeggen on our starboard side, thereafter **Storvika** bay and **Storvika** village in front of the mountain Høgnakken.

66°59'20"N   13°36'28"E   + 0 hrs 52 min ⑧

After Storvika, **Finnes** juts out into the fjord near **Årfjellet** (529 m above sea level).

We are now in **Fugløyfjorden**. On our starboard side we pass Finnes and Årfjellet, **Høgnakken** (1 045 m above sea level) and **Høgstjerna** (820 m above sea level). Between them lies Novika village.

67°00'18"N   13°40'21"E   + 0 hrs 58 min ⑨

At **Novika** near Høgnakken is the only VLF (Very Low Frequency) aerial in Scandinavia, used in communication with submarines. It is owned by the Ministry of Defence and was built in the 1960's. NATO utilised the installation until 2006. Cables run between Høgnakken and Høgstjerna. (The cables are visible on clear days.)

Fugløya

At **Forstranda**, a headland north of Høgstjerna, we find the cave, **Brusteinshola,** an enormous cave system, the so-called "Katedralen" – the Cathedral. In Skauvolldal, on the mainland behind Høgstjerna are also huge, complex cave systems called **Greftkjelen** and **Greftsprek-ken**. These caves are amongst Norway's deepest, 315 m deep with approx. 9 km of tunnels and shafts.

On our port side, we pass a group of islets and skerries called **Floholman**. The name, 'Floholman' is the collective name given to these small barren islets far out in the open sea.

On our port side, we can see **Fugløyvær,** a group of approx. 140 islets, skerries and reefs, in front of the well-known Fugløya. Fugløyvær is registered as an ancient egg and down gathering site (p 333).

To the south we can see the island, **Fugløya** (13 km²), with the now uninhabited former community of **Sørfugløy**. Part of the island is a nature sanctuary. **Hagtinden** is the highest peak (765 m above sea level). Along the shoreline is a ridge where sheep once grazed. Just after the Second World War the island had a population of approx. 200, in 1960 this had fallen to 124 and in 2001 there were only three persons left. Today it is completely uninhabited; however, some of the old houses are used as summer cabins and holiday homes.

Fugløya is an important nesting site for sea birds, especially Puffins. In **Lunddalen**, on the western side of the island, it is estimated that there are approx. 10 000 pairs of nesting puffins. The birds leave the island at the end of August. In addition to the Puffins, many other sea birds also nest here (p 218). Several pairs of White-Tailed Eagles (Sea Eagles) and other birds of prey have also been observed nesting here (p 161).

On the north east side of the island, near the sailing channel, it is possible, with the aid of binoculars, to spot a small figure on the face of the cliff. It resembles a white eagle with spread wings, located a short distance up on the cliff. Some say it has been created by some natural phenomena; however, others say it was made by a German soldier during the Second World War. As the story goes, the soldier was lowered down from above on a rope in order to chisel out the eagle figure. It can be seen between two rocky outcrops just behind the navigation light on the headland.

On the north-easterly side of the island, we find **Nordfugløy**.

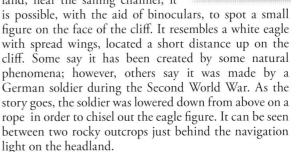

Many legends and stories are associated with Fugløya and Gildeskål. Here is an example:

> The story about "Tjyv-Finn on Sørfugløy".
>
> 99 Many years ago, in Ytre Gildeskål, there lived a couple of thieves, Tjyv-Finn and his woman. The couple had been declared outlaws due to their evil ways, as thieves and kidnappers. They managed to evade capture and lived in a cave on Sør-Fugløy. The cave is still known today as Tjyv-Finnhellaren (cave). Tjyv-Finn and his woman often used a boat on their raids. Their boat was eventually found after they had sunk it on a sandbank on the south side of Fugløy, between a rocky outcrop known as Totmålskjæret and the island itself. After the boat was found, it did not take long to find Tjyv-Finn.
>
> At that time, two brothers, Kristen and Svend Svendsen also lived on Sør-Fugløy, These two were known for their great strength and daring. Kristen and Svend decided they would try to get rid of the thieving couple.
>
> Late one evening just before Christmas, the brothers took their muskets and went out to Tjyv-Finnhellaren. They were careful, as they were in great danger themselves. When they got to the cave, they spotted Tjyv-Finn and the woman, sitting eating their supper by the fire that lit up the inside of the cave. Kristen aimed his gun at Tjyv-Finn and pulled back the hammer on his old musket – then the gun 'clicked' and failed to go off. Tjyv-Finn asked the woman: "What was that clicking noise?", and the woman replied: "Nothing, it was just the fire crackling". Kristen then had time to reload his weapon. He shot Tjyv-Finn and then the woman, and so their saga ended."

After having passed Fugløya and looking back towards the north side of the island it is possible to see an area of gravel and sand that appears as if it is pouring out of an opening in the mountainside like a waterfall.

Ahead and on our starboard side we can see the island, Sandhornøya and the mountain Sandhornet (993 m above sea level).

67°02'N   13°47'N   + 1 hr 12 min ⑩

After passing Høgstjerna and the village of **Vigdel,** on our starboard side we can see the long and low island, **Femris** with its highest point 48 m above sea level.

The village, **Inndyr**, the administrative centre in Gildeskål municipality, is located behind Femris, roughly in the centre of the island. It is difficult to see from the ship. Inndyr is located near the former old shipping channel, but now larger ships sail along Fugløyfjorden. Inndyr has a shipyard with a slipway for larger boats, a mechanical workshop, concrete mixing plant and a number of smaller businesses. Gildeskål Aquaculture Research Station is also located here.

Inndyr, which grew around a natural harbour, was mentioned for the first time in documents from the 17th century and it has been a lively community since the Middle Ages. Inndyr homestead was of great importance to the village, both as a residence for nobility and as a productive farm.

Angellgården (Rødgården) is located in the centre of Inndyr. It dates from 1590 and was originally built as a dowager house. It was moved to its present location in 1760, when it was also extended. Another extension was built in 1807. Angellgården is now refurbished and declared a listed building.

The area around Inndyr is well known for its profusion of wild orchids.

The famous **Gildeskål** Church is located a few kilometres north of Inndyr. However, it is difficult to see from the ship as the islands in front obscure the low-lying area behind. It has two old churches with the rectory standing between.

The old Gildeskål Church is the best preserved of the northern churches built in the Middle Ages. It is assumed that a small wooden church had already been built here in the 11th century, however all traces of it were removed when it was rebuilt as a stone church. The oldest church is dated 12th century and is probably one of the two stone churches King Øystein (1088-1123) (p 9) ordered to be built when he travelled northward in 1114. However, other historical evidence indicates it could also have been built later, in 1170. In pagan times Gildeskål was also a cultural centre where feasts and celebrations took place

© OSCAR BERG/ SALTEN MUSEUMS BILLEDSAMLING

(hence the name, 'Gilde' (feast)). The church is like many other churches built in the 12th century, in simple Roman style with arches and walls almost 1.5 m thick. Carved dragon's heads and gargoyles on the house gutters may have been a way of warding off evil pagan spirits. The old church burnt down in 1710 after being struck by lightning. The church was rebuilt with funds donated by the parish priest of the time and the south wing was added. At one time, the church had a dome; however, this was removed in 1890 as it was in danger of falling down. The church was later refurbished in 1936-37 and 1953-1962. Gildeskål old church is also known as the psalm composer Elias Blix's old church. He was born here in Gildeskål in 1836.

Instead of extending the existing church, a new one was built in the second half of the 19th century and when this was consecrated in 1881, the old church was closed. For this reason, Gildeskål Old Church is one of the best-preserved churches in the north and has retained its original character. It was re-consecrated in 1962.

The new church was a longhouse-style church in Gothic style seating 750. It is situated on a hill overlooking the fjord and Fugløya. In the old rectory we find Gildeskål's collection of relics from the old settlement. The main building is a 33 m longhouse built in the 18th century. All the old buildings here are listed.

❧

After passing the narrow sound, **Røssøysundet** and the island, **Røssøy** north of the island Femris we can now see the approach to **Morsdalsfjorden** on our starboard side. The fjord is located between **Inndyrhalvøya** and the island of Sandhornøya. Gildeskål parish church can be seen from this position.

67°04'N   13°54'E   + 1 hr 27 min ⑪

We have passed the island Fugløya, and the depopulated hamlet **Nordfugløy**. To the northeast and on our port side we can see the relatively low island, Fleina.

Fleina (225 m above sea level) was declared a depopulated area in the 1970's. There are no longer any permanent inhabitants and it is now used solely for recreational purposes.

❧

On our port side, we can see the group of islands, **Fleinvær**. Fleinvær consists of approx. 230 barren, small islets out in the open sea in **Fleinværfjorden**, west of the islands of Fleina and Sørarnøya. In 2001, only six of the islands were home to a total of 31 inhabitants, making a living primarily from fishing.

The islands, **Sørarnøy** (4 km²) and **Nordarnøy** (3 km²) on our port side are connected by a bridge over the narrow sound, **Arnøysundet**. The community of Sørarnøy is a fishing village with fish processing industries. The coastal defence fort on Nordarnøy was built in June 1942. It had been transported from its former site at Memel near the Baltic Sea. It was one of six gun emplacements that were built in order to defend the approach to Bodø. On Nordarnøy alone, four gun emplacements were constructed with ammunition bunkers in the ground below. The 150 mm guns, that originated from the First World War were old but still effective, with a range of 16 000 metres. Three of them remain in place, whilst a fourth is exhibited at Oscarsborg in Oslofjorden.

On Sørarnøy there are 30 burial mounds from the Iron Age (p 83). One of the larger islands south of Sørarnøy is **Hestøya** where there are a further 12 graves. Nearby are another five graves approx. 10-100 m apart. They have all round mounds, 3-4 m in diameter, approx. 50 cm at the highest. Just further north is an oblong mound, 11 x 5 m and 1 m high. Further south there are five more mounds, 4–10 m in diameter and 50 cm high. The last mound in this row is the largest, however it has been partly destroyed.

© ROLF LILAND

Amongst the other islets that face the shipping lane, we can see the small, low **Stangholmen**. Six burial mounds have been discovered here, made with stone linings covered in earth. There are five round graves, 4–8 m in diameter and 0.5–1 m high and one long mound, 12.5 x 3 m in size and quite low. Two of the graves contained the remains of Viking warriors and their iron axes and swords, articles made of bone, bronze scales and sharpening stones. A comb and hairpin made of bone was found in a woman's grave, also from the Viking era.

❧

In the distance and on our port side we can see the island of Landegode and to starboard are the mountains surrounding the town of Bodø.

❧

67°06'N   14°00'E   + 1 hr 39 min

The island of **Sandhornøya** (103.3 km²) is on our starboard side. The island is the largest in Gildeskål. At the foot of the steep, distinctive mountain **Sandhornet** (993 m above sea level), the islands highest, is a relatively wide strip of land with the communities of **Hustad** (behind an island), known for extensive salmon farming and **Lekanger,** with a church. The village of **Våg**, in a bay north of Sandhornet, is known to be an old pagan ritual site. Våg is the birthplace of the poet, Elias Blix.

67°07'28"N   14°01'E   + 1 hr 43 min ⑫

Elias Blix was born on the 24th of February 1836 on the farm **Våg**. His father died when he was three years old and a while later his mother remarried. He studied in Tromsø to become a teacher and taught at a school in the town whilst completing his studies. With financial assistance from a merchant from Nordarnøy he was able to travel to Oslo to study theology. He took his higher exams whilst he was working as a teacher of Latin, French and the old Norse language. During his studies he also studied and learned Hebraic, and was considered especially gifted in this language. In 1866 he took his degree in theology. To work as a priest he also needed to take an examination in practical theology, which he thought would be ideal to take at Gildeskål Church. He was refused permission by the parish priest, who was known to be very conservative, coming from an old family of public servants. The reason for the refusal was that Elias Blix's background was too modest, he came from a mere fishing and farming family and "therefore had nothing to do in a church pulpit". In addition he spoke "landsmål" (New Norwegian) which traditionally had always met with considerable resistance from the bureaucrats, the nobility and middle classes. The day after this refusal, Elias Blix left his birthplace and never returned.

Elias Blix was appointed as distinguished professor of Hebrew in 1879. He was Minister of Church Affairs in Johan Sverdrup's Government from 1884-1888. Thereafter he returned to his professorship. As Minister of Church Affairs he was formally responsible for the decision made in 1885 to have two official equal-status languages in Norway, "landsmål and bokmål".

Elias Blix was best known as a composer of psalms; however he was an able translator of the Bible. He translated a major part of the "Landsmål Edition" of the New Testament, which came out in 1889, including 50 Psalms of David.

His first collection of psalms was printed in 1869, anonymously. Later followed a number of psalm collections, his aim was said to have been to "fill the church year with psalms written in "landsmål" ". In 1892 his work "Nokre Salmar" was permitted to be used in our churches alongside with "Landstads Salmebok". A new psalm collection was introduced in 1900 with 50 psalms, 44 of his own, 6 translated psalms and 10 songs. Two of his best known psalms are; "God bless our Fatherland" and "Nature awakens".

On our starboard side we can see the monument raised on Blixtunet in Våg in honour of Elias Blix.

Ahead and to our port side we can see the Bliksvær Islands west of Bodø. The island of Landegode outside Bodø is straight ahead.

On our starboard side we can see **Mårnesskagen,** the flat headland northwest on Sandhornøya with Mårnesskagen navigation beacon.

67°10'13"N   14°04'E   + 1 hr 55 min ⑬

The village of **Mårnes** is on our starboard side in the bay behind Mårnesskagen. Mårnes has a quartz mine that supplies raw materials to the Elkem plant in Sørfold. South of Mårnes a grave from the Iron Age has been found.

The ship is sailing into **Saltfjorden** towards Bodø. On our starboard side is the northeast point of Sandhornøya with the village of Sandvika and the headland, Skårneset situated to the north of the mountain **Telnestinden** (656 m above sea level).

On our starboard side is Saltfjorden and up ahead is our next port of call, Bodø.

We cross the municipal boundary between Gildeskål and Bodø municipalities

Bodø municipality

Municipal coat of arms, significance: The midnight sun, also that Bodø is the first town north of the Arctic Circle.
Meaning of name: Name of farm, old form for Bådøya, from Bothin, first syllable in Norse; bothi, 'båe', possibly both, 'feast', second syllable vin, 'pasture'.
Municipal seat: Bodø (pop. 35 618).
Position: 67°17'N 14°24'E.
Area: 921 km². **Pop.:** 45 575.
Pop. density: 49.5 /km².
Area distribution: Farming 3 %, forestry 22 %, fresh water 5 %, other 70 %.
Trade and industry: Northern Norway's second largest town. Centre of commerce, services, administration, education and communications. Food processing industry. Metal and machine industries. Graphic design and printing industries. Power generation. Agriculture, including dairy products and meat production. Potatoes and vegetable production. Some fishing.
Places to return to: Saltstraumen (maelstrom). Norwegian Aviation Museum. Kjerringøy trading post. Bodin church. Bodøgård.
Bodø municipality's home page: www.bodo.kommune.no.

Beiarnkjeften, now behind on our starboard side is the northerly approach to **Nordfjorden** and **Holmsundfjorden** behind Sandhornøya. On our starboard side is **Straumøya** (29 km²), the third largest island in the municipality of Bodø. Straumøya and Knapplundøya (6.6 km²), east of Straumøya form the south side of Saltfjorden, which runs eastward to the mainland.

On the northwest side of Straumøya is a marshy and rocky area. This marshy area is a protected nature reserve and is an important nesting area for migratory birds. Near **Seines**, northwest on Straumøya is an area used by the Ministry of Defence with a number of radio antennas that light up at night.

Bodø town is now ahead with the two islands, Lille and Store Hjartøy west of the town. Landegodefjorden is the stretch of water between the mainland and the island, Landegode.

The wide and open **Saltfjorden** is approx. 40 km long. It can be seen on our starboard side and continues as **Skjerstadfjorden** further in, ending at the community of **Fauske** (pop. 5 901) and **Rognan** (pop. 2 498). Fauske is perhaps best known for its marble quarries.

Near **Reitan**, between Bodø and Fauske, a radar station has been blasted into the mountain. The installation houses a radar station, various national control centre headquarters and operation centres for NATO along with an acoustic monitoring station built in the 1950s.

In the distance it is possible to see the glacier, **Blåmannsisen** (1 540 m above sea level, 87 km²) close to the Swedish border. Blåmannsisen is Norway's fifth largest. Not very far away are the historically famous industries at Sulitjelma (pop. 481).

30 km southeast of Bodø is Saltstraumen, which flows between the islands of Straumøya and Knapplundøya/ Godøya.

Saltstraumen is one of the world's strongest tidal currents or maelstroms (p 162). The current is created by approx. 400 million m³ of water that passes through the narrow sound (150 m wide and 3 km in length), every six hours, i.e. four times a day as the tide changes from ebb to flow. The current can sometimes flow at up to 52 km/hr. Eddies are formed up to 10 m in diameter with a depth of 4-5 m.

The narrow sound connects two fjords, Saltfjorden and Skjerstadfjorden, both several hundred metres deep. The sound has a depth of 50-80 m, and underwater rocks that form these treacherous eddies can be very dangerous for boats when the tide is at its strongest, but vessels can safely pass approx. two hours either side of peak tides. Saltstraumen is a popular fishing location amongst Europe's recreational anglers and National Geographic has named it one of the world's most exciting places for recreational divers.

Traces of ancient settlements, probably 10 000 years old and amongst the oldest in Norway, have been found on either side of Saltstraumen. The site was probably chosen because of the abundance of fish, sea birds, seals and whales.

Dramatic events have occurred at Saltstraumen. In 997 King Olav Tryggvason (p 88) ambushed and killed the Viking Chieftain Raud den Ramme ('Raud the Strong') from Godøy (Knapplundøy). The Chieftain's seat, which was located near Saltstraumen, played a role in the reason for Raud's murder. Neither King Olav nor the author of the Sagas, Snorre Sturlason, understood how the maelstrom was created. They believed the phenomena had to be a result of Chieftain Raud's pagan sorcery, and for this reason he was killed.

☙

Saltstraumen Church was built in 1886; however already in 1903 it was dismantled and moved to its present location due to poor ground conditions on the original site. The two church bells are from 1885 and the font, made of marble from Fauske, is from 1953.

☙

On our port side and northeast of Saltfjorden we can see the spectacular mountains, **Mjønestindan** (1 058 m above sea level) and **Mjønesfjellet** (708 m above sea level).

☙

Bliksvær on our port side is comprised of approx. 60 low, treeless islands. The islands have a rich bird life and the area is a protected nature reserve.

In 1999, 1 000 years after King Olav Tryggvason landed here in the year 999 and introduced Christianity to the local people, the only chapel devoted to a saint in Northern Norway, the Maria Chapel, was consecrated. The chapel was built with private funds. Bliksvær had at that time 10 permanent residents

☙

The British cruiser HMS "Effingham" (9 920 gross tons, built in 1921) ran aground on rocks northwest of Bliksvær on 17th May 1940 and sank rapidly in shallow waters. HMS Effingham was on a mission to Norway in April 1940, transporting soldiers from the French Foreign Legion to Narvik that were to take part in operations in the area (p 143). The cruiser had 1 020 soldiers and war materials on board when she ran aground. The soldiers and the ship's crew of 712 were picked up by British warships nearby in a matter of a few hours. Some days later several British ships returned and salvaged the cargo and military equipment and destroyed the guns and fired a torpedo at the stricken cruiser. She was later destroyed by naval units in order to make completely sure she could not be raised. The wreck was broken up after the war and today only rusty sections of scrap metal remain.

☙

The group of islands, **Tennholmen** consists of 25 small islands, west of Bliksvær.

The coastal lighthouse on Tennholmen was built in 1901 in connection with the start-up of the shipping route for iron ore from Sweden via the port at Narvik. The light is 27.3 m above sea level and has a range of 15.5 nautical miles.

☙

67°15'49"N   14°18'E

On our approach to Bodø we pass Bodø Airport and Bodø Main Air Station on our starboard side. The airport is used by both civilian and military aircraft.

Bodø Airport is Norway's largest military airport. It is the home base for 132. Air Wing with F-16 sqns 331. and 332., the 330 sqn with Sea King SAR-helicopters, and several support units.

In the summer of 1951 a new runway was built to accommodate newly commissioned jet planes. The reason behind the move was that the US and Europe feared that the USSR would attack the West after the outbreak of the Korean War in 1950. Bodø Airport hit the headlines in 1960 when the American spy plane, the U-2, was shot down over the Soviet Union and its pilot was taken prisoner. The plane was on its way from Pakistan to Bodø, as Bodø was an important operations base for the U-2 missions over the Soviet Union.

Several European countries and NATO allies have used Bodø Airport as a base for their operational training.

The civilian part of Bodø Airport is the operational base for Widerøe's airline, which is one of Europe's largest regional airlines. The company operates from most of the regional airports that have short take-off and landing facilities. From Bodø they have direct connections with airports in Helgeland, Lofoten and in Vesterålen. Another operator has services to Røst (p 146), whilst the airport at Værøy (p 149) has been closed down since the 1990s following some serious incidents involving passenger aircraft, all caused by bad weather. A helicopter service has replaced the ordinary fixed-wing planes and these now land in a more sheltered area on the island. The concrete runway at Bodø Airport is 2 793 m in length.

☙

The ship docks at the quayside in Bodø CITY MAP P**398**

The town of Bodø grew up around the estate called Hundholmen, which was the original name of Bodø. The town was founded in 1816, as a commercial centre for the local fishing activities in the area, thus effectively replacing Bergen. Bodø

Bodø 1900

was chosen because of its central location in relation to fishing activities and because timber materials were easily available. Already in 1775, Hundholmen (Bodø) had status as a trading centre. Bergen saw this as a threat to their fish trading monopoly and was in strong opposition to Bodø's role in the fish trading business (p 9).

Just after Bodø became a town (with 55 male inhabitants) a prolonged period of inactivity set in. This period lasted until 1864 when a very good herring season led to an upswing in the fortunes of the town. Enormous quantities of herring were caught and in 1874 the population had risen to 1 478 and in 1884 to 2 685. In the mid 1880s the herring disappeared and Bodø had to readjust to harsher times. Bodø Church was built in 1888 and in 1894 the town became a parish. Schools were built; a breakwater and a steamship quay were built in 1904. In 1900 the town had 4 877 inhabitants.

On 27th May 1940, just after British engineers had finished constructing the town airport, most of Bodø was destroyed by German air raids. In the course of two and a half hours fewer than 200 houses were left standing and of the 6 000 inhabitants, 3 500 were left homeless.

The reconstruction of the town began after the war ended in 1945. New development plans had to be made before the rebuilding was started and temporary buildings were not permitted. For this reason Bodø has one of Norway's best-planned town layouts. A new

airport was opened in 1952, Bodø Cathedral was consecrated in 1957 and Bodø railway station was opened in 1962. The station is the northernmost terminal and end station for the Nordlandsbanen.

Today, Bodø is Northern Norway's second largest town with 35 618 inhabitants and is the municipal and regional administration centre. The town is also the region's communications hub for ferries, aircraft and trains. Bodø Airport is the region's main airport and Northern Norway's Defence Command and Bodø Main Air station (military) are located here. Other important institutions include Bodø College (approx. 4 800 students) and the National Norwegian Aviation Museum (1995).

Bodø Cathedral was built in 1956. The Cathedral occupies a complete city block and is built with three basilica naves in Gothic style with a high centrepiece that protrudes beyond the sidepieces. It has a freestanding bell tower. A 12 m high glass painting, 10 tapestries from Nordland and a rose-painted window decorate the interior. The cathedral is an excellent example of modern Norwegian architecture and became a listed building in 2002.

Bodin Church is a stone church from the Middle Ages built, it is believed, by King Håkon Håkonsson (1204-63) in approx. 1240. It was extended in 1784 and later restored. Today the church is termed a long-nave church with smaller side naves and has a square chancel. It is assumed that

the church was originally built as part of a monastery that was located nearby at that time.

Before Norway was christianized the site where the church is today may have been an important religious and assembly place (a 'ting') in pagan times. The first church was small, but as the population grew the church was extended with a nave built with thick heavy stone walls, which were commonly used in stone churches in those days.

Bodin Church has been rebuilt so many times that it is impossible to date the various extensions. It is believed to have had a sharply angled roof and a conical tower. During restoration work remains of an older wall were discovered, probably originating from an older, smaller church located inside the walls of the existing church. The walls in the chancel are nearly 4 m thick and may have had concealed corridors and stairs at one time. Later they were filled in with stones and debris. Due to the use of heavy construction materials the ground under the church subsided and for this reason the church was repaired and rebuilt in the old style. A lot of the old inventory was lost due to all the restoration work carried out.

✍

The ship continues to Stamsund	+ 0 hrs 00 min

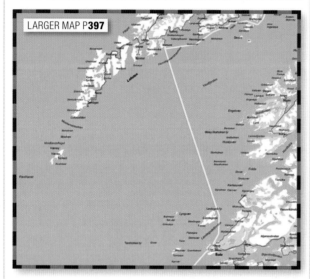

LARGER MAP P**397**

On our port side we can see Saltfjorden.

✍

On our starboard side we pass the small peninsula, **Nyholmen** and the ruins of the fort, Nyholmen Skandse. The fort was built in 1810 during the Napoleonic Wars of 1807-1814 when Denmark-Norway was on the side of the French in the war against England (amongst others) (p 85). English warships formed a blockade along the Norwegian coast and Nyholmen Skandse's mission was to defend Hundholmen/Bodø. Russia was also on the side of the French so that trade between Bodø and Russia via Archangelsk was possible; corn was shipped to Bodø and fish to Russia. This trade lasted until 1812.

The fort on Skandsen was comprised of two parts. The main part was a distorted square with a small opening, with walls that were 1-2 m thick. In addition to this there were gunpowder rooms, guardhouses, storehouses and two platforms with one cannon on each. To the west

of the fort a larger gun platform had been built with four 12-pounders and at least eight 8-pounders. In addition to these guns they had a gunboat with one cannon onboard. In the beginning, 150 men worked here at the fort; some of them were liberated prisoners. Nyholmen Skandse was stripped of its entire armoury in 1815 and closed down altogether in 1835.

Nyholmen Skandse was never attacked but fulfilled its purpose as it kept the British warships at a distance. During the Second World War the German forces constructed artillery units and ammunition bunkers here and in the process many of the old fortifications were destroyed.

Parts of Nyholmen Skandse were restored for Bodø's 180-year jubilee in 1996. Later restoration work was done in stages, following the drawings made by Engineer Captain Friis in 1810. Today the fort is used by Nyholm Skandses Compagnie Historical Group for special salutes, tattoos and open-air concerts etc.

Outermost on the peninsula is Nyholmen lighthouse.

✍

After passing Nyholmen we head northward and we can see **Lille Hjartøya** on our port side. On our starboard side we can see Bodin College of Further Education's training centre that offers students safety and contingency training for maritime operations.

✍

67°18'N 14°22'40"E	+ 0 hrs 10 min ①

We are sailing out into **Landegodefjorden**. Ahead and on our port side is the island, Landegode. On our starboard side we can see some of the suburbs of Bodø along Nordstranda, under the mountain Keiservarden close to Bodø centre all the way to Mjeldefjellet south of Mistfjorden.

✍

Keiservarden (366 m above sea level) was originally called 'Veten', a name often used for peaks where beacons were lit to warn of danger in the community (p 82). On 16th July 1889, on one of his many summer visits to Norway, the German Kaiser Wilhelm II walked up to the peak and after this, Veten, like so many other places the keen mountaineering Kaiser visited, was renamed in his honour by the locals to 'Keiservarden'.

In August 2006, Norway's famous and internationally acclaimed pianist, Leif Ove Andsnes, along with Det Norske Kammerorkester, gave a Mozart concert on top of Keiservarden in magnificent summer weather. A grand piano and many other instruments were transported by helicopter to the top of this mountain and an audience of 3 100 experienced an unforgettable occasion.

A similar event featuring the well-known Norwegian violinist Arve Tellefsen took place the following year.

❧

67°20'N   14°24'E   + 0 hrs 16 min

Ahead and to our port side we can see the island, Landegode. On our starboard side is Bodø's so-called 'north side' – an expanding residential area and a popular place for holiday homes. From here, in clear weather, we can see the beautiful "Lofotveggen" – The Lofoten Wall.

❧

On our starboard side we pass **Løp**, a suburb of Bodø. On Løp we find Løp Gamle Gård, an annex of Salten Museum. Løp Gamle Gård was the bailiff's residence from 1651 to 1837. In 1762 a tax collector/sheriff and his family lived here with a private teacher, clerk, housekeeper, six male servants and several maids. The house was taken over by Bodø municipality in 1984 and the house along with its inventory was totally refurbished. Today it is used for art exhibitions and as a summer café.

On Løp is a medium wave radio transmitter from 1931. It originally served the fishing fleets operating in the north, but was later replaced by a newer transmitter located on the island of Røst (p 146). The transmitter on Løp is under the protection of Norsk Telemuseum and Riksantikvaren (Directorate of Cultural Heritage). Medium wave transmitters are also located on Vigra near Ålesund (p 74) and on Kvitsøy. Together these transmitters cover the entire fishing fleet.

❧

67°21'30"   14°25'47"E   + 0 hrs 29 min

On our starboard side we pass **Vågøya**, a group of islets and reefs. Thereafter we can see the rural districts of **Skau** and **Valvika** on the mainland before we pass the mountain, **Mjeldefjellet** (780 m above sea level), located south of the entrance to **Mistfjorden**. Mjelde peninsula is one of Bodø's popular recreational areas with some very fine beaches.

❧

Ahead, and on our starboard side we can see the mountains, **Breidfjellet** (737 m above sea level) and **Fjærkjerringa.** This area, a peninsula, was incorporated into Bodø municipality in 1964. The peninsula is called **Kjerringøy**, after the small island, **Kjerringøy** in **Karlsøyfjorden**, just off the mainland. Kjerringøy village is located on the island, **Store Kjerringøy**.

Kjerringøy, 40 km north of Bodø is the most famous trading post in Nordland county and probably one of the best known in all of Norway. Many of the trading posts in Northern Norway were established in the late 18th century by boat skippers, shop workers, etc. They generally started with just a small country store, but where trade was good the business was expanded. Some of these traders, "nessekongene" (kings of the headland, a term often used to describe those with great influence over a limited area) became influential figures. From Brønnøy (p 323) to Varanger in Finnmark county (p 223) some 2-300 trading posts existed, mostly located along the shipping channels and close to places where travellers found it convenient to call.

In the 17th century Kjerringøy was already a busy place. The first trading licence was issued at the end of the 18th century. Buying and selling fish and fish products was the basis for the expansion of Kjerringøy. The traders bought fish in Lofoten and other places in Nordland, which they then dried, salted, and sold to the merchants in Bergen. In exchange they brought back various goods, which they sold from their stores on Kjerringøy or in Lofoten. This type of activity peaked around 1820 when a strong upward trend in the market increased the earnings in the fish trade. The merchants on Kjerringøy had ships that transported goods from Lofoten to Bergen, they owned mines and a steam ship company; and were often money-lenders. In the very class-conscious society of that time the merchant was definitely one of the elite. At its peak at the end of the 19th century it was the wealthiest trading centre in all of Northern Norway.

Trade at Kjerringøy lasted until 1937 with varying success. The trading post was taken over by Nordland County Museum in 1959. The trading post is listed property and restored and comprises of the main building;

a typical empire style house, a bakery, a general store with full inventory and artefacts intact, a large boathouse with examples of typical boats used a hundred years ago and a garden. Altogether there are 15 listed buildings with most of the inventory preserved and in good condition. Kjerringøy was awarded the European Rural Districts Development Prize in 2000.

The Norwegian author Knut Hamsun has also contributed to making Kjerringøy famous. As a young man he lived here for some years around 1879 and it was here he was inspired to become a writer. Several of his books have also been made into films here on Kjerringøy. Through his works we have a very good picture of the life and activities surrounding a wealthy fishing village and trading centre. When Hamsun was 20 years old he received economic support from the merchant that owned most of Kjerringøy at that time. It is believed that the merchant became a role model in many of Knut Hamsun's stories and novels.

There has been a church on Kjerringøy since the 16th century and "Kjerringøens church" was first mentioned in documents in 1589. A new church was built in 1763, but was soon found to be too small and was demolished. Another new church was built 1883 with economic support from the merchant on Kjerringøy. The rectory was built in 1889. Some of the items in the church date back to the 17th century. The most valuable treasure is the restored black altar board near the pulpit from 1601. The rectory is today used as a school.

The legend of the Giant in Strandåtinden.
Once upon a time in the mighty mountain called Strandåtinden north of Kjerringøy, lived a Giant that began to feel lonesome in his old days. He cast his eyes on the mountain near the northerly entrance to Mistfjorden, Fjærekjerringa (737 m above sea level), proudly towering up from her location south on Kjerringøy. But she turned her back on him as she was more impressed by the jagged mountains on Landego. The jealous Giant on Strandåtinden took his bow and used a large stone as an arrow. He thought: if he couldn't have Fjærekjerringa, no one else can have her either! But the arrow was too heavy and failed to reach her. The stone landed in a place called Alsos (north of Kjerringøy's stores), it is called Respila (Giant's Arrow), and that is where it rests today.

When the Giant saw that his arrow missed its target he put on his skis and set off down

Strandåtinden. Blinded by rage he sped down the steep mountain far too fast and in order to stop the wild descent he sat down on the sticks - but too late. He tumbled head over heels down the mountain and fell lifeless at the bottom. The tracks from his descent can be seen clearly on the side of the mountain. You will find the Giant's grave at the foot of Strandåtinden, buried under the enormous pile of rocks which is called Resgrava (Giant's Grave).

The ship is now sailing along the island called **Landegode** (30.3 km²) on our port side. The island is a well-known landmark outside of Bodø, with its jagged mountains: from south to north, **Gjura** (705 m above sea level), **Rypdalstinden** (802 m above sea level), **Kvitinden** (788 m above sea level) and **Navaren** (632 m above sea level). In 2001 the island had a population of 62. The largest group of houses is on the island's east side, at Fenes.

In the 'old' days Landegode was called **Gygerøy** (the sorceress' island). The name 'Landegode' ('good land') probably originates from the Viking period. This name is in stark contrast to the harsh weather conditions around it. Superstitious folk at that time said that one should never express anxiety to the open water or use words that could reveal fear of the place or waters because these fears might be realised. The sailors did something rather clever; they referred to these places using friendly and safe words to cover up their worst fears. Hence the name, Landegode, "the Good Land" - where no evil things could happen - in contrast to the original name, Gygerøy, (the sorceress' island).

Today Landegode exports Norwegian redfish to the fish markets in Europe. Landegode has probably the largest population of Sea Eagles in the world (p 161).

On the north side of Landegode are two lighthouses.

67°25'25"N   14°26'25"E   + 0 hrs 48 min

Bjørnøy lighthouse is situated on the small island of Bjørnøya on our port side, just northeast of Landegode. The lighthouse was built in 1890. It was closed down and replaced by an automated beacon in 1972. In 2005 the lighthouse was sold and is now available for recreational use. Bodø municipality is responsible for its maintenance and upkeep.

c/o

67°27'N   14°25'E   + 0 hrs 51 min ②

© RIKSANTIKVAREN

Landegode lighthouse is located on the islet **Store Eggeløysa**, which we can see as we pass Landegode's northerly point on our port side. The lighthouse was built in 1902, when the Hurtigruten had just started, requiring a beacon on the east side of Vestfjorden, on the approach to Bodø. The station has a 29 m high cast iron tower with a light with a range of 17.8 nautical miles. The station had also a foghorn, a diaphone from 1934–1987, and a radio beacon from 1939-92. The houses are placed close together and are comprised of a machine room, living quarters, outhouses, a forge, a boathouse, two landing stages and a garden. The lighthouse was automated in 1988, de-manned in 1993 and listed in 1999. Since then it has been a popular place to hold seminars and courses.

c/o

On 17th July 1924, the old DS "Haakon Jarl", on a northerly course out of Bodø, collided with the southbound DS "Kong Harald". Both ships belonged to the Hurtigruten fleet. The collision occurred in thick fog just north of Landegode, and the ship sank in just 8 minutes with the loss of 17 lives.

c/o

On the 23rd October 1940, southeast of Landegode lighthouse, a powerful explosion tore open the hull of the Hurtigrute ship DS "Prinsesse Ragnhild", which was sailing northwards from Bodø to Svolvær. The ship sank in a matter of a few minutes with the loss of 300 lives. Another ship nearby managed to rescue 142, it is assumed that there were 450 passengers onboard. The cause was never established, but it is believed that DS "Prinsesse Ragnhild" struck an underwater mine.

c/o

Looking behind and to the port side and as we pass the northwest point on Landegode, we can see Landegodekjerringa – a rock formation that resembles a female-like stone figure – centuries-old folklore has it that the figure has been seen climbing up the island from the northern point up to the 830 m high peak.

c/o

After passing the northern point of Landegode we head for Lofoten.

c/o

67°40'N   14°50'E

On our starboard side, after passing Landegode we see Karlsøyfjorden between the mainland near Kjerringøy and Karlsøyvær.

Karlsøyvær (8 km²) is a group of small islands west of Kjerringøy. Karlsøyvær was made a nature reserve in 1977 due to the rich bird life on the island.

c/o

Our course is northwest across **Vestfjorden** to Stamsund in Lofoten. On our starboard side, we see the impressive mountains in the northern parts of Bodø municipality and soon we pass into the municipalities of Steigen and Hamarøy.

c/o

Vestfjorden on our starboard side continues into Ofotfjorden.

c/o

67°44'40"N   14°10'40"E

© THOR-RUNE HANSEN

Narvik is situated at the head of Ofotfjorden and has a population of approx. 13 944. Narvik has an ice-free harbour all year round, which has been an important factor in the development of the town as a major exporter of iron ore from the Swedish Mining Company, LKAB's mines in Kiruna, northern Sweden. Several thousand workers took part in building the railway line ('Ofotbanen') that runs between Narvik and Kiruna in the period from 1898 to 1902. Before the railway came to Narvik there were only a few scattered settlements in the area, but afterwards it grew rapidly. The Narvik-Kiruna railway connects with the Swedish national rail network, which is an important route for transporting other goods as well as iron ore. Narvik's role as a key export harbour for raw materials made it an important strategic target at the start of the Second World War, as the German war machine needed steel for the manufacture of weapons, tanks and artillery.

The "Battle for Narvik" took place from 9th April to 9th June 1940. It was to become one of the biggest battles ever fought on Norwegian soil. Live reports of the battle were broadcast all over the world. This was the reason why, in many other countries, Narvik was the best known town of all in Norway, even several decades after the war had ended.

On 9th April 1940, ten German destroyers, with 2 000 Austrian commando soldiers on board entered Narvik's harbour and sank the two Norwegian battleships, KNM "Norge" and KNM "Eidsvold" with torpedoes. The following day, five British destroyers and more German ships arrived. Two British ships were sunk. In the course of the ensuing sea battle, the entire German invasion fleet was destroyed and the fjord approach into Narvik became the country's largest war cemetery. Many of the battles took place on land. Norwegian troops with support from English, Polish and French Foreign Legion soldiers managed to force the Germans into retreat. The German army was only days away from capitulating in the Narvik area when German forces broke through the French lines. Consequently, the Allied soldiers were pulled out of Narvik and without their support, the Norwegian soldiers were forced to lay down their weapons. The town was recaptured and occupied by the German forces.

After the War, Narvik was rebuilt and again functioned as a transit port for iron ore from Kiruna and took advantage of the general post-war international economic growth. In the 1970s and 80s, like many other towns, Narvik was affected by world-wide recessions, but new areas of investments appeared in the form of mechanical, graphic and printing, and food processing industries. Narvik is the most northerly railway station on the West European rail network with connections to the Swedish, Finnish and Russian rail systems.

Lofoten is the collective name for the many islands west of the mainland that we will soon be approaching. The most important are, as we see them from the south; **Røstøya** (4 km²), **Værøya** (15.7 km²), **Moskenesøya** (185.9 km²), **Flakstadøya** (198.8 km²), **Vestvågøya** (411.1 km²), **Gimsøya** (46.4 km²) and **Austvågøya** (526.7 km²).

From a distance, the islands appear as a solid mass and are often called Lofotveggen (Lofoten Wall). The Lofoten mountains are comprised of extremely hard and old rock types, formed some 2-3 million years ago. During the last Ice Age, that ended approx. 10 000 years ago, the glaciers scoured the rocks and ground and created U-shaped valleys, divided by jagged mountain scars and peaks, the highest of which is 1 146 m above sea level. At that time, the land level was somewhat lower that it is

today, and the sea eroded the weaker zones in the rocks and caves were hollowed out by the pounding waves. There are quite a number of these types of cave formations in Lofoten.

When the first settlers came to Lofoten, approx. 6 000 years ago, forests of pine and birch grew everywhere and the fauna was much more varied than it is today, with bears, lynx, wild reindeer and deer. In the sea, there were large numbers of whales, seals and various species of fish. Traces have been found of Stone Age settlements from approx. 5 500 years ago along with evidence that corn was grown in this area 4 000 years ago. Several Viking chieftain settlements have been discovered (p 83, p 123). Lofotfiske (Lofoten seasonal fishing) has always been, and to a considerable degree still is, the economic backbone of the region.

Today the forests have disappeared. Some small copses remain and some firs have been planted. Apart from relatively small numbers of moose, the fauna today comprises mostly of small rodents, weasels, mink and otter. Bird life is plentiful, in particular on the outer islands. It is estimated that there are approx. 252 species of birds in the area. The flora is also quite varied, considering Lofoten's geographical location.

On the seabed in Vestfjorden, there are 200 different species of kelp and seaweed. In the fjord, there are several types of fish, seals and also killer whales (Orca). Arctic cod come down from the Barents Sea to spawn and the Gulf Stream (p 85) brings fish from the south. Off the coast of Røst, large reserves of oil and gas have been discovered, but due to environmental considerations, the exploitation of this resource has been postponed. In and around Lofoten there are enormous riches, which no longer are just based upon fish.

The unique surroundings attract more and more tourists. Visitors come to enjoy the scenery and to see the quaint fishing villages, or perhaps to take a holiday in a fisherman's cabin. Other popular activities include fishing, sea-rafting, Sea Eagle and whale safaris, trips to Moskenesstraumen and the caves near Moskenes (p 150), mountain climbing on the west side of Lofotveggen and trips to Trollfjorden (p 295). It is also possible to visit the Viking Museum (p 153), to play golf in the midnight sun or take a boat trip to watch the approx. 500 Killer Whales in Tysfjorden during the winter. The range of interesting and exciting activities in the Lofoten region is huge.

From archaeological evidence, it is believed that the annual fishing season known as 'Lofotfisket' has been in existence for approx. 6 000 years. Ancient documents tell us that trade between Sweden and the north of Norway was established already around A.D. 600. There is no doubt that the Vikings were pioneers in the preservation of fish catches; hanging fish on racks and drying them before they went on their journeys as early as A.D. 900. The dried fish is rich in protein and easy to store and transport. Lofotfisket increased in importance at the beginning of the 12th century when King Øystein I Magnusson (1088-1123) (p 10) demanded a tax of five fishes from each fisherman. He built the first church in Vågan (close to what is today Kabelvåg) in 1103. He also built cabins for the fishermen around the year 1120. In the 14th century, the export of dried fish and cod liver oil amounted to ca. 80-90 % of all exports from Norway.

Lofotfisket (literally: 'Lofoten fishing season') is the name given to the seasonal spring cod fishing. The main catch is the northern Arctic species of spawning cod, that make the journey from the vast, nutrient-rich areas in the Barents Sea to the more temperate ocean areas around Lofoten, especially Vestfjorden. At the age of around five, the fish is mature and strong enough to swim the approx. 1 000 km long journey.

The spawning period for the spring cod is from January through April. Previously, many thousand fishermen came to Lofoten each year to take part in the fishing. The boats were open, powered by oars and sails. The life of a fisherman was arduous and dangerous. They could be shipwrecked in storms, or unprotected and wet in their open boats, they could freeze to death in the cold weather; and on land, they sometimes had to sleep under their upturned boats since the cabins were already occupied. If the fish catches failed, it could mean financial ruin for the fisherman. The owners of the onshore facilities leased their cabins to the men, told them where to fish, bought the catch at their price, salted or dried the fish and transported it to Bergen. From here, it was sold and exported to Europe. This system led to many fishermen becoming economically dependent upon the owners of the onshore facilities. In

1816, a law was passed regulating their activities and in 1857, the Lofoten Law was introduced, in order to secure the fisherman's rights. Later, other laws were passed that provided free trade with Northern Norway with the result that the shore facility owners' influence over the fishermen was curtailed.

At the height of fishing activities in the 1800s, approx. 30 000 men were employed in fishing in Lofoten, in some form or other. Men from the north and south flocked to the islands in the hope of making good catches. At the end of the century and at the beginning of the 1900s, the traditional Nordland boats were replaced by larger, motorised fishing boats, a transition that did not happen without a good deal of conflict. The story of the clash between various fishermen's groups at Trollfjorden describes this conflict (p 295). Until 1940, 'Lofotfisket' was the main source of income for the majority of fishermen in Northern Norway, very often combined with another trade, farming or other work. In 1932, 32 000 fishermen took part in the annual 'Lofotfisket'. In 1958 the number had fallen to 12 000. In 1990 the number had fallen even further to 2 000 men - a year with especially poor catches. The most recent available figures from 2006 indicate that 1 424 vessels and 3 082 fishermen took part in the 'Lofotfisket'.

New types of modern vessels and fishing gear are now used during Lofotfisket, which is regarded as one of the world's most effectively organised (and regulated) fisheries. A dedicated fisheries inspectorate maintains control of those taking part and ensures that vessels set out for the fishing grounds at a certain time each day. The fishing grounds are divided into sectors for each type of gear used. The inspectorate maintains strict control that the boundaries are respected.

We are now approaching Lofoten and can see **Lofot-veggen**, which is approx. 110 km long and stretches from Moskenes in the south to Raftsundet in the north. Lofotveggen is Norway's most concentrated jagged rock formation.

Farthest south in Lofoten are the legendary islands of Røst (11.2 km²) with a total of 365 islands, 100 km west of Bodø and 60 km from Lofotodden.

Approx. 67°31'N   12°06'E

Røst municipality

Municipal coat of arms, significance: Illustrates the ancient legend of the cormorants on Utrøst.
Meaning of name: Norse rost, 'mael-strom'.
Municipal seat: Røstlandet. (pop. 358).
Position: 67°31'N 12°06'E.
Area: 11 km². **Population:** 591.
Pop. density: 53.7 /km².
Area distribution: Farming 12 %, forestry 0 %, fresh water 3 %, other 85 %.
Trade and industry: Food processing connected to the fishing season (January-April). Other times of the year, the processing industry is supplied with fish caught by local fishermen. Rock-dried cod which is exported to Italy. Salmon farming. Some farming. A shipyard with slipway, mechanical workshops. Electrical power is transported via a cable from Moskenes over Værøy.
Places to return to: Røst chuch. Skomvær light-house. Church ruins. Sites from early Stone Age. Bird cliff.
Røst municipality's home page: www.rost.kommune.no.

67°64'N   11°52'E

Skomvær lighthouse is one of Norway's most famous lighthouses. It is situated on the island of **Skomvær**, the southernmost of the Røst islands far out in the Norwegian Sea. It is a 31.7 m high iron tower, built in 1887 to assist the timber transport ships sailing from Archangelsk. It was automated in 1979 and finally closed down in 1988. The lighthouse became a listed property in 1999 and is now a cultural monument. During the summer season, daily boat trips are arranged from Røst to Skomvær.

Skomvær was a lively place in its heyday. Several families lived here and the children had their own

governess. The well-known Norwegian artist Theodor Kittelsen lived here for nearly two years at the end of 1880s and he has described his impressions of Skomvær through drawings and words.

Between Skomvær and Røst are a number of small rocky islands, rising between 200 to 260 m above sea level. These are some of the most famous bird nesting sites in Norway. Millions of sea birds come here during the nesting season, especially puffins (p 218). The number of birds was reduced dramatically in the 1970s due to a catastrophic fall in the numbers of herring fry.

Røstlandet is the northernmost island and the municipal seat. The highest point is only 12 m above sea level and most of the islands in the neighbourhood are equally flat.

Southwest of Røst the world's biggest deep-water coral reef was discovered in 2002. It is 35 km long and in some places 3 km wide, in total it covers an area more than 100 km². The reef, of the type 'Lophelia', is located at a depth of between 300 and 400 metres. The age of the reef has yet to be determined, however similar, smaller reefs farther south have been found to be approx. 8 500 years old. Modern fishing methods, such as trawl equipment have damaged and reduced many of these reefs, which should be protected and preserved.

Several settlements and burial mounds dating back to the Stone Age (p 83) have been discovered on Røst. Here we can find sites at which local Viking Chieftains were based, also remains of the island's oldest church from approx. 1400. There are also remains of the church spire from a church built in 1825, which blew down in a storm in 1835. A new stone church was built in 1839, but this was demolished in 1900 as it was too small. The existing church is a wooden structure with an altar cabinet dating from the Middle Ages. The cabinet was brought out to Røst in 1520 and has most probably been part of the inventory of five different churches at some time. The cabinet is one of five donated by Princess Elisabeth of the Netherlands to churches built along the stormy Norwegian coast. These were given in gratitude and as an offering to God for her safe voyage through a storm when she travelled by sea to Copenhagen when she was to be crowned King Christian II's Queen (1489-1551). The Princess had suffered from seasickness!

One of Norway's most famous shipwrecks happened at **Sandøy** near Røst. In the spring of 1431, the Italian merchant and skipper, Pietro Querini, set off from Crete for Flanders with a group of three ships carrying cargoes of spices and casks for the western European markets. The ships sailed into a storm on the west coast of France and became separated. They were probably blown west of Ireland and Scotland. In all 68 seamen were forced to get into the lifeboats. They had to endure the storms and cold for weeks. Some were drowned or died of hunger and exhaustion. The lifeboats drifted with the Gulf Stream (p 85) and just after the New Year 1432, the survivors landed on Sandøya near Røst. Almost a month later local fishermen found them and they were looked after by the people on Røst for about three months, before they returned to Italy in the middle of May 1432. The story of their stormy voyage, their stay on Røst and their journey back home has been recorded by Querini and the men that travelled with him on his ship.

This remarkable meeting between cultures and the description of everyday life amongst the coastal people is one of the few 'eyewitness' accounts from the Middle Ages in Norway. The Italians wrote about primitive people, innocent and content living a dignified and harmonious life. "The people on these islands are the most perfect one can imagine, they are handsome and their women are also beautiful. They are trustworthy and nothing is kept locked. Not even the women are guarded. This we can confirm by the fact that we shared sleeping quarters with the husband, his wife and children without it being strange at all; they would undress and go naked to bed", wrote Querini about the inhabitants of the small island, as he put it, close to "Culo Mundi" – at the edge of the world. He also writes that the people were devout Christians and describes in detail their fishing methods and how they dried the cod.

On 10th June 1932, a memorial stone was raised on Sandøy to commemorate Captain Querini and his men.

Many legends are written about these islands out in the west, the best known of these is as follows:

The Legend of the Cormorants from Utrøst.

On returning home, it is not unusual that the fishermen from Nordland find ears of corn attached to the ship's wheel or find barley in the fish's stomach. It may be that they have sailed over Utrøst or one of the other mythical lands in these parts. These lands appear only to pious and wise people who are in danger at sea, and they can appear where no land is found. The underworld trolls that live here have farms and cattle and they fish and sail their boats just like other people; here the sun's rays shine upon greener pastures and richer cornfields compared to any other place in Nordland. Fortunate are those who can see one of these sunny islands; "he is saved", so they say here in Nordland. An old song by Peder Dass describes in detail one of the islands outside Træna in Helgeland (p 306), called Sandflesa, with rich fishing grounds and an abundance of all kind of wild game. Sometimes, in the middle of Vestfjorden a large, flat, arable land appears only just high enough up from the sea so just so that the ears of corn are seen. Outside Røst, south of Lofoten it is said that there is such a mythical land with green pastures and golden cornfields called Utrøst. The farmer at Utrøst has a boat just like all other farmers in Nordland. At times, they bear down on the fishermen or boat skippers at speed with all sails hoisted, but somehow just before a collison, they simply disappear.

At Værøy, near Røst, there lived a poor fisherman called Isak. His only possessions were a boat and a couple of goats that his wife kept fed on fish scraps and grass found on the hills nearby and his house was full of hungry children. Nevertheless, he was content because that was how the Good Lord wanted it to be. His only complaint was that he got no peace from his neighbour, who was a rich man who always wanted to appear better than poor Isak. The rich man wanted to get rid of Isak so that he could obtain the harbour that Isak had outside his cottage.

One day when Isak was out fishing a few miles offshore a thick fog descended upon him followed by a storm so severe that he had to throw the catch overboard to save the boat and himself. Even then, it was not easy to remain afloat but he managed to skilfully manoeuvre over and between the breaking waves. After sailing like this for five or six hours he hoped he would reach land somewhere. However, the fog and the weather just got worse. Suddenly he realised

© EILIV LEREN

that he was drifting out to sea because the wind had changed and was taking him away from land.

Suddenly, he heard a loud screech up ahead and he thought that it was "Draugen" - the Sea-Troll, singing his last psalm. He prayed to his Maker for his wife and children as he thought his last hour had come. As he sat he saw something shiny and black, and as he came nearer he saw three cormorants sitting on some driftwood. He sailed past them. He was now both thirsty and hungry and did not know what to do next. Almost asleep and with the tiller in his hand, the boat suddenly hit bottom and Isak woke up. The sun drove away the fog and shone over a delightful landscape; the meadows and hills were green and the pastures and cornfields were lush with vegetation and he could smell the sweet fragrance of flowers and grass.

"Thank God, I'm saved, this is Utrøst," said Isak to himself. In front of him was a field of barley with ears so large and full he had never seen the like before. Through the field was a narrow path leading up to a green peat-covered hut and on top of the hut a white goat with golden horns was grazing. It had an udder as large as a cow's and outside the hut sat a small man on a bench, clad in blue, smoking a pipe. He had a beard that reached half way down his chest.

"Welcome to Utrøst, Isak," said the man.

"Praise this meeting, sir," replied Isak. "You know me?"

"That may be so," said the man; "Do you want to stay here tonight?"

"That would be much appreciated, sir," said Isak.

"It is a bit awkward for my sons, they don't like the smell of a Christian man," said the man. "Have you not met them?"

"No, I only met three cormorants sitting screeching on some driftwood," replied Isak.

"Oh yes, that were my sons," said the man. Emptying his pipe he said to Isak: "You had better go as you are both thirsty and hungry, I can imagine."

"Thanks for the invitation, sir", said Isak.

When the man opened the door Isak was quite stunned over what he saw. The table was filled with the most wonderful food Isak had ever seen; Redfish, fish liver with syrup and brown cheese, roast joints, buttermilk pudding, piles of pretzels, spirits, beer and mead and other delights. He ate and drank heartily, but his plate and glass were never empty. The man did not eat much, and when there was a lot of commotion outside the cabin, he went out. After a while, he returned with his three sons. Isak got a fright when he saw the sons but the man had restrained them, as they were smiling and friendly, joined them at the table, and had a drink. But when Isak wanted to leave the table - he was well fed by then - they insisted that he sat with them and had more to drink. Isak did as he was asked and they became very friendly. The three sons insisted that they all went fishing together so that he could bring some fish back to his family.

During their first trip, they were caught in a storm. One of the sons was at the tiller; one sat in the middle and one was up front in the boat and Isak was left to bail out water with all his might. They sailed like madmen, never slacking the sails and when the boat was full of water, they cut a hole in the transom such that the water emptied out like a waterfall. After a while, the storm subsided and they started to fish. They caught so much fish that the sons filled the boat very quickly and returned to Utrøst. As the sons had caught all the fish, Isak complained to the man who promised that he would catch fish the next time out and gave him a pair of fishing lines. This time Isak caught as much fish as the sons did.

Isak became homesick and when he was about to leave the man gave him a new boat filled with flour, linen and many useful things. Isak thanked the man for his kindness who replied: "You must come back when we launch the new boat and come with me to Bergen where you can sell your fish." This Isak wanted to do and asked what course he had to sail in order to come back to Utrøst again. "Follow the cormorant straight out to sea and you are on the right course," said the man. "Have a safe voyage."

Isak set sail and when he turned to look back at Utrøst, he saw only the sea.

When the time came, Isak went to the launching of the new boat. He had never seen such a boat before. It was so long that when the lookout at the bow shouted his instructions to the man at the tiller they needed a man by the mast in the middle of the boat to relay the message, and even then, he had to shout for all he was worth. The part that Isak owned was stowed in the front of the boat. He loaded the fish by himself, but as soon as he carried the fish to the boat more fish filled up his store on shore. So, when he left there was as much fish left behind as was in the boat. This he could not understand.

When he arrived in Bergen, he sold his fish and he had enough money to buy a new fully rigged boat, just as the man had advised him to do. Late that evening before leaving for home the man came on board and asked him not to forget his neighbour's family. Then he predicted success and prosperity for Isak and his boat. "All is well, when it is written in the weather," he said, and by this he meant that there would always be one on board that no one could see, someone who would support the mast with his back if needed.

From then on Isak was prosperous. He understood from where it came and never forgot to send something to those who needed to fish through the winter when he laid up his boat in the autumn. At Christmas, the lights would glow in his boat and there was music, laughter and dancing in the boathouse.

Source: P.Chr. Asbjørnsen og Jørgen Moe, Samlede eventyr.
Første bind, Gyldendal Norsk Forlag, Oslo 1953.

Værøy Municipality

Municipal coat of arms, significance: Puffins, common in the area.
Meaning of name: Norse, vedr, 'weather'.
Municipal seat: Sørland (pop. 542).
Position: 67°39'N 12°41'E.
Area: 18 km². **Population:** 748.
Pop. density: 41.6 /km².
Area distribution: Farming 5 %, forestry - %, fresh water - %, other 85 %.
Trade and industry: Fishing, mainly cod. Fish food factory. Cold storage. Boat yard with slipway and mechanical workshop. Tourism. Sheep farming. Electric power is brought from Moskenesøy via a subsea cable.
Places to return to: Mostad bird cliff.
Værøy municipality's home page: www.varoy.kommune.no

The lighthouse on Værøy was built in 1880 and is situated on a headland on the island's southern point. It has a range of 12.5 nautical miles and was automated and de-manned in 1984.

On the south side of **Værøy** is **Mostad.** It is a de-populated fishing village with an original housing milieu where as many as 150 people lived only just a few years ago. They lived by catching birds on **Mostadfjellet** and fishing. In a deep cavern southeast on Værøy paintings have been discovered that are thought to be 3 500 years old.

On the place called **Nordland**, north on Værøy we can find "gammelkirka" – the old church. The timber church was built in 1714 in Kabelvåg in Lofoten (p 156), but was dismantled and moved to Værøy in 1799 and later restored and refurbished. The church has a characteristic dome and is the oldest existing church in Lofoten. Værøy church, on the south east part of the island, was built in 1939.

Moskenes municipality

Municipal coat of arms, significance:
Illustrates the Moskenes current.
Meaning of name: The farm, Muskenes
or Musnes.
Municipal seat: Reine (pop. 320).
Position: 67°56'N 13°05'E.
Area: 119 km². **Population:** 1 156.
Population density: 9.7 /km².
Distribution: Farming 1 %, forestry - %,
fresh water 7 %, other 92 %.
Trade and industry: Fishing. Lofot fishing. Spring
cod fishing on the coast of Finnmark. Fish food
processing. Power generation.
Places to return to: Maelstrøm at Moskenes-
straumen. Refsvikhula (cave). Fishing village of Å.
Sørvågen Radio.
Activities to return to: Mountain climbing.
Moskenes municipality's home page:
www.moskenes.kommune.no

Moskenesstraumen, also known as "The Big Mael-strom" flows between the south point of Lofotveggen, **Lofotodden** and the northerly islands on Værøy. It is known as one of the worlds most powerful maelstroms (p 162).

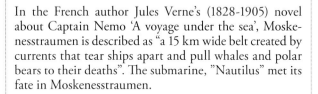

Moskenesstraumen was first described some 2 000 years ago by the Greek histori-an Pytheas, and is marked on many charts, including Arabian, with alarming drawings and warnings.

In the French author Jules Verne's (1828-1905) novel about Captain Nemo 'A voyage under the sea', Moske-nesstraumen is described as "a 15 km wide belt created by currents that tear ships apart and pull whales and polar bears to their deaths". The submarine, "Nautilus" met its fate in Moskenesstraumen.

The American author, Edgar Allan Poe (1809-49) descri-bes Moskenesstraumen in his story about Jonas Rasmus' journey. He wrote that the ocean eddies "rumbled like buffaloes stampeding over the prairie". In 1841 he wrote the following about the current; "Half like a scream, half like a roar so powerful that not even the Niagara Falls co-uld raise its voice higher towards the heavens".

Italian researchers believe that it was Moskenesstraumen the legendary Greek King Odysseus encountered on his voyage.

In 1539 the "Carta Marina", drawn up by the Swedish nobleman, Olaus Magnus (1490-1557) was issued –

complete with drawings of the terrifying Maelstrom. In 1555, he issued a work in Rome, 'The history of the people of the north'. Here he describes the Maelstrom as ocean eddies pumping up and down every day, devou-ring large ships and spitting them out again.

In 1591 a local bailiff wrote "...when the Maelstrom is at its highest then you can see the heavens and the sun through the waves because they roll by as high as mountains…".

The Maelstrom at Moskenes has a natural explanation. Moskenesstraumen is 4–5 km wide and approx. 60 me-tres deep. On either side, in the Norwegian Sea and in Vestfjorden, the ocean bed lies much deeper. As the tidal waters flow into Vestfjorden twice daily, this causes the water level to rise up to 4 metres above normal sea le-vel and when the tide turns, eddies are formed – some with speeds of as much as 6 knots. In the middle of the current, there are skerries where the water is constantly 'boiling', even in dead calm conditions.

This stretch of ocean with its abundance of fish has given rise to settlements in southern Lofoten and on Værøy over thousands of years.

At Lofotodden on Moskenesøya is Refsvik-hula, a gigantic coastal cavern. It is 115 m deep, 12 m wide and 50 m high. Here we see intriguing pictures of human-like figures on the cavern walls, painted by Stone Age people some 3 000 years ago.

***

Moskenesøya (186 km²) is the southernmost island in Lofoten. It is very hilly with a great number of jagged peaks, the tallest being **Hermannsdalstinden** (1 029 m above sea level) on the western side of the island. The west coast is steep and is a favourite place for mountaineering. On the north and eastern sides of the island, there are many deep fjords with several scattered fishing villages. Moskenesøya has a bridge connection with Flakstadøya.

***

Approx. 67°52'N   12°58'E   ③

The fishing village of **Å** on Moskenesøya is the end point of Lofotveien. Once, Å, together with other villages in Lofoten, were full of activity, especially during the fishing season in Lofoten. Many of the buildings are from the 19ᵗʰ century, which are now listed and protected. One of them is Norway's oldest cod liver oil factory from 1850. The main building is from 1840-1860 and there is also an old wharf where they prepared both rock-dried and salted fish. Tourism in Lofoten, also in Å, is growing.

Approx. 67°53'N   13°02'E

The fishing village, **Sørvågen** (pop. 463) is on Moskenesøya. Already in 1861, the authorities invested in a telegraph line to Lofoten, the Lofot Line, which comprised of landlines and sea cables 170 km in length. Nine fishing villages had telegraphic connections with each other; however, this was only 'open' during the yearly Lofoten fishing season from January to April. In 1868, the Lofot Line was connected to the national network and from 1873, it was open all year round.

On 1ˢᵗ May 1906, the world's second wireless connection was commissioned between Sørvågen and Røst. The Italian, G. Marconi was the driving force behind the development of the first wireless signals. He realised the growing need for effective communications between ships and shore due to expanding international commerce. Whilst other scientists in Great Britain were able to send messages by wireless telegraphy over a mere 150 m, Marconi managed to send signals over a distance of 2.4 km. Marconi firmly believed that this could be greatly improved and wireless telegraphy 'took off' around 1900 and reached its high-point when Marconi managed to send a signal across the Atlantic Ocean. The wireless telegraph was established in 1899. Marconi built his land-based station in England shortly after he founded his own company. The Norwegians studied this new communication device and brought it back to Norway and Lofoten in 1902.

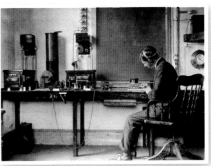

The Lofoten fishing season is the world's largest seasonal fishing and was the reason for the establishment of Sørvågen. As this activity was very profitable for Norway, it was also very important that communications were sound. It was used to order bait, to sell the catch and not least to find out where and when the fish would arrive. For some time surveys were carried out to find a method of installing a telegraph line between Sørvågen and Røst. Moskenesstraumen flowed between the two places and the strong current made the venture very expensive, if indeed it was at all possible. The wireless telegraph solved the problem.

In order to use wireless telegraphy, tall aerials were necessary. Kites with lines were sent up into the air, a method that met with little success. Another method was to string the antennas between tall, 50 m long timber joists anchored with stays. This method proved effective. In 1906, the telegraph station in Sørvågen opened, the second of its kind in the world. Similar installations were built at Værøy and Røst, and thus the wireless communication system in Lofoten was established.

The Norwegian Telecom Museum's collection is at Sørvågen.

***

By Sørvågen is Moskenes Church, a timber cruciform church from 1819, some of the inventory is from 1564.

***

Approx. 67°56'N   13°05'E

The fishing village, **Reine** lies sheltered and protected on a peninsula at the foot of the steep mountain, **Munkan** (775 m above sea level).

© ROLF LILAND

Approx. 67°57'N   13°11'E

The boundary between the municipalities of Moskenes and Flakstad. Flakstad municipality covers the northern part of Moskenesøya and Flakstadøya.

Flakstad municipality

Municipal coat of arms, significance: A sense of belonging for those living along the coast.
Meaning of name: Norse 'flag'-mountainside.
Municipal seat: Ramberg (pop. -).
Position: 68°05'N   13°14'E.
Area: 180 km². **Population:** 1 458.
Pop. density: 8.1 /km².
Distribution: Farming 3 %, forestry - %, fresh water 5 %, other 92 %.
Trade and industry: Fishing, mainly in Lofoten. Fish farming. Agriculture, combined farms with cattle and sheep farming.
Places to return to: Nusfjord fiskevær. Flakstad kirke. Fiskerimuseum.
Flakstad municipality's home page: www.flakstad.kommune.no

The island, Flakstadøya (110 km²) is very hilly, with smooth, scoured rocks and deep fjords. The island's highest point is Stjerntinden (934 m above sea level), located on the east side of the island.

The fishing village of **Nusfjord** was once one of Lofoten's oldest and most active fishing villages. During the Lofot season there could be as many as 1 500 people living here whilst normally there were only 75 permanent residents. The 19th century houses are restored and preserved. They consist of 28 shacks, fish processing works, cod liver oil steam plant, boathouses and a general store. There is still a good deal of fishing activity at Nusfjord, which was one of the pilot projects entered for the European Architectural Preservation prize in 1975.

We are now sailing into Vestvågøy municipality. Nappstraumen, between the islands Moskenesøya and Vestvågøya is another of Lofoten's powerful maelstroms (p 162). These two islands are connected by the 1 776 m long sub-sea road tunnel, Nappstraumen tunnel (68 m below sea level).

Vestvågøy municipality

Municipal coat of arms, ignificance: Symbolises fishing.
Meaning of name:
Municipal seat: Leknes (pop. 2 697).
Position: 68°08'N   13°33'E.
Area: 422 km². **Population:** 10 745.
Pop. density: 25.5 /km².
Distribution: Farming 8 %, forestry 5 %, fresh water 4 %, other 83 %.
Trade and industry: Largest fishing community in Nordland county with a modern coastal fishing fleet. Norway's largest trawler company. Lofot fishing in the winter. Conventional fish processing plants with drying and salting of fish. Fish filleting plant, cold storage, cod liver oil steam plant and fish farming. Boat yards with slipways and mechanical workshops. Farming - including dairy farming, sheep, goats and poultry.
Places to return to: Viking Museum Lofotr at Borg. Iron Age and Middle Ages monuments.
Vestvågøy municipality's home page: www.vestvagoy.kommune.no

The island of **Vestvågøya** (411 km²) is very hilly, with a number of jagged peaks. The highest of these is **Himmeltindan** (964 m above sea level) out towards the Norwegian Sea. There are fjords and inlets surrounding the entire island. A belt of agricultural land stretches in a north-easterly direction across the centre of the island.

Approx. 68°04'N   13°31'E   ④

Ballstad (pop. 749), on our starboard side, is the largest fishing village in Lofoten. Ballstad is located at the mouth of **Buksnesfjorden** and at the foot of **Ballstadfjellet** (466 m above sea level). Ballstad has a good harbour with a cod liver oil steam plant and large fish storage facilities. In the harbour area is Ballstad Slipp (shipyard) which can boast of having the world largest mural on its outer wall. **Kræmmervikan** has one of Lofoten's largest collections of fishermen's cabins.

∞

The village of **Gravdal** (pop. 1 605) is situated approximately halfway along Buksnesfjorden. Gravdal is home to the local hospital, Nordland Fisheries College and Buksnes church which was built in the Modernist style in 1905.

∞

The municipal seat of **Leknes** is located at the head of Buksnesfjorden. Leknes is an important trade and service centre with an airport and a harbour with good facilities. A local chieftain had his residence here in the Middle Ages (p 83).

∞

67°57'N 13°59'E	+ 3 hrs 00 min

The ship is now approaching Stamsund. On our port side and outermost in the bay west of Stamsund, we can see the fishing village of Steine. **Steine** became internationally famous in 1992 when Paul Watson, the head of Sea Shepherd Conservation Society, the international organisation for the protection of marine species, attempted to ram and sink the Norwegian whaler, "Nybrenna" with his ship, "Whales Forever" on Christmas Day. He was also involved in a collision incident with the coast guard ship, KNM "Andenes".

∞

The ship docks at the quayside in Stamsund

We have arrived at the fishing village of **Stamsund** (pop. 998), on the inside of the breakwater consisting of small islands and rocks. Stamsund, at the foot of the jagged mountain **Steinstinden** (509 m above sea level) was built, it is said, in 'sheer defiance of nature' into the mountainside and is one of the larger villages in Lofoten.

The Hurtigruten quay is at Stamneset. The eye-catching mural on one of the warehouse walls was painted by the American artist Scott Thoe in 2003. Stamsund's develo-

ped areas stretch northwards of the quayside along the narrow shoreline between the mountain and the sea.

Stamsund was built up around 1900. Norway's largest manufacturer and exporter of dried cod started a major enterprise here in 1876 and it held the status as the largest employer in the area right up until the 1980s. Today, one of the country's largest fish filleting plants is located in Stamsund, along with various other fish processing industries. Stamsund is also the home port of one of the largest trawler fleets in Lofoten.

At **Helleskjæret** near the Hurtigrute quay is Skjærbrygga, the focal point of Stamsund. The first part was built in 1845 and it has been extended in several phases over many years. It has been home to a number of activities such as a steamship company office and as a landing stage and processing factory for salted and dried fish. There were once many 'fiskehjeller' (wooden fish drying racks) at Helleskjæret (hence the name). Skjærbrygga was restored and refurbished in 2000/2001. The building now houses various activities, such as a restaurant, bar and conference facilities. An attempt has been made to construct the new buildings in harmony with the traditional, original style. However, this has not been a complete success.

Stamsund has a good deal of innovative cultural activity and has amongst other things several permanent theatres and a puppet theatre workshop, galleries and Lofoten Art College. Stamsund arranges an annual theatre and arts festival.

∞

Borg, a former chieftain's seat is situated on the northwest side of Vestvågøya. Some years ago, a few artefacts and wooden objects were found in a mound at Borg. In 1983, archaeological excavations began, and these uncovered what proved to be the largest building dating from the Viking period ever found in Norway and in fact in Europe. The scope and nature of the items found indicated that there was once a rich and influential family that lived at Borg, that there had been considerable activity at the site. Articles found at the site showed that the people here travelled long distances. There are several sites found in the area, indicating that there had been settlements here before and after the time of the great Viking house. This was confirmed by finds originating from a circular courtyard, burial mounds and evidence of the traditional longhouses.

The Viking Museum at Borg is one of Lofoten's most popular attractions. The museum is a replica of the Viking House that was on the same site in the Viking Era (p 83, p 123) with living rooms and a banqueting hall, reconstructed just as the archaeologists believe it was at that

time. The original house, from the Iron Age, erected in the 6th century was 67 m long. The house was rebuilt and extended and at the beginning of the Viking period, it had become 83 m long. The house was approx. 9 m tall.

In the barn, there is an exhibition of relics from the Vikings who lived at Borg and the rest of Vestvågøy. The original cowshed, which was 32 m long, could house as many as 50 cows and there were stables for their horses. The Chieftain's slaves would live in this building.

The reconstructed forge is in working use today and shows us how the Viking blacksmiths produced iron using charcoal fires.

In the bay below the Chieftain's house are three boathouse sites from the Viking period and the Middle Ages. The largest of these is 26 m long. The Viking ship, 'Lofotr', is a copy of the 23 m long Gokstadskipet from the 9th century found in the Oslofjord area. The boathouses at Borg have yet to be excavated, but a 30 m long boathouse has been temporarily erected. This is a copy of a boathouse excavated in the south of Norway.

In the summer of 2006, during the construction of the Viking house, 2 000-year-old cooking pits and house foundations on the slopes up to the Chieftain's house were uncovered. This indicates that Borg was a 'holy' place already in the early Norse period. There are plans to build a large open-air theatre, which will be ready in 2008, however the construction has been put on hold until Tromsø Museum has completed their excavations. The planned start-up date was in 2007.

The ship continues to Svolvær   **+ 0 hrs 00 min**

LARGER MAP P**398**

We are now heading north-east and we cross **Henningsværstraumen** on our port side. Henningsværstraumen continues as two powerful tidal currents between Vestfjorden, where we are now, and the Norwegian Sea on the west side of Lofotveggen. These are **Sundklakkstraumen** between Gimsøya and Vestvågøya, that at its most narrow stretch is only 150 m wide, and the 18 km long and 1-5 km wide **Gimsøystraumen** between Gimsøya and Austvågøya. The marshy island of Gimsøya (46.4 km²) has one of the oldest settlements found in Lofoten, with many relics from the Stone Age and Viking period (p 83). Across Sundklakkstraumen, there is a 276 m long bridge with a clearance of 12 m. Gimsøystraumen Bridge spans Gimsøystraumen, 840 m long, with 9 spans and a clearance of 30 m.

Approx. 68°58'N   14°02'E

We cross the municipal boundary between Vestvågøy and Vågan municipalities approximately in the centre of Henningsværstraumen

Vågan municipality

Municipal coat of arms, significance: Symbolises fishing.
Meaning of name: Norse name of estate, Vågar. 'våg ' – bay.
Municipal seat: Svolvær (pop. 4 177).
Position: 68°13'N 14°34'E.
Area: 477 km2. **Population:** 8 992.
Pop. density: 18.6 /km2.
Distribution: Farming 2 %, forestry 4 %, fresh water 4 %, other 90 %.
Trade and industry: Trawl and net fishing, some in foreign waters. Fishing for herring, sprats, coalfish and minke whales. Shellfish and salmon farming. Fish food- and food processing. Traditional drying and salting of fish. Fillet factories. Cold storage. Canned products. Cod and Herring oil extraction plants. Boatyards with slipways. Mechanical workshops. Some farming combined with production of dairy products. Sheep and poultry farming. Production of electricity
Places to return to: Vågan church. Storvågan old trading post. Lofoten Museum. Skrova.
Vågan municipality's home page: www.vagan.kommune.no

The island, **Austvågøya** (527 km²) on our port side is the largest island in Lofoten, divided between Vågan in the southwest and Hadsel (p 289) in the northeast. The coast is intersected by narrow fjords, steep mountains and compact valleys. Trolltindene, the mountains surrounding the famous Trollfjorden, tower on the island's northern side. People here live mainly along the narrow shorelines and in small inlets or bays.

68°07'N 14°11'E	+ 0 hrs 40 min ①

We are passing the island of **Rødholmen** just outside of the fishing village of Henningsvær, as we head towards Svolvær.

On our port side, we see the fishing village of **Henningsvær** (pop. 428). Henningsvær is located on two small islands on the southern point of Austvågøya, and the sound between them provides a good, sheltered harbour. The village, which is difficult to see from our ship, is often called "The Venice of the North". At the end of the 19th century, Henningsvær became the largest fishing village in Lofoten and an expanding trade and industrial centre. Even today, several thousand fishermen, fish merchants and other workers come here during the Lofoten fishing season. Henningsvær has an important fish processing industry and tourism is increasing.

Henningsvær has a bridge connection over to Austvågøya.

The sheer-sided mountain **Vågakallen** (942 m above sea level) stands behind and northeast of Henningsvær. It

was climbed for the first time in 1885. It is a well-known landmark, and "skårunger"- men and boys on their first time out to Lofoten - had to show respect to the mountain by removing their caps. Vågakallen is a central element in many of the legends of Lofoten and Northern Norway. One of the best-known legends is the tale of the seven sisters (p 315). One story is that "Vågekallen" was the former king in Lofoten who turned into stone when he was exposed to the rays of the sun.

68°11'N 14°19'48"E	+ 1 hr 05 min

The ship is sailing between the small island group known as **Bindingsøyane** on our starboard side and **Austvågøya** on our port side. First we pass the narrow, shallow bay, **Hopen**, thereafter the headland, **Ørsnes** and **Ørsvågen** bay with the mountain **Breidtinden** (731 m above sea level) behind.

Moholmen lighthouse is on our starboard side, located on **Moholmen** just outside of Bindingsøyane. The lighthouse was built in 1914 and the light has a range of 14.5 nautical miles. It was automated and de-manned in 1974 and is today a tourist attraction.

Ahead and to starboard, we can see the islands, Skrova, Litlmolla and Stormolla in front of the mountains on Hinnøya.

68°11'N 14°24'41"E	+ 1 hr 08 min ②

On our port side we pass the village of **Kabelvåg** (pop. 1 614) in the municipality of Vågan. Kabelvåg is the oldest and formerly largest village, now second largest after Svolvær. Kabelvåg has an important cultural history and interesting ancient timber buildings. These buildings have been badly affected by several fires, most recently in 1991 and 1992. Kabelvåg is today an educational and cultural centre with an arts and film academy and Lofoten's Regional Museum that exhibits fishing activities in Lofoten in a historical perspective. Lofoten Aquarium is also located in Kabelvåg. The National Coastal Administration Centre is based here, also some mechanical industry. Tourism is increasing and becoming an important source of income.

The remains of the old Vågan centre are situated near the Lofot Museum, approx. 1 km west of Kabelvåg. From 1985 until 2001, archaeological excavations uncovered evidence of extensive trade and commerce with the south of Norway and foreign countries. This also documented in sources from the Middle Ages.

Rock carvings believed to be 8-9000 years old have been found in the Kabelvåg/Vågan area. Several Stone Age sites have been discovered here, which, like many other places in Lofoten date from the times when hunting and fishing were the main activities. From the Iron Age and onwards people changed from a nomadic lifestyle to a more settled form of existence, in which farming supplemented hunting and fishing. Only a few such places are found here in contrast to the more agricultural areas elsewhere in Lofoten. The reason for Vågan's expansion, in spite of the poor farming conditions and sparse population was its proximity to the important fishing grounds at **Høla** between Vågan, Svolvær and the islands, Skrova and Litlmolla outside of Vågan. The rich fishing at Høla and in Vestfjorden is mainly due to the yearly migration of spawning spring cod from the Barents Sea. The men had to row or sail in open boats out to the fishing grounds; therefore, it was necessary to live close by.

The town of **Vågan** (våg=bay) was the only real town in Northern Norway in the Middle Ages and was the county's commercial, cultural and religious centre in the period from the 12th to the 15th century. Merchants from Bergen and Northern Norway met here in Vågan and exchanged their goods and produce. The town became a hub for merchants sending their goods to Bergen - mainly dried cod in exchange for imported goods from foreign countries.

Vågan was badly affected by the plague, the Black Death. The disease was brought to Bergen by rats on board English ships in 1349 and it quickly spread throughout the whole country (p 10). On Vestvågøya about 80 % of the population died. After the bailiff from Lofoten and Vesterålen visited the town in 1591, he described Vågan as "a pathetic fishing village with only 10-12 poor men living there". Other documents tell us that Vågan continued to be an important fishing village all the way up to the end of the 19th century.

A new centre emerged in 17th century at **Kabelvåg**, approx. 1 km east of Vågan. At the end of the 19th century, Kabelvåg was known as "Lofoten's capital". It had "town-like" buildings and was an active commercial centre, that already in 1895, published three newspapers at the same time. Vågan became once again an important market town although there was a marked reduction in the fish trade - and a definite increase in the social life. There was also a market in Kabelvåg between 1882 and 1939.

As the coastal shipping fleet gradually became more motorised, the facilities at Kabelvåg proved to be inadequate. Svolvær, which had ideal harbour facilities for larger vessels, soon took over as the main harbour and thus became the centre of further expansion in the area. When the Hurtigruten started in 1893, Svolvær also became one of its ports of call in Lofoten.

The first church in Vågan was built by King Øystein (I) Magnusson (1088–1123) (p 9). The King is recognised as being Vågan's founding father.

> The Legend about "The First Church Building in Vaagan":
>
> "When King Øystein Magnusson decreed that a church should be built in Vaagan county he sent priests and craftsmen up to the north in the summer after his brother, Sigurd Jorsalfar had set out on his first pilgrimage. They were told to select the best site for a church; however, it had to be as close as possible to the Place of Assembly ('Ting') at Kjefsøya. After the men had surveyed the area, they agreed that Brettesnesnakken (p 297) was the best site for the church. They laid the foundations and the carpenters laid the timber joists. The next morning the joists were gone and the foundations had been demolished. Nobody understood who or what had caused this. They took a boat and started to look around for clues. As they approached the place where Kabelvåg is situated today they found the joists laid on another newly built foundation. The priest, who was among the search party, said that surely this was just as good a place as Brettesnesnakken. The construction began again, and the carpenters believed that they must have had 'invisible helpers' since the building advanced so fast. This is the reason why King Øystein's church was built here and not at Brettesnakken."

The current Vågan church, or Lofoten Cathedral as it is often called, was built in 1898. It seats 1 200 and is the largest timber church north of Trondheim. This ochre-coloured church replaced the old timber cruciform church from 1798, which had become too small.

Kabelvåg has been a church parish for about 900 years. Five or six churches have been located in the area where the current church stands. The timber used to build the church came from Trondheim, some prefabricated parts came from a factory in Trøndelag, and these were assembled in Kabelvåg. Lofotkatedralen is a cruciform church with a long main nave with short, wide cross-arms situated close to the chancel. In the west, there is a tower with a spire that has an entrance, with special decorative shapes, at the base of the tower. The neo-gothic church is situated on a hill close to the sea.

An unconfirmed story relates to the size of Vågan church. It is said that the church was a gift from a man from Vågan that had emigrated to America and had prospered over there and wanted to give his birthplace a worthy

Yet another mystery concerns the large cross engraved on the stone. One interpretation is the stone was used as an altar during the first sermon during the consecration of the first church built here in the 12th century.

✐

68°12'N 14°32'E + 1 hr 18 min ③

The island, **Skrova** (2.5 km², 281 m above sea level) is on our starboard side as is the village of **Skrova** (pop. 220). The island is said to have one of the last, genuine fishing villages in Lofoten. In addition to the main island, there are several smaller islands, most of these are connected by causeways or bridges. For many years, Skrova was the centre of Lofoten's fishing and whaling activities and for fishing for the winter cod in the spawning grounds between the island, Høla and Kabelvåg/Svolvær. In those times, there could be several thousand men on Skrova. Today, industrial activity is mostly fish food processing and salmon and trout farming.

✐

Skrova lighthouse is located on Saltværholmen on the island's southern point. A smaller lighthouse previously stood on the same site. Skrova lighthouse is a 24.5 m cast iron tower built in 1922. The light is located 41 m above sea level and has a reach of 18 nautical miles. A foghorn was installed in 1922, and an electrically powered siren in 1959. The station was listed in 1999, thereafter automated and de-manned in 2005. The lighthouse has an engine house, living quarters, several outhouses and oil storage tanks. There are remains of German fortifications. Skrova lighthouse was also used as a meteorological station due to its central position in relation to both the fishing grounds in the inner parts of Vestfjorden and the shipping activities in Ofotfjorden and the many harbours in the area.

gift of a new church. The man sent over money to build the church along with a set of building plans. However, as the man now lived in the USA, the dimensions on the plans were in feet, but the church was built in metres!

To the south of the church, there is a large stone, Trollsteinen. There are several legends connected to this stone. One is the story of a Troll that lived on one of the mountains close to Vågan. He was so angry that the people had built a church that he threw a huge stone at the church. However, he missed and the stone landed on the other side of the bay. We can still see the three marks made by his fingers on the stone.

Another legend is that the church verger found a "Black Book" and called upon the Devil. The verger asked him to dig a hole where he wanted to put down a rope. But the Devil dug straight for the church and got nearer and nearer. The verger then called for the priest so he could cast out the Devil. The Devil resisted and held on to the 'Troll-stone' but he lost his grip and fell back to where he came from. He left some easily visible marks on the stone.

The island, **Litlmolla** (9.7 km², 543 m above sea level) lies north of Skrova. The island was once inhabited, however the last residents left some years ago. Near the island, Litlmolla we set course for Svolvær on our port side.

✐

North of the island, Litlmolla is the island, **Store Molla** (p 296).

The ship docks at the quayside in Svolvær

The municipal seat of **Svolvær** is also sometimes called "Lofoten's capital" and is today the largest fishing community and commercial centre in Lofoten. Svolvær was an important trading post in the period 1918-64 and was granted a town charter in 1996. The original houses were situated on a flat headland but these have since spread towards Austvågøya and to islands next to the mainland. There are a number of bridges connecting the islands to the centre.

∞

The bronze sculpture was made by the Norwegian sculptor, Per Ung in 1999. The sculpture is 4.5 m high and symbolises a fisherman's wife, looking out over Vestfjorden, waiting for her husband to return.

∞

On our port side, we can now see a naked rock with a large orange triangular structure. In the rock face behind Svolvær, it is possible to spot a similar orange triangular marker. This is a "fishing area guide", a so-called Mé, designed to assist the fishing fleet. When viewed from the sea, and when they overlap each other they mark the dividing line where different types fishing gear can and cannot be used. On one side, you can fish with nets and on the other side with lines and hooks. These "dividers" can be seen all over Lofotveggen.

The many racks ('hjeller') that you can see around the area are used for drying fish.

∞

Svolvær church is centrally located in the town and was consecrated in 1934. It is a long narrow church in whitewashed concrete with a tower above the chancel and can seat 400.

∞

Svolvær is the arts and cultural centre of Lofoten and is often bustling day and night. The town is known for its fishing and commercial activities. It is one of Northern Norway's largest mechanical and maintenance service centres for the fishing fleet.

∞

Svolvær is located at the foot of **Fløyfjellet,** on our starboard side. In the mountainside, approx. 569 m above sea level, we can see the well-known and remarkable rock formation, Svolværgeita ("The Svolvær Goat"). It is approx. 40 metres high and approx. 1.5 m between the "horns". It can be seen silhouetted against the sky. In the summer, many people climb up the mountain in order to jump from one 'horn' to the other. The view from "Svolværgeita" was voted 'Norway's finest' in 2007.

There are several legends surrounding Svolværgeita ("The Svolvær Goat"). One of the most well known is also associated with Trollfjorden (p 295).

A legend tells of Svolværjura, who lived in Svolværfjellet. She got finely dressed in a pretty frock and hat with ribbons when she heard the Hamarøykallen (p 129) was out to find a wife. But when he arrived, she played a little game of hard-to-get and would not give Hamarøykallen a straight answer. This made Hamarøygubben angry. He grabbed a large stone and threw it at her. He missed, but the stone split into two pieces; one is called Tortelsteinen and the other fell into Svolværvika and was called Gullet. Then the sun rose and Hamarøykallen was turned to stone - into Hamarøystauren, and Svolværjura was changed into Svolværgeita. If you look you can see the ribbons from her hat as the 'goat's' two horns.

∞

In the industrial area in Svolvær harbour and approx. 100 m from land is the wreck of the German steamship, "Hamburg", 5 470 gross tons, which in its time was the most modern factory ship in the world. The ship was hit during an Allied attack on Lofoten in March 1941. The ship was anchored in Svolvær harbour when a group of Allied soldiers attacked the ship with heavy artillery. The German crew abandoned the damaged ship apart from two soldiers who remained behind to scuttle the vessel; shortly after it sank. The wreck lies at a depth of 6–25 m.

∞

31st August 2007 the whaling vessel «Willassen Senior» was scuttled at the quayside in Svolvær. The following day, an American activist group accepted responsibility for the sabotage. No one was on board at the time of the attack and the activists had gone unnoticed on board the boat and removed a pipe from the cooling system, so that seawater entered the engine room. «Willassen Senior» was raised after 12 days.

Svolvær Airport, Helle, is on our port side. It is a civil short take off and landing runway and opened in 1972.

Svolværraidet, Lofotraidet or Operation Claymore, are different names given the British military action that was directed towards parts of Lofoten in the beginning of March 1941. Their mission was to destroy the processing plants and the stores of fish and fish oils. Herring oil could be used to extract glycerine for use in the manufacture of explosives.

In the early morning of 4th March 1941, five British destroyers and two troop ships with approx. 550 British and 52 Norwegian commandos on board sailed into Vestfjorden. The forces were landed in Henningsvær, Brettesnes, Stamsund and Svolvær. The oil tanks were set alight and approx. 4.5 million litres of fish oil was destroyed, along with the fish oil factories and the local power generating plant. Eighteen fisheries were razed and 6 ships were sunk. On board one of the armed trawlers that were sunk in Vestfjorden, a British officer found papers, encoding devices and an Enigma code machine. This find helped the British scientists that were working on breaking the German codes, which enabled them to intercept most of the German maritime communications.

During the raid, 213 German soldiers were taken prisoners. 314 inhabitants of Lofoten followed the ships back to England. Two days later, the German commanders in Norway arrived in Lofoten. Severe reprisals were to be carried out against the local people and Svolvær was ordered to be destroyed. However, some time later the order was revoked and only seven houses were destroyed, however 64 local people were imprisoned. After this event, the Gestapo headquarters for Lofoten and Vesterålen was relocated to Svolvær and many German soldiers were stationed here.

The Germans believed that an invasion was imminent and for this reason, they built a series of bunkers, fortifications and machine gun positions. This work continued right up until the end of the war. Svolvær was the town in Norway that had the greatest concentration of bunkers, gun positions and tunnels within its 2 km² area. In December 1941, British and Norwegian forces raided Reine and Moskenes (Operation "Anklet"). This time 266 Norwegians returned to England with the raiding party.

The ship continues to Stokmarknes

After departing Svolvær, the ship sails towards the narrow channel in Raftsundet. This will be described on Day 9 (p 292).

Nordland county

Coat of arms: Represents a Nordland boat.
Origins of name: In the 16th century 'Nordlandene' and 'nordlandske len' were the terms used for the areas that now are Nordland and Troms counties.   **Area:** 38 463 km².
Population: 236 436.   **County seat:** Bodø.
We pass the following municipalities on our way northwards (in order): Bindal, Sømna, Brønnøy, Vega, Vevelstad, Alstahaug, Herøy, Dønna, Leirfjord, Nesna, Lurøy, Rødøy, Meløy, Gildeskål, Bodø, Vestvågøy, Vågan, Hadsel, Sortland and Andøy.

Topography: Most of the county is made up of mountain ranges that rise quite steeply up from the shoreline. This leads to a narrow band of lowland area along the coast. Lofoten and Vesterålen are well known for their rugged mountains. The highest peaks are along the Swedish border in the east. The mainland is carved up by fjords, some in the main direction of the coast, others cut across.

Nordland is the second largest county in Norway. 13.6 % of the area is between 0-300 m above sea level, 7.4 % is over 900 m. The county has the second largest glacier areas in the country. There are approx. 18 400 islands in Nordland, these represent 28.4 % of the country's total island areas. The coastline on the mainland is 5 087 km long and 17 394 km long on the islands.

Climate: Most low-pressure systems come from the west and head in an easterly direction; wind from the southwest is most prevalent. Cold winds from the southeast and south in the winter, especially at the mouths of fjords. In the summer, the wind usually blows from the north or north west. The coldest winter month is February, when the mean temperature is 0 °C along the coast and -5 to -10 °C in inland areas. The mean temperature in July varies between 11 °C in the coastal regions, up to 14-15 °C inland. The annual precipitation varies from 600-700 mm on the outlying islands to as much as 2 000 mm in coastal mountain areas. On the coast, the greatest amount of precipitation falls in the autumn.

Settlement: Mostly associated with agriculture and fishing along the coast and on the islands. In the inland areas, there are some settlements in a few of the valleys. The annual reduction in the population is around 0.2 % due to the decline in primary industries. There is also considerable population relocation within the county, from the islands, that have fishing and agriculture as their primary industries, to the central areas.

COMMERCE:

Agriculture and forestry: The combination of fishing/farming has long traditions and is of great importance in some municipalities; however, the number of people depending on this type of livelihood has been greatly reduced. Many small, labour intensive and remote farms have been abandoned and the average size of the remaining farms has increased and is now over the national average. Some of the finest agricultural areas are in the south of the county; however, the low summer temperatures limit the agricultural production, to mainly hay and grazing land. Some potato farming, animal husbandry with cattle, sheep and goats.

49 % of the productive forests are coniferous and 51 % deciduous, mainly birch. Forestry is concentrated around the forest villages in the inland areas. Nordland has a limited timber processing industry, however, there are some sawmills and woodworking factories.

Fishing: The number of those involved in fishing as a primary occupation has been greatly reduced and fishing is based on individual fishing boats. Nordland county has the greatest number of fishermen in the country, mainly associated with fishing in Lofoten and Vesterålen. The fishing fleet is largely comprised of smaller boats. Lofotfisket, the seasonal fishing for Arctic cod in February and March is the most important; however, coastal fishing for herring and coalfish (saithe) is also significant. The purse seiners and fresh fish trawlers fish off the coast of Finnmark and in the Barents Sea. The fish is processed into 'tørrfisk' (dried fish, the main ingredient of 'bacalao'), frozen fish, herring oil and herring meal. The county is the second largest producer of farmed fish in the country.

Industry and mining: The foodstuffs industries, especially those associated with fish processing have large seasonal variations. The metal industry is largely based on aluminium smelting that requires large amounts of electricity. Chemical industry in Glomfjord. Smaller shipyards and mechanical workshops. Varied small-scale mining activities. Narvik is an important storage and export port for Swedish iron ore. Small companies in a wide range of industries. A number of decentralised state institutions provide employment. Some electricity production.

Tourism: Tourism is of great importance in the county. Visitors are attracted by the natural surroundings with wild mountains, beautiful coastline and impressive fjords. Lofoten and Vesterålen have many small fishing communities with cabins for hire, and several large bird sanctuaries. The maelstrøm at Saltstraumen just outside Bodø, Svartisen glacier, four national parks and the Arctic Circle are well-known and attractive destinations for tourists.

Communications: Rugged topography and settlements spread over a wide area make communications difficult. The Hurtigrute is the most important mode of transport along the coast, supplemented by fast boats and car ferries. The main highway, the E6, runs from south to north in the inland areas of the county. In the southern part of Nordland, the coastal road (Route 17) runs northwards to Bodø. Lofast, a continuous road connection, without ferries, to Lofoten was opened in 2007. Nordlandsbanen, the county section of the Norwegian national railway, has its end station in Bodø. Ofotbanen from Narvik is connected with the Swedish national rail network. Both Bodø and Evenes have major airports and there are several short take-off and landing airports in the county.

Source: Store Norske Leksikon

© ORCA LOFOTEN AS JOHNNY STORVIK

Polar Circles – Midnight Sun – the 'Dark Period'

The **Polar Circles** are two circles, parallel to the equator at a distance of 23°27'22" from the Poles. The Arctic Circle therefore is at latitude 66°33'38"N. It passes through Norway, Sweden, Finland, Russia, Alaska, Canada and Greenland. The Antarctic Circle is likewise at latitude 66°33'38"S and passes through the Balleny Islands, the Antarctic Peninsula and the Weddell Sea. The Polar Circles are the 'dividing lines' between Earth's temperate and cold zones – the Arctic in the northern hemisphere and the Antarctic in the southern hemisphere.

The Polar Circles also mark the limit of where the midnight sun can be seen in the summer and where the dark period begins in the winter.

Midnight Sun means that the sun is above the horizon for 24 hours. The total number of days of midnight sun increases as we travel northwards from the Arctic Circle towards the North Pole. At the Arctic Circle, there is only one 24-hour period with sunshine whilst the pole itself has daylight for six months, from spring to autumn equinox. The same applies to the southern hemisphere, but in reverse order.

The Dark Period means that the sun remains below the horizon all day. The total number of dark days increases as we move northwards from the Arctic Circle towards the North Pole. At the Arctic Circle, there is only one 24-hour period of darkness. The North Pole has a continuous night for six months, from autumn to spring equinox. The same takes place at the southern hemisphere, but in reverse order.

Sea Eagles (White-Tailed Eagles)

Sea Eagles (Haliaeetus albicilla) belong to the falcon family of birds and are Northern Europe's largest bird of prey. The female is normally larger than the male with a wingspan of up to 2.65 m, a body length of 0.8 to 1.0 m. The heaviest measured weight is 6.85 kg. The chick's feathers are dark brown with white spots, with a dark brown tail and a black beak. They are mature after 4–5 years and by then are mostly dark brown all over with white tail feathers and a yellow beak. They can live to the age of 50 years, but this is rare.

Sea Eagles are found from Greenland and Iceland in the north to Iraq in the south and from the Atlantic in the west, across Central and Northern Asia to the Pacific Ocean in the east. Their numbers were reduced after the Second World War but in Norway, Sea Eagles have been totally protected since 1968 and since then the numbers have increased. Approx. 40 % of the Norwegian birds, some 1 900-2 200 pairs (in 2000) nest in Nordland county.

Sea Eagles build their nests in trees or on rocky ledges and can use the same nest several times. The nest is usually made from twigs and branches and is lined with grass, green plants and kelp. One to three eggs are laid in the period from the end of March to May. It is mainly the female that sits on the eggs. The brooding period is approx. 38 days. The chicks leave the nest after 10–11 weeks. They are mainly fed on fish, sea birds and mammals.

It is said that a Sea Eagle cannot lift prey that is heavier than itself. However the story of the Sea Eagle and the 'kidnapping' on the island of Leka in 1932 is well known and this tells us differently (p 329).

Bodø is regarded as the "Sea Eagle Town" of Norway.

Maelstrom

The definition of a maelstrom is a large whirlpool formed by tidal currents. The most famous maelstrom, Moskenesstraumen, is between Moskenesøy (p 150) and Høgholmene in Lofoten. The word also applies to tidal currents that are intensified in narrow fjords and river estuaries, such as Saltstraumen (p 137).

Through the ages maelstroms have been linked to many myths and legends.

Northern Lights (Aurora Borealis)

The Northern Lights is the name given to a phenomenon that can often be seen in the northern regions. It is also known as "the Heavenly Ballerina". Legends and myths about the Northern Lights are many and varied - from the "souls of dead virgins", "blood light from eternal warriors", "reflections of herring shoals in the sea" and "glowing and fire-spouting mountains in Greenland". In fact, the Northern Lights have existed since the Earth formed an atmosphere. In the southern hemisphere we have the counterpart to the Northern Lights," Aurora Australis".

The Austrian polar researcher, C. Weyprecht (1815-1881) described the Northern Lights rather poetically: "The Northern Lights is a festival of fireworks – unbelievable even for the boldest fantasy. No colours and paint brush could paint this and no words can describe it in its splendour".

Professor in Space Physics at the University of Tromsø, Asgeir Bakke, describes the Northern Lights thus: "The North-

© EILIV LEREN

ern Lights are caused by electrical particles entering the atmosphere, mainly from the sun. The particles are electrically charged and since the earth is enclosed by a magnetic field, the particles are forced to move in a certain way. They are drawn to polar areas where the magnetism is strongest. When the particles approach the Earth, approx. 1 000 km out in space, they start to collide with molecules and atoms (oxygen and nitrogen) in the atmosphere. The nearer the particles come, the more collisions take place until the particles progression is stopped at approx. 100 km above the Earth. Most of the visible Northern Lights are produced at around 105 km above the Earth's surface. The collisions create instability in the atoms and molecules in the atmosphere and their electrons are displaced. They become energized and they seek to get back to their original position and in doing

so they emit light in the form of energy when they "jump" back into place again. It is these billions of light flashes that we see as the Northern Lights.

The light emitted can vary in colour but green light is the most common. Sometimes it can be seen as red or lilac. The colour variations stem from the various atoms and molecules with which the charged particles collide. The oxygen molecule produces the green colour, whilst the violet colour is due to nitrogen. The colour of the Northern Lights can tell us how much of the various gases are in the atmosphere. The "dancing" phenomena stems from the electrical fields around the Earth, which influence the motion of the electrically charged particles. These fields are relatively unstable and turbulent and therefore determine how we see the Northern Lights in the skies.

Norse Gods

Norway was Christianised by King Olav Tryggvason in A.D. 1030. Before then, the Norse Gods dominated. The Icelandic historian, Snorre Sturlason, describes them in his work, Prose Edda, written in the 14th century.

Odin, also called **All Father**, was the head of all gods and the oldest. He would live forever, rule over his kingdom and advise in all matters, important or minor. He created heaven, earth, air, and all things within it. He created man and gave him a soul that would live forever. Everyone that followed this faith should live and remain with him, but wicked people would be sent to Hell. Odin was the father of all the gods. He was also called Valfar (God of Battles) because all those killed on the battlefield (valen), became his dearest sons and allowed to live in **Valhall.** Odin had a spear, **Gunge,** that always hit its target.

Frigg was Odin's wife. Their descendants were the people known as 'Æsir'. They lived in the old **Åsgard**, and were all of godly lineage.

Thor, the God of thunder and war, was son of Odin and Frigg, and was married to **Siv**. Siv was very beautiful with hair of gold. Thor was the strongest of all gods and men. His kingdom was called **Trudvang,**

and his hall was called **Bilskirne**. Thor had two rams to pull his chariot.

Thor's hammer, **Mjolne** was feared, because with Mjolne, he could strike anything, however large, and it would never fail him. When he threw it, it would never miss and no matter how far it flew, it would always come back to his hand. Thor also had a belt that when worn would double his godly powers.

Balder was the son of Odin and Frigg. He was married to **Nanna.** Balder was so handsome and fair that he positively shone. He was wise and eloquent, and was also a good man. He lived at Breidablikk, in the heavens, a place without impurity.

Njord was married to **Skade.** Njord ruled over the weather and winds, oceans and fire. Sailors and fishermen prayed to Njord, to ask for protection and to ensure a good catch. His wife, Skade, came from the mountains, where she wanted to remain. They parted as neither Njord nor Skade could compromise on where they should live.

Frøy was the son of Njord. He ruled over rain and sunshine and thus the riches from the earth and he could be called upon to provide good crops and to maintain peace. He also ruled over man's riches. The ship, **Skibladne** was given to Frøy as gift. The ship was so big it could accommodate all Æsir carrying weapons and armour. As soon as the sails were set, the ship sailed wherever the sailors wanted to go. If the ship was not at sea, Frøy could roll it up like a cloth and carry it in his purse.

Frøya, the Goddess of Love, was Njord's daughter. She was the most noble of all women, after Frigg. When she rode into war, half of the battlefield (valen) was hers, the other half belonged to Odin. Frøya was forgiving and good so prayers were often offered to her, especially in matters of love.

Brage was also a son of Odin and Frigg. He was best known for his wisdom, eloquence, and as a poet. His wife, **Idun** carried apples in her bag, which the gods had to eat when they grew old – they would then become young again.

Loke was regarded as one of the Æsir. He was handsome, but evil, cunning and could not be trusted. He always used his cunning to get the gods into trouble. Thereafter he would again use his cunning to get them out of their dilemma.

Loke had three children with **Angrboda**, a gyger, a giantess from Jotunheimen. These were **Fenrir**, the giant wolf, brought up at Åsgård, **Jormundgand**, the Midgard sea serpent, who was thrown into the ocean depths by Odin, after which the serpent surrounded the world, forever biting his own tail and **Hel**, mistress of the underworld, Nivlheim (the north side of the world, in which there was only frost and mist).

Source: From Snorres Edda.

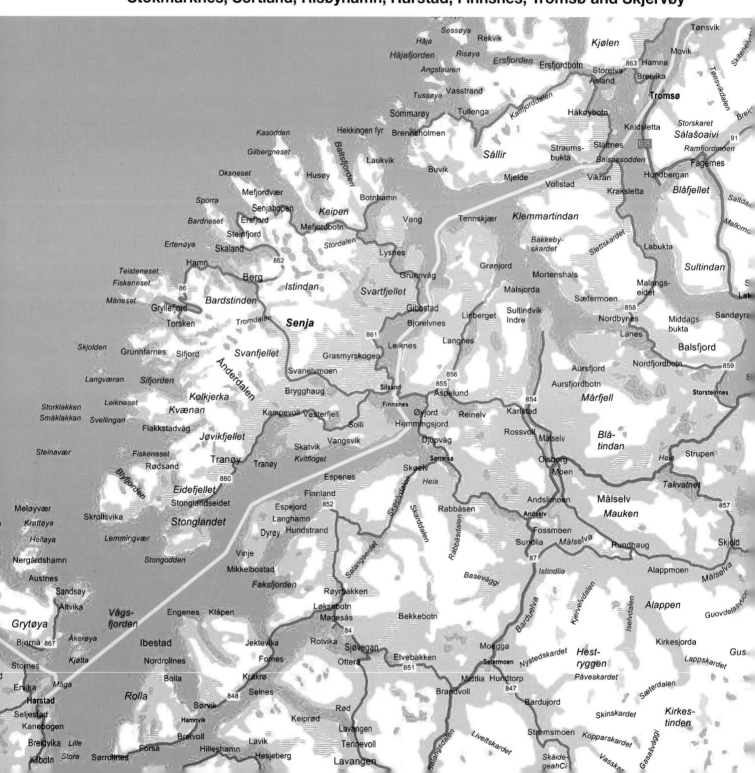

During the night we have passed Hadsel municipality and the port of **Stokmarknes** (68°34'16"N 14°54'44"E, 0045-0100) (p 291), Sortland municipality and the port of **Sortland** (68°42'N 15°25'E, 0215-0300) (p 286), Andøy municipality and the port of **Risøyhamn** (68°58'N 15°38'38"E, 0415-0430) (p 291), and we have also crossed the boundary between Nordland and Troms counties. We arrive at the port in Harstad municipality in Troms county at 0600.

Harstad municipality

Municipal coat of arms, significance: The proximity to the sea.
Meaning of name: Possibly Norse, Hardastadir from man's name, Hordr, gen; Hardar.
Municipal seat: Harstad (pop. 19 573).
Position: 68°47'50"N 16°33'E.
Area: 364 km². **Population:** 23 261.
Pop. density: 63.9/km².
Area distribution: Farming 6 %, forestry 21 %, fresh water 4 %, other 69 %.
Trade and industry: Main emphasis on services. Farming, dairy and meat production. Fish food processing industry. Mechanical industries and shipyards with one of the region's largest dry docks. Important base for the offshore industry in Northern Norway. The oil companies and the Petroleum Directorate chose Harstad because of its good harbour facilities.
Places to return to: Harstad town. Trondenes church. Trondarnes District Museum. 'Slottet'.
Activities to return to: Festival of Northern Norway, International Boat festival.
Harstad municipality's home page: www.harstad.kommune.no

Early in the morning we arrive in **Harstad** (p 271), located northeast on Hinnøya (2 198 km²), Norway's largest and most populated island (p 271).

The ship continues to Finnsnes   + 0 hrs 00 min

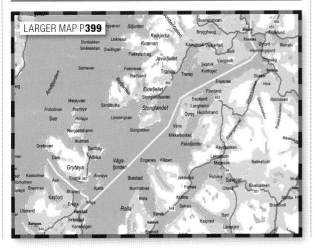

LARGER MAP P**399**

After leaving Harstad, we sail out of **Vågsfjorden,** heading northeast.

68°49'23"N 16°37'35"E   + 0 hrs 11 min

The tiny island of Måga, with a beacon, is on our port side, just outside the peninsula Trondenes with Trondenes church (p 274).

Ahead and on our port side lies the island of **Grytøya**.

On our port side we pass the 3 km wide **Topp-sundet**, located between the islands, Hinnøya with Harstad and Grytøya.

Grytøya (108 km²) is on our port side, with its steep mountainside towards the northeast. The island is divided between Harstad and Bjarkøy municipalities. It is steep and hilly, with the highest mountain, **Nona**, (1 012 m above sea level) located in the middle of the island. Southeast of Nona we see the mountains **Storfjellet** (809 m above sea level) and **Litlgalten** (782 m above sea level) and to their north, **Storgalten** (987 m above sea level). Farmland is mostly found on the south and east of the island where there are also some birch forests. The villages of **For**, **Lundenes** and **Bessebostad** are on the south side of Grytøya (p 275).

East of Grytøya, ahead and to our port side are the two small islands of Kjøtta (3 km²) and **Åkerøya**. Kjøtta is only a 10-minute ferry ride away from Harstad. The island is placed in the centre of the shipping channel and right in the middle of the former herring fishing area. It was an important herring trading post from 1877. In 1929, a herring oil extraction plant was built on Kjøtta. The island is now a popular site for summer cottages, but in 2006 there was only one permanent resident living there.

Behind Kjøtta we see Åkerøya.

The mountain range up ahead and to our port side is located on the island of Senja.

Approx. 68°53'N   16°52'E   ①

We pass the municipal boundary between Harstad and Bjarkøy municipalities on our port side

---

Bjarkøy municipality

Municipal coat of arms, significance: The Bjarkøy family coat of arms.
Meaning of name: Possibly after a Swedish town called Birka on Björkö in Mälaren, 'a market place'. Bjarkøy was also a centre for trade with the Finns.
Municipal seat: Nergård (pop. -).
Position: 69°00'N 16°32'E.
Area: 75 km². **Population:** 523.
Pop. density: 7.0 /km².
Area distribution: Farming 7 %, forestry 70 %, fresh water 7 %, other 21 %.
Trade and industry: Farming and fishing. Some farms are relatively large and combine animal husbandry, beef and mutton/lamb production. Fish farming.
Bjarkøy municipality's home page: www.bjarkoy.kommune.no

Bjarkøy has a ferry connection with Grytøya. In September 2002, 90 % of the people in the Bjarkøy municipality voted for an amalgamation with Harstad municipality as soon as a mainland connection was completed.

The four inhabited islands in Bjarkøy are: Grytøya, Sandsøya, Bjarkøya and Krøttøya/Meløyvær. Between Grytøya and Bjarkøy is the 7 km long Kvernsundet.

Sandsøya (10.8 km²) on our port side is the centre of an ancient church, assembly and trading place. In 1886, the authorities decided that the church dating from 1756 on Sandsøya's west side should be demolished and moved to Bjarkøya, as a Baptist congregation was established there. A new church was built on Sandsøya in 1888, on the same site where the old church had stood. The people on the island obtained the materials for the church by

donating some of their catch from the sea and crops from the land.

Burial mounds from the Stone Age have been found on the island.

As part of the modernisation of Norwegian coastal forts, four 127 mm cannon were installed at a newly built fort on this island in 1964. The cannon came from Denmark at a time when the Danes closed down most of their coastal fortifications.

Bjarkøya (14.6 km²), behind Sandsøya, has an impressive history. The island is well known as an important chieftain's seat in the north during the Viking period. Tore Hund ruled here around the year 1000. He founded the Bjarkøy family's huge estate, and the family was amongst the most influential in the north. In Olav the Holy's Saga (995-1030) (p 88), Tore Hund from Bjarkøya is given high praise. He had been appointed the King's representative in this region, but their relationship soured after the King ordered the execution of one of Hund's close relatives. In the battle at Stiklestad in 1030 (p 98), Tore Hund was one of the leaders of the 'peasant' army that fought against and eventually murdered the King. When the King was later sanctified, Tore Hund went on a pilgrimage and never returned, according to the Saga. A stone monument was raised on Bjarkøya, as a memorial to the chieftain, Tore Hund.

Many valuable discoveries from the Iron Age, the Viking period and up to the 19th century have been made here at Bjarkøya. There are indications that Bjarkøy was an important trading centre as far back as the Migration Period (p 83). A bronze kettle (known as the Bjarkøy kettle), dating back to approx. A.D. 400 was found in a marsh. Several other finds from A.D. 600–700 were also made.

The timber church at Bjarkøya originally came from Sandøya in 1765. It was moved to Nergårdshamn on Bjarkøya in 1886. Some of the inventory remains in the church, e.g. the 17th century font and the pulpit. Some years later, in 1888, Sandsøya built a new church where the old had stood and some of the original interior was returned.

Bjarkøy was also a centre for the trade in furs and leather, as the Sámi paid their taxes with furs and skins. The Norwegian chieftains in the north were active participants in this trade, also with traders from northern Finland and northwest Russia. At that time, skins were valuable and very popular in southern Europe.

Mining was carried out on the island from 1902 until 1910. In 1941 the Germans built a coastal fort on Bjarkøya. The bunkers and one of the cannons still remain.

Sundsvollen, on the north side of Bjarkøya, is a kittiwake nesting colony with over 10 000 birds. They arrive in the area in mid February and depart around the middle of August (p 218).

Krøttøya and **Meløyvær** are the northernmost inhabited islands in Bjarkøy. At one time, a military radar station was in operation here but this has now closed down. On Meløyvær iron ore mining began in 1904 and continued up to 1930. In 2005, only 14 persons were living permanently on the island.

The first of several new, large coastal fortifications to be built in the 1980s was constructed at Meløyvær, as a replacement for outdated fortifications around Vågsfjorden. The modern Meløy fort was completed in 1989. The end of the Cold War and the advent of new precision-controlled weapons that meant that stationary forts became more vulnerable to attack led to the closure of the fort in 2002.

Ahead we can see **Stangnesfjellet** (301 m above sea level) on the low peninsula called Stonglandet in Tranøy municipality. Behind we see Eidefjellet (883 m above sea level) and farther west, Senjehesten (764 m above sea level).

Approx. 68°54'N   16°53'E

We cross the municipal boundary between Harstad and Ibestad municipalities on our starboard side

Ibestad municipality

Municipal coat of arms, significance: Reflects church traditions and archaeological finds from the Middle Ages.
Meaning of name: Named after a farm, Nordic - Ivarstadir.
Municipal seat: Hamnvik (pop. 462).
Position: 68°47'N 17°10'E.
Area: 242 km². **Population:** 1 574.
Pop. density: 6.5 /km².
Area distribution: Farming 5 %, forestry 22 %, fresh water 2 %, other 71 %.
Trade and industry: Ocean-going fishing fleet. Farming as a secondary source of income (sheep and cattle). Public services. Canning factory (shrimps). Fish farming. Ship yards and mechanical industries. Power stations.
Places to return to: Hamnvik Handelssted, Ibestad church and rectory.
Ibestad municipality's home page: www.ibestad.kommune.no

On our starboard side is the island of **Rolla** (106.4 km²) in **Ibestad** municipality. The island has an interesting and varied flora with a number of plants that are not normally found so far north. Here we find two of the largest lime-birch forests in Scandinavia. From botanist's point of view, the island is very interesting – the island has, in fact, 17 different species of orchids.

We see the mountain peaks of **Lasselitind** (896 m above sea level) and **Rolla** (926 m above sea level) in the south and in the centre, the jagged **Stortind/Drangen** (1 022 m above sea level). The many lakes on the island, approx. 70 in total, make Rolla Norway's most 'water-abundant' island in relationship to its size.

The village of **Nordrollnes** is on the island's north side. Most of the population lives on Rolla's east side, near the fjord **Bygda** (14 km long) which separates the two islands, Rolla and Andørja. The population has steadily declined over the last 60 years and a large number have moved to the village of **Hamnvik** on Rolla's south side. Hamnvik Handelssted, founded in 1794, is one of Norway's best-preserved trading centres that has kept its special characteristics, including dwellings, telegraph station, storehouses, bakery, etc. In total, there are 14 buildings. At one time, the place had a sheriff, magistrate and a parson.

Ibestad church, a Neo-Gothic stone church from 1881, is located north of Hamnvik. It is built on the same site as the old church dating from the 12th century. Ibestad rectory, now a protected building, was built in 1758.

Our voyage continues out into Vågsfjorden.

68°55'N   16°58'E   + 0 hrs 51 min ②

Between the two islands of Rolla (which we have already passed) and Andørja is the fjord known as **Bygda** (14 km long), which separates the two islands.

On our starboard side, we can see the island of **Andørja** (135 km²) which is Northern Europe's most mountainous island, relative to its size. There are a total of 14 peaks over 1 000 m above sea level (height in brackets): Langlitinden (1 276 m) on the east side, is Scandinavia's highest island mountain. From the ship we can see **Kråktindan**, **Åtind** (1 108 m), **Snetind** (1 215 m), in the northeast is the 'hat-shaped **Klåptind** (1 179 m), **Vasskardtinden** (1 140 m), **Langlitinden** (1 276 m) and **Snetind** (1 215 m).

The village of **Engenes** is located on a flat piece of land on the north side of **Andørjaråktindan** (829 m above sea level). Andørja church is a timber church built in 1914.

From the north, the 8 km long and narrow **Straumbotnfjorden** cuts deeply into Andørja. A maelstrom is created at its narrow mouth (p 162). There is a bridge over Straumbotnfjorden connecting **Åndervåg** with **Straumen**.

The road system on Rolla and Andørja is well developed including a sub-sea tunnel, **Ibestad Tunnel** (3 400 m long, 112 m below sea level) that connects the islands in the south. Connection to the mainland is over **Mjøsund Bridge** on Andørja's east side. From **Sørrollnes,** on Rolla's southwest point there is a ferry service to Harstad.

Northeast of Andørja, ahead and on the starboard side is the sound, **Mjøsundet** that separates Andørja from the mainland. **Astafjorden**, behind Andørja and Rolla, separates the islands from the mainland. The fjord is 30 km long and has six smaller branches. The biggest of them are the fjords **Gratangen**, **Lavangen** and **Salangen.**

On our port side we can see **Andfjorden**, between the islands of Senja (1 586 km²) in front and **Andøya** (489 km²) farther out on the port side. Senja and Andøya are Norway's second and tenth largest islands respectively.

On port side and on Andørja we can see both Klåptind and Vasskanttinden.

Approx. 68°58'N   17°08'E

On our starboard side, we cross the boundary into Dyrøy municipality

Dyrøy municipality

Municipal coat of arms, significance: Shows a 'platinum fox', first seen here in 1933.
Meaning of name: Nordic; dyr (animal) meaning here; reindeer.
Municipal seat: Brøstadbotn (pop. -).
Position: 69°05'N 17°41'E.
Area: 290 km². **Population:** 1 265.
Pop. density: 4.4 /km².
Area distribution: Farming 3 %, forestry 32 %, fresh water 4 %, other 61 %.
Trade and industry: Formerly farming and fishing, now declining; especially fishing. Farming, including animal husbandry; (cattle, sheep and goats). Dairy produce. Fishing fleet; now mostly small boats. Electronic industries.
Places to return to: Open-air museum, Dyrøy village courtyard. Dyrøy church.
Dyrøy municipality's home page: www.dyroy.kommune.no.

The story behind Dyrøy's coat of arms is as follows: "Dyrøy has long traditions of breeding foxes for furs. The world first 'platinum fox', "Mons" was born at Store Vinje on Dyrøya in 1933. "Mons" was a mutation in a silver fox litter and on his first showing in Harstad he was not viewed as especially valuable. He was therefore sold on to another breeder for only 700 Norwegian kroner. The donation of platinum fox furs to the famous Norwegian skater and film star, Sonja Henie, the Argentine President's wife, Eva Peron and the Norwegian Crown Princess, HRH Crown Princess Märtha, proved to be shrewd marketing. The furs became fashionable and greatly sought-after and prices rocketed. Crown Prince Olav opened the first exhibition of furs from the now so-called platinum fox in Oslo in 1939. Today Dyrøy has a platinum fox in its coat of arms in memory of "Mons" who was born at Vinje – and later became world famous."

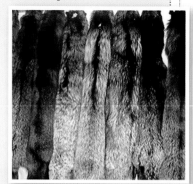

The ship is sailing into **Tranøyfjorden**. On our port side is the peninsula of Stonglandet in Tranøy municipality on Senja, Norway's second largest island. On our starboard side, Dyrøya in Dyrøy municipality.

On our starboard side is the highest mountain in Dyrøy, **Løksetinden** (1 240 m above sea level) which is an excellent landmark for mariners.

We pass the municipal boundary between Ibestad and Tranøy municipalities on our port side

Tranøy municipality

Municipal coat of arms, significance: Fish as food.
Meaning of name: The bird, trane- crane.
Municipal seat: Vangsvik (-).
Position: 69°10'N 17°44'E.
Area: 523 km². **Pop.:** 1 570.
Population density: 3.0 /km².
Area distribution: Farming 1 %, forestry 13 %, fresh water 5 %, other 81 %.
Trade and industry: Combined farming and fishing. Fishing.
Places to return to: Ånderdalen national park, South Senja museum.
Tranøy municipality's home page:
www.tranoy.kommune.no

The island of **Dyrøya** (53 km²) is on our starboard side and is located between the mainland and Tranøyfjorden. On this island we have the mountains, **Dyrøygommen** (491 m above sea level), the highest point, **Bergsheia** (563 m above sea level) and **Holmheia** (450 m above sea level). The east side of the island is the most populated. The west side is more hilly and inaccessible but also here we find many birch forests.

On Dyrøya we find traces of settlements going back to the Stone Age. On **Holm,** on the island's east side there is a church site dating from 1770. The existing church is from 1880, there are traces of a cemetery dating back to the Iron Age. South of Holm is **Dyrøyhamn**, formerly known as Hamn. The farm is mentioned in documents from 1370, the church for the first time in 1589 and it is therefore assumed that it was built in the Middle Ages. In 1770 it was in such total disrepair that it was demolished. At **Mikkelbostad** in the southeast, many relics have been found that indicate that there have been settlements here dating as far back as to the Iron Age and even the Stone Age (p 83). The farm, Mikkelbostad is first mentioned in documents from 1567.

On the southern tip of Dyrøya, near a place called **Hagenes,** remains of houses and farms from the Stone Age have been excavated and these are estimated to be from around 3 000-2 500 B.C. An area with seven burial mounds from the Iron Age was also found on a slope towards the sea.

At Hagenes, the German forces built Hagenes Fort during the Second World War. It had four cannons, bunkers and underground trenches.

69°01'N   17°17'E   + 1 hr 27 min ③

On our starboard side we have the parish of **Vinje** north of the mountain Dyrøygommen. The farm, Lille Vinje, was first mentioned in documents from 1430. Today there are five farms that provide examples of building methods and building history from the middle of the 19th century and up to the 1930s. The farms of Store Vinje and Lille Vinje are mentioned in deeds from 1530. On the farms, traces were found of cultures from the Iron Age and the Middle Ages (p 83). Scientific dating methods show that Store Vinje was inhabited in the Iron Age (7th century). In the tidal zone, near Lille Vinje, 27 round hollows have been found. As yet, no one has been able to determine exactly what they were used for. Perhaps they were building sites, burial mounds or a place to preserve food in wintertime.

Senja (1 586 km²) on the port side, is Norway's second largest island. In the north and northwest it faces the Norwegian Sea. In the southeast is Andfjorden between Senja and Andøya. Senja's western side is mainly mountainous with jagged peaks and deep fjords that cut into the land forming narrow, short valleys. The inhabitants live in fishing villages such as **Gryllefjord** (pop. 407), **Torsken**, **Senjahopen**, **Skaland**, **Fjordgard** and **Mefjordvær**. The eastern side is marshy, with open valleys and quite a number of lakes. Senja has a bridge connection to the mainland at Silsand over to the town of Finnsnes.

The headland at **Stongodden** is located in the southwest on **Stonglandet**, on our port side. In 1983, 1 881 km² of the land area was declared a nature reserve due to its distinctive marshland and special coastal fir trees.

Remains of stone coffins and burial mounds, used by the first settlers on Tranøy in approx. 500 B.C., have been found on Stonglandet. Farming was also carried out during that time.

On the south side lie the villages of **Nylandet** and **Lekangen**.

Sámi people have lived here for several centuries. Most came from Sweden, following their reindeer herds that migrated towards the coast in the summer. It is assumed that these Sámi people from Sweden settled on Senja already before the 18th century. As grazing by the reindeer damaged agricultural land, Stonglandet was protected against grazing in 1910. Recently, the conflict between grazing and land protection has re-emerged and an interim solution between the two parties has been negotiated.

Located on the southernmost tip of Senja and Tranøy is Senjehesten Coastal Defence Museum close to Skrolsvik fort. The fort was built by the German forces in 1941 using forced labour, mainly Russian prisoners of war. The fort was later used by the Norwegian armed forces until it was closed down in 1989. It was armed with four 150 mm cannon, which are still preserved.

© C. M. STIEGLITZ

The fishing village of **Skrolsvik**, also located on the island's southernmost tip, was inhabited as early as the Stone and Iron Ages. This is evident from the many burial mounds that stand on smaller headlands with an open view out towards (and thus visible from) the sea. The fishing hamlet grew up in the 1870s. It had a trading post and fish landing facilities and was operative until the mid-1990s when it was taken over by South Senja museum. Here, a whole section is dedicated to the Halibut – also called "the Holy Fish" – and the myths, mystique and fantasies surrounding this fish.

69°03'N   17°20'E   + 1 hr 35 min

On our starboard side, we have passed **Bergsheia** (563 m above sea level) on Dyrøya and thereafter the parishes of **Sandnes** and **Skogshamn**.

We pass on our port side the village of **Stonglandseidet** located on the narrow neck of land between the peninsula of Stonglandet and Senja. Here is Stonglandet Church, a wooden church built in 1896 seating 240. Right behind is the towering mountain range, **Eidefjellet** (883 m above sea level).

© HELGE N. NILSSEN

We pass on our port side **Vassvika** and **Jøvik** at the foot of **Jøvikfjellet** (596 m above sea level).

Our voyage continues into **Solbergfjorden**. Proposals have been put forward to regulate this fjord and Gisundet (farther ahead), as national salmon fjords, in an attempt to increase the numbers of wild salmon. Regulation would mean a ban on establishment of new fish farms or new landing/processing plants while existing facilities would be able to continue their activities.

68°06'N   17°29'E   + 1 hr 54 min ④

On our port side is the small island of **Tranøy**, which has lent its name to the municipality. It is located by the entrance to **Tranøybotn**, a short, wide arm of **Tranøyfjorden**. There have been settlements here for at least 2 000 years and boathouse sites, ancient relics and burial mounds have been found. There has been a church on Tranøy since the 14th century. The existing timber cruciform church was built in 1775 and seats 210. It has an interior and furniture some 300-400

years old. The church was restored in 1881 and there is a rectory from the 18th century, which is now a protected building and is used as a museum.

Tromsø museum has an ecclesiastical art collection from the old northern churches in Norway. Many of these items are from the church at Tranøy, one being a wooden sculpture of St. Sunniva (p 34) from approx. 1490. The sculpture shows a serene face probably carved after a living model and in all likelihood made in Lübeck in Germany. Another item is an hour-glass that was hung on the wall inside the church. The priests tended to preach very long sermons and some of the congregation would inevitably fall asleep. The hour-glass' function was to remind the priest - when it had run out it was time to end the sermon.

After the small island of Tranøy we pass the **Revsnes** peninsula on our port side and farther south we can see Vangsvik and Rubbestad.

We have passed Dyrøya on our starboard side including the villages of Sandnes, Skogshamn and **Klauvhamn**. In the background and on the mainland we see the mountains, **Børingen** (1 073 m above sea level), and **Børingsfjellet** (1 045 m above sea level).

Dyrøy Bridge was opened in 1994 and spans **Dyrøysundet,** connecting Dyrøya to the mainland at **Finnlandsneset**. Inside the bay are the villages of **Finnland** and **Brøstadbotn**.

U nder Dyrøy Bridge lies the wreck of the German steamship, "Elise Schulte" (4 626 gross tons) from Emden. The ship was on her way from Rotterdam to Kirkenes with a cargo of coal when she ran aground on 11th January 1942. After a few hours the ship sank but no lives were lost. The wreck is still intact and lies at a depth of 5 to 32 meters.

O utside Finnlandsneset lies the wreck of DS "Sirius" (877 gross tons) from Bergen. She was built in 1885, had cabins for 70 passengers, and was chartered by Hurtigruten in 1884-85. Later (until 1927), she sailed on various routes along our coast until she was used between Oslo and Finnmark as a cargo ship. On 18th May 1940, on her way south towards Risøyhamn in Vesterålen (p 283), with a crew of 18, she was discovered by a German plane that attacked with machine guns and seven bombs. "Sirius" broke in two and sank in a matter of minutes. Of the crew, 11 survived and the wreck is located in 45 to 70 metres of water. Despite lying submerged on the seabed for almost 70 years, the wreck is still in reasonably good condition.

After Finnlandsneset and Dyrøy Bridge, we pass **Bettholmen**, **Espenes** and **Forstrand**, situated on the shoreline with the mountain **Børingen**.

69°07'N 17°35'E	+ 2 hrs 04 min ⑤

On our port side is the village of **Skatvik** southeast of **Skatvikfjellet** (466 m above sea level). Further along, we see the village of **Vangsvik** and the village of **Rubbestad** at the foot of **Rubbestadfjellet** (436 m above sea level). At Rubbestad is Holtermanngården Museum. Holtermanngården is a fish/farming estate with houses dating from the 1880s. There are dwellings, a forge, barns, stables and a collection of old tools. The farm was occupied until recently.

At Rubbestad, we find the region's largest land-based fish farm with a deep-water intake at 95 metres. The installation has 14 tanks and nine PVC halls. The farm was closed down in the autumn of 2004 and as of September 2006 it remained closed.

Approx. 69°09'N   17°50'E

We pass the municipal boundary between Tranøy and Lenvik municipalities on our port side

Lenvik municipality

Municipal coat of arms, significance: Fishing and fishing industry.
Meaning of name: Norse Lengjuvik, from the river Lengja, 'the long one'.
Municipal seat: Finnsnes (pop. 4 026).
Position: 69°13'N 17°58'E.
Area: 895 km². **Population:** 11 027.
Pop. density: 12.3 /km².
Area distribution: Farming 4 %, forestry 26 %, fresh water 4 %, other 66 %.
Trade and industry: Public services. Animal fodder production. Farming (milk and meat production). Inshore/offshore fishing. Fish farming and fish food processing. Food processing. Metalworking industries. Mechanical workshops.
Places to return to: Gibostad, Bjorelvnes.
Lenvik municipality's home page: www.lenvik.kommune.no

Approx. 69°10'N   17°53'E

We pass the municipal boundary between Dyrøy and Sørreisa municipalities on our starboard side

Sørreisa municipality

Municipal coat of arms, significance: Sørreisa's oldest municipal seal.
Meaning of name: The river, Reisa, Nordic risa, 'to rise', 'river that rises rapidly'.
Municipal seat: Sørreisa/Straumen (pop 1 435). **Position:** 69°09'N 18°09'E.
Area: 361 km². **Population:** 3 315.
Pop. density: 9.2 /km².
Area distribution: Farming 1 %, forestry 28 %, fresh water 4 %, other 64 %.
Trade and industry: Farming and grass production. Cattle and sheep breeding. Deciduous forestry. Chipboard production. Limited fishing. Armed Forces are an important employer.
Sørreisa municipality's home page: www.sorreisa.kommune.no

On our port side, we see the village of **Solberg**, thereafter **Russevåg** bay and then, Vågan. On our starboard side, we see the villages of **Bjørga, Sildvika** and **Smørsgård**.

The high mountains in the distance are called **Fagerfjellet** (884 m above sea level), **Elveskardtinden** (872 m above sea level) and **Sultind** (1 026 m above sea level).

69°10'N   17°56'29"N   + 2 hrs 36 min ⑥

The short, wide fjord **Reisfjorden** is on our starboard side. Inside the fjord is the village of **Skøelv** at the entrance to the valley called **Skøelvdalen.** Innermost in the fjord we can see the administrative centre, **Sørreisa/ Straumen.** The village has a chipboard factory that uses deciduous wood from throughout Troms county. In addition, there are timber and mechanical industries. The Norwegian Armed Forces has a central laundry station in Sørreisa that provides services to local army camps.

Sørreisa church is located in the bay ahead of the peninsula, **Forøya**, in the centre of the northerly part of Reisfjorden. The church was built in 1992 from steel and timber and can seat 300. The previous, octagonal church was built in 1844, however this burned down in 1987.

One of NATO's most important radar stations, Control and Reporting Centre Sørreisa is located deep inside the mountain, **Høggumpen** near Sørreisa. Construction of the centre began in 1955 and it became operational in 1962. In 1999, a new combat unit was installed.

Sørreisa municipality is behind us, and we have Lenvik municipality on both sides.

Between the village of **Grunnreisa** on our starboard side and **Vågan** on our port side, the ship turns north and into Finnfjorden, heading for our next port of call, Finnsnes. To our starboard side and on the mainland are the villages of **Hemmingsjord**, **Øyjord**, Finnfjorden, and the island of Finnfjordøya, which is a bird sanctuary. Thereafter we see the villages of **Skogen** and **Sandvika.** The mountain behind is Kvittinden (933 m above sea level).

In **Finnfjorden,** partly obscured by the small island, **Finnfjordøya**, is Finnfjord Smelteverk A/S, which is the world's northernmost. Finnfjord produces ferrosilisium and silica, which is mainly exported to Europe's and USA's steel industries. The factory has approx. 100 employees.

On Senja, now on our port side we pass the villages of **Vågan**, **Laksneset**, **Laksfjorden** and **Laukhella**.

The ship docks at the quayside in Finnsnes

The origin of the name, **Finnsnes** is uncertain. It may have come from the man's name, Finn or that a 'Fin' once lived here. Other possibilities have also been suggested. The name was in use before 1400 and a farm by the name Fenneseter was located here in 1567. In a document dating back to around 1400, concerning the properties and farms owned by Trondarnes church, it is recorded that the church was the owner of half of the farm, 'Finznes'. The share of the farm was a gift from a local woman, given so that "the priest, once a year, would include a blessing for her son in his mass".

In a census from 1666, two men and four sons were living at 'Findznæss' (women were not included in censuses at that time). This number hardly changed for more than a hundred years. In 1875, 75 persons lived on the headland. By 1950 it had increased to 1 182.

From the middle of the 19th century, people began to move away from the remote areas on Senja and Gisund. The first trading establishment in Finnsnes was started in 1846. Contact with the surrounding areas increased, sailing ships were gradually replaced by steamships sailing through the sound. Finnsnes was not a regular port of call for steamships until 1883, when ships began calling three times a week. From 1893, Hurtigruten started a regular service to Finnsnes. A new quay was built in 1909; however it fell down just after it was finished. Until another quay was built in 1921 Hurtigruten was serviced using smaller boats. A 17.6 km stretch of road from Finnsnes to the neighbouring municipality of Målselv was opened in 1896 and a coach station was established in 1900, followed by a bus service in 1916. From 1900 to

1930, the population increased by more then 150 %, and it is still on the increase. In the 1950s and 60s, Finnsnes was regarded as a small country village with farms and large fields, now the site of today's commercial centre.

In 1969, the municipality's administration was moved from Gibostad to Finnsnes, which caused a further influx of new residents. Mechanical industries and other activities already established here continued to grow. Finnsnes is today an important industrial, commercial and communication centre. The biggest employer is a fishing gear factory that employs approx. 150 persons. An ambitious extension of Finnsnes centre is underway.

Finnsnes Church was built in 1979 and is a typical 'working-church', built of timber, concrete and bricks and seats 750.

Finnsnes is the regional centre for outer Mid-Troms and received its town charter in 2000.

✎

The ship continues to Tromsø	+ 0 hrs 00 min

After leaving Finnsnes, on our port side we can see the villages of **Laksfjorden** and **Laukhella** and the community of **Silsand** (pop. 1 315) also on our port side, located by the end of Gisund Bridge. Silsand, which is the largest community on the island of Senja, is now regarded as a suburb of Finnsnes. From 1936 to 1972, when Gisund Bridge was opened there was a ferry service between Silsand and Finnsnes.

✎

We are sailing out into **Gisundet**, under the 1 147 meter long Gisund Bridge, here the sound is only 0.5 km wide. Gisund Bridge was opened in 1972. It is a concrete construction with a total of 25 spans. The main span is 142.5 metres in length and the height

above sea level is 41 metres. The bridge connects Senja to the mainland.

✎

69°17'24"N 17°58'E	+ 0 hrs 20 min

On our starboard side we see the three mountains, **Kvittinden** (933 m above sea level), **Kistefjellet** (1 003 m above sea level) and **Nordheia** (655 m above sea level). At the foot of the mountains are the villages of **Trollvika, Leiknes** and **Bondjorda,** directly opposite the small island of **Eggøya** on our port side**,** and farther ahead, **Bjorelvnes,** and Lenvik Church.

✎

On our port side and along the shoreline we see other built-up-areas. On **Brenneset** in Silsand, approx. 1 km north of the bridge a new "fishing village" is to be built to cater for fishing tourists, a popular recreational activity in the area.

✎

Thereafter we see **Finnjorda**, **Grasmyr**, **Neset**, **Kvannåsen**, **Skognes** and the small island of **Eggøya** before reaching the trading centre, Gibostad located on a headland in Gisundet.

✎

69°20'24"N   18°05'20"E   + 0 hrs 36 min ①

On our starboard side, we pass the village of **Bjorelvnes** with Lenvik church and Lenvik Village Museum. The church is a cruciform timber church from 1879. The old church was moved to Roksfjord, behind **Bukkskinn-fjellet** on our starboard side, and used as a chapel. After the 1850s, people relocated from the seaward areas on outer Senja to the areas around Gisundet. The old church was therefore located away from the new settlement and for this reason, Lenvik church was built. Today a modern ski centre is located at Bjorelvnes.

✎

On the other side of Gisundet and on our port side is the village of **Gibostad** (pop. 346), which has a history as an old trading post. Gibostad is situated where the sound

between Senja and the mainland is at its narrowest, (approx. 500 m). Until the middle of the 1980s, a ferry service sailed between Gibostad and Bjorelvnes.

Gibostad was once projected as "the town" in Northern Norway, but in 1794 Tromsø was chosen instead. In 1838, Gibostad already had regular calls by Hurtigruten's forerunner, the postal ship, "Prinds Gustav" on her summer voyages north to Tromsø. This service was of great importance for Gibostad's development as a communication and postal centre that was further strengthened by local shipping activity. The Postal Service established a main office here in 1818 and one of the first telegraph stations in Troms opened at Gibostad in 1876. In common with Finnsnes, Gibostad had a regular Hurtigruten service from 1893.

A commercial and service centre grew at Gibostad along with an open market during the summer. Hurtigruten called here. There were coal bunkers, shipyards and slipways, mechanical workshops, fish traders, a soft drinks factory, a bakery, craftsmen of all kinds and specialised shops, and a hotel. Gibostad was the commercial and administration centre in Lenvik municipality right up to 1969 when it was moved to Finnsnes.

Down by the sea we can see some old buildings from the beginning of the 19th century. Today they are all listed. Unfortunately, many of the fine buildings from the same period were demolished. From 1991, in an attempt to recreate the atmosphere from earlier times, an annual open market, the 'Gibostad Market' has been arranged with great success. Some 3-4 000 people visit the market each year and 60-70 stallholders sell their goods and produce.

Senja's high school, a former agricultural college is located at Gibostad. The school still has large cowsheds

with cows, goats, pigs and horses, a mechanical workshop, a shooting range and a sloop.

On our port side and at the foot of **Bukkskinnfjellet** (507 m above sea level), we see the village of **Bukkskinnet**, thereafter the smaller communities of **Slettnes** and **Hansvoll.**

Up ahead and in the distance we see Kvaløya in Tromsø municipality, with the mountains, from left to right, **Kvitfjell** (566 m above sea level), **Raudfjellet** (542 m above sea level) and **Varden** (345 m above sea level). **Sandvik** and **Greipstad** can also be seen at the foot of these mountains.

69°23'40"N   18°06'E   + 0 hrs 52 min ②

On our starboard side, we have **Kårvika Bay** and the village of **Kårvikhamn.** Located in Kårvikhamn is Stella Polaris, the fish and seafood processing factory that has approx. 50 employees. Due to its proximity to the fishing grounds, the factory has acquired great expertise in processing cold-water shrimps. Exports are mainly to England and Scandinavia.

On the port side of Kårvikhamn, we pass the village of **Grunnvåg** and the fell known as **Vakkerbakkhøgda** (199 m above sea level). **Lysebotn**, a 5 km long branch fjord of Gisundet is located behind the peninsula. The village of **Indre Årnes** is located innermost in Lysebotn.

69°26'33"N   18°07'21"E

We now sail out of Gisundet towards **Malangen** fjord. On our port side we have the villages of **Skardsvåg** and **Vang,** behind them **Skårlifjellet** (323 m above sea level), on our starboard side we see the mountains, **Nakkefjellet** (438 m above sea level), **Kårvikkjølen** (577 m above sea level) and **Vardan** (397 m above sea level), before reaching **Rødberghamn.**

During the Second World War, a German coastal fort stood at Rødberghamn. The fort had 4 gun emplacements and were built to guard the approach to Malangen. The fortifications were reinforced in 1953 and 1967 and their main objective was to train new crews for service at the former German fortifications. As these were gradually decommissioned, the training centre became redundant. The buildings at Rødberghamn were renovated and rebuilt at the end of the 1990s, however just a short time later they were closed down.

The ship is now on a north-easterly course, out in Malangen Fjord.

The fjord **Malangen** is situated in a north-easterly direction between the islands of Senja on our port side, Norway's second largest island and Kvaløya, Norway's fifth largest island. The fjord is 60 km long, and starts on our port side between Hekkingen lighthouse and the island of **Edøya**.

Hekkingen lighthouse is located on the small island of **Hekkingen** on Senja's north-easterly point. The lighthouse is an important marker in the approach to Tromsø. It was built in 1859. The light has a range of 14.6 nautical miles. The lighthouse is now a protected installation and one of the oldest in Northern Norway. Hekkingen island is also protected as a nature reserve. Hekkingen Radio Station was established in 1962. It transmits on 314 kHz, has the identification signal HK (.... -.-), and a range of 50 nautical miles.

There have been settlements on Hekkingen since the Middle Ages. Its most prosperous period began around 1780 and lasted long into the 19th century, when rich catches of coalfish (seithe) attracted fishermen from neighbouring areas to the island.

Approx. 69°30'N   18°16'E

We pass the municipal boundary between Lenvik and Tromsø municipalities

Tromsø municipality

Municipal coat of arms, significance: The reindeer; an important animal in the region.
Meaning of name: Nordic trums, (uncertain), but possibly running water.
Municipal seat: Tromsø (pop. 63 596).
Position: 69°38'N 18°57'E.
Area: 2 566 km². **Population:** 64 492.
Pop. density: 25.1 /km².
Area distribution: Farming 1 %, forestry 11 %, fresh water 1 %, other 87 %.
Trade and industry: Service industries. University. University Hospital. Troms County Administration. Various commercial activities. Agriculture. Fishing. Hunting. Fish farming. Fish food processing. Brewery. Mechanical industry. Graphic design and data industry. Shipping companies.
Places to return to: Sommarøy sea fishing festival, various festivals throughout the year.
Tromsø municipality's home page: www.tromso.kommune.no

The island, of **Kvaløya** (737 km²) ahead (and later on our port side) is, like most of the larger islands in Tromsø quite hilly. The island has a wild and unspoilt nature with deep fjords on the north and west side but a more even and flatter coastline to the south and east. The two deep fjords, **Ersfjorden**, in a south-westerly direction, and **Kaldfjorden**, in a north-easterly direction nearly divide the island into three parts. The islands' highest point is **Store Blåmann** (1 044 m above sea level), located in the northwest. Rock carvings dating back some 2 500–4 000 years have been found on the island.

The small island of **Hillesøya** (1.8 km²) is situated outmost in Malangen, however it is difficult to see from the ship. Previously the island was an important fishing community with its own church. This church was moved to Brennsholmen, south-east of Hillesøya. There is now no farming carried out on the island and the old houses have gradually become summer and holiday homes. On top of the island (210 m above sea level) the Norwegian Armed Forces have installed a coastal radar station.

Hillesøya has a bridge connection to the mainland over the beautiful island of **Sommarøya** (0.9 km², pop. 250). Traces of settlements some 10 000 years old have been found here. Sommarøy fishing village is said to be one of the finest in Norway. The island is a base for the local fishing fleet and has a fish food processing industry. Because of the fine beaches, the island is a favourite recreational area for people from Tromsø and for visiting tourists. On Sommarøy there is a popular Sea Fishing Festival arranged every year at the end of July.

The small island of **Brennsholmen** is situated by the north-westerly foot of **Kvitfjell** (566 m above sea level). Here stands Hillesøya church, which was moved to Brennsholmen from Hillesøya. The timber church was constructed in 1889 and seats 450. The church has two altarpieces of German origin from approx. 1500. Brennsholmen has a large number of sheep farms.

Torsnesaksla (249 m above sea level) juts out into Malangen. There are no roads or houses; however, there are sites of important cultural interest. It is now a protected area.

From Gisundet, our course is east-northeast into Malangen. On our port side we see the villages of **Buvik** (sites and relics from the Iron Age), **Sandvik** and **Greipstad** located at the foot of **Sandviksfjellet** (361 m above sea level). Small sheep and goat farms are very common in this area and it has many fine cultural landscapes of great cultural value.

© EILIV LEREN

69°28'N   18°09"E   + 1 hr 13 min ③

On our starboard side we have the village of **Aglaps-vik**, after rounding the headland known as **Rødbergan** (147 m above sea level), then the headlands **Aglapen** (218 m above sea level) and **Tennskjær** and the community of **Tennskjær**.

Malangen continues in a south-easterly direction on our starboard side between the municipality of **Lenvik** and the peninsula of **Balsfjordhalvøya**. This part of the fjord is 35 km long and splits into four branches: **Rossfjorden**, **Målselvfjorden, Aursfjorden** (with the village of **Aursfjordbotn**) and **Nordfjorden** (with the village of **Nordfjordbotn**). There is an even distribution of small communities along the shoreline.

The ship continues into **Straumsfjorden**, along the east coast of Kvaløya on our port side. At the foot of the mountains, **Varden** (345 m above sea level), **Rismålheia** (646 m above sea level), **Stortuva, Gråtinden** (871 m above sea level) and **Mjeldskardtinden** (952 m above sea level), are the villages of **Bakkejord, Mjelde** and **Skognes**.

We pass the Balsfjord municipality on our starboard side

Balsfjord municipality

Municipal coat of arms, significance: The importance of agriculture in the municipality.
Meaning of name: Uncertain, possibly Norse god Balder, or bals, lump.
Municipal seat: Storsteinnes (pop. 913).
Position: 69°15'N 19°15'E.
Area: 1 494 km². **Population:** 5 569.
Pop. density: 3.7 /km².
Area distribution: Farming 4 %, forestry 26 %, fresh water 3 %, other 67 %.
Trade and industry: Excellent conditions for farming including dairy and meat production, sheep and goats. The country's largest goat farms and goat cheese producer. Limited fishing. Food processing industry. Timber factories and mechanical workshops. Corn silo. Animal and fish food factories. Asphalt and gravel works.
Balsfjord municipality's home page: www.balsfjord.kommune.no

Balsfjord municipality is Northern Norway's largest agricultural municipality. It is also influenced by the two fjords, Balsfjord and Malangen. In Malangen, coalfish and herring fishing has played an important role.

Several rock-carving sites have been discovered in Balsfjord. On **Tennes** near Balsfjord church**,** three sites have been found dating back to 4 600 B.C. and 2 600 B.C. The larger of the three has approx. 40 figures, dating from approx. 2 700 B.C. The sites have rock carvings representing land and sea creatures, which is quite unusual. The oldest and smallest of them, dating back to 4 600 B.C. has only drawings of land animals. At the third site, (2 600 B.C.) the drawings are mainly of animals but also feature two human figures.

✍

69°30'33"N   18°22'41"E   + 1 hr 34 min ④

The westward headland on **Balsfjordhalvøya** (in Troms) we see the place called **Ansnes**, the mountains **Klemmartindan** (1 047 m above sea level), **Blåruttind** (806 and 961 m above sea level), the village of **Brokskard,** the mountain, **Bentsjordtinden** (1 160 m above sea level), the headland, **Vollstad,** the village, **Bentsjord** and the mountain, **Bakaromnstinden**, with **Middagstinden** (1 103 m above sea level) and **Kvitfjellet** (914 m above sea level), followed by the village of **Vikran.**

✍

On our port side we see the villages of **Lauksletta** and **Mjelde,** with Mjelde chapel and cemetery.

✍

After passing Mjelde on our port side and at the foot of **Gråtinden** (871 m above sea level) we can see the small settlements of **Neset** and **Skognes** before Straumsbukta in Vollbukta.

✍

In the distance, we can see a range of mountains before reaching our next port of call, Tromsø. From south, they are named: Itnavárri (788 m above sea level), Bønntuva (766 m above sea level) and Fløya (671 m above sea level).

✍

69°32'33"N   18°37'E   + 1 hr 55 min ⑤

In **Straumsbukta** on our port side and just before the island of Ryøya on our starboard side, we can see the largest continuous cultivated area in Tromsø municipality. The farms have cattle, sheep, horses and plant production. Here we find large woodlands and forests in a cultural landscape with a variety of forestry and farming activities. Elk are here through the winter and there are important grazing areas for reindeer. As this area is fairly close to Tromsø town, many people wishing to live in a more 'rural' area are moving to Straumsbukta.

The farm, Straumen Gård is located in Straumsbukta and is part of the Perspektivet Museum in Tromsø. Straumen Gård, with its 11 buildings is the most complete farm from the 19th century in Northern Norway. In a row along the shore are the houses and the cookhouse, whilst on the other side of the courtyard are the cowsheds, stables and barn. The buildings contain the tools and equipment used on the farm in those days.

✍

On our starboard side, we pass the island of **Ryøya**. Researchers and zoologists from Tromsø University's Department of Artic Biology keep a flock of 17 musk oxen grazing on the island in connection with a research programme into Arctic eco-systems. In ancient times, Ryøya was used as an execution site.

✍

Rystraumen, the channel between Kvaløya on the port side and Ryøya is approx. 500 metres long and 400 metres wide at its narrowest point and the depth varies from 40 to 80 metres. Approx. 90 cruise ships navigate through Rystraumen every year in addition to normal commercial traffic, including Hurtigruten.

✍

The ship DS "Flint" (6.800 gross tons) from Bergen ran aground in Rystraumen 1st September 1928. The ship, a large vessel for its time, was on her way from Kirkenes to Rotterdam with a cargo of iron ore when a strong tidal current in Rystraumen forced the ship off course, across the flow of the current. The crew tried to get the ship back on course but "Flint" ran aground and was stuck for several hours. Another vessel, DS "Frøy", sailing in the same direction through Rystraumen some hours later, was also forced off course by the current and drifted straight into the disabled "Flint". "Frøy" emerged undamaged from the collision but "Flint" capsized and floated on her side. The crew and officers were rescued but when the boilers exploded, the ship broke in two and sank. The wreck of "Flint" is located close to Ryøya in Rystraumen, at a depth of 15-40 m.

✍

To the port side of Ryøya we can see **Hella,** which is a popular recreational area. The strong tidal currents in Rystraumen can reach a speed of 5-6 knots. The currents carry large shoals of coalfish and Hella is a popular place for rod fishing from the rocks towards the channel. Houses from "old" Tromsø have been moved here, which gives the place an air of bygone times. There are rock carvings nearby that tell the story of how people lived and foraged here on Hella 4 500 years ago.

Immediately after Ryøya, we pass the village of **Vikran** on our port side. There is a ferry service between Vikran and the village of **Larseng** on Kvaløya. However, the final decision has now been taken, that a sub-sea tunnel (known as the 'Rya Project') will be constructed. The tunnel wil be due for completion in 2009.

On our starboard side, we can see **Balsnesodden,** Balsfjord peninsula's northeasterly point. On Balsnes, a grave with the remains of a male skeleton was discovered, and found to be from around A.D. 800. The grave contained many artefacts from that period.

We now head into **Tromsøysundet** towards Tromsø. **Larseng** is on our port side.

Astern we can see **Balsfjorden** cutting its way into the mainland. The fjord is 57 km long and 2-7 km wide. It is surrounded by high mountains, some are 1 200 m above sea level on the west side and 1 500 m above sea level on the east side. At the head of the fjord in Balsfjord municipality are the villages of **Nordkjosbotn** (pop. 377) and **Storsteinnes** (pop. 913). The dairy at Storsteinnes is the country's largest producer of goat cheese.

Ramfjorden is the only branch of Balsfjorden, which starts south of the mountain **Itnavárri** (788 m above sea level), the most southerly mountain in this characteristic mountain range in Tromsø. Innermost in the fjord at **Ramfjordmoen,** on the south side of Tromsdalstinden (1 238 m above sea level) we have the installation known as EIS CAT (European Incoherent SCATter), an international scientific organisation that was established in 1975 by research institutions in Finland, France, Norway, United Kingdom, Sweden, Germany, and later Japan.

The Administrative Headquarters for EIS CAT are located in Kiruna in northern Sweden.

EIS CAT's purpose is to investigate the upper polar atmosphere with the help of radar techniques. Advanced technical equipment measures properties such as density and temperature, electrical fields and currents, winds and particle transportation in the atmosphere and the results are used in studies of the Northern Lights

(Aurora Borealis) phenomena, shifting winds induced by sunlight in the atmosphere and the balance of energy in these upper layers (p 162).

Technically, the radar functions around two systems; firstly the UHF (Ultra High Frequency) system operating on a frequency of 933.5 MHz, transmitting from Ramfjordmoen to a receiver at Kiruna in Sweden, Sodankylä in Finland and Ramfjordmoen. The antenna is a 32-metre parabola with an effect of 2 MW. The second system, the VHF (Very High Frequency) system operates on a frequency of 224 MHz, with an effect of 6 MW. The antenna here is parabolic-cylindrical with dimensions 120 x 40 m. Both transmitter and receiver are located at Ramfjordmoen and have been operative since 1983.

The EIS CAT station at Ramfjordmoen includes an installation that is capable of heating the ionosphere by HF (High Frequency) radio waves. This in turn is used in studies of the processes taking place in the plasma in the ionosphere. The radio transmitter operates on frequencies between 4 and 8 MHz, and has an effect of 1 200 MW.

We are sailing past the mountain, Itnavárri on our starboard side, with the village of **Indre Berg**. We then have the mountains called **Bønntuva** (776 m above sea level), **Fløya** (671 m above sea level) and in the background the towering, majestic, **Tromsdalstinden** (1 238 m above sea level).

© BERIT LILAND

69°34'N   18°46'E   + 2 hrs 09 min

The ferry landing at **Larseng** is on our port side. At Larseng is the largest settlement found on Kvaløya dating back to the early Stone Age (p 83). A total of 663 archaeological finds have been made here and of these, 173 were various weapons and tools. Rock carvings, approx. 4 500 years old, were also found here which provide valuable information about the human activity in the area during that period.

Between Larseng and **Håkøy Bay**, on the north side of the mountain **Grønnlibruna** (401 m above sea level) on our port side, are some of the best farms in Tromsø municipality, that produce dairy products, meat and potatoes and in addition some timber, firewood and Christmas trees. The area has a fine cultural landscape with some Sámi culture (p 243) and protected marsh areas with bird and wildlife reserves.

On our port side is the tiny headland of **Tisnes**. Here stands what is believed to be Norway's oldest sea-cable house built in 1869. It is still operative. The cable connects Balsnes on Balsfjord peninsula to Tisnes and then onwards to Tromsøya.

In the background, we can see the mountains on the northern part of Kvaløya and Ringvassøya.

Up ahead we can see the relatively flat island of Tromsøya (21 km²). We see **Sandnessundet** on the west side of the island and the 1 200 meter long Sandnessundbrua (opened in 1974) connecting Tromsøya to Kvaløya and the town district of Kvaløysletta. Tromsøysundet lies east of the island and the 1 016 metre long landmark Tromsøbrua (opened in 1960), connects the town districts of Tromsdalen, Tomasjord and Kroken to the mainland. The centre of Tromsø is on the south side of Tromsøya.

Near the island of **Håkøya**, in the south side of Sandnessundet, between Tromsøya and Kvaløya, are the remains

of the German battleship, "Tirpitz", sunk by British aircraft in 1944 (p 268).

The ship docks at the quayside in Tromsø

CITY MAP P**401**

© LARS TIEDE

Tromsø (2 558 km²) is one of Norway's largest towns, roughly the same size as the Duchy of Luxemburg. The town is also nicknamed "the Gateway to the Arctic Ocean" and "Paris of the North".

Archaeological excavations show that the first settlers came to the Tromsø region some 9-10 000 years ago and finds of Sámi culture go back at least 2 000 years (p 243). Traces of Scandinavian language and culture date back to 4th and 5th century A.D.

According to the Sagas, the first church on Tromsøya was built by King Håkon Håkonsson (1204-63) in the middle of the 13th century. The church known as "Sankta Maria close to the heathens" was dedicated to the patron saint, the Holy Maria, mother of Christ. No traces remain of the church, which is believed to have been a simple wooden building. That the church was located (at the time) at one of Norway's most remote spots supports the theory that the King may have entered into an agreement with the Russian Grand Duke in Novgorod (North West Russia) in 1250/51, in which they drew up the boundaries for the right to collect taxes from the population which were not of Sámi decent. The Norwegian border was then close to Lyngstuva, the northern point of the Lyngen mountains north of Tromsø (p 180, p 264).

Another well-known cultural monument, dating back to the middle of the 13th century is the fortifications (Borgen) at Skansen, also built by King Håkon Håkonsson. The ramparts were built using stones and peat and were constructed as a defence against attacks from the Karelians (from Karelia, an area between the White Sea and the Gulf of Finland) and Russia. Skansen is today a round circular mound with a marked raised outer periphery with a diameter of 50 metres and is a protected site currently under restoration. The church and the fortifications were built about a kilometre apart at Prostneset where Hurtigruten calls today. Between these two buildings from the 13th century, the town of Tromsø emerged 500 years later.

Bergen's trading privileges (dominated by the Hansa merchants from Germany) monopolised all trade north of Bergen (p 11), and Vågan in Lofoten's role as Northern Norway's centre of trade between the west coast and the northern counties (p 156) limited Tromsø's opportunity to develop into a dominating trading centre. The priests however, sailed to Bergen with fish and other goods from the area. According to ancient documents, the first merchants to arrive in Troms came here in 1536.

In the 18th and 19th century and until 1917, trade was carried out between Troms and Finnmark and the coastal regions of northwest Russia - the so-called 'Pomor Trade' (p 241). The first Pomor merchant ship came here in 1725. Tromsø developed into the starting point for the trade routes eastwards and into one of the Pomor Trade Centres in the north. In 1790, when Bergen and Trondheim's trading privileges were abolished, 'free' trade was introduced to "Finnmarkens amt" (Troms and Finnmark counties) and a customs clearance station was opened in Tromsø. In 1794, Tromsø, along with Hammerfest and Vardø, was granted the privileges and status of a town with full trading rights, even though it had only a small population. The town grew in the 19th century and began trading southward with Europe and eastward with Russia. Corn, rope and food were shipped in to Trom-

© POMORMUSEET

sø and rock-dried fish, cod liver oil, goat hides, reindeer hides, fox furs and eider down were shipped out.

The town developed into the administrative and trading centre for the whole of Troms. The new Elverhøy church, built in 1803 became caretaker of some of the items from Tromsø's first church, built in 1252. In 1814, the Chief Administrator for Troms County moved here and the Bishop of Tromsø diocese took up residence here in 1834. However, the population was still quite small; in 1807, the town had less than 100 citizens. In 1830 it had increased to 1 200.

The increase in trade with other countries, the influx of foreigners and visiting summer tourists introduced new trends among the local people. Furniture from Europe, fashions, entertaining and socialising gave new impulses in the development and extension of the town. Tromsø developed a varied cultural scene with various local 'associations' promoting literature, music and theatre. There were also French, German and Russian language societies. Touring circuses, musicians, travelling dance and music teachers came to town. Especially during the light, short summer months, the town was a hive of activity and outdoor life.

PEDER BALKE: TROMSØ

In 1827, Tromsø was described in a tourist guide as follows:
"When one wanders between the handsome houses, observing the well filled warehouses, the harbour full of ships with flags from many nations, listening to the Russian songs from the row boats, viewing the life on the streets, listening to the industrious sound of the smithy hammer, watching the delightfully clad ladies and gentlemen promenade - one could hardly believe one was close to the 70th latitude and at a place that only became a market town in 1794!"

Another travelogue from 1841 states:
"No other place in the far north has impressed us as much as Tromsø. The attraction is not its large population but rather to experience its bustling commerce, its lively company, and its rapid rise; to put it another way - the young and invigorating life that is emerging in this blooming town."

A German tourist who visited the town at the beginning of the 20th century expressed himself thus: "Stockholm is named Paris of the North. If the citizens of the "High North" should have such a place it can only be Tromsø". The nickname for the town has since then been "Nordens Paris" – the Paris of the North.

The commercial and cultural development of Tromsø continued, and in 1838, the postal ship "Prinds Gustav" began sailing to Tromsø during the summer route from Trondheim. Tromsø Shipyard was founded in 1848. In 1867, local ferry routes began sailing from Tromsø to the outlying villages. Tromsø Cathedral was consecrated in 1861 and Tromsø Museum opened in 1872. The first railway planning committee actually met in 1872; however, the town is still waiting for a railway to be built! By 1890 the population had increased to 6 000. In 1893, the first Hurtigruten ship called at Tromsø. This steady development continued into the 1900s. Quaysides and breakwaters were built to provide better, safer facilities for fishing boats and steamships.

Many important explorers, both Norwegian and foreign, used Tromsø as a base from which to set out on various expeditions to the far north and the North Pole and the town became known as "The Gateway to the Arctic". From around 1850, Tromsø assumed the role formerly held by Hammerfest, as the leading commercial centre for Arctic hunting and whaling.

During the Second World War, Tromsø escaped destruction – the only town in Northern Norway to do so. Most of the town's unique, traditional wooden buildings remained intact. Unfortunately, many of these were lost in a huge fire in 1969. It was the largest post-war fire in Scandinavia and it completely destroyed 24 buildings in the centre of town.

As early as the start of the 1900s, almost all of the available land areas on Tromsø island had been used for housing or building. Some municipalities were merged; the

most recent reorganisation was in 1964. The reorganisation processes led to Tromsø becoming one of the largest municipalities in Norway, in terms of area. Tromsø bridge (1 016 m in length) from the island to the town suburb of **Tromsdalen** on the mainland, was opened in 1960. In 1961, the cable car from Tromsdalen to the mountain Storsteinen was opened and Tromsø Airport Langnes began operations in 1964. In 1965, the famous landmark church known as the 'Arctic Cathedral' was consecrated. In 1994, Tromsø bridge, which by this time had become a serious traffic bottleneck, was supplemented by an undersea tunnel, the 3 500 m long Tromsø tunnel (102 m under sea level). The tunnel runs under Tromsø Sound and has two parallel tunnels, each with a dual carriageway.

Tromsø University is the world's most northerly and the third largest university in Norway. It opened in 1972 and in 2007 there were approx. 6 500 registered students and 1 900 lecturers and staff. The university has five faculties: Humanities, Law, Science, Medicine, Fishery Sciences and Social Science. The Norwegian College of Fisheries is an independent college of the university. Tromsø Museum (founded 1872) is also an independent department of the university, as are the Northern Lights Observatory and several research centres, e.g. Roald Amundsen Centre for Arctic Research and the Centre for Sámi Studies.

The town's largest employer is the University Hospital in Northern Norway (UNN). The new hospital opened in 1991. UNN is the regional hospital for Nordland, Troms, Finnmark and Svalbard. In 2007 there were approx. 5 000 employees and 450 patient beds.

In 1988, the Northern Lights Planetarium was opened. In 1998, the Norwegian Polar Institute was relocated from Oslo to Tromsø and in 2005, the town's brand new town hall was opened.

०⁄०

A stroll around town   CITY MAP P**401**

The Hurtigruten quay is in the centre of Tromsø, and a 4-hour call at port on the northbound voyage provides an opportunity to visit some of the sights of the town.

०⁄०

Tromsdalen Church, known as the Arctic Cathedral, is just over the bridge on the mainland. It stands ma-

jestic and proud on the approach to Tromsø and is a famous landmark. The architect's intention was to provide associations with ice and icebergs and with an innovative design, to symbolise the dark winter months and the Northern Lights. The church was consecrated in 1965. The façade towards the west is 35 m high and the long sides are built of concrete elements that reach the ground;

these are clad with flame-lacquered, pearl-grey aluminium plates. The floor area of the church is 900 m². The church has seating for 720 persons.

The Arctic Cathedral has one of Europe's largest stained glass mosaics, created by the well-known sculptor Victor Sparre. The motif is "The glory of the return of Christ". The mosaic was completed in 1972. It is triangular, 23 m high and covers the entire east wall of the church. 11 tons of 2 cm thick, single-coloured and polished glass was used to create the mosaic. The glass is divided into 86 sections that together create the whole pattern.

०⁄०

Tromsø Cathedral is in the town centre. It is the world's most northerly Protestant cathedral and one of Norway's largest wooden churches, with 750 seats. The cathedral was built in 1861 as a longhouse style church in cogged timber, in a Neo-Gothic style. It is situated in a small park, Kirkeparken, that was also a burial site in the Middle Ages and possibly the site of Tromsø's first church, built in 1252. Tromsø cathedral has some fine

detail from the architecture of the period, both inside and on the exterior. The high spire rises in several sections from the porch to the point of the spire.

Elverhøy church is Tromsø's oldest church. It was built in 1803 on the site on which the current Tromsø Cathedral stands; however, it was moved to its present location in 1863. The church is a cruciform construction and it contains a madonna figure from 1252, when King Håkon Håkonsson built the first church in Tromsø. The altarpiece is from the 18th century.

The Catholic church (Our Lady's church), was built in 1861. It is the world's most northerly Catholic Episcopal seat with, of course, the world's most northerly Catholic bishop. Pope John Paul II visited the church and stayed at the Episcopal residence in June 1989. The church and the Episcopal residence are in the centre of Tromsø. The church itself is a longhouse style building with two spires, one over the entrance and another above the chancel.

The Polar Museum in Tromsø is in the listed old customs house from the 1830s. The museum is ideally located close to the harbour near old packing houses and Tromsø's traditional wooden buildings from the 1790s. The Museum has exhibits from the town's Polar exploration and hunting history.

Tromsø's cable car, known as "**Fjellheisen**", takes four minutes to make the trip up to **Storsteinen**, 421 m above sea level. There is a magnificent view of the town and surrounding mountains from the plateau, where there is also a restaurant. "Fjellheisen" was built in 1960 and officially opened in 1961.

Tromsø is today a major centre of education, research and culture in the north. The town is well known for its lively nightlife. Tromsø Film Festival is a major annual event that attracts artists, filmmakers and film enthusiasts from all over the world. The annual Northern Lights Festival presents western classical music and the town hosts many other varied cultural activities throughout the year.

The ship continues to Skjervøy **+ 0 hrs 00 min**

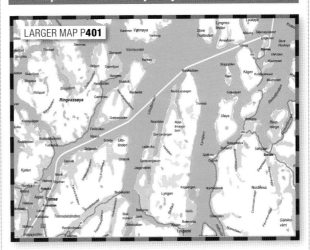

LARGER MAP P**401**

After departing from Tromsø, we sail north-eastwards.

We sail under the Tromsø Bridge, which was opened in 1960. The bridge is built using the cantilever construction method. The longest span is 80 m, the total length is 1 016 m and the height is 38 m above sea level.

On Tromsø island over on our port side, we can see a large red brick building complex – these are part of Tromsø University and the University Hospital in Northern Norway (UNN).

On the starboard side is the oil storage depot in **Kroken**.

69°44'20"N   19°03'40"E **+ 0 hrs 17 min**

Over on the port side near **Krabbenes** we can see an elongated, white building. This is the National Breeding Station for cod, one of the world's most modern research installations for fish farming research. It was opened in 2005. Advanced technology is employed to monitor the fish's genes with the objective of developing robust, healthy breeding fish for cod through natural selection of cod roe. This 'super cod' is not intended to be a genetically modified 'monster' fish, but a progenitor of new generations of thriving farmed fish.

69°45'N 19°04'28"E   + 0 hrs 21 min ①

At **Skarpeneset** near **Tønsnes**, on the port side, there is a former military camp, Grøtsund fort (unfortunately it is hard to see from the ship). The fortifications were built to control and monitor the northerly sea approach to Tromsø, and were armed with three 94 mm cannon, that were left behind by the German forces when they left Northern Norway. Grøtsund fort was finally closed down in the 1990s. The fort was acquired by Tromsø Havn KF in December 2006. The area is to be used for quay facilities, warehousing and industrial units.

The small village of **Tønsvik** is on our starboard side. Due to the fairly close proximity of Tønsvik to the town of Tromsø, the village is now in the process of evolving from a purely agricultural community to a residential area.

> The Norwegian steamship "Kong Ring" (1 994 gross tons) hit a sea mine just outside of Grøtsund fort on the 26th December 1941. The ship was sailing from Kvænangen to Narvik with more than 300 German troops on board. Shortly after the ship had hit the mine, which had been laid by a Russian submarine some 10 days before, the ship's main boiler exploded. Attempts to launch the lifeboats failed and signal flares were not spotted. Just six minutes after the explosion, the ship sank. Approx. 286 men were lost that night.

We have now passed on our port side the mountains **Finnlandsfjellet** (659 m above sea level) and **Kjølen** (790 m above sea level) and the villages of **Nord-Finnes**, Krabbenes and **Krakneset**, under **Kraknesaksla** and the mountain **Austeråsfjellet** (467 m above sea level).

The narrow sound, **Kvalsundet** (20 km long, 1-3 km wide) passes on the port side. The sound divides Kvaløya and Ringvassøya. The two islands are joined by the 1 630 m long undersea tunnel Kvalsundtunnelen (56 m under sea level). The tunnel was opened in 1988 by (then) Crown Prince Harald.

Ringvassøya (656 km², 1 060 m above sea level, Norway's sixth largest island) passes on the port side. The mountainous island is in both Tromsø and Karlsøy municipalities. 223 km² of the south-easterly part of Ringvassøy is in Tromsø municipality. The lake **Skogsfjordvatnet** (13.6 km², 20 m above sea level) in the centre of the island, is Norway's largest lake within an island.

In **Indre Kårvika** on the island's southeast side towards Kvalsundet, is the Norwegian College of Fishery Scien-

ce (NFH). NFH was founded in 1972 and has affiliated colleges in Tromsø, Bergen and Trondheim. The College on Ringvassøya is part of Tromsø University. The college offers international studies and doctorate programmes within most disciplines. The college is well equipped with research facilities and along with the Norwegian Centre for Fisheries and Aquaculture Research, the college has three research vessels and an R & D centre for aquaculture.

The island of Ringvassøy has many interesting minerals. There are deposits of pyrite, copper, gold, lead, iron sulphide and hematite. Gold has even been found on the north west side of the island. Two prospecting companies carried out exploratory mining in 1980. The initial tests were concluded in 1985; unfortunately, however, mining proved not to be viable. International companies still officially maintain prospecting interests in the area.

There is very little agriculture on Ringvassøya. Some areas are being developed for recreational and holiday homes.

Just ahead, we can see the majestic Lyngen Alps.

We have now sailed out into the 4-5 km wide **Grøtsundet**, under the mountains **Skilsmissen** (340 m above sea level) and **Johanfjellet** (438 m above sea level) on the starboard side, and passed the villages of **Åsneset**, **Vågnes** and **Skittenelev** that lie at the foot of the mountain **Svarvarfjellet** (540 m above sea level).

69°47'22"N 19°18'17"E   + 0 hrs 43 min ②

On the port side, we approach **Langsundet**, which is approx. 23 km long and 1.5 km wide at its narrowest point. Langsundet divides the islands of Ringvassøya and the smaller Reinøya. In the northern part of the sound, on Ringvassøya, is the community of **Hansnes**, the administrative centre of Karlsøy municipality. There are several ferries from Hansnes to the neighbouring islands Vannøya, Karlsøya and Reinøya. Ringvassøya church at Hansnes was built in 1977.

The small flat island at the mouth of Langsundet is **Nipøya**.

The German tugboat "Süd Amerika VII" (199 gross tons) sailed into a minefield and sank in Langsundet on her way from the north west side of Reinøya to Tromsø. The wreck lies at a depth of 10 to 15 metres. The tugboat broke in two pieces and the bridge and the funnel can still be seen at the wreck site.

❧

The island of **Reinøya**, (147 km²) is on the port side, after Langsundet. Of the island's area, approx 41.8 km² lies within Tromsø municipality. The remainder is in Karlsøy municipality.

The southern part of Reinøya on the port side is an active agricultural area with sheep and goat farming and plant nurseries. The area has excellent grazing land and productive forests; however, farming is made somewhat difficult by the steep terrain. Reinøya also has fine hunting areas and summer grazing for reindeer. In common with the other islands in Nord-Troms, Reinøya is mountainous. Most of the local population lives along the shoreline.

The old trading post of **Finnkroken** stands on Reinøya's southern tip. Finnkroken chapel, built in 1907, is a longhouse style church with seating for 140. It was restored in 1918 and in 1937.

❧

On our port side, we have the mountains **Gunnarfjellet** (752 m above sea level) and **Oddekollen** (653 m above sea level).

The headland, **Grøtneset**, is the outermost south-easterly headland on Reinøya. Ships sailing from the north in to Grøtsundet may stop briefly here to take a pilot onboard. The fjord continues north-eastwards as Ullsfjorden.

❧

The impressive Lyngen Alps can now be seen up ahead and to starboard.

❧

After the village **Skittenelv** on the starboard side, vis á vis Nipøya, the houses along the shoreline continue to **Snarby**. The outermost mountain, **Ullstinden** (1094 m above sea level) and the headland known as **Blåmannsneset** pass by before we sail into Ullsfjorden.

Ullsfjorden runs between the peninsula and the Lyngen Alps. The fjord is 11 km wide at the mouth (between Karlsøy and Nordklubben, the northernmost point of the Lyngen Alps) and is 82 km long. The 30 km long, innermost part of the fjord is known as **Sørfjorden**.

❧

Approx. 69°52'N   19°50'E

We pass the boundaries of Tromsø, Lyngen and Karlsøy municipalities. On the port side is Karlsøy municipality, over to starboard is Lyngen municipality

Lyngen municipality

Municipal coat of arms, significance: 'Nordland horse' motif.
Meaning of name: Norse fjord Lygnir, from logn 'still'.
Municipal seat: Lyngseidet (pop. 864).
Position: 69°34'N 20°14'E.
Area: 810 km². **Pop.:** 3 199. **Pop. density:** 3.9 /km².
Area distribution: Farming 2 %, forestry 7 %, fresh water 2 %, other area 89 %.
Trade and industry: Agriculture, very often as a supplementary activity. Cattle, sheep and goat farming. Local fishing, especially shrimp fishing. Shrimp factory. Fish processing. Industrial workshops and industrial plastics factories. Production of electricity.
Places to return to: Lyngen Alps.
Activities to return to: Hiking, skiing, mountain climbing.
Lyngen municipality's home page: www.lyngen.kommune.no

❧

Karlsøy municipality

Municipal coat of arms, significance: Sea Eagle colony in the municipality.
Meaning of name: First part is man's name Karl.
Municipal seat: Hansnes (pop. 310).
Position: 69°58'N 19°37'E.
Area: 1 040 km². **Pop.:** 2.372.
Pop. density: 2.28 /km².
Area distribution: Farming 1 %, forestry 8 %, fresh water 3 %, other area 88%.
Trade and industry: Fishing (close proximity to fishing grounds). Smaller fishing vessels for local fishing, larger vessels sail offshore. Fish processing industry. Karlsøy municipality is one of the world's largest exporters of salted cod, mainly to Portugal, Brazil and Spain. Some agriculture with animal husbandry, mainly sheep and goats.
Places to return to: Nordfugløy.
Activities to return to: Sea fishing.
Karlsøy municipality's home page: www.karlsoy.kommune.no

❧

The outermost part of the magnificent **Lyngen Alps** on Lyngen peninsula rises up on the starboard side.

The **Lyngen** peninsula (approx. 1 500 km²) stretches 80-90 km from Balsfjorden in the south to the Norwegian Sea in the north, between Ullsfjorden in the west and Lyngenfjord in the east. The peninsula is just 15-20 km

© JAN HUGO SALAMONSEN / WWW.RYGGSEKK.NET

wide and is divided about halfway in on the east side of Lyngenfjorden by the fjord arm known as **Kjosen**, actually a side fjord of Ullsfjorden. Along the peninsula is the mountain range known as the Lyngen Alps, which are widely known for their majestic beauty.

The glacial mountain **Jiehkkevárri** (1 833 m above sea level) in the Lyngen Alps is Troms county's highest peak, however it is not visible from the ship. From the top of this mountain, it is possible (as a local saying goes) to "gaze upon several municipalities and three nations" (Norway, Sweden and Finland).

Approx. 2 million years ago, there were several alternating freeze-thaw periods. This cycling climate modelled and shaped the landscape. The glaciers gouged out deep valleys and left jagged peaks behind. Furthest along the Lyngen peninsula, several of the peaks have broad plateaus at the top. These are popular areas for more adventurous hikers and glacier walkers.

There are approx. 140 registered glaciers on Lyngen peninsula with a total area of approx. 100 km². The glaciers known as **Gamvikblåisen** and **Strupbreen** are the largest glacier systems, in the outer part of the Lyngen Alps.

The Lyngen Alps were probably not officially climbed before 1897, when a group comprised of an Englishman and 3-4 Norwegians scaled the peaks in the area. In 1898 another group including one Englishwoman and two Swiss guides climbed, explored and mapped the mountains.

© JAN HUGO SALAMONSEN / WWW.RYGGSEKK.NET

The mountains that form the Lyngen Alps are extremely rugged; however, they remain a popular destination for climbers and skiers/snowboarders from all over the world. The area is most popular with skiers during the late winter and in the spring, when the skiing conditions are at their best and with hikers and mountain climbers in the summer. One of the world's most well known extreme skiers has said: "If Alaska is the skiers' Mecca, then Lyngen must be Heaven".

The Lyngen Alps were designated as a protected landscape area in 2004. They cover 961 km² and have great natural science value as a glaciological and quaternary reference area. There is a rich variety of bird an animal life in the area and Sámi, Kven and Norwegian cultural heritage sites are found here.

The municipality of Lyngen has concentrated settlement largely on the western side of Lyngenfjorden and along the north side of the fjord arm, Kjosen. The largest community is Lyngseidet. Skibotn, pop. 476, Storfjord municipality) is at the head of the fjord. The local population has a mix of Norwegian, Finnish and Sámi origins.

The first settlers came to Tromsø and Lyngen approx. 10 000 years ago. Sámi culture goes back at least 2 000 years. From approx. A.D. 300-400, Scandinavian language and culture were evident and from the 18th century, Lyngen experienced considerable migration from Finland. From around 1900, a strong Norwegianizing process took place in former Finnish and Sámi areas in Tromsø and Lyngen along with a great deal of depopulation in the districts.

From the end of the 1800s and for several decades into the 1900s, the cruise ships were almost queuing up to call at Lyngseidet in Lyngenfjord, on their way to the North Cape. Not only did the tourists experience the magnificent mountains that dropped straight into the sea, they were also taken onshore by rowboat and driven in horses and buggies up to the Sámi summer camps to see the reindeer and the Sámi dwellings. The Sámi at Lyngseidet were reindeer farmers from northern Sweden that for hundreds of years had brought their flocks to the summer grazing pastures on the Lyngen peninsula.

The Swedish Sámi and their camps on Lyngen peninsula lasted until 1965, after which they were no longer permitted to cross the border between Norway and Sweden with their reindeer flocks. Today, only ruins and foundations of bothies and tents remain as a reminder of that period.

69°52'N   19°50'E   + 1 hr 33 min ③

Nesodden point stands outermost on the relatively flat **Lenangen** peninsula. Behind Nesodden are the northernmost of the Lyngen Alps. There are several glaciers on these mountains. At 69°48'N 20°12'E is **Kvasstinden** (1 015 m above sea level) with the glacier **Vákkásjiehkki** and at 69°54'N 20°16'E is **Storgalten** (1 219 m above sea level) north of **Gammvikblåisen**, the largest glacier in the outer Lyngen Alps. Towards Lyngenfjorden, the mountains fall steeply into the fjord: (heights in m) **Vákkáscohkat** (1 398), **Stortinden** (1 240), **Rappgamtinden** (1 063), **Tverrbakktinden** (1 390), **Peppartinden** (1 252) east of Gammvikblåisen, **Ruossavárri** (816) and outermost on the cone-shaped peninsula is **Lyngstuva** (391).

Along the western side of the Lyngen Alps is the long, narrow, relatively low peninsula, **Lenangsøyra**, separa-

ted from the Lyngen peninsula by **Sørlenangsfjorden**. The village of **Lattervika** lies north of the small fell, **Nordheim** (355 m above sea level).

69°56'50"N   20°08'E   + 1 hr 34 min ④

The low, narrow headland, **Nordlenangsneset**, passes on the port side, just outside of Lyngen peninsula. The bay in Nordlenangen lies between the headland and the northern part of Lyngen peninsula. Along the western side of Lyngen peninsula, the settlements are spread, including the villages of **Nygårdstranda** and **Straumen**.

The outermost points of Lyngen peninsula are marked by the promontories **Sørklubben** and **Nordklubben**.

When King Håkon Håkonsson built a church and fortification in Tromsø in 1252, it was to mark the northern boundary of the area in which he could impose taxes on non-Sámi residents. The boundary was at Nordklubben (p 179, p 243).

69°59'35"N   19°34'50"E

Over on the port side, on Reinøya, we can see the mountains Rundfjellet and **Nordfjellet** along with the villages of **Søreidet** and **Nordeidet**.

Lyngenfjord, behind the Lyngen Alps on the starboard side, runs in a north/south direction.

We now sail past **Rundfjellet** (713 m above sea level) and **Nordfjellet** (655 m above sea level), before we leave Reinøya behind us.

After passing **Karlsøysundet**, just after Reinøya, we can see the small island of **Karlsøya** (8 km²) on the port side. Karlsøya was the former municipal centre and the site of the old rectory, where the region's largest newspaper, Nordlys, was founded in 1902. The newspaper was written and edited by the parish priest. The original church was built here in 1734 (relocated 1740). The local doctor and sheriff also lived on the island. Near the churchyard stands the old mortuary where the bodies of those who had died during the winter remained until the ground frost had thawed so they could be buried. The mortuary is now a listed building. Historical sources indicate that a church may have stood on Karlsøy as early as the 1300s, as an annex of Tromsø parish. Karlsøy's quay was built in 1830. The local merchants (known as 'nessekongene' – influential owners/traders, p 141) bought and sold fish and other goods. The quay now has a small store, a pub and a restaurant. The island has an interesting flora – several species of orchid grow here, more varied than in any other place in Troms county, and many types of plants have their northern boundary on Karlsøya. The island is linked to Vannøya and Ringvassøya by a ferry service.

&

The sound known as **Vannsundet** divides Karlsøya and Vannøya.

&

The island of **Vannøya** (also known as **Vanna**) (232 km²) on the port side has an elongated form and stretches from north to south. The island is mountainous and the highest peak is **Vanntindan** (1 033 m) above sea level. The name of the island originates from 'Vorn' or 'Varna', 'provider of shelter', referring to the open ocean just beyond. At one time, the island had several large fishing hamlets – most of these are now abandoned. There are several fish processing plants on Vannøya. Sheep, pig and reindeer farming are secondary activities. Settlement is spread around the western, southern and south-eastern sides of the island.

There is a ferry connection to Karlsøya and Ringvassøya.

Several large islands in Karlsøy municipality lie further eastwards out towards the Norwegian Sea. The most westerly of these is **Rebbenesøya** (80.6 km²), that has a car ferry connection to Ringvassøya, further northeast is **Grøtøya** (18 km², uninhabited) and east of Grøtøya is **Nordkvaløya** (85 km²) and **Helgøya** (43 km²).

The fishing ground known as **Fugløybanken**, which has been given its name after the small island of **Sør-fugløya** (70°06'N 18°30'E), lies west of Rebbenesøya. The fishing ground is less than 200 m in depth and is well known for its abundance of cod, haddock and halibut. Fugløybanken was one of the first areas in the north to be opened for petroleum/oil prospecting.

The ship continues north-eastwards, out of **Fugløysundet**. On the port side, we pass **Arnøya** in Skjervøy municipality (p 269).

&

Nord-Fugløy (21.3 km², population 0, approx. 100 000 birds) to our port side. The two highest mountains are the southern **Fugløykalven** (750 m above sea level) and **Rundkallen** (just behind, 740 m above sea level). The island is the northernmost in Troms county and stands in isolation out towards the Norwegian Sea, with Fugløyfjorden and Vannøya to the west and Arnøya in the southeast. The island itself and all skerries within 2 km of the island were designated as a nature reserve in 1975.

One of Norway's largest and most important bird cliffs is found on Nord-Fugløy. The cliffs are home to large colonies of Auks (Razorbills), Common Guillemots and

Puffins. Common Shags, Eider Ducks, Oyster Catchers, Arctic Skuas, Lesser Black-backed Gulls, Herring Gulls, Great Black-backed Gulls, Common Gulls and Black Guillemots also nest here (p 218). The cliffs are also home to one of Europe's largest groups of Sea Eagles (p 161). The island also has a very interesting plant life.

Nord-Fugløy fell into private ownership in the 1660s, when the Danish King sold off crown property. Due to the proximity to the rich fishing grounds, the island was inhabited up to the middle of the 1950s. A school was built and steamships began to call at the island at the beginning of the 1900s. In 1911, the island got its own post office. From the middle of the 1930s the island also had a telephone connection with the rest of the world via radio telephony. At one time, as many as 100 persons lived here and in the fishing season, this number could double with the influx of the seasonal fishing crews. During the stormy winter months, it could sometimes be weeks before boats could land on or leave the island, and so the inhabitants had to be self-sufficient in regard to most things. Some buildings actually had to be tied down with ropes, chains and steel wires to prevent them from being destroyed by the severe weather. Due to the harsh conditions, agriculture was limited, berry picking (cloudberries) and egg collecting were important activities. Egg collecting could be a dangerous activity and several people are known to have been killed whilst looking for eggs on the steep mountainsides.

In the period after the Second World War, Nord-Fugløya fell into decline. The local harbour and facilities were no longer adequate for the motorised fishing fleets. In 1951, the post office was closed down and a short time later, the last of the permanent inhabitants left the island.

&

Fugløykalven lighthouse is north of Stor-Fugløya. The lighthouse was built in 1920 and rebuilt and reinforced in 1956. The light is 41 m above sea level and has a range of 16 nautical miles. It was automated in 2003.

The ship now continues north-eastwards, towards Skjervøy, 22.00. This is covered in day 8 (p 261) on the southerly voyage.

Troms county

Coat of arms: Depicts the Bjarkøy family's coat of arms.
Origins of name: The former Finnmarken county was divided into Tromsø and Finnmarken counties. Today's name is from 1919.
Area: 25 877 km². **Population:** 154 136.
County seat: Tromsø.
We pass the following municipalities on our way northwards (in order): Ibestad, Bjarkøy, Tranøy, Dyrøy, Sørreisa, Lenvik, Balsfjord, Tromsø, Lyngen, Karlsøy and Skjervøy.
Topography: The outermost area and some fjord areas are characterised by a rugged landscape. Inland, there are several gently sloping long valleys. The inland mountain ranges have isolated high peaks. At many of the innermost parts of fjords, there is a low, flat neck of land.

Vegetation is sparse in the outer areas, where the oceanic climate is predominant. The tree line in this area is also relatively low due to the type of climate and latitude, but some valleys are low and sheltered and these have areas of productive deciduous forest.
Climate: There are significant differences in the coastal and inland climates due to complex topography. During the summer, the predominant winds are from north-north-east on the coast. In the fjords and valleys, winds blow towards the warmer valleys inland. During the winter, the wind is cold and blows towards the coast. Along the coast, the wind direction is often from southeast to southwest. The county does not experience stormy weather as frequently or with such intensity as the coasts of Nordland and Finnmark.

The coldest month is February with an average temperature of approx. -2 °C in the outer regions and from -6 to -9 °C in inland areas. The lowest temperature at the coast is approx. -10 to -15 °C and -30 to -40 °C in the inland valleys. During the summer, temperatures can rise to 28 °C at the coast and over 30 °C in sheltered inland areas.

Precipitation varies considerably. Most precipitation falls along the coast and on the coastal mountain ranges. There is relatively little precipitation in the sheltered valleys. Sometimes huge amounts of snow may fall in coastal areas. The outer regions may experience mists in the summer.
Population: About 56 % of the county's population lives on islands; (the towns Harstad and Tromsø are located on islands). The population distribution is very much affected by depopulation of scattered smaller communities and an increase in the larger villages and towns, especially Tromsø. The population growth in Troms county is less than the national average.

TRADE AND INDUSTRY.
Fishing: Fishing remains important for the county's economy. Fishing is very often combined with farming. Fishing is an important contribution to the local fish processing industries, which in turn require goods and services to support their activities. Fishermen take part in the annual fishing season in Lofoten and Vesterålen, and on the banks outside of Troms and Finnmark. All types of fish are landed and Troms is in fifth place in Norway in terms of volume of fish landed. There are also a great number of fish farms in the county.
Farming: Farming has been in decline since the Second World War and the average size of a farm in Troms is slightly under the national average. Many farmers combine farming with other forms of employment, such as fishing and building/construction. The farmers grow mainly grass for hay for animal feed, the animals in turn provide dairy and meat products. Cattle and sheep farming are most common, and the county has some of the largest goat farms in Norway. There is some potato, berry and vegetable production.
Industry: Moderately developed in comparison with the rest of Norway. Food processing industries, based on fish as the raw material are the most important. There is some mining activity (graphite) and a few shipyards, which mainly refurbish and maintain fishing vessels. Other industries include transport services, mechanical industries, metal smelting and metal production plants and a few timber mills.

Harstad is the main support and supply base for petroleum based industries in Troms.
Service industry: Considerable expansion after the Second World War. Mostly concentrated around the larger populated areas. Tromsø is the county seat, with many major education institutions, communications, health services and public and private services both for the county and large parts of Northern Norway. The Norwegian Armed Forces have several bases in Troms.
Tourism: The most popular attractions are the fjords, mountains and the midnight sun. Motorists pass through in large numbers on their way to the North Cape and from Hurtigruten.
Communications: Communications in the county are excellent. The main highway, the E6 runs through Troms. There are bridges, tunnels or car ferry connections between the islands and the mainland. Hurtigruten calls here twice daily. Tromsø has a large national and international airport, which also provides the main connection by air to Svalbard. Harstad's airport is at Evenes. There is a smaller civil/military airport at Bardu and several smaller airfields scattered around the county.
Language: Sámi and Finnish are spoken by minorities. Since 1989, all public signs are written in the Sámi language in addition to Norwegian.

Source: Store Norske Leksikon.

DAY **6**

Øksfjord, Hammerfest, Havøysund, Honningsvåg, Kjøllefjord, Mehamn and Berlevåg

During the night we have sailed passed the municipality of Skjervøy with the port of Skjervøy (72°02'N21°00'E Time: 2215 – 2245) in Troms county and have crossed the county boundary into Finnmark county. We have passed the municipality of Loppa with the port of **Øksfjord** (70°14'25"N 22°21'E, 0200 - 0230), and the municipalities of Hasvik and Hammerfest with the port of **Hammerfest** (70°40'N 23°41'E, 0515 - 0645). We are now in Måsøy municipality, heading towards our next port of call, Havøysund.

The ship continues to Havøysund	+ 0 hrs 00 min

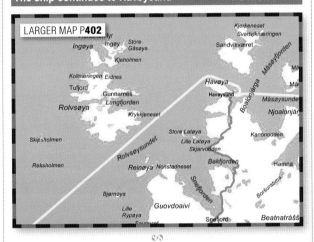

Approx. 70°50'N   23°54'E

We cross the municipal boundary between Hammerfest and Måsøy municipalities

Måsøy municipality

Municipal coat of arm, significance: Fishing.
Meaning of name: From name of the bird; måse, seagull.
Municipal seat: Havøysund (pop. 1 084).
Position: 70°59'N 24°41'E.
Area: 1 134 km². **Population:** 1 319.
Pop. density: 1.2 /km².
Area distribution: Farming 0 %, forestry 0 %, fresh water 6 %, other 94 %.
Trade and industry: Directly or indirectly related to fishing. Havøysund has slipways and a dry dock, mechanical workshops, fillet factory, and cold storage facilities. Extensive fishing fleet equipped for trawling and fishing with nets and lines. Fish farms. Windmill power generation. Sheep farming.
Places to return to: Måsøy museum.
Activities to return for: Sea fishing.
Måsøy municipality's home page: www.masoy.kommune.no

We have crossed an open stretch of sea before heading in to **Rolvsøysundet**.

70°50'N   23°56'E

The small island, **Bjørnøya** (129 m above sea level) is on our starboard side.

Aft and on our port side, we see the two small islands, **Skipsholmen** (175 m above sea level) and **Reksholmen.** Both are nesting areas for sea birds such as gulls and eider ducks. Reksholmen has a rich variety of nesting sea birds.

We are sailing into Rolvsøysundet.

70°53'N   24°04'E   ①

© KETIL OLSEN

On our starboard side is the island, **Rolvsøya** (89.4 km²) the largest island in Måsøy municipality with approx. 60 inhabitants. Before the Second World War almost 1 000 persons lived here during the height of the fishing season. By 1960, this was halved. Several projects have been launched to encourage young families to come and settle on Rolvsøya again. Newly established fishing-related industries may change the situation and perhaps help to increase the population on the island.

Rolvsøya is almost divided in two by **Valfjorden** and **Langfjorden** in the approximate centre of the island, in an east-west direction. We can see the mountain **Valfjordnæringen** (372 m above sea level) on the west side of the island. On the northern half of the island are the fishing villages of Tufjord in the west and **Gunnarnes** in the east. These communities are connected by a road, which is open all year round. A ferry sails to Havøysund and Hammerfest. There is a school and a general store in Gunnarnes, and a small wooden chapel (seating 77) built in 1986. The breakwater provides an excellent harbour.

Fishing has been Tufjord's main commercial activity for practically a thousand years. Most of the fish caught here has been dried and exported to southern Europe. People have lived in the village since the 14th century and have been part of the Norwegian settlement of the coast of

Finnmark. In 1520, 75 persons lived here. Tufjord was badly affected by an economic crisis in 1620 and the village was totally depopulated by 1640. In the years from 1701 to 1734, one or two families lived in Tufjord, but again between 1735 and 1787 the village was uninhabited. However, some time later, in the 19th century, people came back to stay. In Tufjord, there are remains of a church dating from the Middle Ages. It is said that the church was plundered and burnt by Russian pirates early in the 16th century. Immediately after the Second World War, Tufjord was 'adopted' by Tønsberg in an attempt to rebuild Finnmark. Aid in the form of temporary accommodation, ovens, lamps, tables and chairs was transported by boat from Tønsberg to Tufjord.

On Ingøya, near Trollsundet is a place called Djævelleiken. Here is the concise history behind the name and the two churches that were located here in the Middle Ages:
"Norway's religion was Catholicism from 1152 until the Reformation in 1537. The catholic churches were quite richly decorated with valuable inventories and thus they were often targeted by robbers. In Finnmark, the churches were sometimes plundered by Russian pirates.

In the 16th century, there was a church in Tufjord that contained many valuable objects. The Russians knew about the existence of these treasures. One day the Russians sailed into Tufjord and anchored up outside the headland, Kirkeneset, close to the church. At that time, few people lived in Tufjord and they were quite unprepared for such an attack. They fled into the mountains to escape from the pirates. The church was plundered and the valuables were taken on board the Russians' boats. Two men from Tufjord managed to get across to Ingøya to warn the people there that they could also be attacked by the Russians.

On Ingøya, a small force was mobilized, armed with axes, knives and spears. Lookouts were posted where it was thought that that the Russians would land. The Russians rowed across Trollsundet (between Rolvsøy and Ingøy) in stolen boats and came towards Inga, where the church stood. After a while, they met the villagers that lay in wait for them. The Russians quickly saw that they were outnumbered and tried to escape and hide but the villagers followed them and killed them all. Thereafter the place was known as Djævelleiken. The Russian sailors that had remained behind to look after their ships in Tufjord understood that something

had gone wrong and sailed away. The citizens of Ingøy saved their church and no Russians boats were ever seen there again."

A fish processing plant is now established in Tufjord. This is mainly because the fishing industry has modernised and centralised its activities, the fishing fleet is motorised and the fishermen do not have to sail to the nearest harbour to sell their catch. Some of these boats come from Rolvsøya, but boats from many other places deliver their catches in Tufjord during the winter and spring fishing seasons.

The houses in **Trollfjorden** were built around 1650. A whaling station was established here in 1893. The year after it was totally destroyed by high winds but rebuilt the year after that. In **Mafjorden** on Ingøya were two whaling stations, which remained in use until 1904, some say they were in use until the 1920s. The village of **Valfjord** was founded in 1724, and the parish, **Gunnarnes** was permanently settled in the second half of the 18th century.

Rolvsøya is very marshy with a rich bird life in the summer season and an interesting flora and fauna. Here we find the world's northernmost orchid, Royal Helleborine (Epipactis atrorubens) and the Northern Black-Tailed Curlew breeds here. In 1992, a new species of a parasitic wasp (Synara ocularis) was found on the island. Conditions for hunting, fishing, deep-sea angling and berry gathering are excellent. Many houses are empty and their windows are boarded up in wintertime, but during the summer, the population increases significantly. The island is a popular destination for holidays and many of the houses are occupied during the summer season.

Ingøya (18.7 km²) facing the Norwegian Sea just north of Rolvsøya is also nearly bisected by two fjords cutting in from the west and the east. The island is marshy with

high mountains and many smaller neighbouring islands and skerries that have a very special flora and fauna. The island is home to many nesting birds, including a large Sea Eagle (White-tailed Eagle) colony (p 161, p 218).

On Ingøya, traces have been found of settlements from the Stone Age. The finds include weapons made from slate and flint. Several burial mounds have been found, from the Iron Age (p 83).

Five hundred years ago, Ingøya was one of the largest fishing villages in Finnmark and was often described as a town, West-Finnmark's capital city. The most well known village on Ingøy is **Inga** with origins going back to the 14th century, possibly earlier. Around the year 1520, approx. 300 persons lived in this village, which was then populated by ship-owners, masters, ships' officers and the archbishop's representative ('setesvein'). These men managed the commercial activities for the archbishop in the villages in Finnmark and collected taxes on behalf of the church. Inga became the regional centre as most shipping activities had Inga as their end destination.

Ingøy Church was first mentioned in official documents in 1589. The church was the largest in Finnmark, it confirmed Ingøy's importance at that time and the

Town Hall/Assembly Hall was also the largest in Finnmark.

In the 16th century, the market and the price of fish were vital for the island's economy. Around the year 1600, the islanders began farming animals and fishing for their own needs because the market for fish was failing. By approx. 1690 Ingøy was completely uninhabited. In the 18th century, between 5 and 12 families lived on the island. The church was moved to Måsøy in 1747 and until 1866, Ingøy was without a church. A new church was built in 1866 but was destroyed in a storm in the 1880s. It was rebuilt shortly after, but was burnt down by the German forces during the Second World War. The existing church was consecrated in 1957.

Today (2006) approx. 35 persons live on Ingøya. The island has good roads, a church, a general store and a restaurant. New fishing-related industries are being established, which will hopefully lead to further growth on the island.

On the northern side of Ingøy is the fishing village of **Finnes.** It is assumed that this was once a seasonal fishing village, used by the Sámi population from the area during the summer season. The Sámi people traded their valuable products farther south in Norway and Europe. Ingøy was also the centre of the Hansa trade between Bergen and Finnmark. The Sámi settlers left Finnes during the economic depression in the 1600s (p 243).

After 1850, many new settlers came to Finnmark and the village grew once more. In 1895, a steamship quay was built at Finnes and a post office was opened in 1897. Around 1900, 104 persons lived here permanently, or 440 if the migrant fishermen and labourers were included. The village was active until the 1930s when the local economy collapsed due to the general worldwide economic depression. There are still remains of the old Ingøy Coastal Radio Station, which began operating in 1911. It was bombed and destroyed in the Second World War. The station's primary function was to maintain communications with the fishing fleet operating at sea north of Finnmark. It was not rebuilt after the war.

Ingøy Radio started transmitting in 2000. It covers all of the Barents Sea. The mast is 362 m high (one of Europe's tallest constructions) and weighs approx. 300 tonnes including the stays. In total, 44 km of copper cables have been laid in the ground, to provide adequate protection against lightning strikes.

Fruholmen lighthouse, the worlds most northerly, is situated on an islet northwest of Ingøya. It was commissioned in 1866 and rebuilt in 1949. It has an 18 m high concrete tower and the light is located 48 metres above mean sea level. The beam has a range of 19 nautical miles. In 1931, a weather alert station was established on Fruholmen from where the fishing fleet was warned of oncoming storms and bad weather. At the end of the Second World War, all the buildings and inventory were razed to the ground by the retreating German army. An auxiliary lighthouse was erected in 1948 and in 1964, a radio beacon was built that had a reach of 50 nautical miles.

Måsøy museum in Havøysund illustrates how life may have been on Fruholmen station and on all the lighthouses situated along this harsh part of the northern coast of Norway:

" Ingøy and Fruholmen are situated in an exposed area, where people always have had to struggle against the elements. The Gulf Stream (p 85) provides a milder climate than the latitude would suggest. The area is situated in a transition zone between the North Atlantic westerly winds and the Polar regions. Fruholmen is especially exposed – the storms rage with full force on this small island. Statistically, it is probably the country's most stormy location. There are on average 44 storm days per annum and 330 days with strong breezes or even stronger winds.

In addition, tidal variations can cause violent currents and choppy seas. This was the cause of many shipwrecks in the era when boats were powered by sails and oars. It was not just during the winter that the storms created problems; quite often, and suddenly, bad weather could also occur in the summer season and cause considerable damage. On 15th January 1882, possibly one of the worst storms in history raged in the area. A hurricane covered the whole island with sea spray and the windows in the lighthouse shattered due to the violent vibrations caused by the buffeting winds. Boathouses, the forge, shacks and fishing gear were washed away by the waves along with the station's boats, wood supply, dried fish store and equipment. The storm washed a stone weighing 6 tonnes, which they called "Negersteinen", onto the island. The flood wave created by the hurricane washed away fishing gear and equipment, boathouses and boats all over Ingøy. The postmaster lost his house and sheds (the animals were killed) – even the church was moved on its foundations, so much that it had to be rebuilt. Those living on Fruholmen hoisted the emergency flag requesting assistance, as the storm had damaged the fresh water well - however, it took six days before help could reach them due to the violent storm. The lack of fresh water was the greatest hardship for the families living on the station. There was no such thing as insurance cover for such catastrophes in those days, but a nationwide collection was organised so that the lighthouse keeper could be provided with a new boat and overcoat. Only a few days later, another hurricane set in and it felt as if all of Ingøy's foundations were shaken by the enormous waves and the foul weather increased the islander's plight. In another hurricane just four years later, ten fishing boats and two merchant's ships were lost inside Ingøy's harbour.

In the spring of 1932, the storms raged continuously preventing the fishing boats going out to sea. This

© NAM-YOUNG PAK

was disastrous for the island's economy and the situation became desperate for the local people. The worst hurricane in the previous century occurred on 28th December 1936, when the sea washed the beacon and navigation light into the harbour. The flood wave that followed swept away two quays, a cod liver oil production factory, and all the boathouses, resulting in a total loss of all boats and fishing gear.

On Fruholmen, they experienced a flood wave that flooded the station assistant's house and reached high up on the cowshed wall and further on to the boathouse –the whole courtyard was covered with seawater half a metre deep. The storm washed up stones weighing around 500 kg (these are engraved with the date and year). Cellars storing food were damaged and the well was filled with seawater. The lighthouse on the old tower shook so violently that the windows shattered. The same year, in February, they had 26 days with strong winds or worse (19 days with storms of hurricane force) whilst the month of March had "only" sixteen stormy days!

The hurricane of 6th January 1959 is remembered very well by the people living on the lighthouse at the time. The wind was so strong that they had to crawl on all fours between the houses. Facing the wind was impossible, the lungs were filled with air and it felt as if they would burst. There was frost and snow in the air and seaweed was blown up and stuck on the walls. The roar from the hurricane was deafening, the tethered houses groaned and shook as if they had the cramps. The wind speed went off the scale and the hurricane blew relentlessly through the night. The local ferryboat only just managed to stay afloat long enough to reach shelter inside the harbour.

In 1975, a hurricane and accompanying storm waves demolished two boathouses on Fruholmen and caused great damage to the quay and fishing equipment. As recently as in the spring of 2003 a hurricane washed away the steamship wharf in one great blast, including railway tracks and sleepers which it pulverised to matchwood and spread all over the island."

Northeast of Ingøy is the small island, **Store Gåsøya** with the fishing village, **Gåsnes**. Gåsnes was populated as early as the 15th and 16th century. The two fishing villages, Inga and Gåsnes were part of the early Norwegian settlements along this coast dating back to the years between 1250 and 1300. In the years 1701 to 1753, there were between 4 and 11 families living in Gåsnes, but the village was depopulated and lay barren from 1757 until approx. 1790. There were fishing activities on the island until 1970.

The world's most northerly sighting of a sea serpent is at 71°5'N on Ingøy:
In his youth, R. Eliassen, during the summer 1910 was with his father on Ingøy. One day when they were out fishing, they saw something that raised itself five, possibly six feet out of the water. It had a long neck and a narrow head. The creature had two 'humps'; one behind the neck and a larger one on its back. On seeing the beast, they pulled in their fishing tackle and rowed for the shore. The 'serpent' disappeared but re-emerged quickly and swam away with its head bobbing up and down just like a duck. After a while, it went below the surface and was not seen again.

70°53'30"N   24°05'24"E   ②

On our starboard side we pass the mountain **Skoltefjellet** (314 m above sea level) southwest on the island, Rolvsøya. Thereafter the bay, **Sørhamn** and the now uninhabited trading centre, Rolvsøyhamn.

Recent settlements in **Rolvsøyhamn** are from about 1880 and these lasted until about 1944. There was a store and a coalfish processing plant. Coalfish was the main species caught around Rolvsøysundet and the boats delivered their catch in Rolvsøyhamn. The 70 inhabitants were fully employed, and during the high season, extra help was imported. Ships from the so-called Hamburger-route called into Rolvsøyhamn to transport dried fish to the continent. The place remained active up to the time of the Second World War, but was not rebuilt after 1945.

After Rolvsøyhamn is **Dyfjorden** with **Vagnafjellet** (225 m above sea level). In the southeast we see **Krykkjeneset** where the English trawler, "Cardinal" was wrecked just before Christmas in 1925. The whole crew was saved and the members of the rescue party were awarded medals for their bravery.

On our port side, we have just passed the narrow, oblong island, **Reinøya** (142 m above sea level) and up ahead we can see the small island, **Reinøykalven** (94 m above sea level**)**. Reinøykalven is a designated nature reserve and an important nesting place for sea birds and for this reason, hunting on the island is restricted.

Reinøysundet separates the islands from Porsanger peninsula, which is a mountain plateau, typical of Finnmark (p 217).

We have already passed the wide fjord, **Revsbotn** (aft and on our starboard side). The village of **Kokelv** (pop. 230) is located at the head of the fjord. The majority of the inhabitants are Sámi (p 243). The chapel in the parish was raised by German peace groups in 1960 as a token of reconciliation from the German people for the damage caused by the German army throughout most of Finnmark during the Second World War.

"The Road to Havøysund" (Vegen til Havøysund) is fast becoming an independent concept. Route 889 that connects Kokelv to Havøysund is very special due its picturesque coastline. From the road, it is possible to see magnificent mountains and rock formations, beaches and valleys with trees and wooded slopes with rich bird and animal life. For this reason, it has been nominated to become a "National Tourist Road".

Outmost on the peninsula known as **Kvalnesklubben** just inside Reinøya we see the mountains, **Vestre Burstadfjellet** (471 m above sea level) and **Nordfjellet** (314 m above sea level). We are passing **Nonstadneset.**

At the head of **Snefjorden** is the small parish with the same name**.** During the summer, the Sámi bring their reindeer down to the area to graze.

After the mountain **Finnkonetoppen** (367 m above sea level) and the headland **Avløysinga** on our starboard side, the next bay is **Bakfjorden**. This beautiful but exposed place is now isolated. Today there is only a small quay and a few cabins left. Bakfjorden became famous

due to the support given to the Russian partisans by the local people during The Second World War. The houses were razed to the ground by the German forces in 1944 and the population fled into the mountain areas and remained there until the area was liberated in 1945.

Route 889 also passes a huge rock formation on the lower side of the road, known as Håkonstabben. When the road was built, it proved impossible to blow up this rock, even when they set the most powerful charges.

On the stretch from Bakfjorden to Havøysund are many remains of settlements more than 6 000 year old.

After having passed the mountain **Skjarvefjellet** (360 m above sea level) and **Skjarvodden** the next bay in Havøysund is Selvika, with a popular beach. During the War, some Russians hid from the German forces in a cave, which is now known as "Russerhulen" – "the Russians' Cave". It can easily be reached from the road. Outside and to the north of Selvika are the small islands of **Lille Latøya** and **Store Latøya**.

One of the many stories about sightings of a sea serpent along the Norwegian coast is from Store Latøy.
"Some fishermen from Kvænangen had been fishing in Havøysund. Near Knipen, they came across a serpent. They immediately rowed their boats to shore

and pulled them onto land. They sat a whole day on the shore, waiting for the beast to swim away. The serpent vanished when the wind turned northeasterly. The men decided to hoist sails and continue in spite of the heavy winds. Soon after, the serpent returned. The boats sailed side by side but the serpent came closer so they tacked towards Store Latøy into Sandkjeila on the inside of the island and thus escaped from the sea creature".

We are passing the mountain **Hestefjellet** (384 m above sea level), the headland **Nebben**, **Myrfjorden**, the headland **Nipa** (294 m above sea level), then the mountain **Nipfjellet** (388 m above sea level) and into Havøysundet and our port of call, Havøysund.

Ahead we can see Havøya with the windmills on its ridge.

70°58'N   24°20'E   ③

On our port side, we see **Kalvodden** on the east side of Rolvsøya.

On our port side we see Ingøya northeast of Rolvsøya. Far up ahead we see the depopulated island, Hjelmsøya and in front on our starboard side, Havøya with the windmills on its northern point.

71°00'N   24°27'E   ④

The narrow sound **Havøysund** is on our starboard side, between **Havøya** (7.2 km²) and the mainland. The island is connected to the mainland by a bridge built in 1988.

We are sailing along the northern shores of Havøya.

Stories of shipwrecks along this coast abound. In Rolvsøysund, just south of the windmill park the following tragedy occurred in 1941:
The steamship, "Richard With", named after the founder of Hurtigruten, was built in Trondheim in 1909. The vessel was registered to carry 300 passengers. On Saturday, 13th September 1941, "Richard With" was sailing southwards with 135 passengers onboard when she was hit by a torpedo and sank within one minute. A total of 102 persons lost their lives, including the ship's captain. The small Norwegian vessel, "Skolpen" was at anchor close by. Miraculously, the crew managed to save the remaining persons that were swimming in the icy water. "Richard With" was torpedoed close to Rolvsøya, bet-

ween Hammerfest and Honningsvåg by the British submarine, HMS "Tigris", which did not give the crew or the passengers onboard the ship any chance to leave the ship before it was torpedoed. The commander of HMS "Tigris" tried to bluff his way out of the situation by claiming that the ship was part of a convoy. However, the truth was soon discovered and the he was eventually given a verbal warning.

The wreck of "Richard With" now lies at a depth of 55 m."

On the northeast side of Havøygavlen, another ship was lost:
"The steamship "Hera" sank in a storm near Havøygavlen northwest of Havøysund on 18th March 1931. The ship was on its normal route southwards from Honningsvåg towards Hammerfest with 67 passengers on board when the accident occurred. The only means of navigation onboard were a compass and a clock and on this particular night, things went badly wrong. "Hera" ran aground on Havøygavlen and was damaged. Water gushed into the ship, which started to list so badly that the funnel fell overboard. In the collision, the lifeboats were smashed and the ship began to break up just in front of the wheelhouse. Captain Loose was an experienced sailor and took firm command of the rescue operations. 3rd officer Ramm volunteered to take a rope onshore, so that evacuation of the ship could begin. Six lives were lost in the freezing cold water that night in March 1931. The ship eventually broke up and in five metres of water, we can see "Hera's" motor and propeller. Most of the remaining wreck lies at a depth of ten metres. At the deepest point, approx. 30 metres down are her two enormous boilers. At Hurtigruten's quay in Havøysund a memorial stone has been erected to commemorate those who lost their lives that night."

Just outside Havøygavlen, close to the windmill park, a third ship was wrecked. The English trawler, "Ian Fleming" grounded on Gavlen on Christmas Day 1973 at 20.00, despite reasonably good weather at the time. Several boats from Havøysund took part in the search for the ship and its crew. During the rescue, 15 crewmembers were picked up from a life raft while four others, wearing only life vests, were picked up from the sea. One was picked up from the boat. Of the 20-man crew, three lost their lives. The crew was taken in to Havøysund. It was later found that if the trawler had maintained its course eastwards for just two more minutes, the vessel would have rounded Havøygavlen and the tragedy would not have occurred.

The island, Hjelmsøya with the steep mountains, **Knarr-viktindane** (297 and 274 m above sea level) plunge into the fjord up ahead and the silhouette of Hjelmsøystaven can be seen against the sky on the west side of Hjelmsøya. Thereafter we can see Måsøyfjorden between the islands, Hjelmsøy and Måsøy.

On the northern tip of Havøya we see the headland, **Havøygavlen** (285 m above sea level). In August 2002, the construction of the windmill park at Havøygavlen began and the park - the first of its kind in Finnmark - was officially opened in June 2003. The windmill park has 16 triple-bladed windmills, each 80 m high with a blade length of 38.8 m. Together they will produce approx. 120 GW of electric power, enough to provide electricity for 6 000 homes. The park is owned by Norsk Hydro (now StatoilHydro) and the Dutch energy company Nuon. Several more similar projects are planned along the coast of Finnmark. The greatest problem in building windmill parks so far north is in transporting the generated electricity to the largest group of consumers in the south.

The ship passes Havøya and enters Breidsundet and will soon be at the quayside in Havøysund.

The cave, Russehula, is located near the headland, which we pass as we enter the sound. The name has its origin from the Pomor trade (p 241). A Russian Pomor captain had been on a trade mission to Finnmark. He did not manage to sell all his goods and consequently a fair amount of unsold merchandise was on board his ship, which he did not want to take with him back to Russia. He decided therefore to store the entire cargo in the cave, which later was given the name, Russehula. It is said that Russians hid there during the Second World War. Today the cave is mostly visited by school classes.

During the War, both Soviet and Norwegian undercover agents operated along the coast of Finnmark reporting on shipping activities, military or civil, to bases in Murmansk. From Murmansk, actions were organised in the form of aerial or submarine attacks on shipping (p 220).

The ship docks at the quayside in Havøysund

The municipal centre and fishing village of **Havøysund** is located on the smallest of the five larger islands, **Havøya** (7.2 km²) in Måsøy municipality. Havøya is separated from the mainland by the narrow sound, **Havøysundet**. A bridge connection across the sound was opened in August 1988.

Havøysund was first mentioned in documents dated 1666, when a tax return form showed that two persons in Havøysund paid taxes that year. In the 18th century, 3 to 7 families lived here. The first trading licence was issued to a merchant in 1811 and at the turn of the century, a boat slipway was built that remained in operation until 1926. In 1928 a fish landing depot was established on the mainland side and a new slipway was constructed. Around that time another fish depot opened, with export of fish products as its main activity. In 1940 there were three fish processing plants in Havøysund. The fish was mainly prepared as salted or dried product and the first ever cold storage warehouse for fish was built in Havøysund.

Havøysund has expanded rapidly since the Second World War. In 1940, 300 people lived here – however their homes were burned to the ground by the German army as they retreated from Finnmark in 1944 (p 221). Havøysund was quickly rebuilt in the typical post-war rebuilding style that is so characteristic for Finnmark.

In the 1950s, Havøysund became an important fishing community once again and eventually had an impressive fleet of small and large fishing boats. Today, there are several factories, cold storage warehouses, fillet factories, fish salting plants, fish oil plants and a covered dock. Depending on the fish stocks, Havøysund harbour can be packed with boats and teeming with people or just a few boats off-loading their catch.

Havøysund church seats 300 and is a longhouse-style church built in 1960 in concrete and wood. Havøysund has a rich social and cultural community.

From 1838 until 1944, a bronze statue of the last French King, Louis Philippe was placed here in Havøysund. He visited Norway and Finnmark in 1795. He was pronounced as King of France after the July Revolution but for political reasons had to live in exile for many years in America and Europe, from 1793 to 1817.

In 1795, when Louis Philippe was 22 years old his travels took him to the Scandinavian countries and all the way up to the North Cape. From Trondheim he travelled in an open boat to Alta, overland to Hammerfest and from there again in an open boat to the North Cape and finally back to Alta - then on to Kautokeino and to Sweden. He travelled incognito, as did his companions. In Norway Louis Philippe enjoyed great hospitality and assistance from the locals, especially in Finnmark; "where such hospitality was very welcome in a country where comforts were so lacking".

Later, and as King of France he did not forget his friends in Finnmark. He sent them gifts and letters as a token of his gratitude. He also equipped three

expeditions that in the years 1838, 1839 and 1840 carried out scientific research along Spitsbergen's (Svalbard) west coast and the sea between Norway and Spitsbergen. The ship used for this purpose was the "La Recherche", carrying with her many scientists. In 1838 he sent a bronze bust of himself and other gifts as a reminder of his earlier visit as young prince. There is some uncertainty how the bust arrived at Havøysund, as his hosts were actually from Måsøya. It is assumed that by 1838 they were deceased and that 43 years later their next of kin had moved to Havøysund. The bust was given to the right people but placed on the wrong island.

Today the bronze bust is kept in Måsøy Museum in Havøysund. It has clear marks from the fire caused by the German soldiers' retreat in 1944.

The ship continues to Honningsvåg	+ 0 hrs 00 min

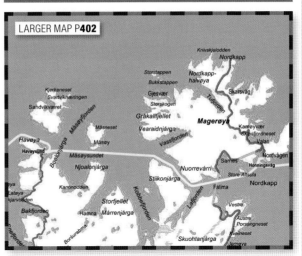

LARGER MAP P**402**

After leaving Havøysund the ship sails into **Breidsundet**.

Heading eastwards, we sail through Breidsundet and pass the island of Hjelmsøya on our port side. Måsøya is ahead and on our port side. Between the two islands is **Måsøyfjorden.**

Hjelmsøya (39 km^2) is second largest and most northerly island in Måsøy municipality. The island is totally depopulated and there are no public communications.

Like so many other places here in Måsøy, settlements on Hjelmsøya can be traced back to the times of the Vikings (p 83, p 123). The fishing village, **Keila** facing

© GERD-WENCHE BROCHMANN

the Norwegian Sea and **Knarvik** on the inside facing Breidsundet, were settled already in the late Middle Ages. The first settlers and seasonal fishermen came here probably in the 14th century. In 1522 there were 85 inhabitants living in Keila and 10 in Knarvik.

The fishing village of **Svartvik** on the north side of Hjelmsøya was founded in 1735 and has been populated up to the time of the Second World War. The fishing village, **Sandvikvær** in **Akkarfjorden** on the west side of the island was the last important fishing village on Hjelmsøy. After the collapse of the economy in 1970 the village was abandoned and Hjelmsøya became uninhabited.

© EILIV LEREN

The most northwesterly point on Hjelmsøya is the rock, **Hjelmsøystauren** (219 m above sea level), one of Europe's northernmost nesting sites (p 218). The rock face plunges 200 metres almost vertically into the sea below. At the foot of the large rock a finger-like piece of rock rises vertically out of the sea where Guillemots, Cormorants, Puffins, Gulls and Auks nest. Here we also find Finnmark's largest Sea Eagle (White-tailed Eagle) colony (p 161). This rock has always been very important for local people. They had the rights to local resources but disagreements were common, especially between the locals and the seasonal fishermen from farther south.

A legend from Hjelmsøy goes like this:
"On the northern side of Hjelmsøy is a small bay called Keila. On some old charts the bay is named Fuglevik (Bird Bay). The reason may be that the bay is close to the famous bird nesting rock known as Stauren. Immediately west of the entrance to Keila is a cave with its entrance at the tidal zone. This cave is called, Daumannsrevna (Dead Man's Cave) and it is associated with a story from when Russian pirates were raiding and plundering along the coast of Finnmark.

At that time there was a church in Keila. Like so many other churches in Finnmark it was full of valuable gold and silver. The priest and his family lived in Keila. One day the local people observed four Russian ships sailing into Svartviksnæringa towards Keila. However, a storm blew up and the Russians had to turn back. The priest was told of the ships, so he took all the valuables out of the church, and hid them in the cave near Keila.

Everyone believed that the Russians would return. Indeed they did, and anchored up on the east side of Hjelmsøy, as there was less chance of being discovered there. The raiders walked over the mountain to Keila. The priest was warned in advance of the threat from the Russians. He therefore brought his family, wife and four children to the cave and hid them there. The rest of the inhabitants escaped up into the mountains as they were outnumbered and had no weapons with which they could defend themselves.

The priest had a large pet dog that he was very fond of. The priest's wife asked him to kill the dog in case it barked at strangers and betrayed their hiding place. The priest refused and the dog went with them into the cave. When the Russians arrived at the church they found it had been emptied of all items of value. They realised that they had been observed and that the valuables were probably hidden somewhere. They began searching in Keila and the surrounding mountains. After a while they approached the cave where the priest and his family were hiding. The entrance was close to the sea and was difficult to find for those who were not familiar with the area. But when the dog heard that there were people outside the cave he began to bark and the family was discovered. The Russians then realised that the priest had hidden the church's valuables in the cave. However, they did not dare to enter the cave, as the entrance was so narrow that they could only pass one at a time. They decided to build a fire at the entrance. The smoke from the fire blew into the cave and suffocated the family and the dog. The Russians later found all the church's valuables and took them away with them. The bodies of the murdered family were left in the cave. In 1900, their remains were found, along with buttons and other personal items. The cave was after this named Daudmannsreva (Dead Man's Cave)."

Kulfjorden is now on our starboard side. There are two short bays at its head, **Vesterbotnen** and **Austerbotnen**. These have been declared "contingency harbours" in Finnmark in the event of an oil tanker spill along the coast of Finnmark. Several of these contingency harbours have been established along the Norwegian coast due to the expected increase in shipping activities to and from West Siberia and the gigantic Russian gas field, the Sjtokman (often called Stockmann) Field.

70°59'40"N   24°52'03"E   + 0 hrs 16 min ①

Måsøya (13.9 km²) has lent its name to Måsøy municipality. Today (2006) there are approx. 60 people living on the island, which has an active fishing community with a well-sheltered harbour, a fish processing plant, a church, school and a general store. The island is also home to a herd of approx. 40 wild reindeer.

© ROY ALLAN HANSEN

On Måsøya, facing Måsøysundet, the remains of a Stone Age settlement have been discovered (p 83). Permanent settlers came to Måsøy around 1660 to 1670. They had their own church as early as 1668. In the 18th century, 3 to 15 families were living here and by 1750, the population on the island was the largest in the district of Måsøy. For this reason, Måsøya became the main parish in 1746 and the church was moved here from Ingøya in 1747. The church was moved once again shortly after this, to Havøysund, mainly due to a decline in the local economy. In the 1850s, the economy had recovered and in 1865, the church was finally relocated on Måsøy. Now it is located in **Vestervågen**, and we can see it from the ship.

The well-known Norwegian psalm writer, poet and local historian, Magnus Brostrup Landstad was born on Måsøy in 1802. His father was the parish priest there from 1797 to 1804.

One of the most well known merchants around 1780 was Cort Peter Buck. He was host to the French Prince Louis Phillipe a few months in 1795, without actually being aware of the true identity of his guest. When Louis Phillipe later became King of France, he sent a bronze bust of himself to Buck, in 1838. However, in the meantime

Buck had died. The bust was handed over to the mayor of Måsøy municipality and placed in Havøysund (p 199).

Måsøya has a ferry connection with Havøysund.

There are many local stories of life here in Finnmark in former times, here is one of them:

From July to August, during a short period known as the 'worm' period (so called because of the seasonal infestation of fish by parasites) Russians often came to the coast of Finnmark to buy fish, mostly halibut, wolf fish and coalfish. During these particular months, the fish merchants would not (and could not) process the fish because parasites had infested the fish. The trade with the Russians was part of the so-called Pomor Trade (p 241), which lasted until the Russian Revolution in 1917.

During the spring fishing season, the local merchants would also buy the wolfish and halibut from the fishermen but they could also sell their catch on to the Russians. The price the fishermen got for their fish was poor - 10 øre per kilo for halibut and 50 øre per wolf fish, no matter the size. The fishermen chose therefore to sell directly to the Russians because they could get a better price when they exchanged fish for flour and corn. The Russians had other goods as well, such as timber logs and planks. Sometimes they would have textiles such as wool cloth and something they called 'klaverduk'- a thick linen cloth that was much sought after. These goods were very often sold on to local merchants.

Many years go, a Russian ship arrived at one of the fishing villages in Måsøy municipality. The captain was a handsome young man. Whilst their ship was docked at the village, he went ashore, as usual, in order to make personal contacts. The people in Måsøy enjoyed the visits; the visitors sometimes brought them food and came to visit them occasionally.

A young girl from the village, along with her friends, rowed out to the ship to buy nuts and sweets, which they knew the Russians always brought with them. This girl was exceptionally beautiful and the handsome captain fell deeply in love with her and frequently came to visit her at her home. She, however, would not have anything to do with him since she was already engaged to a boy from the village. Her widowed stepmother would rather that the captain courted the girl. She tried to talk her into accepting the handsome Russian but without success. The girl refused.

When the ship was ready to leave, it was customary to invite the local people on board for a farewell drink. The captain invited the widow and her stepdaughter, along with many others, on board for drinks the day his ship was ready to leave the village. The captain and the widow had secretly agreed the widow would get a whole roll of linen cloth if she managed to bring the girl on board with her. The girl came with her stepmother to the ship. When they were leaving, the stepmother got into the rowing boat first and the girl went to follow her. The captain embraced the girl thus preventing her from getting into the rowing boat. The girl cried in vain for help and the captain carried her down to his cabin. Immediately thereafter, the captain ordered the ship to set sail and the Russian ship left the harbour. The stepmother told the villagers that the girl had become engaged to the captain. They were to marry when they were back in Russia, she said. That was the end of a sad story!

Porsanger peninsula on our starboard side has few inhabitants. The landscape is rugged and vegetation is sparse. However, there are a large number of fresh water lakes, some are stocked with fish and in the summer season reindeer graze here. The area was formerly owned by the state, but the ownership has now been transferred to "Finnmark Estate". Finnmark county and the Sámi Parliament appoint a committee that is responsible for the management of the estate on behalf of the public.

We sail onwards in Breidsundet and continue into **Måsøysundet** between Måsøya on our port side and the peninsula, **Njoalonjárga** (336 m above sea level) on our starboard side.

On our port side, we see the island, Magerøya with the North Cape. The wide fjord, **Vassfjorden** cuts into the island's south-westerly side. On the north and on the east sides of the fjord respectively, we see the mountains, **Vassfjordnæringen** (257 m above sea level) and **Straumsnæringen**.

On our starboard side, after the headland, **Njoalneset** (336 m above sea level), we see the fjords **Ryggefjorden** and **Kobbefjorden** on either side of **Marreneset** with the mountain **Storfjellet** (376 m above sea level). The island, **Store Kobbøya** is in the middle of Kobbefjorden, thereafter we see the peninsula, **Stikoneset** (322 m above sea level). Both Ryggefjorden and Kobbefjorden are now uninhabited.

70°59'15"N   25°19'47"E   + 0 hrs 52 min ②

At the foot of the outermost point on **Stikkelvågnæringen,** on our port side as the ship passes the mountain, we can see a small rock formation. It resembles the figure of a woman looking in a westerly direction out towards the shipping channel.

The ship continues into **Magerøysundet**, the narrow sound that separates Magerøya from the north-eastern part of Porsanger Peninsula.

After passing Stikkelvågnæringen, on the starboard side we see the deserted community of **Stikkelvåg** with a few remaining scattered houses. A census from 1865 shows that six persons lived here; a fisherman, a merchant, his wife and four small children.

One of many "Finnmark-labyrinths" was found in Stikkelvåg. It is assumed that they date from A.D. 1000 to 1600. The "labyrinths" consist of stones laid in a certain pattern. One theory is that the stones were used in connection with Sámi rituals, in cemeteries, where the concept is of moving through the labyrinths towards the centre. The sites face the sea and are close to good fishing grounds.

On our port side, we pass the deserted village of **Finnvika**.

After Finnvika, we pass the bay, **Gaissevagge,** a distinctive, remote bay with mountains surrounding it in a kind of U-shaped ring.

Approx. 70°58'N   25°25'E

We cross the municipal boundary between Måsøy and Nordkapp municipalities

Nordkapp municipality

Municipal coat of arms, significance: Depicts the profile of the North Cape. **Meaning of name:** Last part from the Latin; caput 'head', used in the sense;' headland, point'. **Municipal seat:** Honningsvåg (pop. 2 417). **Position:** 70°59'N 25°57'E. **Area:** 925 km². **Population:** 3 274. **Pop. density:** 3.54 /km². **Area distribution:** Farming 4 %, forestry 0 %, fresh water 4 %, other 92 %. **Trade and industry:** Fishing and fish processing. Food processing industry. Service industry for the fishing fleet. Mechanical workshops. Tourism. **Places to return to:** North Cape, North Cape Museum. Gjesværstappan. **Activities to return for:** Deep sea rafting. Fishing. Diving. Bird watching. Various winter activities. **Nordkapp municipality's home page:** www.nordkapp.kommune.no, www.northcape.no.

On our port side is the island, **Magerøya** (436.6 km², 417 m above sea level). The island has a steep rocky coastline with a relatively flat, plateau-like summit. Like most of the larger islands in Troms and Finnmark, it has deep fjords stretching out towards the Norwegian and Barents Seas. The North Cape is located on Magerøya.

Our voyage takes us through the relatively narrow, barren Magerøy Sound. On both sides of the sound, we can see characteristic rock formations. At its most narrow point, the sound is only 1.8 km wide. Each spring thousands of poorly nourished reindeer would swim across the sound from the bleak Porsanger peninsula to their summer pastures on Magerøya. The military used their special landing craft to assist with the transportation, as many of the animals were so weak that they could not swim across. In the autumn, the animals would swim back, but now they had grazed on the rich pastures all summer and were well nourished. The landing craft were built in Bergen in 1972 and were sold in 2002 to private interests on the condition that they offered transportation to the reindeer farmers on a commercial basis.

The North Cape Tunnel was opened in 1999, and now most of the reindeer are transported on trucks to their summer pastures on Magerøya.

The ocean current in Magerøy Sound is amongst the ten strongest in Norway (p 162).

70°55'35"N   25°33'31"E   + 1 hr 18 min ③

On our starboard side we pass **Lafjorden** situated between the mountains **Stiikogáisa** (400 m above sea level) and **Slimmenjárga** (394 m above sea level). **Skatternjárga** (347 m above sea level) is on our port side. We are heading towards Honningsvåg.

Ahead and on our port side atop the mountain **Honningsvågfjellet** (389 m above sea level), we see a round radar dome. This is one of the newly-installed NATO-financed early warning stations, SINDRE II, which began operating in 2003. It is also used by Avinor for civilian air traffic control in parts of Finnmark and surrounding areas. The radar can be retracted into the mountain and completely sealed in the event of an attack.

70°56'15"N   25°43'N   + 1 hr 32 min ④

On our port side we see the headland, **Veidnes/Slimmenjárga** and on starboard side, **Vesterpollen/Guvllanjárga** bay.

On the headlands on either side of the ship, we can see two yellow-coloured square buildings. These are the transformer stations for the sub-sea power cables from the mainland to Magerøya. They also mark the location of the North Cape Tunnel.

Along Porsanger peninsula's east side (our starboard side) we see Route E69 heading southward, later it becomes the E6. In Norway, the E6 goes all the way to the Swedish border, to Svinesund Bridge near Halden in Østfold county. From there the road continues down through Europe. Route E69 continues north through the North Cape Tunnel to Magerøya and on to the North Cape.

The entrances to the tunnel on both sides of the sound are on the hidden sides of the headland. The tunnel was opened in 1999 after a construction period of four years. It was then Europe's longest and the second longest sub-sea road tunnel in the world. The tunnel is 6 875 m in length and runs 212 m under the sea level at its deepest point. The width is 8 m and it has a maximum gradient of 9 %.

70°56'32"N   25°47'E   + 1 hr 39 min

At the head of **Sarnesfjorden** on our port side, is the small, now depopulated community of **Sarnes**, which at one time had a trading post and a boarding school. Remains have been discovered of what could be one of

the earliest settlements in Finnmark, possibly in Norway. It is believed that the settlers lived in small family groups, in tent-like shelters and they would wander over quite large areas, hunting and fishing. The finds are approx. 10 300 years old. It is possible that these people came from the east, some historians claim they must have come from the south. They settled in these inhospitable areas when the mainland was still covered by ice (p 243).

For a period, Sarnesfjorden is to be used as a transit port for oil brought from Russia. The oil will be transferred to large oil tankers to be shipped out to the world's markets. Bøkfjorden, near Kirkenes (p 227), was originally selected as a transit port; However, Bøkfjorden is designated a national salmon fjord and so a conflict of interest arose between conservationists and the oil industry.

On our starboard side is the fjord **Kåfjorden,** the mountain **Slimmenjárga** (394 m above sea level) and the headland **Vestre Porsangneset** (57 and 46 m above sea level). The fjord is approx. 5 km long. Thereafter we reach **Porsangerfjorden**, Norway's fourth longest fjord, 123 km in length. At the innermost part of the fjord is the community of **Lakselv** (pop. 2 169).

The island, **Store Altsula** (175 m above sea level) on our starboard side, is located in front of the headland near the mountain Honningsvågfjellet, where there once was a fishing village, now no longer inhabited. Altsula is a nesting site for sea birds and a popular place to collect eider down (p 218, p 333).

Honningsvågfjellet passes on our starboard side, and our heading is set towards our next port of call, Honningsvåg. East of Honningsvåg is the smaller community of Nordvågen, which has now become part of Honningsvåg.

The ship docks at the quayside in Honningsvåg

Honningsvåg became the municipal seat in 1895, when new and larger motorised fishing vessels required better harbour facilities than the older Nordland boats (these used oars and sails). Close proximity to the fishing grounds was no longer a condition when choosing the municipal centre. Honningsvåg had a much better harbour than the fishing village of Kjelsvik (p 208), which had been the previous centre. The population increased all through the 20th century but was greatly affected by the peaks and declines in the fishing activities. Honningsvåg was granted a town charter in 1996.

Like so many of Finnmark's built-up areas, Honningsvåg was razed and burnt in 1944 during the retreat of the German forces. Only the church was left undamaged. It is a longhouse-style wooden church built in 1885. After the Second World War, the church provided shelter to the population who were busy rebuilding their homes. Honningsvåg is a good example of the prevailing architecture and town planning in the years from 1945 to 1960. Scattered around the town are a number of information boards suggesting walks around the town.

Honningsvåg is one of northern Norway's largest fishing ports. It has expanded and become merged with the former fishing village of **Storbukta**, further along the same inlet. In Storbukta, there are some large storage tanks. Some of these belong to the Hordafor Barents Company, which specialises in processing  waste products from the fishing industry. Honningsvåg is the last pilot station in Norway before the Barents Sea for shipping heading north and northeast.

With approx. 110 cruise ships calling annually, with approx. 63.000 passengers, Honningsvåg is amongst the five largest cruise ports in Norway. A limiting factor is the dimensions of the quaysides. Due to the ever-larger cruise ships and the small quays, the ships must anchor in the fjord and ferry passengers on land in smaller boats. The majority of cruise ships arrive during the summer, to enable passengers to see the midnight sun. Honningsvåg is a regular port of call for Hurtigruten with two calls a day, and the port is used by many coastal cargo freighters.

Honningsvåg is Finnmark county's centre for fisheries studies. The college building is close to the Hurtigruten quay.

Only approx. 40 % of visitors to the area arrive by sea. Most travel by car or by air. Honningsvåg has a short take-off and landing strip that is notorious for its frequent bad weather and difficult landing conditions. In October 1990, a Twin Otter belonging to the Norwegian Air Force crashed here due to extreme turbulence. Three people were killed in the accident. The nearest large airport is Banak airport in Lakselv, at the head of Porsangerfjorden.

Honningsvåg, in common with many other harbours along the route, has what appear to be 'fences' on the steep slopes and mountainsides behind built up areas. These are 'snow-stoppers', designed to prevent avalanches from falling onto the houses located in the most exposed areas.

Close to the Hurtigruten quay in Honningsvåg is the North Cape Museum, a local museum for the municipality of Nordkapp that has exhibits illustrating the coastal culture and fishing history of Finnmark county.

The German battleship, "Tirpitz" was severely damaged whilst anchored at Alta (p 268). The battleship was later bombed and sank near Tromsø (p 179). Tirpitz had 12 auxiliary engines (diesel motors/turbines and generators). One of these is located in Honningsvåg and another in Havøysund. The engine given to Honningsvåg was to provide extra electric power to the fishing industry after the war.

From Honningsvåg it is possible to take a guided bus tour to the North Cape (71°10'21"N), the 307 m high cliff best known as Europe's most northerly point. This is not quite true as the exposed point 4.5 km west of the Cape, **Knivskjellodden** (71°11'08"N), is technically the northernmost point. There is a marked tourist path to Knivskjellodden. The hike along the path is a return journey of 18 km.

No farming is carried out on Magerøya, but each year six Sámi families from Karasjok drive their reindeer flocks, approx. 6 000 animals, to graze here on the North Cape plateau in the summer. The plateau appears barren and bleak but approx. 200 different plants have been discovered growing here, some unique to the area. Along the cliffs, there are millions of nesting birds and the sea around the island is teeming with life. Marine species include Killer Whales (Orca), Minke Whales, Dolphins, Porpoises, and various

species of seals. Because of their vulnerability, all plants and animals on the plateau are protected.

On the way to the Cape we pass the fjord, **Skipsfjorden**, on our starboard side and the headland, **Skipsfjordneset** with the fishing village of Kamøyvær to the east. Thereafter the peninsula, **Fuglenæringen** (381 m above sea level) with the northernmost fishing village, **Skarsvåg** (pop. 140). After Skarsvåg is the fjord, **Vestfjorden** before the North Cape. Those taking the bus journey may also visit a Sámi summer camp.

The fishing village of **Kamøyvær** (pop. 130) was first populated in 1900. People came here from the rough coastal weather areas in Finnmark, and Sámi fishing families moved here as well as Finns from the forests across the border. Three cultures and three languages were melted together, but today Norwegian is the common language and the ethnic divisions are practically non-existent.

The fishing village of **Gjesvær** (pop. 190), located northwest on Magerøya, was connected by road to Honningsvåg in 1976. Cold storage facilities, fishing and fish-food processing are the main industries. The area around the village was populated in the Viking period (p 83, p 123), with a trading post and fishing activity. It was probably the first permanently settled site on Magerøya. From the Middle Ages and up to the 19th century, Gjesvær was one of the largest and wealthiest fishing villages in Finnmark. One of Europe's two most northerly birch forests is located near Gjesvær.

Gjesværstappan bird nesting cliffs is a group of nearly one hundred islands of various sizes. Among them are the steep, once inhabited islands of **Bukkstappen**, (92 m above sea level), **Kjerkestappen** (166 m above sea level) and **Storstappen** (283 m above sea level) just off the coast of Gjesvær. The islands are excellent land markers, and well-known bird nesting sites. The cliffs are home to Sea Eagles, Puffins, Fulmars, Auks, Eider Ducks, Cormorants, Sea Gulls and Frigate Birds. Approx. three million birds are believed to nest on the islands (p 218).

Nordkapphallen (the North Cape Hall) at the outermost tip on the **North Cape Plateau** was officially opened in

© EILIV LEREN

1990. The hall has 6 000 m² of floor space and contains a museum and historical exhibitions, a video show, restaurants, post office, chapel and a large metal globe placed at 71°N. In addition, there is a Thai pavilion and a souvenir shop. In 2005, there were 207 000 registered visitors to the Cape. A guided bus tour is arranged from the ship.

The North Cape was first named and placed on a map in 1553. In an attempt to find the North East Passage, the northerly sea route from Europe to China, the English explorer, Richard Chancellor, passed by the Cape. He was the Captain and Chief Navigator on the ship, "Edward Bonaventure", one of the three ships taking part in the expedition. He did not find the North East Passage but his was the only ship to return to England the year after; the two others were lost at sea. Chancellor had left his ship south of the Kola Peninsula in Russia and travelled overland by sledge to Moscow, where he negotiated a trading treaty with Tsar Ivan (the Terrible) before returning to his ship and so to England the following year. As a result of this expedition, "The Muscovy Company" (the English Russian Company), the first large British trading company was founded. On a similar expedition in 1555, Chancellor lost his life when his ship was wrecked on the homeward voyage in an autumn storm off the coast of Scotland.

The Italian priest and scientist, Francesco Negri, visited the Cape in 1664 and he later wrote in his diary about his experience and impressions from "the extreme north". The journey was partly made on horseback, on skis and in open fishing boats but his destination, the North Cape he describes as the most exciting place on earth.

From 1836 the paddle steamer, "Prinds Gustav" (124 feet, 215 tons, driven by two 40 HP steam engines) started her regular service between Trondheim and Hammerfest. From Hammerfest, it was relatively easy to get to the Cape. In the beginning, the paddle steamer sailed only during the summer months and called at Hammerfest every third week. In 1851, "Prinds Carl" also a paddle steamer, was commissioned to provide a service from Bergen to Hammerfest. In the course of the 1850s, the steamships also began operating through the winter months. Due to the poor navigational equipment at that time, these ships would only sail

PEDER BALKE: NORDKAPP

during the day. Later, several operators started regular steamship services to Finnmark.

Hurtigruten was established in 1893, with weekly sailings from Trondheim to Hammerfest. For the next two years, one new ships was added annually to the service, the last of these now started its journey from Bergen. Although none of these ships actually sailed all the way to the North Cape, they did bring tourists close to the famous plateau. The North Cape road from Honningsvåg to the Cape was first opened in 1956. From the time when the first tourists arrived in 1882 on the British cruise ship, "Ceylon", and up to the time of the opening of the North Cape road, visitors had to climb up the steep path from the jetty at Hornvika, southeast of the plateau. In the beginning, mostly Norwegian and British ships made this voyage. But from the 1890s and onwards, several German cruise ships made the trip up north. Amongst them were the Atlantic steamer, "Kaiser Wilhelm II" from Norddeutscher Lloyd and "Augusta Victoria" from Hamburg-Amerika Line. In the years leading up to the First World War, ships from many countries visited the Cape. Naturally, the outbreak of the war put a stop to tourism and it was not until 1921 that visitors began to visit the Cape again. The cruise ship, "Emperor of India" brought American tourists directly from New York. Famous visitors to the North Cape were Prince Louis Philippe of Orléans, King Oscar II of Sweden/Norway, Kaiser Wilhelm II of Germany and King Chulalonkorn of Thailand.

In 1925, Den Norske Amerikalinjen began operating cruises carrying Norwegian and American tourists to Bergen and the North Cape. The first ship was "Stavangerfjord", later came "Bergensfjord". In 1926, 32 cruise ships called at Hornsvika. Two reasons for the increasing interest in these cruises was the over-capacity in the American passenger market, due to stricter immigration laws into the USA, and another reason was the economic depression that meant the middle classes were less well off. Both the German Hamburger-Amerika Line and the British Cunard Line had expensive, exclusive sailings from New York to the Cape each year. In addition, first

German tourists, and later Norwegians became interested in "no-frills" tours to the North Cape.

The outbreak of the Second World War once again halted cruise traffic to the North Cape. In 1948 the Norwegian passenger ship, "Stella Polaris" returned to regular cruises and the first foreign cruise ship returned in 1951. MS "Oslofjord" belonging to Den Norske Amerikalinjen started cruises in 1955. After the opening of the road out to the Cape in 1956, passengers began to be taken out to the plateau by bus. By 1972, the last of the cruise ships had called at Hornvika.

The ship continues to Kjøllefjord	+ 0 hrs 00 min

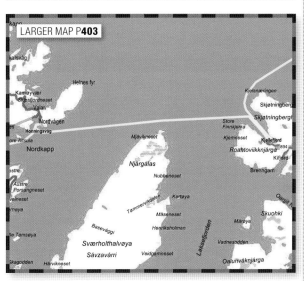

LARGER MAP P**403**

The ship leaves Honningsvåg heading for the next port, Kjøllefjord. Ahead we can see the near vertical cliffs on the peninsula, Sværholthalvøya. Over on our starboard side we can see Porsangerfjorden.

70°58'N 26°00'E	+ 0 hrs 10 min

After rounding the first headland after leaving Honningsvåg, we pass the village, **Nordvågen** (pop. 414) on our port side. Nordvågen is the largest fishing village in Nordkapp municipality. The economy is largely based on fishing and fish food industries along with mechanical workshops and boat slipways. The village was rebuilt after the Second World War

Porsanger Peninsula and Porsanger Fjord are on our starboard side and Sværholthalvøya is straight ahead.

70°58'N   26°09'50"E   + 0 hrs 12 min ①

The now uninhabited village of **Kjelvik** is on our port side. It was at one time the largest and most important fishing village in Finnmark. Kjelvik was the municipal seat up to the beginning of the 1890s when the new motorised fishing fleet required better port facilities. The centre was therefore moved to Honningsvåg, which had a better harbour. Kjelvik was partly rebuilt after the Second World War. The houses that remain are mainly holiday cottages.

Helnes with Helnes Lighthouse on our port side is the most easterly point on Magerøya. The lighthouse was built in 1908, to guide shipping from Archangelsk in to Magerøy Sound, and to assist the increasing shipping activity along the coast of Finnmark. Until 1966, families with children lived at the station. Today the station is de-manned and has become a tourist attraction.

In the Middle Ages, Helnes was an active and prosperous fishing village. During the spring cod fishing, many visiting fishermen would row out to the fishing grounds from here. The census of 1865 states that people spoke Finnish, Russian and Sámi languages, also Norwegian dialects from Trøndelag, Romsdal and Nordland. The harbour conditions were poor and often the Nordland boats had to be pulled on land after use. At the turn of the century, fishermen demanded that the harbour conditions should be improved. In 1905, Helnes got its first post branch and in 1911 its first proper post office. Steamships called here and a there was also a general store.

One of the first churches in Finnmark was built at Helnes, the date of the actual construction is unknown but we know that it was demolished (or moved) in 1694. The lighthouse is erected on the site of the old church and during rebuilding work carried out after the Second World War, human remains were found in the old cemetery.

Helnes lighthouse is a coastal station erected in 1908.

© KYSTVERKET.

It has a beam with a range of 17.2 nautical miles. The foghorn, a nautophone, was installed in 1949. Helnes radio beacon was installed in 1955. The station was modernised in 1996 and

equipped to broadcast calibration signals to the satellite navigational system Navstar GPS. The lighthouse was automated in 2004.

In the autumn of 1944, the German forces burned down the village of Helnes and Helnes lighthouse. The lighthouse was rebuilt in 1946 and re-commissioned in 1948; however, the village was not rebuilt after the war.

Nordkapp during the Second World War has also its place in the history books. The following is extracted from a lexicon article: "The Battle for the North Cape":

"The Battle for the North Cape" was a marine battle between the German Kriegsmarine and the British Royal Navy during the Second World War, fought in the waters around Norway's North Cape.

"On the 26th December 1943, the German 'Gneisenau'- class battle cruiser "Scharnhorst", and the destroyers "Z-29", "Z-30", "Z-33", "Z-34" and "Z-38", commanded by Rear Admiral Erich Bey, left Altafjord (p 268) on an operation codenamed 'Ostfront' ('Eastern Front'). Their orders were to intercept the Arctic convoys "JW 55B" and "RA 55A" on their way to Russia. The convoy, that had in fact been spotted three days earlier by a Luftwaffe aircraft, was comprised of 19 cargo ships and 10 destroyers. However, unknown to the German Kriegsmarine, the British Royal Navy had intercepted and decoded the orders and lay in wait for the German ships. The Royal Navy ships, under the command of Rear Admiral Robert Burnet, comprised of the cruisers "Norfolk", "Belfast" and "Sheffield". In addition, Admiral Sir Bruce Fraser's Home Fleet, comprised of the battleship "Duke of York" and the cruiser "Jamaica" and four destroyers followed at a distance.

The following day, the weather was stormy with heavy seas. Due to the weather, Luftwaffe aircraft could not patrol the area effectively and Rear Admiral Bey was unable to locate the convoy. Believing that he had sailed past the enemy, he ordered the destroyers to head southwards in an attempt to widen the effective search area. Admiral Fraser, who had expected a German attack, had split the convoy to the north outside of the area in which they were expected to sail.

The "Scharnhorst", which was now alone, met Burnett's cruisers shortly after 0900. At a distance of almost 12 km (6.5 nautical miles), the British ships opened fire. "Scharnhorst" returned fire. The cruisers were not hit; however, the German ship was hit twice – destroying the radar equipment thus leaving Scharnhorst sailing relatively 'blind' in an approaching snowstorm. Due to the lack of radar, the gunners on board the battleship could only sight their guns on the enemy's muzzle flashes – this was made difficult as two of the British cruisers used non-flash ordnance. Rear Admiral Bey, now completely outgunned and believing he faced a battleship, turned his ship south-eastwards in a attempt to escape.

Shortly after 1200, "Scharnhorst" once again encountered the convoy's escorting cruisers, including the British battleship the "Duke of York". Despite suffering major damage, "Scharnhorst" set a course southwards and temporarily increased the distance from its pursuers. After several hours on the run, being hunted the whole time by Burnett's cruisers, the "Scharnhorst" was finally caught up by the British battleship the "Duke of York". "Scharnhorst" came under fire at a range of 11 920 yards. The 'A' turret of the German ship was destroyed, which also detonated the charges in the 'A' turret ammunition magazine. A short time afterwards the cruisers "Norfolk" and "Belfast" opened fire. Despite the fact that Admiral Bey was able to put some distance between his ship and the Royal Navy, his luck ran out at 1820, when a grenade pierced the ship's armour and destroyed the main boiler room. "Scharnhorst"'s speed was thus reduced and the ship could only sail at 22 knots. The ship was now vulnerable to the Royal Navy's smaller destroyers. Five minutes later, in a desperate situation, Admiral Bey sent a radio message to the German Kriegsmarine Command: To: Der Führer! We shall fight until the last grenade is fired!" At 1850, Fraser's destroyers closed in and fired four torpedoes at the "Scharnhorst"; one struck the ship on the starboard side and three on the port side. Despite the immense damage caused, the German ship continued to maintain a speed of some 20 knots. The torpedo hits were followed by

four successful barrages from both the "Duke of York" and "Norfolk". "Scharnhorst" returned fire from its remaining guns. The Royal Navy subjected the battle cruiser to intense fire, and the cruisers "Jamaica" and "Belfast" fired their remaining torpedoes at the "Scharnhorst" that by now had lost speed. The "Scharnhorst"'s fate was sealed when the British destroyers fired nineteen more torpedoes at the ship. Severely damaged and unable to escape, the "Scharnhorst" finally capsized and sank at 1945. Of a crew of 1 968, only 36 survivors were picked up from the freezing water. Rear Admiral Bey was not among those who survived.

⚓

We cross the fjord **Porsangerfjorden,** on our port side. The fjord is Norway's fourth longest (123 km from Sværholtklubben to Lakselv in the inner part of the fjord). Like many of the fjords in Finnmark, Porsangerfjorden is different from the fjords in western Norway, in that it resembles more of a wide sea bay. The fjord is 17 km wide at the mouth, 20 km further in towards the head. In the innermost part of the fjord, there are a number of small islands and islets. At the head of Porsangerfjorden is the community and communications centre of **Lakselv** (pop. 2 159), Banak airport and Banak fort. The original airstrip at **Banak** was built by the German forces in 1941-42, to provide a base for aircraft that flew to attack the convoys sailing to Murmansk. It was expanded after the war and is now used by civil and military aircraft.

Porsangerfjorden is no longer rich in fish resources; however, there are great numbers of seals. A commercial sea urchin project is now in progress. In the inner, shallow part of the fjord, there are extensive wetlands that are used as stop-overs by flocks of migrating waders in the autumn and spring. The entire inner fjord area is worthy of protection and is considered one of the most important wetland areas in Scandinavia.

⚓

The island of **Store Tamsøy** is in the outer part of Porsangerfjorden.

⚓

Sværholthalvøya peninsula, on our starboard side, is between Porsangerfjorden and **Laksefjorden**. The steep mountainsides are characteristic of the area. The mountain plateau above is relatively flat. **Saufjell** (577 m above sea level) is the highest point. The outermost part of the peninsula is uninhabited.

⚓

70°58'50"N   26°41'20"E   + 1 hr 03 min ②

Sværholtklubben (166 m above sea level) stands as a separate headland outermost on Sværholthalvøya peninsula. It is a designated nature reserve and a well-known landmark in the area. 'Klubben' is regarded as Norway's third largest bird cliff. One of the world's largest bird colonies is found here. During the breeding season there are as many as 55 000 breeding Kittiwake pairs (p 218).

The village of **Sværholt** is on the northeast side of the low isthmus between Sværholtklubben and the mainland. It has a varied history as an old fishing village and defence post during the English blockade of the Norwegian coast between 1807 and 1814 (p 85). During the Second World War, the German forces built a large coastal artillery fort on the top of the cliff, to cover the approach to both Porsangerfjorden and Laksefjorden. The German commanders believed that an invasion of Northern Norway was imminent, a belief that was confirmed by the many air raids carried out by Allied aircraft against targets in Lofoten (p 159). The fort's various sections were connected by tunnels constructed inside the mountain. The fort was constructed using forced labour, mainly Russian prisoners of war. Remains of the fort can still be seen. Sværholt was destroyed in 1944, however the population returned after the war had ended. The village is now uninhabited.

Approx. 70°59'N   26°41'E

We cross the municipal boundary between Nordkapp and Lebesby municipalities at Sværholtklubben. The boundary is also the demarcation of West and East Finnmark regions

Lebesby municipality

Municipal coat of arms, significance: Mountain range of Finnkirka, west on Nordkinn peninsula.
Meaning of name: From Norse Lidvards-byr, Lidvard farm, or from Sámi læibes, 'older'.
Municipal seat: Kjøllefjord (pop. 919).
Position: 70°57'N 27°21'E. **Area:** 3 459 km².
Population: 1 357. **Pop. density:** 0.4 /km².
Area distribution: Farming 0 %, forestry 0 %, fresh water 6 %, other area 94 %.
Trade and industry: Fishing and fish processing. The fishing fleet is largely made up of smaller vessels. Fish farms. Some agriculture in villages near Laksefjord. Grazing and calving areas for reindeer.
Places to return to: Kjøllefjord.
Lebesby municipality's home page: www.lebesby.kommune.no.

Laksefjorden (75 km in length) on the starboard side is a typical Finnmark bay/fjord and the 13ᵗʰ longest in Norway. It is wide and open and has several 'arms'. One of these is **Adamsfjorden** with the spectacular 37 m high

Adamsfossen waterfall. The village of **Kunes** is innermost in the fjord. At the head of the fjord and on the peninsulas on either side are areas used for herding reindeer and for grazing and calving.

Ahead is the bleak **Nordkinn** peninsula with its steep coast. The peninsula is connected to the mainland at **Hopseidet**, a narrow isthmus between Eidsfjorden in the west and Hopsfjorden in the east. The isthmus is 2 km wide at low tide, 500 m wide at high tide and the highest point is 2.5 m above sea level. In the 17ᵗʰ century, there were settlements here and a church near Hopseidet. The population today is very

© ROLF LILAND

sparse. There have been many debates and discussions concerning the construction of a ship canal across the narrow isthmus, so that boats may avoid the exposed sea round Nordkinn peninsula.

Nordkinn road, Route 888, runs from Mehamn on the northern end of the peninsula, over Hopseidet to **Bekkarfjord** in Laksefjord. Route 888 is widely accepted as Norway's most difficult stretch of road during the winter. Motorists must use the ferry between Kjøllefjord and Bekkarfjord when the road is closed.

On the mountain **Gartefjellet** (303 m above sea level) ahead, there are 17 generator windmills, erected in 2006. The annual amount of electricity produced by the generators is approx. 150 GWh, which is equivalent to the average consumption of 7 500 households.

Europe's northernmost mainland point Kinnarodden, is on Nordkinn peninsula. The North Cape is on an island, Magerøya.

We will soon arrive at the municipal centre and village of Kjøllefjord at the head of Kjøllefjorden (10 km in length). The fjord is surrounded by the peninsulas of Dyfjordhalvøya in the south and Skjøtningberghalvøya in the north.

70°59'N   27°08'E   + 1 hr 42 min ③

On the shoreline of the steep headland close to the mountain **Vindhamran** (313 m above sea level), near the southern mouth of Kjøllefjorden, are the spectacular cliff formations **Store Finnkjerka** and the more well known **Lille Finnkjerka**. The cliffs, formed by the sea, are reminiscent of cathedrals with spires and towers and

are often referred to as 'the most distinctive cliffs on the coast'. The cliffs were first climbed in 1955. It is said that Finnkjerka may once have been used by the Sámi as a place of sacrifice.

The ship docks at the quayside in Kjøllefjord

The community and administrative centre of **Kjøllefjord** is one of the largest fishing communities in Finnmark. As early as the 16th century, trading took place here. In 1690, Finnmark was divided into seven trading districts. The district known as Omgang (on the northeastern end of Nordkinn peninsula) and Kjøllefjord traded with the Sámi in the areas south of the peninsula, in Laksefjord and Tana. The Norwegian author Jonas Lie (1833-1908) wrote in one of his novels from Kjøllefjord about the way of life here around 1750: "Kjøllefjord is a gathering place for the goods and produce of Finnmark, that are loaded onto ships from Bergen and Denmark, and the village is a port of call for Russian sloops trading along the coast and as a refuge for foreign ships sailing the seas to Archangelsk. The place is always a hive of activity". At that time Kjøllefjord was a larger trading port than both Vardø and Vadsø further east.

In 1944, when the German occupying forces retreated from Finnmark, the trading post was burnt to the ground. Only four houses remained. All the residents of Kjøllefjord (approx. 700 persons) were evacuated. Most of them returned when the war ended. A new town plan was drawn up and the rebuilding started. Nine new fishing wharves were established, business began to thrive and the fishing fleet quickly expanded.

Kjøllefjord church was consecrated in 1951. The fine stone church with seating for 300 was the first church

to be rebuilt after the war. The church was a gift from Danish church communities, and was built "in gratitude for Denmark's escape from the destruction of the war and as a symbol of a deep sympathy for our brethren in the north". The church is a somewhat larger version of the original 200-year old church that was burnt down in 1944. There has been a church on the site from around 1670. The church has King Fredrik II's bible from 1589 that was rescued when the last church was destroyed.

In 1974, an airfield was built for the air ambulance service near Kjøllefjord.

Today, activities in Kjøllefjord have declined. The fishing fleet has also been reduced. However, the remaining boats are varied and quality is good. There are two fish processing plants – their future depends on the availability of raw materials, something that varies considerably. The municipality itself is the largest employer. Kjøllefjord has all the facilities required of a small, modern community, such as schools, swimming pool, large sports hall, library, local cinema and a hotel.

The ship continues to Mehamn   **+ 0 hrs 00 min**

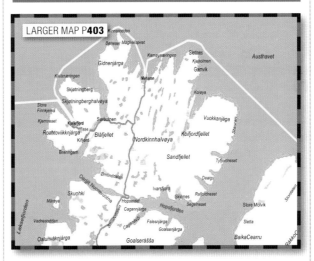

LARGER MAP P**403**

Just after leaving Kjøllefjord, we pass the restored **Foldalsbruket**, said to be the largest wooden building in the region. The wharf was built in 1917 as a conventional fish and oil processing plant. The cod was hung on racks and dried, the cod liver was used to make cod liver oil. The final products were then sent to the south of Norway. Foldalsbruket had its own quayside that was in use between 1927 and 1959. In 1987, Foldalsbruket went bankrupt and gradually became derelict. Recently, the plant and quayside have been restored and it is now used as a centre for coastal culture.

Foldalsbruket shows just how the fishing industry worked and has wharves/packing houses and sheds used to clean the fish, the fisherman's cabins and bait sheds, the cod liver oil processing plant and the offices/house. In front of the building are the large wooden quaysides, and the slope behind the plant is where the large fish drying racks once stood.

The building has 4 storeys. On the ground floor is where the fish was salted. On the first floor, packing cases were made and on the second floor, fish was dried. Much of the equipment used in production, such as the crushed ice machines, dried fish press, machines for manufacturing packing cases, saws, ice pincers etc. remain and these illustrate the production process from landing the fish until the final product.

On the port side, at the outermost headland near the mountain Vindhamran we can see the silhouettes of Store Finnkjerka and Lille Finnkjerka.

We sail past two peninsulas - **Dyfjordhalvøya** on the port side and **Skjøtningsberghalvøya** on the starboard side.

71°00'N 27°12'E	+ 0 hrs 22 min ①

Bøneset, Sandfjorden and Kinnarodden.

We pass **Svartnakken** and **Kvitnakken** two cone-shaped, wide, monumental cliffs formed of an especially hard type of stone, one white and one black. The cliffs are on either side of a narrow cleft. Just beyond is the rock projection known as **Alteret.**

The ship now turns around the sheer headland of **Kjøllefjordneset** (324 m above sea level), before heading north east.

71°08'40"N 27°39'26"E	+ 0 hrs 38 min ②

We round the mountain known as **Kjelsnæringen** (298 m above sea level), with its characteristic outer 'horn', at the mouth of Oksefjorden. The word 'næring' in this context is defined as "high, steep rock face (on a headland) out towards the sea".

Just inside the mountain of **Kjelsnæringsfjellet** is **Skjøtningsberg,** a now uninhabited fishing village from the 15th century. At that time, the village was a major fishing centre with a population of 200-250. In 1589, the main church on Nordkinnhalvøya was located here. In 1903, there were 703 active fishermen. As long as fishing vessels were rowed and sailed, Skjøtningsberg remained a central place. During periods of bad weather, the boats could be taken ashore. However, this was not possible with the larger, motor powered boats. The poor harbour facilities led to the relocation of the fishing fleet, along with most of the fishing activities.

In recent times, **Oksefjorden** has been associated with whaling. In 1898-1903, whaling was carried out from land-based stations. The entire place was burnt to the ground in 1944. The remains of the whaling station, a 3 m long steaming vessel, is still visible. Close to Oksvågen Land Station, further inside the fjord is one of the world's two most northerly birch forests (the other is near Nordkapp).

71°06'N 27°26'50"E	+ 0 hrs 55 min

On the north side of Oksefjorden are the characteristic cliffs near **Engelsnæringen**.

71°07'31"N 27°33'38"E	+ 1 hr 05 min ③

We pass the headland **Bøneset** (310 m above sea level). Behind the headland, the fjord **Sandfjorden** opens up. Ahead we can see the cliff, **Kinnarodden**.

Innermost in Sandfjorden, at the end of the last Ice Age, large masses of rock and gravel were pushed down from the mountains. These were then levelled by the sea waves. This flat area later rose to form a 'terrace'. Sandfjorden has been populated at one time, these people traded and sold fish and other goods. The area is now a protected area and has a rich bird life and colonies of seals.

71°08'39"N 27°39'52"	+ 1 hr 13 min ④

We round the cliff at **Kinnarodden.** At 71°08'31"N this is the northernmost point of the European mainland. The cliff is 234 m above sea level.

© BERIT LILAND

The area before Kinnarodden is bleak and is only accessible on foot or by boat. As the area is becoming a popular place for tourists, a path marked by stone cairns has been created. It was officially opened in 2004. The path begins near Mehamn airport and is approx. 23 km in length.

At the Kinnarodden plateau, two Junker JU-88 aircraft crash landed during the Second World War. In 1999, the aircraft remains were transported to Bodø to be preserved and rebuilt. Of the approx. 1 500 aircraft of this type that were built, only five remain in existence.

We cross the municipal boundary between Lebesby and Gamvik municipalities as we pass Kinnarodden

Gamvik municipality

Municipal coat of arms, significance: Depicts fishing.
Meaning of name: Probably Gangvik, from Norse gangr, 'grazing for farm animals'.
Municipal seat: Mehamn (pop. 688).
Position: 71°02'N 27°50'E.
Area: 1 414 km². **Population:** 1 046.
Pop. density: 0.7 /km².
Area distribution. Farming 0 %, forestry 0 %, fresh water 3 %, other area 97 %.
Trade and industry: Fishing and fish processing. Fishing fleet comprised of mainly open, coastal boats along with some larger, offshore vessels. Grazing grounds for reindeer from Karasjok. Tourism.
Places to return to: Brodtkorb wharf. Gamvik Museum. Kinnarodden. Slettnes lighthouse. Slettnes nature and cultural heritage area.
Activities to return to: Hiking to Kinnarodden. Bird watching.
Gamvik municipality's home page: www.gamvik.kommune.no

| **71°08'N   27°37'E** | **+ 1 hr 15 min ⑤** |

We now head south-eastwards towards the fishing community of Mehamn. Ahead we can see the headlands of Kamøynæringen and **Vadnesodden**.

| **71°07'36"N   27°45'E** | **+ 1 hr 22 min** |

We now pass the characteristic **Magkeilspiret** (300 m above sea level) in **Magkeilfjorden** (starboard side). The Coastal Administration authority has decided that the fjord is to be one of 15 'contingency harbours' in Finnmark that will be used as emergency harbours for stricken vessels and for landing of wrecks etc. The reason for the decision is the increasing transport of petroleum-based products along the Finnmark coast, from West Siberia to Europe and the USA.

| **71°06'41'N   27°47'E** | **+ 1 hr 29 min** |

Ahead is the headland on the mountain **Smørbringen** (179 m above sea level), and further ahead on the eastern side of **Mehavnfjorden** is Kamøynæringen.

We round Smørbringen and sail into Mehamnfjorden.

The ship docks at the quayside in Mehamn

The administrative centre and fishing community of Mehamn is one of the communities in Finnmark that is totally dependent on the supplies of fish from the sea. Mehamn is regarded as having one of the best harbours in Finnmark. In the 1960s, there were approx. 10 fish processing plants in Mehamn; only one of these remains today. Fish, fish processing and associated industries are still the most important commercial activities in Mehamn.

Today, new commercial ventures are in progress or planned. Catches of Red King Crabs are exported to Spain and Japan, dried fish is exported to Eastern Europe and

were powerless. They saw that the reduction in the number of whales, due to over-exploitation, could lead to a reduction in the fish catches. Appeals to the authorities to stop the exploitation of the whale stocks were not heard. Hearings and discussions in Parliament were repeatedly postponed. In 1903, after yet another delay, the fishermen took the matter into their own hands. 1 200 fishermen stormed the whaling station in Mehamn. The buildings were demolished, machinery destroyed and the oil tanks were emptied. What was left was in ruins. The fishermen threatened to repeat their actions at the whaling station in Oksfjord (we have just passed the area). Military forces were called in to restore law and order. Several of the leaders of the uprising were jailed. Whales were protected by law the following year; however, the whales had already almost disappeared in the area.

In modern times, Mehamn has become well known in Norway due to the 'Mehamn air tragedy'. In March 1982, a Twin Otter aircraft with 15 persons on board crashed southeast of Gamvik (p 216). All those on board were killed. The Accident Investigation Board's original report was not accepted by some people, however a new independent investigation commissioned by parliament found in 2005 that the accident was caused by a fault in the aircraft's elevator, combined with strong turbulence in the area.

Mehamn airport was opened in 1974. It is a short take-off and landing airport with tarmaced runway, 800 m in length.

The ship continues to Berlevåg	+ 0 hrs 00 min

Mehamn is behind us as we head out into Mehamnfjorden. We pass the steep headland **Kamøynæringen** (137 m above sea level), then **Bispen** (230 m above sea le-

Africa, fresh and frozen fish is sold in Scandinavia and Europe and salt fish to Spain

The dependence on fish supplies was the underlying reason for the famous Mehamn-uprising in 1903. There were a considerable number of whales in the area and the fishermen saw their own advantages in the relationship between whales and fish stocks. They believed that the fish, in escaping from the huge, greedy fish-eating whales, swam to safety into shallow waters, where the fishermen could reap huge catches of fish. When whaling began to develop in the 1870s and wealthy capitalists from southern Norway began to build specialised whaling stations, also here in Mehamn, the fishermen

vel), **Sandfjorden** and **Vadnesodden**, with Slettnes lighthouse.

In **Sandvågen,** just before Vadnesodden, under the mountain **Steinvågaksla** (220 m above sea level) is the now uninhabited trading post of **Steinvåg**. The small bay has been inhabited since the 17th century and Sámi burial sites indicate a coastal Sámi history. Steinvåg was one of six places in Finnmark that were centres of Pomor trade. This trade began in 1720 and continued up to the time of the Russian Revolution in 1917 (p 241).

Two of the small inlets before Vadnesodden have remarkable names, such as **Hollendervika** (Dutch Bay). The name is said to originate from a Dutch ship, loaded with a cargo of timber that was wrecked here around 1860. It may also be from the time Dutch whalers visited the site. Another place is **Daumannsvika** (Dead Man's Bay), that, as the name readily indicates, received its name due to the many shipwrecked and drowned sailors that washed up on shore in the bay.

Slettnes nature reserve, approx 12 km², between Vadnesodden and Slettnes lighthouse is inland of the coast. The flat coast area distinguishes itself clearly from the remaining mountain terrain found elsewhere on Nordkinn peninsula. As many as 95 different species of birds have been observed in the nature reserve, 53 of these species breed here every year. Slettnes nature reserve is one of Scandinavia's most important, both as a stop-over point for migrating birds and as a breeding area for waders, gulls and ducks. Norwegian and foreign researchers come here every year to register and observe the bird life and the results of their research contribute to international studies of wading birds. Slettnes nature reserve is a protected area.

Slettnes lighthouse was commissioned in 1905 and is the world's most northerly mainland lighthouse. It has a 39 m high cast iron tower, the only one of its type in Finnmark and it is one of Norway's tallest lighthouse towers. There are 130 steps up to the top of the tower. The light is 44 m above sea level and the range is 17.6 nautical miles. A foghorn installed in 1922 was in operation until 1944. As is the case with other lighthouses in Finnmark, Slettnes lighthouse was destroyed by the retreating German forces in 1944 and the lighthouse was bombed in November the same year. Apart from the lower section of the tower, the lighthouse was destroyed, including all the auxiliary buildings. Four years later the lighthouse was rebuilt, even taller than before. After the war, a new two-tone fog warning signal was installed that could be heard at a distance of 5-6 km. A radio beacon was installed in 1955. The radio signature is SN (... _.), and it is broadcast on a frequency of 295.0 kHz with a range of 50 nautical miles. The lighthouse was automated in 2005.

Slettnes lighthouse is a popular tourist attraction and it is possible to stay overnight there.

The area around Slettnes lighthouse, as in the case of Sarnesbukten near Honningsvåg, is an area with traces of some the oldest settlements in Finnmark along with traces of old fishing village settlements.

Between Slettnes and the fishing community of Gamvik is an almost intact fort from the Second World War with well-preserved bunkers, cannon emplacements and trenches. The fort was built in 1942 and was strategically placed with a view to the north, south, east and west. At the most, there were 130 men stationed at the fort. During the retreat of the German forces in 1944, the bunkers were blown up and materials removed.

71°05'N   28°24'E   + 0 hrs 58 min ⑥

On the way to our next port of call, Berlevåg, we pass the fishing community of **Gamvik.**

Gamvik church was built in 1958 on the same site as the former church that was burnt down in 1944. The church is a concrete structure, with seating for 224.

The first church to be built in Gamvik, known as the 'Lapp church' or the 'Sámi chapel' was consecrated in 1858. It was a missionary church. It stood until 1914, despite a new church being built in 1894 – this was burnt in 1944.

The municipal centre and fishing community of Gamvik is characterised by the typical post-war architecture that prevailed during the rebuilding process after 1945. The population was forcibly evacuated in 1944 when all the houses were burnt down and the quaysides and boats were blown up or burnt.

In the centre of the community is the Brodtkorb fish processing wharf, which was rebuilt after the Second World War, on the same site as the original wharf from the 1840s. The wharf was owned by the Brodtkorb trading dynasty in Vardø (p 234). The wharf was closed down in 1969 because of the collapse of the market for

© GAMVIK MUSEUM

dried fish. Brodtkorb wharf is included in the Directorate of Cultural Heritage's preservation plan for technical and industrial cultural heritage sites and is currently the only site of national interest of its type. It is now used as a museum by Gamvik Museum 71°N, that also preserves and exhibits fishing and coastal culture.

The population of Gamvik has declined considerably during the last few years, due to the closure of the local fishing industries.

At the end of the 1980s, representatives of a Norwegian organisation claimed that the Norwegian Armed Forces had installed listening devices to pick up signals from Soviet submarines in the Gamvik area. The organisation published the highly controversial allegations in the media.

We head for our next port of call, Berlevåg. We pass the fjord, **Koifjorden**, then the peninsula **Vuokkanjága** and the now uninhabited fishing village of **Omgang** and **Russevika** bay. Omgang was once a place of exile for prisoners. It had a church as early as 1589. Omgang is also mentioned as one of the places along the Finnmark coast that was once a site of witch burnings. Omgang also has a large bird cliff (p 218).

We cross the fjord **Tanafjorden.** The fjord is 65 km long and 8-12 km in width. It has several side 'arms', the outermost of these is **Hopsfjorden** to the rear of Nordkinn peninsula, **Langfjorden** and **Trollfjorden.**

Finnmark county

Coat of arms: Depicts Vardøhus fort and border fortifications to the east.
Origins: From Finnmork, from finner, 'Sámi people', and mark. Likely meaning is 'populated border area'
Area: 48 618 km². **Population:** 72 655.
County seat: Vadsø.
We pass the following municipalities on our way northwards: Kvænangen, Loppa, Hasvik, Hammerfest, Måsøy, Nordkapp, Lebesby, Gamvik, Berlevåg, Båtsfjord, Vardø, Vadsø and Sør-Varanger.
Topography: About 95 % of the area is under 600 m above sea level. Finnmarksvidda (the Finnmark plain) is approx. 300 to 500 masl. It's very marshy with many lakes, wide valleys, quiet rivers and undulating landscape with gentle slopes. The coast is broken up by long, wide and deep fjords mostly in north-south direction and present wide bays with many islands and large peninsulas jutting out between the fjords. The coast in West-Finnmark (west of the North Cape) is protected by islands; in East-Finnmark the coast is unprotected. There are 1,888 islands along the coast.
Geology: The particular landscape in large parts of Finnmark is due to the fact that the bed-rock here is very different to the bed-rock farther south in North Norway. South of Varangerfjorden (p 230) and in a line running south-westward the predominant bed-rock is gneiss forming an undulating plateau which is approximately 2,500 million years old. In the north this bed-rock is covered by sandstone reaching as far out as to cover Varangerhalvøya. The sandstone has probably been pushed in large flakes over the bed-rock with a narrow strip of slate between the sandstone and the bed-rock. These layers are relatively horizontal such that most of North and East Finnmark has a plateau like landscape. Slate and sandstone offer little resistance to wind and wave forces, therefore the coast from Porsanger and eastward to Varangerfjorden has no skerries or beaches, but rises straight up from the sea like a wall to heights of 150 to 300 masl. The coast to the west has smaller, narrower fjords and larger islands. The mountains are jagged, some covered by glaziers.
Climate: Climatic conditions vary greatly between the different regions in the County. Mild air comes in from the west and the mountains by the coast give shelter from the sea to the areas behind. Temperate waters brought up by the Gulf Current (p 85) makes the coast virtually ice-free all year round. Storm conditions are frequently experienced due to low pressure regimes along the coast. In January wind forces of strong breeze or more will occur 30-40 % of the time. February is the coldest month with an average temperature of -2 to -7 °C, coldest in the east. The average temperature in the interior -10 to -15 °C. On Finnmarksvidden the average temperature has been measured as low as -40 to -45 °C, in the months November - March. The lowest temperature measured was -51,4 °C, 1st January 1886. The winds will often come in from the east and north along the coast mid-summer. Average temperature in July is 10 to 12 °C along the coast and 14 °C in the interior. The warmest weather is brought in by winds coming up from the south-east and in the summer the maximum temperature can be as much as 25 to 30 °C by the coast and over 30 °C in the valleys inland.
Population: The inhabitants live mainly in the coastal areas and mostly concentrated in larger villages with good harbour facilities since their income is very much dependent on fishing activities. After WW2 most of the burnt down villages were rebuilt, but many of the smaller villages have later been vacated. In the interior almost only the villages of Karasjok and Kautokeino are populated. The population has varied over the last 60 years. The consequences of periodic decline in the main economic activities, like fishing and mining has resulted in a reduction in the population along the coast. In the period from 1970 to 2004 it was reduced by as much as 25 % in the County as a whole. It is mostly the younger generation that leave after completing their education which has resulted in shortcomings in filling key positions in industry

TRADE AND INDUSTRY:
Farming and Forestry: Finnmark is the County in Norway with the least arable land. Only 0.2% of total area is cultivated. The climate limits the use of land for animal fodder. Cattle are the most important farm animals for their milk and meat production. The County can not provide all their needs of agricultural products. Few are employed in forestry.
Reindeer Production: From an employment point of view, not very significant in Finnmark. In 2002 there were approximately 2.000 units in the County that had this as their main source of income; total number of domesticated reindeer was estimated to approx. 126 000. The reindeer flocks roam seasonally over large areas and most reindeer owners live permanently in a village and don't move with the flock anymore. This is now done by reindeer shepherds. The reindeer graze up on the plateau wintertime and move down to the coast to calve and graze in summertime. There have been many conflicts with farmers, hydro-electric power schemes, mining projects and the Armed Forces over the use of reindeer pastures. The problem is however, that there are too many animals for the available grazing areas.
Fishing: Fishing has been the main source of income from old and took place in the fjords, along the coast and on the fishing grounds some 15 to 20 nautical miles offshore. Some of the larger boats venture farther away to fish. Cod is the main catch and takes place along the coast in the months May and June. Coastal cod is caught all year round and trawlers fish cod farther away from the coast. The fish is filleted and frozen and there are many such factories in the County. Some fish is dried and salted. Haddock and coalfish are also important and in the latter years trawling for shrimps and catching kingcrabs have increased significantly.
Mining: The County's biggest employer has been Sydvaranger ASA who operated Norway's largest mine in Bjørnevatn close to Kirkenes. Iron ore was extracted and pellets were produced until closure in 1997. In Alta we find Norway's largest accumulation of slate and many quarries. On Stjernøya "nefelinsyenitt" is quarried for export.
Industry: The County has the lowest industrial employment of all counties in Norway. The fishing industries are dominating and therefore employ the most. These industries are located along the entire coast and due to its seasonal nature and varying supply of fish it can't guarantee permanent employment.
Tourism: Tourism, which started in the 1800s, is mainly to visit the North Cape and to see the Midnight Sun and takes place summertime. Hurtigruten has been important for tourism in Finnmark and in the latter years so has the airlines and the motorist.
Communication: The E6 connects Finnmark to the South and good roads connect the many villages in the County. Hurtigruten is very important and ferries and local shipping tie the many islands to the mainland. Air transport is also important both inside the County and connecting Finnmark to the rest of the Country.
Language: Sámi and Norwegian are used side by side and can be seen by the fact that all official signs are in both languages.

Source: Store norske Leksikon

Bird nesting cliffs in Norway

ORKNØYENE

All of the larger nesting cliffs in Norway are in the north of the country, except for the cliffs on the island of Runde (p 46). Usually these nesting sites are situated on rocky islands located far out to sea or on steep, inaccessible rock faces along the coast. This very inaccessibility protects them against predators and the proximity to the sea provides easy access to food. The birds come onto land to nest, sometimes forming huge colonies. In the breeding period from March/April to August, they display distinct social behaviour and the different species occupy separate parts of the cliffs. Each species has a different method of building their nest. Outside of the nesting period, the birds remain away from the cliffs. Some species look for food far out at sea (like the Fulmars and Kittiwakes), others closer to shore (like the Cormorants and Auks). Some species begin making their nests as early as April, but seldom lay their egg(s) before May. Most eggs are hatched in late June and the fledglings generally leave their nests in July, some as late as August. The nesting period begins somewhat earlier in the southern parts of the

country than in the north. The different species of birds specialise in catching different kinds of food. The Kittiwake catches insects and small fish on the surface whilst the Auks dive for herring and capelin. Gannets plunge into the water to catch fish deeper in the water. The different species of Auks avoid competition for food in that they prefer different species or a different size of fish.

The Gannet is a large, white seabird with a wingspan of approximately 170 cm and weighs from 2 to 3.5 kg. The wing tips are black and the neck and head is yellow. The blue and white pointed beak is approximately 10 cm long. The young are speckled greyish-brown in colour until they mature at about the age of five. They dive from a height and with great speed into the water to catch their food. This species only nests in northwest Europe and around Newfoundland in Canada.

© ANDREAS TREPTE

The Cormorant is approximately 90 cm long and has black plumage with a bluish metal lustre, white throat, white 'cheeks' and a large white spot on the outside of the leg from January to July. They nest in colonies and their nest is made from twigs and kelp. Both parents brood on three to five light blue eggs for about 28 to 31 days. The fledglings leave the nest when

© EILIV LEREN

they are approximately seven weeks old. The Cormorant nests on both sides of the Atlantic and in many other parts of the world. Cormorants are common in Norway, along the coast from Trøndelag and northwards.

The Shag is approximately 75 cm long and has black plumage with a greenish metal lustre with a noticeable plume on its head during the mating season. They also nest in colonies and the nest is generally found in screes or in rock crevices. Both parents take turn in brooding on two to four eggs for about 30 days and the fledglings leave the nest after approximately 30 days. They nest along most of the European coastline.

© EILIV LEREN

The Fulmar nests on shelves and projections on the face of steep cliffs. They have the appearance of a large seagull but without the black and white wing tips. Their back is bluish-grey and their underside, neck and head is white. An adult Fulmar weighs approximately 500 to 900 g. They are mature at the age of eight and nest in large colonies. They lay only one (white) egg, which both parents will brood for seven to eleven days each for approximately 50 to 55 days. The birds are very clumsy when they walk on land. They nest in most Arctic waters and in Europe as far

south as the south coast of England. Outside of the nesting season, they live far out at sea.

Kittiwakes, **Auks**, **Guillemots** and **Black Guillemots** often choose the steepest cliffs to build their nests.

The Kittiwake is a migratory bird, about the size of a seagull. They have a grey and white plumage, the tips of the wings and feet are black and the back toe is practically absent. Fledglings and mature birds have a black spot behind their eyes when in their winter plumage and the young birds have a black band around their necks. Kittiwakes nest in huge colonies and usually build their saucer-shaped nest on a narrow, protruding rocky shelf. They lay two to three greyish-brown black speckled eggs which both parents brood for 26 to 28 days. The young leave the nest after 40 to 45 days.

The Guillemot, a member of the Auk family, has black and white plumage, a pointed beak and weighs about 600 to 1 000 g. They nest in colonies of varying size. One egg is laid directly on a rock shelf, often side by side with a neighbour. The eggs take approx. 32 days to hatch with both parents taking turns to brood. The young fly the nest after approx. three weeks. The numbers of Guillemots have fallen dramatically in recent years, mainly due to a lack of their preferred food and due to oil pollution.

The Black Guillemot also belongs to the Auk family of birds. The summer plumage is jet black with a large white patch on its wing, a black beak and crimson feet. Their winter plumage is white with dark spots and a white underside. They weigh around 400 to 500 g and are around 34 cm long. They normally lay two eggs, which are kept well hidden in rocky crevi-

ces and they generally nest separately as pairs or in small colonies.

Puffins are the most distinctive and numerous of all the birds on the cliffs. They also belong to the Auk family and nest in large colonies. The Puffin is also known as the Parrot Bird. They have a black back and white underside, white cheeks and a very large, flat, multi-coloured beak and red feet. The eyes are remarkable; there is a red ring around the eye, a blue triangle above the eye and a small white square under the eye. Puffins weigh about 400 to 500 g. Each year, on the same date and at the same time, normally on 14th March they come in from the sea to nest. The female lays her egg inside a crack in the rocks or in a burrow, sometimes 2 m long that they dig out with their beaks. The egg is hatched after 40 to 45 days and the chick leaves the nest after six to ten weeks. The numbers of Puffins has been reduced dramatically due to a lack of their preferred fish, and to some degree due to oil pollution. They often become stuck in fishing nets and drown. A ringed Puffin has been documented as reaching the age of 36 years.

The Barents Sea

The dividing line between the **Norwegian Sea** in the west and the **Barents Sea** in the east is at the North Cape. The Barents Sea covers an area of approx. 1.3 million km², and stretches all the way to the Russian island of Novaya Zemlya. The demarcation line between Norway and Russia remains a topic of discussion, but the Norwegian part is at least 650 000 km². Negotiations concerning the demarcation have been ongoing since 1974. The outcome of these is important, since it concerns the rights to fishing grounds and the right to prospect for oil and gas in the area

The Barents Sea is named after the Dutch explorer, **Willem Barents** (1549-97). He set out on three expeditions to find a navigable passage, the so-called Northeast Passage from Europe to East Asia. Difficult ice conditions prevented the expedition from achieving its goal, but large areas were charted between the northern coasts of Norway/Russia and the seas in that region, including Bear Island and Svalbard/Spitsbergen. On the final expedition, their ship became frozen in the ice. During the winter that followed, some of the expedition's crew, including Willem Barents, died before the ship reached the

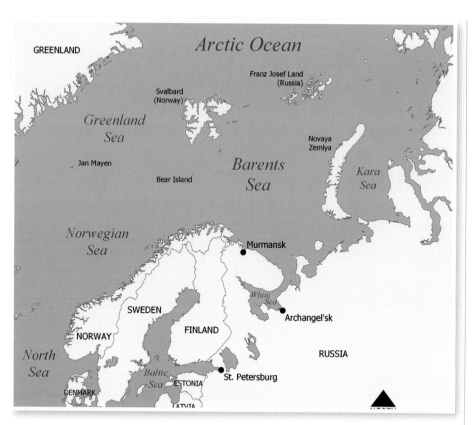

Russian coast. The survivors were eventually rescued by another Dutch expedition. **Barents** has lent his name to Barentsburg (the Russian mining town on Svalbard, pop. approx. 95), the **Barents Sea** and **Barents Island** (an island in the Svalbard archipelago, 1 288 km²).

Convoys in the Second World War

The German battleships, "Tirpitz" and "Scharnhorst" were stationed in Finnmark (p 268) in order to attack convoys heading for Murmansk carrying vital war supplies to the Eastern Front.

Aircraft, weapons etc. were transported by rail from Murmansk, to southern Russia. Sailing in the convoys was extremely hazardous and many Allied ships were sunk, mainly by submarines and in air attacks by the Luftwaffe, which were sent from their bases in Lakselv and Bardufoss. During the summer, the convoys could sail further north, out of range, however in winter the ice shelf forced the convoys further south, where they were more ea-

sily found and attacked by the Luftwaffe and the Kriegsmarine. The German admiralty did not want to send warships northwards to Finnmark, as most of their larger battleships had been sunk or destroyed in Allied air attacks on German ports in Europe. The loss of a ship would therefore be disastrous, not only for the Kriegsmarine but also for German prestige. Only

36 German sailors survived the sinking of the "Scharnhorst" (p 208), almost 2 000 men were killed.

The "Tirpitz" was severely damaged in an attack, first by British mini-submarines and later by several long range bombing raids that eventually destroyed the ship.

The burning of Finnmark in 1944

© GJENREISNINGSMUSEET IN NORD-TROMS AND FINNMARK

© GJENREISNINGSMUSEET IN NORD-TROMS AND FINNMARK

In June 1941, Germany attacked the Soviet Union, which led to the Soviet Union joining the Allies in the war against Germany. Hitler's plan was to attack the Soviet Union in the north and south. As Kirkenes was the northernmost German stronghold in Europe, a huge military build-up took place in Finnmark, especially in the area around Kirkenes.

The war was fought on several fronts. The northernmost of these was the so-called Litsa Front, between Kirkenes and Murmansk. Further south and east was another front line, the Salla Front.

The battles along the Litsa Front were hard-fought. In addition to the fighting between opposing troops, both armies had to fight against a common enemy - the Arctic winter. The late winter of 1942 was especially severe and a large number of soldiers on both sides froze to death, especially the German troops suffered greatly in the conditions and lost many men.

Despite intense fighting, the German forces could not break through the front to reach Murmansk. In the late autumn of 1944, the Soviet forces broke through the German defence lines at the Litsa and Salla Fronts and began to move forward towards Sør-Varanger and Kirkenes. The German army was forced to beat a hasty retreat.

The German army had received orders from Hitler that the 'scorched earth' tactic was to be employed in Finnmark. The retreating army, which was largely made up of engineer divisions, was ordered to raze everything to the ground and the people left were to be forcibly evacuated. With very few exceptions, the order was carried out. The fishing village of Bugøynes (p 226) was spared, as the German officer in command refused to obey the order. Some years after the war had ended, the officer returned to the village, this time as a tourist. He was very well received.

A summary of the catastrophe revealed that approx. 10 563 houses had been burnt down, along with approx. 4 711 barns and cowsheds, 27 churches, 141 chapels and other places of worship, 19 medical clinics, 417 businesses, 61 public administration buildings, 106 schools, 229 industry and trade buildings and 54 banks – all were completely demolished. On farms, all sheep and cattle were slaughtered.

The people of Finnmark were given very short notice of evacuation and many refused to leave. Approx. 50 000 persons were forcibly evacuated and removed to other places in Norway, among them Vesterålen and Lofoten. 23 000 remained behind. Many of these lived in terrible conditions, without food and proper shelter against the rain and cold. Some escaped into the mountains and others onto the Finnmark plains. They sought refuge in cabins, caves and turf huts. They had to remain vigilant all the time, as the German troops patrolled the coast, looking for those who had refused to obey the evacuation order.

After the war, the whole county of Finnmark had to be rebuilt in a relatively short time. This is apparent in the large numbers of buildings and homes that have very similar architecture.

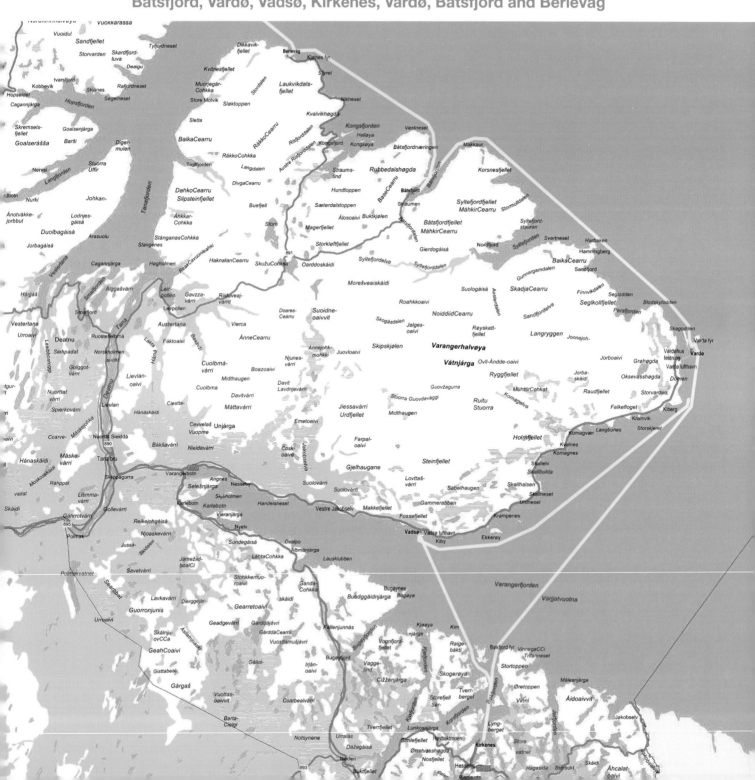

During the night we have sailed by the ports of **Berlevåg** (70°51'26"N 29°06'45"E, 2215-2230) in Berlevåg municipality, **Båtsfjord** (70°37'42"N 29°43'12"E, 0030-0100) in Båtsfjord municipality and **Vardø** (70°22'33"N 31°06'19"E, 0400-0415) in Vardø municipality.

The **Varanger Peninsula** lies between Tanafjord in the Barents Sea and Varangerfjord. It is comprised of rolling fells rising up to 633 metres above sea level. The terrain is barren and bleak and is used as summer grazing for reindeer. The municipalities of Berlevåg, Båtsfjord, Vardø and Vadsø are within the peninsula.

Vadsø municipality

Municipal coat of arms, significance: Represents the county.
Meaning of name: Norse Vatsøy, Vassøy, where the oldest inhabited area is found. The name Vassøy is found at several places along the coast. The name indicates to seamen that they could find fresh water at these locations.
Municipal seat: Vadsø (pop. 5 073).
Position: 70°04'N 29°44'E. **Area:** 1 258 km².
Population: 6 124. **Pop. density:** 4.86./km².
Area distribution: Agriculture 1 %, Productive forest 0 %, Fresh water 2 %, other areas 97 %.
Trade and industry: Service industry (Vadsø is the county seat of Finnmark). Fish processing. Herring oil factory. Fishing/farming in combination.
Places to return to: Vadsø Museum, Kvænbyen. Tuomaine farm.
Activities to return to: Crab fishing safari.
Vadsø municipality's home page: www.vadso.kommune.no

We have already passed several interesting places in Vadsø municipality.

70°11'N 30°22'E

Skallelv was originally one of several purely Finnish communities in the area, populated at the end of the 19th century. The local people were known as Kvens, the North-Norwegian name for people of Norwegian-Finnish descent. Skallelv is one of very few remaining areas with buildings that were constructed before the Second World War.

The State has granted permission to build a windmill farm with 8-16 windmill generators at Skallhalsen close to Skallelv.

70°05'N 30°18'E ①

Krampenes is one of the few more populous communities in Vadsø municipality. The island **Lille Ekkerøy** is just outside Krampenes. The island is full of cultural heritage and also has some smaller bird cliffs. Lille Ekkerøy was most likely populated before the neighbouring island of Store Ekkerøy, which lies further to the south-west.

Store Ekkerøy was an island until 1750. The narrow road that links the island to the mainland is built up from the sea. The fishing processing plant on the island, which was built up in the period from 1900-1960, had several landing piers, shops, a school, shrimp factory, oil processing plant and a dried fish store. There were approx. 270 persons living here. Today the population has fallen to fewer than 50.

The first certain evidence of what is thought to be the first, permanent settlement on Store Ekkerøy is from the late Middle Ages (p 83). In 1922, a grave from approx. year 900 was discovered. This is known as the 'Ekkerøy find' which is regarded as the finest Viking age find in Northern Norway.

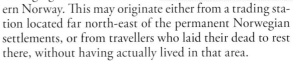

This may originate either from a trading station located far north-east of the permanent Norwegian settlements, or from travellers who laid their dead to rest there, without having actually lived in that area.

Parts of Store Ekkerøy were declared a nature reserve in 1983. The island has a small (40-50 metre high) bird cliff (p 218) on the west side of the island, which is a nesting area for many rare species. In the breeding season from March to August/September the cliffs may be home to as many as 20 000 kittiwake pairs. The settlements on Store Ekkerøy were not destroyed during the Second World War and therefore several fine old houses have been preserved. The German troops built bunkers and ammunition stores in the mountains on the outer part of the island.

70°04'N 29°51'E

Just east of the town of Vadsø is the community of **Kiby**, a typical fishing-farming community with some buildings that were constructed before the Second World War. Especially worthy of preservation is the well-known Elisseuss building which is now listed. The house was probably built in the first half of the 19th century.

The ship docks at the quayside in Vadsø

The ship docks at the quayside on the inner side of **Vadsøya** - the island has a bridge over to the mainland.

The municipal centre of **Vadsø** is the county seat of Finnmark. The town is also called the 'Kven capital' of Norway, (Kvens are an ethnic minority, of Finnish descent) as there was considerable migration from Finland in the 18th and 19th centuries. The migrants came to Norway to escape the famine and harsh conditions in their home country. Excavations have shown that there were settlements in the area as long as 9 000 years ago. In the 16th century there was considerable Norwegian settlement on Vadsøya, that was at that time a large fishing community

© ROLF LILAND

with its own church. Vadsøya was separated from the mainland by a 750-metre wide sound that could be walked across at low tide (still possible today). During the 17th century the population gradually relocated to the mainland, and in 1717 the church was moved. The current church, the "Ishavskirken" is the fourth church and was consecrated in 1958.

Vadsø received its town charter in 1833 and the municipality became an important centre of trade. The Pomor trade was especially important (p 241).

Close to the quayside in Vadsø, towards the stern of the ship is a 60 m tall mast. This was constructed in 1926 by the Italian aviation engineer Umberto Nobile and was used as a mooring mast for the airships "Norge" in 1926 and "Italia" in 1928. The mast respresents an important era in Norwegian and European polar history. The two airships left Vadsø for Ny-Ålesund on Svalbard when they embarked on their famous expeditions to the North Pole.

The famous Norwegian polar explorer and scientist Roald Amundsen (1872-1928) had already achieved worldwide recognition through his expeditions to the Arctic and Antarctic. He felt that exploration of uncharted areas in the Arctic could best be accomplished by using airships. His first attempt with 2 aircraft from Tromsø in 1922, ended in crashes, however the pilots were rescued. The next attempt, with two new aircraft, which also began in Tromsø in 1925, ended in considerably more dramatic circumstances in the ice at 87°N 10°37'W. After three weeks, members of the expedition managed to repair one of the aircraft and get it airborne and reached a safe haven, after first clearing a runway in the inhospitable icescape.

A year later, in 1926, Amundsen and the American multi-millionaire Lincoln Ellsworth left on a new expedition to the Arctic. This time they flew on the airship "Norge" which was built in Italy by the engineer Umberto Nobile, who was also the pilot. The expedition left from Rome, via Oslo, Leningrad and Vadsø, crossed the Barents Sea and flew onward to Ny-Ålesund on Svalbard. From there they reached the North Pole on the 11th May 1926 and later landed at Teller, Alaska on the 14th May. The Arctic had been explored, and the crew returned to Norway as heroes.

Unfortunately, Amundsen and Nobile later became bitter rivals. However, when Nobile disappeared on a flight with the airship "Italia" north of Svalbard in 1928, Amundsen flew the aircraft "Latham" from Tromsø to search for

him. The last signals from Amundsen's plane "Latham" were received three hours after takeoff. The plane probably crashed close to Bjørnøya and all six crewmembers were killed. One of the aircraft's pontoons was washed ashore in Troms, and this is on display in the National Maritime Museum in Oslo. Nobile and several of his crew survived, however, and were found on the ice during the biggest ever search and rescue operation in the Arctic at that time, in which over 1 500 men from seven countries took part.

During the Second World War, Vardø was at times the headquarters for approx. 2 000 German troops. The centre of town was badly damaged when the Allies bombed the town in 1944. In spite of the bombing, almost one-third of the town's buildings were left standing. In Vardø, there are more preserved pre-war buildings than anywhere else in Finnmark county.

On Vadsøya there is a 1.8 km long cultural heritage trail, with interesting information on ancient sites from the Middle Age settlements in Vadsø, the cemetery, the airship masts and other war memorials. Vadsøya also has a very active bird life.

The ship continues to Kirkenes	+ 0 hrs 00 min

LARGER MAP P**404**

Varangerfjord on the starboard side is the most easterly fjord in Norway. It is approx. 90 km long and 55 km wide at the estuary, however it narrows at the inner part of the fjord to about 1 km. In terms of area, Varangerfjord is Norway's largest fjord with an area of 2 260 km². The south side of the fjord has several shallow side 'arms', among them the one that leads into Kirkenes. At the inner part of the fjord are **Varangerbotn** and **Karlebotn,** where there are remains of a number of settlements from the early Stone Age (p 83). These have been

excavated, and there are approx. 90 remains of dwellings. The settlement has been used for several hundred years in the early Stone Age and there have been as many as 10-20 dwellings in use at the same time.

The Red King Crab – Kamtsjatka – has become established in Varangerfjord. The Red King Crab's natural habitat is the Kamtsjatka Peninsula in the northern Pacific Ocean. Russian researchers released the crab at several places on the Murmansk fjord during the 1960s and it has since spread southwards along the coast of the Kola Peninsula and north-westwards along the coast of Finnmark. The Red King Crab has no natural enemies in the area and has therefore been able to spread almost unchecked. In the Varangerfjord it appeared in such great numbers in the winter of 1992 that it began to create problems for the traditional coastal fishing fleets in the area. From 1994, fishing of crabs for research purposes was permitted and from 1997 registered secondary fishing of Red King Crabs was introduced. The information obtained via registered catches showed that the problems with the crabs were greatest in connection with net fishing of cod, in that the crab gets tangled in the nets and destroys them. The crab eats the bait in the case of line fishing and often the catch itself.

The Red King Crab, that normally has a claw-to-claw span of approx. 1.5 m and can weigh up to 12-14 kg, is not only regarded as a problem. The meat in the large claws is edible. This is considered a delicacy and much of it is exported to Japan. Only male crabs over a certain size are caught. Catches of crabs and export of crabmeat has become an acceptable secondary source of income for fishermen that are otherwise affected by the Red King Crab's presence around the Finnmark coast.

For some time, Norwegian and Russian fishery authorities have tried to prevent the spread of the Red King Crab. West of 26°E, close to the North Cape, there are no restrictions on catches of Red King Crab. East of 26°E the catch is regulated. These restrictions are provisional, dependent on the spread of the crab in the future. Permission has been granted for catching of a certain amount of Red King Crab by tourists.

© ROBERT LAURILA

Approx. 70°0'N 29°49'E

We cross the municipal boundary between Vadsø and Sør-Varanger

Sør-Varanger municipality

Municipal coat of arms, significance: The motif is a symbolic representation of the number 3.
Meaning of name: Originally the name of a fjord, Norse Ver(j)angr, from ver, 'fishing community' and angr, 'fjord'.
Municipal seat: Kirkenes (pop. 3 267).
Area: 3 967 km². **Position:** 69°44'N 30°04'E.
Population: 9 490. **Pop. density:** 2.39/km².
Area distribution: Farming 0 %, forestry 12 %, fresh water 13 %, other areas 75 %.
Trade and industry: Shipyard. Trade and commerce development with North-West Russia. General animal husbandry (cattle). Some forestry. Some fishing as a combined enterprise, mostly in the north-west.
Activities to return to: River safari. Hunting.
Sør-Varanger municipality's home page: www.sor-varanger.kommune.no

Sør-Varanger municipality has a border with Russia in the south-east (196 km long) and with Finland in the south-west (140 km long).

On the starboard side and ahead is the island Skogerøya, to port is Kjelmsøya and Holmengråfjellet/ Uhca Vindas. The community of Bugøynes is also on our starboard side.

69°59'N 29°50'30"E   + 0 hrs 34 min ②

The fishing community of **Bugøynes** (pop 295) on the starboard side is the only one of its kind in Sør-Varanger municipality. It was established by Finnish immigrants in the 19th century. They had left their own country due to political unrest and poor living conditions in Finland at that time. The Finnish influence is still evident, as most of the population are Kvens, the name given to Norwegians of Finnish descent. The buildings show signs of Finnish architecture and style, many of the local people have Finnish names and Finnish language is still quite actively used. The immigrants brought knowledge of agricultural methods with them from Finland, and quickly learned local knowledge of fjord fishing. The Finns also brought their religious traditions with them, a conservative Christian movement known as Læstadianism. This still holds a firm footing in Bugøynes and is evident in the everyday life in Bugøynes which is marked by sobriety and moderation.

© ROLF LILAND

Bugøynes was saved from the ravages of 1944, when the whole of Finnmark was to be razed to the ground ('scorched earth policy') in connection with the retreat of the German forces. The original Finnish architecture has therefore been preserved.

Bugøynes was affected by the crisis in the fishing industry in the 1980s, but managed to pull through. The fishing community had the first salmon farms in East Finnmark and managed to utilise commercially the invasion of the Red King Crab from Russia. Today, the catching, processing and export of Red King Crab products is under considerable development at Bugøynes. The annual production in 2005 was approx. 120 tonnes and the enterprise employs 17 persons. Approx. 60 % of the production is exported to Japan, 20 % is exported to various European countries and another 20 % is exported to the USA. In addition there are salmon farms and a salmon processing plant at Bugøynes.

At the bay **Ranvika** in the Bugøynes fjord on the mainland south-east of Bugøynes, lie Sør-Varanger's largest bird cliffs (p 218).

69°55'N 29°57'E   + 0 hrs 51 min ③

Our course continues towards the town of Kirkenes and on the starboard side we have the sparsely populated and partly tree-covered **Skogerøya** (132 km²), with the mountain **Skogerøytoppen** (445 m above sea level) as its highest point. The island (132 km²) is the only island of any size in Sør-Varanger municipality. It is used for summer and autumn grazing land for reindeer.

The ship sails into **Kjelmøysundet** with **Kjelmøya** (5.6 km²) on the port side and **Skogerøya** on the starboard side. There have been settlements on Kjelmøya from the Stone Age and there have been several discoveries of prehistoric ornamental arrowheads and lances dating back 3000 years. It is assumed that these finds originate from Sámi settlers. During the Second World War there were major gun positions located on Kjelmøya. The German forces built a small railway system that transported ammunition to the gun batteries. Kjelmøya, and Kiberg and Store Ekkerøy on the north side of Varangerfjord were the main sites for the German defence positions at the mouth of the fjord.

69°51'24"N 30°01'41"E   + 1 hr 07 min ④

South of Kjelmsøya (on the port side) we pass **Sølferbukta** on the starboard side, with Oksebåsneset up ahead.

69°50'25"N 30°05'E   + 1 hr 13 min

As we pass **Oksebåsneset** (196 m above sea level) on the eastern side of Skogerøya to starboard, with the peninsula of **Holmengrålandet** and **Stortoppen** (408 m above sea level), the ship enters **Bøkfjorden**. Bøkfjorden has a rich variety of bird life with breeding areas for many species. The fjord is also designated a national salmon fjord.

On the rear side of Stortoppen is **Holmengråfjorden** with **Holmengrå** summer fishing community, originally used by Eastern Sámi for sea salmon fishing. It has a special and individual milieu with connections to several ethnic groups, their culture and traditions. The fishing community was given protected status in 1998. There is also one of the best preserved labyrinths in Norway (p 202).

69°48'N 30°06'E   + 1 hr 22 min ⑤

With the island **Reinøya** on the port side, Bøkfjorden is divided, to starboard is **Korsfjorden**, leading in a southeast direction.

Between the southern headland of Reinøya and the mainland at **Ropelv**, permission has been granted to construct a landing 'stage' for smaller oil tankers to transfer oil from the oil fields near Murmansk and north-west Russia to the larger supertankers, for further transport to the world markets. The project is somewhat controversial, as Bøkfjorden is a national salmon fjord and the transfer of oil is regarded as a risky operation. (Pending approval from the Norwegian authorities, the trans-shipment site has temporarily been relocated to Sarnesfjorden west of Honningsvåg (p 204).

Bøkfjorden narrows at **Tømmerneset** on the starboard side and the mountain **Lyngberget** (222 m above sea level) on the port side. At the headland on which Kirkenes is located, the fjord splits into **Langfjorden** to the south and Bøkfjorden continues to the south.

The ship docks at the quayside in Kirkenes

CITY MAP **P405**

The Russian ships moored at the quayside in **Kirkenes** are the first sight to greet passengers when sailing into port. They are the most important sign of the current and most important commercial basis - shipyard services and other commercial trade with North-West Russia.

On the slope near Kimek Skipsverft, on the starboard side, we can see several buildings that formerly housed warehouses, loading machinery and conveyors for iron ore extracted from the now closed mines at Bjørnevatn. The iron ore was transported by rail from the open cast mines, approx. 10 km from Kirkenes, to the storage warehouses. From there is was transported on conveyor belts on board bulk carriers that brought the iron ore to the world market.

The areas around Kirkenes, especially the inland areas, were summer residences for the Sámi from the east for many hundred, perhaps many thousands of years. During the summer months the Sámi were based here with their reindeer flocks on the Varangerfjorden,

© ROLF LILAND

and in the winter in Northern Finland. During the 1830s, when the winter frost was too severe in Northern Finland, the area began to be populated by farmers and foresters from this area. For several decades Finns were the dominant group of settlers in Sør-Varanger.

Neiden, 45 km west of Kirkenes, bears the greatest witness from that period. Neiden is regarded as the centre of Eastern Sámi culture in Norway and a large proportion of the population are of Finnish descent. St. George's chapel is to be found at Neiden, a Russian-orthodox chapel, which is said to have been built in 1565. Neiden chapel was built in 1902, requested by the local people, possibly also as a mark of confirmation of the Norwegian state's sovereignty in Eastern Finnmark.

Kirkenes, which was granted a town charter in 1998, was "discovered" in 1902 in connection with the discovery of ore deposits in the mining settlement of Bjørnevatn, 10 km south of Kirkenes. Up to that time, the community was comprised of a few small houses and a church on a headland (Norwegian "kirke" and "nes" – Kirkenes).

The mining operations at Bjørnevatn began in 1906. Kirkenes was the shipping port, and the town experienced a steady increase in prosperity and importance. Many different languages were spoken in the community and the commercial premises that were constructed were inspired by Russian architectural traditions (typical features are the large cupola). After the First World War the demand for iron ore increased, as many places were rebuilt.

Kirkenes was severely affected during the Second World War. The Russian city of Murmansk was just over the border and its port was ice-free, the only port in the European part of Russia that was not under control by the German forces. Large Allied convoys (p 220) carried supplies of food and war materials via Murmansk. These were sent on to Moscow, to prevent the fall of the capital and occupation by Nazi Germany. Kirkenes was therefore of enormous importance for the German war campaign in Finnmark. Over 30 000 troops were stationed in the area and supply depots for 100 000 men were built. Kirkenes was subjected to repeated bombing from Soviet aircraft during the war years. Air-raid warnings sounded over 1 000 times and there were over 300 bombing raids. It is claimed that Kirkenes was one of the towns in Europe that was subjected to the most intensive bombing, in terms of the number of raids, during the whole of the Second World War.

The fighting at the front between Kirkenes and Murmansk cost the lives of many tens of thousands of soldiers on both sides. They either were killed in action or froze to death in temperatures as low as -30 to -40°C. The rugged terrain made it difficult to establish supply chains and the

Russian forces brought the planned advance to the railway between Murmansk and Archangelsk to a halt. The war then turned into a standoff. In October 1944, after Finland and the Soviet Union agreed on a cease fire, the Germans intensified their plans for a retreat from Finnmark, and Kirkenes, which by now had been bombed to ruins, was liberated. There is a statue in Kirkenes that honours the Russian soldiers that lost their lives in Finnmark.

During the retreat, the German forces employed the "scorched earth" tactic, as in the rest of Finnmark (p 221). Apart from a few houses, all buildings remaining after the bombing were burned own. The local people that had avoided forced evacuation hid in mine tunnels and caves. Approx. 2 500 persons sought refuge for up to two months in one of the mine tunnels near Bjørnevatn. In fact, 10 children were born in the tunnels. Many of them were forced to live in the ruins and cellars of bombed and razed houses before the rebuilding of Kirkenes could begin. The general shortage of timber in Finnmark made it necessary to transport materials great distances.

In North Troms and Finnmark, approx. 25 000 people escaped the forced evacuation. People lived in caves, tents and in turf huts. In all, 45 000 persons were forcibly evacuated.

Kirkenes was rebuilt after the war and the mines began operating again in 1952. Iron ore from Bjørnevatn was very much sought after throughout Europe, to be used in reconstruction work and this brought in a good income. The infrastructure in the municipality was once again restored and the town got its own air station, Kirkenes Airport. This was originally built to enable the transport of supplies to the battle front and as a starting point for German fighter aircraft and bombers. A modern town centre was built and there are good museums that contain exhibitions of the varied cultural history. There is also a separate art museum that is dedicated to one of the country's most famous Sámi artists, whose work illustrates Sámi reindeer herding culture and the fascinating natural surroundings in the North.

The Russian corporation, Shtokman Development Company, is poised to develop the enormous Shtokman gas field that lies just off the coast of North-West Russia. The company signed an agreement with the Norwegian oil company StatoilHydro that gives StatoilHydro a 24 % equity interest in Shtokman Development Company. This has led to considerable optimism in Kirkenes which is now looking forward to increased commercial and industrial activity, due to the geographic proximity of the development area.

The community of **Bjørnevatn** (pop. 2 419), also known as "the mining town" has been of strategic importance for the development of the Kirkenes area. Bjørnevatn lies 10 km south of Kirkenes. The mine, which is Europe's largest open-cast mine, was opened in 1906 and finally closed down in 1996. Mining workers and engineers from all over Scandinavia came here to work. Ore extraction at Bjørnevatn became gradually less profitable and from the 1980s the mines were gradually downscaled until 1996 when they were finally decommissioned and closed for good.

In Bjørnevatn stands the Rallar monument, which has been erected in memory of the first mine workers at the site. A distinctive music pavilion with a typical Russian cupola was erected in 1953, as a monument to the liberation of Sør-Varanger and to 90 years of mining operations.

The small village of **Grense-Jakobselv**, 60 km east of Kirkenes, on the edge of the Barents Sea, is separated only by the 55 km long Jakobselva river that runs into the sea close to the village. The river is a well-known salmon river. Both Norwegian and Russian border guards patrol the border. During the Cold War the patrols' objective was to ensure that agents from either side did not cross over the border, especially defectors from the Soviet Union. Nowadays the patrols are more concerned with illegal immigration and trafficking. It is still forbidden to take photographs in the area and there are strict penalties for private persons who cross the border.

The village's attractions are first and foremost the Kong Oscar II chapel, which is a stone chapel from 1869 that was constructed as a border post and marker, and Prestestua, built in 1867. These two buildings represent an important part of the colonization history of the border in Sør-Varanger.

Pasvikdalen (Pasvik valley) stretches along the border between Finland and Russia for approx. 100 km in an easterly direction. The Pasvik River that runs through the valley forms most of the 196 km long border with Russia. Pasvikdalen is widely known for its special flora and fauna and forms a botanic 'boundary' between Europe and Asia. In Øvre Pasvik there is undisturbed pine forest (virgin forest) with some spruce. An area of 67 km² in Øvre Pasvik is a protected national park. Norway's largest group of brown bears (Ursus arctos arctos) is found in Pasvikdalen.

Kirkenes is a suitable starting point for a trip to Russia – the border crossing at Storskogen is only 15 minutes from the town centre. A visa is required for all visitors, for all nationalities, that wish to cross the border. A visa may be obtained from travel agents in Kirkenes, however the office should be contacted in plenty of time before making the trip.

Despite Kirkenes being located up in Norway's furthest north-east corner, only 40 km from the town it is possible to take a train on the Russian railway network that, if you so desire, can take you all the way to Vladivostok on the northern Pacific coast.

The ship continues to Vardø	+ 0 hrs 00 min

LARGER MAP P**404**

The ship leaves the quayside at Kirkenes, towards Bøkfjorden, with Vardø as the next port of call. We sail partly along the same passage as we took when sailing into Kirkenes.

69°44'34"N 30°04'35"E	+ 0 hrs 06 min

On the port side is the bay **Gamnesbukt** just before the headland **Tømmerneset** (98 m above sea level).

Behind Tømmerneset is **Korsfjorden** in a south-easterly direction. On the starboard side is **Lyngberget** (222 m above sea level). In the bay you can see **Ropelv**, and the small island of **Reinøya**.

At the southern tip of Kjelmøya on the port side up ahead at the mouth of Bøkfjorden, we continue along the steep mountain, **Stortoppen** (408 m above sea level) on the starboard side.

Bøkfjord lighthouse is on the tip of the **Holmengrålandet** peninsula on the starboard side. It was constructed in 1910 to provide a beacon for the approach. The original building was built of timber with a standard light as

© KYSTVERKET

the light source. The lighthouse was totally destroyed in 1944 and was rebuilt in 1947-48 with a new light tower and a machine room, accommodation, outhouses and two boathouses with landing stages. The lighthouse has a 10 m high concrete tower. The elevation of the light itself is 33 m and the range 16 nautical miles. The foghorn signal from 1910 was replaced with a nautophone in 1948. This was decommissioned in 1990. A radio beacon was built in 1955 and decommissioned in 2000. A radar beacon was installed in 1992. Bøkfjord lighthouse is of great architectural value and was granted listed status in 1998. Remains of the old lighthouse can still be found on the site. As late as December 2006, the last lighthouse keeper left the site and it is now fully automated. The Norwegian Coastal Administration carries out any necessary site maintenance.

Bøkfjorden lighthouse was fortified during the war years. Close to the lighthouse buildings there are remains of a German coastal fort with guns, gun emplacements, bunkers, trenches and machine gun positions. These were probably built to protect the lighthouse against attacks and attempts at sabotage from the sea. During the dark time of the year, navigation without beacons and lighthouses was extremely difficult and dangerous.

Now we are in the outer part of Varangerfjord. On the mainland on the port side you can see The Varanger Peninsula with the communities of Vadsø, Kiby, Store and Lille Ekkerøy, Krampenes and Komagnes in Vadsø municipality (p 223). The interior of Varanger peninsula is hilly, barren and almost uninhabited. The highest point is Skipskjølen (633 m above sea level) in the middle of the peninsula. The area is used as a summer grazing area for reindeer.

On the starboard side is the Barents Sea (p 220).

The ship continues to the town of **Vardø** on the outer point of the Varanger peninsula. On the port side is Varanger fjord, approx. 90 km in length, 55 km at the mouth of the fjord.

Approx. 70°10'N   30°48'E

We cross the municipal border between Sør-Varanger and Vardø

Vardø municipality

Municipal coat of arms, significance: In black letters is: VARDØENSIS INSIGNIA URBIS. CEDANT TENEBRÆ SOLI (The seal of the town of Vardø. "The dark shall give way to the sun") and the year 1787, when Vadsø was granted a town charter. The shape is somewhat like a banner, which is unique among Norwegian municipal coats of arms
Meaning of name: In the 14th century the name was written Vargøy, from the Norse varg, 'wolf, outlawed person', later changed to Vardøy, from varde, 'cairn'.
Municipal seat: Vardø (pop 2 012).
Area: 600 km². **Position:** 70°22'30"N 31°06'14"E.
Population.: 2 286. **Pop. density:** 3.8/km².
Area distribution: Farming 0 %, forestry 0 %, fresh water 3 %, other 97 %.
Trade and industry: Fishing, with relatively large vessels. Fishing industry with filleting and freezing. Some processing (smoking) and fresh fish for export. Shrimp factory.
Places to return to: Vardøhus fort. Vardøhus Museum. Pomor Museum.
Activities to return to: Pomor festival. Crab fishing safari.
Vardø municipality's home page: www.vardo.kommune.no

70°11'31"N   30°52'26"E   + 2 hrs 17 min ❶

Between the towns of Vardø and Vadsø lies **Komagvær,** which is an area mainly comprised of cabins and recreational dwellings. The 45 km long Komagelva River, is a well-known salmon river. The area is also popular with ornithologists.

Kramvik has an active and varied bird life and is a very popular spot for bird watching.

70°16'N   31°03'E   + 2 hrs 41 min ❷

We pass the community of **Kiberg** (pop. 241) the second largest community in Vardø municipality, on the port side, just south-west of the headland Kibergneset. In the 16th-17th century Kiberg was one of the largest fishing communities in the area and it played a central role in the Pomor trade period with Russia and their fishing industry. Kiberg is still important as a fishing catch landing stage. The community escaped destruction during the German forces' retreat of 1944 and many of the original buildings and architecture still remain.

With its strategic location, Kiberg played a central role during the Second World War. The geographical proximity to the Soviet Union had, over several years, brought Russian and Norwegian people together. When Kiberg became important to the German forces, many left Kiberg and moved southwards, over the border to the Soviet Union. Some returned and worked for the Soviet military intelligence services. It is thought that there were as many as 45 partisans in the Kiberg area. One of the most important tasks was to monitor and pass on radio communications about the German shipping fleet. Around half of the partisans were killed in battles or were executed during the war. It has been calculated that some 80 German merchant ships on their way to Kirkenes were sunk due to their operations. After the war ended, most of the remaining partisans returned to Kiberg. The Cold War and the tense political situation in the 1950s and 60s, during which the Soviet Union was considered the main enemy, led to suspicion being directed towards those who had been partisans during the Second World War. It was widely known that East European intelligence services were active in Norway, because of the country's NATO connections and strategic location in regard to the Soviet Union and its access to the Northern Atlantic.

King Harald honoured the partisans in a speech held at the partisan monument in Kiberg in 1992. For many, this was the first official recognition of their efforts on behalf of their country during the Second World War.

Kibergneset, or Østkapp on the port side, is Norway's most easterly point on the mainland. During the Second World War the area around Kiberg had some of Europe's largest gun positions and gigantic fortifications towards the Barents Sea. The fortifications were known as "Fort Kiberg" and were one of eleven fortifications on the Varanger peninsula.

On rounding Kibergneset you can see the sound of Bussesundet and the island of Vardøya up ahead and to starboard. On the port side we pass the bay of **Melvika**, just before **Domen** mountain (164 m above sea level), with its flat peak and sheer drop into the ocean. At the foot of the mountain is a deep cave that is currently open for visitors. The cave was known locally as "The gateway to Hell".

The mountain Domen has its own very special history. It is known as "Heksefjellet" (Witches Peak). In the 17th century, between 1593 and 1669, there were approx. 140

"witch cases" in Finnmark. Roughly 100 of these 'witches' were burned at the stake. In a European context, the Vardø area was among the worst in regard to the scope of brutal witch-hunts. In the winter of 1662/63 more than 30 women were accused of having plagued others with their witchcraft and sorcery. According to the history of that time, many of the women admitted to the inquisitions that they had danced, drunk and consorted with the Devil himself on the mountain called Domen, between Kiberg

and Vardø. On Domen, the women held their ceremonies and sabbaths and they gained power for their witchcraft, having taken an evil oath to Satan. They were given the command of smaller devils that streamed out of a cave at the bottom of the mountain when darkness descended over the area. The small devils were used to carry out evil and magic. The Devil himself also lived in the cave. All form of contact with the Devil and his demons was regarded as a heinous crime. Confessions by the women often came after manipulation, prolonged torture and abuse. To extract a confession the women often had to endure the notorious "water test". They were tied by their hands and feet and thrown into the sea. If they were guilty, they floated and were thus declared a witch. If they were innocent they sank and drowned!

The ship is nearing the town of Vardø on Vardøya. Behind the island you can see the small island of Hornøya with Vardø lighthouse, also Reinøya. Hornøya, at 31°10'14"E, is Norway's most easterly point.

© EILIV LEREN

Vardø lighthouse on **Hornøya** was built in 1896 and is Norway's most easterly lighthouse. The square tower is 20.5 m in height, made from steel girders, clad with sternite plates. The height of the light above sea level is 77.2 m, and the range is 23 nautical miles. The lighthouse has a fog warning signal. From 1910 this was a conventional foghorn until 1937 when it was replaced by a diaphone (a signal device driven by compressed air that generates a powerful, penetrating low tone, ending in a short deep tone, a so-called "grunt") and later by a nautophone in 1976 (sounds are generated by alternating current that is fed into an electromagnet and to a steel plate fitted with a vibrating membrane).

The lighthouse buildings were rebuilt after the Second World War, but were demolished in 1959 and completely reconstructed. The lighthouse today is comprised of a light tower, an engine room, accommodation, outhouses, a machinery room for the cableway and two boathouses. The area shows clear evidence of earlier German fortifications. The site is of architectural value - among other things, the tower is only one of three in Norway with this special type of design. The lighthouse was automated in 1991 and the remaining lighthouse keepers left. It was granted listed status in 1998. The lighthouse is located in a protected nature reserve. There is a rich bird life on Hornøya.

Vardø radio beacon was built in 1953, the call signal is VD (..._ _..), broadcast at 307 kHz. The range is 70 nautical miles. After 1994, the radio beacon's function has been to send out correction signals to the satellite-based navigation system, Navstar GPS.

© BERIT LILAND

The ship sails along the outer side of Vardøya (3.7 km²) to approach the quayside from the west. On the port side you can see the characteristic round antennae that are part of the Norwegian Defence Forces' radar system Globus II. The radar systems are a joint project between the Norwegian intelligence services and the US Air Force Space Command. The radar systems were formerly installed at Vandenberg Air Force Base in California. The construction work for the radar installation in Vardø began in 1998 and the systems were finally on-line in 2000. At that time, the radar was the only one of its kind in the world. It has a mechanically-controlled parabolic reflector antenna with a diameter of 27 metres, which is fed through a feed horn, protected by an inflatable dome with a diameter of 35 metres. The antenna is mounted on a rotating platform so that it is able to follow objects in the sky as far as 40 000 km above the earth. The systems can pick up satellites in earth orbit. It is said that the radar can "see a tennis ball over Rome". The radar systems at Vardøya are politically very controversial. Officially, the goal of the radar is to keep track of "space junk" and satellites that orbit around the earth and also to help monitor Norwegian territorial interests. However, the USA has invested over a billion Norwegian kroner in the construction of the radar systems. Russia on the other hand, claims that the project is merely an extension of the American missile defence systems and is therefore a threat to their national security (Vardø lies very close to the Russian border).

Vardøya is in fact comprised of two islands, **Vestøya** and **Østøya**, that are connected by a low neck of land, **Valen**. The islands are separated from the mainland by the 1.7 km wide **Bussesundet**. An undersea tunnel (2.89 km long, 88 m under sea level) runs underneath the sound. The tunnel, which was the first undersea road tunnel to be built in Norway, was opened in 1982.

After rounding the outside of Vardøya the ship turns southwards and passes the outer breakwaters, then docks at the quayside in the bay of **Vestervågen** between Vestøya and Østøya.

The ship docks at the quayside in Vardø CITY MAP P406

Vardø is Norway's most easterly town and is known as "The Gateway to the Barents Sea and the North-East Passage". It is the only town in Western Europe that lies within the Arctic climate zone, i.e. that average temperature in the summer months does not exceed 10°C. The limits of the zone extend to Bussesundet. The winter climate is harsh, with strong winds and low temperatures. It is said that in the old days the children had to carry rocks in their pockets in order to prevent being blown away on especially windy days!

Archaeological excavations show evidence of settlements in Vardø that are approximately 4 500 years old. In 1307, Vardø was mentioned as a 'fishing port' in official documents, and the same year the first church was consecrated by Bishop Jorund at Nidaros (Trondheim). At about the same time, the first Vardøhus fortification was built by King Håkon 5 Magnusson (1270-1319). The fortifications were built at the beginning of the 14th century and were then known as Borgen. It was partly a defence fortification, as Finnmark and Hålogaland were subjected to a great deal of plundering and

attacks by Russians and Karelians (from Northern Finland). It was also the residence of the local feudal overlord. The fortifications were later relocated and the new fortifications, called Vardøhus Slott ("castle") were completed around 1460.

Vardø is said to be the world's northernmost fortified town. Vardøhus fortifications, such as they stand today, were built during the period 1734-1738, as the third set of fortifications in Vardø. It is built as an octagonal star-shaped entrenchment with four bastions and four star-formed quoins. The building is constructed from granite, the spandrel wall is of earth and turf with a dry moat.

The Hungarian astronomer and Jesuit Miksa (Maximilian) Hell was the director of the observatory in Vienna. He left in 1768, on an assignment for King Christian VII of Denmark/Norway (1749-1808) to Vardø to follow the planet Venus' passing in front of the sun, such that it would be possible for the first time to calculate the exact distance from the Earth to the Sun. He built an observatory in Vardø and calculated the site's exact longitude and latitude with great accuracy - as far as the methods available at that time allowed.

Vardø is one of Norway's oldest towns. It received a town charter on the 17th July 1789 when King Christian VII signed a document that gave Vardø rights as a market town. The town was also the centre of the Pomor trade (p 241) at that time and Russian fishing traders until the First World War in 1914.

OBSERVATIO
TRANSITUS VENERIS
ANTE DISCUM SOLIS
DIE 3. JUNII ANNO 1769.
WARDOËHUSII,
AUSPICIIS
POTENTISSIMI Ac CLEMENTISSIMI
REGIS DANIÆ ET NORVEGIÆ,
CHRISTIANI VII.
FACTA,
ET
SOCIETATI REGIÆ SCIENTIARUM HAFNIENSI PRÆLECTA
à
R. P. *MAXIMILIANO HELL*, è S. J.

Fridtjof Nansen (1861-1930), the famous Norwegian polar explorer and diplomat, sailed on the 24th June 1893 with 12 men, from the port at Vardø in the specially-constructed polar vessel "Fram". The goal was to confirm the theory that the polar ice drifted from Siberia over the Polar Sea to Greenland. Nansen wanted to allow "Fram" and its crew to drift with the ice, in order to - if possible - cross over the North Pole. Foreign polar researchers were sceptical; however, the Norwegian authorities eventually granted financial support to the project. "Fram" followed the coast of Siberia, and arrived on the 22nd September 1893 in the ice at 78°50'N 133°37'E, whereupon the ship froze fast and was driven with the drifting ice slowly north-west. On the 14th March 1895, Nansen and Lieutenant Hjalmar Johansen left the ship, to try and reach the North Pole on skis and with dog sleds. After massive efforts they reached as far as 86°14'N, further north than any previous expedition. The return journey was hazardous and they were in great danger several times. However, on the 15th August they reached Frants Josefs Land where they decided to make camp and stay through the winter. Exactly a year later, on 15th August 1896 they left their winter camp. A month later they were lucky and happened upon another expedition that brought them back to Vardø, where they arrived on the 13th August, one week before "Fram" reached land at Skjervøy, north of Tromsø (p 263).

Fridtjof Nansen was welcomed as a hero and later embarked on a number of lecture tours in Europe and America and was showered with honours. At Fridtjof Nansens Plass in Vardø there is a statue of Nansen, unveiled in 1993, during the jubilee year for his epic journey from Vardø towards the North Pole with the ship "Fram". Later, Nansen also made great humanitarian efforts in connection with the famine that ravaged the Soviet Union, and in establishing the so-called "Nansen-passport", used by refugees that did not have official papers. The "Nansen-passport" was accepted as an official passport by over 50 countries and made it easier for refugees to apply for entry into each country.

Until 1850, Vardø was a small fishing community, however during the years 1850–1910 the population increased dramatically, expanding to 3 023 in 1910. Finnmark became an expanding county, and was for many an alternative to emigrating to the USA. The good fishing stocks and the Pomor trade gave grounds for optimism and was the reason behind the rapid population of the area.

From the middle of the 1850s, the Pomor trade (p 241), which had its origins in bartering for goods, gradually became more associated with regular trade with monetary exchange. Much of the trade was organised via professional traders. The largest trade house in Vardø was run by the Brodtkorb family. Approx. 20-30 Russian guest workers were employed at the trading house. In the 1890s, an average of 384 Russian ships docked at the town's ports annually, whilst 361 ships left Vardø for Russia to ply their trade. Vardø was also an important transit port for goods that were to be sold on the Russian market. Wealthy Pomors came to Vardø to buy goods and produce, and the people from these ships – with their colourful costumes and their beautiful, harmonic choral singing and the ring-style dancing at the quayside – became a charming attraction in the town. After the Russian Revolution in 1917 the Pomor trade ceased, the Russian ruble became worthless and in the subsequent

period of economic and social depression, many of the traders in Vardø went bankrupt. After the Cold War ended, the contact between Vardø and Archangelsk was re-established and the towns became twin towns in 1989. Each summer since 1991, a special Pomor day has been arranged in Vardø.

Vardø was of great importance to the German forces during the Second World War. The town was in a strategic location for monitoring the movements of Allied shipping sailing to Russia. Two-thirds of the town was destroyed during the war years. Vardø was subjected to several Soviet air attacks, both against German installations on land and against shipping that transported supplies to Kirkenes and to the war front. Vardø suffered severe destruction during the retreat of the German forces in 1944 (p 221).

Vardø church is the fourth to be built in the town, and was consecrated in 1958. The first was built in 1307 and stood approx. 1 km from the current church. The second was built in 1714 and the third in 1869. This was burnt down in 1944, but was not rebuilt until 1958. The town also has a chapel, built in 1907, close to Vardøhus fortifications.

Vardø is built up around the fishing and fish processing industries. The population has declined after the fall in the market for fish products. The town is currently in a transitional phase and new jobs are being created. One of the new enterprises is the establishment of a new shipping traffic control centre that will monitor the increasing numbers of tanker ships that sail along the Finnmark coast and the open ocean beyond, between north-west Russia and the west. This coastal monitoring station is to be built near Vardøhus fortifications, along with Var-

© POMORMUSEET

dø radio coastal communications centre. Vardø is also a favourite destination of birdwatchers. The development of tourism is also an important industry. At the end of each winter season, an extended snowmobile race is arranged. The aim of the race is to achieve the fastest time to complete the demanding 100 km trail.

Vardø Airport is at **Svartnes** on the mainland within Vardøya, and is connected to the Norwegian national air network. European highway E75, which starts on Crete in Greece, has Vardø as its end point.

The ship continues to Båtsfjord	+ 0 hrs 00 min

LARGER MAP P**407**

The ship sails from Vardø and heads west, past the breakwater that protects the harbour against the Barents Sea. The next port of call is the fishing community of Båtsfjord.

Laukvika can be seen on the port side on the mainland. Also to port is Vardøya's northernmost point, **Skagodden**.

On the starboard side you can see **Reinøya** and **Hornøya** with Vardø lighthouse. Both islands are protected areas, due to the rich bird life. In the 1970s the numbers of Great Black-backed Gull and Herring Gulls were thought to be around 30 000 pairs. Reinøya is one of Norway's largest egg sites (p 333). The collection of eggs has been controlled and organised by the Commander of Vardøhus fortifications since the 1960s and continues to this day. In 1971, approx. 40 000 eggs were collected. When the newly-laid eggs are removed from the nests the gulls lay more eggs. Other bird species such as Kittiwakes, Puffins, Razorbills,

Guillemots, Arctic Guillemots, Black Guillemots, Great Cormorants and Shags also nest here (p 218).

Vardø is on the same degree of longitude as the Great Pyramid of Cheops in Egypt. This has been marked by the erection of a small pyramid on the top of Reinøya, at the exact same longitude as the Egyptian pyramid.

Hornøya is Norway's most easterly point, 31°10'14"E, with a protected bird cliff on which approx. 80 000 pairs nest during the breeding season. The island has a policy of restricted access, however trips can be arranged with the harbour boat from Vardø.

We continue north-westwards, up ahead on the port side is Kavringen and the point of Blodskytodden.

70°26'40"N 31°00'44"E	+ 0 hrs 20 min ①

At the foot of the mountain **Blodskythøgda** on the port side lies the now uninhabited **Kavringen**, which was a living fishing community right up to the end of the 1960s. **Blodskytodden** is the last point in Vardø municipality. The point is a nature reserve and a breeding site for many kinds of birds, especially wetland species.

The bay of **Persfjorden** is on the port side along with the headland **Prestnæringen** at the southern approach to the bay.

Approx. 70°29'N 30°52'E

We cross the municipal border between Vardø and Båtsfjord

Båtsfjord municipality

Municipal coat of arms, significance: Symbolises fishing and the importance of the fishing industry for the municipality. **Meaning of name:** Probably from 'botn', meaning the inner part of a fjord. Also estate name, Sámi "Báccavuodna" or "Báccevuodna".
Municipal seat: Båtsfjord (pop. 2 099).
Position: 70°38'N 29°34'E. **Area:** 1.434 km².
Population: 2.113. **Pop. density:** 1.47/km².
Area distribution: Farming 0 %, forestry 0 %, fresh water 1 %, other areas 99 %.
Employment: One of Norway's largest fishing communities. Fish processing plants. Filleting factory with freezing plant. Shrimp factory. Production of capelin roe and capelin. Aquaculture. Smaller shipyards for the fishing fleet. Summer grazing land for reindeer. Lifeboat station.
Places to return to: Hamningberg. Makkaur Peninsula nature reserve.
Båtsfjord municipality's home page: www.batsfjord.kommune.no

70°31'30"N 30°46'E	+ 0 hrs 50 min

On the port side you can see the bay of **Sandfjorden**, ahead on the port side is the fishing community of Hamningberg. Well ahead are the two mountains Syltefjordklubben and Korsnesfjellet.

70°32'48"N 30°42'E	+ 0 hrs 58 min ❷

Hamningberg passes on the port side, in the small bay before the point of **Harbaken** (81 m above sea level). The European highway E75 from Vardø, that originates on Crete, reaches its end point here. Along the road, which resembles a moon-like landscape, you can see clear geological traces of the influence of the ice masses from the different ice ages.

Hamningberg is an uninhabited fishing community with a Russian-inspired architecture and a fascinating landscape. It was built as a traditional fishing community in Finnmark. On the shore, quays were built with landing stages, packing sheds and boathouses. The houses were situated along the road and up towards the mountain. Fish drying racks were erected where there was any space available. The Pomor fishermen were here from the 18th century and dried fish was previously exported to Russia and Europe from Hamningberg. Before the Second World War there were approx. 700 residents. After the war, Hamningberg was one of the few traditional fishing communities left in Finnmark, and it avoided most of the systematic razing during in the German forces' retreat of 1944 (p 221). However, great damage had been done to the buildings – the chapel was burnt down and most of the quays were destroyed. The population declined to approx. 200. Many left, however at a somewhat slower rate than many other places along the coast. The three last permanent residents left in 1978. Hamningberg is now inhabited during the summer months when the road is re-opened. The buildings are regarded as a part of cultural heritage and have been restored.

After Hamningberg is **Syltefjorden** on the port side.

Nordfjord, a few kilometres along the fjord's north side was the last fishing community in Båtsfjord to finally become uninhabited, in 1989. Nordfjord has many summer houses that are owned by people in Båtsfjord. There is a 25 km road that joins the two communities.

In **Ytre Syltevika** further out in the fjord, remains of a church building and several groups of remains of dwellings from the Middle Ages and more recent times have been found. There are also traces of Stone Age dwellings.

70°36'38"N 30°30'E	+ 1 hr 20 min ❸

Between Syltefjorden and the neighbouring fjord ahead, Båtsfjorden, lies **Makkaurhalvøya** Nature Reserve with **Syltefjordfjellet** (403 m above sea level) and Makkaurfjella. The nature reserve was established in 1983, and covers an area of 113 km². Its goal is to preserve the characteristic area of the Arctic coast of Øst-Finnmark and one of the country's most important bird cliffs, Syltefjordstauran.

The bird life in most of the nature reserve is sparse. In the mountain plateau the usual species to be found are the high mountain species such as the Snow Bunting and Rock Ptarmigan, however they have spread breeding patterns. The contrast between the monotonous coast and mountain landscape and the teeming bird life at Syltefjordstauran is enormous.

Syltefjordstauran (220 m above sea level) is most likely Norway's biggest bird cliff - approx. 4 km in length. The cliff is close to the north-westerly mouth of Syltefjorden. Nesting in the steep cliffs are a great number of Kittiwakes, also Guillemots, Arctic Guillemots and Northern Gannets (p 218). It is not known exactly how many Kittiwakes nest here, however the colonies have been estimated as the largest in Norway – the numbers have been previously calculated to be as great as 1 500 000 pairs. The bird cliff is a protected nature reserve.

On one of the inaccessible rock piles on the outside of the cliff itself – **Store Alkestauran** – is Finnmark's only, and the world's northernmost, breeding colony of Northern Gannets. The Northern Gannet first became established here in 1961. In 1982, the colony had 250 breeding pairs and the numbers are still on the increase. The Northern Gannet has an impressive size, with a wingspan of approx. 2 metres and it is Norway's largest seabird. The Northern Gannet is always the last species to leave the bird cliff in the autumn.

On Store Alkestauran and on other places on the bird cliffs there are also Razorbills, Guillemots and Arctic Guillemots. The Guillemots are the most numerous; however, the exact numbers are not known, possibly around 10 000 pairs. Between 100 and 1 000 Arctic Guillemots pairs breed on the cliff. This species mainly breeds in Arctic areas. In Norway (apart from Svalbard) it is found almost exclusively in Finnmark. The other auk species, the Black Guillemot and the Puffin, are also observed near Syltefjordstauran. The characteristic Puffin probably breeds on the cliffs, however there have been no confirmed instances (p 218).

The rich bird life in Syltefjordstauran is an eldorado for predatory birds and carrion eaters. Ravens and Crows are the most common, Sea Eagles are also often seen. Great Black-backed Gulls and Herring Gulls are greedy egg thieves and also take young chicks that are unprotected on the cliffs. Both species of gull breed at Syltefjordstauran.

Apart from at the bird cliffs, the greatest number of bird species is found at **Makkaursandfjorden**, which is a common feather moulting area for the Common Merganser. Up to 1 000 Common Mergansers collect here for a few weeks in July and August, when the moulting takes place.

70°39'40"N 30°20'22"E	**+ 1 hr 38 min**

Just after Syltefjordstauren, the distinctive shape of **Stormolldalen** appears as a deep cleft in the mountain, like a vertical valley.

As we sail along Makkaurhalvøya Nature Reserve, we pass Makkaursandfjorden, depopulated in the 1950s, with the mountain Korsnesfjellet to the rear.

70°42'32"N 30°08'E	**+ 1 hr 59 min** ④

At the top of **Korsnesfjellet** (296 m above sea level), formed in silhouette against the sky, you can see a building which is the remains of one of the State Telegraph's link stations.

Makkaur lighthouse can be seen up ahead. The lighthouse was built in 1928 and is one of the country's most distinctive, with great architectural value. It was declared a

listed building in 1998. The lighthouse is constructed as a white concrete building with a curved roof and a tower on the roof. The height of the light above sea level is 39 m and the range is 17.6 nautical miles. The fog signal, a diaphone, was installed in 1922 and was decommissioned in 1989. The machine room and pressure tanks for the diaphone, the fog signal apparatus and the power generators are still intact.

The lighthouse building and the keeper's quarters are preserved and date from before the Second World War. The light installation itself, which was used by the German forces during the war, was destroyed. It was however, rebuilt later. The remaining buildings were accommodation and outhouses and these were demolished in the 1980s. A poorly-constructed building that is currently used as accommodation and machine room, was erected outside the site. A cast concrete path leads down to the boathouse and landing stage.

Makkaur is an uninhabited fishing community and trading post at Makkaur lighthouse. The area was populated from the Middle Ages, at the end of the 16th century and during the two first decades of the 17th century it was one of the largest fishing communities in Finnmark, with approx. 100 inhabitants. From 1620, Makkaur found itself in a period of crisis, with extreme depopulation. This was due to declining fish stocks, a poorer climate and a fall in prices on the fish markets.

Makkaur was inhabited up to the start of the Second World War, however it was one of the few fishing communities that were not rebuilt after the war. The buildings were moved to Båtsfjord and Syltefjord (among them, the church). At Makkaur, in addition to Makkaur lighthouse, there is a fortification from the Second World War, shipwrecks, remains of dwellings and two cemeteries.

Makkaur is the municipality's oldest church parish and was mentioned in documents as early as 1521. The last chapel in Makkaur was consecrated in 1934. This was moved to Syltefjord in the 1950s.

The geologist B.M. Keilhau, who travelled to Finnmark in 1827/1828 describes the kind of accommodation he experienced in the fishing villages in Finnmark:
"The turf huts, as the Norwegians have constructed them, are, in regard to the climate, the most effective

kind of housing. There are fairly small wooden timber houses, sealed and covered in stones and turf. The stalls for the beasts are connected to the main buildings and it is possible to go between them via a corridor or chamber to the door of the inner room, through which the air from outside cannot access. The living room is as sealed and warm as any man could wish - but by no means damp. Apart from the chimney they also have a bricked annexe which is heated from the living room, with perhaps an iron stove. This has a small window that provides adequate light. In the turf hut it was possible even in the deepest winter to work by daylight for an hour in the afternoon."

© EILIV LEREN

70°43'N 29°58'E	+ 2 hrs 14 min

In front is the headland **Rossmålen** (242 m above sea level). Before we round the headland you can see a grotto in the mountainside.

Our heading is towards the fjord of **Båtsfjorden** (13 km), towards the community and centre of Båtsfjord. On the port side, the steep slopes of **Makkaurfjella** (383 m above sea level) and **Båtsfjordfjellet** (445 and 214 m above sea level) descend into the sea.

On the west side of Båtsfjorden you can see the peaks of Båtsfjordnæringen and Hamnefjell. The valley between them is known as **Austre Rubbedalen**.

At the top of Hamnefjell towers a massive telecommunications mast. With a height of 241.8 m this is Norway's tallest mast of its type.

70°41'28"N 29°53'E	+ 2 hrs 24 min

The approach to Båtsfjord is colourful. The steep mountain slopes of Makkaurfjell on the port side, in the right light setting, can be seen as a fascinating colour palette of red, green, black and white. The headland, **Rødbergneset**, is distinctive with a rust-red colour and a small cave just over the waterline.

The ship docks at the quayside in Båtsfjord

Båtsfjord is regarded as Norway's largest fishing community and is one of Finnmark's largest fishing ports with 7 000 vessels calling annually. At the fish processing factories there is a multi-national community, with Norwegians and guest workers from Russia, Finland, Sweden, The Faeroe Islands and formerly many from Sri Lanka.

The current Båtsfjord was most likely populated around or later than the beginning of the 19th century. In 1852 there were 26 inhabitants registered in Båtsfjord. During the years 1865–68, many Finns moved into eastern Finnmark due to the famine and economic depression in their homeland. In 1900, the population had

increased to 54. At the same time that Hamningberg (p 236) experienced stagnation due to poor conditions in the harbour, much of the activity was moved to Båtsfjord that had a much more suitable harbour. During the fishing season the sale and trading of fish increased considerably. In 1909, there was also a coal fuel depot for the fishing fleet, located in the inner part of Båtsfjord. Several landing stages and quays were also built. For motor and steam ships it was no longer necessary to remain so close to the fishing grounds. It is said that in the spring of 1909, as many as 3-400 boats with 3-4 000 men were moored at the harbour at Båtsfjord.

There have been three whaling stations at Båtsfjord. The first was built in 1884. There are also several uninhabited fishing villages that are now used as summer residences.

The variation in the fish stocks and catches throughout the years, the variable climate, economic booms and recessions and wars influenced Båtsfjord in the same way as they influenced other places in Finnmark. Båtsfjord was not completely destroyed in 1944, as the German forces withdrew very quickly from the area (p 221). The combined schoolhouse and chapel that was consecrated in 1923, was one of the buildings left standing, even though it had been occupied by the German troops during the war. After liberation, the fishing community has experienced rapid development – however the commercial basis, i.e. the stocks of fish in the sea, have varied greatly. In common with most fishing communities in the north, the population and economic activity has varied in accordance with available resources.

Today (2006), Båtsfjord has four fishing plants, two of them are engaged in full activity, one of them operates at reduced capacity and another processes waste products from fish processing. The fishing community has an open year-round road connection over Båtsfjordfjell and a short-runway airport with four daily flights.

The new Båtsfjord church is from 1971. It is a so-called 'working' church built from concrete, with seating for 300. The church has one of Europe's largest stained-glass windows (85 m²).

The ship continues to Berlevåg	+ 0 hrs 00 min

LARGER MAP P**407**

70°39'N 29°47'31"E	+ 0 hrs 09 min

The ship sails out of Båtsfjord, heading for our next port, **Berlevåg**. On the port side we sail just under **Hamnefjellet** (368 m above sea level) with Norway's highest telecommunications mast, rising 241.8 meters from the top of the mountain, We then continue along **Rubbedalshøgda** (427 m above sea level), past **Rubbedalsneset** and the valley of **Rubbedalen.** The ship then sails under the steep face of **Båtsfjordnæringen** (354 m above sea level), towards Seibåneset (with lighthouse).

We round **Seibåneset** and our heading is set in a northwesterly direction. In front is Kjølnes lighthouse, just south of Berlevåg.

Approx. 70°44'N 29°46'E	

We cross the municipal border between Båtsfjord and Berlevåg

Berlevåg municipality

Municipal coat of arms, significance: Symbolises the municipality's dependence on the sea.
Meaning of name: The first part may be the Sámi 'perle' and may indicate finds of pearls. The name has also been said to correspond to berle, meaning to 'move carefully'
Municipal seat: Berlevåg (pop. 1 040).
Position: 70°51'N 29°07'E. **Area:** 1.120 km².
Population: 1 086. **Pop. density:** 0.97 /km².
Area distribution: Farming 0 %, forestry 0 %, fresh water 3 %, other areas 97 %.
Trade and industry: Fishing, several industrial fishing plants. Mechanical workshops and slipways. Production of electricity.
Places to return to: Berlevåg Museum.
Activities to return to: Fishing, diving.
Berlevåg municipality's home page: www.berlevag.kommune.no

70°45'N 29°45'E	+ 0 hrs 37 min ①

At the point **Vestneset** the wide fjord bay of **Kongsfjorden** can be seen on the port side.

Kongsfjord fishing community, on the west side of Kongsfjord and with its 60 inhabitants is the second largest community in Berlevåg municipality. The peninsula of Veidnes in the inner part of the fjord provides protection from the storms coming from the north and a breakwater protects the harbour. Kongsfjord chapel is a longhouse timber building, dating from 1927 and seats 200.

A German fort was built on the western part of the peninsula of Veidnes during the Second World War. In the outer part of Kongsfjord lie three islands teeming with bird life: **Kongsøya**, **Skarvholmen** and **Helløya**.

In the inner part of Kongsfjord lies **Straumen**, an eldorado for divers, with several shipwrecks. In the sound between **Straumsneset** and **Storneset**, a strong current is formed that leads into the small skerries at Straumen. Several seal species are to be found here, all year round.

Kongsfjord and Kongsfjordelva have been given status as national salmon fjords and salmon rivers. This means that fish farming installations for salmon are not permitted in this area. The shore in the inner part of Kongsfjord is protected as a special landscape area.

70°49'N 29°28'E	+ 1 hr 05 min ②

After Kongsfjord, on the port side is the point **Nålneset,** and the beautiful **Sandfjorden** with its wide sandy bay, then we can see **Sandfjordfjellet** (288 m above sea level). Towards the rear is **Laukvikdalsfjellet** (381 m above sea level). Sandfjorden was declared a special landscape area in 1983, it covers a land area of 4.8 km² and a sea area of 0.6 km². The special landscape area was formed because of its quarternary geology (the most recent, geological period that covers the last 2 million years (approx.) of the Earth's history).

Kjølnes lighthouse is on the port side on a low peninsula out towards the Barents Sea. The first primitive lighthouse on the headland was erected in 1900, with a range of 7.2 nautical miles. This was powered by paraffin, brought to the lighthouse by boat, a method that was used until 1959.

The need for a larger and more effective lighthouse was obvious and in 1916 a new lighthouse was constructed - a black-painted cast iron structure, 20.8 metres in height with a secondary beacon with two levels. The lighthouse was driven by oil. After the retreat of the German forces in 1944, Kjølnes lighthouse was bombed and left partly in ruins.

The people of Berlevåg built a provisional lighthouse in the form of a construction with a strong lantern. The new lighthouse was completed in 1949 with two sets of accommodation, four outside toilets, four outhouses and four boathouses. The lighthouse has a 22 metre high concrete tower and has a range of 15 nautical miles. It was not before 1957 that Kjølnes lighthouse was supplied with electricity and at the same time the first fog signal was installed. Two years later, a road was constructed all the way up to the lighthouse. Kjølnes lighthouse was automated in 1989 and became unmanned from 1994. It was given protected status in 1998. The lighthouse is now in private hands and offers accommodation for overnight stays.

We pass the outer side of the breakwater before we enter the fishing harbour at Berlevåg.

The ship docks at the quayside in Berlevåg

The community and municipal seat of Berlevåg is one of the largest fishing communities in Finnmark, with industrial fishing plants, boatyards and mechanical workshops. Berlevåg lies as far east as Istanbul and is located almost as far north as the North Cape and Barrow in Canada.

As the German troops retreated in 1944, Berlevåg was left in ruins. The buildings were burned to the ground, livestock was slaughtered and the people were deported or evacuated. The buildings in Kongsfjord, however, were not destroyed. During the 1950s the fishing community was rebuilt, in the same post-war architectural style that was typical for the period, around the harbour as its natural centre.

The sea around Berlevåg is comprised of shallow fishing banks and previously the fishermen had not far to go to get to their fishing grounds. Berlevågs location, out towards the Barents Sea, exposed to extreme weather, has previously led to great problems for the community. In 1882 most of the fishing fleet was lost in a massive storm. Throughout the years several breakwaters have been built to try and protect the harbour. During the period 1875 to 1975, four breakwaters were constructed - all of them were destroyed by fierce storms. The current outer breakwaters are built from approx. 10 000 four-armed cast concrete blocks (known as 'tetrapods') each weighing 15 tonnes. These are joined together in a certain pattern. They have withstood waves up to 9.8 metres in height. The harbour is continually dredged and deep-water berths have been created in order to allow larger vessels to dock.

Berlevåg church is a marker point for approaching ships and boats and is built on a slight rise. It was consecrated in 1960. It has been built as a longhouse construction and has seating for 300. It has a beautiful altar and a 9-voiced pipe organ.

Berlevåg has a very active cultural scene – some of this was documented in the acclaimed cinema film documentary "Heftig og begeistret" (English title: "Cool and Crazy").

The ship continues to Mehamn

We pass the headland of **Valen** and Berlevåg airport, a short-runway airport with a tarmaced 800 m runway, which lies just west of Berlevåg. As the final point on the Varanger peninsula before the fjord **Tanafjord**, on the port side you can see **Russehamn** lying beneath **Dikkavikfjell** and **Tanahorn** mountain at the mouth of Tanafjord. Tanahorn is a steep mountain peak (270 m above sea level), known as a site of former Sámi sacrifices.

Tanafjord, on the port side, is 65 km long. It is 8-12 km wide and has several large fjord arms. The largest of these is **Hopsfjorden** that cuts into the **Nordkinn** peninsula to **Hopseidet** (p 210), **Langfjorden** which runs 24 km southwest further in Tanafjord, and **Trollfjorden** leading north-east into the **Varanger** peninsula. The population along these fjords is sparse.

Approx. 70°58'N   28°51'E

We cross the municipal border between Berlevåg and Gamvik, in the middle of Tanafjord (day 6)

The Pomor Trade

The word 'Pomor' in Russian means 'one who lives near the sea'. The Pomors were from the White Sea coast. The capital was the town of Archangelsk by the mouth of the River Dvina. Archangelsk was founded in 1584 as a centre of trade between North West Russia and Western Europe. The trade started after the English explorer Richard Chancellor, on an expedition to find the Northeast Passage, arrived at the White Sea (p 206).

The Pomors were fishermen and hunters and travelled as far as Svalbard. Many of them traded from their boats. They lived in large family communities and were organised as village communes and cooperatives. Many Pomors were followers of the so-called 'old faith' – they had severed ties with the official Russian Orthodox Church in the second half of the 17th century and retained their old religious traditions. They had their own churches and monasteries in the Pomor area and owned huge tracts of land by the middle of the 18th century. These people took part in the Pomor trade in Northern Norway.

Even though trade between Northern Norway and North-West Russia took place as early as in the Viking period, the era of the Pomor trade is regarded as lasting from approx. 1740 until the Russian revolution of 1917. The trade between those living along the coast in Northern Norway and Russians from the White Sea/ Archangelsk took place during the summer months. Some of the trade was barter, some involved monetary exchange. The goods that the Russians brought with them were mainly rye flour, however they also brought a variety of other goods; tar, canvas, ropes, bark, wheat flour, oatmeal, meat, dairy products and luxury items such as sweets, porcelain items and fine wooden carvings. In exchange for these goods, the Russians took all kinds of raw fish, especially halibut, seithe (coalfish), haddock and cod that they salted on board their ships. They had a special reason for wanting to obtain fish from Norway. The Russian church had decreed

Vadsø

a number of fast days on which they were only permitted to eat fish and vegetables. In return, Northern Norway was assured important supplies, independent of those that came from the south of Norway.

The Pomor trade was actually illegal. The trading authorities in Bergen, Trondheim and later Copenhagen had a monopoly on the trade with Northern Norway. The Pomor trade, however, proved difficult to monitor and control and was eventually made legal in 1796.

In the 1800s, the most important period for the Pomor trade, as many as 300-400 ships from Russia came to Norway, with crews totalling some 2 000 men. The captains had their regular contacts and supply points and returned to the same fishing villages year after year. The Russians were popular and spoke to the Norwegians in a specially developed mixed language known as 'russenorsk'. Via the Pomor trade, the people of Northern Norway gained an insight into a colourful and alternative culture, with harmonious songs, vivid clothes and renowned hospitality.

Vardø, the nearest customs post on the Norwegian side of the border, was regarded as the 'Pomor Capital'. Vadsø, Hammerfest and Tromsø were also large Pomor ports. On some occasions, as many as a hundred ships could be moored in the harbour in Vardø.

Both in Northern Norway and in Archangelsk, there are museums that have preserved items and information about the Pomor trade. The most well known of these museums, the Brodtkorb museum in Vardø, has some of the oldest preserved wharves in Northern Norway. The museum has detailed documents from the Pomor times. The listed buildings, which were built between 1840 and 1900, have three storeys, built from solid Russian timber and wide planks of Russian larch. The buildings were the centre of the Pomor trade and many Pomors worked here each summer until 1917. In several of the ports that were visited by the Pomors, there is evidence of their presence, e.g. the 'Russian cabins' in Hamningsberg (p 236) and Indre Kiberg (p 230).

The Sámi

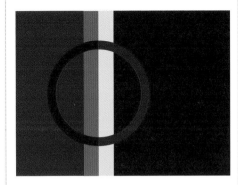

The Sámi are an ethnic minority group in Norway; however, they are a part of the Norwegian population. Most Sámi originally settled in Troms and Finnmark counties; however historical sources show that they also lived in the interior and southern parts of the country. An official definition that a person is a Sámi is "when the person regards himself as a Sámi, or if a parent or grandparent has spoken the Sámi language as their mother tongue".

The descendants of the Sámi were semi-nomadic hunters and fishermen. They were known as the "indigenous people of the North Calotte" and lived in the northern parts of Norway, Sweden, Finland and Russia. Some of the first archaeological traces of settlements in Northern Europe have been discovered at Sarnes on Magerøya close to the North Cape (p 203) and at Slettnes near Gamvik on the Norkinn peninsula (p 215). Archaeological evidence shows that people lived in the area approx. 10 000 years ago. The people lived by hunting and fishing and they followed the reindeer flocks that grazed on the edges of the glaciers that at that time covered the land. It is uncertain where these settlers originally came from – they may have come from the south and travelled up the Norwegian coast, they may have come from Russia in the east or from Bottenviken between Northern Finland and Northern Sweden.

In 1925, archaeological excavations revealed finds from the early Stone Age near the mountain of Komsa in Alta municipality (p 268). The people that lived here belonged to the so-called "Komsa

culture" which existed around 10 000-4 000 B.C. The area of the Komsa culture stretches from the boundary between Troms and Finnmark and the Fisker peninsula in Russia.

The Komsa culture is divided into three phases: The oldest, from approx. 10 000-7 000 B.C., shows evidence of the use of certain tools and this tells us that the people hunted whales and seals along the coast, and carried out hunting and trapping in the inland areas. The absence of any evidence of permanent dwellings indicates that they were nomadic and lived in tents and moved along with the flocks of game.

The middle phase, from 7 000-5 500 B.C., shows that dwellings (turf bothies) had become more permanent. People still followed the wild game; however, they returned to the same settlements year after year. Finds of various alternative tools from this period indicate that whales and seals were no longer hunted to the same extent.

In the third phase (5 000-4 200) B.C., the ice was beginning to recede and it

was possible to travel inland across the Finnmark plains. The pine forests began to spread and along with these, elk and small game such as otter and squirrels began to become established.

In the early Stone Age (4 200-1 800 B.C.) most tools were made from slate. The main settlements were in the innermost part of the fjords, where people lived during the winter months. In the spring, the people went to the coast to hunt seals and small whales. During the summer they remained in the inland areas, fishing in the rivers and gathering berries. In the autumn they hunted reindeer on the plains.

After 1 800 B.C. the climate once again became colder. The pine forest and wild game retreated and the wild reindeer remained. A pattern became established, of grazing on the plains in winter and at the coast in the summer. The people followed the reindeer flocks and developed various hunting techniques. Among others, one method was to set up a fence to block the reindeers' path and drive the animals over a cliff or into a pit. When the number of wild reindeer dwindled, people began to keep domesticated animals and over the centuries reindeer husbandry became more and more of a regular practice. However, the established pattern of summer and winter grazing continued. During the winter the Sámi lived on the plains along with the reindeer. The animals survived on lichen that they dug from beneath the snow. When spring came the Sámi moved along with the reindeer, which live in large flocks, down to the coast where the grazing was better and the plants more nutritious. The movement of the flock each spring took place just before the calving season and the sites where the annual calving took place were the same every year for each reindeer flock. The calves were marked with the owner's special brand mark before they were taken from their mothers.

This pattern has continued right up to modern times.

The oldest known written text about the Sámi was written by the Roman historian Tacitus. He described a tribe of people he called "fenni" in a book from A.D. 98. The people he referred to lived in the far north, wore clothes made of hides and did not live in permanent dwellings.

In A.D. 555, the Greek historian Procopius described a war between the Romans and the Goths. He referred to Scandinavia as "Thule", and among them were a group of people he called "Skridfinns".

The Roman Paulus Diaconus wrote around A.D. 750 about the "Skridfinns". He described them as hunters and skiers that kept animals that looked somewhat like deer (reindeer). Some of the Icelandic sagas also confirm these observations.

Snorre Sturlason's King's Sagas, that mainly describe the period from the 10th to the 13th century A.D., tell of traders that did business with the Sámi and levied taxes. At that time, animal skins were among the most popular trade goods. During the preceding Viking

period and the later Middle Ages (p 83), furs were the most prized items. The Viking Ottar (p 123) made possibly the best observation of the Sámi and their way of life when he visited King Alfred the Great and his court at the end of the 9th century.

The coastal Sámi lived along the coast and in the innermost parts of the fjords, and fished and kept livestock. Originally, they settled along the coast as far south as Trøndelag. The coastal Sámi were active traders and they constructed ships that carried goods to Vågan in Lofoten and to Bergen. They traded with the Hansa in Bergen, selling furs, walrus ivory and waterproof textiles that were woven using traditional Sámi techniques.

Snorre Sturlason's King's Sagas tell of the Sámi and their knowledge of magic and sorcery. The Sámi religion was closely associated with nature; the sun, moon, wind and thunder all had divine powers. A tree, a stone or a mountain had a life and a soul. By offering sacrifices it was possible to appease the gods. Drumming on rune drums and singing songs known as a 'joik' were important elements in this respect. The shaman, or 'noaiden' was a very important figure in Sámi culture – he could travel into the realm of the dead and bring back lost souls. He could also see into the future.

Christian missionary efforts among the Sámi began in the 1550s; however, it was not before the 1700s that the indigenous Sámi religion began losing ground. Churches and missions were built in the Sámi areas and missionaries were sent out to convert Sámi people to Christianity. The missionary work was also a way of demonstrating the ownership of Norwegian territory. The land areas in the north and the sea further beyond became steadily more important, both politically and in regard

to trade. The borders between the Nordic countries were established in 1721. The Saami Codicil was written in 1751. This guaranteed Sámi the same rights to freedom of movement over borders and to use the same ancient Sámi routes, regardless of actual nationality – they were however to pay tax to just one country. Formerly, the Sámi had been gravely exploited by tax collectors and had been required to pay taxes to Russia, Finland, Sweden and Norway at the same time.

The exploitation of the natural resources in the Sámi areas had great influence on the lives of the Sámi in the north. The rich fishing grounds off the coast of Troms and Finnmark drew many fishermen from the south. Later, the newly established prospecting and mining enterprises contributed to the population of the inner areas of Finnmark, which led to a partial alteration of the Sámi way of life. The migrants brought new agricultural techniques with them from the southern parts of the country and it became more difficult for the Sámi to live by their familiar, traditional methods.

The pervasive activities of missionaries and the school system led to the increased integration of the Sámi into the Norwegian population and its culture. At that time the schools were mostly residential, the teaching language was Norwegian and the teachers spoke Norwegian to the pupils. Teaching of Sámi culture and language was given low priority. It was first in 1930 that the Sámi language was accepted as a second language in some schools. In some other areas Sámi language was actually forbidden until as recently as the 1950s.

The Sámi language belongs to the Finn-Ugric language group and is thus 'related' to Hungarian and Finnish. It has three distinct dialects – southern, northern and eastern Sámi.

The Norwegianization policy began to influence the politics of agriculture, national defence, school policies, communi-

© DESTINATION TROMSØ

cations and the media. For example, the Norwegian Land Act of 1902 states clearly that "land was only to be managed by Norwegian nationals and to those who could speak, read and write Norwegian". Even though the Norwegianization program eventually ended, the damage done to the Sámi people's knowledge of their own language, history and culture was considerable.

Reindeer husbandry has always been an important part of the economy for Sámi. It has become steadily more industrialised and now only approx. 5 % of Sámi are actually involved in the industry. The number of reindeer, however, has increased and the damage caused to the Finnmark plains by overgrazing is considerable. The former trade and barter system in which reindeer meat was exchanged for other goods has been replaced by a monetary trade system. The sale of reindeer meat has become regulated and modern abattoirs and sales organisations for reindeer products have been established, ensuring stable prices and turnover.

The conflict that arose from the development of the Alta-Kautokeino water course in the 1970s and 1980s led to greatly increased awareness of Sámi culture and various other issues among Norwegians and even the Sámi themselves. The first development plans were so extensive that the Sámi village of Masi would have been placed under water along with large areas of grazing grounds on the Finnmark plain. The development schemes were later moderated and Masi was saved. The conflict led to a separate Sámi Parliament being established in 1989.

The Sámi Parliament is today the most important, elected Sámi institution in Norway and has been delegated responsibility for making decisions that previously were taken by special government committees and boards, concerning Sámi language, culture and communities. The Sámi Parliament is elected by a Sámi population that in 2006 included approx. 10 000 registered voters. A certain amount of funds are transferred annually from the Norwegian Storting which is used to reinforce and develop a sustainable indigenous peoples' culture in Norway. The Sámi Parliaments in Norway, Sweden and Finland joined together to establish a common parliamentary committee, to promote the interests of Sámi in all Nordic countries.

Another organisation that works for the rights of Sámi in Norway is the Norwegian Sámi Association, established in 1968. The organisation works to unite all Sámi and for better cultural, social and economic conditions for the Sámi people.

After 25 years of cooperation between the Norwegian Storting, the Sámi Parliament and Finnmark county administration, the new Finnmark Act was introduced in 2005. The Act grants Sámi and other Finnmark residents rights to land and water in Finnmark. An area larger than Denmark is to be transferred from national to local ownership. Existing rights are to be evaluated and officially recognised.

The aim of the Finnmark Act is to provide a basis for the management of Finnmark's natural resources in a balanced and ecologically sustainable manner, in the best interests of the population of the county and especially concerning Sámi culture, reindeer husbandry, use of grazing areas, enterprise development and communities (Royal Norwegian Ministry of Justice and the Police, fact sheet on the Finnmark Act 24.06.2005).

Source: http://tovesiv.stud.hive.no.
Store norske Leksikon.

DAY 8

Mehamn, Kjøllefjord, Honningsvåg, Havøysund, Hammerfest, Øksfjord, Skjervøy and Tromsø

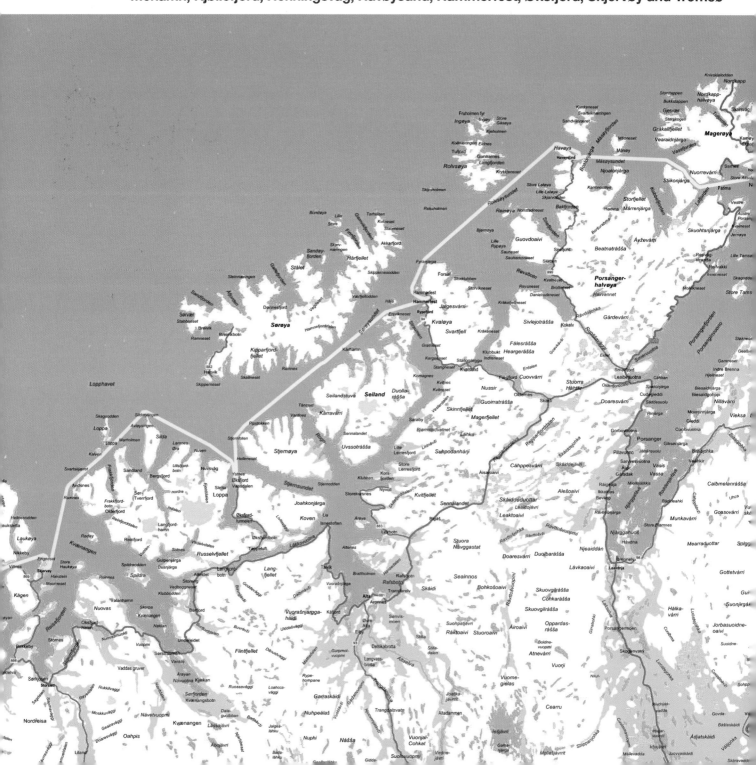

We are now in Nordkapp municipality (p 203). During the night, we have sailed by the ports of **Mehamn** (71°02'N 27°50'E, 0100-0115) (p 213) in Gamvik municipality and **Kjøllefjord** (70°57'N 27°21'E, 0315-0330) in Lebesby municipality (p 211).

The community of **Honningsvåg** (p 204) is now behind us and we set a course for our next port of call, Havøysund (p 198).

70°58'N   24°21'E   ①

The ship sails along the east coast of **Magerøya**, through the narrow **Magerøysundet** (p 202).

At the foot of the outermost headland on **Stikkelvågnæringen/Stiikorássa** on the port side, for a brief moment, as the ship passes close to the mountain, you can see two small cliff formations – one at the water's edge and another further up the cliff face. The topmost formation can be interpreted as the figure of a woman that looks out over the channel in a westerly direction.

After rounding Stikkelvågnæringen we head westwards in **Måsøysundet**. On the port side are the two fjords **Kobbefjorden** with the large island **Store Kobbøya**, and **Ryggefjorden**. The headland of **Marreneset** with **Storfjellet** (356 m above sea level) divides the two fjords. The island of Havøya, the tongue of land known as Havøygavlen with its characteristic windmills, and the community centre Havøysund are up ahead. On the starboard side is the mountain known as **Vassfjordnæringen** (267 m above sea level).

Approx. 70°58'N   25°25'E

We pass the municipal boundary between Måsøy (p 191) and Nordkapp

70°59'N   25°00'E   ②

The ship sails by **Måsøya** (13.9 km²) on the starboard side (p 201). North-west of Måsøya is the uninhabited island of **Hjelmsøya** (39 km²) (p 199).

The following often-told legend is allegedly true: "On Helmsøy there is a mountain known as Spenselfjellet. A man named Spensel died on the mountain many years ago - hence the name. There was a young girl called Barbro who worked as a domestic servant for the priest on Måsøy. She was engaged to be married to Spensel. No one really knew where Mr. Spensel came from, but according to ru-

mours, he was supposed to have come from a fine family. One day, the priest heard that Barbro was expecting a child. The girl was summoned to see the priest. She had to explain her situation. The discussion ended with the girl being hounded out of the house by the priest. As if that was not enough, the girl was also ordered to leave Måsøy, and never to set foot in the priest's parish again. Barbro did not know what to do. She went to her fiancé and told him of her dreadful situation. They had to admit that they had no choice but to leave Måsøy. However, the question was: what were they to do in the wintertime? No one in the village would take them in, for they dared not defy the orders of the priest. One evening the weather had eased a little. Barbro and Spensel got hold of a boat and they planned to row over the fjord whilst the weather was still good. However, a short time after they had started out from Måsøy, the weather turned against them. Gales from the northeast and high waves and snow made the conditions terrible.

On Måsøy, the local people believed that Spensel and Barbro must have capsized - it seemed impossible that they could have crossed the fjord to Helmsøy in such foul weather. When no one had heard from them throughout the entire winter it seemed clear that they had been drowned crossing the water.

The winter ended and spring arrived. The snow began to melt away. On Helmsøy, towards Svartvik, or Svartvikhalsen, the body of a man was found. No one knew who he was. On his clothing were embroidered the initials "P.S.". The body was left where it lay, as no one dared to move or touch it. It could have been the body of a fugitive, who had moved on from place to place to avoid capture. As spring went on, almost in the summer, the bodies of a woman and a newborn baby were found under a rock face at Svartviknesset. No one knew the identity of the woman. When the local people of Helmsøy came to Måsøy later in the summer, they heard the tale of Peter Spensel and his fiancée and their journey to Helmsøy across the fjord. They understood straight away that it must have been the bodies of Spensel and Barbro that had been found. The initials on Spensel's clothes told them as much. So their tragic journey was reconstructed – the couple had managed the first part of their journey across the water; however, when they reached Svartviknesset the wind had become too strong. Spensel and Barbro had most likely landed their boat there, and sought shelter under the rock face. It was possible that they had waited there for the weather to improve, and then tried to cross the mountain to Keila. However, Barbro had become terribly sick, she had been unable to cope with the effort of rowing the boat so far and Spensel had decided to go over the mountain alone. The storm continued to rage and had combined with a terrible snowstorm. Spensel, who was unfamiliar with the area, had probably got lost on the mountain. Instead of heading for Keila, he had set off in the direction of Akkarfjord, and had finally collapsed of exhaustion. When Barbro did not receive any help she and the child became weaker and both of them died there under the rocks."

To port is the headland **Njoalneset** (337 above sea level) between **Ryggefjorden** and **Kulfjorden** (p 200). On the port side, up ahead is the headland **Trollfjordneset**.

We begin to approach the next port of call, the community of Havøysund. Ahead, we can see the bridge that connects the island of Havøya (7.2 km²) with the mainland. On the port side is Breidsundet between Havøya and Rolvsøya (89.4 km²).

The ship docks at the quayside in Havøysund (p 198)

Many places in Norway have their own legends. This is a legend from Havøysund concerning the sound at Havøysundet. The previous generations of coastal ships were smaller than today and were able to pass easily through the sound. They could see the headland Øraodden (70°59'40"N 24°39'48"E) from the ship. The place is a few minutes walk from the current port, and is the scene of the following legend:

"A long, long time ago, a Sámi family lived in Havøysund. The family had many children and was quite wealthy. The eldest child – a girl – grew up to be very beautiful and it was said that she was the prettiest girl in the whole of Finnmark county. One day a young Sámi came to Havøysund. He had a fine blue Sámi costume and was quite  wealthy, however he was not very handsome. Straight away, he was very taken by the beautiful Sámi girl and he believed that she would be his bride as he was the only suitor for many miles around. Time went on, but the girl did not give her consent.

And so, one day, another Sámi in a red costume came to stay at Havøysund. He was a fine young man, and wealthy too. It was not very long before he and the Sámi girl were spending most of their time together. The Sámi in the blue costume did not appreciate this at all. He was consumed by jealousy and one day he cast an evil spell on the other Sámi in the red costume, and turned him into a rock on the cliff face just above the sound. This made the Sámi girl extremely angry and so she cast a spell on the blue-costumed Sámi and he too was turned into a part of the same cliff. This cliff is just above the sound from Øraodden. When the cliff is wet from rain and the evening or midnight sun shines at an angle, you can see the contours of both Sámi – the one in the red costume just to the east of the 'blue' Sámi."

The ship continues to Hammerfest   **+ 0 hrs 00 min**

LARGER MAP P**408**

The ship leaves Havøysund, sails back along the same course to Garpeskjæret, enters Breidsundet and rounds Havøya. On the starboard side is Hjelmsøya. Further along is the windmill park at the headland Havøygavlen.

71°00'N   24°27'E

We pass Havøygavlen (287 m above sea level) and the windmill park (p 198). On the starboard side, just ahead is **Rolvsøya** with the sandy beach at **Gunnarsnes** and the short **Langfjorden**, then the small neck of land between the northerly and southerly parts of Rolvsøya (p 191). Furthest out is **Ingøya** (p 192). We sail into the sound **Rolvsøysundet**. Several ships have been wrecked in this area (p 197).

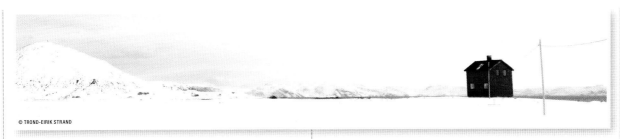

© TROND-EIRIK STRAND

Ahead is Sørøya, behind Rolvsøya. On the port side up ahead is Kvaløya - both of these islands are in Hammerfest municipality.

70°58'N 24°20'E	+ 0 hrs 46 min ③

On the port side we pass the islands **Store Latøya** and **Lille Latøya** (p 196), behind them are the two fjords **Bakfjorden** and **Snefjorden** (p 196).

70°55'N 24°11'E	+ 1 hr 02 min ④

The bay of **Sørhamn** and the mountain **Skoltefjellet** (314 m above sea level) on the southernmost part of **Rolvsøya** are over on our starboard side. Before the ship enters the leeward side of Sørøya in Hammerfest municipality, you can see the open Norwegian Sea.

The mountains **Vestre Burstadfjellet** (471 m above sea level) and **Vestre Middagsfjellet** (445 m above sea level), outermost on the peninsula **Kvalnesklubben** on the **Porsanger** peninsula can be seen on the port side, up ahead. In front of the mountain are two islands, **Reinøykalven** (94 m above sea level) and **Reinøya** (142 m above sea level) (p 196) both of these islands are breeding sites for seabirds. On the port side is Vestre Middagsfjellet.

The bird island of **Bjørnøya** (p 191) lies ahead on the port side, behind the two smaller islands **Lille** and **Store Rypøya** at the entrance to the fjord bay of **Revsbotn** (p 196) between Kvalnesklubben, Kvalsund municipality at the bottom of the fjord, and the island of Kvaløya up ahead in the distance.

© STATOIL

"The Road to Havøysund" is gradually becoming a concept in its own right. The road that runs between the community of Kokelv innermost in Revsbotn is especially picturesque and has achieved the status of 'national tourist road' (p 196).

Kokelv (pop. approx. 230) is a coastal Sámi village and the second largest local community in Kvalsund municipality. The chapel at Kokelv was built by German peace workers in 1960 during the "Action for Atonement". The community earns its living from fishing in combination with other commercial activities.

Approx. 70°50'N   23°54'E

We pass the boundary between Måsøy and Hammerfest municipalities

Hammerfest municipality

Municipal coat of arms, significance: Hunting in the Polar region.
Meaning of name: From Norse hamarr, 'steep cliff face, and festr, 'mooring rope for boats'.
Municipal seat: Hammerfest (pop. 6 832).
Position: 70°40'N 23°40'40"E.   **Area:** 848 km².
Population: 9 391.   **Pop. density:** 11.1 km².
Area distribution: Farming 0 %, forestry 0 %, fresh water 3 %, other area 97 %.
Trade and industry: Fish processing. Oil and gas industry. Oil supply base. State Oil Spill Contingency Agency. Mechanical workshops. Fishing gear manufacture/repairs. Service base for the fishing fleets in the Barents Sea. Fishing trade organisations and fish exporters. Commercial and service industry for West Finnmark. Regional offices of several state institutions and companies.
Places to return to: Ishavsklubben. Finnmark Restoration Museum. Meridian monument. Hammerfest church.
Activities to return to: Sea fishing.
Hammerfest municipality's home page: www.hammerfest.kommune.no

Hammerfest municipality lies within parts of the three islands of Kvaløya, Seiland and Sørøya. Sørøya and Seiland have steep, rugged coastlines.

In front you can see Kvaløya and the town of Hammerfest. In front on the starboard side is Sørøya.

Between the large islands of Sørøya (starboard, ahead) and Kvaløya (port, ahead) and Seiland behind Kvaløya, is **Sørøysundet,** which is 70 km long and 4-17 km wide.

Sørøya (816 km², 659 m above sea level) ahead on the starboard side is Norway's fourth largest island and the largest in Finnmark. The coastline is steep and rugged, especially on the north side of the island. The northern part of the island lies within Hammerfest municipality and is very sparsely inhabited. The southern part lies within Hasvik municipality.

Kvaløya (336 km²) on the port side, is treeless with a steep coastline and rounded mountains. The mountain **Svartfjell** (630 m above sea level) in the centre of the island is the highest point. Hammerfest town lies on the north west side of Kvaløya. Most of the population lives along the island's western coastline. Kvaløya with Hammerfest town has a mainland connection over Kvalsundet via Kvalsund bridge on the eastern side of the island. The bridge is the world's northernmost suspension bridge, with a main span of 525 m and a total length of 741 m. The bridge was opened in 1977. The three largest islands in the municipality are connected by a ferry service.

70°49'24"N   23°52'E   + 1 hr 35 min ⑤

Sørøya on the starboard side has innumerable inlets and headlands. There is a great deal of history connected with these, both on the north east side of the island (that cannot be seen from the ship) and on the south east side which faces Sørøysundet. The northernmost point of the island is the headland of **Tarhalsen** (129 m above sea level) and thereafter Kjøtvikfjellet, that drops steeply into the ocean.

Kjøtvikvarden is an 11 m high navigation marker built of stone on the peak of **Kjøtvikfjellet** (319 m above sea level). The cairn was built in 1854 and is the only one of its kind in Norway that is constructed at such a height – all the others are built upon skerries and islets. The cairn is one of the few constructions that survived destruction by the German forces during the Second World War. The Kjøtvik cairn is also the oldest stone block construction in Finnmark.

After the headland at **Bismavik** on the starboard side, we can see the fishing community of **Akkarfjord** (pop. 83 in 2001), innermost in **Akkarfjorden.** Thereafter, also on the starboard side are **Borvikklubben** (271 m above sea level) and the bay **Borvika,** then **Høgnova** (385 above sea level), **Skippernesodden** and **Skippernesfjorden.** Further, the well preserved **Hellefjord** where there are now only a handful of permanent residents left, **Værfjellodden, Langstrand** and **Langstrandfjorden** within the

island of Hjelmen. The division between the various bays and inlets can be somewhat difficult to spot.

70°47'N   23°44'E   + 1 hr 48 min

For a while, we have been able to see the north end of Kvaløya on the port side, with the mountain **Miilet** (364 m above sea level). In the bay **Kirkegårdsbukta** near the village of **Forsøl** on the north east side of the mountain, stands one of the most well known cultural heritage sites in Finnmark. This now protected area has evidence of ancient settlements from the Stone Age, the Iron Age and recent times. The most well known site is of a house from the early Middle Ages (p 83), which measures 23 x 25 m with six rooms and three entrances.

On the port side up ahead is the bay of **Myllingbukta,** before the mauntain **Storfjellet** (384 m above sea level). In front is Melkøya.

In front, further forward, you can see the island of Seiland and the glacier Seilandsjøkelen.

70°42'N   23°34'E   + 2 hrs 12 min ⑥

On the starboard side up ahead, in the middle of Sørøysundet, are the two islands of Håja and Hjelmen. Håja is up ahead with the smaller Hjelmen behind.

The island of **Melkøya** (port side, ahead) has lent its name to the Melkøya major gas installation project in Hammerfest and Finnmark. The massive project began in 1980, when licences for prospecting for petroleum in the Barents Sea were first granted, with Hammerfest designated as a base for supply ships, oil spill contingency services and helicopter traffic. After the discovery of the gas fields of Snøhvit, Askeladden and Albatross just outside of Hammerfest, it was decided to construct a LNG (Liquid Natural Gas) plant on Melkøya. Gas is brought on land to the production and export installations on Melkøya before being shipped to Europe and the USA. The construction of the plant began in 2002 and production began in 2007 (p 266).

The ship docks at the quayside in Hammerfest

Hammerfest port was known as the best in Northern Norway, well before it was populated between 1250 and 1350. The origin of the name Hammerfest is hamarr, the

Norse name for 'steep cliff face' and festr, which means a 'rope for mooring boats'. The ice-free harbour was close to the sailing channel, and was therefore well suited to commerce and trade. The famous explorers that set out to explore the Northeast Passage, to chart the northerly sea route to China and India, stopped here to take on fresh water before continuing on their journey.

Both Hammerfest and Vardø (p 232) received their town charter in 1789, the first towns north of Trondheim. They were central locations for the Pomor trade with North West Russia (p 241). The same year,

PEDER BALKE: FROM HAMMERFEST

the trade monopoly held by Bergen for commercial trade with the north of Norway was abolished. The local people learned about polar hunting skills from the Pomors and the first polar sea expeditions from Hammerfest set out in the 1790s. During the following years polar hunting increased considerably and at the beginning of the 1900s, Hammerfest was widely regarded as the "Polar Capital" of Norway.

Several major powers set up consulates in Hammerfest, among them Russia, England, Holland, France, the German town of Hamburg and the principality of Mecklenburg. The United States opened a separate consulate in 1865. The reason for this was Hammerfest's connection to the rich fishing grounds in the north. Hammerfest had direct export of fish to Germany and Italy and trade connections with the Spanish towns of Malaga, Barcelona and Bilbao.

In 1809 Hammerfest became involved in the Napoleonic Wars (p 85). The town was central in the corn trade between the towns of Archangelsk and Denmark and for that reason it was attacked by two British naval vessels, besieged and plundered for almost a week. The land defences comprised of 28 men with four small cannons!

In 1825 the town had a population of 341, and the port was visited by 150-200 vessels. In 1865 the population had risen to 1 547. Today (2007) the town has 6 832 inhabitants and approx. 4 000 vessels call at the port annually – not including the fishing fleet.

In 1856, Hammerfest was left almost in ruins by a savage hurricane. Funds for the rebuilding of the town came in via contributors as far away as Stockholm and Copenhagen.

In 1890, two-thirds of the town was destroyed by fire. In the rebuilding phase after the fire, Hammerfest, as the first town in northern Europe, had electric street lighting installed. The electric power required for the street lights came from a separate hydroelectric power station.

Hammerfest 1890

In February of 1945, during the retreat from Finnmark and Northern Norway, the German forces burned Hammerfest as part of their 'scorched earth' tactic (p 221). Only one building was left standing.

After the Second World War, Hammerfest became Finnmark's most important centre for fishing and the fishing industry. The proximity to the fishing grounds in the Norwegian Sea and The Barents Sea, along with the excellent port facilities, has always been the very basis of Hammerfest's existence. As an international polar port, fishing harbour and maritime centre the town has developed a commercial centre, skilled milieu and services within these fields. Hammerfest is a natural service centre for the fishing fleet of the Barents Sea.

In addition to the commercial fishing industries, including fish farming, there are also many companies and institutions that operate within travel/tourism, commerce and service, education, public administration and communications.

The port of Hammerfest has been designated as the regional port for the county of Finnmark, and is the largest within the county. Most of Finnmark is connected via Hammerfest by daily catamaran services. The port is visited by a large number of cruise ships during the tourist season.

The airport at Hammerfest is one of Norway's busiest short-runway airports. The airline company Widerøe has its base here for its activities in Nord-Troms and Finnmark and the town is the major hub for Widerøe's network of flights in the north.

The Meridian Monument was erected in 1854. The Russian scientist Fredrik G.W. Struve started a survey project in 1816, to determine the degree of flattening of the earth's surface that occurs at the poles. The information would enable cartographers to draw up more precise charts and maps. The survey was carried out at a number of separate points along a meridian from the town of Ismail on the Black Sea and northwards to Fuglenes in Hammerfest. Struve's meridian curve passes through ten countries: Norway, Sweden, Finland, Russia, Estonia, Latvia, Lithuania, Belarus, Moldova and Ukraine. These countries worked together to preserve the 34 points that were used when the survey was carried out. Four of these survey points are in Finnmark, of which one is in Hammerfest.

In 2005, UNESCO accepted the application to include the survey points on the World Heritage List. The basis was that Struve's meridian curve is a "scientific work that is unsurpassed in dimension and scope". Due to the precise nature of the survey, the results have remained extremely useful in charting and mapping sciences, right up until the advent of satellite technology made further advancement possible.

The Hurtigruten remains at the quayside in Hammerfest for approx. 1½ hours, allowing a good opportunity for a little sightseeing.

"Isbjørnklubben" (The Polar Bear club) is a museum exhibition that shows the long history of the town and its proud heritage of fishing and hunting in polar regions. It is possible to become a member of the club

The "Restoration Museum" for Finnmark and Nord-Troms holds an exhibition that deals with the history of forced evacuation, burning and restoration of Finnmark and North-Troms during and after the Second World War.

The "Ishavsporten" statue stands before the town hall and indicates the meridians that lead towards the north, crowned with Hammerfest's coat of arms. The ice floes with polar bears symbolize the town's history as a polar town.

The fountain known as "Mother and Child" on the town square symbolizes a family on land that waits for their husband and father to come home from the sea. The statue was a gift from an American ambassador to Norway, whose mother came from Hammerfest.

The smaller fortification, "Skansen", that was used in the Napoleonic Wars stands close to the Meridian monument. "Skansen" was restored in 1989.

The sculpture "Polar vessel in the ice" on the square is a symbol of the activities that shaped Hammerfest, namely polar hunting and fishing.

The "Blue music pavilion" stands in the park just above the square and exhibits the best of building architecture from old Hammerfest. The pavilion was presented as a gift during the town's 200th jubilee in 1989.

The first church in Hammerfest was built in 1620. The town has previously had five churches. All were destroyed by fire.

The present church in Hammerfest was consecrated in 1961, as the previous church had been burned down during the retreat of the German forces in 1944. The church is a longhouse construction in which the roofline is brought down towards the ground giving the church a distinct triangular shape. The triangle shape is repeated in the tower and in the windows along the sides of the

building. The church is somewhat special in that it does not have an altar, but a large glass mosaic at the front. The church seats approx. 500 persons.

The Catholic church in Hammerfest, St. Michaels, is the world's most northerly Catholic church, and was built in 1958.

Behind Hammerfest is the local mountain known as **Salen**, on which stands restaurant Turistova. On Salen there is a cairn, a copy of the original cairn that was built before the Second World War.

On the southern side of Kvaløya, close to the bridge to the mainland, is **Stalloen**, an ancient Sámi sacrificial site that was used until the 19th century. Coastal Sámi culture has been present here throughout history.

The ship continues to Øksfjord	+ 0 hrs 00 min

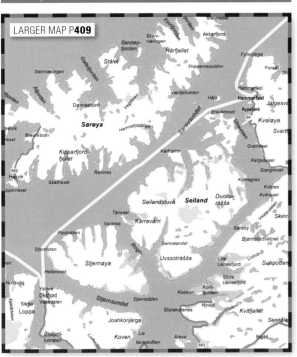

LARGER MAP P**409**

© INGUS

The hat-shaped and beautiful island of Håja and the smaller Hjelmen on the starboard side in Sørøysundet lie outside of Hammerfest. The islands are characterised by the special topography in and around Hammerfest which has been formed by glaciers, weather and ocean currents.

On the starboard side and in the distance to starboard you can see Sørøya and Sørøysundet. On the port side we will see the sound of **Straumen** between Kvaløya and the island of Seiland ahead on the port side.

70°39'27"N   23°35'33"E   + 0 hrs 14 min ①

The bay **Rypefjord** is on our port side, under **Tjuven** (418 m above sea level). The mountain was given the name Tjuven ('thief') as it covered the sun and 'stole' the light during the winter. A television mast (Tyven main transmitter) dominates the peak of the mountain.

The community of **Rypefjord** (pop. 1 745) lies behind the small peninsula of **Rypklubben** and is a suburb of Hammerfest. Rypefjord has an oil supply base, mechanical workshops and fishing industries.

Kirkegårdsøya is one of the small islands south of Rypefjord. The island is believed to have been used as a cemetery before the 17th century and was used as a Sámi burial ground between 1650-1750.

The island of **Håja** (296 m above sea level) passes on the starboard side, followed by the island of **Hjelmen** (142 m above sea level). The headland **Ersvikneset** (224 m above sea level) is on the port side.

70°38'N   23°22'E   + 0 hrs 27 min ②

We pass the headland **Grunnvågklubben** (216 above sea level) with a beacon set into the mountainside and the journey continues into Sørøysundet.

To starboard, we can see the central part of Sørøya with the village of **Slettnes** and the steep mountain **Klubben** north of **Slettnesfjorden**. Thereafter **Sandvikfjellet** (608 m above sea level).

At Slettnes a large and historically valuable cultural heritage site was discovered in the 1960s. When the site was found to be suitable as an alternative for construction of a new LNG-terminal, to bring gas ashore from the Snøhvit field, several archaeological surveys were conducted during 1991-92. More than 180 archaeological finds were registered, most of them provided evidence of ancient settlements. These finds date back some 11 000 years and cover a period lasting 10 000 years from approx. 9 000 B.C. to approx. A.D. 1 000. Remains of dwelling foundations from the early Stone Age have been discovered, however most of the finds were of settlements and dwellings from the recent Stone Age and early Iron Age (p 83). Five stone blocks with ancient carvings were also found, which are the world's northernmost rock carvings. These have been found to be from the transitional period between the early and more recent Stone Age and are thus more than 6 000 years old. These finds confirm that Northern Norway became populated at the same time as the south of the country. In addition, remains of dwellings and sacrificial pits were found, dating from the first millennium A.D. These are part of Sámi culture (p 243).

The northern part of the island of **Seiland** is ahead on the port side. The island has been given its special name because of the huge amounts of "sei" fish (seithe  or coalfish) that are caught there every year. Seiland is Norway's seventh largest island. It is almost treeless, but has a good deal of green vegetation. The island is split between the municipalities of Hammerfest, Kvalsund and Alta. The coast is rugged and has both deep and shallow fjords. The mountains drop steeply in most places directly into the sea. The sheerest terrain is found on the western side of the island, with a number of peaks that are more than 800 m above sea level. Norway's two most northerly glaciers, **Nordmannsjøkelen** (approx. 2 km², 1 079 m above sea level) and **Seilandsjøkelen** (approx. 12 km², 950 m above sea level) are in the centre of the island. Both of these glaciers have retreated considerably during the last 60-70 years due to the effects of global warming. The inhabitants of the island are spread around several smaller communities – the population was reduced considerably when the fishing industry began to fail and several smaller fish-

ing communities are now completely uninhabited. Seiland has very interesting geological formations with many types of mineral resources that may be possible to extract in the future. Archaeological excavations show that people have lives on Seiland for over 7 000 years.

Most of the transport to and from the islands is by boat, as there are few roads. In the summer the island is used as summer grazing ground for reindeer. These are brought to the island on barges in the spring and the animals swim back to the mainland in the autumn, when they are fit and nourished after the summer grazing.

The authorities are currently working on a proposition to declare Seiland a national park.

70°36'20"N   23°17'E   + 0 hrs 39 min

The islands of **Lille Vinna** (158 m above sea level) and **Store Vinna** (390 m above sea level) can be seen to port, after the mountain and peninsula of **Grunnvågklubben** which is now behind us. Store Vinna is used as a grazing area for male reindeer in the summer. These are most often brought to the island on barges in the spring. The reindeer swim back to the mainland in the autumn.

The mountain **Hønsebyfjellet** (556 m above sea level) is seen to port, behind Lille and Store Vinna, **Hønsebyfjorden** and the village of **Hønsebybotn** at the bottom of the fjord. The mountain **Veggen** ('the wall') (589 m above sea level) on the port side when passing Hønsebyfjorden, has an appropriate name – it falls almost vertically straight down into the fjord.

70°33'30"N   23°06'45"E   + 0 hrs 50 min

After Veggen is the fjord **Jøfjorden** that cuts 11 km into the island of Seiland.

At **Kårhamnneset** on the west side of Jøfjorden is the tiny fishing village of **Kårhamn** (pop. 35) at the foot of

the mountain **Stortinden** (627 m above sea level). The population of Kårhamn has remained stable during the last few years. There is a modern fish processing plant at Kårhamn. Traces of Stone Age settlements have been found here.

We continue to sail along Sørøysundet, an area rich in wild and beautiful nature, high peaks and numerous fjords. The coastline on the starboard side is difficult to describe in detail, as the scenery changes rapidly. As we sail along Sørøysundet, the mountains and the fjords appear one after another. One of the peaks is **Komagaksla** (659 m above sea level), the highest point on Sørøya.

The fjord **Skreifjorden** is passed after Kårhamn. In 1997, a Leatherback Sea Turtle had 'got lost' on its way northwards, guided by the Gulf Stream (p 85) and swam into the fjord. It collided with a boat belonging to two reindeer herders. The herders shot at it with a rifle and hit the animal several times, but could not kill it. The Leatherback Turtle was towed to land and later died of its injuries. The argument over the ownership of the turtle became so heated that the police had to intervene.

Lossefjellet (845 m above sea level) rises up on the port side. Behind the mountain is the glacier **Nordmannsjøkelen** (approx. 2 km², 1 079 m above sea level). This has retreated considerably during the last 100 years and has now split into several smaller glaciers.

Behind Nordmannsjøkelen you can see the larger glacier **Seilandsjøkelen** (approx. 12 km², approx. 950 m above sea level).

© ROLF LILAND

| 70°30'N   22°54'E | + 1 hr 16 min ③ |

Further out of Sørøysundet on the starboard side we pass Komagaksla, and then ahead is the headland of **Gåshopen**, the southern tip of **Strandafjellet** (459 m above sea level), and the peninsula of **Ramnes** (382 m above sea level), between these lies **Kobbefjorden.**

Still heading southwestwards, we pass **Nordre Bumannsfjord** on the port side, then the mountain **Sjutalet** (737 m above sea level) and **Søre Bumannsfjord**. Ahead, on the port side, we approach the mountain **Ytre Bårdveggen** (881 m above sea level), **Bårdfjorden** and **Tåneset**, the most south westerly point on Seiland.

| 70°28'N   22°45'E | + 1 hr 31 min |

We continue, with Sørøya on our starboard side. Soon we cross the municipal boundary between Hasvik and Hammerfest municipalities. The part of Stjernøya we can see on the starboard side lies within Hasvik municipality. The stretch of open sea across **Lopphavet** opens up west of the island. The mountains up ahead are within Loppa municipality.

| Approx. 70°27'N   22°39'E |

We cross the municipal boundary between Hasvik and Hammerfest municipalities

Hasvik municipality

Municipal coat of arms, significance: The gull is a common bird in the municipality.
Meaning of name: Likely from Norse hár, 'boat oars'.
Municipal seat: Breivikbotn (pop. 305).
Position: 70°35'44"N 22°18'20"E. **Area:** 559 km².
Population: 1 005. **Pop. density:** 1.8 /km².
Area distribution: Farming 0 %, forestry 0 %, fresh water 4 %, other area 96 %.
Trade and industry: Fishing and fish processing based on the flounder and halibut fishing grounds around the island and supplies from foreign fleets. Salmon and cod farming. Reindeer herding. Tourism.
Places to return to: Hasvik church. Dønnesfjord church.
Activities to return to: International fishing festival.
Hasvik municipality's home page: www.hasvik.kommune.no

| 70°24'N   22°29'16"E | ④ |

At the village of **Hasvik** (pop. 363) to starboard southwest on Sørøya, traces of settlements have been found that can be dated back 11 000 years. Similar finds have been made around the fjords on the west side of the islands. (Hasvik cannot be seen from the ship).

The two churches, Hasvik church (in Hasvåg) and Sørvær church were mentioned as early as 1589, in an overview of churches in the municipality that was written at the time. (Sørvær church was demolished in 1697 after it became derelict and was further destroyed by storms). The foundations of Hasvik church were constructed from whale-

bone. Dutch sailors built whaling stations on Sørøya in the 16th century and whalebone was more readily available than timber. The fence around the old cemetery was also built from whalebone. In 1756 a new church was  built in Hasvik, partly built from materials recovered from the old church. In 1861 Hasvik again received a new church - a longhouse style church built of timber. This was destroyed in 1944. The new Hasvik church was consecrated in 1955.

Dønnesfjord church on the northwest coast of Sørøya is a unique church building of great cultural and historical value. The church was built in 1888 in **Dønnesfjord**, which was at that time a major fishing community. It is a simple, white timber church with 150 seats and is the only building in the area that was left intact after the Second  World War. An attempt was made to burn down the church; however, the fire went out. On the steps of the church you can still see scorch marks from the arson attempt. As the fishing community was not built up again after the war, the church was moved to **Øya** in Dønnesfjord in 1951 and rebuilt there.

During the most active period for the fishing industry in the 19th century, with the rich fishing grounds just off the west coast, Hasvik and Sørøya were much more densely populated than today. From any one of these places, as many as a hundred boats with 500-600 fishermen on board sailed out to sea and followed the fish stocks. The famous Norwegian whale hunter Sven Foyn had a whaling station on the northwest side of Sørøya.

On the mountain **Håen** outermost on the southwest tip of Sørøya, close to the community of **Hasvik,** the German forces built a fortification, with a network of bunkers, gun emplacements and trenches. The work was carried out by forced labour teams comprised of civil Norwegians and Russian prisoners of war. The fortifications were strategically placed, as the German forces had established a fleet base in **Altafjorden**, behind the island of Stjernøya on the port side, where among others, the battleships "Tirpitz" and "Scharnhorst" were anchored (p 268). From the fortifications on Håen, the approach into Altafjorden could be monitored. To

prevent sabotage attacks the German forces had laid approx. 700 mines around the area. After the German retreat of autumn 1944, the installation was destroyed and the batteries of guns were relocated to Andøya (p 279).

In common with many other places in Finnmark, Sørøya and Hasvik municipality were victims of the forced evacuations during the German forces' retreat of 1944. With the exception of Dønnesfjord church, every single property was burned down. A large group of local people refused to be evacuated, however, and went into hiding. Of 1 650 inhabitants, 1 100 were forcibly evacuated. Approx. 550 went into hiding, in various caves, of which there are a number on Sørøya. This operation was carried out on orders from the governing authorities in exile in London. Their stay in hiding was originally meant to last for a few weeks; however, it lasted considerably longer.

The cave Kvithellhula lies north of the community of Hasvik. 35 persons went into hiding in the cave for 99 days during the winter of 1944/45. The cave is shallow and was very exposed to the weather. The children were therefore placed innermost in the cave and the adults protected them when the sea threatened the cave entrance. They remained within the cave most of the time and rarely went outside, for fear of being discovered.

The cave Nordsandfjordhulen lies on the northwest side of the island and can be difficult to locate. Approx. 100 persons lived here through the winter of 1944/45.

In the February of 1945, 502 persons who had been hiding in caves and other places were picked up by four British destroyers and taken to Murmansk, where they were then transferred to Allied merchant ships. They arrived in Glasgow on 28th February 1945, two weeks after they had been rescued from Sørøya.

More recently, other military forces have also made their mark on Sørøya. When the church bells began to ring in the Christmas of 1994, the population of Sørvær (pop. approx. 201) on the west side of the island was 'presented' with a special Christmas gift. The Russian cruiser "Murmansk" sailed out of control towards the village. On its way to India to be broken for scrap, the ship had broken its tow lines and began drifting just off the coast of Senja (p 169). It then drifted without captain or crew through four days and nights of gales and storms. The cruiser was not halted by the Coast Guard or the Navy and ended up, ironically enough, as a close neighbour to the NATO-radar installation on Sørvær. Now the ship "Murmansk" lies aground just under a steep rock face and only a very short distance from the beautiful natural surroundings of Sørvær. The rusting hulk, that is 211 m long and weighs 17 000 tonnes, has become an undesirable landmark for the tiny coastal community, lying aground in 15 m of water. It lies solidly anchored, as the keel has bored its way firmly into the sea floor.

✂

70°26'40"N 22°34'44"E	+ 1 hr 43 min

The island of **Stjernøya** (248 km²), a star-shaped island that is within Hasvik, Loppa and Alta municipalities, is without roads and is uninhabited. Stjernøya is very mountainous and the highest peak is **Kjerringfjordfjellet** (904 m above sea level.). The island is rich in the much sought-after mineral neph-elene syenite, a mineral that is used in the manu-facture of glass, porcelain and ceramic tiles. Each day, about 100 employees from Alta and Øksfjord commute to **Lillebukta** on the south west side of Stjernøya, to work in the mines. The annual production and export is close to 330 000 tonnes (2000).

✂

70°21'N 22°18'E	+ 2 hrs 18 min ⑤

Vardnes lies to port, the most north easterly point on Stjernøy. Between the next outcrops of Kjerringfjord-fjell, which can remind one of starfish arms or toes on a foot, there are several fjords. Up ahead we can see **Store Kjerringfjorden, Lille Kjerringfjorden, Smalfjorden, Nordfjorden** and **Sørfjorden**. The headland of **Stjern-foten** is on the north western part of the island.

✂

The ship approaches the next port, Øksfjord. Our head-ing takes us into the sound **Stjernsundet** on the port side, at the rear of Stjernøya and we sail into **Øksfjorden** (25 km long).

✂

The southern part of Seiland and Stjernøya and Stjern-sundet are in Alta municipality. Alta municipality is not included in the route for the Hurtigruten (p 268).

✂

Ca. 70°20'47"N   22°17'33"E

We pass the municipal boundary between Hasvik and Loppa municipalities

Loppa municipality

Municipal coat of arms, significance: Symbolises fishing.
Meaning of name: Uncertain.
Municipal seat: Øksfjord (pop. 495).
Position: 70°14'30"N 22°21'12"E.
Area: 691 km².
Population: 1 150. **Pop. density:** 1.7 /km².
Area distribution: Farming 0 %, forestry 0 %, fresh water 3 %, other area 97 %.
Trade and industry: Mining. Fishing. Fish farming. Filleting factory and freezer plant. Herring oil factory. Slate quarry. Agriculture is a secondary activity, mostly based on sheep farming.
Loppa municipality's home page: www.loppa.kommune.no

✂

As we approach Øksfjord we sail alongside the steep mountains **Eliassen** (939 m above sea level) (on our port side) and **Helletinden** (890 m above sea level) with the headland **Helleneset**. On the port side, between **Stjernøya** and the mainland, is Stjernsundet. (The sound continues behind Stjernøya and ends at **Altafjorden**, 38 km long, with the town of **Alta** in the inner part of the fjord).

After passing **Klubbnestinden** (707 m above sea level), the outermost headland on this part of the mainland in Loppa municipality (on our starboard side), the bay **Klubbnesvika** and Ystnes (port side), we arrive at Øksfjord. From here we can see parts of the glacier Øksfjordjøkelen, which lies innermost in a valley on the other side of the fjord.

✂

Øksfjordjøkelen (41 km², 1 204 m above sea level) is the ninth largest glacier in Norway and the largest in Finnmark county. The glacier is a plateau glacier with several arms that lead into nearby valleys, among them Nuvsvåg, which we will be sailing by later. Øksfjord-

© ROLF LILAND

jøkelen is the only glacier in Norway that leads directly into the fjord, at **Jøkelfjorden** on the south side of the glacier.

～

The ship docks at the quayside in Øksfjord

© EILIV LEREN

The fishing community and administrative centre of Øksfjord lies at the foot of the mountain **Grasdalsfjellet** (830 m above sea level). Almost half of the municipality's population lives in Øksfjord. Øksfjord was connected via an open year-round road connection with the rest of the mainland municipality, by a 4 252 m long tunnel in 1986. The rest of the municipality's population lives in smaller communities along the coast of Lopphavet.

Most of Loppa municipality's industry is in Øksfjord, which includes a fish fillet factory with a freezer warehouse and a herring oil factory. As the outer parts of the municipality have very poor road connections, most transport is carried out by boat. Øksfjord is the communications hub for local boat connections.

～

The church at Øksfjord is a longhouse style church, built in 1954.

～

The ship continues to Skjervøy   + 0 hrs 00 min

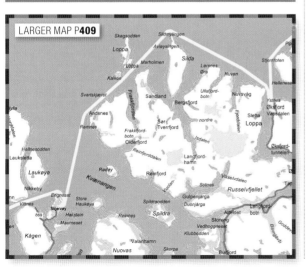

LARGER MAP P**409**

We set course for the open fjord, the next port of call is Skjervøy. Behind us on the port side is the small bay **Tverrfjorden** and **Bukta** under the mountain **Skatviktinden** (1 025 m above sea level). Up ahead and in the distance is Hasvik on Sørøya. On the starboard side we pass Stjernsundet, behind Stjernøya.

～

The ship rounds the headland at **Klubbnestinden** (707 m above sea level) and heads northwest, out onto the open sea, Lopphavet.

～

Lopphavet, between Sørøya in Finnmark and Nord-Fugløy in Troms (p 188) is one of the six open stretches of sea along the Hurtigrute sailing route. This stretch, which is 70 km wide, is notorious for being exposed to extreme weather. "Go and sail on Lopphavet!" is a well-known Norwegian expression, sometimes used in frustration.

～

70°19'N   22°11'N   + 0 hrs 30 min ①

The coastline on Lopphavet is marked by shallow fjords that cut inland on the north side of islands and the mainland. We pass the headland **Samuelsnes** and the mountain **Kollaren** (954 m above sea level), thereafter **Nuvsfjorden** with the community of **Nuvsvåg** in the fjord. Nuvsvåg has a population of approx. 140, a chapel and a school. In Nuvsfjorden the climate and environmental conditions are ideal for farming of the Arctic Catfish (Wolf Fish), considered a delicacy by many.

～

At the inner part of Nuvsfjorden we can see Øksfjordjøkelen, and on the port side you can see the steep, outer mountains of Sørøya.

～

On 17th October 1941, the former Hurtigruten ship DS "Vesteraalen" was torpedoed by a Russian submarine just off Nuvsfjorden. The ship was built in 1890 and had a capacity of 40 passengers. She was later rebuilt to be able to carry up to 200 passengers and was the first ship in the Hurtigruten fleet. The ship sank in 1913, but was raised and repaired and was taken into service again in 1914. In 1932 she was replaced by a newer vessel, and remained in dock in Trondheim in 1940, when war broke out in Norway. The ship was then taken over by the occupying German forces and was again used in coastal service. It is thought that approx. 60 persons perished when the ship was torpedoed.

～

On the port side we pass **Nuvsnes** under the mountain **Nuven** (688 m above sea level), we then have the fjord **Ullsfjorden** on the port side. At the inner part of the fjord, just northwest of Øksfjordjøkelen, we can see **Svartfjelljøkelen** (1 166 m above sea level). Further on we pass **Rokkenes** (806 m above sea level) with the village of **Gammelvær** and the headland, **Lørsnes**.

70°21'20"N   21°58'N   + 0 hrs 52 min ②

On the port side is the fjord **Nordre Bergsfjorden**, which divides the northern mainland part of Loppa municipality from the island of Silda, on the forward port side.

The island of **Silda** (48 km²), to port, is very mountainous and is uninhabited. Both the east and north sides of the island have deep, wide valleys. The highest peak, roughly in the middle of the island, is **Sunnacohkka** (628 m above sea level). There were formerly smaller fishing communities along the outer edges of the valleys – one of them was **Ivervær,** which was the former 'centre' of the island. In 1926 approximately 60 persons lived on bleak Silda, most of them were coastal Sámi.

After rounding the headland **Sildmylingen** (334 m above sea level) on the northern point of Silda, we head south west, towards **Leisund**. On the port side, Silda's vertical cliffs stretch along the length of the island, broken up only by **Avløysingen** to the north west.

We sail south westwards on Lopphavet, between the north westerly mainland part of Loppa municipality and the island of **Loppa** (12 km²), which has given its name to the municipality. Traces of Viking settlements have been found on this island and remains of a church from the Middle Ages at **Kraken,** in the north east. The former trading post in Loppa became the natural centre of the municipality. Loppa was at one time a major trade hub in the area.

The island's highest mountain, the protected bird cliff of **Rektind** (289 m above sea level), lies on the southern part of the island and has a rich variety of bird life. At one time, slate was quarried on the island. The now uninhabited fishing communities of **Mevær** and **Mønes** on Loppa pass on the starboard side. These were important fishing ports in the Middle Ages and archaeological sites have revealed several important finds. The church, a longhouse-style timber building, was built in 1953. In 2006 there were only six persons living on Loppa.

On the southern tip of Loppa, on the port side we pass the tiny **Marholmen**. The fjord, **Søre Bergsfjorden** continues along the steep west face of Silda and runs into the fjord, **Nordre Bergsfjorden** at Silda's southern tip.

Hurtigruten has a so-called 'request-stop' at the mouth of Søre Bergsfjorden. The old fishing community of **Bergsfjord** (pop. 142) on the mainland, has an active fishing fleet and its own landing stages and produces salt fish and caviar. The fishing community is one of many smaller places in the municipality that does not have a road connection. Passengers that wish to embark or disembark the Hurtigruten, can request the ship to stop here. A smaller boat is used to transfer passengers to shore, boarding or disembarking is via the pilot's gangway.

South west of the mountain **Seavssnjárga/Isfjellet** (278 m above sea level) on the port side, our course continues into the sound **Leisund**.

70°18'30"N   21°25'47"E   + 1 hr 43 min ③

To starboard, the sound **Kalvsundet** leads between the islands of **Loppa** and the smaller **Loppekalven**.

The fjord of **Frakfjorden** (11 km long) passes on the port side, just before Kalven. Thereafter we pass the headland of **Kjæresnes** and the mountain **Skavnakk** (893 m above sea level).

70°16'05"N   21°17'33"E   + 2 hrs 03 min

To port is the bay **Trollvika,** and the islet of **Svartskjær** on the starboard side.

70°15'N   21°13'23"E   + 2 hrs 10 min ④

The village of **Andsnes** passes by on the port side. Andsnes has a fish catch landing stage and a school. Only four persons were resident in the village in 2006.

The tiny island of **Brynilden** is on the port side. This is Finnmark's most westerly point.

Approx. 70°13'30"N   21°08'45"E

We cross the county boundary between Finnmark (p 217) and Troms counties (p 189)

70°11'N   21°07'E   + 2 hrs 30 min ⑤

On the port side is **Nakkefjellet** (749 m above sea level). South of the mountain lies the mouth of the fjord arm **Olderfjorden**, with the village of **Olderfjord**.

To port you can see the glacier **Langfjordjøkelen** (1 062 m above sea level, 8,4 km² in 1994), one of the northernmost glaciers on the mainland. Langfjordjøkelen is a plateau glacier that stretches up to 1 050 metres above sea level with an eastern arm, descending to approx. 300 m above sea level. The glacier has gradually retreated during the last few years.

The island of Arnøya in Skjervøy municipality is on the starboard side.

Approx. 70°10'N   21°06'E

Skjervøy municipality

Municipal coat of arms, significance: The cormorant is a common bird in the area.
Meaning of name: From Norse skerfr, 'bare rocks'.
Municipal seat: Skjervøy (pop. 2 350).
Position: 70°02'N 20°59'E. **Area:** 478 km².
Population: 2 966. **Pop. density:** 6.2 /km².
Area distribution: Farming 0 %, forestry 1 %, fresh water 2 %, other area 97 %.
Trade and industry: Fishing and fish processing industry (shrimp factory and fish fillets). Fishing port. Fishing gear manufacture. Shipyards. Steel and metal construction.
Places to return to: Maursund farm.
Activities to return to: Grouse hunting (Skjervøy was voted as Norway's best grouse island in 2004). Mountain climbing.
Skjervøy municipality's home page: www.skjervoy.kommune.no

We head southwards, into the fjord **Kvænangen,** approx. 72 km long. At the mouth of the fjord between Brynilen and Arnøya is Kvænangen, approx. 15 km wide.

Arnøya (274,8 km²) to starboard, is the largest island in Skjervøy municipality. The highest peak is **Arnøyhøgda** (1 168 m above sea level) on the islands east side. The scattered settlements lie on the south and east sides. A total of 198 farms on the island were burned down during the German forces' retreat from Northern Norway; only two farms were left standing.

The fishing community of **Årviksand** (pop. 446) on the north west side of Arnøya has a fish landing stage and a fish processing industry. More than 50 % of the inhabitants are engaged in the industry. Årviksand also has a slipway for repairing and servicing the local fishing fleet.

At Årviksand there is a monument erected in remembrance of the Arnøy tragedy. One of the stories from the war years concerns several Norwegians that shortly after the German invasion of 1940, left for Russia to train in espionage. They returned to continue their fight against the Germans in Northern Norway. A secret radio transmitter was installed in a cave close to Årviksand. The radio transmissions relayed the positions of German ships so that they could be targeted and torpedoed by Russian submarines. When the radio transmitter was discovered, the punishment was severe - eight persons were executed. The three men present in the cave when the transmitter was found were also killed.

The headland of Klubben passes on the starboard side, thereafter the steep peak **Flutinden** (833 m above sea level).

70°08'N   21°05'50"E   + 2 hrs 42 min

The island of **Rødøya** (266 m above sea level) is on the port side. The fjord, Kvænangen, continues on the port side, with the community of **Kvænangsbotn** innermost in the fjord.

© ANITA OLSEN

The island of **Laukøya** (36 km²) passes on the starboard side. The island is divided from Arnøya by the narrow channel of Lauksundet, with a scattered population along the sound. The northernmost point is the headland known as **Hellnesodden**. Following are the steep mountainsides before the community of **Nikkeby** under **Nikkebytinden** (770 m above sea level) on the south side of the island. Laukøya has a ferry connection to Arnøya.

The island **Store Haukøya** (506 m above sea level) on the port side is now uninhabited.

The island of **Skjervøya** (12 km²) approaching on the port side, has lent its name to the municipality. Here lies the day's final port of call, **Skjervøy**, which is well protected by mountains and large islands.

The ship docks at the quayside in Skjervøy

© ROLF LILAND

Skjervøy church is centrally located, close to the harbour. It is a cruciform church with a long nave and somewhat smaller cross-arms. The church has been extended several times. The first church on Skjervøy

was mentioned in written sources as early as 1589; however the church was probably actually built around 1539. The current church was built in 1728, when the old

church became too small. In 1778 it was made larger, the walls were raised to make room for a gallery – creating more seating places, a new roof was laid and the church was given new exterior cladding.

A legend has it that the choice of church site was determined by the forces of nature. The timber for the building was cut in one of the nearby forested valleys and was brought along the river course out into the fjord. The timber drifted with the wind and weather and wherever the timber came into land – the church was to be built. Most of the timber drifted and came on land on Skjervøy and therefore the church was built here.

When the first church on Tromsø island, known as "Saint Maria close to the Pagans" was built by King Håkon Håkonssøn in the middle of the 13th century (p 179), it was to mark the outer border of Norway, which was then at Lyngstuva, the northernmost part of the Lyngen Alps (p 185). The area north-east of Lyngstuva was regarded as Sámi land. The church was therefore seen as a missionary church that was to practice Christian teaching, baptise children and bury the dead according to church practices. Located at the entrance to three large fjords, Reisenfjorden, Kvænangfjorden and Lyngenfjorden, Skjervøy was strategically placed for this type of function. A census of the permanent population in 1666 showed a population of 14 Sami tax-payers, i.e. 14 Sami families - there were no Norwegians.

The church also functioned as a church for travelling Norwegian fishermen and later became a parish church for a Norwegian congregation when Norwegians began to settle in the area.

Skjervøy was known as a good area for fishing and many people gathered here during the fishing seasons. Most of them were fishermen; however there were also merchants and other trademen. There was a barter trade, with fish exchanged for various goods. Travellers came from Sweden and Finland. Kvens also came to trade goods with the fishermen and ships' crews. Authorities that were to provide for law and order also came to Skjervøy. Skjervøy had a district court in 1586. Persons who had committed crimes could be arrested and be s entenced; they could be fined or even imprisoned. Taxes were collected, sometimes in the form of fish catches. Around this time, a regular market was held that attracted a considerable number of people, from as far away as Sweden. The market, by the standards of the day, was quite large and laid the foundation for the original settlement of Kvens. Up to 1914 there was a good deal of Pomor trade (p 241) on Skjervøy.

Skjervøy developed from a small shoreline hamlet into more of an idyllic town with a church, a local authority

administration and various traders. From a population of 2 410 in 1895, this increased to 4 410 in 1946. The shipping route known as the Hamburger Route, which was a large cargo vessel that sailed between Vadsø and Hamburg to bring fish to Germany, called at Skjervøy, and from 1896 the Hurtigruten began to dock at Skjervøy. The main telegraph line was extended as far as Tromsø in 1869 and in 1890 the line was extended to Skjervøy. A bank was established in 1865.

Skjervøy is well known as the first port of call for the polar exploration vessel "Fram" after the 3-year North Pole expedition carried out by Fridtjof Nansen in 1893-1896 (p 234). The expedition was called the first "Fram" voyage, during which the ship drifted with the ice over the Polar Sea. Nansen and one of his closest colleagues, Lieutenant Johansen, left "Fram" frozen in the ice in March 1895 and travelled northwards on skis and with dog sleds. The captain of "Fram", Otto Sverdrup, sailed the ship out of the ice, southwards and arrived at Skjervøy on the 20th August 1896, eight days after Nansen and Johansen were brought to Tromsø by another vessel.

During the German forces' retreat in 1944, some parts of Skjervøy escaped the Germans' "scorched earth" policy and were left intact.

Troms county municipality has designated Skjervøy municipality as the official maritime centre for North-Troms, which has generated an upswing in activity within the fishing industry. The community is an important fishing port - Skjervøy has shrimp factories and fish processing plants, aquaculture and engineering companies associated with shipbuilding and maintenance of fishing vessels.

The ship continues to Tromsø	+ 0 hrs 00 min

We head towards our next port of call, Tromsø, and round **Ramnneset** just outside the harbour, then

Engneset with the fell **Brusen** (289 m above sea level), the northernmost point of Skjervøya.

70°03'35"N 20°56'E	+ 0 hrs 21 min

On the port side is the narrow and shallow **Skattøyrsundet** between the islands of Skjervøya and Kågen.

There have been several archaeological finds of ancient settlements between Kågen and Skjervøya, spanning a period from the Stone Age up to the time of the destruction that took place in the Second World War. There are traces of both reindeer herding Sámi and coastal Sámi settlements.

Skattørsundet bridge connects the two islands. The bridge has one lane with a meeting point in the middle and is 805 m long in total. The centre span is 32 m long, the remaining spans are 20 m long. There are 40 bridge spans in total. The bridge was opened in 1971.

70°03'10"N 20°51'25"E	+ 0 hrs 26 min

Heading westwards, on the starboard side we pass the southern point of Laukøya, the community of **Nikkeby** with the peak **Nikkebytinden** (770 m above sea level), and thereafter the mouth of the sound **Lauksundet**, a narrow sound between Laukøya and Arnøya. There are some scattered houses on both sides of the sound. The islands and Kågen (to port) are connected by a ferry service.

We sail into **Kågsundet** between the sheer mountain cliffs of **Singeltinden** (742 m above sea level) to starboard on the south east side of Arnøya and **Storstein** (683 m above sea level) with the headland **Vittnes** and the peak **Kågtinden** (999 m above sea level) on the port side, on the north side of Kågen.

The island of **Kågen,** (85,7 km²) on the port side is the second largest island in Skjervøy municipality. It is a hilly island with the high peak of **Store Kågtindan** (1 163 m above sea level) in the north, the islands highest point. There are also several other peaks over 1 000 m. On one of these, **Storsandnestiden** (1 091 m above sea level), is the small glacier known as **Blåisen**.

Kågen has a mainland connection by a road tunnel through the mountain Kågtinden, and an undersea tunnel, Maursundtunnelen, on the south side of the island. Maursundtunnelen was opened in 1991 and is 2 122 m long, descending to a depth of 92.5 m below sea level. The steepest climb in the tunnel is 10 %.

Maursund farm on the east side of Maursundet was a well-known and wealthy trading post for several hundred

years. Written sources identify the farm as early as the 17th century. The location was central for the trade routes of that time and the sailing routes for shipping, and the owners of the farm traded in fish, transport services and commerce. Maursund farm received status as a traveller's inn in 1776. An overview of the estate from the middle of the 19th century shows that it comprised of 20 buildings, among them boathouses, two barns, a storehouse, a quay, herring oil production and a mill.

Maursund farm had its golden age in the 19th century. The current farmhouse, a large building with a façade in the Louis-Seize style, was built at the end of the 18th century and was granted listed status in 1944. The farm is now owned by the Nord-Troms Museum.

70°02'N 20°40'E	+ 0 hrs 41 min

The sound of **Kjølmangen** is on the port side, between the islands of Kågen and Vorterøya.

To starboard we have passed **Grunnfjorden** with the community of **Arnøyhamn** between **Draugneset** and **Stakenes.**

In front we can see the northern part of the beautiful and rugged **Lyngen Alps**. The glaciers **Gammvikblåisen** (1 252 m above sea level) and **Vakkåsbreen** are to the south.

On the port side up ahead is **Vorterøya** (12 km², 235 m above sea level). Only a few people live here permanently, however the flat and marshy island is a popular summer resort and the population may then increase to as many as 100.

70°01'N 20°35'E	+ 0 hrs 49 min

The headland of **Haugnes** is on the starboard side, and the mouths of the fjords **Akkarfjorden** and **Langfjorden**, with the community of Akkarvik. **Store Trolltinden** (850 m above sea level) west of Akkarvik.

70°01'N 20°32'E	+ 0 hrs 53 min ⑥

We head towards the headland of Nordklubben and Lyngstuva (391 m above sea level), the northern tip of the mighty Lyngen Alps in Lyngen municipality (p 185). The journey continues into Ullsfjorden (p 185) towards our next port of call, Tromsø (p 179).

A French lady's impresssions of Finnmark in 1838

The French King Louis-Phillipe, who was exiled for political reasons, spent a period of his youth on the island of Måsøya in Måsøy municipality (p 199). He became very fond of and interested in Måsøya and during the years 1838-40 he sponsored three scientific expeditions that sailed to the area. In 1838, Leonie d'Aunet accompanied her husband who was a scientist and artist on one of the expeditions. In 1867 she published a travel journal in which she recounted her experiences and impressions.

"...The journey was through......., in Norway to Hammerfest with the Norwegian steamship "Prinds Gustav" and then from Hammerfest to Spitsbergen with the French expedition vessel "la Recherche" that was sailing on a scientific expedition to Spitsbergen". She wrote of the wonder of the light nights in Hammerfest, where she arrived in the middle of June: "It is less than one year," she wrote, "since it took a month to travel between Trondheim and Hammerfest – now it is possible to make the journey in eight days, thanks to the steamship that has been introduced on the route, the "Prinds Gustav"…".

Hammerfest had a population of approx. 500 and comprised of about 60 wooden houses painted with yellow ochre. At the most, a dozen of these were inhabitable. The rest were ramshackle cabins that were erected by the poorer Norwegians, or

caves in which the coastal Lapps lived. Four of the wooden buildings had two levels and were painted white, decorated with green and blue lines, rather like the side plates seen in small restaurants. In these lived the merchant aristocracy. The small cabins were built from logs and the spaces in between were filled with moss or old unravelled rope. Each cabin was divided into two rooms. The entrance served as a kitchen, lounge and dining room. An impossibly large oven built from stone blocks, primitively formed, rose up to the ceiling. The rear room was used as a bedroom for the whole family and also served as a storeroom for clothing and groceries. This was somewhat similar to the "homestead" of southern Norway, but smaller, poorer and more dismal, due to the barren soil and an appalling climate. The roofs were covered with turf, which formed the only green areas on the whole landscape. It was a strange sight to see the women, each morning, lifting their goat onto the roof so that the poor animals could graze fresh grass. Under the storehouses lay fishing nets, fuel, wagons and all kinds of items that were not suitable for storage indoors.

The population of Finnmark managed to combine the greatest honesty with their great fondness for making a profit. They charged three times as much for their goods but you could stay with them without locking the door – no one would ever steal anything. Many foreign ships arrived in the summer. Russians brought flour, timber, butter, the Dutch brought with them potatoes, wine and groceries, ships from Hamburg brought clothes, soap and furniture.

The physical height of the Lapps was said by the author to be somewhere between 4 feet 4 inches and 4 feet 10 inches. It was rare to find a man that was 5 feet tall. The clothes of the Lapps were described as follows: "underneath the clothing was a sheepskin with the wool side turned inwards. This item of clothing, when worn in winter, was covered by a jacket made of reindeer hide, in summer by a jacket made of a type of felt, grey or dark blue, edged with ribbons of various hues. The collar of the jacket was always stiff, it stood straight up and was decorated with strands of red material and with pewter decoration. All Lapps had copper plates, buttons made of pewter or woven silver plate. The men wore their hair long, falling to the shoulder. They wore headgear made from material decorated with multicoloured fabric, and boots made from reindeer hides and leather shoes with the same shape as our wooden shoes.

The Lapp women wore a helmet-shaped hat; this martial headgear made the Lapp women look rather like burlesque Minervas. All women older than very young girls smoked tobacco. In the winter a broad hat made from reindeer skin with the fur on the outside was added to the clothing. Both men and women then took on the appearance of large bears that walked around on their hind feet. The most important personal item for men was a leather bag, worn around the neck, hung by two white ribbons, that rested on the chest between the first and second layers of jackets. One Lapp showed the author the contents of the bag: it contained a knife, one large, old pistol without a hammer - to which he attached special importance; four coins, a quantity of smoking tobacco, a box made of birch bark filled with butter made from reindeer milk, a piece of smoked fish and a pile of fine hay to fill his shoes and boots with; this particular hay had been well used so it was rather pungent.

A few Lapps had recently settled in Hammerfest and their pathetic 'cabins' formed the lowest standard of dwelling in the town. The dwellings were cone-shaped and their bases were dug down into the ground. They seemed to be built from the remains of old boats and of compressed moss covered by soil and they gave the impression of tents made of earth. The interior was not divided; the fireplace was in the centre of the cabin on flat stones and the smoke rose through a hole on the roof. A few branches that formed a bed were filled with dried seaweed. A few wooden vessels were all the household items needed. The Lapp did not eat bread and did not own linen, he knew nothing of the arts and sciences, and he did not sing or have any form of music…".

Source: Leonie d'Aunet – the first woman on Spitsbergen and her account of the journey from Finnmark, Hammerfest and Lappland. By A.B. Wessel ("Tromsø" 8/12-30).

Melkøya and the Snøhvit Field

In 1980, oil and gas prospecting started in the Norwegian Sea/Barents Sea. Test drilling began on 1st June 1980. Since then a large number of test wells have been drilled and several operator licences have been approved in the area. Most of these are in the Hammerfest basin, which lies north west of Hammerfest town. The gas fields of Askeladden, Albatross and Snøhvit were discovered between 1981-1984. These three gas fields represent the Snøhvit field. The Norwegian oil companies Hydro and Statoil were involved in

the prospecting process. The name 'Snøhvit' means 'Snow White'.

Hammerfest was chosen as the base for supply ships, oil spill contingency and helicopter transport. The choice of Hammerfest was influenced by the town's strong maritime traditions within fishing and hunting and its history as a starting point for polar expeditions. After gas was discovered in the fields, a decision was made to build a LNG (Liquefied Natural Gas) processing plant on Melkøya just outside of Hammerfest port. Gas from the plant is transported in specially constructed tankers to Europe and USA. The construction process began in 2002 and production began in 2007.

In advance of the construction of landing sites and process terminals for gas from Snøhvit to Melkøya, 50 archaeologists from Tromsø University carried out site excavations during the summers of 2001 and 2002. They made a number of discoveries from the period when the ice melted along the coast at the end of the last Ice Age, up to modern times. The oldest traces that were found are probably 10 000 years old. Several ancient house remains, from the transition between the early and late Stone Age (p 83) have been found, along with many types of tools and artefacts from later periods.

The Snøhvit project in the Norwegian Sea is a milestone in the extraction of oil and gas off the coast of Norway and is the first production and export plant for LNG (Liquefied Natural Gas). It is the largest industrial project ever undertaken in Northern Norway (as of 2007). The Snøhvit field is approx. 140 km west of Hammerfest, at 71°30'N, and is the first lar-

ge project on the Norwegian continental shelf without installations on the sea surface.

The production plant is located on the sea bed, between 250 m and 545 m below the surface. There will be no conventional platform marking the extraction site. On the sea bed, 20 gas production wells have been drilled to extract a product called 'wellstream'. This is transported from the undersea production installations to Melkøya in multi-phase pipes (length 143 km, inner diameter 63.5 cm). This is a world record for transporting gas in an untreated well stream.

At the production plant on Melkøya, the wellstream is processed and the carbon dioxide (CO_2) that is extracted is sent back to the Snøhvit field in a separate pipeline. It is then stored in the sea bed to reduce the amount of CO_2 emissions to the atmosphere. Wellstream also contains condensate (natural gasoline) as well as the liquid gases butane and propane. These are extracted and sold as separate products and exported from Melkøya.

After the wellstream is processed, the natural gas is cooled via a specialised process to minus 163 degrees under normal atmospheric pressure in the processing plant on Melkøya. In that the natural gas takes on a liquid form, the volume is reduced by a factor of approx. 600, which simplifies the storage and transport of the gas. At the receiving terminal, the cooled gas is heated and in gaseous form is later used for heating or domestic use or for the production of electricity.

Specially constructed LNG tankers transport the gas from Melkøya to the receiving terminals in various countries. Approx. 70

such transports will take place annually. Each tanker ship carries an amount of energy corresponding to the amount used by 35 000 households in one year. USA is the largest purchaser of the gas. 2.4 billion m³ of liquid gas will be exported to the receiving terminal at Cove Point in Chesapeake Bay, Maryland, on the east coast of USA. Spain will receive 1.6 billion m³ and France 1.7 billion m³ annually.

The production period is expected to last approx. 25-30 years.

The process installation on Melkøya was built at the Dragados shipyards in Cádiz in southern Spain. In May/June 2005, the ship "Blue Marlin", the world's largest heavy lifting vessel, transported the 33 000 tonne plant on deck over a distance of 5 000 km (2 700 nautical miles) from Cádiz. The journey to Hammerfest and Melkøya was completed in 11 days. In Spain, the processing plant was built on a giant barge, 160 m x 60 m x 9 m, which was an integral part of the plant. The unloading of the barge and processing plant was carried out by evacuating the forward and aft ballast tanks of the

heavy lifting vessel, so that the loading deck sank below the surface. The barge then floated and was towed away from the vessel. A dock had already been prepared on Melkøya and the foundation for the plant had been constructed. The barge was brought into position in front of the dock. At high tide (3-4 m above normal sea level), the 9 m high barge carrying the processing plant was pulled into the dock by powerful winches and six large tugs and lowered onto the completed foundations.

The Snøhvit field is located in an area that is of great importance to the fishing industry in Norway. It has therefore been essential to construct the field in cooperation and understanding with the industry and the local population. The installation on the sea bed is constructed so as not to present an obstruction to fishing vessels. The installation is constructed so that trawlers in the area will not become entangled and all pipelines, as far as possible, have been laid outside the important fishing zones. Environmental considerations that require zero emissions, a 'clean ocean' policy and co-existence with other commercial enterprises have

been specified and demanded of the companies involved throughout the project. In the course of 25 years of prospecting in the Barents Sea, there have been no incidents causing damage to marine life or the environment.

*Among many other major assignments, the "Blue Marlin" was also used to transport the US Navy destroyer USS "Cole" back to the USA after the ship was attacked and bombed in Aden, Yemen in October 2000.

Alta Rock carvings

In Alta are Northern Europe's largest rock carvings, which depict hunting scenes. The rock carvings are included on the UNESCO list of cultural and natural heritage sites. The first rock carvings were discovered in 1972. Since then over 5 000 figures have been found in different areas - most of these are located at Hjemmeluft, approx. 1.5 km west of Alta. Hjemmeluft is thought to have been a site of ritual assemblies for over 4 000 years. The rock carvings depict several of the species of animals that inhabited Finnmark, both land, marine and flying creatures. They also depict boats and human figures engaged in rituals, also hunting and fishing. The rock carvings originate from four historical periods: 4200-3600 B.C., 3600-2700 B.C., 2700-1700 B.C. and 1700-500 B.C. Alta Museum, opened in 1991, is located near the Hjemmeluft carvings.

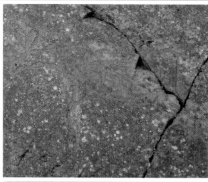

"Tirpitz"

The 42 900 ton German Battleship, "Tirpitz" (named after Admiral von Tirpitz) was launched in 1939 and went into service in 1941. When fully equipped the ship had a displacement of 56 000 tons, and a crew of 2 340. She was the sister ship of the "Bismarck", and both ships, along with the "Scharnhorst" were sent to hunt and destroy the Allied convoys in the North Atlantic, that were én route to Murmansk with supplies to the Soviet armies in Russia. The presence of these three battleships forced large numbers of Allied and British naval units to be present in the North Sea.

The German Navy's largest naval bases in Norway were in Altafjorden and Kåfjorden. Having been moved several times between fjords in Trøndelag and Lofoten, "Tirpitz" eventually arrived in Kåfjorden in the spring of 1943. The German Navy was anxious not to lose the "Tirpitz" and made great efforts to protect the ship. The battleship was only used twice in combat, one attack was aborted and in the second, she was used in action near Svalbard. "Tirpitz" was under constant surveillance by Allied agents and every movement was reported to London.

Despite the fact that "Tirpitz" had not participated in many combat operations the ship's very presence in the area was a deterrent. From Altafjorden to the Allied convoy routes to Murmansk (p 220) was only 15 hours sailing and the ship could be mobilised for war at very short notice. In addition to "Tirpitz", the German Navy had a number of vessels at the base in Altafjorden, amongst them the battleship "Scharnhorst" (p 208), the battle cruiser "Lützow" and several destroyers. The German headquarters for the war in Northwest Russia was also located in Kåfjorden. Some 15-20 000 German sailors and soldiers either were on board ships or stationed at the land-based fortifications in and around Altafjorden. The presence of this large German naval fleet in the fjords interfered with the important supply route to Russia via the Barents Sea.

Without these supply lines reaching the Soviet troops, the German armies could have won the Second World War.

The British Prime Minister, Winston Churchill, wrote in 1942: "The biggest single operation that must be carried out to establish the balance of naval strength will be to destroy "Tirpitz", or inflict such damage that she is incapacitated. No other goal is comparable, since the whole naval situation throughout the world will be altered by this achievement". He added: "All our global strategies are concerned with this ship. Four British battleships are occupied in the Atlantic - not to mention the new American battleships that have to be held back to patrol in the Atlantic. I regard this matter to be of the utmost significance and importance".

Several attempts were made to sink the battleship, but she escaped serious damage each time. Based on detailed radio reports sent by Norwegian agents, British aircraft attacked the ship in April 1943 and struck 14 times. The attack severely damaged "Tirpitz" and rendered the ship inoperative. The British Admiralty decided to build six special mini submarines to solve what came to be known as "the Tirpitz Problem".

The mini-submarine, or X, as it was called by the British, was a 15 m long steel cylinder with a diameter of 1.7 m, which could transport two specially-constructed mines, each containing two tons of Amatex explosives attached to the submarine's hull. As soon as the mini-submarines were inside the enemy's base, the mines could be placed on the seabed under the hull of the targeted enemy ships.

The six mini-submarines were towed to Sørøya by ordinary submarines. Unfortunately two of them sank underway. Three of the six were to attack "Tirpitz" where she was moored, well protected behind anti-submarine nets and a torpedo-proof enclosure; two were to attack "Scharnhorst", and one was to attack the battle cruiser "Lützow". The four remaining mini-submarines managed to pass through the dense minefields into the base. The three that were to attack "Tirpitz" arrived on 22nd September 1943

and placed the explosives on the seabed directly underneath the battleship. The charges were set to detonate one hour later. However, the submarines had been detected and after the crew had destroyed all secret documents, they were forced to surface, and were taken prisoner. One submarine was destroyed and the crew lost their lives. The unit that was on its way to attack "Scharnhorst" had problems and failed to accomplish its mission.

"Tirpitz" was lifted 7 feet into the air by the explosion, which tore a hole in her port side, said to be the 'size of a barn door'. There was also other serious damage; water rushed in and flooded the lower decks. The surviving British sailors were sent to a prisoner of war camp in Germany for naval personnel and all returned to England after the war. Many rate this mission as the most daring of the Second World War.

"Tirpitz" remained in Altafjord for repairs for five months. An aerial attack in April 1944 caused serious damage but she remained afloat. After further attacks that autumn, "Tirpitz" was declared no longer seaworthy and was towed to Tromsø, to serve as a floating fortress. However, the Allies were not certain if the ship had been made seaworthy, so on 12th November 1944 the RAF attacked the battleship near Kvaløya just outside Tromsø. The ship capsized and sank. More than 1 200 sailors died. 806 survived - amongst these were 82 that were rescued through a hole that had to be cut in the hull.

As a curiosity, it should be mentioned that the wreck was bought by a ship breaker after the war for 100 000 Norwegian kroner. Oslo municipality bought some of the steel armour plates taken from the hull, which they still use today to cover road works in the city streets. The plates remain in good condition to this day, despite being exposed to the Oslo traffic for so many years.

DAY 9

Finnsnes, Harstad, Risøyhamn, Sortland, Stokmarknes, Svolvær and Stamsund

© STEVE NILSEN

During the night we have passed the municipality of Troms with the port of **Tromsø** (69°40'N 18°58'E, 2345-0130) (p 179), the municipality of Lenvik with the port of **Finnsnes** (69°13'47"N 17°58'19"E, 0415-0445) (p 172). We have then past the municipalities of Sørreisa, Dyrøy, Tranøy, Ibestad and Bjarkøy. We are now in Harstad municipality.

The ship docks at the quayside in Harstad

Harstad municipality

Municipal coat of arms, significance: The coat of arms signifies the town's maritime connections.
Meaning of name: Possibly from Norse Hardastadir, from the man's name Hordr, Hardar.
Municipal seat: Harstad (pop. 19.573).
Position: 68°47'50"N 16°33'E. **Area:** 364 km².
Population: 23 261. **Pop. density:** 63.9 /km².
Area distribution: Farming 6 %, forestry 21 %, fresh water 4 %, other area 69 %.
Trade and industry: Service industries, many based on agriculture. Dairy and meat processing. Fish processing. Mechanical workshops. Shipbuilders and dry docks. Oil industry administration and large oil depot. Petroleum Directorate regional headquarters.
Places to return to: P 272.
Harstad municipality's home page: www.harstad.kommune.no

Harstad municipality lies mainly on the island of Hinnøya. 69.3 km² of the municipality is on the island of Grytøya (p 165).

Hinnøya (2 198 km²) is the largest and most populous island in Norway. Several of the municipalities that we will sail by during the day are wholly or partially on the island. Wide, deep, narrow and short fjords cut into the hilly island. The highest peak is Møysalen (1 262 m above sea level) in the south. The mountains are steep, however on the northwest of the island there are low, marshy valleys between the peaks. Hinnøya's population lives along the coast, mostly in the northeast around the

town of Harstad. The island is connected to the mainland at the southern end.

The town of **Harstad** lies close to the boundary between the northernmost part of Nordland county and the southernmost part of Troms county. Harstad is the commercial and administration centre for these areas. The communications are excellent, whether travelling by air, boat or by car. The town is known as the "Culture Town of the North" – in June, there is a major culture festival known as "Festspillene" which attracts a great number of visitors, and there are concerts and musical events in concert halls and churches throughout the town. In addition, there are many other cultural events taking place the whole year round. The architecture in the town reflects a mixture of restored buildings, well-maintained town houses and modern buildings.

The area around Harstad was of major importance in Norwegian history, due to the chieftain seat on Bjarkøya (p 166) and the nearby parish and chieftain seat of Trondenes (p 273).

© HARSTAD TIDENDE

In common with many other communities that we pass by along our voyage, the excellent harbour conditions and fishing activities, especially in the latter part of the 19th century and the beginning of the 1900s, were the basis of the town's development. In 1844 the steamships began to call at Harstadhamn instead of Trondenes, and then later at Harstadsjøen. This was the first step in the establishment of Harstad as a town.

The town really began to expand at the start of the 1870s, when large catches were landed from the rich herring fishing grounds in Vågsfjorden, north of Harstad, In 1888, Harstad built its first large quayside suitable for steamships, at about the same time that annual trade fairs were held. These drew many people to the area. In 1890, there were approx. 88 houses in Harstad and the population was approx. 540. The same year, the first newspaper in Harstad was established. The creation of new jobs and the increase in population led to the division from Trondenes municipality, into a separate municipality. In 1895, a shipyard was opened and this provided many new jobs for the local people. The fact that Harstad was chosen as the headquarters of the Regional Armed Forces and as the site of the officers' training college in the new military district of Northern Norway was also of major significance in the further development of the town. In addition, Harstad was centrally located in one of the region's finest and most populous agricultural areas. Harstad was designated a separate town municipality in 1904. In 1907, the town had a population of 1 735 and 156 wooden houses. The town was the headquarter for Hålogaland Steam Company; there were mechanical workshops, shipyards and boat builders, a tobacco factory, a wool mill, a herring oil factory, an animal feedstuffs factory, and two soft drinks factories.

The rich herring catches led to the construction of herring oil factories along the coast of Norway. The first one was built at Brettesnes in Lofoten in 1870 (p 297). The first one to be built in the Harstad area began production in 1919. This gradually developed into the country's largest and became a well-known landmark in the area. Several other herring oil factories were built in the districts around Harstad. Salting of herring and storage in barrels was also an important commercial activity.

Just after the invasion by German forces in April 1940, a large Allied fleet sailed into Harstad harbour to provide a defence against the expected German attack on the town. However, the fleet withdrew after approx. two months, after which the German forces moved in and occupied the town. Harstad survived the war years without extensive damage. During the winter and spring of 1944-45, the town had a vital function as a reception camp for evacuated Norwegians from Finnmark and North-Troms and for Russian prisoners of war.

Harstad continued to grow after the war. The current boundaries were set in 1964 and the total area is 722 km², of which the land area is 364 km².

Harstad was formerly a "military town". The officers' college for the infantry in North-Norway was at Trondenes camp until it was closed in 2003. The Coastal Ranger Command still uses the camp at Trondenes.

In 1976, Norway's largest oil company, Statoil, established its administration centre for Northern Norway in Harstad. The town is now the region's oil 'headquarters', with a well-established professional milieu within prospecting, research and development.

The most well known sights in Harstad are:

Trondenes church (p 274).

Harstad church was consecrated in 1958, and stands on the headland west of the centre of town. The distinctive church tower is easily visible and is an important landmark. The church was one of the first 'working churches' in Norway, in that it has several other functions than purely liturgical. The exterior is quite distinctive, as it has been constructed from several different materials. For example, there is a slate roof and rendered concrete has been used on several facades.

Harstad Culture Centre lies approx. 800 m north of the quayside. The Centre was opened in 1992. From the ear-

ly 1900s, the area had a good deal of industrial and maritime activity, however from the 1980s this type of activity was greatly reduced, and the area fell into decline. This trend was reversed after the Culture Centre was built. Four years later the new Harstad College was built nearby.

Harstad Culture Centre is Northern Norway's largest concert hall, with an area of 12 000 m². This includes industrial units (approx. 8 000 m²) that were integrated into the new construction. The largest hall has a seating capacity of 1 000. The building also contains a library and a hotel. The Culture Centre's façade towards the sea is dominated by a huge glass wall. A narrow, high wing that is reminiscent of a tower divides the building's façade.

Trondenes district museum (p 274).

Trondenes Historical Centre (p 274).

Adolf Gun (p 275).

Altevågen (p 274).

Røkenes Gård og Gjestehus (p 276).

Skjærstad herring oil factory (p 275).

The ship continues to Risøyhamn   **+ 0 hrs 00 min**

LARGER MAP P**410**

As we leave Harstad harbour, on the starboard side we can see the peninsula and suburb of **Stangnes**. Harstad is the main base for oil prospecting activities in the region. A larger oil base with port and industry enterprises has been built on the east side of Stangnes. This is not visible from the ship.

On the starboard side are the islands of **Rolla** and **Andørja** (p 167). Ahead and to starboard, we can see the low islet **Måga,** and behind is **Vågsfjorden**.

On our port side is the peninsula of **Trondenes** with Trondenes church. The church is an easily spotted and well-known landmark when approaching and leaving Harstad harbour. Trondenes has a long and colourful past, and features both in Norse and ecclesiastical history.

Trondenes is an ancient chieftain seat and administrative district. Archaeological excavations carried out in the 1960s indicated remains of a large farm that may date from 200 B.C. During the Viking period (p 83, p 123) it became a chieftain base.

In Snorre Sturlason's Saga of King Olav the Holy (995-1030) (p 88), we read for the first time about the chieftains that ruled at Trondenes and Bjarkøy at the beginning of the 12th century. Sigurd Hund was the chieftain at Trondenes. He was the brother of Tore Hund from the island of Bjarkøy, north of Trondenes (p 166). Sigurd Hund was married to Sigrid Skjalgsdotter, the sister of the famous Erling Skjalgsson from Sola (975-1028. He belonged to a powerful clan line from the West that supported King Olav). Sigurd Hund died when his son Asbjørn was 18 years old. To quote from the Saga:

"Here is the story of the young clan leader Asbjørn from Trondenes (Asbjørn Selsbane) who defied the King's orders and sailed southwards to buy corn from his uncle, the mighty Erling Skjalgsson at Sola. Along his journey Asbjørn came into conflict with the King's man on Karmøy, Tore Sel. The conflict la-

ter led to Asbjørn killing Tore Sel. On the advice of his uncle, Tore Hund from Bjarkøy, Asbjørn refused to accept the punishment meted out to him. Consequently, he was killed by the King's soldiers during his journey home from Vågan (in Lofoten) (p 155). The Saga tells how his mother, Sigrid, blamed Tore Hund for giving Asbjørn the fatal advice, which led to his death. She asked Tore Hund to avenge his death by killing the King, Olav Digre (Olav the Holy). The saga tells of how Tore Hund gathered a peasant army and travelled to Trøndelag, where he met the King in a battle at Stiklestad (at the inner part of Trondheimsfjorden (p 98). The King was killed in the battle and the saga tells of how Tore Hund took care of the King's body. This is the tale of Tore Hund and the clan at Trondenes."

In the bay **Altevågen** at the rear of Trondenes peninsula, excavations carried out in 1952 and 1995 have uncovered the remains of two large boathouses that, with their size and location, correlate with the stories in Snorre's sagas. The boathouses are connected to the story of Asbjørn Selsbane and his two ships. The largest boathouse, some 30 m long, appropriate for a chieftain, has at one time housed a large ship. There are also remains of five graves, which are the only preserved grave remains from the pre-Christian era at Trondenes. The excavations also revealed a wine cellar from the 17th century that belonged to Trondenes church, and the remains of an open-hearth room from the 13th century.

Before the easily recognisable Trondenes church on the port side, we can see the low, turf-covered building of the Trondenes Historical Centre and Trondarnes District Museum.

Trondenes Historical Centre was built in 1997 and has been adapted to the

historical surroundings and the cultural heritage landscape, by visually blending in with the local landscape. The building houses a permanent exhibition about Trondenes through history, also various changing art and cultural history exhibitions.

The first church built at Trondenes was a small wooden church built around A.D. 1000, just outside the chieftain homestead. There was possibly another church also on the same site, before the current Trondenes church was constructed. The sagas tell that King Øystein (1) Magnusson (1088-1123) (p 10) built churches at Agdenes on Trondheimsfjorden (p 338), Vågan in Lofoten (p 156) and at Trondenes in Harstad. There is some discussion as to when the current church was built. Some say it was built in the 13th century, however more recent research suggests that it was completed much later, in approx. 1440.

Trondenes church is the world's most northerly stone-built church, and one of Norway's most important churches from the Middle Ages (p 83) and the only one of its kind in Troms county. The church is surrounded by a thick cemetery wall, which is between three and five metres high with two small towers that face eastwards out to sea. It is built in the Gothic style, with three altars with a triptych from the late Middle Ages, most likely of German origin. The church originally held seven triptychs, which indicates its wealthy and important status in Catholic times. It has six stone altars - the main altar is free-standing, but is connected to the wall behind by an arch. Documents show that the main altar was consecrated in 1476. Several hundred skeletons have been discovered under the floor of the church. Burial under the church floor was often the privilege of the wealthy.

Trondenes church is regarded as the region's most important item of cultural heritage and contains many art treasures. Around the time of the Second World War the church was restored and returned to the form that it was believed the church had in the Middle Ages. During the restoration work, a ship's sail was discovered in the roof construction – this is thought to be Norway's oldest example of its type.

Trondenes played an important role during the Second World War. The German occupying troops built a large fortification in 1943, Trondenes fort, with cabins, roads and smaller buildings between the church and Altevågen at the rear of the peninsula. A Russian prisoner of war camp was also built here. On the fort were four "Adolf guns", the world's largest land-based cannon, with a calibre of 40.5 cm and a range of up to 56 km. These guns, of

which one has been completely restored, remain at Trondenes as a memorial. After the war the soldier's former quarters were used to house refugees from Finnmark and Nord-Troms. In total, 930 persons lived in just 100 of these cabins. The camp, which was very well organised, remained in use until 1951.

The low islet **Måga** passes by on the starboard side, with a small lighthouse on the southern tip of the island. There is an old stone cairn on the islet.

In front on the starboard side are the islands of Kjøtta, **Kjøttakalven** and Åkerøya.

The small island of **Kjøtta** (3 km²) is only 10 min. by fast boat from Harstad. The island is centrally located in the shipping channel, in the middle of the former herring fishing grounds. It played an important role in the herring trade as early as 1877. In 1929 a herring oil factory was built here. The island is a popular summer destination.

The hilly island of **Grytøya** (108 km²) lies up ahead. The island is split between Harstad and Bjarkøy municipalities – we sail alongside the part of the island that is in Harstad municipality. The village of **Bessebostad** lies southeast on the island, just inside the island of **Åkerøya** behind Kjøtta. The neighbouring village of **Lundenes** is on the southern tip of Grytøya.

Lundenes church is a longhouse-style church built of timber in 1974. The church has seating for 200 persons.

Grytøya Village Museum at Lundenes is one of the finest old village courtyards in Northern Norway. It comprises a collection of six antiquarian buildings and over 3 000 artefacts that document the traditions and way of life on the coast. The main building was built in 1770 and extended

in 1824. The buildings are listed and remain as they were originally erected. In addition, the courtyard has a pillared storehouse, a byre with stalls and a barn with traditional farm implements. The museum has a fine collection of old musical instruments from the village, an interesting collection of weapons, sables and bayonets and a large collection of handicrafts. On the shore there is a boathouse with Nordland boats and older boat engines and a small fisherman's cabin. Some of the ancient finds from Grytøya are exhibited at the museum, including flint knives and arrow heads from the Stone Age and bronze jewellery from the Viking period. Grytøya Village Museum is part of Trondanes District Museum.

After rounding the northern tip of Trondenes peninsula, we head towards the 3 km wide **Toppsundet.**

68°50'51"N   16°33'23"E   + 0 hrs 22 min ①

The small island of **Kjeøya** passes by on the starboard side, south of Lundenes. The island is known for its cave paintings from the hunting culture of ancient times. These are painted on a steep fell wall on the southwest side of the island. The paintings comprise around 10 human figures, a geometrical pattern and a figure that possibly represents an elk, painted in red. There are also grave markings from the Iron Age.

The bay **Bergsvågen** and the village of **Ervika** lie at the inner part of the bay on the port side of the ship, which is now in Toppsundet.

At the inner part of Bergsvågen is Skjærstad herring oil factory. Even though Harstad lay in an area rich with herring, the first herring oil factory was not built until 1919. Several others were built later. Skjærstad herring oil factory was built in 1922 and was in production for just six years, until 1928. The factory was

small, but had fairly advanced technical equipment for the time. The production process was driven by a 17 HP steam engine. From 1928 until the 1990s, when it was turned into a museum, the factory remained intact and untouched. The herring oil factory is the only completely preserved factory of its kind in Norway from that particular period. It has been granted status as a site of national technical and cultural heritage.

*

On the west side of Bergsvågen is the renowned, traditional and beautiful Røkenes Gård that was founded during the migration period (p 83). The old homestead, which is mentioned in writings from the Viking period and the Middle Ages, was an ancestral home as early as the 14th century and was granted status as a trading post and inn by Royal decree in 1777. The current listed main building is thought to be from around 1750. This is believed to have been built by church building workers that were also repairing Trondenes church. The 20 m long façade is traditional with its many small-paned windows and a rococo portal. The current hosts are the 10th generation of owners.

Røkenes Gård and Gjestehus has been renowned through many hundred years for its fine location and buildings and the varied cultural activities that take place there. This excellent reputation continues today. Many guests from Norway and abroad (which have included Mikael Gorbatsjov, King Harald, well-known politicians, clerics and cultural personalities) enjoy the sport and recreational facilities and the old traditions that are so reverently maintained.

*

We pass the headland **Stornes** on the port side, with the ferry to the village of **Bjørnå** on the starboard side, followed by the village of **Vaskinn**, with the 4 km long road tunnel through the mountain Toppen.

*

The island of **Grytøya**, to starboard, is steep and hilly. The highest peak, **Nona** (1 012 m above sea level) lies approx. in the centre of the island. Southeast of Nona there are two other peaks, 809 m above sea level and 782 m above sea level. The most productive agricultural areas are found on the eastern and southern parts of Grytøya. There is some birch forest also growing here.

*

68°53'N 16°30'18"E	+ 0 hrs 27 min

The steep and characteristic mountain known as **Toppen** (759 m above sea level) on the starboard side is said to have a hole running straight through it. According to the legend of "Tore Hund's arrow" the hole was made by the Viking chieftain Tore Hund from Bjarkøy (p 166). At Borkenes in Kvæfjord (one of the fjords to the south of Toppsundet), there is a stone monument in the churchyard, near Kvæfjord church. The stone monument is 1.50 m high and points northwards. The legend tells of the Viking chieftain Tore Hund, who is said to have turned himself into a pagan troll and fired an arrow to destroy the newly-built church in Kvæfjord. The arrow hit Toppen mountain in Toppsundet and made a hole in the mountain. This slowed down the arrow so that it hit the ground 20-30 m from the church. According to the legend, the stone monument is said to be the arrow head (p 278).

*

68°53'40"N 16°23'40"E	+ 0 hrs 40 min ②

The ship sails alongside the steep-sided mountain **Aunfjellet** (498 m above sea level) on the port side and we pass the village of **Aun**. Research on place names in Norway has revealed that the word 'aun' was used for farms that were left derelict, e.g. after plagues such as the Black Death in the 1350s (p 10). This is thought to be the origin of the name. The village was well populated before the Black Death; however, later it

DETAIL FROM **PESTA** BY THEODOR KITTELSEN 1904

became almost deserted. For that reason the village was also given the name Ødegård ("deserted farm"). In the 16th century the population returned and the village has been growing ever since.

The main activities in the village have always been fishing and agriculture, mostly in combination. Aun had its own landing stage between 1946 and the 1980s. Large amounts of fish have been traded during this active period. A number of fur farms (mink and fox) were in operation between 1955 until 1970. Several of the old farms are now derelict. In 1972 Aun was connected to the rest of Harstad municipality by a road over Aunfjellet. Previously, the only access to the village was by boat.

*

The church community, Aun Baptist Church was founded in 1887. The chapel was built in 1857 and is the oldest independent chapel in Northern Norway. The church community has approx. 20 parishioners.

*

North west of Aun there are remains of an ancient Sámi settlement with approx. 14 sites (p 243).

ᐧᐧ

68°54'20"N   16°21'30"E   + 0 hrs 43 min ③

The mountain **Elgen** (534 m above sea level) is on the port side.

ᐧᐧ

The headland known as **Ytre Elgsnes** on the port side is the northernmost headland, on the northeastern part of Hinnøya. At **Elgsnes**, extensive archaeological excavations have been carried out, revealing finds of quartz axes and flint tools, dating back to the early Stone Age (p 83).

ᐧᐧ

At Elgsnes stands Elgsnes chapel, built in 1985 as a memorial to Hans Egede, a minister who travelled to Greenland to practice as a missionary. He is also known as the "Greenland Apostle". Hans Egede was at one time the resident curate at Vågan church in Lofoten (1707-1718) (p 156).

ᐧᐧ

There are many wrecks all along the coast of Norway. On the 11th July 1941, the Norwegian steamship "Landego" hit a mine and sunk quickly in Kasfjorden in Toppsundet, just outside of Indre Elgsnes at the rear of Elgsnes peninsula, on the port side. The ship had been requisitioned by the German occupying forces, for use in laying undersea cables in the sound; however, the Captain did not check the list of minefields in the area. 7 of the 14 Norwegian crew and 2 of the 4 Germans on board were killed. The wreck is still in relatively good condition and lies at a depth of 50 m.

ᐧᐧ

The village of **Dale** is on the starboard side, across from Ytre Elgsnes at the mouth of the valley of **Dalsdalen**, between the mountains of Toppen and **Flyndretinden** (828 m above sea level). The road between Dale and Alvestad, further north west, is known somewhat laconically as Norway's "most often closed road" – due to the great danger of avalanches along that particular stretch of road.

ᐧᐧ

68°56'N   16°16'E   + 0 hrs 52 min ③

The village of **Alvestad** on the starboard side lies at the southwest foot of **Flyndretinden.** The village has many grave sites and remains of settlements dating from several

thousand years ago. These are mainly on the short headland of **Veneset** that projects into Toppsundet. On the shore at Alvestad are several old boathouses, forming a historical collection of old buildings.

ᐧᐧ

In front is the island of Andøya in Andøy municipality.

ᐧᐧ

On the starboard side, just above Elgsnes is the fishing hamlet of **Grøtavær** (pop. 170), outermost towards the north west of Grytøya, at the foot of the mountain **Hattfjellet** (856 m above sea level). The fishing hamlet is the northernmost settlement in Harstad municipality. Just outside of Grøtavær are over 100 small islands, islets and skerries, among them the islands of **Skipperøya** and **Smaløya.** Halibut farming is carried out in Grøtsundet, between the islands and Grytøya.

Grøtavær is a fishing community with many important archaeological finds dating from the Iron Age (p 83). Grøtavær is one of the fishing settlements that flourished in the Middle Ages, along with many others in Lofoten, Vesterålen and further north along the coast of Troms and Finnmark. The fishermen lived in small cabins during the hectic fishing season. Fishermen came from many other places to fish here, while their wives stayed at home, tended the farms, and fished to provide food for the family. Many generations in Grøtavær have made their living through fishing and small-scale farming.

ᐧᐧ

The Norwegian Armed Forces maintained a coastal fort at Grøtavær for many years. This was decommissioned in the 1990s. One of the guns at the fort, a massive cannon from the German aircraft carrier "Graf Zeppelin", had a somewhat unusual history: The cannon first stood at Store Korsnes in Alta (p 268). Later it was moved to Karlsøy in Troms (p 185). In 1962 it was relocated to at Grøtavær fort, where it remained until 1998 until it was finally sold abroad.

ᐧᐧ

Grøtavær chapel is a longhouse-style church built in 1915 with seating for 200 persons. The chapel also has a cemetery.

ᐧᐧ

Grøtavær Baptist Community was officially founded in 1944; however, the community was active for many years before that time. The community has a small church outermost on Grøtavær.

ᐧᐧ

68°57'36"N 16°09'E + 1 hr 05 min ④

We continue on and into the fjord **Andfjorden**, to the open sea crossing between the island of Andøya up ahead, the island of Senja (p 169) in the north east and Grytøya. Andfjorden is approx. 30 km wide and is 517 m at its deepest point.

A short stretch towards the next port of Risøyhamn brings us (port side) into the municipal boundary of Kvæfjord municipality.

Kvæfjord municipality

Municipal coat of arms, significance: Agriculture.
Meaning of name: First part of the name of the island Kvidja, from the Norse kvidr, "stomach, belly", from Kvæøya, an island in the fjord that has the appearance of a stomach.
Municipal seat: Borkenes (pop.1 510).
Position: 68°46'40"N 16°10'E. **Area:** 522 km².
Population: 3 048. **Pop. density:** 5.8 /km².
Area distribution: Farming 2 %, forestry 16 %, fresh water 2 %, other area 80 %.
Trade and industry: Agriculture, cattle farming with dairy production. Sheep and pig farming. Poultry farming Vegetable, potato and strawberry farming. Salmon farming. Mechanical workshops. Many of the local people commute to work in Harstad and Tromsø.
Places to return to: Hemmestad quay.
Kvæfjord municipality's home page: www.kvafjord.kommune.no

The wide bay on the port side splits into the fjords Kasfjorden, Kvæfjorden, Gullesfjorden and Godfjorden.

Kvæfjord church at **Borkenes** in Kvæfjord municipality was originally built in 1220. The church was rebuilt in 1867. The many stone monuments at the church and the surrounding area indicate that there was quite a large population here during the Iron Age. One of the stone monuments has a legend associated with it – the legend of the Viking chieftain Tore Hund from Bjarkøy (p 166, p 276). Burial mounds have been found further out in the fjord.

Hemmestad quay, in outermost **Gullesfjorden** was known as a trading post for those travelling to and from Trondheim as early as the 16th century. The trading post developed through the years and was granted official trading status in 1799. Hemmestad quay became an economic hub in the region, and trade was car-

ried out with countries throughout Europe and Russia. The trading post, at its peak, had fleets of boats, sailing ships and Nordland boats that sailed on merchant voyages. A ship made a voyage to Bergen twice a year, sailing with a cargo of dried fish, herring oil, poultry and cloudberries and on the voyage home they brought back coffee, spices, sweets, textiles and spirits. The boats were equipped for the annual fishing season in Lofoten at Hemmestad. This 'golden age' at Hemmestad continued until the end of the 19th century.

Hemmestad quay is now a museum, in which some of the traditional buildings around the quayside have been recreated. Hemmestad quay is part of Trondanes District Museum (p 274).

68°58'30"N 16°00'E + 1 hr 18 min ⑤

The headland of **Kinneset**, the mountain **Nilsandersatinden** (831 m above sea level) and the community of **Sletten** can be seen on the port side. Kinneset is the northernmost point on Hinnøya. In the front is the sound between Hinnøya and the southern part of the island of Andøya.

To starboard we can see our next port of call, Risøyhamn. On the starboard side is the village of Åse.

Approx. 68°59'N 15°53'E

We pass the boundary between Troms (p 189) and Nordland (p 160) counties

We pass the municipal boundary between Kvæfjord and Andøy municipalities

Andøy municipality

Municipal coat of arms, significance: Represents a wave that symbolises the municipality's maritime connections.
Meaning of name: From the Norse Ond, originally Omd which is the ancient name of Andøya.
Municipal seat: Andenes (pop. 2 636).
Position: 69°19'36"N 16°07'36"E. **Area:** 659 km².
Population: 5 152. **Pop. density:** 7.8 /km².
Area distribution: Farming 2 %, forestry 5 %, fresh water 5 %, other area 88 %.
Trade and industry: Fishing. Fish processing industry. Graphic design and production. Tourism, whale safari. Agriculture, based on dairy and beef cattle. Sheep farming, reindeer farming.
Places to return to: Andenes, Bleik. Andøy Museum. Polar Museum. Åse. Bjørnskinn.
Activities to return to: Whale safari.
Andøy municipality's home page: www.andoy.kommune.no

The island of **Andøya** (489 km²) on the port side is the 10th largest island in Norway. It is comprised of large areas of marshy ground (263 km²) that form a belt in the centre of the island and dominate the landscape in the north. Some areas of the island are only 10 m above sea level; however, especially in the north west and southern half of Andøya there are steep mountains up to 700 m above sea level. In the marshy areas there is peat production and cloudberry harvesting. The only Norwegian deposits of coal outside of Svalbard have been found on the island; however, mining the coal is not seen as economically viable. The island is well known for its many fossils. Among others, a fossil of a 3 m long fish-lizard has been discovered. Finds of 11 000 year old charcoal deposits indicate that the island has been inhabited since the Stone Age (p 83).

The administrative centre of Andenes is one of the largest in Vesterålen (p 284) and has been the largest community on Andøya for many hundreds of years. It lies close to rich fishing grounds and there is evidence of fishing settlements from as long ago as A.D. 500. Fishing took place all year round and for many years Andenes was regarded as the largest fishing community in Norway. Andenes' location means it is very exposed to the weather. On the northern tip of the island, however, it is protected from the worst storms from the Arctic Ocean by the largest breakwater in northern Europe, which is 2.5 km long. The oldest part of the breakwater, a 488 m long section, was built between 1895-1904. The breakwater contains over 306 000 m³ of rock.

Andøya is mentioned in Snorre Sturlason's King's Sagas, with the ancient Norse name of **Omd,** both in the 'Ynglingsaga' and the saga of Olav Trygvason (p 88). Omd was the original ancestral land of the earls in Hålogaland (which was an independent kingdom before 1030. It covered the area, which is currently Nordland and Troms). Some of the first Norwegian Viking expeditions started from here.

Andenes was once a wealthy fishing community. In the Middle Ages (p 83) traders from Germany and Holland came to buy dried fish and the fishermen encountered the powerful German Hansa (p 11). It is claimed that the fishermen also caught a species of shark, the Greenland Shark. Some say the fishermen used dead calves and dogs that had decomposed in barrels as bait. After a few weeks the carcasses were placed in baskets woven from juniper. The rotten odour was said to attract the shark, whereupon it could be caught.

In 1520, it is estimated that 590 persons lived on the island. 50 years later that number had increased to 7-800. Andenes had its 'golden age' around the year 1600, before a steady decline set in that continued until around the 19th century. Andøya had previously been integrated into the Bergen trading monopoly in Northern Norway and now the commercial voyages to Bergen were stopped. The formerly wealthy fishing community was reduced to a few fishermen' cabins near Andenes. In 1831, 1 127 persons lived on the northern part of Andøya. At that time and up to 1917, Pomor trading also took place at Andenes (p 241).

In 1921, at the site where the fishermen's cabins stood, a stone monument was erected, on the 100th anniversary of a tragic event that took place in 1821: On Sunday the 6th February 1821, 30 fishermen were lost at sea. In the morning on that day the weather was good. For some time, poor weather had prevented the boats from going out to fish. As the conditions had improved, the fishermen went out to sea. However, the weather changed suddenly and dramatically, and a fierce storm blew up. Some of the boats sank straight away, others capsized after a while. In Hammerfest in Finnmark (p 250) six men were found dead on the shore some days later. They had managed to escape the actual storm, but had later frozen to death. Only one boat survived. The boatman on board said that they had sailed in total darkness - he managed to save the boat and crew because he knew the coast extremely well and had listened for the breaking waves and currents. For several days after that tragic Sunday, people lit fires along the coast so that any survivors would be able to see them and sail to shore. It is said that the owner of the fishing plant was visited in the night by the ghosts of dead fishermen who tried to take him with them out to sea. Finally, he had to move away from the area – and was found drowned some time later!

There have been five churches in Andenes. The first was built during the 15th century. It was richly decorated, with a triptych and sculptures made in Lübeck, Germany. One church is said to have been demolished in 1600 and a new one built in 1607. The next was built in 1734 and stood until 1830. It was said of this particular church, that in 1820 it was so draughty that fishermen dried their fishing nets in the church. The current church at Andenes was built in 1876 and was restored in 1966. It is a longhouse construction with seating for 400 persons.

Andenes lighthouse stands near the harbour at Andenes and is a part of the local architecture. It was built in 1859 and is a 40 m high red iron tower, one of the country's tallest, with a 148-step interior staircase. The range of the lighthouse is 18 nautical miles. The lighthouse was fully automated in 1978 and was officially granted listed status in 1999. It is equipped with a radio beacon that can be used both by shipping and aircraft. Previously, a pilot station was also located at the lighthouse, with eight pilots. Ships had to sail along the outside of Andøya until Risøyrenna was opened in 1922.

Fishing still takes place all year round at Andenes, nowadays with modern trawlers. There are freezer plants and a filleting factory. Export of fish and fish products is a major industry and the fishing trade is still the main commercial activity in the municipality.

It is possible to go on a whale safari from Andenes. No other place in Norway has the Atlantic Ocean shelf so close to land and the ocean is a rich feeding ground for sperm whales, which often gather here.

The Royal Norwegian Air Force, and Andøya Air Base which lies just southeast of Andenes, are the municipality's largest employers. The Air Base is a military area and is the main air base for the Air Force's maritime aircraft. It is also used for civil air traffic. The construction of the Air base began in 1952 with the help of NATO funds.

The world's most northerly permanent firing base for research rockets, Andøya Rocket Range (Oksebåsen), which is officially a department of the Norwegian Space Centre, lies just southwest of Andenes. In addition to being a rocket range it is also a base for geophysical observations, as it lies in the southern outer region of the zone of maximum Northern Lights (Aurora Borealis)

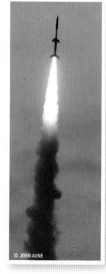

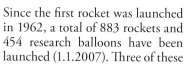

activity and has a special location in regard to the Northern Lights and the polar atmosphere (p 162). The range has eight firing ramps. It is possible to fire rockets weighing up to 20 tons and to send up research balloons. Data can be received from several rockets and balloon instruments at the same time. Researchers from more than 80 research institutions in Europe, USA, Canada and Japan have been involved in rocket launches from Andøya.

Since the first rocket was launched in 1962, a total of 883 rockets and 454 research balloons have been launched (1.1.2007). Three of these were over five tons in weight and one of them reached a maximum height of approx. 1 450 km.

On the east side of the island, out towards Andfjorden, is Europe's first commercial firing range, used in the development of military weapons systems. The test area covers 1 850 km^2.

The following article is taken from The Norwegian Astronautical Society newsletter, No. 1 1995.

Near-apocalypse on Andøya:
"It caused a worldwide sensation when the Russian news bureau Interfaks announced on the 25th January 1995, that a rocket from a Northern European country had been shot down over Russian territory. In reality it was a civil research rocket that had been launched from Andøya in Vesterålen that, without actually going anywhere near Russian territory, had fallen back to earth 300 km north of Svalbard after a successful flight that lasted 23 minutes. Interfaks announced some time later that the previous notice about the rocket being shot down was incorrect, but that the rocket had set off a defence security alarm at Russian military radar installations. This was in spite of the fact that Norway, as is normal procedure, had notified the Russian authorities of the launch in advance. Even more sensational was an announcement the day after the incident by Russia's president Boris Jeltsin, who almost boastingly declared that for the first time he had used his so-called 'black briefcase' which contains the equipment necessary to give the order to release Russia's nuclear weapons arsenal. This time, however, Jeltsin limited his

use of the equipment to communicate with the military leaders while they followed the flight of the rocket. Several conflicting statements have been made as to actually how close the world had come to a Russian retaliatory attack. The Andøy rocket, which was an 18.45 m long 3-stage Black Brant XII, weighing 6 tons, was twice as heavy as the heaviest of the 606 rockets that have previously been launched from Andøya. It reached a height of 1 453 km, approx. 500 km higher than the previous record. The 113 kg instrument payload carried out measurements of fields and particles in the so-called polar cleft over Svalbard, where the lines in the Earth's magnetic field are perpendicular to the Earth's surface."

Source: Øyvind Gulbrandsen

Who would have thought anything like that could have happened here, when passing by this "anonymous" island on the starboard side!

The community of **Bleik** (pop. 465) lies on Andøya's west coast. On Bleik there are listed, special courtyard-style buildings that remain as they were first constructed in the Middle Ages. **Bleikstranden** near Bleik is northern Europe's longest sand beach.

The island **Bleiksøya** (160 m above sea level) just outside of Bleik has one of the largest bird cliffs in Norway.

68°58'40"N 15°48'E	+ 1 hr 35 min ⑥

The community of **Åse** on the starboard side of the ship, lies at the foot of the fell **Åseåsen** (190 m above sea level), with the mountain **Steinheia** (405 m above sea level) in the background. Åse was one of the main clan seats in the Viking period, near the sea route to Bjarkøy and Tore Hund, who was the chieftain there (p 166).

Just south of Åse, in a muddy marsh, remains of one of the region's few preserved star-shaped courtyards from the Iron Age (p 83) have been discovered. The courtyard was built approx. 1 800 years ago to protect the people of Andøya against enemy attacks. Only the foundations remain. The courtyard was deliberately built some distance away from the other settlements at Åse. There was a good view out to sea, and the courtyard was difficult to spot for those arriving at Andøya via the sea route. The Åse settlement comprised 14 houses built in a circle, with a courtyard in the middle, approx. 40-44 m in diameter. The houses were built in a row, wall-to-wall. They varied from 5 to 10 m in length, and were 2-3.5 m wide. Earth and turf were used to build the houses. The people of Åse probably had boats down by the shore further away, or

at Åse river, a few kilometres further north. It is thought that the last Andøy clan chieftain to use the Åse settlement as a fortress was forced to escape to Iceland at the end of the 9th century, as the King's earls wanted more power and banished the local chieftains.

The village of **Myrset** near the mountain Bjørnskinnfjellet and the community of Risøyhamn can be seen up ahead, to starboard. At Bjørnskinn, on the southern side of the mountain is Bjørnskinn church, consecrated in 1885. Another church, built in 1740, once stood on the same site. This was found to be too small and was demolished to make way for the current church. The church contains an old altar taken from one of the previous churches. There once was another church closer to the mountain at Bjørnskinn, however this was destroyed by an avalanche in the 18th century.

On the port side, after **Kinneset,** are the marshes on **Lovikmyra,** also the peninsula and the community of **Lovika** under the fell **Gardsheia** (465 m above sea level)**.**

68°58'40"N 15°47'40"E	+ 1 hr 38 min

We approach **Risøysundet,** the shallow sound between Andøya and Hinnøya, and **Risøyrenna.** Risøyrenna is a part of the channel for ships that sail on the inside of Andøya when sailing along the coast, or those that have ports of call in Vesterålen. The channel is 4 850 m long, 6 m deep and is 50 m wide measured along the ocean floor. Navigation along the channel requires some skill - in addition to being narrow, it has two changes of direction on the route to Risøyhamn.

The first dredging operations in Risøyrenna were carried out from 1876-81 when a 1 800 m long channel with a bottom width of 31 m and a depth of 3 m was excavated. Despite the sound being adequate for the chieftains

© EILIV LEREN

mentioned in the sagas (which is reflected in the discoveries of ancient settlements along the channel) and for the ships sailing to Bergen, it was necessary to carry out deeper and deeper dredging operations as more modern, larger ships demanded greater channel depth. From 1911 to 1922 work continued to create a bottom width of 50 m and a depth of 5 m. Only after these dimensions were reached could the ships in the Hurtigruten traffic (which began sailing in 1893) and other similar sized vessels use the channel, without depending on the high tide for passage.

© FAVRE

At 11.00 in the morning on the 22nd June 1922, with great jubilation, Risøyrenna was officially opened. The Hurtigruten ship "Finnmarken" had been painted white for the occasion and had the Norwegian King Haakon VII (1872-1957) and other prominent guests on board. The ship crossed two banners decorated with the Norwegian flag colours that were hung across the channel in the southern and northern ends. After MS "Finnmarken" came a cortege of boats that had come from many places in Norway.

A few years ago, Risøyrenna was widened and dredged once more, to accommodate modern ships and an increase in shipping in general.

ᘒᘓ

68°58'36"N   15°46'36"E   + 1 hr 38 min

The ship sails into Risøyrenna, on the way to our next port of call, Risøyhamn, just before the bridge, Andøybrua.

ᘒᘓ

68°58'44"N   15°43'13"E   + 1 hr 44 min ⑦

Just before Risøyhamn, on the starboard side towards the centre of Andøya are Northern Norway's best-preserved farms from the Iron Age (p 83). Close to the foot of the mountain **Bjørnskinnfjellet** (638 m above sea level), in an approx. 300 m wide and 500 m long belt along the edge of the marsh, there are two Iron Age farms and a Middle Ages farm – in total 16 foundation remains and 43 graves. There is also several hundred metres of stone wall. The area is very well preserved and almost untouched. It indicates that the people here survived on agriculture, hunting and fishing. Pollen analysis shows that corn was grown here more than 3 000 years ago and there are traces of farming activity from around 400 B.C. until modern times.

Just south-west, at **Slettan**, there is an area with eight small house remains from the Middle Ages and six graves from the pre-Christian era. There are also three larger house foundations from the Iron Age, six graves and stone walls. In the eastern part of Slettan, five house foundations have been found, 28 burial mounds and a large rectangular-shaped cobblestoned area. The largest foundation is 45 long. The graves vary from smaller stone piles to larger rounded heaps.

The ship docks at the quayside at Risøyhamn

The community of **Risøyhamn** (pop. 213) at Risøysundet was formerly an active trading post for the many flat-bottomed ships and boats that sailed through the sound. Currents and tides brought sand and deposits and gradually the depth of Risøysundet decreased. At one time it was less than 1 m over a 125 m stretch. This area became a bottleneck, preventing modern ships sailing through Vesterålen (p 284). The number of ships thus gradually decreased.

Trafostation
© SIRI LØKEN

Captain Richard With, the founder of the Hurtigruten, bought the trading post and moved to Risøyhamn in 1875. He began to restore Risøyhamn and organised the first dredging operations in the sound. In 1902, the trading post was sold once more and Risøyhamn expanded during the next few years - a boatyard was established and the road through to Andenes was built between 1898-1910.

The family that had bought the trading post in 1902 still owns the store and general office here. Risøyhamn had its 'golden age' in the 1950s and 1960s and at one time had a hotel, bakery, mineral water factory, timber factory and dairy. Risøyhamn is currently a municipal administration centre. Andøy Museum has a smaller branch here.

The ship continues to Sortland   + 0 hrs 00 min

LARGER MAP P410

The ship departs from the quayside at Risøyhamn and sets sail for the next port of call, Sortland. We sail under Andøy bridge, which spans Risøysundet from Andøya to Hinnøya. The bridge was opened in 1974. The bridge is 750 m in total length and the main span is 110 m. It is built according to the cantilever (hollow box) principle.

68°57'40"N   15°37'32"E   + 0 hrs 10 min

Our voyage continues, we sail into Risøysundet On the starboard side we pass the fjord **Tranesvågen,** the only fjord on Andøya and the only sea approach to the characteristic **Bjørnskinnfjellet** and the remains of the farm from the Iron Age at the innermost part of the fjord. The village of **Tranesvågen** is at the southern mouth of the fjord.

68°57'N   15°36'34"E   + 0 hrs 12 min

The community of **Tranes** passes on the starboard side, then **Nygård** under the mountain **Kvasstinden** (705 m above sea level).

On the port side we have sailed past the flat land area of **Dragnes,** before **Reinhaugsheia** (485 m above sea level and 561 m above sea level), then the village of **Buksnes,** at the southern foot of the fell.

68°52'20"N   15°33'34"E   + 0 hrs 33 min ⑧

The village of **Skjoldehamn** and the headland **Gavl-neset** on the starboard side are the most southerly points of Andøya. The village lies at the base of the mountain of **Gavltinden** (662 m above sea level).

During extraction of peat in a marsh at Skjoldehamn in 1936, a body was found. The body was wrapped in a

We pass the municipal boundary between Andøy and Sortland municipalities

Sortland municipality

Municipal coat of arms, significance: Reference to Sortland as Vesterålen's 'port' both from the ocean and land sides.
Meaning of name: From the Norse S(v)ortuland, first part of the name of a river, Svarta, from svart.
Municipal seat: Sortland (pop. 4 679).
Position: 68°42'N 15°25'E. **Area:** 722 km².
Population: 9 703. **Pop. density:** 13.4 /km².
Area distribution: Farming 2 %, forestry 16 %, fresh water 3 %, other area 78 %.
Trade and industry: Service enterprises. Agriculture and cattle farming (Langøya). Fishing, largely from smaller vessels. Food industry. Canned produce and herring oil factory. Production of marine oils. Mechanical workshops. Concrete fabrication.
Places to return to: Jennestad quay.
Sortland municipality's home page: www.sortland.kommune.no

woollen blanket, and laid upon birch sticks and twigs. It was covered with a layer of birch bark and was in relatively good condition. It was later dated to approx. A.D. 1 200.

The clothing, which came to be known as the "Skjolde-hamn costume", was preserved and restored at Tromsø Museum. It comprised a shirt, a jacket and trousers, an ankle bracelet, ankle gaiters and socks. Of the shoes, only the soles remained. The clothes were old and ragged and it was obvious that the individual had not been a wealthy person. The costume is Norway's only complete find from the Middle Ages and is regarded as a national treasure as it provides valuable information and contributes to understanding how 'common' people dressed during that period.

In the foreground on the starboard side are the mountains on the island of Langøya.

To port is the village of **Fornes** and **Fornesfjellet** (589 m above sea level) on Hinnøya. Then we sail past the shallow fjord **Forfjorden.** Forfjorden, the valleys of **Forfjorddalen** and **Finnsæterdalen** further in the bay are protected nature reserves due to their U-shaped valley formations, created by the inland ice that at one time filled the valleys and also due to their moraine ridges. These are unique in Norway. In Forfjorddalen there is a protected virgin pine forest area. Some of the trees are over 700 years old.

The municipality of Sortland lies on both sides of **Sortlandssundet**, with an area of 308 km² on Hinnøya to port, and 269 km² on Langøya to starboard (sea area not included).

The region of **Vesterålen** is the common name for the district, which covers an area between approx. 68°25'N and 69°20'N. The islands of Langøya (860 km²) to starboard, Andøya (490 km²) to startboard (behind), Hadseløya (102 km²) ahead and to starboard, western part (1 275 km²) of Hinnøya to port, northern part (202.8 km²) of Austvågøya up ahead, and some smaller islands, are all part of Vesterålen.

Other areas at the same longitude have an Arctic climate, such as Alaska, Greenland and Siberia. The reason for the amelioration of the temperature is the Gulf Stream (p 85) that runs along the Norwegian coast.

A poet has described Vesterålen as "...a wonderland that fell into the Arctic Ocean from the heavens when the earth was created, a landscape formed from an incredible fantasy, one of the unknown creator's great masterpieces. Vesterålen is a unique, rich and remote world...".

68°51'30"N 15°30'E   + 0 hrs 37 min ⑨

The fjord **Gavlefjorden** (20 km long) to starboard opens up towards the Norwegian Sea in the north, 11 km wide. At the mouth towards Sortlandssundet the fjord is 4 km wide. It divides the islands of Andøya (up ahead) and Langøya. The village of **Alsvåg** lies in the fjord, on Langøya.

The island of **Langøya** (860 km²) to starboard is the third largest island in Norway and is a part of Vesterålen. Out towards the Norwegian Sea are the municipalities of Øksnes in the north and Bø in the south, and western parts of the municipalities of Sortland and Hadsel. The island has many fjords, the longest is the 25 km long Eidsfjorden which runs along the length of the island from the south and almost splits the island in two (p 289). Langøya is very mountainous, especially in the west, with steep peaks. However there are also wide, populated shore areas. On the eastern side, towards the Hurtigruten's sailing route, the shore areas are wider and more densely populated. Between the coastal strips there are marshy areas with rivers and small lakes. Archaeological site excavations indicate that Langøya has been inhabited since the Stone Age (p 83).

✂

68°50'40"N 15°29'E	+ 0 hrs 41 min ⑨

The headland of **Bremnesodden** is on our port side, with the fell **Bremneskollen** (244 m above sea level), thereafter the small island of **Bremnesøy** and the village of **Bremnes.**

✂

68°50'N 15°28'10"E	+ 0 hrs 44 min ⑨

After Forfjorden, which passes on the port side, we see the island of **Rogsøya** outside of the village of **Rogsøy,** and the flat marshy valley of **Rogsøydalen**, thereafter **Nordneset** and the smaller fell, **Stamnes** (217 m above sea level) and the mountain **Høgfjellet** (711 m above sea level).

✂

To port, up ahead is the bridge Sortlandsbroen.

✂

The flat headland with the village of **Bogen**, the fjord **Gåsfjorden** and the headland **Fagerneset** is on our starboard side. **Gåsfjorden** is a well-known and popular area for bathing in the summer months and a recreational area for the population of Sortland. There are also sites from the Stone Age and remains of old Sámi settlements.

Further along are **Vik**, the bay **Vikbotn** and the island of **Vikøya.** Vikbotn is a marsh, which is used as a stopover by various species of geese on their way to and from Svalbard. The pointed peaks in the background on the starboard side are on the western part of Langøya, out towards the Norwegian Sea.

✂

68°46'N 15°18'E	+ 0 hrs 54 min ⑩

The old trading post of Jennestad lies just east of Vikbotn on the starboard side. The trading post, which had its golden age during the first ten years of the 1900s, was first established in 1830 as a small business; however, it received a boost in 1863, when the construction of Brygga (a large quayside building that housed a store, post office, warehouse, landing stage, salt store, offices and workshops) was completed. Jennestad was granted official status as a trading post in 1870. It was said that 'anything' could be bought - or sold - at Jennestad. In total there were almost 14 000 varieties of goods for sale, kept in drawers and on shelves, under the eaves or stored in the warehouse. In the 17 m long counter alone, there were 153 drawers for weighed goods and a total of 222 drawers in the whole store. The assortment of goods varied tremendously, from chewing tobacco, coffee, shirt laps and collars to nails, gunpowder, fishing gear, hairpins and eau de cologne. The local transport boats anchored just outside the headland, and were tended by smaller craft. The boats were rowed to the gable end of Brygga and the goods were lifted up and down by a hoist. In 1911 a steamboat pier was built with a warehouse and rail tracks to make loading and unloading easier.

✂

Graphite deposits were found here at the beginning of the 19th century. The graphite ore lay open on the shoreline and could be cut loose with a pick and shovel. The ore was sent on to Bergen, where it was used as a lubricant and as a dye additive. Later, the graphite was used for pencils, batteries, seals and paint. In 1902 the operating rights were sold to the company Norwegian Mining Co. Ltd, Middlesbrough, England, which operated the mines until 1912, when they were sold to the owner of Jennestad trading post. Up to 1978, when the company was closed down, there was occasional activity in the mines. Other times the mine was inoperative.

NORSK KULTURARV
NORWEGIAN HERITAGE

In the beginning, the graphite was easy to extract; however, later it became difficult to access, with long mineshafts and tunnels dug out manually, sometimes with dynamite, mining drills, picks and shovels. The ore was transported using wheelbarrows and was hoisted up to the surface in boxes using a horse-driven elevator. The ore was then hand-sorted on a long workbench before the sorted ore was exported abroad. The operations continued until 1914. When the mining operations stopped, the mines were soon filled with water. In 1931 operations began once more in the first mines. The work was now more mechanized. At the most there were up to 30 men working in the mines, working in three shifts. The mining operations were halted several times until 1978 when they stopped for the last time and production finally ceased.

Jennestad trading post lost its central role when the Risøyrenna ship channel was opened to larger ships in 1922. The community of Sortland became a port for the Hurtigruten and developed as the new central traffic hub for the area. The larger motorized fishing vessels required better quayside facilities than those offered at Jennestad.

Effective farming was also carried out at Jennestad until the end of the 1970s.

Today, Jennestad trading post is a thriving museum and cultural heritage centre.

68°47'35"N   15°26'E   + 0 hrs 58 min

On the port side are the villages of **Reinsnes** and **Maurnes,** before and after the fell **Svellingen** (439 m above sea level). After the village of **Liland** the bridge crosses the narrow **Hognfjorden**, at **Finnset** that continues south eastwards into **Sørfjorden**.

The flat headland of **Kringelneset** passes on the port side, with the mountain **Kvalsauktinden** (767 m above sea level) behind.

Sortlandsbroen can be seen up ahead. Further forwards we can see the wild peaks on Hinnøya, among them the high mountain of **Møysalen**.

The community of **Ånstad** passes on the port side, just before the bridge.

68°42'28"N   15°25'40"E

The Coast Guard Headquarters in Sortland passes on the port side. It was opened in 1984 and is the base for the Coast Guard Squadron North, the Coast Guard vessels that operate in the northern ocean regions. The leader responsible for the Coast Guard services carries the rank of

Commodore and is a member of the Naval Chiefs of Staff in Oslo. The Coast Guard officers have police authority and the right of inspection in their daily work in enforcing the Fisheries Acts in areas under Norwegian jurisdiction.

© BERIT LILAND

The Coast Guard was established in 1977 and is a continuance and expansion of the Naval Military Fishery Inspection. It carries out various tasks, such as protecting Norwegian maritime sovereignty and authority at sea and it contributes to a reliable control and monitoring of fishing resources and fishing grounds. The Coast Guard's objective is to enforce the laws and regulations that apply at sea, contribute to ocean research and be able to offer fast response to persons and vessels in distress by offering technical and practical assistance, and help to prevent accidents and pollution. The Coast Guard also assists other national organisations that are responsible for monitoring coastal zones.

To carry out their duties, which include monitoring Norwegian territorial waters in the Norwegian Economic Zone, in the protected zones around Svalbard and Jan Mayen, the Cost Guard has a fleet of vessels, aircraft and helicopters. The Coast Guard operates according to their motto "Always Present" and has contributed greatly in the prevention of serious international economic criminal activities in connection with fishing vessels' illegal fishing in Norwegian territorial waters.

The ship docks at the quayside at Sortland

After sailing under the bridge Sortlandsbroen, the ship docks at the quayside. Sortlandsbroen, which was opened in 1975, is a hollow box construction in concrete with three spans and 18 side spans. The total length of the bridge is 948 metres and the longest span is 150 metres in length.

The town of **Sortland**, which is also the regional centre for Vesterålen, received its town charter in 1997. It has been given the name "The Blue Town on the Sound" after the (originally private) initiative to paint all of the buildings in different shades of blue, an initiative which

© KARL LAURITS OLSEN

was eventually adopted by the municipality. Not all of the property owners agreed and there are currently ten or more buildings painted blue in the centre of town.

Archaeological finds indicate that the area may have been inhabited as long as 5 000 years ago, at as many as eight different settlements. The hunter-gatherer population moved from settlement to settlement (p 83). 270 graves have been located, from the Iron Age, in and around Sortlandssundet and over 30 house remains have been found. Written sources from 1370 indicate a "Swartalandes" church, and in documents found in treasure chests dating from 1567, several farms are mentioned. However, the numbers of permanent settlers were not great, for several hundred years the total number did not exceed 2-300. In 1769 the number had increased to 600 and 100 years later there were over 1 000 persons registered in the area. These lived on farms on both sides of the sound or on single isolated farms. Approx. 10 % of the population was Sámi (p 243); most of these lived in the innermost parts of the fjord. The broad shorelines around the sound provided excellent conditions for agriculture.

For many years, especially at the end of the 19th century, there were large herring catches in the waters around Sortland (p 289). However, although the fishing grounds were nearby, most of the population made a living from a combination of fishing and agriculture. The first cannery in the area was built in 1912. At one time there were as many as 120 employees working at the factory, canning meats and fish products. Based on products from agriculture and fishing, many other large food processing factories were also built. The seines (fishing nets) could be seen all along Sortlandssundet and several boatyards were established

in the municipality. The settlements gradually became denser around the church in Sortland. Around the 1900s, Sortland was known as "the church parish with 33 inhabited houses and 250 local inhabitants".

The development of Sortland received a boost after the Risøyrenna ship channel was dredged in 1922 (p 281) and was opened for larger ships. It became a port of call for the Hurtigruten. Before this time much of the shipping sailed along the outer side of the islands in Vesterålen, using Stokmarknes (p 291) as the natural stopping point. Sortland also overtook many of the functions of Jennestad trading post, which then became less central and did not have adequate quayside facilities for the larger ships.

Sortland became the busiest trading post in Vesterålen, schools were built and it became a traffic hub for the local area. The arrival of the Hurtigruten in 1922, the car ferry across the sound in 1948, the opening of the bridge in 1975, the establishment of the Coast Guard Headquarters in 1984 and the proximity of several airports, both large and small, have all contributed to the development of Sortland. Trade and services are the most important commercial enterprises today, followed by agriculture, fishing and aquaculture. Sortland has a wide range of cultural activities; one example is the Musical Society which was established in 1893.

As early as 1370, there are references to a church in official documents. The current church in Sortland is probably the 5th or 6th to be built. It is a long cruciform church in a new-gothic style and was consecrated in 1901. The architect, who died before the church was completed, also designed the Lofoten Cathedral (Vågan church) (p 156) in Kabelvåg. The church has seating for 840.

The old church was demolished when the current church was constructed. The spire from the church is preserved and stands at the entrance to Minnelunden on the old church site in Sortland. It is one of the oldest preserved church spires in Norway. The spire clock has an inscription dating from 1474.

The ship continues to Stokmarknes   + 0 hrs 00 min

LARGER MAP P**411**

The community of **Strand** (pop. 550) can be seen on our port side.

In front are the mountain peaks of the northern part of the island of Austvågøya (p 155) and the southern part of Hinnøya. Among them is the peak of **Møysalen** (1 262 m above sea level) which is the highest point in Vesterålen. The peak is a well-known landmark for sailors and has smaller glaciers close to the summit. Møysalen National Park (51.2 km²) was established in 2003.

68°39'28"N   15°24'28"E   + 0 hrs 16 min ①

On the port side is **Kjerringnes**, home of Vesterålen's first golf course. The course has 9 holes and was opened in 2000. Thereafter we can see the two small islands **Kjerringnesøya** and **Åserøy** (111 m above sea level), just outside the community of Sigerfjord (pop. 776) on the north side of the mouth of Sigerfjorden.

Around 1920, **Sigerfjord** was the third largest community in Vesterålen with a population of approx. 700. Sigerfjord had good harbour facilities and lay in a central location in relation to the rich herring fishing grounds. Sigerfjord was the headquarters of one of the area's most successful shipping companies, which was established in 1899 and had approx. 300 employees in 1920. The shipping company was a pioneer, adapting the old fleet and developing new types of boat according to the transport needs of the market and competition. The shipping company developed, among other things, a transport ship for fish for use in Northern Norway. During the 1920s, the economic situation became more difficult for the whole country and the shipping company went bankrupt in 1930.

After a difficult period after the Second World War, Sigerfjord has once again become a dynamic and thriving community.

During the night between the 6th and 7th March 1956 a massive avalanche occurred in Sigerfjord, one of the biggest in Norway's history. After a heavy snowfall followed by mild weather, a 5 km wide avalanche swept away four houses. 13 persons were killed, 9 of them were children. The press and media from all over the world came to Sigerfjord to report on the tragedy.

Sigerfjord church is a longhouse-style wooden building. It was consecrated in 1933 and has seating for 280 persons. The church contains a St. Olav figure from the 15th century. Close to the church is a monument to those that were lost in the Second World War, erected in 1947.

On the port side of Sigerfjord, we pass **Steiro** and **Bø** at the foot of the mountain **Bøblåheia** (810 m above sea level), and then the communities of **Holand** and **Rise**.

68°38'38"N   15°22'50"E   + 0 hrs 20 min

The mountain **Middagsbogtinden** (721 m above sea level) on the port side rises up between the fjords **Sigerfjorden** and **Djupfjorden**. Then follows the village of **Blokken**, before passing the peaks of **Rødsandheia** and **Blokktindan** (866 m above sea level).

Innermost in Djupfjorden is a hydroelectric power station.

We cross the community boundary between Sortland and Hadsel municipalities

Hadsel municipality

Municipal coat of arms, significance: Forms a stylised map of the municipality. **Meaning of name:** From the Norse *Hofðasegl*, from *hofði*, 'high headland, crag', and 'segl 'sail (meaning a mountainside lit such that it resembles a sail).
Municipal seat: Stokmarknes (pop. 3 081).
Position: 68°34'N 14°54'E. **Area:** 556 km².
Population: 7 907. **Pop. density:** 14.2 /km².
Area distribution: Farming 4 %, forestry 13 %, fresh water 2 %, other area 81 %.
Trade and industry: Agriculture with meat and dairy production. Cattle and pig breeding. Fishing, Vesterålen's largest trawler fleet. Fishing industry. Fish farming. Fish processing and foodstuffs industries. Services. Hurtigruten's administration office. Mechanical engineering and workshops. Boatyards and docks. Graphic design and production. Timber supply industry. Production of oil booms. Energy and electricity production.
Places to return to: Raftsundet. Trollfjorden. Hurtigruten Museum. Hadsel rectory. Vesterålen Museum.
Activities to return to: Hunting.
Hadsel municipality's home page: www.hadsel.kommune.no

Hadsel municipality's area is spread over four islands: Hadseløya (102 km²), part of Langøya (98 km²) to starboard, part of Austvågøy (203 km²) up ahead, part of Hinnøya (150 km²) to port.

The fjord **Fiskefjorden** and the village of **Kvitnes** is under the mountain **Kvitnesheia** (384 m above sea level) on the port side. In the valley innermost in Fiskefjorden there is a power station, built in 1937. There is also a former iron ore mine.

At one time, one of the largest homesteads in Vesterålen was located at Kvitnes. It had a post office, administration office for local transport boats and a boatyard. This is now derelict; however the farm is still active.

On the starboard side we pass the villages of **Gjerstad**, **Grytting** and **Hauknes** under the fell **Ol-Hansatinden** (748 m above sea level). Remains of a chieftain settlement have been found at Grytting, from the latter part of the Viking period, along with several grave sites. This stretches along the eastern side of Langøya, is regarded as one of the finest agricultural areas in the whole of Nordland county.

The ship approaches the next port of call, Stokmarknes, with Hadseløya on our port side up ahead. We can see the bridge, Hadselbroen, up ahead and to starboard is **Skagen**, with its long flat headland on the south east tip of Langøya.

We pass the short take-off and landing runway at Stokmarknes Airport at Skagen. The airport was opened in 1972 and has a tarmaced runway 870 m in length. In 2006, approx. 93 000 passengers travelled via the airport.

© KARL LAURITS OLSEN

The ship sails into **Langøysundet**, which divides Langøya and Hadseløya. We round the south eastern tip of Langøya, with Hadseløya and Stokmarknes on the port side. In the distance up ahead we can see the mountains in Bø municipality in Vesterålen.

Ahead and to starboard, **Eidsfjorden** cuts into Langøya, parallel with Sortlandssundet that we have just left behind. In 1890, the world's largest herring catch was caught here. The amount of herring was so great that the entire fjord was blocked until the herring could be landed from the sea. Approx. 400 000 barrels of herring were salted after the massive catch – however much of the herring was left to rot, as there was not enough capacity available at the time to process all of the fish.

The legend of Eidsfjorden:
There is a fjord called Eidsfjorden, which is about 20 km long from southwest to northeast, cutting into Langøen in Vesteraalen. According to the legend it was created thus: A good-natured giant, who lived on one of Langøens mountains, thought that a part of the island, lying between Sortlandssundet and Vestbygden in Øksnes, was just too big, and in any case unsuitable for building houses on or to live in. Therefore, he decided to remove it and make a fjord, so that people could build houses there and live along the shoreline. On the island's south coast, where the sea comes in, he began to dig

large areas of flat marshy terrain between the fells. The coastal area in the south west is cultivated.

Hadseløya, at the end of the 19th century and the first ten years of the 1900s, was known nationally and internationally as Rypeøya (Ptarmigan Island). The island was well known for its rich hunting and fishing grounds. Englishmen were especially frequent visitors. Many books were written about the 'hunter's paradise' in Northern Norway. The first ptarmigan hunt in Norway using dogs took place on Hadseløya. Hunters from England brought their dogs with them and used the area to train their English Setters as hunting dogs. During this period the island was almost cleared of ptarmigan. Many VIPs visited the island, from France, Germany, England and Norway, among them Kaiser Wilhelm II of Germany in 1892 and King Haakon VII of Norway. This era lasted until the start of the First World War.

out the nearest mountains and as a tool he used an enormous shovel. With the shovel he removed huge lumps of land. But when he got to the place where Kjeldraget stands now, the handle of the shovel split, and the giant could not dig as easily as before. So the fjord was smaller than he had planned, and Eidsfjorden's south eastern and north western sides were very narrow and small. He carried on working, but the split in the shovel got larger and larger, and so Bjørndalsfjorden, the continuance of Eidsfjorden towards the west, is also very narrow and shallow. Only a bit of land remained, before the fjord could be joined with Skjærfjorden on Langøen's north west side. However, the shovel handle finally broke off and the giant, in his rage, threw the shovel blade up onto a rock face, where it still stands in the form of a hundred foot high peak, known as Ræka, where it is shaped like a long square spade with a broken handle just above the blade. The rest of the handle was thrown into the fjord, and this created a long flat island, which is known as Rækøen. The part of the ground that was left behind, where the handle had broken, is a low, flat neck of land that is known as Skjærfjordeidet. The giant complained of his bad luck and said that the fjord was so narrow that a snow bunting could fit through the gap.

As a way of mocking the giant, many of the local people in Vesterålen still say, about something open and wide: "It's as if a snow-bunting squeezes into Eidsfjorden".

Source: Legends and tales from Nordland, compiled by O. Nicolaissen, published in Kristiania in 1879.

We sail under the bridge Hadselbroen that stretches across **Langøysundet**. The bridge is a cantilever construction and the main spans are 75 m + 150 m + 75 m. The remaining 24 spans are cast using a steel framework. The total length of the bridge is 1 011 m and it was finally opened in 1978. The bridge leads over to the small island of Børøya, and from there a smaller bridge, built in 1965, leads over the narrow sound known as **Børøysundet** to Stokmarknes.

Hadsel bridge is equipped with a high-frequency sound barrier, to prevent foxes crossing the bridge from Langøya to Hadseløya.

The island of **Hadseløya** (102 km²) is the largest island in Hadsel municipality. The island is hilly – the highest peak is **Lamlitind** (657 m above sea level) in the west. In common with the rest of the Vesterålen area, there are

The ship sails around the small island of **Børøya** (52 m above sea level), that lies just outside Stokmarknes. In addition to a fair amount of housing, there is also a timber pro-

SORTLAND · STOKMARKNES · SVOLVÆR | **DAY 9**   **291**

duction factory, fish feed factory, salmon farm and salmon processing plant, a recycling unit and a smaller shipyard on the island.

On the island there is a boat that has been brought onto land, N97VV. The boat is called MK "Isqueen", and was built in 1954. It was originally 66.4 feet long – later extended to 84 feet – and is 19.6 feet wide. "Isqueen" was an active whaling ship from 1955-1985. According to the boat's log, during this period the catch was 1 475 Minke Whales, 10 Killer Whales (Orca), and 2 Bottlenose Whales. The boat whaled along the coast of Nordland, Troms and Finnmark, in the Norwegian Sea between Norway and Svalbard and off the coast of Svalbard. The boat was sometimes away at sea for many months. The boat was also used for cod and herring fishing.

At the end of the 1980s the engine room caught fire and "Isqueen" was brought up on land and was rebuilt as one of the country's most original restaurants. The boat has a restaurant with seating for approx. 60 persons and a pub/bar. A new tourist centre close to "Isqueen" is being planned - a 900-bed development with 50 brand new shoreline cabins and a hotel with spa.

The ship docks at the quayside in Stokmarknes

Stokmarknes is the community and administration centre in Hadsel municipality, also known as the 'birthplace of the Hurtigruten'.

There are traces of ancient settlements in the area around Stokmarknes, with sites from the Iron Age, also burial sites and boathouse remains. In 1776 the town received official status as a 'privileged trading post'. Stokmarknes was strategically placed for vessels sailing along the outer side of Vesterålen, before the shallow Risøyrenna was dredged and opened for shipping in 1922. An annual market was held here from 1851 until 1935. Stokmarknes was granted a town charter in 2000.

Around 1900, many industrial and commercial innovations occurred in Stokmarknes, within communications, trade and public services. Captain Richard With from Stokmarknes founded the company Vesteraalens Dampskibsselskap AS in 1881 and the first Hurtigruten ship, "Vesteraalen" left the quayside in Trondheim for Hammerfest in 1893. Stokmarknes was the ship's home port. Richard With later became widely known as 'the father of the Hurtigruten' (p 299). The shipping company retained its headquarters at Stokmarknes until 1988.

"Hurtigrutens Hus" the building containing a museum and gallery, was opened in 1999. There are exhibitions of photographs, paintings, boat models, historical films and videos that detail the history of the Hurtigruten and its importance for those living along the coast, through more than 100 years, and the development of the ships from the start of the company, right up to the present day (p 298).

MS "Finnmarken", a Hurtigruten ship that has been brought ashore close by, is the museum's biggest attraction. The ship was built in 1956 and sailed along the Norwegian coast until 1993. It was brought ashore in 1999, and is probably Norway's largest and heaviest museum artefact. MS "Finnmarken" is open to the public. As part of the continuing development of the museum, a larger building, which is to be built around the entire ship, is currently being planned.

At "Hurtigrutens Hus" there is also a hotel, convention centre, culture centre and gallery.

The regional hospital for Vesterålen is located at Stokmarknes.

The ship continues to Svolvær   + 0 hrs 00 min

LARGER MAP P**411**

In front is the village of Kvitnes under the fell Kvitnesheia (384 m above sea level).

We set a course for Raftsundet (26 km long). On our port side up ahead is the southern part of Hinnøya and the mountains **Middagstinden** (667 m above sea level) and **Hennesheia** (405 m above sea level) near to the villages of **Hennes** and **Kaljord.**

68°33'N   15°04'E   + 0 hrs 22 min ①

Hadsel church is on the top of a hill near the community of **Hadsel** to starboard. It is a red-painted octagonal church built of notched timber in 1824, with a pulpit altar. The church was restored in 1935. It contains a triptych and an Olav figure from the early 16th century. The triptych is probably made in Utrecht, Holland and is one of five that are found in Lofoten and Nord-Trøndelag, in the churches at Røst (p 146), Grip (p 347), Leka (p 328), Ørsta and Hadsel. A legend tells of a Spanish/Dutch princess that gave the triptych as a gift, as thanks to God after she survived a stormy voyage over the ocean from the Netherlands to Denmark (it is said she actually suffered from seasickness).

The parish of Hadsel has been in existence since the Middle Ages and at least three churches have stood on the same site since the 14th century. One of these was dedicated to St. Stefanus, the first Christian martyr, and it is thought that the triptych was built for this particular church as Stefanus is one of the persons depicted in the carvings.

Hadsel Cultural Heritage Park is also at Hadsel. It covers an area that includes Hadsel rectory, three cemeteries and an area of agricultural land. Skipsnausthaugen is located here, one of the largest Iron Age barrows in Northern Norway.

It is believed that Hadsel was the regional and political chieftain seat during the Iron Age (p 83) and had a settled population. Skipsnausthaugen probably has some connection with this fact. So far, nine archaeological finds have been made here; one of them is the largest star-shaped sacrificial monument that has been registered in Norway.

The community of **Melbu** (pop. 2 097) is on the southern side of Hadseløya and can be seen from the ship. A large farm was found here during the saga period, as well as an ancient trading post. Melbu began to expand considerably in the 1880s, and up to 1930 the population grew from 70 to over 1 000. Melbu became an industrial centre, with a dairy, spinning, wool and margarine factories and a large fishing industry.

Vesterålen's largest village museum is in Melbu, with one of the country's finest collections of traditional costumes from the 18th century, a culture centre with several preserved buildings, among them the main building, which is from the 1830s with a garden created in the Romantic style. Melbu is also the home of the Norwegian Fishing Industry Museum. Melbu once had Vesterålen's largest trawler fleet, however this is now somewhat reduced. There are also fish processing plants and mechanical workshops.

Each year, in the first half of July, a week-long festival known as Summer Melbu is arranged. This is a significant cultural festival that attracts many participants from Norway and abroad.

From Melbu there is a car ferry service over Hadselfjorden to Fiskebøl on the island of Austvågøya.

The fjord **Hadselfjorden** opens up to starboard towards the Norwegian Sea. It divides Hadseløya and Austvågøya.

The ship sails further towards the famous sound, Raftsundet. On the starboard side up ahead we can see the steep mountains in Austvågøya (p 155), to port are the mountains on Hinnøya (p 271).

68°29'40"N   15°11'37"E   + 0 hrs 38 min ②

The island of **Brottøya**, to starboard, is a beautiful small agricultural island, with farms, pastures for the farm animals and beautiful sandy bays, especially on the southwestern side of the island.

On the port side are several smaller islands.

The fjord **Ingelsfjorden** can be seen on the port side and the steep mountain **Nipa** (678 m above sea level) descends into the fjord at the northern mouth.

The project known as **LOFAST** (Lofoten's mainland connection) is a large road project that connects the existing road network in Lofoten with the rest of the country. A new road has been built along the east side of Ingelsfjorden. The road runs from Fiskebøl, west of Raftsundet, over **Raftsund bridge**, and has a total length of 53 km. The road opened in December 2007 and runs through several unspoilt areas, among them Møysalen National Park. The road is a part of European Highway no. 10.

Seven tunnels, of which the two longest are 6 370 m and 3 337 m in length, also three bridges, including the 711 m long Raftsund bridge are a part of the LOFAST project.

From **Fiskebøl** on the starboard side the ferry crosses to Melbu on Hadseløya.

The small island of **Hanøya** can be seen on the starboard side, just before the approach to Raftsundet. Behind the island, on the north eastern tip of Austvågøya, we can see the idyllic and peaceful bay of **Hanøyvika**.

On the 22nd September 1954, the Hurtigruten ship MS "Nordstjernen" ran aground close to the mouth of Raftsundet. The ship was sailing northwards from Svolvær to Stokmarknes with 163 passengers and a crew of 46 on board. The time had just passed midnight, the radar had been switched off and the ship was navigating by compass and by visual means. The dark shadows from the land that reflected in the water led to an error in navigation by the bridge officer and the ship sailed off course. Just as she passed Hanøy, the ship ran aground and was severely damaged on the starboard side. She began to take in water. The alarm was sounded and the lifeboats were made ready. Two of the lifeboats were launched; however, some of those on board attempted to swim to shore. The passengers and crew were well looked after on Hanøy and were later rescued and taken on board another of the company's ships.

Hanøyvika was formerly a lively, if somewhat isolated trading post with a school, church, store and landing stage. The bay is now used by summer guests and has few permanent inhabitants.

The current Hanøy church was built in 1912 and has seating for 100 persons.

On the port side, on Hinnøya at the entrance to Raftsundet is tiny **Hattvika**. We then pass the small island of **Gunnar-skjåen**.

The ship approaches Raftsundet bridge, which is a part of the LOFAST project that connects the Lofoten islands with the mainland. The bridge, which is a cantilever construction, has a total length of 711 m. The main span is 298 m. When the bridge was opened in 1998, it was the world's second largest span of its type. The longest span is on another bridge which is also constructed in Norway.

On the road along the 26 km long Raftsundet we pass several small, uninhabited hamlets. Just after the bridge,

we can see **Nordnes** on the starboard side, then the bay **Stenbakken** on the port side.

68°26'21"N 15°10'E   + 0 hrs 56 min

To port is **Kongselven**, then the headland of Åsnes.

Nilsvik is on the other side of the sound.

The ship passes to starboard of the small islet **Nordholmen**, in the middle of Raftsundet.

68°25'32"N 15°08'25"E   + 0 hrs 59 min

The partially enclosed **Tengelfjorden** can be seen on the port side. We sail into a narrower part of Raftsundet, which is known as **Trangstrømmen**. **Raftstrand** is on the port side.

68°24'N 15°06'24"E   + 1 hr 08 min

To port is the bay of **Raften** and **Langnesvik** after the headland **Langneset.**

To starboard are **Faldet** and the inlet, **Faldviken.**

In front we can see the island of **Ulvøya**, which lies at the mouth of the famous fjord **Trollfjorden**. Before Ulvøya is the small islet of **Rognholmen**.

68°21'40"N 15°02'55"E   + 2 hrs 01 min ③

On the port side of Ulvøy are **Tennstrand**, **Tennstrandnes** and **Langnes**.

© EILIV LEREN

South of the island of **Ulvøya** is the smaller island **Brakøya**, with the short **Lauksundet** in between the two. We round **Brakøya** before sailing into the famous **Trollfjorden**. (The ship sails into the fjord when there is no longer a danger of avalanches in spring; the all-clear is given by the shipping company.)

The trading post of **Lauksund** was formerly a well-known beauty spot in the middle of Raftsundet, but has now become derelict. The local general store had everything that the fishermen needed, as well as a post and telegraph office and telephone services.

On some voyages the ship enters Trollfjorden through the narrow sound between the northern part of Ulvøya and the mainland.

We are now just outside the mouth of Trollfjorden.

The voyage into **Trollfjorden** is thought to be one of the highlights of the Hurtigruten voyage. The fjord is one of Norway's most popular photographic subjects. Trollfjorden, which is a side arm of Raftsundet, is approx. 2.5 km long and is just 100 m wide at the mouth. The mountains known as Trolltindene rise up to the heights close to

1 000 m above sea level. At the inner part of the fjord is a small hydroelectric power station.

Trollfjorden is known for the so-called 'Battle of Trollfjord' that took place here in 1890. The conflict is a central element in Norwegian fishing history and is described in Johan Bojer's book "The Last Viking". The conflict arose between the traditional fishermen that fished from open rowing boats with oars and sails and the owners of new, larger boats with covered decks and engines. The traditional fishermen felt that it was unfair that a few fishermen had the right to use steam-powered boats and to fish large catches in Lofoten, whilst most of the fishermen still used rowing boats. They also feared that noise of the boats' engines would drive away the fish and that they would eventually leave their breeding grounds, leading to serious consequences for future catches.

The Trollfjord conflict was actually sparked off by one particular event. A large shoal of spring cod had entered Trollfjord. When the fishermen with their traditional rowing boats arrived at the fjord, they found that the way was blocked by the motor-driven boats, and the crew and owners of these boats refused to allow the rowing boats into the fjord. Fights broke out and some of the motor-

driven boats were damaged – the traditional fishermen meant that they should not have been there, as they threatened their very livelihood. The traditional fishermen eventually won the 'battle'.

At the inner part of the fjord, the ship turns 'on a sixpence', with the help of the bow propeller and we set sail out into the fjord again.

Throughout the country, there are many legends associated with various geographical areas that tell the tale of how the landscape was created. The following legend is about how Trollfjorden and Svolværgeita (p 158) came to be:

"Several thousand years ago, Trollfjorden was a lake known as Trollsjøen.

One summer, the herring fishing in Vesterålen was exceptionally good, and Vågakallen (p 155) hastily left in his boat to take part in the fishing. His cows were left to wander about as they wished while he was away. So, the cows ended up grazing near Trollsjøen, as the grass there was green and lush. However, this grazing area was reserved for the cows belonging to the one-eyed Hinnøy troll. One night, when the daughter of the Hinnøy troll had gone out to milk the cows, she saw two unfamiliar cows. She jumped over Raftsundet and began to roar, waving her arms and drove the cows to the west. The same thing happened the next night, and also on a third night – after this she ran home to complain to her father.

The Hinnøy troll was angry and gathered up some giant boulders and tramped off to sort out the problem once and for all. He banged the rocks together with such force that sparks flew and the echo roared like thunder in the mountains. The cows heard the noise from far away and began to run towards the west. The Hinnøy troll threatened them with his clenched fist and swore that if they ever came back he would make mincemeat out of them. A whole week went by before the cows from Vågan eventually turned up again at Trollsjøen.

However, suddenly one night the girl came running home and shouted that the cows from Vågkallen were back again! The troll became so angry that he took his largest axe and made his way to Trollsjøen. He had made up his mind to stop this business once and for all. But when he arrived at Raftsundet, he tripped over a mountain ridge and fell over. In his fall, he drove the axe into the mountain between Raftsundet and Trollsjøen with such force that the axe blade went under the surface of the ocean. When he eventually got up, he pulled the axe free and the level of the water in Trollsjøen fell to the same level as the sea. Trollsjøen had become a small fjord arm which later became known as Trollfjorden. The frightened cows belonging to Vågakallen had disappeared by the time the troll had come to his senses. The only animal he found was a goat that had been killed by the flying stones from the mighty axe blow. In his anger he took the dead goat and threw it as far as he could. It fell down on the mountain to the north of Svolvær and turned to stone, and is now known as Svolværgeita (geit=goat)".

Approx. 68°20'N   14°58'E

We cross the boundary between Hadsel and Vågan municipalities (p 154)

68°19'N   14°58'15"E   + 2 hrs 17 min ④

We head south once again, towards our next port of call, the fishing community of Svolvær. On the starboard side is Digermulen, to port, up ahead is the island of Stormolla.

Digermulen (approx. pop. 330) is known as the 'capital' of Raftsundet, with the fell **Digermulkollen** (384 m above sea level) in the background, which was

Raftsund, Digermulen, Lofoten

the oldest tourist spot in Lofoten. In July 1889, the German Kaiser Wilhelm II came on the first of many visits and he is thought to have founded the basis of Lofoten tourism. Other royalty came to Digermulen, and in the summer of 1900 the first cruise ship arrived, Digermulen began to be quite well known abroad. Tourist traffic to Digermulen was greatly reduced after the Second World War.

Digermulen church stands in a majestic location on a central rise. The local people demanded a church as ear-

ly as 1900; however, the first church was not built until 1951, after a year's construction. The octagonal church is built of concrete and has seating for 250 persons.

Digermulen's archaeological history indicates that there were settlements here 6 000 years ago. There were also settlements here during the Viking period.

Up ahead, on the port side, is the distant mountain chain in Steigen municipality, on the other side of Vestfjorden. In the inner part of Vestfjorden is the town of Narvik. (p 143).

68°17'50"N   14°58'20"E   + 2 hrs 22 min ⑤

We sail into the sound between the large islands of Årsteinen to port and Store Molla to starboard.

Årsteinen (10.5 km², 530 m above sea level) on the starboard side is only separated from Hinnøya by a narrow channel. South of the island are small skerries and islets.

Store Molla or **Stormolla** (34.4 km², 751 m above sea level) lies to port. The ferry quay at **Finnvik** on the island's north east tip provides the connection to the mainland, to Digermulen on Hinnøya.

68°16'40"N   14°57'40"E   + 2 hrs 29 min

The idyllic village of **Ulvåg** is on the port side, south east of the mountain **Grønåsen** (629 m above sea level) and has a population of approx. 20. The village has prospered after the connecting road was opened in 2002.

68°14'18"N   14°55'E   + 2 hrs 38 min

Gullvika is a popular spot for boats, with quiet bays and weekend cabins.

68°13'13"N   14°50'36"E   + 2 hrs 44 min ⑥

At the southern tip of the island is the headland of **Brettesnesnakken**, here we head west-north-west. We pass **Brettesnes** on the starboard side, between the mountains **Løvnakken** and **Stor-Sveinen**.

At the turn of the century a ship sailed the fixed route between Brettesnes-Bergen-Newcastle in England, which was the first route between Norway and England. A school and a power station were built at Brettesnes, and the first herring oil factory in Norway was built here during the 1870s, with English capital. The factory maintained production until 1892, when the herring catches were insufficient for a while. Later, the factory was taken over by various owners, with varying degrees of commercial success. Throughout the decades of the 1900s the factory began to experience problems, and in

1990 it was finally closed own. The factory that had been the very heart and soul of the area was shut, machinery and equipment was sold off and all the employees were made redundant. The large tanks remain as witnesses to the former activity.

Now (2006) there are only approx. 20 permanent residents left at Brettesnes. However the village is far from dead, the houses are kept maintained by their former owners or by their families. Many return here during holidays and in the summer the local 'population' increases to a few hundred. The permanent residents look after the village during the remaining part of the year with a store, post office, and maintenance of buildings, roads and quayside.

In the village of **Våtviken**, after Brettesnes, there are several salmon farms. At one time there was a ferry connection to Svolvær. This was closed in 2001 after the new road was opened and the ferry route from Finnvika on the north of the island to Digermulen on Hinnøya was opened.

68°13'09"N   14°52'50"E   + 3 hrs 08 min

To port is the island **Lille Molla** (**Litlmolla**) (9.7 km²) on our port side. The island is uninhabited.

We set sail for our next port of call, **Svolvær** in Lofoten. Just ahead are the sharp, jagged peaks of the mountains on **Austvågøya** (p 155).

In front is Svolvær airport, Helle, a civil short take-off and landing airport. It was opened in 1972 and has a runway length of 800 m.

The rest of the day's sailing, including Svolvær is described in Day 4 (p 158), on the voyage northwards.

Hurtigrutemuseet (Hurtigruten Museum) and MS "Finnmarken"

The Hurtigruten Museum Association was formed in 1989 with the aim of establishing a Hurtigruten museum at Stokmarknes. The Hurtigruten Museum was eventually opened in 1993, 100 years after the Hurtigruten first sailed in 1893. For the first few years, the museum was located in the old director's villa that belonged to the shipping company 'Vesteraalen Dampskibsselskab' in Stokmarknes. In 1994 the museum took over the former Hurtigruten ship MS "Finnmarken", which had been donated by Ofotens & Vesteraalens Dampskibsselskap, one of the two companies that merged into Hurtigruten Group ASA in 2006 (renamed Hurtigruten ASA in 2007). MS "Finnmarken", was part of the Hurtigruten fleet from 1956 to 1993.

The original intention was to bring MS "Finnmarken" onto land, to become a part of the museum and to build a protective building covering the ship.

In 1999, the Hurtigruten Museum relocated to the newly-built Hurtigrutens Hus that, in addition to the museum, houses a cultural centre, a hotel and a conference centre. The museum leases 600 m² of the building and the collection comprises approx. 3 000 artefacts. Of these, approx. 60 % have been registered. The museum also contains various exhibitions, photographs, ship's drawings, documents, paintings, models of boats and historical films. In addition there is the ship itself, MS "Finnmarken" and a cabin section preserved from the

old Hurtigruten ship DS "Finnmarken" that was built in 1912.

The foundation "Hurtigrutenskipet Gamle Finnmarken" was established in 1994. The foundation was assigned the responsibility for the operation and maintenance of the landed Hurtigruten ship. The Hurtigrutenmuseet foundation was established in 1999 and became responsible for the operation of the museum. In 2005, the two foundations were merged to form the foundation known as 'Stiftelsen Norsk Hurtigrutenmuseum BA'. The foundation's aims were outlined in eight points, with the main aim being to maintain and collect historical artefacts associated with the Hurtigruten enterprises along the Norwegian coast.

MS "Finnmarken" was brought on land in June 1999. The process involved a simple, yet ingenious solution: Two angled cast concrete joists were constructed from the quayside into the sea, approx. 4 m under the surface at high tide. The concrete joists were designed to align with two "sleds" that had been welded to the hull of the ship, fore and aft, during the last dry dock inspection. At high tide the ship was manoeuvred in place and when the tide went out the ship was left resting on the joists. With the help of steel cables and hydraulic winches attached to the sleds, the ship was slowly hauled onto land. It now stands 1.5 m over the normal water level, resting on the sleds that in turn rest on the joists.

MS "Finnmarken" weighs 2.189 gross tons and has a hull 266 ft. in length. There were 205 berths on board – 63 in 1st class, 114 in 2nd class with another 28 convertible cabins. The ship was certified to carry 585 passengers. The main engine was a 10-cylinder MAN engine generating 2 960 HP that could sail at 16.6 knots.

The Maritime Museum in Oslo and the Bergen Maritime Museum have comprehensive exhibitions on the Hurtigruten. A saloon and a cabin section from DS "Finnmarken", built in 1912 are on display at Bergen Maritime Museum.

The history of the Hurtigruten

For several hundred years there had been considerable boat traffic along the coast between Bergen and Northern Norway. The sea was the "main highway" of the time (p 27) and many boats, fully loaded with cargoes of fish and other goods sailed to the Hansa town of Bergen, carrying necessary provisions and luxury goods on their return journeys. In 1838,

the state introduced the first paddle steamer, "Prinds Gustav", which sailed the summer route between Trondheim and Tromsø. A few years later, another ship was introduced, "Prinds Carl", also a paddle steamer. Both ships only sailed during the summer months. In the years that followed, private shipping companies were also granted permits to sail along this route.

In 1891, a call for tenders was issued by The Department of Internal Affairs to establish an express sea route for passengers, goods and post between Trondheim and Hammerfest. However, no tenders were submitted by any of the shipping companies. One year later, the Department issued a new call for tenders, this time with an amended contract. The new contract was for sailings once a week in each direction and the ship was to carry post. Vesteraalens Dampskibsselskap drew up

an agreement with the state authorities, submitted their tender and was granted a licence. The owner of the shipping company, Captain Richard With, signed a four-year contract with the state. The route was to sail to Tromsø during the winter and to Hammerfest in the summer and the ship was to call at nine ports. Two of the larger shipping companies of that time, Det Bergenske Dampskibsselskap in Bergen and Det Nordenfjeldske Dampskibsselskab in Trondheim had been asked to sail the route, however they declined due to the necessity of sailing through the dark winter months and storms, something they considered impossible to do. At that time there were only two nautical charts and 28 lighthouses along the coast north of Trondheim.

On the 2nd July 1893, the ship DS "Vesteraalen" sailed on her first journey from

Trondheim on what was now called the Hurtigruten, and reached Hammerfest 67 hours later. Post that had taken as long as a month to reach Tromsø in the summer and five months in the winter, now took only a week to arrive. Today, the ship takes 41 hours and 15 minutes to cover the distance.

The fact that this could be achieved was largely due to the efforts of the pilot mariner Anders Holte. For several years he had kept systematic records and drawings in his private log with meticulous details of the ship's route along the coast. By using a compass and with exact notation of hours

and minutes, he knew the position of the ship in the sailing channel at any time and when and where to make adjustments to the ship's course. The system was developed during daytime sailings but could also be used to sail at night and even in fog. In 1888, the shipping owner With, pilot Holte and their families and several of the crew had relocated to Bergen and started a private enterprise sailing along the coast – mostly carrying goods; however there was also room for a few passengers. The pilot's knowledge and notes were the basis for Captain Richard With's later journeys between Trondheim and Hammerfest, as all navigational data, sailing distances and times had been noted in detail. Tables of headings had been carefully recorded to make it possible, under most conditions, to sail using just a watch and compass. After the first winter it became clear that the newly acquired ship "Vesteraalen" (1891)

was just as punctual during the winter as it was in summer. The shipping company had carried out detailed planning before sailings began. The timetable and the route had been reviewed in detail by Captain Richard With and pilot Anders Holte.

The following year a joint licence was granted to the above named shipping companies in Bergen and Trondheim and in the summer of 1894, a second ship began sailing along the route. A third ship was introduced in 1898 – the first of the fleet to sail from Bergen. When the contract came up for renewal in 1898, all three of the steamship companies made a joint application. Between 1898 and 1907 a separate route between Tromsø – Hammerfest - Vadsø was established, known as the 'Finnmarksruten' and from 1907 a continuous route from Bergen to Vadsø sailed twice weekly. From 1914, the route sailed five times a week between Bergen and Kirkenes. From 1926 this increased to six times a week and finally in 1936 daily sailings each way were introduced. Of these, five journeys started in Bergen, one in Stavanger and one in Trondheim. It was not before 1953 that all the sailings began in Bergen. The route, which soon came to be known as the Hurtigruten, was originally intended to be a postal ship with a

few passengers. However, due to the large quantities of fish that were transported along the coast it soon acquired status as a goods route.

The first ships in the Hurtigruten fleet had three passenger classes, an open bridge and were steam-driven. The standard of comfort on board, both for the passengers and the crew, gradually improved through the years – however the first diesel powered ships were not introduced until after the Second World War.

All Hurtigruten sailings were cancelled after the outbreak of the Second World War in Norway in 1940. The sailings started up again a few months later. Several tragic shipwrecks occurred during the war years. The first was in October 1940, just off the coast of Bodø, when DS "Prinsesse Ragnhild" probably hit a British-laid underwater mine and 230-280 persons were killed. The majority (150-200) were German soldiers. Other major shipwrecks included DS "Barøy" carrying 107 passengers, that was sunk in Vestfjorden by a British air-launched torpedo in September 1941 and DS "Richard With" that was torpedoed by a British submarine just off the coast of Havøysund, also in September 1941 (p 197). Despite the fact that the Hurtigruten sailed throughout the war, after this last tragedy the ships no longer sailed north of Tromsø and an alternative route began sailing between Tromsø and Hammerfest. Several of these ships were attacked and sunk by the Allies, either due to misunderstandings or because they were believed to be carrying German troops. The standing order was that all civil transport ships sailing alone were not to be attacked; however, this order was not always followed.

In the post-war years the Hurtigruten received competition from a steadily improving road and air network. Passenger and

goods transport along the coast declined and the boats became old and outdated. The first new ships were built in Italy at the end of the 1940s and were financed by 'klippfisk' ('bacalao') exports – they were therefore known as the "Italian ships" or the "Klippfisk ships". The modernisation of the fleet continued until 1964.

Later, it was considered whether the Hurtigruten should concentrate exclusively on goods transport, or whether it should be abandoned altogether. After a resolution was passed by the Norwegian Storting, three new ships were built in 1982. The Hurtigruten was to mainly concentrate on goods and freight. The new ships were rebuilt with a new forward section and a large open deck with a large crane astern. When the potential of the Hurtigruten in regard to passenger transport became clear, the cranes were removed and the holds were rebuilt. A new, large passenger section was built astern with a saloon with a panoramic view on the top level.

New types of ships, on which passenger comfort was given priority over freight volume were built during 1994-2002; these were aimed at comfortable passenger transport and especially tourism. A central loading ramp and reasonably large freight holds made for an effective combination of passenger and goods services. Some of the ships were rebuilt in 2005 with fewer, larger cabins.

Several of the major coastal shipping companies have at some time been operators of the Hurtigruten; most of these were eventually discontinued. In 2006, OVDS (Ofoten & Vesteraalens Dampskibsselskab) and TFDS (Troms Fylkes Dampskibsselskab) merged into Hurtigruten Group ASA with the corporate head office located in Narvik. The company name was changed to Hurtigruten ASA in May 2007.

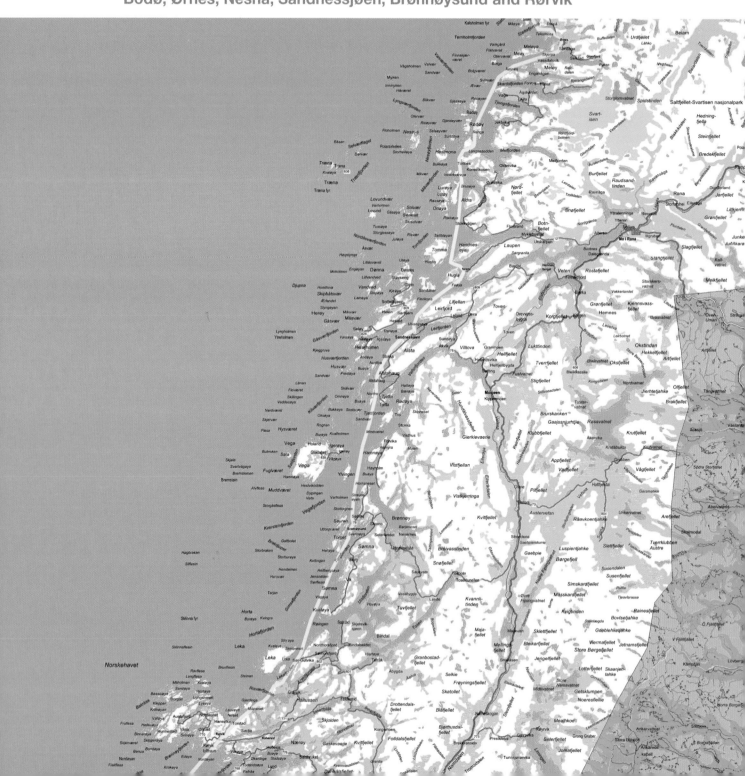

During the night we have passed **Bodø** municipality (p 137) with the port of Bodø (67°17'N 14°21'30"E, 0130-0400) (p 139), Gildeskål municipality (p 132) and Meløy municipality (p 125) with the port of **Ørnes** (66°52'06"N 13°42'E, 0650-0715) (p 130). We are now in the county of Nordland, (p 160).

We are now in the county of **Nordland** (p 160).

The ship continues on to Nesna	+ 0 hrs 00 min

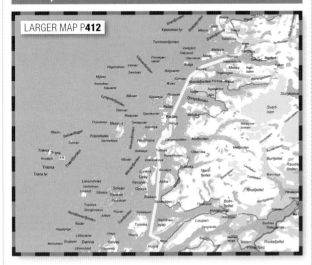

LARGER MAP P**412**

The ship leaves behind the old trading post of **Ørnes** (p 130). On the starboard side is the island of **Messøya**. On the port side, up ahead, just after departure we can see the glacier **Glombreen** (p 130). We sail through the sound **Eidet** and then out into the fjord **Meløyfjorden** (p 126).

© ROLF LILAND

66°50'N 13°40'E	+ 0 hrs 10 min ❶

Behind the long, narrow headland **Glomneset,** on the port side we pass the mouth of **Glomfjorden** and the industrial site, **Glomfjord** (p 129). Ahead on the port side is the village of **Vassdalsvik** (p 129) with a ferry connection to the island **Bolga** up ahead, the ferry quay **Meløysund** on **Meløya** and **Ørnes,** further on is the village of **Valla**

(p 128). On the starboard side, after **Messøya**, the small island of **Skjerpa** (275 m above sea level) comes into view, followed by **Meløya** (21.8 km², 582 m above sea level) with the ferry quay Meløysund to starboard. In the distance, we can see the island of Bolga with its characteristic shape.

66°48'30"N 13°27'E	+ 0 hrs 29 min

Up ahead on our port side is the village of **Jektvika** (p 127) on the island of **Grønnøya** with its forest of coastal pine trees. In the summer season, on the northward journey, the ship stops just outside Jektvika to transfer passengers that are taking the trip to the Svartisen glacier, onto a local tourist boat. There are several local legends about Svartisen (p 128).

To starboard is the mountain **Meløytinden** (582 m above sea level), then **Meløy** and Meløy church (just visible behind the trees). The island, the location and the church have an interesting history (p 126).

After Grønnøya on the port side, we see the larger island of **Åmnøya**, which has ancient rock carvings (p 126).

On the starboard side, just up ahead is the island of Bolga.

66°47'40"N 13°22'42"E	+ 0 hrs 40 min ❷

On the port side is the village of **Åmnes** and the jagged peaks of **Skardstinden** (648 m above sea level) and **Snødalstinden** (640 m above sea level) (p 126).

Up ahead on the starboard side is the island of **Bolga** (2.4 km²) (p 126). The mountain **Bolgtinden/ Bolgbørra** (338 m above sea level), in common with the more famous mountain **Torghatten** further south

© TONE-LISE LYNGENG

on the Helgeland coast, has a hole running straight through the mountain. The stone block, Ruggesteinen is also one of the attractions on the island. The block, despite weighing 60 tons, is so finely balanced that it can easily be moved 10 cm with one hand.

The fishing village of **Bolga** (pop. 141) can be seen when looking out towards the channel, it is the outermost island with permanent inhabitants in Meløy municipality. At Bolga, there is a slipway, mechanical workshops and one of the region's largest fish farms. Bolga has hosted many festivals and is a popular spot for aerial sports such as hang gliding and paragliding. There is a ferry connection to the mainland.

The small islands and skerries southwest of Bolga are part of the group of islands known as **Bolgværet**. It is said that there are 365 islands here, one for every day of the year.

66°45'45"N 13°13'32"E   + 0 hrs 54 min

We pass by the village of **Åmnøyhamna** on the port side, then **Skardsfjorden** (p 125). It is possible to see the glacier **Svartisen** from here. We are now in the fjord Rødøyfjorden.

Approx. 66°44'N 13°12'E

We cross the boundary between Meløy and Rødøy municipalities

Rødøy municipality

Municipal coat of arms, significance: The motif and colour represents the mountain Rødøyløva.
Meaning of name: First part raud 'red', often indicating red stone.
Municipal seat: Gjerøy (pop. -).
Position: 66°40'N 13°03'E. **Area:** 712 km².
Population: 1 343. **Pop. density:** 1.9 /km².
Area distribution: Farming 1 %, forestry 11 %, fresh water 3 %, other area 84 %.
Trade and industry: Fishing is the most important industry, mostly with smaller vessels. Small fishing hamlets. Modern freezer plants. Shrimp factory. Fish farming. Salmon processing plant. Agriculture with cattle farming, also sheep and chickens. Boat slip-way. Mechanical workshops. Foodstuffs industry.
Places to return to: Myken. Svinvær. Selsøy.
Rødøy municipality's home page: www.rodoy.kommune.no

The group of islands, Svinvær (p 126), on the starboard side is a group of islets and skerries, the largest of which is **Svinvær** (73 m above sea level). Svinvær is one of the oldest trading posts along the Helgeland coast. Archaeological finds indicate settlements from the Stone Age (p 83). From 1620, the same family – for many generations – ran various trades, including selling spirits. The regional courthouse was also located on Svinvær. The trading post was sold at auction in 1850, after it no longer could compete with other neighbouring (but slightly better located) traders. The buildings have been owned by the same family since 1879. The old building burned down in 1958, but was rebuilt.

Svinvær has about 60 neighbouring islands and skerries. Many of these are ideally suited to agriculture with rich soils and many successful farms have operated here. Seabirds have nested on the islands and given the owners a useful extra income from the collection of eggs and down (p 333).

MS "Skramstad" was built in Hamburg in 1925, and had a weight of 4 300 gross tons. "Skramstad" was under German command and was sailing from Trondheim to Narvik with 850 German soldiers on board when she was attacked by Allied aircraft near Rødøya in October 1943. The ship caught fire; however, the crew managed to run the ship aground close to Svinvær where the ship then burned out completely. An unknown number of soldiers were killed. However, most of those on board managed to get ashore.

© BJØRN SKAUGE

Out towards the Norwegian Sea, approx. 32 km from the mainland, is the fishing hamlet of **Myken** (66°30'N 12°28'E), on one of the outermost islands of the hundreds in Rødøy municipality. In 2003, there were just 20 permanent inhabitants on the island, which is the largest of the many islands and skerries in the group. Fishing was formerly the main commercial activity, especially fishing for spring cod and herring. In the autumn of 1915, there were as many as 1 500 fishermen active on the herring catches around Myken. Myken, which is the only remaining fishing community in the region, is now used as a base and as a landing stage for fishing vessels. The catches are then sent on to Jektvik on the mainland. In the summer months, a number of training courses and conferences are held in the old, well-preserved buildings on the island. There is a fast boat providing a connection to the mainland.

Myken lighthouse lies on a small island in the sea just off Myken. The lighthouse is a channel beacon constructed from timber with a low tower, built in 1918. The height above the ocean is 40.3 m and the range 16.8 nautical miles. It was automated in 1975. The lighthouse was granted status as a cultural landmark in 2000.

66°43'30"N 13°11'24"E   + 1 hr 04 min ❸

On the port side, we pass the headland of **Sleipnesodden,** the outer point of the peninsula between the fjords

© ROLF LILAND

Skardsfjorden on the port side aft, that continues into **Holandsfjorden** in to the glacier Svartisen. **Tjongsfjorden** (17 km in length) is up ahead, with the community of **Vågaholmen**. The highest peaks are **Rismålstinden** (699 m above sea level) and **Kjølen** (841 m above sea level). In the distance, on the port side, we can see the glacier Svartisen.

DS "Narvik" (241 gross tons) was sunk just outside of Sleipnesodden in March 1944. The ship, which was originally built as a fishing vessel in Aberdeen, Scotland, had been rebuilt and extended several times and sailed during the war as a combined merchant and passenger ship between Narvik and Trondheim. "Narvik" was torpedoed by the British submarine "Syrtis", and sank rapidly. 16 men were killed in the attack, 9 survived and were rescued.

The fabled island of **Rødøya** (8.2 km²) with the mountain **Rødøyløva** lies on the starboard side up ahead. With its peak 443 m above sea level in the centre of the island, Rødøyløva has long been a landmark in the channel. Seen from the south, the island has the appearance of a lion lying down, or possibly an Egyptian sphinx. Part of the lion is a red-coloured stone known as serpentine. This has led to the name Rødøyløva ('red island lion'). The lion is represented in the municipal coat of arms of Rødøy.

For some time is has been said that if Tromsø is the "Paris of the North", Rødøya must be Hawaii! The island is one of the islands named in the saga "The Seven Sisters" (p 315).

66°40'N   13°07'32"E   + 1 hr 18 min ④

On the port side is **Værnes**, outermost on the peninsula between the fjords Tjongsfjorden and **Værangen,** with **Jektvika** outermost in Værangenfjorden. On the peninsula are the mountains of **Værnestinden** (688 m above sea level) and **Værangstiden** (665 m above sea level).

Rødøy church and rectory are on the southern tip of Rødøya, on the starboard side. Rødøy is one of the area's oldest parishes, with a history dating back to the early Middle Ages (p 83). The current church is from 1885, and is a combination of a cruciform and octagonal construction.

After Rødøya is the small island of **Flatøya**. After this, we can see **Gjerdøya** (9.3 km², 168 m above sea level) on the starboard side up ahead, which has a population of approx. 130. **Gjerdøya** is the largest island in the municipality.

To port, up ahead, vis-à-vis Gjerdøya is the island **Renga** (190 m above sea level) with its characteristic ridge crossing the island diagonally. The Hurtigruten passes by the island.

66°35'28"N   13°04'E   + 1 hr 39 min

Ahead and to starboard is **Rangsundøya** with the mountain **Rangsundtuva** (267 m above sea level).

West of Rangsundøya is the smaller island of **Selsøya**, which cannot be seen from the ship, with Selsøyvik trading post dating from the 18th century. The trading post is the oldest of its kind in Norway that is still in normal business. The most important commercial activity on the island is salmon farming. The island is connected by a bridge to Rangsundøya.

66°35'15"N   13°04'33"E   + 1 hr 40 min ⑤

On the port side, after the headland of **Telnes** and the mountain **Telnestinden** we can see the mouth of the fjord **Melfjorden**. Melfjorden is further divided into **Nordfjorden** with very steep mountainsides, and **Melfjordbotnen**. Melfjorden and Nordfjorden are known as Northern Norway's answer to the famous Geiranger fjord. **Sørfjorden** (30 km long) runs in a southeasterly direction behind the headland **Langnesodden**.

66°33'17"N   13°02'37"E   + 1 hr 49 min ⑥

The ship changes course and we now sail along the foot of **Tonnesfjellet** (471 m above sea level) on the port side.

The island **Hestmona** (or **Hestmannøya**) lies ahead to starboard. In the north and east, the island is flat and marshy. The Arctic Circle, at 66°33'N (p 161), crosses the northern part of the island. The municipal boundary between Rødøy and Lurøy municipalities also runs across the island. The island has been inhabited since the latter part of the Stone Age. The main commercial activity is agriculture. There is a ferry connection to the neighbouring islands and to the mainland.

Many legends are associated with the mountains along the Helgeland coast, including Hestmona/Hestmannøy (see the legend of the Seven Sisters, p 315). On the island is the mountain **Ambotá** ('servant woman') (571 m above sea level). According to local people, Ambotá looks northwards and her long hair flows to the south. "Hestmannen" pulls Ambotá by her hair and it is popularly said that "he never really has been too kind to her".

66°32'N   12°58'42"E   + 1 hr 57 min

The islet known as **Vikingen** passes on the starboard side. On Vikingen, there is a globe that marks the latitude of the Arctic Circle. The previous globe blew down during hurricane Narve in January 2006. In the middle of December the same year, a new globe was ready to be erected on the islet. The 7-metre high globe with a base is lit and is visible from the Hurtigruten when crossing the Arctic Circle.

When crossing the Arctic Circle, we also pass through the point dividing the regions with and without the Midnight Sun.

66°31'32"N   12°58'E   + 1 hr 57 min

Hestmona passes on the starboard side with the mountain **Skagfjellet** (246 m above sea level) on our port side. The village of **Tonnes** is south of Skagfjellet, with the famous grotto **Tonneshulen**. We are now in the fjord known as **Måsværfjorden**.

It is difficult to become orientated within the group of islands that we now sail through due to the many islets, skerries and headlands that pass by.

Out in the ocean, west of Hestmona is the island municipality of Træna.

Træna municipality

Municipal coat of arms, significance: Symbolizes fishing.
Meaning of name: From the Norse thrion, probably connected to the number 'three', possibly after three of the peaks on the largest island.
Municipal seat: Husøy (Pop. 360).
Position: 66°30'N 12°06'E. **Area:** 16 km².
Population: 446. **Population density:** 27.9 /km².
Area distribution: Farming 1 %, forestry 0 %, fresh water 0 %, other area 98 %.
Trade and industry: Dominated by fishing, mostly with smaller vessels. The group of islands is surrounded by rich fishing grounds. Fishing industry and fish processing. Boatyards with mechanical workshops. Some agriculture and sheep farming. Electric power is supplied via an undersea cable from the mainland. Fast boat connection between Træna, outlying islands and the mainland.
Places to return to: Sanna and Kirkhelleren.
Træna municipality's home page: www.trana.kommune.no

The municipality of Træna is regarded as possibly the most distinctive of all island communities along the Norwegian coast. The Arctic Circle runs through the municipality. The largest island, **Sanna** (3 km²), has steep mountains, the highest of which is **Trænstaven** (336 m above sea level) and is a well-known landmark for sailors. The archaeological finds known as the 'Træna finds', with caves, houses and burial mounds indicate ancient settlements that span from the late Stone Age to the late Middle Ages (p 83). On the cave floor at Kirkhelleren on Sanna, a 3.5 m deep layer of cultural history was discovered. The cave is 45 m deep, 20 m wide and 30 m high and was used by the hunter-gatherer peoples during the Stone Age. The house remains found on Sanna are some of the oldest that have been discovered in Norway.

Træna lighthouse is on one of the islets in the municipality. It was constructed in 1877 and is a stone building with an iron tower. The lighthouse is 37.7 m high and has a range of 17.0 nautical miles. The lighthouse was automated in 1974.

Approx. 66°30'40"N   12°58'E

We pass the municipal boundary between Rødøy and Lurøy

Lurøy municipality

Municipal coat of arms, significance: Illustrates the coast and the importance of fishing in the municipality.
Meaning of name: From Norse Ludrøy, from ludr, 'stave'; from the pointed Lurøy-fjellet on Lurøya.
Municipal seat: Lurøy (pop. 336).
Position: 66°25'N 12°51'E. **Area:** 262 km².
Population: 1 970. **Pop. density:** 7.5 /km².
Area distribution: Farming 3 %, forestry 9 %, fresh water 3 %, other area 85 %.
Trade and industry: Agriculture and fishing. Fishing is important in the island communities, mostly smaller vessels. Local and Lofoten fishing. Fish farms. Limited processing. Large agricultural areas in the inner areas of the municipality. Milk and beef production. Half of the farms are located on the islands. Mechanical industry (maritime). Some timber production. Boat connection between the islands and the mainland.
Places to return to: Grønsvik fort. Lurøy rectory.
Lurøy municipality's home page:
www.luroy.kommune.no

In **Lurøy** municipality there are 1 372 islands.

66°30'N 13°00'E   + 2 hrs 05 min

We are now in the fjord known as **Kvarøyfjorden.** Ahead and to starboard is the small, flat island of **Innerkvarøya,** with the hillier **Ytterkvarøya** to the west. A burial mound was discovered here and was later excavated, revealing a rich find of weapons, jewellery and artefacts dating from A.D. 600-800.

On the port side are several small islets, just outside the village of **Konsvikosen,** thereafter the bay **Kvina,** and the headland **Valen,** north west of the mountain **Okstinden**.

66°28'N   12°58'E   + 2 hrs 14 min ⑦

We sail into **Stigfjorden** with the relatively flat island **Stigen** (13.5 km²) and the mountain **Stigen** (380 m above sea level) to starboard.

Behind Stigen lies the island **Lurøya** with **Lurøyfjellet** (685 m above sea level). On the west side of **Lurøya** is Lurøy church, a fine wooden cruciform church from 1812, which was chosen as the municipality's finest cultural heritage site in 1997. There has been a church on this site since the 14ᵗʰ century. The listed and preserved Lurøy rectory is from 1827. Lurøy farm is also from 1827. Lurøy farm is

© LURØY FOLKEBIBLIOTEK

near the church and has one of Northern Norway's best-preserved Renaissance gardens.

The island of **Aldra** (24 km²) can be seen on the port side, with the mountains **Aldertinden** (737 m above sea level) and **Hjarttinden** (967 m above sea level). On the island's northern tip is the village of **Stuvland**, and on the southern tip is **Hjart.**

The sound, **Aldersundet** runs between the back side of Aldra and the mainland. The mainland mountains behind Aldersundet, seen from the north are: **Okstinden** (791 m above sea level), **Rundtinden** (947 m above sea level) and **Strandtindan** (1 173 m above sea level).

The southern tip of Aldra passes by on the port side (at the southern mouth of Aldrafjorden), then the mountains of **Nonstinden** (995 m above sea level) and **Stordalstinden**.

The island of **Onøya** (7.7 km²) lies to starboard, just south of Stigen. South of **Onøya** are two small islets, **Sjonøya** and **Rokkøya.**

66°21'N 12°57'35"E	+ 2 hrs 42 min ⑧

Grønsvik coastal fortifications on the mainland (on our port side) were built by the German forces during 1942-45 as a part of the German construction the 'Atlantic Ocean Wall' and were operative from the autumn of 1942. They were built to control the traffic along the shipping channel, especially into the industrial area of Mo i Rana. At the most, over 200 German troops and approx. 100 prisoners of war were stationed on the headland. The coastal fortifications were destroyed after the war, the guns were dismantled and sent to be smelted and parts of the bunker system were demolished.

The coastal fortifications have been partly restored and have now been opened as a museum with exhibitions on the war in general with comprehensive information about the history of the fortifications. The museum also has an exhibition on Omega, a worldwide navigation system for American submarines that was operational from 1966 until 1997. The only Norwegian station for the navigation system was in Aldersundet.

On the port side, at the foot of Nonstinden/Stordalstinden (955 m above sea level) lies the village of **Selnes.**

66°19'N 12°56'E	+ 2 hrs 51 min ⑨

Up ahead and to starboard is the island Tomma, east of the island Dønna.

In the **Norwegian Sea** to starboard lies the group of islands Solvær and the island Lovund.

The **Solvær** islands are a group of many small and flat islands. Some of them are inhabited, with small fishing hamlets. The bedrock here is largely comprised of marble.

The island of **Lovund** (4.9 km²) with **Lovundfjellet** (623 m above sea level) lies west of the Solvær islands. The largest attraction on the island is the bird cliff **Lundeura** on the south side of Lovundfjellet, where it is said that on the same date each year, the 14th April, approx. 70 000 puffins arrive at the same time to nest here. The puffins leave the island sometime in August (p 218). Salmon farming takes place at Lovund. North of the islands is the group of islands known as **Lovundvær.**

© LURØY FOLKEBIBLIOTEK

66°19'N 12°57'E	+ 2 hrs 51 min

The fjord **Sjona** (26 km in length) opens to port, the mountain **Pollatindan** (1 019 m above sea level) is on the north side of the fjord. Handnesøya with Stokkatinden (599 m above sea level) is on the south side, and **Botnfjellet** (737 m above sea level) is at the innermost part of the fjord.

We cross the boundary between Lurøy and Nesna municipalities

Nesna municipality

Municipal coat of arms, significance: Stylistic depiction of a headland.
Meaning of name: From Norse Nesnar, from nes, 'headland'.
Municipal seat: Nesna. (pop. 1 229).
Position: 66°12'N 13°00'E. **Area:** 183 km².
Population: 1 776. **Pop. density:** 9.7 /km².
Area distribution: Farming 8 %, forestry 23 %, fresh water 1 %, other area 68 %.
Trade and industry: Agriculture with milk production. Sheep farming. Fishing was formerly an important industry but is now somewhat reduced, mostly local self-supply. Fish farming. Boatbuilding. Fabrication industry. Foodstuffs industry. Developing tourism.
Places to return to: Husby mansion. Nesna Village Museum. Nesna church.
Nesna municipality's home page: www.nesna.kommune.no

© ROLF LILAND

66°18'N   12°55'43"E   + 2 hrs 55 min

The northern tip of **Tomma** (47.3 km²) passes on the starboard side. The mountain **Tomskjevelen** (922 m above sea level) towers above us. The island is the largest in Nesna municipality. On the west side are several caves and burial mounds. The majority of the inhabitants of the island live in the village of **Husby** on the east/west tip. Husby farm, an old mansion house, is also found here.

On the port side is the island **Handnesøya** (34.4 km²) and the mountain **Stokkatinden** (599 m above sea level) in the centre of the island. Most of the houses are located along the narrow shoreline in the southeast and west.

We pass through the sound between the islands of Tomma and Handnesøya. In the centre of Tomma, on the starboard side is the village of **Forsland**. Northwest on Handnesøya (on the port side) is the village of **Handstein**.

On the southern tip of Handnesøya, close to the village of **Handnes**, we head towards our next port of call, the community of Nesna. Handnesgården in Handnes has origins going back to the Stone Age. The farm was a chieftain seat during the Iron Age and in Viking times (p 83, p 123). It has also been a major trade point and the seat of the local judiciary in the recent past.

On the starboard side, we pass the mountainous island of **Hugla** (17.8 km²), with **Hugltinden** (624 m above sea level) as the highest peak. The inhabitants of Hugla live mostly on the southeast side of the island, towards Nesna. We pass an industrial area, with large tanks. This is a plant for treating waste products from the salmon farming industry. The final products, oil from the process, are stored in the tanks.

The ship docks at the quayside in Nesna

The ship docks at the quayside for a short stop at the community and municipal seat of **Nesna**. Nesna is an old college community and has been a seat of learning for almost two hundred years. Klokkargarden is probably Norway's oldest schoolhouse and Nesna College of Further Education is Northern Norway's second oldest higher educational institution. It has approx. 1 200 stu-

dents and approx. 130 staff members. From 1918 and up to 1994 the school was known as Nesna Teacher Training College. The College has played a large part in the development of the community.

Nesna church is a wooden cruciform church from 1879. The priest and poet Petter Dass (p 318) was the curate at a former church at Nesna from 1672 until 1689.

Nesna now has a modern marina and a large fabrication company that supplies custom made products manufactured from steel, stainless steel and aluminium to customers in Norway and abroad.

The ship continues to Sandnessjøen   + 0 hrs 00 min

LARGER MAP P**412**

We head out into the fjord, with the island **Hugla** to starboard up ahead. The ship passes between Hugla and the small island of **Feøya**. To port we can see Leirfjord with the long mountain chain of **Lifjellan**.

On our starboard side, we pass the villages of **Vik** and **Ytterhus** on the island of Hugla.

Approx. 66°08'N   12°51'E

We cross the boundary between Nesna and Leirfjord municipalities

Leirfjord municipality

Municipal coat of arms, significance: Symbolises agricultural activity.
Meaning of name: Norse fjord Lein, from the river Leira.
Municipal seat: Leland (pop. 598).
Position: 66°04'N 12°56'E. **Area:** 444 km².
Population: 2 123. **Pop. density:** 4.8 /km².
Area distribution: Farming 5 %, forestry 14 %, fresh water 2 %, other area 79 %.
Trade and industry: Leirfjord is an agricultural municipality. Cattle and dairy production. Some forest, however limited timber production. Fishing is of little importance, some seasonal fishing. Fish farms. Fish processing plants. Industry connected with fishing and processing. Mechanical workshops. Boatyard with production of wooden boats.
Leirfjord municipality's home page: www.leirfjord.kommune.no

Leirfjord municipality is a mainland municipality, as distinct from the island municipalities we have just passed on the starboard side.

We sail into the outermost part of the fjord **Ransfjorden** (68 km in length) that cuts into the land in a north-easterly direction. The outer part of the fjord has steep mountainsides, further in it becomes wider and lusher. The community of **Hemnesberget** (pop. 1 227) lies approx. in the centre of the fjord and in the inner part of the fjord is the industrial town of **Mo i Rana** (pop. 17 830).

On the port side, we can see the characteristic Lovund-fjellet on the island of Lovund (p 308).

Approx. 66°08'N   12°51'E

On the port side is Dønna municipality

Dønna municipality

Municipal coat of arms, significance: Waves striking the beach, breakers.
Meaning of name: Norse dynja, 'thunder, shake, rumbling'.
Municipal seat: Solfjellsjøen (pop. -).
  Position: 66°07'N 12°28'56"E. **Area:** 193 km².
Population: 1 489. **Pop. density:** 7.7 /km².
Area distribution: Farming 9 %, forestry 5 %, fresh water 3 %, other area 83 %.
Trade and industry: Limited industry. Fish farming (salmon, cod and halibut). Salmon processing. Fish processing industry for fresh, frozen fish, also traditional 'lutefisk'. Timber production.
Places to return to: Dønnes mansion. Dønnes church. Gleinsneset.
Activities to return to: Bjørnsmartnan.
Dønna municipality's home page: www.donna.kommune.no

66°08'40"N   12°51'40"E   + 0 hrs 20 min ⑩

The island of **Løkta** (17.4 km²) passes on the starboard side. **Sandåkerfjellet** (238 m above sea level) is the highest peak on the island.

At **Hov**, on the north part of Løkta, the remains of buildings were uncovered in 1981. These were a ring-shaped collection of dwelling foundations, dated to the Merovingian/Viking period (p 83). The site is strategically placed at the mouth of Ranfjorden, in the middle of the channel. In common with most of these types of sites, it was also located close to the best arable land. The site is thought to have been part of a larger chieftain seat. One theory is that it may have been the centre of a chieftain territory. Relatively elaborate and finely decorated burial mounds have been found in the area. Some of them are 'boat graves', i.e. the deceased and his personal possessions were placed in a boat on land before the boat was buried. Three larger, unopened graves are in mounds that are 26-28 m in diameter and up to 3 m in height. There are also remains of a 40 m long burial mound. In 1963, five 20-30 m long boathouses were registered in the area, these may at one time have housed longships.

The name 'Hov' means 'pagan temple'. It is likely that the site has been used as a religious place in pre-Christian times, especially in the early Stone Age. The phallus at Glein on Dønna island, on the other side of the sound **Skipsfjorden** between the two islands may also indicate this, as does Dønnes church just north of Glein.

We are now in the fjord **Ulvangen**. On the starboard side is the mountain **Sandåker**. In the village of Kopardal on the south west tip of **Løkta** there is a liquor cellar dating from approx. 1790, one of the very few remaining in the region.

66°07'N   21°46'E   + 0 hrs 30 min ⑪

The islet of **Finnkona** passes by on the starboard side. On the port side are the villages of **Fagervika** and **Naustholmen** under the mountain range of **Lifjellan**.

Dønna (137 km²) on our starboard side is the largest island in Dønna municipality. It is relatively flat and marshy, except in the south. The island is a popular hunting area for deer, small game and for fishing. The island has a rich and proud history. Historical sources say that Dønna has been a seat of power and influence since the migration period and right up to the 1900s. There is much evidence contained in cultural history and heritage to support this theory.

At **Dønnes,** on the north east part of the island is Dønnes farm, or Dønnes mansion house. The mansion house was at one time Northern Norway's largest land property and included most of the property from Salten in the north to Namdalen in the south – in total more than 500 farms, not including outlying fields totalling several million decares. All of the farms were later sold.

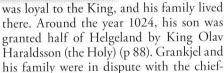

The farm was first mentioned in the early 11th century, when the chieftain Grankjel who was loyal to the King, and his family lived there. Around the year 1024, his son was granted half of Helgeland by King Olav Haraldsson (the Holy) (p 88). Grankjel and his family were in dispute with the chieftain Hårek at Tjøtta, further south in Helgeland (p 319). The conflict ended in the death of Grankjel and many of his men, burned to death by Hårek. When Hårek, many years later visited the reigning King in Trondheim, Granskjel's son was also present. He avenged his father by cleaving Hårek's skull with an axe. In the years following the incident there were many bitter feuds between the two clans.

Dønnes was mentioned once again around the year 1200 when the extremely wealthy Pål Vågeskalm, the governor of Alstahaug was resident there. He probably built Dønnes church as a private chapel close to the farm. It was originally built from stone with cornerstones made of soapstone. His descendants were also rich and powerful and owned the Dønnes mansion house until 1273, when the owner died whilst on a pilgrimage to the Holy Land. The new owner was part of the Bjarkøy clan from north of Harstad (p 166). The Bjarkøy farm was included in an inheritance from the later owners of Dønnes, along with the Giske farm just outside of Ålesund (p 73). The property, rank and status of three of Norway's most powerful families were thus gathered at the Dønnes mansion house, the home of Erling Vidkunnson Dønnes. When the royal line died out in Norway in 1323, he was chosen to be Norway's national leader and became, in practice, Norway's prime minister. He held this position until his death in 1355. Powerful and wealthy family members continued as owners. In 1490, the Dønnes mansion house was taken over by a female descendant and on her death in 1526, the mansion house and part of the Bjarkøy farm were taken over by another relative, Erik Ottesen Rosenkrantz. Rosenkrantz was a governor at Bergenhus and the founder of the Rosenkrantztower. The ownership continued down the family line, to the Danish nobleman Frantz Rantzau. The mansion was owned by the Rantzau family until 1651 when it was sold once more. In 1679, P.C. Tønder bought the farm and made it the seat of his family. Around the 1720s, the farm burned down twice but was rebuilt. In 1751, through marriage, the Coldevin family became connected with the farm. The main building was then completed, with four buildings all connected as a square. In 1796, the private church was sold to the missionary collegium. In 1892, the old main building burned down and much of the valuable inventory was destroyed.

The Dønnes farm continued to be owned by the same family. From 1803, new owners took over. They were diligent and visionary farmers who introduced new ideas and thoughts on scientific agriculture, livestock farming, corn harvesting and mechanized production methods. The owner was the first in Norway to acquire a tractor, in 1908. However, his complex reorganisation of the management of the land and farm led him into economic difficulties and in 1916, the farm was sold outside of the family. The new owner's family remains at Dønnes to this day.

Dønnes church is on the north east side of the island. In 2006, it was chosen as Northern Norway's finest church. It was built in the 12th century as a private chapel for the Dønnes mansion and is one of three remaining churches dating from the Middle Ages in Helgeland – the others

are on Nord-Herøya (p 317) and Alstahaug (p 319). The church has a distinctive architectural style and is built from stone. At the end of the 17ᵗʰ century an annexe was built that functioned as a mausoleum for the owner's deceased family. This is the largest and best preserved mausoleum in Norway, with 22 family caskets. The church was rebuilt in the 1860s; however, it was returned to its original state in the 1960s. There are many cultural treasures in the church.

At **Glein,** south of Dønnes church, with Hov (likely an ancient site of sacrifice) on the island of Løkta on the opposite side of the fjord (p 310), is one of the largest grave mounds in Northern Norway. It has a diameter of 35 m and is 5 m in height. The burial mound is thought to be from Roman times or from the migration period (p 83) and has been excavated in several stages. On top of the mound is Northern Europe's largest stone phallus. The sacred white stone is hewn from marble. It is 89 cm tall and 50 cm in diameter and probably dates from the migration period. In Norse saga literature there is evidence that it was common to offer a sacrifice on burial mounds in pagan times. The white stone is a phallic symbol of power that is also associated with fertility rites and worshipping of the Norse god Njord – the god of fertility, wealth and shipping (p 163). The fact that this type of stone is placed on a burial mound or in places in which churches were later built, is often interpreted as an expression of the protective powers that the stone was thought to have.

On the headland of **Gleinsneset** at Glein, there is a burial site with finds dating from the Iron Age. The site has 21 graves that have been left open, so that the actual construction of the graves can be seen.

Dalsvågfjellet (379 m above sea level) is in the south western corner of the island of Dønna. Then we see the village of Bjørn with fish farms and fish processing companies. There is also a ferry stage.

66°04'32"N 12°40'E	+ 0 hrs 44 min ⑫

At **Bjørn** the annual market held here, known as Bjørnsmartnan, was at one time Norway's largest coastal market. On the site of the old market, finds of Norwegian, Swedish and Russian coins have been made, dating from the 16ᵗʰ century. Bjørnsmartnan was officially opened by royal decree in 1754. In the peak of summer, there was a great deal of activity with sale and trade along with cultural events – Italian musicians, strange animals, giants and dwarves, carousels and a circus. The market had its 'golden age' in the 1870s, when there could be as many as 3 000 visitors and 160 houses were in use as trade stalls. Foreign visitors also came to the market, especially from Sweden and Finland. A major fire in 1889 destroyed 160 houses – about half of the houses in Bjørn. The market was officially discontinued in 1882. However, it continued as a regular market until 1939. The old traditions were revitalised in 1981, with the market as a cultural arrangement with an emphasis on popular entertainment and coastal heritage. The event is still arranged every second year at the beginning of July.

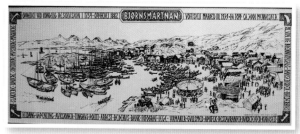

It is thought that the forerunners of the Bjørnsmartnan were the old courthouse assemblies. Bjørn was a district seat of the judiciary and taxation authorities and here the taxes were levied, fines were imposed and legal disputes resolved. The island was a suitable meeting place along the coast with good harbour facilities and a strategic location. There were just a few locals living there all year round, which was an advantage when the noise and bustle was at its worst!

The west side of Dønna, which cannot be seen from the ship, also has sites of cultural heritage. At **Nordvik**, in the middle of the island is Northern Norway's probably oldest preserved trading post with a history that goes back to the 17th century. The trading post had a trade route with Bergen and was granted official guesthouse status. During its golden age in the 1880s, there were 16 buildings on the site. Nordvik church, which was founded on the trade at Nordvik, was completed in 1871.

The north side of Dønna is comprised of long stretches of land and low marshy ground. Altervatn Nature Reserve is located here, a protected landscape, home to many species of breeding birds.

On the north west side of the island is **Rølvåg**, the birthplace of the author Ole E. Rølvaag (1876-1931). Rølvaag was a fisherman and farmer's son who emigrated to America as a 20 year-old, and became one of the USA's leading immigration authors.

West of Dønna is the island of **Vandved** with several surrounding islets. Vandved has around 60 permanent inhabitants. The island is relatively flat and has fish farming as its main commercial activity.

The small group of islands with the uninhabited fishing hamlet of **Åsvær** lies outermost towards the Norwegian Sea. On one of the islands is Åsvær lighthouse from 1876. The lighthouse has an 18.5 m high iron tower. The light is 24.5 m above sea level and the range is 15 nautical miles. The lighthouse was automated in 1980. It was granted protected status in 2000.

On the port side, we have passed the villages of **Naustholmen**, **Forneset** and **Løkvika**, outermost on the headland, **Angerneset**. The narrow, elongated peninsula **Ulvangsøya** juts out into the fjord. Between Ulvangsøya and the next long narrow headland, **Leinesodden**, the narrow fjord **Melsfjorden** runs in a north easterly direction.

We approach the community of **Sandnessjøen**. In the background the legendary 'Seven Sisters' tower above.

On the starboard side is the island of **Skorpa**, in front of Dønna.

The bridge Helgelandsbroen on the port side brings together the northern tip of the island of Alsta and Sandnessjøen with the mainland in Leirfjord municipality. The bridge is one of the largest cable-stayed bridges in the world, with a main span of 425 m and a total length of 1 131 m. The height of the towers is 127 m. The bridge was officially opened in 1991.

Approx. 66°02'N   12°38'E

We cross the boundary between Leirfjord and Alstahaug municipalities

Alstahaug municipality

Municipal coat of arms, significance: Mountain range, the 'Seven Sisters' and its mirror image in the sea.
Meaning of name: Norse Alastarhaugr, first part from Alost (now Alsten), last part is from the name of the farm, Haug.
Municipal seat: Sandnessjøen (Pop. 5 662).
Position: 66°01'N 12°38'E. **Area:** 215 km².
Population: 7 225. **Pop. density:** 33.6 /km².
Area distribution: Farming 6 %, forestry 10 %, fresh water 1 %, other area 83 %.
Trade and industry: Agriculture. Dairy and beef cattle. Grazing fields. Potatoes, corn and vegetables. Fishing now has less importance.
Places to return to: Petter Dass Museum. Alstahaug church. War cemetery. Tjøtta.
Alstahaug municipality's home page: www.alstahaug.kommune.no

Alstahaug is principally an island municipality with 917 larger and smaller islands.

The ship docks at the quayside in Sandnessjøen

© ROLF LILAND

We arrive at **Sandnessjøen** on the north east tip of the island of **Alsten** (153 km²). Alsten's western part has low, cultivated shores. In the eastern part, the famous mountains tower above – the 'Seven Sisters'. On the island's north west tip is the community of Sandnessjøen and on the south west tip is the well-known church parish of Alstahaug. Sandnessjøen had an upswing in its fortunes in the 1870s, when the telegraph company, a bank and a steamship company all opened offices here. The Hurtigruten began to call regularly in 1893 and the municipal administration was relocated from Søvik to Alstahaug in 1899. The community, that received a town charter in 1999, is the service and communications hub for the local region. There are fishery-related companies and a dairy, and a supply base for the oil enterprises located off the Helgeland coast. Helgeland Commercial Park has a number of companies that manufacture offshore equipment and steel fabrications etc.

The Viking Torolv Kveldulvsson, who is mentioned in Egil's Saga, was a man-at-arms at the court of the King Harald Hårfagre (Harold Finehair), and the uncle of the renowned court poet Egil Skallagrimsson, from Tjøtta (p 319). After a friend had fallen in the battle of Hafrsfjord near Stavanger (approx. 885), Torolv took over the farm Torget just outside of Brønnøysund (p 324) and also his friend's wife, Sigrid.

Torolv and Sigrid later moved into Sigrid's former childhood home, Sandnesgården, now known as Sandnessjøen, and achieved great power in the region. He was also granted the right to levy the "Finn tax" for the King, taxes and duties that the Sami in the North Calotte had to pay to the authorities. Torolv was the first known exporter of dried fish from Northern Norway. He sent his men to Vågan in Lofoten (p 155) to fish for spring cod around the year 875 and transported the fish to England. Egil's Saga tells the story that he "had cod and skins and ermine furs carried on board" and sailed westwards to England to "buy clothes and other things that he needed". Torolv and Sigrid had their own islands where they collected eggs and harvested feathers and down, an important trade product with long traditions (p 333). After a time, King Harald Hårfagre lost faith in Torolv Kveldulvsson, and had him assassinated around the year 900. Sigrid later married the chieftain at Tjøtta (p 319). It was said that the descendants of Torolv were among the Vikings that later settled on Iceland.

Today there are no remains of Sandnesgården. A church once stood on the site, however this was moved to Stamnes, further south on the island, in 1768.

In 1899, the municipal administration in Sandnessjøen was moved from Søvika to the parish of Alstahaug (p 317).

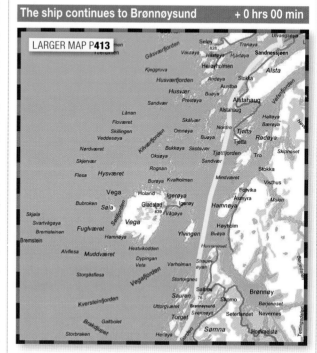

The ship continues to Brønnøysund   **+ 0 hrs 00 min**

LARGER MAP P**413**

From Sandnessjøen, we sail into the fjord Ulvangen. In front of Dønna, on the starboard side, is the island **Skorpa** (224 m above sea level), behind this is the village of **Hestad**. On Dønna is the mountain **Høgtuven** (736 m above sea level) and further south **Dønnmannen** (858 m above sea level). Dønnmannen has been given its name because from a distance the mountain seems to depict a man lying on his back with his arms folded across his middle. Viewed from the north-east the mountain has the profile of a man's face (p 311).

66°00'50"N   12°34'E   **+ 0 hrs 12 min**

On the starboard side are the small islands of **Lauvøya** and **Tranøya,** before **Dønnessundet** between Dønna and Nord-Herøy.

On the port side, we can see part of Sandnessjøen community.

On the port side, we will sail by the 'Seven Sisters' for quite a distance. Along with other well-known Nordland coastal mountains, they are a part of a dramatic legend.

The legend of the mountain range "The Seven Sisters" is one of the most famous legends connected with Norwegian mountains and nature. It goes something like this:

"In the far north of Hålogaland, two old trolls sat on either side of Vestfjorden and glowered at each other. They were not especially good friends, as one of them was a mountain-dweller and the other lived by the sea. The troll in the west, Vågekallen (p 155), sat in his great chair, a thousand metres over the sea at Henningsvær. The whole of Lofoten was his empire and especially Vestfjorden with its huge shoals of millions and millions of codfish. Around the Vågekallen, wild mountains towered above and with his mighty gaze, he looked out over the ranges and the ocean. For thousands of years he had weathered storms and waves – and Thor's hammer (p 163) – and he could take whatever he wanted.

Across the Vestfjorden, at Landego (p 142), the Landegomøya (Landego maiden) sat and gazed over at Vågekallen who was her secret lover. She was carrying his child, despite being engaged to Blåmannen (p 137). She was besotted with Vågekallen and gazed longingly northwards. In the morning sunlight, she saw his purple cape and in the evening light, she saw the reflection of the sun on his golden crown. Vågekallen had a son, called Hestmannen (Horseman), because he always rode a horse. He was a wild and unruly child, and after an argument with his father, he ran away from home and went to live in the mountains of Svolvær with the Svolværgeita (p 158). He grew to be much bigger than his father, and it was not advisable for anyone to get on the bad side of Hestmannen and his fierce temper.

In the east, the Sulitjelma (p 137) troll sat and looked out on his kingdom. He was king of the wide mountains and the ranges of forests and lakes. Every now and then, he would chuckle to himself, because no-one, apart from him, knew that the mountains under his feet held unlimited treasures of copper ore and other precious metals. The two old trolls agreed, however, about one thing – that youngsters were impossible. The Sulitjelma troll had seven daughters that made every day a misery for him. Finally, he could see no other way out than to send them out to Landego to stay with the Landego maiden as housekeeper and to get a strict governess known as Lekamøya sent from the south, who could keep control of the unruly girls. The girls lived well and had a quiet life in the sun, with the Northern Lights twinkling over the idyllic scene.

However, one night in May, Hestmannen sat on his mountain in Svolvær, and with his sharp eyes, he spied over Vestfjorden to Landego. He saw Lekamøya and the seven sisters who were out bathing in the waves. He became wildly enamoured and the 150 kilometres over Vestfjorden were nothing to him – he clambered onto his horse in full armour, threw his cape over his shoulder and set off at a gallop. His helmet plume swayed in the wind as he rode southwards and the sea spray from the horse' hooves glistened like sparks. Hestmannen's eyes shone even brighter and Lekamøya saw him approaching. She saw that neither prayers nor sheer might would be able to stop him, so she gathered the seven sisters around her and they ran to the south in a panic. Rødøyløven (p 305) lay at the approach to Saltenfjorden, and the lion raised his head to hear the remarkable noise and commotion coming from the north. But the seven sisters from Sulitjelma talked and said that it was stupid and foolish of anyone to run away from such a suitor. Hestmannen was, despite everything, an extremely manly and fine example. So the seven sisters threw off their capes and these capes fell down and created Dønna island (p 310). Then the seven sisters lined up on Alsten island, and made themselves appear as beautiful and as attractive as they could, first the youngest and slimmest Botnkrona, then Grytfoten, Skjeringen, Tvillingene, and Kvasstiden, and furthest south the eldest, Breitinden with a child in tow….

The dreams of romantic adventure lit up in their eyes, however the sisters could have saved themselves the effort – Hestmannen was not the slightest bit interested in them. It was Lekamøya he wanted. She ran further south until she came to Tjøtta where she threw her baking board, rolling pin and spoon away (p 319) and ran with giant strides, faster and faster southwards. When Hestmannen realised he could no longer catch her, he was furious. He arched his bow and shot an arrow after her.

In the mountains close to Brønnøy, sat another troll and had great fun watching the whole scene. When he saw the arrow flying southwards, he threw his hat into the path of the arrow. The arrow went through the hat and fell down, creating Torghatten with a hole straight through (p 326). Lekamøya ran until she came over to Trøndelag and was saved.

However, just at that moment, the sun shone on the landscape, as the spring nights are short in Nordland, and all the trolls turned to stone where they stood. And there they will stand until the end of time: Lekamøya at Leka (p 329), Torghatten near Brønnøysund, the Seven Sisters at Alsten, Hestmannen on Lurøy, Rødøyløven on Rødøy, Landego near Bodø, Sulitjelmatoppen on the Swedish border and Vågekallen on his throne looking over Vestfjorden. The baking board, spoon and rolling pin lie as giant stones at Tjøtta."

The geographical data for the mountain chain on the port side are, from the north (height above sea level, in metres): **Botnkrona** (1 072), **Grytfoten** (1 019), **Skjæringen** (1 037), **Tvillingene** (945 and 980), **Kvasstinden** (1 010) and **Stortinden** (910). The mountains are of granite and were created when small glaciers forced their way down from the peaks. They have been famous landmarks for generations.

The communities on the shore along the mountain range are: Stamnes with a church, **Urda**, **Porsmoen**, **Sørnovika**, Stokka with airport, Lund and Søvika.

Approx. 66°00'N   12°30'E

Herøy municipality passes on the port side

Herøy municipality

Municipal coat of arms, significance: Symbolizes boat crewmen.
Meaning of name: First part herr, likely meaning skipaherr, 'gathering of the fleet'.
Municipal seat: Silvalen (pop. 665).
Position: 65°58'24"N 12°17'43"E.
Area: 62 km².
Population: 1 682. **Pop. density:** 27.1 /km².
Area distribution: Farming 8 %, forestry 3 %, fresh water 2 %, other area 87 %.
Trade and industry: Coastal fishing, also Lofoten and Finnmark fishing, mainly with smaller vessels. Landing stage. Fish processing plant. Mechanical workshops and boatyards. Aquaculture. Limited agriculture.
Places to return to: Herøy church. Herøy Village Museum. Nord-Herøy farm.
Herøy municipality's home page: www.heroy.kommune.no

66°00'N   12°31'E   + 0 hrs 16 min ①

On the starboard side is the small island of **Hjartøya**. Behind this island is **Nord-Herøya** (8.9 km²), the largest island in Herøy municipality. Just south west of this island is Sør-Herøya.

The farm Nord-Herøy gård was formerly one of the largest in the area. It was crown property and from 1618 was the residence of the local justice. Throughout hundreds of years, it has been owned by various well-known and wealthy families. The only remaining building from the original construction is the larger main building from around 1900 and part

PETTER DASS
PREST OG DIKTER
I NESNA
1673 - 1689

of the garden. The famous poet and priest **Petter Dass** (p 318) was born at Nord-Herøy gård in 1647.

The community of **Silvalen** near Herøy church is the municipality's administrative centre.

On **Sør-Herøy** stands Herøy church, also known as the Helgeland cathedral. The church is one of three sister churches in Helgeland. The others are at Dønna (p 312) and Alstahaug (p 319). A wooden church has at one time stood on the site. The next church to be built was a longhouse style build-ing in soapstone, construct-ed in the Romance style in 1150. It had 350 seats and 1.5 m thick walls. It is the only church north of Trondheim with an apse (semi-circular extension). The triptych and the pulpit are from 1760. The church was extended in 1880 and later restored.

Herøy Bygdesamling, is also located here, a collection of antiquarian buildings and artefacts. The collection has a complete courtyard with seven houses and over 8 000 artefacts that provide an interesting insight into ancient fishing and hunting traditions along the coast.

Herøy municipality is well known for its traditional fish-ing hamlets and its fabulous natural islands, which com-prise approx. 1 700 low-lying islands and islets. Anti-quarian finds show that there have been settlements here since prehistoric times. The population is mainly concen-trated on the larger islands close to the mainland. These are connected by a number of bridges.

The island of **Sandsundvær** is one of the many islands out in the ocean, approx. 11 nautical miles from the mu-nicipal seat. On the 22nd January 1901, 34 people lost their lives here. The following story illustrates how harsh the life on the islands could be:

> 99 The tragedy was caused mainly by the spring tides combined with a strong wind. On the day of the tragedy, 254 persons were out on the is-land. Only one family were permanent residents – the others were there for the winter fishing and they lived in fishermen's cabins. The destruction be-gan two hours before the high tide, which was due at 13.00. The first thing to be blown down by the storm was a pile of logs. The wind then began to

pluck at the cabins and the boats broke free from their moorings and were dashed against the rocks on land. As Sandsundvær is for the most part comprised of low-lying islets, there were few places that people could shelter. Those that were left on the most ex-posed islands held onto ropes and chains. However, after a while the freezing sea became full of dange-rous flotsam. It is said that many of those who died were struck by pallets and planks that they could not avoid.

The tragedy happened in the morning, in daylight. About half of the cabins were destroyed by the storm. The dead were laid in one of the cabins. People helped one another as much as they could, out on the storm-bound islands in the open ocean. They all feared that they would be taken by the sea and the storm when the tide came in again during the night.

It is unimaginable, the conditions that prevailed on Sandsundvær during the three days that the storm raged, before people could escape inland and sound the alarm.

34 persons died in the Sandsundvær tragedy. Of the 25 that were found, 21 of these are buried in a sepa-rate burial site at Herøy old cemetery. Four are bu-ried in Leirfjord municipality. Nine people were ne-ver found."

65°58'N 12°26'E	+ 0 hrs 28 min

To starboard, we pass the small islands of **Svinøya** and **Valløya**. On the port side is the community of **Stokka** with Sandnessjøen airport, a civil short takeoff and land-ing airport with a 1 087 m long tarmaced runway. The airport was opened in 1968.

We continue into **Alstahaugfjorden.**

Søvika is on the port side at the foot of the "Seven Sisters" mountain of Stortinden. Søvik was the former centre of Alstahaug municipality until 1899, when it was relocated to Sandnessjøen.

On the starboard side, we can see the flat island of **Altra** (0.24 km²) with the village of **Austbø** to the north.

South of Altra are the islands of **Blomsøya** and **Hestøya.** A road runs from south to north that connects the islands.

The islands **Husvær** (0.7 km²) and **Brasøya** to starboard lie west of Altra. This area is regarded as one of the world's finest areas for farming cod, salmon and other fish species.

The group of islands that lie further west, **Husvær**, **Måsvær**, **Gåsvær** and **Skipbåtvær** is comprised of innumerable smaller islets and skerries between the mainland and the larger islands and the Norwegian Sea.

65°53'44"N 12°22'E   + 0 hrs 48 min ②

The community of **Alstahaug** at the foot of the low mountain **Vettfjellet** (244 m above sea level) passes on our port side. The name 'veter' (wooden pile) indicates that, many years ago, timber cairns were lit as beacons to warn of approaching enemies (p 82).

The poet and priest Petter Dass and Alstahaug are closely connected in Norwegian history. The last 18 years of his life (1689–1707), Petter Dass was the local priest at Alstahaug. Petter Dass was born on Nord-Herøya on the opposite side of Alstenfjorden in 1647, the eldest of five children. His father was Scottish, living in Bergen and his mother was the daughter of the tax inspector in Helgeland, which at that time was based on Nord-Herøy. His father died when the boy was just 6 years old. Along with his younger siblings, Petter Dass was raised by relatives. He was sent to live with his uncle, who was the parish priest at Nærøy, south of Rørvik (p 120). Around 1660, he was sent to live with his father's sister in Bergen, in order to attend the Latin School there (p 17). In 1666, he began studying theology in Copenhagen, where he remained for 3 years.

As a newly trained theologian, Patter Dass worked for a time as a teacher in Vefsn, the neighbouring municipality east of Alstahaug, then later as an assistant to the priest at Nesna, north of Sandnessjøen (p 309). His fiancée, Margrethe, became pregnant before they were married; however, in 1673 he was granted 'the merciful pardon of the King' so that he could be ordained as a priest, get married and take over the priest's duties at Nesna, where he remained for 17 years, both as an assistant and from 1681 as the resident curate. It was at Nesna that he began to write his main literary work 'The Trumpet of Nordland'.

In 1689, Petter Dass was appointed as the parish priest in Alstahaug, Northern Norway's wealthiest parish that was the main diocese for nine other churches. He remained here until his death in 1707, 60 years old. He is possibly buried under the floor of the chancel in Alstahaug church.

The majority and the most important of his literary works were written during the last 30 years of his life. The only work that was printed in his lifetime was "Norwegian Valley Songs". His main work 'The Trumpet of Nordland', that describes the life of the people of Nordland, the relationship between people and nature, lay unpublished for 32 years after his death, despite several attempts to have the work published when he was still alive.

Petter Dass wrote poetry about everyday life and life's milestones, births, weddings, funerals, especially tragic or uplifting events. He wrote evangelical songs with themes taken from the four gospels in the New Testament and wrote texts for each Sunday in the church year based on well-known melodies. He also wrote songs with material taken from the Old Testament. His psalm "Lord Thy Name and Glory" is his best known.

In 1999, Petter Dass was chosen as the 'Nordlander of the Millennium' by Northern Norway's largest newspaper.

Recent research into the life of Petter Dass claims that the almost undividedly positive image that has been put forward does not have any basis in fact. His personality and his mission had many negative aspects. However, these claims are highly controversial among historians.

The farm known as Belsvåg Gård stands in the bay close to Alstahaug church. The oldest buildings are from around 1650. The farm was the episcopal residence of the first bishop of Nordland and Finnmark, Mattias Bonsach Broch, who was bishop between 1804 and 1812.

The main building was constructed in 1804. The farm was sold to private owners in 1864 and some parts of the building were demolished. The main building and a store were granted protected status in 1928 and in 1984, this status was extended to the remaining buildings. The Petter Dass Museum with exhibitions and interior from the 17th century and 18th century is located in the old rectory and the surrounding buildings. In October 2007, a new Petter Dass Museum was opened

in Alstahaug. The building, has a gross area of 1.350 m2, spread over 3 floors. The building has large glass-covered areas and is constructed from steel and concrete, clad with zinc plates.

A statue of the poet and priest stands nearby.

Alstahaug church is one of the three churches from the Middle Ages in Helgeland. The two other 'sister churches' are on Sør-Herøya (p 317) and Dønna (p 311). The churches at Alstahaug and Dønna have characteristic 'onion shaped' cupolas. The first stone church was built at Alstahaug at the end of the 12th century, most likely as a farm chapel, in a Romance style. The church was rectangular (12.2 m x 9.3 m) with a narrow chancel and was richly decorated. Without making too many alterations to the Middle Age church, Alstahaug church was restored in the 1960s. The church has a wonderful altarpiece from 1649 and Middle Ages chalk paintings with motifs from the story of the suffering of Christ. In connection with the restoration, archaeological excavations were carried out at the church.

At Alstahaug cemetery there is one of Northern Norway's largest burial mounds. It is said to be the grave of the Viking chieftain Ølve.

On the headland **Haugsneset**, the outermost southern point in the island of Alsten on the port side, is **Kongshaugen** burial mound, which is probably one of the largest in Nordland. It is 30 m in diameter and 8 m high. In one of the smaller mounds, an archaeological dig found items dating from the late Bronze Age (p 83).

The flat agricultural islands of **Offersøya** (6.7 km²) and **Tjøtta** (11.3 km²) lie south of Alsta. The two islands are connected by a bridge.

The Viking chieftain Hårek of Tjøtta had his base at Tjøtta Gård. He inherited the farm from his father, the courtier Øyvind Finnson Skaldespiller, who resided

here during the 10th century. Hårek eventually became Hålogaland's most powerful figure and adopted Christianity in 999.

The story of Hårek from Tjøtta is one of Viking conflicts, battles between mighty Viking chieftains, of murder and revenge. For a time Hårek was the King's authority, under Olav Tryggvason (968-1000) and Olav Haraldsson (the Holy) (995-1030) (p 88), however he eventually came into conflict with them. He also came into conflict with members of the Chieftain clan of Grankjellsson (p 311) at Dønna due to dispute about the harvesting of eggs and feathers on the islands off the Helgeland coast (p 333). In 1028, after being caught poaching and humiliated in a dispute about rights, Hårek took his revenge by burning down the mansion house at Dønna - the chieftain Grankjellsson and several of his men were killed in the fire.

During the battle of Stiklestad in 1030 (p 98), Hårek of Tjøtta was one of the leaders of the peasant army that rose up against the King Olav Haraldsson (the Holy) and his army, when the peasants killed the King. Six years later when Hårek was in Trondheim, paying visit to the reigning King, Hårek was killed by an axe blow from Åsmund Grankjellsson, whose father had died in the arson attack at Dønna. In true Viking tradition, justice had been done.

Tjøtta is steeped in history; no other place in history has so many ancient historical sites preserved within such a limit area. Evidence of 16 star-shaped courtyards from the first settlers, one of the largest and oldest Iron Age settlements in Norway, has been found on the island. There are also a large number of visible burial mounds and four stone monuments, some of them are connected to the legend of the "Seven Sisters". Lekamøya, in her escape from Hestmann is said to have "thrown a spoon, baking board, baking form and rolling pin, which are now turned to stone at Tjøtta".

The site known as the 'Golden Mound' at Tjøtta is one of the largest burial mounds in Northern Norway and is 70-80 m in diameter. Between the graves are hollows, much like the graves of today. These are from the early Iron Age, dated to A.D. 600-1000. They have been in use for 400 years.

Tjøtta farm has formerly belonged to the Bjarkøy clan (p 166) and was the archbishop's seat in the middle of the 14th century. After the Reformation in 1537, Tjøtta farm became crown property and later became the official residence of the tax authorities in the area. From 1666, the farm passed into the hands of various private owners. In 1930, it was bought by the state, and it was turned into a sheep breeding station and a research farm working on the growth of plants suitable for Northern Norway.

In 1995, it became the professional headquarters of the Nordic Institute for Agricultural Research.

From approx. 1800, the farm at Tjøtta comprised 380 tenant houses. These were shared out by four brothers in 1865. The main farm at Tjøtta had approx. 20 smallholder plots. The main building is a two-storey house from 1873, built after the older building from 1756 was demolished. The farm also includes Tjøtta church from 1851.

The church at Tjøtta is the third to be built on the site. There was most likely a church on the same site from when the Viking chieftain Hårek was alive. Hårek and his family allowed themselves to be christened in 999, under the threat of death if they did not comply. The church was probably destroyed by fire, as was a second on the same site.

At the war cemetery at Tjøtta, north east on the island, there are 6 725 war dead buried in a fenced-in common grave and 826 others buried in individual graves. The war cemetery is also known as the Russian cemetery. Soviet prisoners of war were buried in public cemeteries during the Second World War. After the war, it was decided to move the graves and bury them together on state land at Tjøtta. The cemetery was opened in 1953.

Tjøtta International War Cemetery was opened in 1970. Approximately 2 457 casualties of war are buried here, in unmarked graves, all from the German troop transport ship "Rigel" that was sunk on the 27th November 1944, just west of the island Tjøtta. The ship was about to evacuate 2 248 Russian prisoners of war during the retreat from Narvik and Bodø, as well as 103 German prisoners, a few Serbs, Czechs and Norwegians. In addition, there was a German escort ship, and a Norwegian crew – in total 2 838 persons were on board. Allied aircraft attacked the ship and it was sunk, 2 457 persons were killed. It is thought to be one of the world's largest ever shipping disasters.

To starboard of Tjøtta we have sailed along the islands of **Nordre** and **Søndre Rosøya**.

65°48'N 12°20'E	**+ 1 hr 11 min** ❸

The fjord **Vefsnfjorden** (51 km in length) on the port side cuts into the land first in a north easterly, then south easterly direction, between the islands of Tjøtta and Rødøya. On the eastern side of the fjord is **Aspvikfjellet** (521 m above sea level). At the inner part of the fjord is the industrial community of **Mosjøen** (pop. 9 784).

The island, **Rødøya** (7.3 km²) on the port side with **Rødøyfjellet** (307 m above sea level) is on the southern side of the entrance to Vefsnfjorden. The red colour comes from the deposits of serpentine and chrome.

In 1927, at **Tro** on the southern tip of Rødøya, 4 000 year old rock carvings were found hewn into a rock face.

One of the figures in the carvings depicts a skier. This figure has become internationally famous. The skier from Tro on Rødøy was the inspiration for the pictograms used during the Lillehammer Winter Olympic games in 1994.

The island **Mindlandet** (13.8 km²) is an agricultural island, south of Tjøtta and Vefsnfjorden and south west of Rødøya. At **Brakstad,** in the middle of the island's west side lies one of Helgeland's oldest settlements. Most of the archaeological finds from here are roughly hewn stone tools, which are thought to be from the early Stone Age (p 83). There are also smaller flint items from more recent times.

We are now in the fjord **Mindværfjorden**, and have passed the island of Mindlandet. On the port side, south of Mindlandet, is a small group of islands and skerries known as **Mindværet**.

Approx. 65°43'N   12°16'46"E
We cross the boundary of Alstahaug and Vevelstad municipalities

Vevelstad municipality

Municipal coat of arms, significance: Symbolizes the name of the municipality, a 'V'.
Meaning of name: Likely from Norse Vifilstadir; combination of Norse man's name Vifill, and stad.
Municipal seat: Forvik (pop. -).
Position: 63°43'N 12°28'E. **Area:** 530 km².
Population: 504. **Pop. density:** 1.0 /km².
Area distribution: Farming 1 %, forestry 7 %, fresh water 4 %, other area 88 %.
Trade and industry: Agriculture. Cattle, dairy and beef production, sheep farming. Some forestry. Some smaller timber mills. Fishing, in combination with farming. Landing stage and timber manufacture.
Vevelstad municipality's home page: www.vevelstad.kommune.no

65°43'N   12°17'E   + 1 hr 32 min ④

The island of **Hamnøya** (16.4 km², highest point 278 m above sea level), passes by on the port side. In the middle of the island's west side, near the village of **Hesstun** at the foot of the mountain, remains of ancient settlements have been uncovered, dating from the Stone Age and the early Iron Age.

The sound **Vevelstadsundet** lies between **Hamnøya** and the mainland. On the mainland, behind Hamnøya is the

© HELGELAND MUSEUM

municipal seat of **Forvik**, with the restored Forvik trading post from 1792.

Close by is Vevelstad church, built in 1796. The triptych has been painted by the Italian artist Joseph Pisani. The church was extended in 1871.

Vevelstad courtyard, close to the church, has 10 buildings and a comprehensive collection of artefacts from the municipality. The courtyard is a presentation of Vevelstad's recent history.

There is a 3-4 000 year old rock carving site in the municipality.

The range of mountains that we now pass is, from the north: **Forvikfjellet** (841, 849 and 840 m above sea level), **Høyholmstindan** (1 015 and 996 m above sea level) and **Hornstinden** (885 m above sea level).

On the port side is Vega municipality

Vega municipality

Municipal coat of arms, significance: Boats and the sea.
Meaning of name: Norse Veiga, from veig, 'strong drink', poss. from the original meaning 'liquid'.
Municipal seat: Gladstad (Pop. 290).
Position: 65°40'37"N 11°57'28"E. **Area:** 159 km².
Population: 1 299. **Pop. density:** 8.2 /km².
Area distribution: Farming 9 %, forestry 4 %, fresh water 2 %, other area 85 %.
Trade and industry: Agriculture and fishing. Cattle farming with dairy and meat production, sheep farming. Some vegetable growing. Fishing along the coast with smaller vessels, Lofoten fishing season. Limited industry. Mechanical workshops. The electricity is supplied via an undersea cable from the mainland. Fast boat connection to Brønnøysund.
Places to return to: Vega islands. Rørøy farm. Bremstein.
Activities to return to: Egg and down islands.
Vega municipality's home page: www.vega.kommune.no

Only about 15 of the 6 500 islands here are inhabited and only three of these are inhabited all year round. The population is spread and there are no large communities.

65°40'N 12°15'E	+ 1 hr 44 min

The small, flat island **Igerøya** (6.6 km²) passes by on the starboard side. The island has a bridge leading over to Vega and a boat service to the mainland.

The island of **Vega** lies behind Igerøya. It is relatively flat, apart from the south western part. **Trollvasstinden** (800 m above sea level) is the highest peak. The community of **Gladstad** (pop. 290) in the central part of the island is the administrative centre. The church at Gladstad is from 1863. In the middle of the island, in a sandy area, remains of a Stone Age settlement have been found, dated at 9 000 years old. This is one of the oldest traces of any settlement in Northern Norway. Remains have also been discovered in other places on the island. On the eastern part of the island there is a stone monument. The earliest traces that we know of permanent settlements on the many low-lying Vega islands are approx. 1 500 years old. The islands are mentioned in writings from the Middle Ages, especially the outermost islands that were important for their egg, feather and down resources (p 333). The fishermen-farmers that lived here were tenants or servants associated with the large and wealthy mansion house at Tjøtta (p 320).

Close to the sound between Vega and Igerøya are the old trading posts Rørøy and Veigstein.

Rørøy trading post on the east side of the island of Vega was an old farm and commercial centre. The main two-storey building, as it stands today, was built in approx. 1800. Trade began here in 1727 and the farm had 118 tenant plots in Vega, Brønnøy and Velfjord on the mainland. The farm was sold in 1800 and all of the tenant plots were sold off. A new owner who bought the land in 1840, merged 60 tenant plots together under Rørøy farm. In 1924 the land was sold to the tenant farmers.

© MORTEN PETTERSEN

In 2004, Vega was added to UNESCO's prestigious World Heritage List, a list of the world's finest natural and cultural treasures. The basis of the UNESCO committee's decision was:

- Unique traditions of duck down harvesting that have existed for over a thousand years.
- a landscape created by people that bears witness that a special and simple way of life has been developed in an extremely exposed area just south of the Arctic Circle.
- the long and continuous relationship between the people and the landscape that reflects an unusual continuity in the culture, and
- the key role played by women in the duck down harvesting and the following manufacture of a high-value product that became a part of the Hanseatic trade.

Other values that were noted in the nomination were:

- the geological and topographical form (shoreline with thousands of islands, islets and skerries) that is unique both in form and scope.
- the quaternary geological history that offers a unique opportunity for research into the history of settlement and cultural development.
- The traditional combinations of farming and fishing have contributed to the fact that biological diversity is greater than a comparable landscape in a natural state.
- the area's international ornithological and marine biological significance is the basis for the development of the varied cultural landscape with unique traditions, and
- the area is a unique example of the significance of the Gulf Stream for settlement in the areas along the northern coast in this particular area of the world.

The flat island of **Ylvingen** (7.6 km², 68 m above sea level) passes by on the port side. The main commercial activities here are agriculture and fishing. There is one landing stage on the island. In the south of the island is a fortification from the Second World War.

A group of islands known as **Bremstein** is out in the ocean, approx. 20 km west of Vega. The islands have rich fish, egg and feather/down resources (p 333).

At **Geiterøy** on the Bremstein islands stands Bremstein lighthouse, constructed as a coastal lighthouse in 1925. It was reinforced and electrified in 1961. Bremstein lighthouse is 27 m high, and has a red cast iron tower with a typical white 'belt'. The beacon is 41.5 m over the sea and the range is 18 nautical miles. It was automated in 1980. It was declared a listed building in 1990. There is an auxiliary light on the same site; this has a height above the sea of 28.5 m.

65°39'N   12°15'E   + 1 hr 48 min

On the port side are the villages of **Høyholm** and **Lauknes** in Vevelstad municipality, before **Velfjorden** cuts inland some 31 km, in a south easterly direction. The fjord has many 'arms'. The north westerly point for the mouth of Velfjorden is Hornsneset.

Approx. 65°36'N   12°14'E

We cross the boundary between Vevelstad and Brønnøy municipalities

Brønnøy municipality

Municipal coat of arms, significance: Reflects the connection of the local people with the sea.
Meaning of name: From Norse Brunnøy, which is comprised of 'brønn'(well) and 'øy'(island), as sailors knew they could obtain fresh water here.
Municipal seat: Brønnøysund (Pop. 4 464).
Position: 65°28'32"N 12°12'39"E. **Area:** 1 040 km².
Population: 7 548. **Pop. density:** 7.3 /km².
Area distribution: Farming 3 %, forestry 18 %, fresh water 4 %, other area 75 %.
Trade and industry: Agriculture with cattle and sheep farming, also dairy production. Forestry is a secondary industry in the inner areas. Fishing, especially on the islands. Aquaculture. Limestone industry.
Places to return to: Torghatten. Torget. Skarsåsen coastal fort.
Activities to return to: Sea fishing.
Brønnøy municipality's home page: www.bronnoysund.kommune.no

65°35'36"N   12°13'38"E   + 2 hrs 02 min

The southern tip of the island of Ylvingen in Vega municipality passes on the starboard side. The northern tip of Brønnøy municipality, with the headland **Hornsneset** and the community of **Horn** are on the port side

The ship sails into **Tilremsfjorden,** on the port side we pass the flat **Straumøyane** islands and the small village of **Mo.**

65°31'45"N   12°09'35"E   + 2 hrs 18 min ⑤

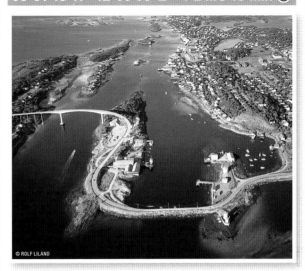
© ROLF LILAND

To starboard is the long, narrow headland of **Stortorgnes**, the northernmost point on the island **Sauren** (7.4 km²), and several smaller islands. On the port side are the villages of **Myra** and **Vikran**.

We approach the quayside at Brønnøysund. To starboard is the north end of the island of Torget. In front is the Brønnøysund bridge.

The ship docks at the quayside in Brønnøysund

The town of **Brønnøysund** is now on a peninsula, however it was originally on an island, separated from the mainland by a narrow sound. As the land rose and the ice retreated, the sound became gradually shallower until it could be crossed at low tide. Stone, gravel and earth were filled in to join the island to the mainland in 1850.

In a historical context, Brønnøysund has almost just been a "narrow sound where sailors were close to fresh water". Snorre Sturlason's King's Saga tells the tale of the men of Duke Skule (Bårdsson, 1189-1240), that they "pirated ships and killed the people of Brønnøy". Brønnøy has been a church parish for 700-800 years. In 1321 it was noted by church scribes that "a priest from Brønnøy attended the service". The increase in the population cannot have been exactly explosive, for in 1701 it was noted that "the priest and his family of ten were the only people in Brønnøysund". In 1801 there were 44 inhabitants, and six families. During the subsequent years some migrants came from the eastern part of Norway, from Trøndelag and from Jämtland in Sweden. In 1838 the steam ship "Prinds Gustav" docked at Brønnøysund for the first time. The local priest was also the post and goods administrator.

Brønnøysund's first "town plan" was drawn up in 1887 when 38 properties were divided from the rectory property. Brønnøysund did not become the regional centre until after the First World War; until then most of the trade went via Kvaløya, somewhat further south. However, Brønnøysund grew steadily and in 1890 the new quay was constructed. In 1893 Brønnøysund was chosen as the permanent port of call for the Hurtigruten. This led to a major turning point in the history of the town. At the end of the 19th century, within a short time the population more than doubled.

Around 1900, several businesses started up in Brønnøysund. A beer and wine store was opened, two hotels were built and doctors and solicitors began to open surgeries and offices. The building trade began to expand and in 1915 Brønnøysund had a post office, a customs office, a harbour office and a county clerk. Electricity was introduced and a bank was opened, as well as a newspaper and a bookstore. Between 1900 and 1930 the population quadrupled, from 305 to 1255. In 1923 Brønnøysund became a separate town municipality, a status it held until 1964, when it was joined together with other areas to create a larger single municipality, Brønnøy.

During the last few decades, the importance of Brønnøysund has increased and in 1981, it was decided that a helicopter and supply base for the oil industry off the coast of Nordland should be established in the town. In 1988 the Brønnøysund Register Centre was established. The Brønnøysund Register Centre is comprised of 19 different state registers, all of them electronic. Among them are the Property Register, Company Register, Accounts Register and the Bankruptcy and Insolvency Registers. Brønnøysund has an airport and was granted town status in 2001.

Brønnøy has been a church parish for 7-800 years and it is likely that the churches have all stood on the same site. The foundations of St. Knut's church, originally a soapstone church from the 1350s, were excavated in 1934. The current church from 1870 is a stone building, with a chancel wall and entrance dating from the Middle Ages. The church was built after the previous burned down in 1866. The church before this one also burned down in 1770, according to available information.

Skarsåsen Coastal Fortifications were constructed during the Second World War. The fortifications were equipped with 15.5 cm cannon, 4.96 m long with a range of 17 000 m. During the war, Brønnøysund was known as "Little Berlin" because of the large number of German soldiers in the area (400-600 men). The construction of the fort was complex, and was carried out by German troops,

Russian prisoners of war and other forced labour. The fortifications were protected by a large number of anti-personnel mines and several rows of barbed wire.

At the end of the 1970s, parts of the fortifications were demolished and filled in. During the 1990s, some parts of the site were reopened and the area is currently an attractive recreational area with a fine view.

The ship continues to Rørvik	+ 0 hrs 00 min

LARGER MAP P414

In front is the curved Brønnøysund bridge, a concrete span bridge with a main span of 110 m and a total length of 550 m. One of the main spans and a side span has a horizontal curve of 100 m.

We sail between a number of small islands and into the fjord, **Torgfjorden**. On the port side is the long, low island of **Torget** (16.4 km²), and several small islets.

To starboard we can also see some small islands and on the mainland the villages of **Kråknes**, **Rodal**, **Trælnes** and **Strand**. The mountains in the background are **Sæterfjellet** (599 m above sea level), **Ryptinden** (586 m above sea level) and **Trælneshatten** (567 m above sea level).

65°25'21"N 12°09'E	+ 0 hrs 19 min ❶

The village **Torget,** close to the mountain of Torghatten has an interesting history. In Viking times it was the site of one of the most famous chieftain seats. There was a large farm and a trading post. Torget was the seat of power, strategically placed in the middle of the sailing channel. The owners, during the time of Harald Hårfagre's (Harold Fairhair's) reign, held the right to demand a "Finn tax" from the Sami on behalf of the King. The chieftain seat's history is connected to the Viking chief-

tain Torolv Kveldulvsson and his wife, the chieftain's daughter Sigrid, who was the widow of the former owner of Torget farm. After a time, she moved with her new husband Torolv to her birthplace, Sandnes in Sandnessjøen (p 314). When she became a widow she married the chieftain of Tjøtta farm (p 319).

Later, the farm was owned by several well-known noble families. It became crown property during the Reformation and was used by several senior officials before it was split into three tenant plots and sold at the end of the 19th century.

At the south east end of the island of Torget is the famous 'holed mountain' **Torghatten** (258 m above sea level). Torghatten is one of the most well-known tourist attractions in Northern Norway. The hole, which is 112 m above sea level, is rectangular, 160 m long, 25-35 m in height and 12-15 m in width. Petter Dass from Alstahaug, the poet and priest (1647-1707) (p 318), described the mountain in his work "The Trumpet of Nordland" as "the unsleeping eye, an eye that looks over Nordland's people and it's riches – one that never sleeps."

Torghatten has been visited by the old and the young, by artists and kings and has been mentioned in writings published far beyond the country's borders. In 1838 the steamship "Prinds Gustav", began sailing regular routes along the coast of Nordland, passing Torghatten along the way. The Swedish King Oscar II visited the mountain both in 1873 and in 1903, the German Kaiser Wilhelm II in 1889 and several times after that, and the Norwegian King Haakon and Queen Maud in 1907, guided by the polar explorer Fridtjof Nansen. King Chulalonkorn of Siam (now Thailand) visited in 1907.

In 1930, a journalist went through the hole on skis and was mentioned in the American press. In the 1950s there was a plan to fly through the hole in a light aircraft – however, (and some may say fortunately) nothing ever came of the plans. After a bridge was built across to the island in 1979, Torghatten has had approx. 20 000–40 000 visitors annually.

Torghatten is regarded as one of the world's most distinctive and well-known mountains. The geological reason for the "Torghatten-hole" is that it has been created by a weak zone in the mountain, in an area with many fissures and cracks. During the Ice Age several million years ago, the land mass was compressed by the weight of the ice. In the period between the Ice Ages the ocean level rose once more. Torghatten was formed in a time when the land in this area was 140-160 m lower than it is today. Waves, tides, ocean currents, ice and frost eroded the mountain in the area with fissures and cracks. The rock slowly crumbled and the hole in Torghatten gradually formed.

> The legend of the hole in Torghatten is connected to the tale of how some of the mountains in Nordland and the Helgeland coast were created (p 315). Lekamøya escaped southwards from the amorous and lovesick Hestmannen, and the Sømna troll threw his hat in the path of the arrow that Hestmannen fired at Lekamøya. The hat was holed through by the arrow and fell down onto the island of Torget. Thus the name Torghatten came about.

Around Torghatten there are several visible Stone Age settlements. Several of them are in the scree zone around the mountain

> In May 1988, one of Norway's most serious aviation accidents occurred at Torghatten. A four-engined Dash 7 aircraft with 36 persons on board flew too low when coming in to land at Brønnøysund airport and the aircraft crashed into the mountain. All those on board were killed. The minimum height when approaching the airport is 400 m. The aircraft was flying at 170 m. A plaque in memory of those who were killed has been erected at the site.

The ship continues along the route, sailing between the many small islands.

Approx. 65°22'N   12°05'E

We pass the municipal boundary between Brønnøy and Sømna municipalities

Sømna municipality

Municipal coat of arms, significance: Symbolizes agriculture.
Meaning of name: From Norse Søfn, possibly from sveifa, 'wind, swing', i.e. a place where ships are turned, possible from svefja, 'quiet, still, i.e. a place where the wind calms. **Municipal seat:** Vik (pop. 364).
Position: 65°18'N 12°09'E. **Area:** 193 km².
Population: 2 047. **Pop. density:** 10.6 /km².
Area distribution: Farming 15 %, forestry 28 %, fresh water 2 %, other area 55 %.
Trade and industry: Agriculture. Corn harvesting. Mill and corn silos. Some vegetable growing. Dairy with production of milk products and butter. Beef cattle and pig farming, limited sheep farming. Plant nursery, some fishing. Cement factory.
Places to return to: Sundspollen burial mounds. Vik village courtyard.
Sømna municipality's home page: www.somna.kommune.no

Archaeological finds indicate that the history of the municipality dates from the late Stone Age. The oldest find is a leather shoe dating from 300 B.C.

On the starboard side we pass by several small islands and several villages on the mainland.

65°23'08"N 12°06'20"E   + 0 hrs 28 min

Between the headland of **Trælnesodden** and the island of **Sømnesøya** on the port side is **Sømnesvika**. The village of **Berg** is in the inner part of the bay, one of the two larger communities in Sømna municipality. On the south side of Sømnesvika is the old farm, Sømnes. Sømnes has been well known since the Middle Ages and at one time was divided into many tenant plots that formed a collective under the main farm on Torget in Brønnøy municipality, until the beginning of the 18th century. The farm was given to the archbishop in 1330 and became crown property during the Reformation in the 16th century. From 1741 and until the present it has been privately owned by several families. During one period there were 123 tenant plots belonging to the main farm. There has also been a guest house, large forests and salmon fishing rights. From 1895 until 1948 there was a large cannery at Sømnes.

65°19'N   12°00'E   + 0 hrs 49 min ②

In the inner part of the bay **Vikvågen** on the port side is the municipal seat of **Vik** (pop. 364). At Vik is Sømna village courtyard, a collection of 12 antiquarian buildings that serve as exhibits of the local cultural history with an emphasis on the farmer and fisherman's everyday lives in the period from 1800-1950. The collection is comprised of agricultural and fishing artefacts, handicrafts and household items, and a complete cobbler's workshop.

Vik church, a wooden building, was consecrated in 1876.

65°17'N 11°58'E + 0 hrs 58 min ③

We pass the small islands of **Lyngvær** and **Vågøya** on the port side, just outside of **Lyngværfjorden.** To port up ahead is the island of Kvaløya.

The community of **Vennesund** lies further south on the Sømna peninsula, close to the narrow sound to the island of Kvaløya. At Vennesund is the old, well-known Vennesund trading post. The water spring Olavskilden at Vennesund is said to have healing properties after Olav Haraldsson (the Holy) (p 88) visited the spring on one of his many journeys. There is also a mound from the Bronze Age at Vennestad.

65°15'N 11°55'E + 1 hr 08 min

Kvaløya (9.6 km², 308 m above sea level) passes on the port side, after **Lyngværfjorden.** The island is connected to the mainland by a bridge. The small community of **Røssvika** is on the northern tip.

To starboard up ahead is the island Leka.

Approx. 65°12'49"N 11°53'40"E

We cross the boundary between Sømna and Bindal municipalities

Bindal municipality

Municipal coat of arms, significance: Symbolizes boatbuilding traditions. The number six refers to the number of school districts.
Meaning of name: From the name of the river, Binna, older form Birna 'female bear'. May also be of Sámi origin.
Municipal seat: Terråk (pop. 576).
Position: 65°05'12"N 12°22'45"E. **Area:** 1 262 km².
Population: 1 692. **Population density:** 1.3 /km².
Area distribution: Farming 1 %, forestry 15 %, fresh water 4 %, other area 80 %.
Trade and industry: Agriculture and forestry. Cattle and sheep farming, also some pig farming. Wooden boatbuilding. Saw mill. Timber industry, manufacture of doors. Fish farming and salmon hatchery. Reindeer farming in inland areas.
Places to return to: Solstad church. Melsteinen.
Bindal municipality's home page: www.bindal.kommune.no

Bindalsfjorden (60 km in length) opens up on the port side. It has several deep side fjords towards the north-north west, north west and south west. The longest is Bindalsfjorden/Tosen that cuts inland in a north easterly direction. At the mouth of the fjord is the island of **Gimlinga**.

Solstad church stands on **Holmhalvøya** peninsula (with **Holmsfjellet,** 620 m above sea level), that juts out into Bindalsfjorden. The church is from 1888. The first church on the site was built in 1642-43. It was 8.2 x 16.7 m, had three windows, but did not have a spire. In 1715 it was decided to build a new church, as the older one was in poor repair. The new church was completed in 1734. It was a panelled and red painted longhouse-style church without cross-beams and had a square spire with a cupola. This church was moved in 1888, when the current church was built.

In the same area there is a burial ground from the Iron Age (p 83) that comprises 22 burial mounds and two burial piles. The area has been used for several hundred years. It is difficult to date exactly, as archaeological excavations have not yet been carried out. Another find is a rune-decorated item of chain mail dated from A.D. 600.

65°11'20"N 11°52'E + 1 hr 25 min ④

On the starboard side we pass the small island of **Melsteinen.** It is said that the island is cursed…. According to superstition it is the very reason why there have been so many drowning accidents on or near the island. During the last century, thirteen persons – all of them with connections to the island – have drowned. A well-known murder case is also connected to Melsteinen, one of the most infamous in the area. The incident took place at the end of the 17th century and has even been made into a film.

In February 1692 a boat with four travelling traders came in to Melsteinen. They were in unknown waters and asked for lodgings at a tenant farmer's house. After that, no one heard from them again. Some time later, a rumour of a boat wreck on the island reached the local sheriff. The tenant farmer in that area, Sjur Paulsen, had not reported a boat wreck of any kind. However, when questioned, Sjur Paulsen and two other tenant farmers from a neighbouring island admitted that they had found a capsized boat and some flotsam. They had shared some of the goods they had found and burnt, broken up or destroyed the rest.

The men were arrested. During the subsequent court case, Sjur and his wife Anne's foster daughter aged 13 or 14 told what she had seen when she had woken and heard screams one night. The four tradesmen had called and asked for lodgings and were shown to the barn. During the night, Sjur and Anne had beaten them to death with an axe. One of the men had managed to scream. Thereafter the four bodies were dragged to the marsh and dumped there. A large sum of money had been stolen, along with the goods they had with them. Later, Sjur and Anne had broken up the boat so that it would look as if the boat had capsized and been washed ashore. Sjur admitted the murders, but Anne refused to admit anything for a long time. Finally, she confessed to taking part in the crime. The two other tenant farmers that had taken part in the theft of the goods from the men, but not the murders were also found guilty.

Sjur and Anne appealed against the verdict to the crown court and were transferred to a prison near the town hall in Trondheim. These prisons were often walled holes in the ground or dark, dank and draughty cellars. Often the prisoners died from starvation or from the cold, some even committed suicide. Before the case came up again both Sjur and Anne had died. According to the legal process at that time the sentence meant that they, after their deaths, were to be 'laid out', i.e. the bodies were laid out either whole or disembowelled on a horizontal wheel and left to the birds. This was often in a public place to serve as an example and a warning to others who might have criminal intentions.

Approx. 65°13'N   11°50'47"E

We cross the boundary between Bindal and Leka municipalities

We cross the boundary between Nordland (p 160) and Nord-Trøndelag (p 122) counties

---

65°10'30"N   11°51'E   + 1 hr 29 min ⑤

The peninsula of **Austra** (88 km²) is on the port side. We pass the headland known as **Oterneset** on the northern tip of the peninsula with the mountains **Vettafjellet** (448 m above sea level) (p 82) and **Grovafjellet** (588 m above sea level). The western part of the island is in Leka municipality, the place is known as Gutvik.

We are now in **Lekkfjorden**. On the starboard side is the island **Leka**.

Leka municipality

Municipal coat of arms, significance: The story of an eagle taking a 3½ year old girl in 1932.
Meaning of name: From Norse Leka, may be associated with the verb lekke (leak), possibly from 'gravelled earth', that seeps water.
Municipal seat: Leknes/Leka (pop. -).
Position: 65°05'18"N 11°42'55"E. **Area:** 108 km².
Population: 583. **Pop. density:** 5.4 /km².
Area distribution: Farming 8 %, forestry 3 %, fresh water 1 %, other area 88 %.
Trade and industry: Agriculture with animal husbandry, cattle and chicken farming. Fishing, fish farming. Salmon processing plant. Boatyard.
Places to return to: Leka island. Herlaugshaugen. Solsemhulen cave. Town fort remains. Leka church.
Activities to return to: Bird watching.
Leka municipality's home page: www.leka.kommune.no

The island of **Leka** (57 km²), with its red serpentine rock, is regarded as one of Norway's most beautiful and distinctive islands. It is a saga island, steeped in Norwegian history. Settlements date back 10 000 years, which is probably due to the early retreat of the ice in this area. The western side of the island is completely different from the eastern side that can be seen from the channel. It is said to be much like an arid American desert landscape with barren but beautiful mountain formations.

65°08'24"N   11°49'41"E   + 1 hr 38 min

The headland **Skeineset** is the most north easterly headland on the island of Leka, with the low islands of **Storøya**, **Leknesøyan** and several smaller islands to the north west. This is one of Norway's largest and most species-rich shore meadows with over 90 different species of birds and more than 300 plant species registered in the area. There are also traces of 5-6 000 year old Stone Age settlements, 40-50 burial mounds from the Bronze and Iron Ages and house remains from the Middle Ages. Skeineset is regarded as one of the most important remaining coastal heather moors in Nord-Trøndelag.

65°05'30"N   11°47'16"E   + 1 hr 51 min

At the burial mound at Herlaugshaugen, on the port side of the island of **Madsøya** is Norway's second largest king's grave from the Viking era, and the country's largest 'boat grave' i.e. the deceased was laid out in a boat before burial. It was originally 55 m in diameter and 12 m high, and was constructed around A.D. 870. There are also 160 stone burial mounds, spread around the area.

The legend has it that the local king, King Herlaug 'went into the mound' because he refused to subject himself to the rule of Harald Hårfagre (Harold Fairhair) (865-933) when the country was united as one kingdom. King Herlaug is said to have said that "It is better to die standing, that to remain on your knees for the rest of your life" as he handed over his kingdom to his brother. Then he is said to have voluntarily allowed himself to be buried alive along with his servants in a large mound that had taken three years to build. Finds of ship's nails in the mound confirm that the ship that the King was buried in was much larger than the famous Oseberg and Gokstad ships.

Now we can see the village, the harbour and the ferry quay at **Skei** with the ferry to Sør-Gutvika on the port side and the village of **Leka,** where the church stands. Outside of the village of Leka is the islet of **Havneholmen.**

65°04'50"N   11°47'56"E   + 1 hr 53 min ⑥

Leka church on the starboard side is from 1867. It is a longhouse-style church built of timber. The village of Leka has been the local parish on the island since 1634. An altarpiece made in Holland around 1535 is one of the treasures in the church, in addition to the tempera-paintings from the 18th century. It is claimed that the altarpiece was a votive gift (a gift given as thanks for a prayer answered) from Queen Elisabeth, the wife of King Christian II. The altarpiece was loaned to the World Fair in Amsterdam in 1958. The five paintings were rescued when the old church burned down in 1864.

The bay **Gutvika** passes on the port side. Several ships have run aground and sunk in the area. The most well known of these is the French privateer "L'enfant de la Patrie", that sank on the 17th February 1798. The French corvette, a large sailing ship with 18 cannon and a crew of 230, had set sail from Dunkerque in France in January 1798. The ship got caught up in a violent storm and after a hard journey the ship ran aground on the rock face at Gutvika. Most of the sailors on board the ship managed to get ashore. They later marched over 300 kilometres to Trondheim under terrible winter conditions. An open-air play has been created to commemorate the shipwreck. The 'Privateer's March' is a hike that has been arranged every year since 1988. The marked trail passes the spot at which the ship went aground, at **Raudhammeren** (approx. 65°08'27"N   11°49'42"E) where a commemorative plaque has been erected. Two of the cannon from the ship have been raised from the sea and are now in the museum at Leka.

In the distance we can see the islands Inner-Vikna, Mellom-Vikna and Ytter-Vikna in Vikna municipality.

65°04'39"N   11°46'06"E   + 1 hr 54 min

On the port side we sail beneath the mountain **Rossvik-fjellet** (538 m above sea level) and the bay **Rossvika**.

The island of Madsøya lies to starboard up ahead, with the village of **Haug** behind Madsøya.

Further on, to starboard is the island, Dolma.

On the starboard side, on Leka, is the low mountain **Lekamøya** (124 m above sea level), a well-known landmark and one of the most legendary mountains in Norway. Seen from the south west the mountain appears to represent the shape of a woman with long, flowing, loose robes, running southwards. The legend tells that Lekamøya was running away from Hestmannen who had become besotted with her and had chased after her. When the sun's rays shone, all of the trolls involved in the legend were turned to stone. They now stand as well-known mountains along the coast of Nordland (p 315).

At Solsem on the island's southern part, the Finnish three-master "Fedrelandene" ran aground in a fierce storm on a February night in 1848.

The island of Leka also has other places of interest that are unfortunately not visible from the channel. **Solsemshulen** is an almost 40 m long, 4-6 m wide and 8 m high cave, that in ancient times was possibly a site of religious sacrifices. It is in an inaccessible location, approx. 78 m above sea level. In the inner part of the cave, two of the rock faces have been painted and show figures of approx. 20 dancing men and a cruciform figure. The figures are painted with a red colour and are 0.3–1 m high. These were discovered by local youths in 1912, and are the first cave paintings discovered in Northern Europe. The floor of the cave has been excavated and finds have been made of fish bones, seabirds, seals, goats, cows, horses, adult and infant humans, also tools and weapons. The finds have been dated to the early Stone Age or the Bronze Age (p 83).

On the island's north west side is **Kvaløy**. The place is best known for the famous "eagle incident". In 1932, a three year-old girl playing outside her home was taken by an eagle and taken to the eagle's nest on a mountain several hundred metres away. A huge search operation was mounted, and after eight hours of searching, the girl was rescued alive.

The mother of the Viking Gange-Rolv (Rollo), who founded the dukedom of Normandie in 911 (p 74) is said to have come from Leka. Gange-Rolv was the ancestor of William the Conqueror and is therefore distantly related to the British royal family.

On two of the mountain peaks on the island's west side there are remains of several village fortifications from the migration period (p 83). These are most likely village defences.

65°02'N 11°42'E	+ 2 hrs 07 min

On the starboard side we can see the southern tip of the islands of Leka and Madsøya. The island of **Dolmen** is to starboard up ahead. On the port side, after the southern end of the island **Austra**, is the mouth of the fjord **Råsa**, continuing behind the island **Austra** that we have just passed.

Approx. 65°01'40"N   11°41'16"E

We cross the boundary between Leka and Nærøy municipalities

We sail through the narrow sound **Dolmsundet** between the island of **Dolma** on the starboard side and the mainland, along the side of **Eiternestind** (239 m above sea level) and pass the headland of **Eiterneset**. The mouth of the fjord **Eiterfjorden** is on the port side just after the headland.

To starboard up ahead is the group of islands known as **Risværøyane.**

Next is the island of **Gjerdingen** with the small community of **Gjerdinga** that has a ferry connection to **Måneset** on the mainland, on the port side.

We continue along our journey along the narrow channel towards our next port of call, Rørvik.

In common with many other communities and towns found along the Hurtigruten voyage, **Rørvik** grew after the shipping fleet became motorised and permanent ship routes were established along the Norwegian coast. Rørvik was strategically placed along these routes and had good harbour facilities for this new type of ship. Rørvik was centrally located in the active fishing grounds and there were many larger fishing villages on the surrounding islands, not least on the islands of **Ytter-Vikna**, **Mellom-Vikna** and **Inner-Vikna** (p 120).

In 1862 it was decided that Rørvik should be developed as a local port of call for ships sailing along the coast. At that time there were only four property owners, however this was deemed as being sufficient to provide board for those travelling by boat. Rørvik was a port for the Nordlandsruten from 1863 and the Hurtigruten from 1893. The ships, carrying post, were served by rowing boats that went out to the ship that was anchored in the middle of the sound. At the same time the merchant Johan Berg established an enterprise at Rørvik and 'Bergsgården' became a centre of Rørvik's further growth. The main building was located such that it was visible to sailors and prominent visitors came to stay at Bergsgården. The store sold fishing gear, equipment and consumer goods. The homestead had a fine garden looking out towards the sea.

The post office and the postmaster's quarters were built and as early as 1876 the community had a telegraph office, largely due to the relatively frequent shipping traffic. A national telephone exchange was installed in 1896. During the years following 1860 and up to the turn of the century Rørvik grew considerably and gradually became the most important communications centre along the coast of Nord-Trøndelag. The community became a traffic hub, connecting ships sailing along the coast, the local boats that connected the districts, and a road network that was steadily improving. The Hurtigruten, that was established in 1893, arrived at the port once a week during the first few years, later this increased to daily routes. The ship had good cargo capacity and refrigera-

The ship docks at the quayside in Rørvik

tion facilities, which was of great importance to the development of the fishing industry in the area. It was not before 1920 that Rørvik had a suitable quay, until then all handling of shipping had been carried out via smaller 'transit boats'.

The current Rørvik is the municipal seat in Vikna municipality and the largest centre in Ytre Namdalen. Enterprises include: Fish processing industries, aquaculture, shipbuilding and telecommunications and sea rescue services. Rørvik also has a coastal museum, Norveg. The museum building is regarded as the coast's most spectacular landmark. The building was nominated for a prestigious European architecture prize in 2005.

In addition to collections and exhibitions at Rørvik, the museum also has the responsibility for Berggården in Rørvik, for the fishing hamlet Sør-Gjæslingane (p 118), Vågsengtunet and Woxeng's Collection, founded by the local historian Paul Woxeng (1883-1967), the restored ketch "Søblomsten" (1864) that sailed with cargoes of fish and timber along the Norwegian coast and the museum buildings at Rørvik.

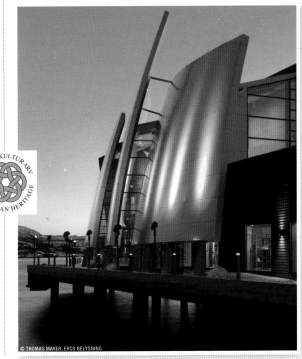

© THOMAS MAYER, ERCO BELYSNING

Nord-Trøndelag county

County coat of arms: Represents Olav the Holy's shield
Origin of name: From Norse *thændal*, combination of *thændr* and *log* 'law, jurisdiction'.
Area: 22 396 km². **Population:** 129 069.
County seat: Steinkjer.
We pass the following municipalities on our way southwards (in order): Leka, Nærøy, Vikna, Fosnes, Namsos and Flatanger.
Topography: The county has a great number of fjords and valleys that largely run in a south west to north easterly direction. At the end of the last Ice Age, large amounts of sand and clay were deposited on the shallow sea bed. This rose approximately 100 m along the coast and 200 m inland when the ice retreated. It formed wide, continuous arable areas, especially around Trondheimsfjorden. Inland of the coastal areas are wide, forested valleys and low mountain areas. Towards the Swedish border in the east, the mountains reach up to 1 200-1 500 m above sea level. The coastline is rugged, with many fjords and a large number of islands. 38 % of the area is under 300 m above sea level, 22 % over 600 m, of which 2 % is over 900 m. 7 % of the area is fresh water.
Climate: The inland areas are sheltered by the mountains and have a typical inland climate with moderate precipitation and cold winters. Outer, northern parts of the county are influenced by the Norwegian Sea and experience frequent high winds, especially in the open sea stretch at Folda. The annual average for the incidence of gales is 20 % and for storms 1 %. Fosen peninsula provides shelter for the lowlands in the south from the influence of the Norwegian Sea. The coldest month at the coast is February, with an average temperature of just over 0°C. The average temperature in summer is 13-15°C. Most precipitation falls along the coast in the autumn and in early winter.
Settlement. Densest in the lowlands around Trondheimsfjorden and in the lower part of Namdalen. Approx. 55 % of the population lives in larger communities, which is slightly below the national average.

TRADE AND INDUSTRY
Agriculture and forestry: The villages along Trondheimsfjorden have some of the country's finest agricultural land. Some areas in the north of the county also have excellent agricultural areas. Farms are mostly larger than the national average. Approx 33 % of agricultural land is used for growing corn, mostly barley. Only 8 % is used for other arable land. Cattle and dairy production. Potato and vegetable farming. 2 % of the area is productive forest, mostly spruce.
Fishing: In the coastal municipalities, fishing is an important activity. Approximately one-third of catches are of cod. Fish farming is of local significance.
Industry: Mining was formerly a major industry (iron ore and pyrites). However, operations ceased in the 1980s and 90s. Industry based on agricultural products and forestry are important, more recently major ship and oil installation yards have developed (Aker Verdal, oil rigs). Industry is largely concentrated around inner parts of Trondheimsfjorden. Timber processing and transport industries. Rubber and plastics industries.
Energy: There are a total of 33 hydroelectric power stations in the county.
Tourism: Large numbers of tourists visit or pass through the county during the summer months. Internationally renowned salmon rivers (Namsen and Stjørdalselva). Historical plays with the theme of Olav the Holy and the Battle of Stiklestad in 1030. Several Middle Ages churches and monastery ruins. Two national parks.
Communications: E6 and railway (Nordlandsbanen) connect the county to Northern Norway and the southern parts of the country. Branch lines connect smaller communities to the railway network. The largest islands all have connections to the mainland. Main airport at Trondheim Airport, Værnes. Smaller airstrips at Namsos and Rørvik.

Source: Store Norske Leksikon.

© LARS FORSETH

Egg and down gathering

The oldest written reference to egg and down collecting is found in Snorre Sturlason's King's Saga. The Viking adventurer Ottar (p 123) traded eggs and down with the Sámi in Finnmark. The Saga also tells of the Viking chieftain Hårek from Tjøtta (p 319). Hårek's men came into conflict with members of the chieftain clan Grankjellson (p 311) at Dønnes estate. The estate owned many of the islands islets and skerries along the Helgeland coast. Hårek's men felt so humiliated when they had their spoils taken from them after they were caught stealing on the islands, that they burned down the Dønnes mansion and

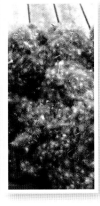

killed the chieftain and some of his men. Hårek himself was killed by the following generation of Grankjellson, as revenge for their murder. The Viking temperament was not to be underestimated when it came to eggs and down.

Egg and down gathering has always been an important part of coastal culture. The eggs were an important food source and down was a valuable export product. Traces of Eider ducks have been found in dwelling remains from the Stone Age and Eider are also depicted in cave paintings. Old land documents from the 15th-16th centuries often mention eggs and down as part of the assets of the farms and this had an effect on the scope of settlement on the islands. During the latter part of the Middle Ages the demand for down increased in Europe. The increasing value of down led to the regulation and protection of the collection sites in the 17th and 18th centuries.

The down was gathered from the female of the Eider duck. In February/March, the Eider ducks came in large flocks to breed on the outermost islands. The females often returned to the same nesting site each year. The birds built their nests on seaweed, along the shore or under a rocky slope. When the nest had been made, the female ducks would line their nests with down plucked from their breast, to make the nest comfortable and warm. The females laid 5-6 eggs during May/June. One or two of these were removed. When some of the down was collected from the nest, the females plucked new down and lined the nest again. The relationship

between birds and people was a good one – the birds were almost regarded as domesticated. People built small 'houses' of wood or stone and placed dried seaweed in and around them, to provide materials for nest building. They also fed the birds and protected them from predators. In the 1900s, some of the large farms had as many as 800 Eider ducks. Smaller farms could have as many as 200-300.

Today the business of down collection has declined considerably. People have moved away from the outermost islands and the process of caring for the birds and cleaning the down has become too expensive. Now that the people have left, the numbers of birds has also dwindled. They have many natural enemies, such as wild mink and otters.

The 'Dutch Trade' period

As early as the 10th century, fish was the most important export product from Norway. However, during the 17th century, timber became gradually more important for Norwegian exports. Most timber was exported to the Netherlands and later, to England. Timber from Norway was very much sought after in Europe, due to the proximity of the export harbours to the market and because the ports remained ice-free during the winter months. Not least, the Norwegian timber was of a high quality. The timber was cut in the large inland forests and floated down on rivers to the sawmills. Most of the export harbours were in southern Norway. However, some were located in Møre and Romsdal and Sør-Trøndelag. Timber was in great demand in the Netherlands, both for ship and boatbuilding and for the construction of towns and harbours throughout the country.

The timber export trade continued until the end of the 19th century, after which the export of cellulose and wood pulp took over.

Trondheim, Kristiansund, Molde and Ålesund

During the night, we have passed the municipalities of Nærøy, Vikna, Namsos and Flatanger, thereafter the boundary with Sør-Trøndelag county (p 122). We then sailed past the municipalities of Osen, Roan, Åfjord, Bjugn, Ørland, Agdenes and Rissa. We arrive in Trondheim at 06.30.

Trondheim history (p 87)

A walk around the centre of Trondheim (p 91)

The voyage between Trondheim and Agdenes lighthouse is described on the northbound route, Day 3 (p 87). This text includes positions, times and place names, with a reference to the relevant page in the guide containing more information.

The ship continues to Kristiansund	+ 0 hrs 00 min

LARGER MAP **P415**

The small island of **Munkholmen** (0.013 km²) passes to starboard shortly after leaving **Trondheim** (p 97).

We leave Trondheim behind us and sail out into **Trondheimsfjorden** (130 km in length and Norway's third longest). Trondheimsfjorden has several 'branches' (p 98)

63°27'22"N 10°19'34"E	+ 0 hrs 12 min ①

Trolla Brug passes on the port side (p 99).

Leksvik municipality lies up ahead, on the north side of Trondheimsfjorden.

Leksvik municipality… (p 100).

The community of **Vanvikan** (pop. 748) is on the starboard side, on the north side of Trondheimsfjorden (p 100).

We approach Rissa municipality on the starboard side.

Rissa municipality… (p 100).

After Vanvikan… (p 100).

The ship continues into Flakkfjorden… (p 100).

63°28'N 10°03'E	+ 0 hrs 40 min ②

The village of **Rein,** to starboard, is just before Raudbergneset and can be seen just ahead of the ship… (p 100).

Raudbergneset lies ahead and to starboard

The village of **Stadsbygda** lies just inside of **Raudbergneset**… (p 100).

Ahead, on our port side, is Agdenes municipality.

Agdenes municipality… (p 101).

63°29'39"N 9°56'04"E	+ 0 hrs 54 min

Ahead on the port side is the village of Ingdalen, in Agdenes municipality, on the western side of Trondheimsfjorden. Ingdalen chapel is from 1960, a wooden longhouse-style chapel with seating for 140.

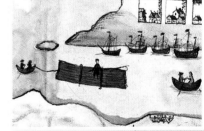

Ingdalen is an old industrial location. The Ingdal river system leads out into Ingdalen. The river runs through a large forested area and was therefore important for the lumber trade. The river was used for floating timber. A dam was built above the waterfall and a log channel was built to direct the timber safely past the falls. A water-driven saw was constructed in the 17th century and for quite some time the Ingdal sawmill produced timber for the Dutch market (p 333).

Water from the Ingdal waterfall powered a corn mill during the middle of the 17th century. In the middle of the 19th century, a mill for the manufacture of textiles was also in operation at the waterfall, producing hard-wearing woollen cloth.

We can see the village of **Tennel**.

The village of **Brøskift** (**Brødreskift**)… (p 101).

On the port side is the municipal centre of **Selbekken** (pop. 376) and the village of **Lensvik** in Agdenes municipality (p 101).

Over on the starboard side is the village of **Reinsgrenda** in Rissa municipality (p 102).

On a mound down towards the lake **Botnen** (5.6 km², 2 m above sea level), (not visible from the ship) is the historic mansion known as **Reinskloster**…(p 102).

63°32'N   9°52'E   + 1 hr 06 min ③

The industrial site of **Kvithylla** is on the starboard side, then Reinskloster, followed by **Sundsbukta**. The lake, Botnen, is just inside Kvithylla.

Rissaraset… (p 102).

Fosen Mek. Verksted (FMV) is at Kvithylla before Sundsbukta (p 102).

63°37'23"N   9°47'04"E   + 1 hr 28 min ④

We see Hambåra fortifications, on the port side, just before the headland of Selvnes (p 103).

Selvnes is over on the port side, with the village of **Selva** in the bay.

The former fortifications at Hysnes are on the starboard side at **Hysnes**, before Hasselvika… (p 103).

Hasselvika, a village in Rissa municipality, over to starboard, followed by Hysneset.

The old Brettingen fortifications at **Brettingsneset** stand north of Hasselvika. The fortifications date from 1898 and are part of military history. The site has been listed as being of 'special cultural interest'.

63°38'26"N   9°46'28"E   + 1 hr 32 min

Djupvika in Agdenes municipality is on the port side. (p 104).

Agdenes lighthouse stands on the port side, at the mouth of Trondheimsfjorden… (p 105).

63°39'16"N   9°43'E   + 1 hr 40 min ⑤

We change course and head towards the southwest. On the port side is **Agdenes**, and the sound **Trondheimsleia**.

According to historical records from approx. 1540, there is a valuable treasure, known as 'the Olav treasure' in the depths of the ocean just off Agdenes lighthouse... (p 105).

To starboard, up ahead is Ørland municipality with the municipal centre of **Brekstad**. **Stjørnfjorden** can be seen on the starboard side. In the innermost part of Stjørnfjorden is **Råkvåg** (pop. 255) (p 106).

In Stjørnfjorden on the starboard side, east of Brekstad, stands **Austrått** farm and Austrått fortifications. The spire on Austrått farm can just be seen through the trees, just to the left of a large barn (p 106).

63°39'13"N   9°45'25"E   + 1 hr 40 min

Austrått Manor, ahead on the starboard side is one of the oldest and most well known homesteads in Norway, and one of Norway's most important cultural heritage sites from the Middle Ages (p 106).

The mighty fortifications at Austrått fort at the mouth of Trondheimsfjorden were constructed by the German forces during the Second World War (p 107).

Agdeneståa, is the most northerly point of Agdenes municipality.

Through historical sources, Ørland church at Brekstad can be dated back to 1342.

Hovde is on the headland, south of **Brekstad** (p 107).

The villages of **Grande** and Beian pass by on the port side.

63°38'15"N 9°37'E	+ 1 hr 51 min

Beian (pop. approx. 100 in 2001), had been granted status as a guesthouse and coaching inn as early as 1799 (p 107).

"King Øystein's Harbour" is situated in a bay on the western side of Agdenes, southwest of Agdenes lighthouse (p 105).

63°39'N 9°42'E	+ 1 hr 52 min

On the starboard side are three islands: Garten (1.5 km²), behind is Storfosna (11 km²), and even further beyond is Hitra (571.5 km², with windmills).

63°39'10"N 9°41'31"E	+ 1 hr 54 min

As the ship turns south-westwards in the Trondheim channel, we pass the community of **Bcian** on the starboard side, then the island **Garten** (pop. approx. 210), with a bridge leading over to the mainland.

South of Garten, we can see the island of Storfosna. The sound running between the islands of Garten and Storfosna has rich shoals of fish, due to the strong tidal currents that run between the islands.

The island **Storfosna** (11 km², 158 m above sea level) is on the starboard side (p 108).

Just outside of Storfosna, we can see the northern tip of Fjellværsøya in Hitra municipality.

63°38'N 9°35'39"E	+ 1 hr 54 min

On the port side, we have passed the ferry quay at **Valset** where the ferry leaves for **Brekstad** in Ørland, the islet of **Meholmen** and the village **Vassbygda**.

Up ahead and to starboard is the large island of Hitra with Fjellværsøya and Ulvøya. Further west is the island **Frøya**.

Ahead, on the starboard side, we approach the two small islands of Nordleksa and Sørleksa.

63°36'N 9°28'46"E	+ 2 hrs 04 min ⑥

On the port side, we sail by the community of **Værnes** with Agdenes church.

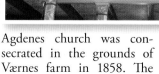

Agdenes church was consecrated in the grounds of Værnes farm in 1858. The church, which is a wooden longhouse-style construction, originally had 329 seats. The altarpiece is from 1918.

At the outermost point of **Vernestangen**, out towards **Trondheimsleia,** a burial site has been discovered containing 10 large and some smaller burial mounds, with diamctcrs from 2.5 up to 20 m.

Between Vernestangen and **Seterneset** is the mouth of the narrow fjord **Verrafjorden**, with the steep mountain **Terningsheia** (533 m above sea level) in the background.

Approx. 63°35'34"N   9°27'E

On the port side, we cross the municipal boundary between Agdenes and Snillfjord

Snillfjord municipality

Municipal coat of arms, significance: Symbolizes agriculture.
Meaning of name: First part from an ancient name of a river, from Norse snild, from snjallr, 'quick', meaning 'fast-flowing river'.
Municipal seat: Krokstadøra (-).
Position: 63°23'N 9°30'E. **Area:** 508 km².
Population: 1 021. **Pop. density:** 2.0 /km².
Area distribution: Farming 3 %, forestry 21 %, fresh water 4%, other area 73 %.
Trade and industry: Agriculture. Cattle and sheep farming, combined with forestry or fishing. Fish farming. Some full-time forestry. Timber and furniture industry. Mechanical workshops. Rubber and plastics industry.
Places to return to: Hemnskjell coastal fort/museum.
Snillfjord municipality's home page: www.snillfjord.kommune.no

63°34'50"N   9°24'37"E   + 2 hrs 16 min

On the starboard side, we pass the islands of **Nordleksa** and **Sørleksa** in Agdenes municipality. We can also see he ferry quay, **Gjerdet**, on the northern part of the island Nordleksa, with the connection to Vernes, the islands of Garten, Sørleksa and to Kongensvollen.

On the north side of the island Nordleksa, there is an undersea reef at a depth of 175 m. It is 500 m in length, 35 m high and 200 m wide.

The Leksa islands are mentioned in Olav Tryggvason's Saga and in Snorre Sturlason's King's Saga. According to the Sagas, there was a large burial site from prehistoric times on Sørleksa. It was placed such that it could be seen from both sides of the island. On the Leksa islands, several ancient monuments have been discovered, including a cairn dating from the Bronze Age. There are also remains of a Stone Age settlement that is comprised of 10, possibly more, circular dwelling foundations from the early Stone Age (p 83).

To port is the small, flat island of **Moldtun** before the mouth of the short fjord **Imsterfjorden.** The island **Åsøya** lies at the outermost point of the fjord. The village and ferry quay at **Kongensvollen** are on the southwest side of Imsterfjorden. The ferry provides a connection to **Leksa** on the island of Sørleksa

Approx. 63°33'N   9°17'29"E

On the starboard side is the boundary between Ørland and Hitra municipalities

Hitra municipality

Municipal coat of arms, significance: Depicts the deer found in the area.
Meaning of name: From Norse Hitrar, likely meaning 'split, divided'.
Municipal seat: Fillan (pop. 485).
Position: 63°36'20"N 8°58'41"E.
Area: 680 km². **Population:** 4.028.
Pop. density: 5.9 /km².
Area distribution: Farming 3 %, forestry 14 %, fresh water 5 %, other area 78 %.
Trade and industry: Agriculture. Fishing (crab, cod). Fish farming (salmon and rainbow trout). Fishing industry. Kelp factory. Boatyard with slipway. Dairy. Cement factory. Windmill park.
Places to return to: Dolmen town. Terningen lighthouse.
Activities to return to: Deer hunting.
Hitra municipality's home page:
www.hitra.kommune.no

© DARIJUS STRASUNSKAS

Most of Hitra is flat marshland. Some of the marshes are up to 100 m above sea level. Rocky outcrops rise from the marshes; these are highest in the southwest and in the middle of the island. In total, the municipality is comprised of 2 500 islands, islets and skerries, most of these lie north of Hitra. There is a large flock of hart (deer) in the inner part of the island.

Frøya municipality is West of Hitra, out in the ocean.

Frøya municipality

Municipal coat of arms, significance: Historically, fishing has always been the most important commercial activity in the municipality, and remains so today.
Meaning of name: From the god, Frøy, gothic frauja, 'man, foremost'.
Municipal seat: Sistranda (pop. 690).
Position: 63°43'N 8°50'E. **Area:** 231 km².
Population: 4.052. **Pop. density:** 17.5 /km².
Area distribution: Farming 4 %, forestry - %, fresh water 4 %, other area 92 %.
Trade and industry: Fishing, fish processing. Fish and shell farming (salmon, rainbow trout, scallops and mussels) Some textile, plastics and mechanical industry. Agriculture as a secondary activity. Sheep farming. Wind power generation.
Places to return to: Frøya Village Museum.
Frøya municipality's home page:
www.froya.kommune.no

Frøya municipality is comprised of approx. 5 400 islets and skerries. The island of **Frøya** is the largest (151.9 km²). The extended archipelago provides shelter from the ocean to the west. The landscape is hilly and treeless. The marshland areas provide an ideal environment for birds and the island is a stopover, breeding and winter home for many species. Approx. 20 % of the Norwegian stocks of Cormorants breed here - approx. 30 000 Cormorants stay throughout the winter (p 218).

The group of islands known as Sula is comprised of a group of barren islets 15 km northeast of Frøya. Some of the islands have landing stages and a minor amount of fish processing is carried out, as well as fish farming. The islands have a fast boat connection with Frøya and Trondheim.

63°33'48"N 9°20'17"E + 2 hrs 23 min

In the background of Sørleksa is **Fjellværsøya** (26.7 km²), northeast of Hitra, with a bridge connecting the island and the smaller island **Ulvøya** (6.4 km²) that lies just north. The main commercial activities here are agriculture, fishing, fish farming and processing.

The island of **Hitra** (571.5 km²) is Norway's seventh largest island and the largest island south of Nordland county. The community and administrative centre is **Fillan**, which is in **Fillfjorden,** southwest of Fjellværsøya. Fillan church is a cruciform church dating from 1789.

On the mountain **Eidfjellet**, north west of the municipal centre of Fillan, 24 power generator windmills were erected in 2004. They have a maximum output of 55 MW and a supply line 10 km in length that runs to Fillan.

Hitra has Northern Europe's largest stocks of hart (deer) and offers excellent opportunities for hunting.

The community of **Hestvika** (pop. 231) is on the starboard side, in the north west on Hitra. The islands **Utsetøya, Børøyholmen, Stora** and **Vedøya** lie just off the headland. In Hestvika there are various industries, fish farms and landing stages. A new industrial area is being planned.

Børøyholmen lighthouse at Hestvika, was constructed in 1874. The lighthouse was closed down and replaced by an automated beacon in 1970.

The island **Dolmøya** (14.5 km², 63 m above sea level) lies between Frøya and Hitra, with a bridge built across the narrow sound, **Dolmsundet.** On Dolmøya there are ruins of a stone church from the early Middle Ages. The island also has a miniature town known as "Dolmen Town" with approx. 700 houses, boats and a harbour.

The Frøya Tunnel, 5.3 km in length, 164 m under sea level, runs under Frøyfjorden, between Dolmøya and the island Frøya. The tunnel was opened in 2000.

63°33'N 9°17'E + 2 hrs 30 min

In Snillfjord municipality on the port side, we can see the village of **Vingan**, west of the mountain **Blåfjellet** (526 m above sea level). There is an interesting story about the islet, **Storholmen**, in the bay. Queen Elizabeth II of England went ashore here in 1969, with her children Anne, Andrew and Edward, to swim and to take lunch. They were sailing with the royal yacht "Britannia" when they discovered this beauty spot. Since then Storholmen has also been known as **Dronningholmen** (Queen's Islet).

A whaling station was in operation at **Vingvågen** near Vingan, between 1917-1925. In 1905 a ban on land-based whaling operations was introduced. Norway remained a neutral country during thc First World War (1914-1918), however the Norwegian Merchant Marine suffered great losses, supplies could not reach the country and there were food shortages. To help the situation, the ban on whaling stations (p 214) was repealed and five land-based whaling stations were established - one of them was the station at Vingvågen. Three whaling boats used the station as a base; 50 men worked at the station and each of the three boats had a crew of 10.

The whales provided meat for food and useful oil products. Both of these products were in short supply. Much of the whale meat was sold in Trondheim and a motor boat had a fixed route to Trondheim carrying products to the markets in Trondheim as long as the station remained in operation.

Vingvågen lay a little too far from the whaling grounds and the pollution from the whaling station was excessive. In 1925 it was decided to move the station to outer Hitra. During the eight years it was in operation, 2 249 whales of various species were caught and brought to the whaling station at Vingvågen.

We see the mountain **Kamvikfjellet** before the narrow mouth of the fjord **Valslagvågen,** with the mountain **Aunhesten** and the headland **Trollvikskjeret.** Just outside the fjord is the small islet of **Svansholmen.**

63°32'12"N   9°13'51"E   + 2 hrs 39 min

On the starboard side, after the islands of **Storøy** and **Vedøya** we sail by the villages of **Strand** and **Badstuvika,** before the community of **Sandstad** and the island **Jøsnøya.** Sandstad church was built in 1888 and has seating for 350.

To starboard up ahead is the low island of **Hemnskjel,** and we can also see the eastern end of the Hitra tunnel.

An old legend has it that at one time there was a forest on Hemnskjel. However, the forest was burned down in order to capture some robbers that had hidden among the trees. Large, old roots have been found in the marshes on the island, which is proof that in fact there were once trees on the island.

Flint axes and arrowheads from approx. 8 000 B.C. have also been discovered on the island, as well as the 'Hemnskjell treasure', an item of decorative Bronze Age jewellery dated from approx. A.D. 900.

On the 19th July 1929 the yacht "Naz-Perwer" ('Beautiful Lady') sank close to the uninhabited island of Ystholmen, approx. 1 nautical mile north east of Hemnskjel. The yacht, which was 235 ft. long, 29 ft. wide and had a draft of 17 ft., was built in Leith in Scotland and was launched in 1924. The owner was the Egyptian Prince Yousouf Kamal from Cairo.

The yacht was on a trip to Norway with a relative of the owner, the Egyptian Prince Amr. Ibrahim, his wife, some friends and a crew of 30. In total there were 39 people on board, including two Norwegian pilots. On the way to Nordkapp the yacht ran into thick fog at Terningen lighthouse. Just after 6 o'clock in the morning the yacht ran aground. All of those on board were rescued, apart from one of the crew. crew. All were taken to Trondheim by ship.

The operation to salvage the "Naz-Perwer" was complicated and took two months, despite the efforts of three salvage tugs and a steamship. The yacht proved to be seriously damaged and was towed to Trondheim. It was later sold to a company in Sweden to be broken for scrap.

During the Second World War, Hemnskjel was heavily occupied by the German forces. At one time there were as many as 600 troops stationed on the island. There are still gun emplacements and bunkers, trenches and remains of walls and barracks remaining. A bunker that was used as a communications base has been restored as a small museum with pictures, artefacts, maps and charts showing the location of former minefields.

63°30'32"N   9°07'27"E

Hitra tunnel (5 645 m in length) connects the islands Hitra, Frøya and Fjellværsøya with the mainland. An undersea tunnel runs under Trondheimsleia from Sandstad (to starboard) to the island Hemnskjel (4.4. km²) on the port side, and from there is a bridge to the mainland. The tunnel was, at the time, the world's deepest tunnel when it was opened in 1994.

The easily recognisable Terningen lighthouse passes on the starboard side. The lighthouse was constructed in 1833 and has a 12 m high concrete tower. The light itself stands 17.8 m over the sea and the range is 13.4 nautical miles. The lighthouse had a foghorn from 1923, replaced by a compressed air siren from 1958-82. The lighthouse was automated in 1991.

We continue sailing in Trondheimsleia.

Approx. 63°29'N   9°03'E

We cross the boundary between Snillfjord and Hemne municipalities on the port side

Hemne municipality

Municipal coat of arms, significance: Indicates that hazel forest is found in the municipality.
Meaning of name: From Norse Hefni, probably fjord name meaning 'harbour'.
Municipal seat: Kyrksæterøra (pop. 2.499).
Position: 63°17'17"N 9°06'E. **Area:** 659 km².
Population: 4 247. **Pop. density:** 6.3 /km².
Area distribution: Farming 3 %, forestry 21 %, fresh water 5 %, other area 71 %.
Trade and industry: Agriculture, forestry. Cattle, livestock. Smelting plant for ferrosilicon, silisium and silica. Foodstuffs and timber companies. Shoe factory. Transport companies. Windmill park.
Places to return to: Magerøya Guest House.
Hemne municipality's home page: www.hemne.kommune.no

The fjord **Hemnefjorden** (25 km in length) lies to port of Terningen lighthouse. The boundary between Snillfjord and Hemne municipalities is in the middle of the fjord. The fjord has three 'branches', **Åstfjorden** in a north-easterly direction, **Snillfjorden** that runs parallel with Åstfjorden, with the community of **Snillfjord** at the innermost part, and **Hemnefjorden** with the industrial area **Kyrksæterøra** (pop. 2 499) innermost in the fjord.

| 63°29'03"N 9°00'42"E | + 3 hrs 04 min |

On the port side we pass the island **Stamnesøya** and the headland **Kråka**, out towards Trondheimsleia.

| 63°28'22"N 8°57'34"E | + 3 hrs 10 min |

The small island of **Magerøya** (6.7 km²) can be seen on the port side after passing the headland. The island has most likely been inhabited since before the Viking era. Up to 1537, it belonged to the Archbishop of Nidaros; however, in 1684 the tenants on the island were granted official inn status by royal decree, with a "duty to provide their guests with good beer and spirits, light and warmth". The island had its 'golden age' as a trading post in the latter part of the 19th century. Descendants of the same family lived on the island for 250 years, until 1929 when the trading post was compulsorily auctioned. The island became uninhabited in 1965. Today, there is a small guesthouse on the island, which is open during the summer season.

We continue to sail by Hitra's sparsely populated shores. On the starboard side is **Ballsnes**, and to port is Røstøya.

The island of **Røstøya,** after Magerøya, is currently uninhabited. It was purchased by the state as a recreatio-

nal area and in 1992 the whole island became protected under the Conservation Act.

Between Røstøya and the mainland is **Tannsundet**.

At **Taftøy**, on the mainland on the port side, an industrial site has been developed in connection with the petroleum industry operations at Tjeldbergodden.

The industrial area at Tjeldbergodden can be seen ahead on the port side.

| Approx. 63°26'N 8°44'E |

We cross the boundary between Hemne and Aure municipalities, on the port side

Aure municipality

Municipal coat of arms, significance: Symbolizes the traditional dried fish industry.
Meaning of name: From Norse place name, *Aurar*, originally plural of aurr, 'gravel'. Refers to the large gravel masses located at river mouths.
Municipal seat: Aure (pop. 599).
Position: 63°15'51"N 8°31'12"E. **Area:** 503 km².
Population: 3 515. **Pop. density:** 7.0 /km².
Area distribution: Farming 3 %, forestry 32 %, fresh water 3 %, other area 62 %.
Trade and industry: Landing stage for gas brought ashore via the pipeline from the Heidrun field. Methanol and air gas plant. Agriculture in combination with other trades. Cattle farming, dairy production. Sheep farming. Fishing. Two traditional boat builders.
Places to return to: Stutzpunkt Melland.
Aure municipality's home page: www.aure.kommune.no

The municipality is comprised of a mainland area and the larger islands of Ertvågsøya, Skardsøya, Lesundøya, Grisvågøya, Stabblandet, Tustna and several smaller islands.

| 63°26'13"E 8°47'09"E | + 3 hrs 33 min |

Up ahead on our port side is the bay and the village of **Kjørsvik**, then the industrial area Tjeldbergodden. Behind them is the mountain **Fonna** (722 m above sea level).

The Kjørsvik sawmill, at **Kjørsvikbugen** has a history that goes back to the 17th century. It is one of the oldest and most traditional sawmills in Aure. During the 'Hollander period', a period of trade with the Netherlands, many Dutch ships anchored here, waiting to load their cargo of timber (p 333).

An aquaculture installation is situated at Kjørsvikbugen. Heated water from the cooling plant is piped approx.

1 km from the methanol plant at Tjeldbergodden, to supply a lobster hatchery and a salmon farm.

63°26'03"N 8°41'54"E   + 3 hrs 38 min ⑧

When the industrial area at **Tjeldbergodden** was constructed in the middle of the 1990s, it was one of the largest industrial projects in Norwegian history. The large industrial area is located on a shelf on the low landscape, which has been excavated down to the level of the fjord. The site, which was officially opened in June 1997, is comprised of four plants, gas landing stage, methanol plant, air gas plant and LNG (Liquefied Natural Gas) plant. The site is operated by the Norwegian oil company StatoilHydro.

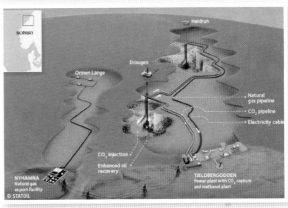

Tjeldbergodden is the landing stage for gas brought ashore from the Heidrun field, located on the Halten bank in the Norwegian Sea, approx. 50 nautical miles off the coast of Flatanger in Nord-Trøndelag (p 116). The petroleum field, which is at a depth of 350 m, was discovered in 1985. A development plan was approved in 1991 and production began in 1995. Extracted oil is brought onshore from a storage buoy by ships. The gas is transferred in a separate pipeline, Haltenpipe, to Tjeldbergodden. The pipeline became operative in December 1996. It is approx. 250 km in length. 35 km of the pipeline runs close to shore. The pipeline has an inner diameter of 16" (40.6 cm) and can transport approx. 7.2 million m^3 of gas per day. Only a fraction of the gas is used at the methanol plant at Tjeldbergodden.

The methanol plant is one of the largest in the world and one of the most energy-efficient. When the plant became operative, it was the first time that natural gas had been used for large-scale industrial production in Norway. The capacity of the plant is approx. 900 000 tonnes of methanol annually, which corresponds to approx. 25 % of Europe's collective production capacity for methanol and 13 % of Europe's requirements. The methanol produced from the natural gas at Tjeldbergodden is frequently used in the chemical industry, as fuel, as a solvent and antifreeze. There are plans to expand the plant, which will increase the production capacity to 1 200 000 tons of methanol per annum.

The air gas plant at Tjeldbergodden is the largest in Scandinavia. Air gas is a common term for gases that are extracted from air (often called industrial gases). The air gas plant liquefies air so that it can be distilled, i.e. fractionated to oxygen, nitrogen and argon. Oxygen and nitrogen are used in the plants at Tjeldbergodden and all three of the gases are exported to customers in Norway and Scandinavia. Oxygen is used in industry, for welding, fish farming, medical use etc. Nitrogen is used as an inert gas (i.e. it does not have a tendency to form compounds with other substances) and argon is used as an inert gas for welding and in the metallurgy industry.

LNG (Liquefied Natural Gas) is natural gas that has been liquefied at a low temperature. From Tjeldbergodden the gas is transported to consumers in the Trondheim area.

StatoilHydro and Shell cooperate on the "Halten CO2-project", and are one of the 12 selection candidates for the pilot project for the development of technology that will help the EU states reduce discharges of CO2 to the atmosphere. The project is now (2007) in a phase of technological and commercial development and evaluation (concept phase).

To starboard we can see the southern tip of Hitra and several small islands – the largest of these are **Værøyan** and **Ramsøya**. On the starboard side just ahead is the low island Smøla. **Ramsøyfjorden,** which opens out into the Norwegian Sea, is between Hitra and Smøla.

63°25'30"N 8°38'E	+ 3 hrs 45 min

On the starboard side we pass the sound **Dromnessundet**, then the island **Skardsøya** (52.3 km² 390 m above sea level), with the village of **Skipnes** that is on the north eastern side, then **Finnset** and **Livsneset** on the north western tip of the island. On the headland of **Dromnes** after Tjeldbergodden, before the mouth of Dromnessundet, there are many burial mounds from the Bronze Age. The farm at Dromnes is mentioned in ancient documents and was probably the oldest in the area (early Iron Age).

63°23'N 8°34'41"E	+ 4 hrs 04 min

At the farm **Finnset** on Skardsøya's south western side, there is a German fortification, built during the Second World War, known as "Stutzpunkt Melland". The fortifications had eight gun and anti-aircraft emplacements, sanatorium, barracks, prison camp, bunkers and an electric generator. A local railway line was built leading to the fortifications.

On the mountain behind Finnset, **Vettaheia** (390 m above sea level) was the site of a cairn built by King Håkon I (Håkon the Good) (918-961) (p 82).

Further in the fjord is the farm Melland, which is mentioned in written sources as long ago as the 16th century. The farm was crown property until the 18th century.

Skardsøya has two bridges connecting it to the mainland, one in the south and another in the east.

We then follow, on the port side the smaller islands of **Lesundøya** and **Grisvågøya** (13.9 km²). **Lesund,** on the

western side of Lesunøya has one of the oldest settlements in the municipality, dating from the early Iron Age. The settlement probably extended over both islands.

The islands are connected by a bridge. Another bridge provides a connection to the mainland. Behind the islands are the fjords **Gjerdavika** and **Torsetsundet.** Torsetsundet bridge, completed in 1976 is 355 m in length.

The mountainous island Ertvågsøya (140 km², 694 m above sea level) can be seen after Grisvågøya, followed by the islands of Stabblandet and Tustna.

Behind the south eastern tip of Hitra, to starboard, we can see the western tip of Frøya (p 339). Slettringen lighthouse on the island of **Slettringen**, is the tallest lighthouse in Norway, with a height of 45 m. The lighthouse was constructed in 1899 and has a range of 18.5 nautical miles. The lighthouse also has an auxiliary light that was built the same year. It has a fog signal, a siren installed in 1923; this was replaced by a compressed air-operated horn in 1968. The lighthouse was automated in 1993. It was granted listed status in 2000.

South-west on Frøya, close to Slettringen lighthouse is the traditional fishing village of **Titran** (pop. approx. 130), formerly one of the most important fishing communities in the area. During the peak season the excellent harbour could be filled with scores of boats and hundreds of fishermen.

The Titran disaster is one of the greatest catastrophes to occur in Norwegian fishing history. On the 18th October 1899, 29 fishing boats with a total of 140 fishermen on board sank in a fierce storm that had moved northwards along the coast. The unsuspecting fishermen had set out for the herring grounds when the weather was still calm - however, at around midnight the storm hit them with hurricane force winds and lashing rain. A warning of impending bad weather had been issued further south along the coast, but because there was no telephone line to Frøya it had not been possible to warn the fishermen on the island. Even though a telephone line had been planned for several years, it was not installed until a month after the disaster. Some time later, an extremely successful national charity fund was set up for the dependents of the victims. Near the church on Titran, a memorial monument has been erected with the names of the 140 fishermen who died in the disaster.

Titran has a landing stage, a fish processing factory and a land-based fish farm. Titran has the first wind-driven power station to be built in Norway (1986). A second one was built in 1989.

Approx. 63°22'N 8°23'E

We cross the boundary between Hitra and Smøla municipalities on the port side

Smøla municipality

Municipal coat of arms, significance: The close relationship of the municipality with the coast and ocean.
Meaning of name: In the Middle Ages written Smyl, like smule, 'crumbled', likely to reflect the many islets and skerries around Smøla.
Municipal seat: Hopen (-).
Position: 63°27'57"N 8°00'34"E. **Area:** 282 km².
Population: 2 165. **Pop. density:** 7.7 /km².
Area distribution: Farming 5 %, forestry 1 %, fresh water 4 %, other area 90 %.
Trade and industry: Agriculture and fishing. Dairy production. Vegetable growing. Fish farming. Production of dried fish. Foodstuffs industry connected to fishing. Mechanical industry. Window manufacturer.
Smøla municipality's home page: www.smola.kommune.no

© FLICKR

On the western side of the island of Smøla is Smøla windmill park. When the second construction phase was completed in 2005 it became Europe's largest windmill park with 68 turbines. The windmills are up to 70 m high and have a blade span of up to 80 m. The windmill turbines produce electricity corresponding to the normal consumption of 20 000 households.

In the Norwegian Sea north of Smøla lies the idyllic island of **Veiholmen** (0.6 km², pop. approx. 250) which is rich in culture and tradition. The community of **Veiholmen**, with the neighbouring community of **Innveien**, is the largest active fishing community in Norway south of Lofoten, with an extensive fleet of fishing vessels. The fishing communities have a road connection via bridges and breakwaters, over islets and skerries, to Smøla.

There were probably permanent settlements on Veiholmen around the year A.D. 1100 or earlier. In the latter half of the 14th century a church was built here. The altarpiece from the church, which has been kept at Oslo University's ancient artefact collection since the 1870s, has been dated to the 16th century. It was probably made by artisans from the Hansa town of Lübeck in Germany. The church was demolished in 1749, as it was in poor repair. A new church was consecrated at **Hopen**, in the north of Smøla in the same year.

The oldest existing building on Veiholmen is a stone cairn at **Verket**. The cairn was used as a landmark for sailors and was probably erected before the 15th century.

Haugjegla lighthouse stands on a flat island north of Veiholmen. The lighthouse was built in 1905, and has functioned as a channel beacon since 1922. The lighthouse tower is a 28 m high cast iron tower on a 7 m high concrete base. It has a range of 15.3 nautical miles. Haugjegla lighthouse was automated in 1988. The lighthouse has listed status under the Cultural Heritage Act.

Skalmen lighthouse, a white house with a low tower, stands northwest of the island of Smøla. It stands 24 m above sea level and was built in 1907. It has a range of 14.8 nautical miles. There is an auxiliary light in the same building. The lighthouse was automated in 2002. The first lighthouse keeper was the Second Officer on Roald Amundsen's Gjøa expedition (p 224). He brought one of the sled dogs back with him from the expedition. At the lighthouse there is a paw print in the concrete, which is said to have been made by this dog.

63°20'N 8°18'41"E   + 4 hrs 24 min ⑨

Up ahead on the starboard side, in the fjord **Edøyfjorden** before the low and marshy island of **Edøya** (7.5 km²). We pass the two small islands of **Glassøya** and **Lauvøya**. On both of these islands, several relic sites have been discovered.

To starboard we pass Tyrhaug lighthouse, built on the islet **Ringholmen**. The lighthouse was built in 1833 and has a range of 13.4 nautical miles. The lighthouse was automated in 1967.

On the port side we can see the island **Tustna**. Just before Tustna is the island **Stabblandet** (40 km²) with the mountains **Storøra** (905 m above sea level) and **Stabben** (908 m above sea level). The low island **Solskjeløya** lies north of Stabblandet. A cable ferry runs between the two islands.

According to Snorre Sturluson's King's Sagas, two battles were fought on Solskjeløya, in connection with the unification of the country during the reign of Harald Hårfagre (Harold Fairhair) who was king from 865-933. The battles took place 9 and 8 years before the battle at Hafrsfjord in approx. 885, when Norway became united as one kingdom. Tustna was also the site of a battle in 1208.

63°18'N   8°08'45"E   + 4 hrs 37 min

The low island **Edøya** (7.5 km², 41 m above sea level) on the starboard side is largely marshland. It is the second largest island in Smøla municipality. Many ancient relics have been discovered on the island, from the Viking era and earlier (p 83). The proximity of the cultural relics is said to be the densest in Norway. The most well-known and visible monument is Edøy old church, a stone church dating from approx. 1190. The church also functioned as a meeting place for sailors and local residents for many hundred years. The shore close to the church was known as a good place to weigh anchor.

Edøy old church is one of the two oldest stone churches in Nordmøre. It was probably built as a private chapel for the commissioner on Edøya and was somewhat smaller than today. The front of the church has been built some time later, probably before 1695. In 1887, the timbers of the church were burned away by a fire caused by a lightning strike. Only the altarpiece, two candelabra, a stool and a counter were saved. The altarpiece was later moved to a museum in Kristiansund where it was destroyed during the bomb raids on the town in 1940 (p 350). The church lay in ruins until 1946. The German occupying forces used the ruins of the church as a munitions store. During the construction of the new church, a bunker

from the war was used as the church floor. This is one of the few wartime bunkers in Norway that have been granted protected status. Edøy church was finally restored and consecrated in 1950. The church bells are tuned in the key of E and G, in deference to the initials of the forenames of the benefactor's parents. The church was redecorated in 1990 in connection with the 800th anniversary and a new organ was installed.

Every summer, during the island's cultural activity week, the outdoor play "Madam Guri from Edøy" is performed. The play tells the story of everyday life at Edøy farm as it was 800 years ago

On the southern side of Edøy there are many bunkers and gun emplacements from the Second World War. A large battery of guns was strategically placed at the mouth of **Trondheimsleia,** which we have just sailed through. Several ships were sunk here.

Edøya is connected by road to Smøla.

Near Edøya is the island of **Kuli** (70 m above sea level), that has traces of Stone Age and Iron Age settlements (p 83). On Kuli there are several burial sites from the Iron Age. There is also a copy of the Kuli Stone, the most famous of the rune stones discovered in Norway. The original, dating from 1034, was moved in 1913 to the Science Museum in Trondheim. The vertically-carved inscriptions on the original stone were first discovered in 1956. The vertically-carved inscriptions on the original stone were first discovered in 1956. The discovery was a sensation at the time. They were interpreted as "Tore and Halvard erected this stone" and "Christianity has existed in Norway for twelve summers". The stone is the oldest, Norwegian written source that mentions Christianity in Norway. The language symbols used indicate that the inscription was made by a bilingual missionary, who used both Nordic and Anglo-Saxon languages.

Most of the small islands in Smøla municipality were depopulated in the 1950s and 60s. Some of the houses are now used as holiday homes.

On the port side we pass the three larger islands Ertvågsøya, Stabblandet and Tustna. The sound Aursundet separates these from the mainland.

On the eastern side of **Aursundet** is Aure church. The first church on this site is thought to have been one of the oldest in Norway, mentioned in Snorre Sturlason's King's Saga, when it was said to have been burned by Trondheim

hordes about 1 000 years ago. The Maria church in Aure was mentioned in documents from the 1430s. A later stave church was demolished in 1725. It was replaced by a cruciform church with seating for 750 – this burned down after being struck by lightning in 1923. In 1924 the largest wooden church in the county was completed, with 800 seats. It has an altarpiece from the Middle Ages.

The farm Aure has lent its name to the whole municipality. There have been settlements on this site since the early Iron Age and the site is one of the oldest in the municipality.

On the small island of **Ruøya** in Aursundet, lay Hamna, a central trading post from the early 18th century until 1830. The guesthouse and the general store were active at Hamna until 1829, when the houses were demolished and the business was moved to **Lurvika**, on the peninsula **Rottøya** in the south east. In the 17th century, the bay at Ruøya was used by Dutch ships that arrived to load timber from area (p 333). There were probably already buildings on land to service the boats. Later, a coaching inn, post office, bakery, general store and guesthouse were opened. In the 1870s Lurvika comprised of 23 buildings. Later, a steamship administration office was also opened.

The rocky, but lush Ertvågsøya (140 km²) with **Korsbakkfjellet** (694 m above sea level) can be seen further on the port side. In the middle of the island, behind the small island of **Jøssøya**, the long and narrow 7 km long fjord Follfjorden cuts into land in an easterly direction. The sea has to pass two narrow channels in the fjord at high and low tide. This makes Foldfjordstraumen one of

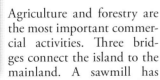

Northern Europe's fastest flowing ocean currents (p 162).

Agriculture and forestry are the most important commercial activities. Three bridges connect the island to the mainland. A sawmill has been in operation in various guises at the former ferry quay at **Vinsternes** on the western side of the island since 1614. Several new bridges connecting the islands, new roads and a new ferry service to the mainland are collectively known as the 'Imarsund roadway' that links the islands in Aure municipality and connects them to the mainland. The Imarsund roadway was opened in 2006.

63°15'33"N   8°05'E   + 4 hrs 57 min

Further south in Edøyfjorden, on the port side is the rocky island of **Tustna** (89 km²), with the mountains **Skarven** (896 m above sea level) and **Jørenvågsalen** (857 m above

sea level). At the side of Tustna is the island Stabblandet, between Stabblandet and Tustna is the narrow sound **Soleimsundet.** Most of the houses here are built along the shoreline. Agriculture and livestock farming along with fishing are the most important commercial activities. The production of dried fish ('klippfisk') is an old tradition on Tustna. On the island's southern side there are pine forests.

The island **Golma** is the largest of the smaller islands that lie south west of the island Tustna. On the port side is the small island **Møyslåtten**, and other small islets.

Behind the islands Stabblandet and Tustna are the fjords **Talgsjøen** and **Vinjefjorden**, with the municipalities of Tingvold and Halsa on the mainland.

Approx. 63°10'N   7°45'E   ⑩
We cross the boundary between Aura and Kristiansund municipalities

Kristiansund municipality

Municipal coat of arms, significance: From town charter. Current symbol from 1900.
Meaning of name: Origin Christian VI, who granted the town a trade charter. Previously called Fosna, from Norse Folgsn, 'hiding place'.
Municipal seat: Kristiansund (pop. 16 820).
Position: 63°06'48"N 7°44'17"E. **Area:** 22 km².
Population: 17 094. **Pop. density:** 777.0 /km².
Area distribution: Farming 2 %, forestry - %, fresh water - %, other area 98 %.
Trade and industry: Foodstuffs industry, fish processing, canning and freezer plants. Operations and supply base for offshore activities in central Norway. Oil industry-related commerce. Chemical and graphic design industries.
Kristiansund municipality's home page: www.kristiansund.kommune.no

1.1.2008 Kristiansund and the neighbouring municipality of Frei were merged into one municipality.

The group of islands known as **Grip** is over on the port side, 14 km north west of Kristiansund. The 82 islands are low, flat and almost without soil. The islands' cemetery is therefore on the island of Averøy (p 352). From 1897 to 1964 Grip was a separate municipality, the smallest in Norway.

The island **Gripholmen** (0.04 km²) has been inhabited since the Middle Ages, possibly as early as the 9th century. Grip stave church stands on the island, dating from

the 1470s. It is one of Norway's smallest and simplest of its type. The church was restored and rebuilt in 1621. The decorative painting is from the time of the rebuild. The altarpiece is from approx. 1515 and probably originates from Northern Germany, a gift from Princess Elisabeth of The Netherlands, who was the wife of King Christian II (1481-1559). Grip church was restored once more in connection with the construction of a new porch and vestry in the 1860-70s. In 1932-33 an attempt was made to restore the church to its original state, as it was in the 17th century. In 2006 a new restoration started. Due to the lack of soil on the island, the cemetery for Grip was at Bremsnes church on Averøy (p 352). The houses on the island are built closely arranged around the stave church.

At one time there were more than 400 persons living on Grip; however, during the fishing season there could be as many as 2 000 fishermen from Nordmøre on the island. The group of islands has been hit by a number of natural disasters - in the Grip church records there is a record of the fierce storm of November 1796 that raged across the island, destroying approx. 100 houses. Three persons were killed.

In 1964, 70 persons lived on the island. The pilot station on Gripholmen was closed down in 1969. The last permanent residents moved from the island in 1974. During the summer the island is a popular recreational area. Many of the houses are summer homes and the island attracts a considerable number of tourists.

Grip lighthouse, north of Grip, was constructed in 1888. The iron tower stands on a high base of hewn stone and the total height is 44 m. The lighthouse is the second highest in Norway. The range is 15-19 nautical miles. Grip radio beacon was in operation from 1947-86. The lighthouse was automated in 1977. It was granted protected status in 2000.

63°09'26"N   7°44'21"E   + 5 hrs 41 min

The ship approaches the next port of call, Kristiansund. The town stands on three islands: **Kirkelandet** (5.9 km²), **Nordlandet** (14.3 km²) and **Innlandet/Gomalandet** (0.7 km²). Kirkelandet is almost divided by the 1 km long bay Vågen, where the harbour is located. The north eastern side of the island is known as **Gomalandet**. The islands are connected by bridges.

We approach the north side of Kirkelandet, the town district of **Karihola** is on the port side up ahead.

The masts at Kristiansund's airport, known as Kvernberget can be seen on the port side. The airport itself is not visible from the ship.

We round Kirkelandet. There are several churches on the island, these cannot be seen from the ship.

On the starboard side is Stavenes lighthouse in Averøy municipality.

The ship sails into **Sørsundet**, between Kirkelandet and Innlandet and under Sørsund bridge, which joins the islands. The bridge was opened in 1963. It is 408 m in length, with a main span of 100 m.

Nordlandet church stands magnificent and proud on the slope on the starboard side. The decision to build the church was made in 1875, however the foundation stone

was not laid until 1913. The church was consecrated in 1914. Granite from the local area has been used in the construction, and each stone has been hand-cut. The church has extremely good acoustics. The organ is recent, from 2000, however the organ façade is unaltered from the original organ that was built in 1914. It is said to represent one of the finest examples of Nordic organ building traditions and artwork.

During the bombardment of the town in 1940, most of the houses on Nordlandet were laid in ruins. The church was one of the few buildings that remained standing.

© EILIV LEREN

Kristiansund received a town charter and trade rights from King Christian VI in 1742. The town was previously known as **Fosna** and is one of the places that lays claim to being the earliest settlement in Norway. The Fosna culture goes back to approx. 8 000 B.C., and it is thought that people have lived on the coast here since before the end of the last Ice Age, approx. 10 000 years ago. At Nordlandet in Kristiansund, traces of settlements dating from the early Stone Age have been discovered. (p 83).

At places all along the Norwegian coast, good harbours are often the basis for commercial expansion, this is also the case in Kristiansund. Even though the fishing community of Grip (p 347) was more important for the boat traffic sailing along the coast, the significance of the harbour between the three islands increased, and the small community grew rapidly from the 17th century onwards. The state opened a customs office for control of the Dutch traders' timber trade (p 333) in Nordmøre, and having been given the status as a transit port the community was allowed to trade a limited range of goods.

Kristiansund is said to have been 'founded on klippfisk' (dried cod). Knowledge of the process involved in the production of this type of dried fish is said to have been brought to the town by the Dutchman Jappe Ippe in the 1690s. He received a royal 'letter of privilege' entitling him to produce and trade 'klippfisk' in 1691. After a few years the Scotsman John Ramsay overtook the enterprise and during the 18th century the production of 'klippfisk' became a major industry. Boats came in from the sea with salted fish that was first washed before being taken to be salted once more and to be hung to dry on the rocks. The fish was then put into a press for two weeks to allow the salted water to drain.

After Kristiansund had been granted a town charter in 1742 the town expanded, due in a large part to the fish trade. A large fleet of ships was built up in the years following 1776 and several shipyards and rope works

were established. Commerce in the town developed considerably during the following decades and the town prospered. The demand for 'klippfisk' increased so much that the local fishermen could not supply enough fish and to meet the demand, in the middle of the 19th century raw fish was brought from Lofoten and Finnmark. The market for 'klippfisk' continued to grow and the town's tradesmen became extremely wealthy. From the 1820s, salted herring also became an important export product. At the end of the 19th century Kristiansund was a fine town with many large merchant mansions, quaysides and wharfs.

A curious fact: the ships that brought 'klippfisk' to Spain brought back soil as ballast. The area around Kristiansund had little soil and the Spanish soil was, among other things, used in the town's first public cemetery. The deceased of Kristiansand therefore rest in soil brought from south-west Europe.

Due to the limited scope of the commercial activities in the town, i.e. based on one product in particular, Kristiansund was greatly affected by the economic crisis that occurred after the First World War. During the 1930s an attempt was made to find various alternatives, however it was not until after the Second World War that more varied industries became established.

At the end of April 1940, Kristiansund was subjected to almost four days of continual bombing by the German Luftwaffe and the town was laid almost in ruins. The reason for the intensive bomb raids was that the German forces believed that the Norwegian King and the government were in the town. Five people were killed and approx. 800 buildings were destroyed by fires that raged for several days, and most of the old wooden houses were destroyed.

Post-war Kristiansund is distinguished by the typical post-war reconstruction architecture that can be seen in many towns along the coast. Some of the old farms from the 18th century and 19th century still remain, some of them are listed buildings. The food industry, based on fish as a raw material, is still important, however the town has become a central operations and supply base for the offshore industry off the coast of central Norway. Oil industry-related business is now the main commercial basis of the town. In 2008, Kristiansund and the neighbouring municipality of Frei were combined into one municipality.

The ship's stay in Kristiansund is brief and does not give much time for sightseeing. Most of Kristiansund's public buildings, hotels, businesses and schools and the quayside are on Kirkelandet.

Kristiansund is known as the "opera town". In 1928, 32 years before the National Opera was founded in Oslo, the Norwegian people's opera was established in Kristiansund. The aim of the people's opera was to create a collaboration between professional and amateur opera singers. Each year, in February, there is an opera festival in the town that has now been extended into a two to three-week long event.

The ship continues to Molde   **+ 0 hrs 00 min**

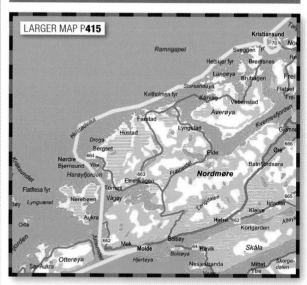

Our voyage continues along Sørsundet once more, past Nordlandet church and under Sørsund bridge. Up ahead we can see the community of Bremsnes in Averøy municipality.

South of Kristiansund is the island of **Frei** (65 km²), that until 01.01.2008 was a separate municipality.

Furthest south on the island of Frei, a battle took place in 955 between King Håkon (the Good) and the sons of

Eirik Bloodaxe. Several ship graves in the area are associated with the battle. There are many burial mounds on the island (p 83).

Kvalvik fortifications stand on the north-eastern part of Frei. The fortifications are some of the most well-preserved from the war. Construction began in the spring of 1942. Prisoners of war from many different countries took part in the construction, among them 50 Russian prisoners of war. The fortifications were still not completed when the war ended in 1945 and were never actually used for war purposes. The fortifications are strategically located at the mouth of the fjords **Vinjefjorden**, **Tingvollfjorden/Sunndalsfjorden** and **Halsafjorden/Stangvikfjorden**. They were, among other things, intended to prevent the movement of Allied troops. The fjords cut deep into the mainland and provided the opportunity for rapid movements of troops in the event of an invasion.

Freifjord tunnel on the south side of Frei, connects the Kristiansund islands to the mainland. The undersea tunnel was opened in 1992. It is 5 086 m in length and 130 m under sea level at its deepest point.

Approx. 63°07'N 7°41'E

We cross the boundary between Kristiansund and Averøy municipalities

Averøy municipality

Municipal coat of arms, significance: Denotes the many archaeological finds in the municipality. More recently, interpreted as a peace symbol.
Meaning of name: Possibly from Norse afr, 'large', or from ave, meaning 'shallows, bay', shallow sounds and fjords in the north west of the island.
Municipal seat: Bruhagen (-).
Position: 63°04'20"N 7°38'34"E. **Area:** 174 km².
Population: 5 367. **Pop. density:** 30.8 /km².
Area distribution: Farming 12 %, forestry 19 %, fresh water 1 %, other area 68 %.
Trade and industry: Most commercial activity is connected with the fishing industry. Modern fishing fleet. Fish farming. Other industries connected with the fishing industry: Foodstuffs, fish feed production and manufacture of machinery and equipment. Dairy and beef production. Tourism.
Averøy municipality's home page: www.averoy.kommune.no

On the south western side of Averøy is Kvernes stave church, which is thought to have been built in the 14th century. In 1633, the old chancel was demolished and replaced and the church was redecorated and new windows and pews installed. The Cultural Heritage Society has owned the church since 1893, when a new church was built close to the old one.

© FRODE INGE HELLAND

Close to the stave church is Old Kvernes Local Museum, which is an open-air museum with 11 houses from Averøy and neighbouring municipalities. The museum has a maritime section with a boathouse, fisherman's cabin, boats and maritime artefacts, and an archaeological section with relics from the Fosna culture, which was one of the first settlements in Norway after the last Ice Age, approx. 9 500 B.C. Close to the museum are approx. 70 graves from the Bronze and Iron Ages.

63°07'33"N 7°38'30"E   + 0 hrs 18 min ①

As we sail under the bridge and out into **Bremsnesfjorden**, we can see the community of **Bremsnes** (pop. 382) on the starboard side up ahead, on Averøya.

The ancient chieftain seat and the homestead of Bremsnes existed here from approx. A.D. 600. Historical records indicate that Harald Hårfagre (Harold Fairhair), who was only a lesser king in A.D. 872 , while he was visiting Ragnvald Mørejarl, promised to let his hair and beard grow until he had united Norway under one kingdom. When he had achieved his goal, after the battle at Hafrsfjord in approx. 885, the King returned to Bremsnes and cut off his hair and beard at the ancient sacrificial site at the homestead. Both the site itself and the central sacrificial stone have been preserved.

The mountain **Bremsneshatten** (130 m above sea level) and the cave Bremsneshola, are close to Bremsnes homestead. Bremsneshola is the largest grotto in Nordmøre. It is 80 m deep and 25 m high. Several Stone Age dwellings have been discovered in the area along with traces of the first settlers in Nordmøre (p 349).

As early as before the year 1300, a longhouse stave church stood at Bremsnes. This burned down to the ground in 1770 and was replaced by a new church in 1771. This was built from round timber and clad with panelling. The church underwent major restorations in 1886 and at the end of the 1960s. It has a fine altarpiece from 1771. During restoration work in 1869 the altarpiece was painted over with ordinary paint, but was restored with its original decoration in 1932. Around the church there are fine deciduous trees, beech, larch, chestnut and oak, which were brought from Scotland and planted around 1790 by the then owner of the homestead at Bremsnes.

Historically, both the town of Kristiansund and the group of islands at Grip (p 347) have had their cemeteries at Bremsnes church.

The ferry that currently sails between Bremsnes and Kristiansund will be decommissioned in 2008 when the new road project the "Atlantic Tunnel" is completed. The tunnel will join Averøy and Kristiansund. In addition to new roadways at each end, a 5.7 km long tunnel will be constructed under Bremsnesfjorden. This will provide a road connection between the municipalities of Averøy, Kristiansund and Frei.

Stavenes lighthouse passes on the port side. The lighthouse was built in 1842. It has a range of 14.3 nautical miles and was automated in 1976.

After we pass the lighthouse, we set course for Ramnefjorden towards our next port of call, Molde. The community of **Øksenvågen** is on the port side. Øksenvågen has been a fishing community since the 19th century. Due to the good harbour facilities, it was one of the places that were considered for the construction of a landing stage for natural gas from the Ormen Lange field in the North Sea. The mouth of the Atlantic Tunnel is at Øksenvågen.

The low island of **Ekkilsøya** (4.5 km²) can be seen in the wide bay on the port side. Fish farming takes place here and one of the world's leading aquaculture rese-

arch stations has an ocean-based station on the island. Ekkilsøya is joined to Averøya by a bridge.

On the port side is Hestskjær lighthouse.

63°05'24"N   7°28'40"E   + 0 hrs 37 min ②

Hestskjær lighthouse passes on the port side. The lighthouse was built in 1879. It was rebuilt and reinforced in 1960. The lighthouse is a white concrete construction and has a range of 15 nautical miles. The lighthouse was manned until 1986, when it was automated.

© RIKSANTIKVAREN

Ahead, on the port side, we can see the mountains in Eide and Fræna municipalities.

The ship now sails in foul waters alongside a number of small islands in Averøy and Eide municipalities. The islands are difficult to distinguish from one another.

63°04'N   7°25'E   + 0 hrs 49 min ③

Lauvøyfjorden begins on the port side. From here and on to Kvitholmen lighthouse we sail parallel with Atlanterhavsveien (the Atlantic Road, Route 64). During the voyage we will be able to see some of the bridges on the port side.

The unique and spectacular Atlanterhavsveien was chosen in 2005 as the 'construction of the century in Norway 2005'. It is regarded one of the greatest tourist attractions in the area and has been given the status of a "National tourist route". The British newspaper The Guardian has crowned the road "The World's Finest Car Journey".

The road connects the municipalities of Eide and Averøy and was opened in 1989. Construction began in 1983. The road construction workers experienced 12 hurricanes during the construction period before the Atlantic Ocean Road was finally opened. As early as the 1900s, plans were made to build a public transport connection on the same site as the new road. However, the plans were finally shelved in 1935. The former plans were for a railway and not a road! New plans for a highway were reconsidered in the 1970s.

Atlanterhavsveien is 8.27 km in length and has eight bridges, a total of 891 m. The road swings between and over islets and skerries. Some of these islands were inhabited around the 1900s, but these are now vacated. Along the road are cabins, camping sites, cafes, restaurants and a diving centre.

The bridges along the road, in our sailing direction are: Lille Lauvøysund bridge, 115 m, height 7 m, Store Lauvøysund bridge, 52 m, height 3 m, Geitøysundet bridge, 52 m, height 6 m, Storseisundet bridge, 260 m, height 23 m, Hulvågen bridge, 3 bridges in total 293 m, height 4 m, and Vevangstraumen bridge, 119 m, height 10 m.

Near the north end of the Atlanterhavsveien is the fishing community of **Håholmen**, with 20-30 buildings from the 18th and 19th centuries. The fishing community was active until 1960. The course and conference centre Håholmen Havstuer is located on the island.

The owner of Håholmen, Ragnar Thorseth (b. 1948), is an accomplished explorer and author who began his expeditions by rowing alone from Måløy (p 30) to Lerwick in Shetland in 1969. Thorseth sailed along the same route taken by many of the Norwegian Vikings and polar explorers, in a vessel that was almost identical to one of the original boats. He has also made other epic voyages: In 1975 he spent five months crossing the Atlantic, by the same route as the first Viking ships that sailed to Vinland. In 1979-80, in a 20-foot boat, he allowed himself to be driven by the polar ice and passed through the Northwest Passage, as did Roald Amundsen. Thorseth was the captain on board a copy of the Viking ship "Gaia" that completed the voyage from Norway to New York harbour in 1991. The ship received a jubilant reception.

63°02'25"N   7°13'17"E   + 1 hrs 08 min ④

Kvitholmen lighthouse passes on the port side. This lighthouse, at the northern end of Hustadvika, was built as a channel beacon in 1842. Approx. 100 men worked on the construction. These men came from all over the country. The lighthouse tower is 16 m tall and was built from granite brought from a nearby quarry. 39 000 stones were used in the construction. The rest of the buildings form a courtyard and include a machine room, quarters and outhouses. In 1902 an auxiliary beacon was lit at Kvitholmen. The lighthouse was rebuilt in 1906, and the auxiliary beacon's light was moved to the old stone tower and the lighthouse continued as a channel beacon. In 1956 the light was again moved to a new 12 m high concrete tower and it was electrified with power supplied by a genera-

tor. The lighthouse has a range of 15.1 nautical miles. The old stone tower still stands and a proposal has been made to declare the tower a listed building. In 1977 a radar installation was added at Kvitholmen lighthouse. It was automated in 1990 and is now unmanned. The site is protected under the Cultural Heritage Act.

The mountain range behind Kvitholmen lighthouse is in Midsund and Haram municipalities (p 77, p 75).

Approx. 63°03'N   7°17'E

We cross the boundary between Averøy and Eide municipalities

Eide municipality

Municipal coat of arms, significance: Denotes the many marshes and the presence of Whooper Swans in the municipality. **Meaning of name:** From Norse eid, 'neck of land'. **Municipal seat:** Eide (1 181). **Position:** 62°54'22"N 7°27'"E. **Area:** 153 km². **Population:** 3.365. **Pop. density:** 22.0 /km². **Area distribution:** Farming 13 %, forestry 30 %, fresh water 4 %, other area 53 %. **Trade and industry:** Agriculture and livestock farming. Some fishing. Stone quarry. Production of textiles, clothing and timber. **Eide municipality's home page:** www.eide.kommune.no

Approx. 63°01"N   7°10'38"E

We cross the boundary between Eide and Frøya municipalities

Fræna municipality

Municipal coat of arms, significance: Symbolizes the sea. **Meaning of name:** From Frænfjorden, uncertain meaning. **Municipal seat:** Elnesvågen (2 133). **Position:** 62°51'N 7°10'E. **Area:** 368 km². **Population:** 9 131. **Pop. density:** 24.8 /km². **Area distribution:** Farming 17 %, forestry 20 %, fresh water 2 %, other area 61 %. **Trade and industry:** Agriculture, large areas of fertile land. Dairy and corn production. Fishing. Fish processing and foodstuffs industry. Timber and plastics industries. Limestone production. Mechanical engineering. Approx. 25 % of the working population works in Molde (2001). **Fræna municipality's home page:** www.frana.kommune.no

The notorious **Hustadvika,** on the port side is the open ocean stretch between Kvitholmen and Bjørnsund lighthouses. This stretch is approx. 11 nautical miles in length and has innumerable skerries and islets. With the Norwegian Sea just beyond, this is regarded as one of the most hazardous stretches along the Norwegian coast. Several ships have run aground and been lost here. Hustadvika is often associated with storms and tragedies, brave sailors and heroic rescues. The sea here is regarded as 'foul water' as far as 1.5 to 2 km nautical miles from land.

One of the many shipwrecks near Hustadvika, occurred at Kvitholmen lighthouse in July 1909. The passenger ship MS "Olav Kyrre", built in 1886 in Bergen, ran aground on one of the many skerries in the area. The ship remained aground on the rocks for a time before being broken up by storms and it eventually sank. The wreck was discovered again in 1987.

The Norwegian ship MS "Kongstind" sank in January 2003. A 'Mayday' signal was sent out around midnight on the 4th January 2003. Ships and helicopters were sent to search for survivors. The ship was found late in the night, she was afloat but only the bow was showing above the waves. Of the crew of four, one was found drowned and the others could not be found. The ship was on its way to Kristiansund with a cargo of fertilizer. The wreck lies at a depth of between 36 and 47 m.

The mainland inside of Hustadvika is comprised of large, cultivated marsh areas. Further in, the terrain becomes very steep.

63°01'13"N   7°06'08"E   + 1 hr 20 min

We round Nordneset lighthouse on the port side, before we pass the bay **Breivika** and the village of **Farstad.** The mountain providing the backdrop is **Sjurvarden** (667 m above sea level).

In the next bay is the village of **Hustad** with Hustad church, built in 1874. Hustad was formerly a royal homestead and noble seat, mentioned in documents from 1122. It is said that King Øystein (I) Magnusson (1088-1123) (p 9) died here. In the 16th century, the homestead was owned by the Danish noble family Rosenkrantz, and later by the Governor Christoffer Urne. In 1713 the homestead was taken over by Reknes

Leper Hospital in Molde and later became a sanatorium for tuberculosis patients. The farm was divided into a number of smallholdings and all traces of the royal homestead are now gone.

Behind Hustadvika is a range of mountains, among them are **Raudtua** (950 m above sea level), **Talstadhesten** (913 m above sea level) and **Skalten** (692 m above sea level).

The lighthouse at Vikan can be seen to port, at the approach to the fishing port and village of **Vikan.** On the wide, low shore is the village of **Bergset.**

At Storesundet lighthouse, built in 1915, we change course and head towards the south east.

Bjørnsund lighthouse on the island of **Moøy,** north west in the group of islands, was built as a channel beacon in 1871, and was rebuilt and reinforced in 1886. The lighthouse is important for shipping that navigates in the hazardous area around Hustadvika. The height of the beacon is 26 m and the range is 15 nautical miles. In 1917 a foghorn was installed that emitted a signal every 10 seconds. The lighthouse was electrified in 1948. A super-siren that gave a stronger signal, and a special fog detector was also installed. This did not function as expected in the exposed climate out in the ocean. When the manufacturer was told of the problem, he could not understand – as the "prototype of the detector has performed for many years without a single problem, in the Gobi Desert!". A radio beacon was installed in 1959, this was replaced by a radar beacon in 1977 (as one of two in the country at that time). The lighthouse was automated in 1994. It was granted protected status in 2000.

© STEVE RØYSET / WWW.STERK.NO

The uninhabited, idyllic fishing hamlet of **Bjørnsund** is up ahead. Around the year 1900, 5-600 persons lived on these islands; however, Bjørnsund is now uninhabited, the last residents left in 1971. The fishing hamlet is a popular holiday destination during the summer months.

The houses cling to skerries and islets and many have been restored as holiday cottages. In Bjørnsund there is a statue of a polar bear that is a monument to fishermen lost at sea.

62°54'32"N   6°50'E   + 2 hrs 07 min ⑤

The old, traditional fishing village of **Bud** passes on the port side, outermost on the headland. The name 'Bud' comes from the old fishing cabins. The first settlers may have been farmers from the inland areas of the fjords who came to fish during the season. During the Hansa period in the 14th-15th century, the great demand for fish for export and the proximity to the fishing grounds made ideal conditions for fishing and it became a year-round activity. The fishing village increased in size and importance. In the 15th-17th century Bud was one of the largest trading places between Bergen and Trondheim.

In 1530 there were 130 inhabitants, in 1801 there were 278 and 548 in 1901.

The final Norwegian state meeting was held at Bud in 1533. The archbishop Olav Engelbrektsson (p 89) called the meeting when the Norwegian state committee and the Norwegian catholic church felt threatened by the Danish King and the Reformation. Important state issues were discussed, but this did not lead to any decisions being made. The Reformation was introduced, the Norwegian state committee was dissolved and Norway became further incorporated into the Danish state. This was the final blow for the hope of an independent Norway.

A monument has been erected to commemorate the meeting. It was removed by the German occupying forces in 1941, but was replaced again on the 17th May 1947.

Bud church is a wooden building from 1717 with seating for 250. The cupola-shaped spire was formerly a landmark for fishing vessels returning home. During the Second World War the spire was in the line of fire for the  German guns placed at Ergan coastal fortifications. The local people of Bud took down the spire, hid it in the neighbouring village and replaced it after the war.

Today, Bud is still an active fishing hamlet with export of fish products and a mechanical workshop. It is a popular and charming recreational area with several good fish restaurants.

Ergan coastal fortifications near Bud were built during the Second World War between 1941-1943. The fortifications were the largest that were built by German forces during the war and were a part of a comprehensive defence system known as the "Atlantic Wall". In addition to the 350 German troops, there were also 150 Russian and Polish prisoners of war in Bud during the war. The fortifications could monitor the busy shipping lanes at Hustadvika, the approach to the towns of Ålesund, Molde and Kristiansund and the fishing hamlets of Bjørnsund and Ona. The fortifications have been restored and there is a command centre, gun placements, a sanatorium and water reservoir in the mountain.

Close by the fortifications is a bird cliff, on which hundreds of Kittiwakes nest during the breeding season (p 218).

To starboard up ahead is the island Gossen in Aukra municipality.

We are now in **Harøyfjorden**. The two small islands of **Ytre** and **Indre Harøya** can be seen, just before the fishing hamlet of **Harøysundet**.

Approx. 62°53'N   6°54'41"E   ⑥

On the port side is Aukra municipality

Aukra municipality

Municipal coat of arms, significance: A bracelet from The Middle Ages symbolizes solidarity and roots.
Meaning of name: Aukra, older form akerø, after the farm and parish of Aukra east on the island, from Norse Aukrin, from akr, 'field', and vin, 'natural meadow'.
Municipal seat: Aukra (pop. 770).
Position: 62°47'45"N 6°55'37"E. **Area:** 58.5 km².
Population: 3 142. **Pop. density:** 53.7 /km².
Area distribution: Farming 14 %, forestry 11 %, fresh water - %, other area 75 %.
Trade and industry: Agriculture with fields and meadows, cattle farming. Fishing fleet with varied types of fishing. Shipbuilding. Aquaculture and fish farming. Nyhamna at Aukra is the landing stage for gas transported from the Ormen Lange field.
Aukra municipality's home page:
www.aukra.kommune.no

The island **Gossen** (46.5 km²) is the largest in Aukra municipality. 80 % of the local population lives on the island. Gossen has a marshy shore area, the highest point is 99 m above sea level.

Rindarøya is a small island at the north western tip of Gossen, which is now connected to land. The stone sculpture "Rokta monument", stands here as a memorial to the cargo boat "Rokta" that sank in a hurricane, near Galleskjærene west of Bjørnsund on the 3rd April 1938. Due to the storm, the rescue boats were unable to reach "Rokta" until the day after the shipwreck. Six of the crew of 12 were lost, the survivors were taken on board a lifeboat. The shipwreck and the rescue efforts were broadcast live on the radio and people all over the country sat intensely and followed the rescue hour by hour. It was one of the most dramatic rescue operations in Norwegian coastal history. The rescuers showed bravery and heroism that was later described in a book and in poetry about the incident. In 1988 the Rokta monument was erected in memory of the tragedy.

On the north eastern tip of the island is **Nyhamna**, the site chosen in 2002 as the landing stage for the natural gas brought ashore from the Ormen Lange field. In advance of the construction of the industrial area at Nyhamna, major archaeological excavations were carried out, some of the largest operations of this type in recent times. At the peak there were 57 archaeologists working in the area. They examined 32 different sites, 60 cultural relics were found and registered. Under thick layers of peat, gravel and sand they found traces of 11 000 year old settlements within the designated area. Around 320 000 finds were collected and 167 000 were catalogued. Of these, around 50 000 were tools or parts of tools. The remains of a jawbone and cranium of a small child were found; these were found to be between 7 000 and 4 500 years old. In addition, approx. 10 dwelling remains, with fireplaces, supports, ovens, graves and walls from the Stone Age were found (p 83).

The Ormen Lange field was discovered by Norsk Hydro in 1997. The field lies approx. 100 km west of Kristiansund, and up to 2006 was the second largest field to be discovered in Norway. The field is named after the Viking ship of Olav Tryggvason (968-1000) (p 88). The plant began operations in October 2007.

The development of the field has been complex and has involved innovative construction technology and design techniques, as the field is at a depth of 800-1100 m, in a dangerous area created by the Storegga undersea landslide (p 85). The gas reservoirs lie approx. 1 500 m beneath the sea bed. Two wellhead templates, each with room for eight undersea wellheads, have been located on the sea bed without visible surface installations. These are attached to a multi-phase pipeline that will bring the gas to the process plant at Nyhamna. 720 km of pipeline has been laid from the undersea wellheads to Nyhamna, two 30" pipelines for gas, two 6" pipelines for glycol and two umbilicals (control cables) to operate the well templates. The undersea terrain on which the pipelines are laid is extremely rugged and demanding. Hydro has therefore had to prepare the site by digging out areas using a remote-controlled excavator at a depth of approx. 850 m, then placing large amounts of crushed rock to support the pipes. The pipes run in lengths without support for up to 1 000 m. At Marintek (the Norwegian Marine Technology Research Institute, that carry out research and development work in marine environments) in Trondheim, calculations were made and tests carried out to determine how long the pipes could run unsupported without being damaged. There is a harsh

climate in the area, with high winds, powerful waves and sea currents. The currents are strong and the temperature on the sea bed is below freezing. Huge sums have been invested in exploring the sea bed to evaluate the danger of a new Storegga landslide.

After the natural gas has gone through the process plant in Nyhamna, it is sent through the world's longest undersea gas pipeline, the 1 200 km long Langeled, to **Easington**, south east of Leeds in England. The gas from the Ormen Lange field is calculated to be able to supply approx. 20 % of the gas requirements for the whole of England. The daily output production is calculated at 70

million m³ gas and the field will be able to supply gas for approx. 30-40 years. In addition a proportion of the gas will be refined into gas condensate (gases in liquid form that contain butane, propane and pentane).

During the Second World War, Gossen was an active community, despite 800 of the 2 000 inhabitants being forcibly evacuated. At the most there were 5 000 German troops, prisoners of war and evacuated Norwegians on the island. The German occupying forces built several airstrips along the Norwegian coast, to allow German bombers to fly on their missions. One of these was built on Gossen. The airstrip was to function, among other things, as an emergency landing strip between the airport at Herdla north of Bergen (p 384) and Trondheim. From 1943 it became a fighter base. The fighter aircraft were used to attack Allied planes and ships with bases in Scotland and Shetland, who in turn attacked German ships that transported troops from Norway to the continent, where the Germans were beginning to be worn down on several fronts. It was said that there were plans to develop the airstrip into one of the largest airports in Northern Europe, if the war had continued. The 1 650 m long runway was completed in 1944. It was covered with gravel and timber planks. Today, it is only 500 m long and is used as a light aircraft landing strip.

The community and municipal centre **Aukra** lies south east on the island.

The first church at Aukra was most likely a stave church from the 1430s. In 1648 it was extended with a half-crucifix church, however the church burned down after being struck by lightning in 1709. Before the present octagonal wooden church was built in 1843, Aukra had two other churches, built in 1712 and 1772. However, these also burned down due to lightning strikes. The present church has part of an altarpiece, a counter, chalice and an antependium (decorated front of an altarpiece) that were saved from the fire of 1712.

On the port side of Gossen, we pass the village of **Tornes** (pop. 899) before **Frænfjorden** with the municipal centre of **Elnesvågen** (pop. 2 133) in Fræna municipality. Elnesvågen is the second largest community in Romsdal and has various types of industry. The famous Jarlsberg cheese is made here.

On the southern side of Gossen, we pass Aukra ferry quay with the car ferry to **Hollingsholmen** on the mainland on the port side. The village of **Eiskrem** is on the port side.

Approx. 62°45'N 6°57'37"E

We cross the boundary between Aukra and Molde (p 79)

Just ahead is Julsundet, between the municipalities of Molde and Midsund with Otterøya (p 78).

On the voyage through Julsundet we can see the majestic mountain peaks and the mountain ranges that make the Romsdal Alps so different to other mountain areas.

At **Setet** on Otterøya, on the starboard side, we pass a salmon farm, close to the car ferry quay at **Solholmen**.

After passing Julsneset we set sail towards the town of Molde that stretches like a 10 km wide 'belt' along the north side of Moldefjorden and Fannefjorden. To starboard we can see the Romsdal Alps. The fjord **Isfjorden** with the communities of **Isfjorden** (pop. 1 246) and **Åndalsnes** (pop. 2 067), **Langfjorden** with the community of **Eidsvåg** (pop. 882) and **Fannefjorden** with the communities of **Hjelset** (pop. 1 003) and **Kleive** (pop. 483) open into **Romsdalsfjorden** and **Moldefjorden**, where the town of Molde is located. The fjords in the northern part of Møre and Romsdal county have always played an important role in the interaction between the inland valleys and the coastal areas.

The small island of **Veøya** (1.1 km²) ('the holy island', most likely because in pre-Christian times there was a pagan worship site here) lies in a central location between Isfjorden, Langfjorden and Romsdalsfjorden, east of the island of **Sekken** (18.45 km²). The Vikings sailing to eastern Norway or to Nidaros (Trondheim) often sailed into the inner parts of fjords before continuing over land. Veøya was the first community in the area and was mentioned in Snorre Sturluson's King's Sagas in connection with the battle on the neighbouring island of Sekken in 1162 (p 79).

Veøya was one of the larger trading posts along the coast that had trade relations with the Hansa town of Bergen (p 11) and Vågan in Lofoten (p 156). Archaeological excavations revealed finds that date back to 1100-1200. The trading post has probably had a population of as many as 350-400 during its 'golden age', which was around 1050-1350.

Towards the end of the Middle Ages (p 83), much of the trade was moved to the fishing village of Bud (p 356). The reason for this was the increase in activity in the fishing industry and the shipping of dried fish and other products along the coast. The amount of ships sailing to Veøya and the surrounding fjords was still of some importance. The "Hollender period" in the 16th and 17th centuries was the peak of the trade in timber that took place between Norway and Europe. The majority of ships came from Holland, but there were also vessels from England, Scotland, Germany, France and Portugal (p 333).

The island no longer has any permanent residents; however, the old Veøy church and rectory remains and is now owned by Romsdal Museum. Both buildings are listed and protected under the Cultural Heritage Act. The church is a longhouse-style building of stone, built in the romance style from approx. 1200, dedicated to St. Peter. It has seating for 400 persons and has undergone several extensions and rebuilds. The interior is from the period after the Reformation in 1537. The church, which still holds services on certain days of the year, became inactive in 1901, but remained a parish church until 1907. The rectory is thought to be from 1750, and comprises two

log houses with vertical panelling over two floors. The last priest moved from Veøya in 1898.

The ship docks at the quayside in Molde CITY MAP P417

Molde was also 'founded on fishing' and the herring shoals could sometimes come far into Moldefjorden. Salting plants and herring exports were the reason Molde was officially granted town status (but without full trading rights) in 1612. Molde received a town charter from Christian VI (1699-1746) in 1742 and thus gained free trade status compared with Bergen and Trondheim. Molde had long been a central town in the timber trade. The town gradually developed as the administrative centre, as it was strategically located between the fjord and the sea. The merchants in the town had considerable economic interests in the fishing industry and the nearby fishing hamlets of Bud and Bjørnsund (p 355, p. 356).

At the end of the 19th century the majestic fjords in Romsdalen were 'discovered' by foreign tourists, and Molde, with its quaint, small, wooden houses and the fine flower gardens, as well as the so-called 'Molde panorama' with 'a view over 222 mountain peaks reaching over 1 000 m', became one of the leading tourist towns in the country. The German Kaiser Wilhelm II (1859-1941), a great admirer of Norway, paid annual, week-long visits to Molde in the period between 1889 and 1913. He called the town "Nizza des Nordens" – a kind of Nordic Nice. In addition to his yacht, "Hohenzolleren", a fleet of 10-12 other German vessels also arrived in Molde. Several other

© FRODE INGE HELLAND

royal guests and prominent people followed the Kaiser's example, and the town attracted many visitors and regular tourists. Kaiser Wilhelm II visited Molde for the last time in 1913, the year before the outbreak of the First World War. A fire in January 1916 destroyed 225 houses and a number of gardens in the eastern part of the town. These were rebuilt, this time of brick. When one of the two large hotels burned down in 1919 and was not rebuilt, this was an indication that Molde's golden age as a tourist town was over.

Much of Molde was destroyed at the start of the Second World War. The reigning monarch, King Haakon VII, along with Crown Prince Olav, central government ministers and Norway's gold bullion stocks were moved to Molde. The German forces subjected the town to massive bombing. After a week of drama, the King, the Crown Prince and others, and their precious cargo went on board the cruiser "Glasgow" that was to take them to safety. The famous picture of King Haakon and Crown Prince Olav under the Kongebjørka ('King's beech tree') was taken during these dramatic days. The bombing of the centre of Molde, with its distinctive small houses, left the town in ruins. After the war these were replaced by large tenements built along wide streets.

Molde has experienced considerable growth in the population and in land area since the war and the town boundaries have been moved several times. The town is no longer dependent on fishing and fish export. In addition to being the administrative centre for the county of Møre and Romsdal (p 81) and a number of state institutions, the town also has Molde Hospital (the town's biggest employer) and a college of higher education. Molde is also the largest industrial town in the county, with a lighting and heating systems manufacturer, mechanical industry, commerce and service industries. The clothing industry was at one time a major enterprise, however this is now almost completely absent.

Even though Molde is no longer a holiday destination for the aristocracy of Europe, the town is still popular destination for tourists. Molde is close to well-known tourist attractions such as the scenic, winding mountain road Trollstigen. The rock faces at Trollveggen are internationally famous among climbers, Atlanterhavsveien (the Atlantic Road), the 'construction of the century in

Norway 2005' (p 353), and Ergan coastal fortifications (p 357).

Molde is famous, both nationally and internationally, for the annual Molde International Jazz Festival or "Moldejazz". The festival first took place in 1961 and has consistently attracted an impressive number of international stars from the jazz world. The week-long festival takes place during week 29 each year. The jazz festival is a member of IJFO, a cooperation between the 14 largest jazz festivals around the world. During the 2006 festival, 140 concerts were held on 17 stages, 25 000 tickets were sold and between 80–100 000 visitors came to Molde to experience the festival atmosphere.

The renowned Norwegian author Bjørnstjerne Bjørnson (1832-1910) spent his childhood years in Romsdalen and in Molde. The Bjørnson festival, named after him, has been arranged each year since 1991 and is the country's largest international literature festival. Well-known Norwegian and international writers and literary guests meet with the aim of "promoting an interest in literature and the art of writing".

A number of monumental buildings, both old and new are visible before the ship docks at the quayside in Molde:

"Seilet" ("The Sail") is the name of the hotel with a mirrored façade that resembles a large sail. The 16-storey, 170-room hotel is also a culture and conference centre and was completed in 2002. Part of the hotel is built on pillars out in the fjord.

Aker Stadium (formerly Molde Stadium, opened in 1998) is another major building that stands close to "Seilet". It was a gift to the town from two well-known businessmen, former residents of Molde. The stadium, an all-seater, has a capacity of 11 167.

Molde Cathedral was consecrated in 1957. It has been designated a cathedral from 1983. It is a double-naved longhouse-style church made of stone, with seating for 900. The free-standing spire is 50 m tall and has a carillon of 26 bells that are controlled electronically. Three other churches have previously stood on the same site. The first was a wooden cruciform church, built in 1661. The second was built in the same style in 1841; however, this burned down in 1885. The third wooden church was built in 1887 in a new-gothic style. This church was destroyed during the German bombardment in 1940. The altar cross from 1661 and the altarpiece from 1887 are preserved in the current cathedral. The attractive Kirkeparken park is adjacent to the cathedral.

The old homestead, Moldegård, is comprised of an elegant building from the 17th century with wings from the 18th century. Moldegård was the county governor's residence from 1704 and is said to be the model for Henrik Ibsen's (1828-1906) play "Rosmersholm". The farm has been owned by the same family since 1788.

The ship continues to Ålesund (p 68)

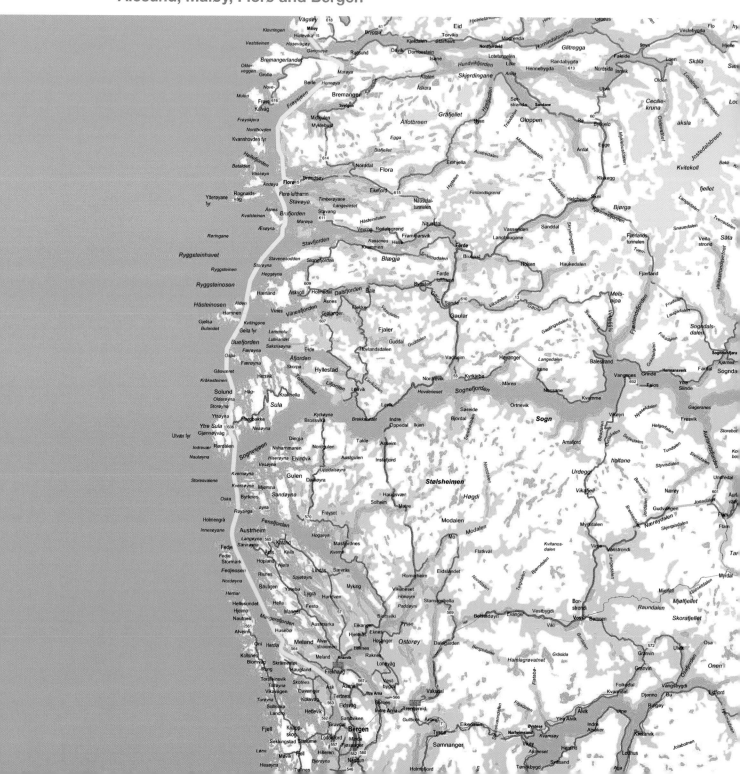

fter departing from Molde we have passed the municipalities of Midsund, Haram, Giske, Ålesund and the port of **Ålesund** (62°28'30"N 6°09'10"E, 0000-0045) (p 68), followed by the municipalities of Sula, Hareide, Ulstein, Herøy and the port of **Torvik** (62°20'10"N 5°44'E, 0200-0215) (p 44) and Sande municipality. These municipalities are in Møre and Romsdal county (p 81). After crossing the county boundary into Sogn and Fjordane (p 386), we pass by the municipalities of Selje and Vågsøy, also the port of **Måløy** (61°56'20"N 6°07'25"E, 0515-0545) (p 30).

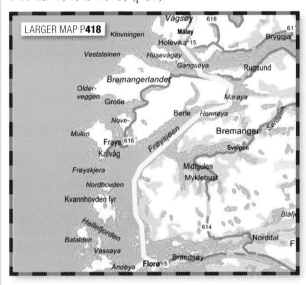

LARGER MAP P**418**

LARGER MAP P**418**

Approx. 61°52'40"N 5°11'20"E

We cross the municipality boundary between Vågsøy and Bremanger municipalities

Bremanger municipality

Municipal coat of arms, significance: Reflects the local connection with the sea.
Meaning of name: -
Municipal seat: Svelgen (pop. 1 164).
Position: 61°46'N 5°18'E.
Area: 176 km².
Population: 3 930.
Pop. density: 34.8 /km².
Area distribution: Farming 4 %, forestry 14 %, fresh water 3 %, other area 79 %.
Trade and industry: Fishing and fishing industry. Fish exports. Mechanical engineering in connection with fishing fleets. Agriculture and livestock (cattle and sheep), often in combination with fishing.
Places to return to: Rugsund Trading Post, Rugsund Church, Kalvåg.
Bremanger municipality's home page: www.bremanger.kommune.no

On the starboard side, we have passed the island of **Gangsøya,** (1.1 km², 80 m above sea level) (p 29). The island is mentioned in documents from the 14th century and there has been a working farm on the site since before 1650. It is a popular summer destination.

On the port side is the small island of **Risøya**.

The ship sails into the narrow sound, Skatestraumen. On the port side is Rugsundøya (10.7 km²), separated from the mainland by the narrow Rugsundet behind the island.

❶ **Skatestraumen,** a rapid tidal current that runs between the islands of Bremangerlandet on the starboard side and Rugsundøya to port, is the main shipping channel between Bergen and Nordfjord. On both sides of Skatestraumen, there are several cultural heritage sites and remains of Stone, Bronze and Iron Age dwellings. The oldest are from the early Stone Age, the most recent are from the migration period (A.D. 300–700) (p 83). Approx. 151 dwelling remains have been found, with some house foundations and tents. The finds indicate that agriculture, fishing, hunting and animal husbandry were common in the area. Among other things, approx. 40 small buttons made of amber have been found. These were precious decorations on a costume found in a grave. The buttons probably originate from the Baltic region.

© ALF KÅRE LEFDAL

On the 13th September 1909, the Norwegian cargo ship "Sterk" sank at Skatestraumen. The ship ran into a violent storm and ran aground around midnight and sank quickly. The ship was carrying limestone and had a 16-man crew. Nine of these were rescued. The ship now lies at a depth of 25 to 37 m.

On the port side, we can see **Rugsundøya.** Tongane Coastal Fortifications stand on the western tip of the island. The fort was one of the largest German fortifications to be constructed in Norway during the Second World War. It was strategically located, with a good view over the shipping channel in to Måløy, the approach to Nordfjord on the port side and Skatestraumen ahead. The fort was first involved in conflict during the Måløy raid (Operation Archery) during Christmas 1941 (p 31). Large parts of the fortifications, the main guns and the soldiers' quarters are still standing.

The fort originally had two 130 mm guns that had a somewhat remarkable history before they were installed at the fortifications. To the great surprise of the German forces, the guns were found in the hold of a Finnish cargo ship that was docked at Bergen harbour, on the 9th April 1940. The guns had originally been mounted on a Russian battleship that was built in 1914. After the Russian Revolution of 1917, the ship then came under German command, then British command as part of war repatriations in 1918. The ship was then used by White Russian forces in 1919, before being interned in France in 1920. The battleship fell into disrepair and sank in 1931; however, it was raised in 1932 and finally scrapped in 1933-1936. The guns from the ship were removed and given as war material support to Finland in the war against Russia. However, the guns only got as far as Bergen before the war began in Norway. The 18 original Russian 130 mm guns were installed at six fortifications along the coast of Norway in 1940.

The fortifications were included in the Norwegian coastal artillery and known as 'Rugsundøy Fort'. The fort was closed down in 1950. A 1940-model Russian gun still remains at the fort.

Rugsund Trading Post on the island's northeast tip was a well-known and important trade hub as early as the 17th century. It was the home of the local courts, had a herring salting factory, store, spirits trade and a church. Even before the trading post was established, there had been considerable boat traffic between Nordfjord and Bergen through Rugsundet. Rugsundet is mentioned in the Sagas from the 13th century, including the account of the conflict between the Bagler and Birkebeiner factions.

Rugsund Trading Post had its 'golden age' in the 1800s. From 1850, Rugsund was the staging post for the post route from Bergen to Trondheim, operated by steamships. By 1870, Rugsund was an important port of call for both steamships and local routes. Around 1919, a new quay was built on the mainland and most of the ships and boats began to use the improved facilities there. Rugsund Trading Post was granted listed status in 1924.

Today, Rugsund is a popular harbour for recreational boats with guest piers and a service building. There is still an old store, preserved in the old style, with traditional over-the-counter service. Some of the buildings are rented out to tourists and there is also a diving centre. There are excellent opportunities for scuba diving in this area.

Rugsund old church stood on Rugsundøya as early as the Middle Ages (p 83) and priests lived in the parish before 1338. The church became privately owned from 1723; however, it burned down after being struck by lightning in 1834. The foundation wall from this church is still visible. A new church was built on the mainland in 1838, built according to plans drawn up by the architect Linstow, the same architect responsible for the design of the Royal Palace in Oslo. The reason that the new church was built on the mainland was the shallow soil and poor ground conditions at the site on Rugsundøya (for burials, soil had to be brought to the island). The church was rebuilt and extended in 1911 and is regarded as the finest church in Nordfjord. It has been beautifully decorated with rose painting, murals, glass mosaics and carvings.

The island of **Bremangerlandet** (153 km²) lies on the starboard side. The island is quite mountainous, the highest peak is Klubben. Most of the population lives in the village of **Bremanger** (pop. 405) in the bay known as **Bremangerpollen** on the island's western side.

The Bremanger road, that runs between Klubben on the starboard side and Bremangerlandet on the mainland, via Rugsundøya, was opened in 2002. The total length of the road is 8 050 m and includes Rugsund bridge (length 311 m) between Rugsundøy and the mainland. It also includes Skatestraumen tunnel (1 890 m, 80 m under sea level), which runs between Klubben and Rugsundøya. The tunnel was the first of this type to be built in Sogn and Fjordane county.

We sail alongside the well-known mountain **Hornelen** (860 m above sea level) on the starboard side. The mountain is often described in Norwegian prose and several legends have their origins here. Hornelen was first climbed in modern times in 1897.

Hornelen is thought to be the highest sea cliff in Northern Europe. The peak juts slightly outwards and according to a legend, there is a crack in the peak. It is said that if sailors sound their ship's horn here, the vibrations could loosen the rock and the peak could fall into the sea, resulting in a massive flood wave.

Several legends are associated with Hornelen, some of them are included in Snorre Sturlason's King's Sagas. In these, the mountain is known as Smalsarhorn.

According to one legend, King Olav Tryggvason (968-1000) (p 88) climbed the mountain and placed his shield at the top of the cliff. When one of his men climbed up to get the shield, he was unable to get down. The King then climbed up once more, took the man (and the shield) under his arm and climbed down again!

Another legend tells of Juratinden, the topmost vertical cliff on Hornelen. It is said that the cliff is shaped like a female troll with a child under her arm. The legend claims that this is the "troll that Olav the Holy (995-1030) (p 88) turned to stone when he sailed so hard into the mountain that it broke off a huge stone block that fell into the sea and became what we now know as Marøya."

Yet another legend claims that Marøya was once joined to Bremanger. Olav the Holy commanded the mountain to part, so that he could sail through. Thus, the two land areas became separated and Marøy became an island.

every Christmas Eve and Midsummer Night to dance and consort with the Devil. The same superstitious beliefs are associated with other mountains: **Lyderhorn** just outside Bergen (p 24), **Dovrefjell** in Oppdal and **Domen** in Vardø (p 231). Witches from these areas are said to have come together to dance and cast evil spells.

Behind Hornelen is Klubben (889 m above sea level).

The small island of **Marøya** passes by on the port side. The island is mentioned in several sagas, in connection with the mountain Hornelen that we have just sailed by.

The ship rounds the southeast headland of Bremangerlandet on the starboard side. Over to port side, on the mountain **Blålida,** a coastal fortification was built in 1944, with four 105 mm guns. This type of gun had a range of 11 000 metres.

61°50'N　5°15'30"E　②

The bay known as **Botnane** is behind Marøya, to starboard, just before the mountain **Hesten** (823 m above sea level). Eight burial mounds have been found in the area. It is thought that these are from the early Bronze Age (p 83). The graves are probably those of chieftains, built as a sarcophagus from stone blocks in which the deceased were laid, often along with their weapons and private possessions. These were then covered with huge piles of stones, until they stood as large, visible stone mounds on the landscape. The largest grave, which stands on the outer point on the northern side of the bay, is 36 m in diameter and 3-4 m in height. It has a wide overhang and a 10 m crater on top. On the southern side of the bay, there are several other graves that are also easily visible from the sea. The largest of these is 30 m in diameter and 4 m in height. The burial mounds at Botnane are typical 'coastal mounds', i.e. they are not covered with earth and have an additional function as landmarks for sailors at sea.

Over to starboard are the bay **Vingenpollen** and the village of **Vingen,** between the mountains **Bortneskora/Hesten** (823 m above sea level) and **Vingekvarven** (940 m above sea level). The first stone carvings found in the "Vingen carvings" area were discovered here in 1910. The area has one of Northern Europe's largest stone carving sites and Norway's second largest, with almost 2 000 carvings, from both the early and late Stone Age. Approx. 1 500 of the carvings have been found in

© ALF KÅRE LEFDAL

Hornelen is one of the two most infamous "witch mountains" in Sogn and Fjordane county. According to superstition, witches gathered on the mountain

© ARVE KJERSHEIM

Vingen, the remainder were discovered in the surrounding areas. Most of them show carvings of deer-like animals. These animals may have been seen as symbols of fertility. Some depict snakes, dogs and male and female human figures. It is assumed that the carvings were created over a period of some 2 000 years, from approx. 4 500-3 000 B.C. Archaeological analysis of the Vingen carvings is still being carried out and it is believed that there are many that still remain undiscovered. Vingen Special Landscape Area was established in 1980 and covers an area of 5 km². The Vingen carvings and the surrounding area were granted listed status by the Directorate of Cultural Heritage in 2002.

There are various interpretations of the carvings. One of them is that Vingen has at one time been a larger community and cult worship site in connection with deer hunting. The method of hunting was the group chase, i.e. a large number of hunters gathered over a large area and drove the deer over a cliff. Others stood at the bottom of the cliff to trap the animals when they fell down.

The ship sails into the fjord **Frøysjøen,** (25 km in length, 2-4 km wide).

To port, we pass the tiny island of **Hennøya**. Behind the island, we can see the village of **Hennøya** and the mountain **Aksla** (592 m above sea level).

❸ The village of **Berle** passes by on the starboard side on the island Bremangerlandet. Berle is known to have been a Viking settlement as early as the year 750 (p 83, p 123). The name 'Berle-Kåre' is mentioned in Harald Hårfagre's (Harold Fairhair's) saga and Snorre Sturlason's King's Sagas. Berle-Kåre joined the crew of Rangvald Jarl on his longship when the Jarl was in the Flora area in the latter half of the 9th century, in connection with the unification of Norway into a single kingdom. Berle-Kåre later became the King's envoy. He was known as a tough, strong and brave man who often went on Viking raids. His two sons fought on the front line for King Harald Hårfagre (865-933) during the battle of Hafrsfjord in approx. 885.

During the Second World War, German fortifications were built in the mountain near Berle. These included a number of tunnels and grotto-like caves. The fortifications were built in order to attack any Allied ships sailing into Frøysjøen. Four guns were relocated to Skarstein in 1943. These have now been removed. Today, the grottoes are used to hold concerts.

A German gun emplacement was also built in the village of **Skarstein** (on the starboard side) during the Second World War. The battery was installed in 1943 with four 105 mm guns.

61°46'28"N 5°03'E   ❹

After the headland of **Ospeneset** and the village of **Høfledal** (port side), we can see the fjord, **Gulen,** that divides into the fjords **Sørgulen**, **Midtgulen** and **Nordgulen**. At the innermost part of Nordgulen is the municipal seat and industrial area **Svelgen** (pop. 1 174) with Bremanger Smelting Plant.

South of the fjord Gulen is the headland **Gulestøa,** at the foot of the mountain known as **Skudalsnipa** (670 m above sea level). In 1991, the remains of a Stone Age settlement were found at Gulestøa. This settlement is known as "Litlesommaren".

The southern tip of the mountainous island of Bremangerlandet and the village of **Smørhamn** pass on the starboard side, followed by the island of Frøya (17.5 km², 378 m above sea level) also on the port side.

Frøya church, on the eastern tip of the island is a longhouse style church with seating for approx. 400. It was consecrated in 1865. For the first few years, the church had a tall spire; however, during stormy weather the spire became unstable, causing the roof of the church to leak. The spire was removed in 1933 and a shorter, broader spire was erected in its place. The church's old altarpiece is dated 1752 and another is from 1865.

On the island's south east side is the traditional fishing hamlet of **Kalvåg** (pop. 335) that grew up as a result of the large winter herring catches at the start of the 1860s. The (now well-preserved) milieu of fisherman's cabins, landing stages and the road to Bremangerlandet helped to maintain activity in the fishing hamlet.

It had a good, still harbour for the open fishing boats and was close to the fishing grounds. When the catches were at their peak in the 1860s, as many as 7 000-10 000 fishermen gathered at Frøya and Kalvåg. During the 1870s, there were 52 salting factories in Kalvåg, with a total production capacity of over 35 000 barrels. The herring shoals, which had returned to the area every year since 1811, disappeared for a time in 1873.

The quay, good harbour facilities, steam ships, transport administration, postal service, telegraph and telephone office led to a steady increase in the population of Kalvåg. From 1866, it also became the administrative centre for Bremanger municipality. The herring returned to the area in great numbers for a few decades before 1960, after which the catches dwindled once more. This led to reduced activity and the population declined. Kalvåg no longer has the capacity to take in the newer, larger boats and their catches. However, Kalvåg is still an important trading area for both trading and processing of fish. Some of the old fisherman's cabins have been rebuilt and these are now rented out to tourists. The island has a road connection with the mainland via the smaller islands to the neighbouring island of Bremangerlandet, and from there the undersea tunnel links the island to the mainland. The Bremanger road was opened in 2002 and runs via Rugsundøy to Rugsund on the mainland.

© VIVVI

The small village of **Liset** near the southern tip of Frøya has traces of settlements dating back to the early Stone Age (p 83). It is thought that farmers from inland areas came to stay here for shorter periods to fish.

The bay **Botnen** passes on the port side, with the villages of **Nordbotnen** and **Sørbotnen** on each side.

61°42'N   4°57'30"E

We cross the boundary between Bremanger and Flora municipalities

Flora municipality

Municipal coat of arms, significance: Refers to the former herring fishing in the area.
Meaning of name: Possibly original name Florelandet, western part of Brandsøya, from Norse *flódr*, or *flór*, 'current or channel', most likely a reference to the channel with strong currents that divides Brandsøya.
Municipal seat: Florø (pop. 8 296).
Position: 61°36'N 5°01'37"E. **Area:** 693 km².
Population: 11.341. **Pop. density:** 16.4/km².
Area distribution: Farming 3 %, forestry 20 %, fresh water 4 %, other area 73 %.
Trade and industry: Flora is an industrial municipality with shipbuilding, fishing industry and oil-related industry. Oil supply base. Agriculture. Fishing and fish feed. Fish farming. Tourism.
Places to return to: Florø, Kinn, Svanøy.
Flora municipality's home page: www.flora.kommune.no

On the starboard side is the small island **Nordhovden** and the larger, mountainous and treeless island of **Hovden** (14.6 km²). Hovden is the largest island in Flora municipality. In 1991, a family from the Netherlands moved to the island and was quite taken by the area. They spoke warmly of Hovden in the Dutch media and several more Dutch families moved to the island and the surrounding area. Today, some of them have moved away, either back to the Netherlands or to other places in the municipality.

The largest colony of Bearded Seals in the municipality is found at Nordhovden (approx. 20), also the largest Herring Gull colony south of Stad (approx. 1 500 pairs). On the western side of the island, 4 000 year-old cave carvings, depicting boats, have been discovered.

Kvanhovden lighthouse stands on the North West point of Hovden. The lighthouse was built in 1895 and is the municipality's 'newest' lighthouse. It is the channel and coastal lighthouse for vessels that approach from the sea to Frøysjøen on the northern side of Hovden. Much of this area is foul water.

The lighthouse is comprised of the keeper's quarters - the light itself is installed on the western gable end – and approx. 300 m from the lighthouse there is a boathouse, landing stage and a swing crane. The lighthouse stands 40.3 m over the sea and the range is 17.7 nautical miles. The lighthouse keeper lived here with his family and ran a smallholding in addition to maintaining the lighthouse. Kvanhovden was automated in 1980.

On the port side on the mainland is the village of **Husefest**, at the foot of the mountains **Grønegga** (634 m above sea level) and **Tverrdalsnipa** (533 m above sea level), followed by the villages of **Sunnavåg** and **Ura**.

The ship sails between the low **Nærøyane** islands on the starboard side and the mainland, with the villages **Årebrotet** and **Vaulen** to port. Part of the Nærøyane islands is a bird sanctuary. The island also has fish farms for cod.

To port ahead we can see the factory buildings of EWOS fish feed factory, that produce feed for fish farms. EWOS is among the world's leading companies in their field.

Several larger islands and groups of islands can be seen to starboard. These island communities around Florø have been of major importance during the periods of rich herring catches in the area (p 369). South of Hovden is the island group known as **Batalden**, comprised of 30 islands, the largest of which is **Store-Batalden** (1 km², 492 m above sea level). Only the two larger islands south and southwest of Store-Batalden, **Fanøya** and **Vevlingen** are inhabited.

Stabben lighthouse and the island of Skorpa can be seen to starboard, ahead. Further west is the group of islands known as Kinn and the island of Reksta.

The ship docks at the quayside in Florø

Florø is mentioned in written texts from around A.D. 1 300. However, traces of settlements have been found in the area, including rock paintings and burial mounds, dated as early as 6 000 B.C.

The town's proximity to the shipping channel has influenced Florø throughout history. Many of the Viking Kings' voyages outside of Norway are believed to have started from the fjords east of Florø, and several infamous Viking chieftains lived in the area. One of them was Kvedulv from the island of Batalden, one of the outermost islands north west of Florø. Kvedulv is described in Snorre Sturlason's King's Sagas and in the Sagas of Egil Skallagrimsson. In the Saga he is referred to as a 'ruthless and fearless' Viking and his description reinforces the popular reputation of the Vikings, of being tough and merciless warriors:
"…Kvedulv approached them from the rear. He went alone from his group of men, straight at Einar and struck

him between the shoulders with his axe, just as Einar hit Simon across the head with his axe. Kvedulv turned and stabbed Tord in the throat with the tip of his axe blade, and Tord was slain instantly…"

Another story about the Vikings from the area, one that also very much confirms their violent reputation, tells of how Inge, the son of King Harald Gille (1103-1136) (p 92), avenged his father's death: "…they broke his (Sigurd Slembe, d. 1039) arms and legs with axe-heads, then tore off his clothes and began to skin him alive. They broke his head with axe blows; but they could do no more because he was bleeding so much. Then they took their knives and cut him so that he looked as if he had been skinned. Then they hit him with a log and broke his back. After that, they dragged him to a tree and hanged him; later they cut off his head and buried his body in a mound. This happened in 1139…"

More than 800 years later the descendants of these Vikings have been given the honourable task of awarding the Nobel Peace Prize and have become known as peace negotiators in conflicts all over the world!

Florø was granted a town charter in 1860. The Storting had decided that another trade centre between Bergen and Ålesund was necessary. Florø was chosen because it had good harbour facilities, access to fresh water and large available land areas. Florø was also centrally located in the sailing channel. The merchants in Bergen were fiercely opposed to the new town, they saw it as a threat to their own commercial activities in Bergen and their economic dominance. Traditionally, they had always maintained full control of all fish trading in the west of the country.

A saying is that "the herring was the foundation of Florø". The town is located in the middle of the former herring grounds. The ocean areas around the islands in the west have been a spawning area for herring for hundreds, possibly thousands of years. Winter herring fishing has been carried out here from 1699 up to recent times. However, the herring stocks have not been particularly stable. They have disappeared many times, only to return some years later. During good fishing periods, there was a great deal of activity on the islands off the coast of Florø – in some seasons there were as many as 13 000 fishermen taking part. They found space and bedded down wherever they

© EILIV LEREN

could, in the traditional small cabins and even under their boats, despite the cold winter nights in February and March, for as long as the fishing season lasted. During the years from 1873-1880, the herring catches failed. This lead to a major economic crisis and great hardship among the fishermen. Some of them emigrated to America, or they moved to other areas in Norway. Around 1875 the situation had become so serious that a national charity fund was set up to help the affected fishermen in Kinn and Florø. Fishermen also took part in fishery activities in other European countries, in order to learn more effective, modern techniques.

The world's largest herring catches are said to have been taken here on the west coast between 1945 and 1957. In a 12-year period, approx. 105 million hectolitres of herring were caught. In 1956 alone, 12.3 million hectolitres of herring were landed. In one 24-hour period, as much as 340.000 hectolitres of herring were landed from a total of 227 herring boats. The main centres of activity were Florø and Måløy (p 30). In 1959, the stocks of fish dwindled once more.

The uncertainty of the herring fishing trade, which varied from extreme peaks of activity to almost nothing, led to the establishment of alternative industries in Florø. In 1949, the industrialist Ole A. Aaserud opened a small mechanical workshop in the town. In the course of 30 years, he built up two large shipyards in the county, one in Florø and another in Førde (p 375). The shipyards employed as many as 1 000 workers and generated considerable activity via sub-contracts with other enterprises in the area. The shipyards built mostly fishing boats for the first 20 years. Later, the yards also constructed larger tankers in cooperation with the yards at Førde. Unfortunately, the shipyard eventually got into financial difficulties and finally went bankrupt in 1985. Subsequently there have been several owners. In 1996, a new, covered dry dock was built which has become something of a landmark in Florø. Since 2006, the yard has been owned and operated by Aker Yards (p 77).

Florø is also known as "the fish farming capital" in Sogn and Fjordane county. Several of the largest operators in the salmon farming industry have concentrated their business here and during the 1980s, many large salmon processing factories were constructed. At Svanøy Foundation on Svanøy (p 374) there is a research centre dedicated to farmed fish species and on some of the islands, there are large installations for smolt and fish breeding. The fish feed manufacturer EWOS is one of the largest operators in the market. A worldwide salmon farming concern has opened its Norwegian headquarters here. Florø port has been developed and has Norway's largest freezer container capacity.

Many oil-related industries have services and factories at 'Fjord Base', a multi-enterprise industrial complex that was established in Florø in the 1980s.

Florø has a short take-off and landing airport, which was opened in 1971. It has an 820 m long tarmaced runway. The airport also has a helicopter base for the transport traffic to and from oil platforms in the North Sea.

The ship continues to Bergen   **+ 0 hrs 00 min**

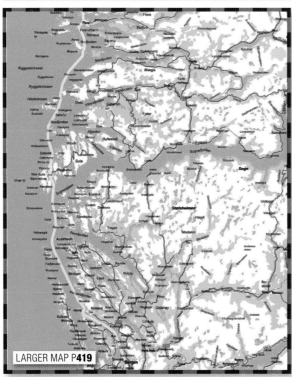

LARGER MAP **P419**

Shortly after leaving Florø, we pass **Stabben** lighthouse. There is a considerable amount of shipping in the waters around Florø and these are treacherous waters and difficult to navigate. When the herring fishing industry experienced a new surge in the middle of the 1860s, it was decided that several more lighthouses should be built in the area.

Stabben lighthouse, on the small islet on the starboard side was the first of these lighthouses to be constructed and the first in Sogn and Fjordane county. The lighthouse was completed in October 1867. Stabben lighthouse has been given its name because the islet it stands on rises straight up from the sea and is shaped rather like a chopping block (stabbe=block), with deep water on all sides. It is so small that there is only room for the lighthouse building itself. The foundations had to be built higher than normal so that all the facilities that would normally be built outside could fit into the cellar. The light itself had to be placed on top of the roof of the lighthouse. A tiny vegetable patch was laid in the narrow strip between the lighthouse and the sea – this had to be removed every autumn to prevent the soil being washed into the sea during the winter storms. It was impossible to approach the lighthouse by boat unless the weather conditions were favourable.

Two months after the lighthouse was completed, a balcony was destroyed by heavy seas. The following year, a plough-shaped deflecting wall was built on the northwestern side of the lighthouse building.

In 1899, the lighthouse was rammed by a sailing ship. The ship hit the deflector wall and the prow went through the lighthouse. In 1905, the lighthouse underwent alterations, a new tower was built and the light capacity was increased. The lighthouse keepers and their families lived on Stabben lighthouse until 1975, when it was automated.

North east of Stabben lighthouse is the islet **Grasskjær**. In 1910, the then ten-year-old Hurtigruten ship DS "Astrea" ran aground here and sank. There were no fatalities. The ship was sailing northwards and was intending to turn into Florø. DS "Astrea" was the largest ship in the Hurtigruten fleet at that time (765 tonnes).

Ytterøyane lighthouse is another lighthouse built outside of Florø, west of Stabben on the outermost island towards the North Sea. A decision was taken to build

the lighthouse in 1851; however, it was not completed until 1881. The red iron lighthouse tower is 31 m in height and has a typical white 'belt'. The range is 20.4 nautical miles and the light stands 57 m above the sea during high tide. At the side of the lighthouse, there are keepers' quarters and outhouses. The light was upgraded in 1913. In 1950, the lighthouse was electrified and a diesel generator was installed in the concrete machine room. Lighthouse keepers and their families lived here permanently, until 1965 when the lighthouse began operating a shift system. Ytterøyane lighthouse was granted protected status in 1999 and was only automated as recently as 2004, as one of the last in Southern Norway.

Most of the lighthouses along the coast have their own special stories. At Ytterøyane, there is a tale from the late 1800s, of the midwife that came to assist with a birth and became weather bound on the island for several weeks. The lighthouse was attacked and damaged by Allied aircraft in 1940 and 1941.

Northeast of Kinn and just west of Florø is the island **Skorpa** (9.0 km²). The highest point is **Blåkollen** (393 m above sea level). In common with many other islands in the area, Skorpa had its 'golden age' during the years of the rich herring catches in the 1880s and the 1900s (p 371). During the boom period there were approx. 15 000 fishermen on Skorpa and the surrounding islands during the herring season. In 2001 there were approx. 60 persons living on Skorpa.

The island **Kinn** (7.3 km², 315 m above sea level) is the outermost of the larger islands between Ytterøyane lighthouse and Florø. Kinn is regarded as one of the most historic islands in Norway and is associated with Selja and the legend of St. Sunniva. According to the Kinn legend, three ships sailed from Ireland with the Christian princess Sunniva on board, who had fled from a pagan suitor. Two of these ships, on one of which Sunniva was a passenger, are said to have gone aground at Selja (p 34). The third ship, with Sunniva's sister Borni on board, ran aground at Kinn. People on board the ship were said to have found shelter under an outcrop on the island known as Byrjehellaren. Traces of a building have been found there. Close to Kinn church on the west side of the island is Bornihellaren. However this story is a legend. It is most likely that it was not the daughter of a king, but Celtic missionary monks that escaped from religious persecution and chose to settle on the island.

Kinn church was built in the 12th century. It is believed to have been built by King Øystein (1088-1123) who also built the church on Selja (p 35). The church is constructed in the romance style in two phases; first the chancel, 7.2 m x 7.65 m, followed by the main room 10 m x 17.7 m. The church has an altar made of soapstone with a marble slab from the 12th century, an altarpiece from 1641 and an altar cloth from 1739. The carved wooden chancel arch is believed to be from approx. 1250. It depicts the apostles and is one of the most valuable examples of Norwegian Middle Age art. It also has three saint figures from the Catholic period. The church was a site of pilgrimage in the Middle Ages (p 83) due to the association with St. Sunniva and Selja.

Since 1985, the church grounds have been the stage of the annual Kinna plays. The theme is built around the Reformation period in 1537; however, the story of the king's daughter's flight from Ireland is also included in the play. Professional actors and local amateurs take part in various roles.

The famous mountain **Kinnaklova** near Kinn church is a well-known landmark that can be seen from some distance.

| 61°35'10"N | 4°57'25"E | + 0 hrs 14 min ❶ |

We pass between the smaller islands **Nekkøyane**, to starboard and **Færøya** on the port side. Southwest of Nekkøyane we can see the island **Reksta** (220 m above sea level). On the western part of Reksta is the fishing village of **Rognaldsvåg** (pop. 170). Rognaldsvåg has a rare collection of buildings with farmhouses, boathouses and fisherman's cabins. The village has two harbours, joined by a specially constructed canal, on which the boathouses stand wall-to-wall. Several burial mounds and remains of ancient dwellings dating from Viking times have been found on the island (p 123).

61°34'N   4°58'10"N   + 0 hrs 18 min

The fjord **Solheimsfjorden** is on the port side. This splits into the long, narrow **Eikefjorden** with the village **Eikefjord**, and the shorter, wider **Høydalsfjorden.**

At the southern mouth of Solheimsfjorden, is **Stavøya.** The island was connected to the mainland by a bridge in 1990.

On the mainland, behind the island is the village of **Stavang**, with Stavang church, that was relocated here from Svanøy around 1870 (p 375). **Skålefjellet** (765 m above sea level) is in the background.

We continue our voyage, into **Brufjorden**.

61°34'N   5°00'E   + 0 hrs 24 min ②

On the starboard side are the small islands known as **Oddane**, before the island **Askrova**. In 1936, the largest known herring catch was made on the western side of Askrova, in **Vallestadvågen**. Some people on the shore saw that huge amounts of herring were moving towards the bay. As quickly as they could, the fishermen set out their nets, laying them out double, and with a long stretch of net they enclosed the herring in the bay. When they discovered after a few days that the herring were escaping through an undersea gap in the rocks, divers were sent down to close the hole with rocks. Herring were fished from the fjord for several weeks. The official catch was between 100 000 and 120 000 hectolitres of herring, however those who were present claim that the catch was actually closer to 200 000 hectolitres.

61°31'N   5°00'E   + 0 hrs 33 min ③

The lush island of **Svanøy** (10.3 km², 235 m above sea level) on the port side, has an interesting history. Besides Kinn, Svanøy is the island in the area that receives the most visitors. The flora is diverse and includes most of the types of plants that are to be found in the western part of the country and there is a pine forest that is several hundred years old. The bird life and fauna is also very varied and, for example, both White-tailed Eagles and deer can be observed here.

Archaeological excavations have found that Svanøy has been inhabited since the Stone Age. The island had quite a number of settlements during the Viking period (p 83). History indicates that the Viking King Eirik Bloodaxe (895-954), the son of Harald Hårfagre (who united Norway as one kingdom) grew up here. The local farm was named after him, and is now known as Erikstad.

The island and the farm on the island were originally known as Bru. They became crown property after the Reformation. In 1662 it was sold to the archbishop Hans Svane in Copenhagen, however Svane died in 1668 and his widow was granted permission to change the name of the farm and island to Svanø. Despite no one from the owner's family ever visiting the island, it was still owned by the family up to 1718, when it was sold. After several changes of ownership it was sold to Severin Seehusen, whose great ambition was to become recognised as a peer. When he finally achieved his aim in 1720, under the name Severin de Svanenhielm, Svanø farm became a noble's residence. Svanenhielm fell into debt with the king and the farm was sold by auction on his death. The Svanenhielm family bought back the property around 1730; however, it was sold once more when the owner died.

In 1804, the island and the farm were sold to the revivalist preacher Hans Nielsen Hauge (1771-1824). At that time there were 28 houses on the farm, including the main house and a church. Ole Torjussen, a good friend of Hauge, overtook the management of the island and the properties. He grew corn, built a flour mill, ran a sawmill and opened a shipbuilding yard. Some time later he built a salt mill. Svanøy became a central community in Sunnfjord. In 1812 he took citizenship in Bergen as a merchant. As one of four representatives from Nordre Bergenhus, Ole Torjussen Svanøe was one of those called to Eidsvoll to form the new Norwegian constitution. He was a member of parliament from 1821 to 1842.

Ole Torjussen
Svanøe

His eldest son Christoffer, who also became a member of parliament, overtook the farm in 1840, and developed it into a model enterprise. His youngest son overtook the Erikstad farm. From the 1870s until 1923 copper mining was carried out. At the peak, around the time of the First World War, the company employed as many as 100 men.

The Svanøe family is now one of several landowners on the island. The listed main building, built in 1750, was rebuilt with its current façade around 1820. Svanøy homestead and its surrounding areas were handed over to Svanøy Foundation in 1972. The independent foun-

© J. T. SOLHEIM, WWW.SVANOY.COM

dation Svanøy Hus was established in 1992. Local and national businesses contribute financially to maintain the upkeep of the buildings.

Bru church, later renamed Svanøy church, was built long before the 14th century as a secondary church to the one at Kinn (p 373). It is thought to have been in use until it was taken down and relocated to Stavang on the mainland, around 1870 (p 374).

© J. T. SOLHEIM, WWW.SVANOY.COM

Close to the former church site is the well-known St. Olav's cross. Legend has it that the stone cross formerly stood on Brandsøya west of Florø, but was moved and erected here by Olav the Holy (p 88). The cross, which is one of the few of its type remaining in the country, is approx. two metres in height. On the one side are rune inscriptions that can be read from above and downwards. From these inscriptions, the words "Tordr raised this cross for…" can easily be deciphered. This type of cross was used as an assembly point for the congregation when church services were held.

Behind Svanøya is the mouth of the narrow and winding Førdefjorden (36 km in length). The villages of Naustdal (pop. 1 078) and Førde (pop. 8 942) are approximately at the midpoint and the innermost part of the fjord respectively.

61°27'N 4°55'E

We cross the boundary between Flora and Askvoll municipalities

Askvoll municipality

Municipal coat of arms, significance: Reflects the Korssund cross, a stone cross from the early Middle Ages associated with the legend of Olav the Holy.
Meaning of name: After the farm of Askvoll, from Norse *Askvollr*, combination of the names of the trees 'ash' and '*voll*', grassy mound.
Municipal seat: Askvoll (pop. 591).
Position: 61°21'N 5°04'E. **Area:** 322 km².
Population: 3 143. **Pop. density:** 9.8/km².
Area distribution: Farming 6 %, forestry 10 %, fresh water 2 %, other area 82 %.
Trade and industry: In coastal areas, fishing. In inland areas, agriculture based on dairy production and sheep farming. Metalworking industry. Fish processing. Summer tourism.
Askvoll municipality's home page: www.askvoll.kommune.no

We pass the fjord **Stavfjorden** on the port side. Behind Svanøy it continues into Førdefjorden.

The characteristic island of **Alden** can be seen to starboard ahead. The island is also known as "The Norwegian Horse". Just beyond Alden is the island of Tvibyrge. Its profile is reminiscent of a dog lying down.

Then we see the headland **Stavenesodden**, with the village of **Stavenes**. Along the shore, outermost on the southern side of the headland, 30 burial mounds have been discovered along with 11 rock carvings from the Bronze Age (p 83). The carvings represent mostly boats or ships; however, there is another that depicts two horses in front of a two-wheeled 'sun carriage'. This type of motif is rare. According to legend, the burial mounds may originate from a Viking battle in Stavenesvågen, which took place between the Viking chieftains Håkon Grjotgardsson from Selva (p 103) and Atle Jarl from Atløy. The battle was over territory and the control of the western areas.

Behind Stavenesodden is the fjord **Stongfjorden**.

The small group of islands **Storøyna** on the starboard side and **Heggøyna** on our port side pass by, before we arrive at the island **Atløya** (38 km²) with the mountain **Skredvarden** (636 m above sea level) on the port side. Rock carvings have also been found on Atløy with motifs of boats and sun-figures. On the western part of the island is the village of **Hærland** with an old trading post and landing stage. On the southern tip is the village **Vilnes** with Vilnes church, a wooden log-built church from 1674 with seating for 130. The church was restored in 1959.

The island **Tvibyrge** (193 m above sea level) passes to port outside of the western tip of Atløya.

The ship continues into **Aldefjorden** between Alden and Tvibyrge. The steep, mountainous island **Alden** (3.4 km²) with the mountain **Norskehesten** (460 m above sea level) are well-known landmarks. The farm of **Alden** stands on the southern side of the island.

The low lying island **Værlandet** (9 km², 165 m above sea level) and the group of islands known as **Bulandet**,

which is made up of approx. 300 small islands, islets and skerries, lies southwest of Alden. About 15 of the islands are inhabited (total pop. 260). Bulandet is the most westerly active fishing hamlet in Norway, with fishing, fish processing and tourism as the most important commercial activities.

The stretch between Bulandet and Værlandet is 6.7 km long and six bridges with a total length of 986 m connect the two communities, which are Norway's most westerly. The road project was completed in 2003 and was the recipient of the "Picturesque Road" prize in 2006. A car ferry and fast boat connect the islands to the mainland.

The mouth of **Vilnesfjorden** opens up south of Atløya. The fjord continues into the narrow **Dalsfjorden** and has a total length of 40 km and is 3.5 km in width (0.5 - 1 km at its narrowest point). The villages of **Holmedal**, **Dale** and **Bygstad** are on the fjord.

Legend has it that the first settler on Iceland (874), Ingolf Arnason, came from the village of **Rivedal** in the outer part of Dalsfjorden. A monument has been erected here in his honour.

Geita lighthouse passes on the port side. The lighthouse was built in 1897, rebuilt in 1961, automated in 1980 and the last keepers finally left in 1982. The lighthouse has a height of 42.8 m. The lighthouse was granted listed status in 1999.

65°15'11"N   4°44'17"E

Fjaler and Hyllestad municipalities pass by on the port side

Fjaler municipality

Municipal coat of arms, significance: Reflects the "Trondheim postal route" and the bridges along the route.
Meaning of name: Plural of Norse fjol, 'board', meaning 'edge', possibly connected with the 8 km long Helleberget, that has a sheer drop into Dalsfjorden.
Municipal seat: Dale in Sunnfjord (pop. 987).
Position: 61°22'N 5°24'E. **Area:** 418 km².
Population: 2 870. **Pop. density:** 6.87 /km².
Area distribution: Farming 6 %, forestry 31 %, fresh water 7 %, other area 56 %.
Trade and industry: Fish farming. Agriculture with sheep farming and dairy production. Leather goods industry, footwear manufacture. Shipbuilding.
Fjaler municipality's home page: www.fjaler.kommune.no

Hyllestad municipality

Municipal coat of arms, significance: Symbolises agriculture and millstone manufacture.
Meaning of name: First part from fjord name Hylli or Hyllir, from Norse hylli, 'calm, friendly place', or hylli, 'goodwill'.
Municipal seat: Hyllestad (pop. -).
Position: 61°10'30"N 5°17'46"E. **Area:** 259 km².
Population: 1 492. **Pop. density:** 5.76 /km².
Area distribution: Farming 6 %, forestry 31 %, fresh water 3 %, other area 60 %.
Trade and industry: Fishing of minor importance, several fish farms. Agriculture with cattle, sheep and chicken farming. Shipyards. Building and construction. Production of electricity.
Hyllestad municipality's home page: www.hyllestad.kommune.no

As early as the 11th century, millstones were cut at Hyllestad and sent to mills along the entire coast. Large stone crosses, up to several metres in height were made from the same type of stone as the millstones. These can be seen in several places in the west of the country (p 375).

We cross the boundary between Askvoll and Solund municipalities

Solund municipality

Municipal coat of arms, significance: The background of the motif is found in the Losna clan's coat of arms.
Meaning of name: First part from Norse sol, 'groove, furrow' and und, 'provided with', original name of island of Sula.
Municipal seat: Hardbakke (pop. 244).
Position: 61°04'N 4°50'E. **Area:** 229 km².
Population: 871. **Pop. density:** 3.8/km².
Area distribution: Farming 1 %, forestry: 2 %, fresh water 4 %, other area 93 %.
Trade and industry: Fishing, some cattle and sheep farming and smallholdings. Boat construction and repair.
Places to return to: Sula. Utvær.
Solund municipality's home page: www.solund.kommune.no

61°14'47"N   4°43'40"E   + 1 hr 50 min ⑨

The group of islands **Ospa** with the main island, also known as **Ospa** (111 m above sea level) passes on the port side. Just beyond Ospa is the group of islands **Færøyna**, the northern tip of the island Sula and the mouth of **Åfjorden**, which continues into **Hyllestadfjorden**. The village of **Hyllestad** lies at the innermost part of the fjord.

During the Second World War, Ospa was a centre of illegal operations. Due to its location, Ospa became a hiding place for Norwegian and Allied military vessels. In June of 1943, the Norwegian motor torpedo boat "MTB 345" was discovered by the German forces and after a short skirmish the crew of seven was forced to surrender. They were taken prisoner, interrogated and tortured. They were subsequently found guilty of sabotage and executed. 60 years later a memorial was erected in memory of the officers and crew of "MTB 345".

61°10'23"N   4°44'E   + 2 hrs 09 min

We continue sailing between the many islands in this island municipality, Solund. Out towards the Norwegian Sea to starboard we can see the small islands **Gåsværet** and **Kråkesteinen**.

61°00'N   4°45'21"E   + 2 hrs 52 min ⑩

The largest island in Solund is **Sula** (117.8 km², 569 m above sea level) which is separated from the other islands by narrow fjords and sounds. The voyage continues through the sound **Ytre Steinsund** between the islands of **Ytre Sula** (34.7 km², 202 m above sea level) to starboard and **Steinsundøyna** (18.7 km², 315 m above sea level) on the port side. The islands are steep and rocky. Out of the sound, we sail along the southeastern side of Ytre Sula, with the village of **Trovågen**.

West of Ytre Sula is the small group of islands **Utvær** with the island **Utvær** (0.2 km²) and Utvær lighthouse. Utvær is Norway's most westerly island. It is now uninhabited, but until the 18th century it was a fishing hamlet with its own chapel.

The former Utvær chapel is often mentioned in old texts in context with Selje monastery (p 34) and Kinn church (p 373). Historical documents indicate that one of the three ships that left Ireland with the fleeing king's daughter Sunniva and her companions ran aground at Utvær. The chapel is mentioned in texts from 1320; however the exact date of the church is unknown. It was built from timber, measured 7.3 m x 6.5 m and had seating for 130 persons. The church received its income from donations and tithing from fish catches. In the 17th century it was robbed by Scottish pirates. Four church services a year were held at the chapel. The priest came by boat from Eivindvik on the mainland and was often weatherbound on the islands closer to the mainland. In 1718 the chapel was moved from Utvær.

© RIKSANTIKVAREN

Utvær lighthouse was constructed in 1900. It is a 31 m high cast iron tower with an auxiliary beacon, built on a base of concrete. The height of the light is 45 m and the range is 18.6 nautical miles. The lighthouse was granted listed status in 1999. Utvær radio beacon began transmissions in 1954 (radio signal VR (...._ .-.) and broadcasts on 300.0 kHz. The radio beacon sends correctional data to the satellite-based navigation system Navstar GPS.

Utvær lighthouse was damaged by fire during an Allied attack in February 1945. It was rebuilt in 1948, with a different design to the original. The lighthouse station includes a machine room, keepers' quarters and outhouses around the tower and stands in an area that is designated and protected as a nature reserve.

In October 1989 the Brazilian bulk carrier «Mercantil Marica» (15 000 gross tonnes) lost engine power during a severe storm. The ship ran aground near the skerries just off the small island group known as Storsvalene (starboard side). 350 tonnes of fuel oil spilled into the sea. The wreck later broke in two and now lies at a depth of 25 to 30 metres.

Approx. 60°58'N   4°45'E

We cross the municipality boundary between Solund and Gulen municipalities

Gulen municipality

Municipal coat of arms, significance: Reflects the two stone crosses in Eivindvik, some of the first Christian monuments in Norway.
Meaning of name: From Norse *gul*, 'gust of wind', possibly from German root *geul*, Norse *gjól*, 'cleft'.
Municipal seat: Eivindvik (pop. 284).
Position: 60°59'N 5°04'30"E. **Area:** 596 km².
Population: 2 406. **Pop. density:** 4.04/km².
Area distribution: Farming 4 %, forestry 19 %, fresh water 3 %, other area 74 %.
Trade and industry: Agriculture with cattle, sheep and poultry farming. Fish farming. Some coastal fishing. Waste handling depot. Cement factory. Tourism.
Places to return to: Eivindvik. Skjerkehamn.
Gulen municipality's home page: www.gulen.kommune.no

We are now in **Sognesjøen**, which continues into **Sognefjorden** (205 km in length), which is Norway's longest fjord and one of the longest in the world. The fjord has many 'branches', most of these are in the inner part of the main fjord

Several municipalities border on Sognefjorden. Solund and Hyllestad municipalities lie north of the outer part of the fjord. The short **Bøfjorden** with the communities of **Heggebøen** and **Leirvik** with the shipyard Havyard Leirvik are all in Hyllestad municipality. South of Sognefjorden is Gulen municipality with **Risnefjorden** and the villages of **Brekke** and **Instefjord**.

Høyanger municipality follows, on both sides of the fjord. On the northern side of the fjord is the short **Vadheimsfjorden** with the village of **Vadheim**. Sognefjorden's deepest point, 1 308 m is just outside of Vadheimfjorden. Then we see **Høyangerfjorden** with the industrial community of **Høyanger** (pop. 2 204). South of Sognefjorden is the short **Fuglsetfjorden** with the villages of **Osland**, **Bjørdal** and **Søreide**.

Balestrand municipality is just after Høyanger on the northern side of Sognefjorden. The short **Lånefjorden** with the village of **Låne** is the most westerly in the municipality, then the 25 km long, narrow side fjord **Fjærlandsfjorden,** with the tourist village of **Balestrand** (pop. 834) and the village of Dragseid at the mouth of the fjord. **Fjærland** is at the innermost part of the fjord. At Fjærland there is a glacier museum, opened in 1991, with information about and exhibits from Jostedalsbreen National Park (1 310 km²). **Jostedalsbreen** is Norway's largest glacier.

On the eastern side of Sognefjorden is Vik municipality with two short fjords, **Finnafjorden** and **Arnafjorden,** and the village of **Vikøyri** (pop. 1 076). Next is Aurland municipality with the beautiful **Aurlandsfjorden** that cuts in towards the east. Further along is **Aurlandsvangen.** The well-known railway line between Myrdal-Flåm (Flåmsbanen) ends at the innermost part of Aurlandsfjorden. The beautiful, narrow 20 long **Nærøyfjorden** is on the UNESCO World Heritage List, along with Geirangerfjorden (p 62).

On the north side of Sognefjorden, the short **Sogndalsfjorden** cuts into Sogndal municipality, with the community of **Sogndalsfjøra** (pop. 3 108) at the innermost part. The village of **Kaupanger** (pop. 825) lies out towards Sognefjorden.

The village of **Lærdalsøyri** (pop. 1 105) lies at the innermost part of Lærdalsfjorden in Lærdal municipality, on the south side of Sognefjorden.

Innermost in Sognefjorden, the fjord divides into two smaller fjords - the 43 km long picturesque **Lustrafjorden** that runs north in Luster municipality, with the villages of **Gaupne** (pop. 1.017) and **Luster**. The other fjord, **Årdalsfjorden** continues eastwards in Årdal municipality, with the village of **Årdalstangen** (pop. 1 455).

✍

60°57'N 4°45'E	+ 3 hrs 10 min

Our voyage continues through the outermost part of Gulen municipality, with approx. 1 500 small islands on the port side that are somewhat difficult to distinguish from one another.

East of the southern tip of Ytre Sula we pass the island of **Hille**, the most northerly of the larger islands in Gulen municipality. Just beyond the island is **Hisarøy** (18.7 km²). South of Hille the larger island of **Byrknesøy** (18.7 km²) passes slightly further south. Just beyond are the islands of **Mjømma** (10.3 km²) and **Sandøy** (31.9 km²). The largest islands are connected by bridges. In 2008 a bridge will be constructed to link these to the mainland.

✍

© DAN YOUNG

At **Skjerjehamn**, on the north west tip of Sandøy is the site where the much-debated new statue of King Olav V is to be placed. The statue was originally commissioned by Oslo municipality and was to be placed near the town hall in the capital. However the municipality rejected the statue when it was completed in 2006. Skjerjehamn is an old trading post and communications centre. It is mentioned in written texts dating from 1641, however it is believed to have been a trading post on the island long before this time. From 1839, Skjerjehamn was a port of call for regular boat routes and there was a general store and a post office (from 1866), telegraph office, guest house, timber yard and an oil storage warehouse. Skjerjehamn is now being renovated and rebuilt to become a local arts centre.

Gulen has a great deal of cultural heritage, with archaeological finds of Stone Age settlements, burial mounds from the Bronze Age and many finds from the early Iron Age (p 83). In the village of **Eivindvik** on the mainland, there are two stone crosses that are believed to have been erected in connection with the introduction of Christianity in Norway (p 377).

© JARLE WESTERVIK

Gulating tingsted (ting=place of assembly) was said to have been located in the area, possibly at Eivindvik. Gulating was a joint court for the western counties in Norway. The court's task was to make judgements in cases and to pass new laws and regulations. The court was probably established before the year 930. All free-men could meet at the common court. Later, the court was extended and became a representational court. Each year, approximately 400 farmer representatives or committee members met, also royal ombudsmen and parish priests. The number of representatives was later greatly reduced. In the 14th century the Gulating was moved to Bergen, it became Bergen Lagting in 1604.

Approx. 60°51'N 4°46'E

We cross the boundary between Gulen and Austrheim municipalities

Austrheim municipality

Betydning av kommunevåpen: Symboliserer de mange broene som binder kommunen sammen.
Betydning navn: -.
Kommunesenter: Årås. **Innb.:** 560.
Posisjon: 60°47'10"N 4°55'13"E.
Areal: 56 km². **Innb.:** 2.520.
Befolkningstetthet: 45,13 innb./km².
Arealfordeling: Jordbruk 10 %, produktiv skog 13 %, ferskvann - %, annet areal 77 %.
Næringsliv: StatoilHydros oljeraffineri er hoved-arbeidsgiver, Servicebedrifter og verksteder innen industrien.
Austrheim kommunes hjemmesider: www.austrheim.kommune.no

The mouth of the fjord Fensfjorden passes on the port side. The fjord runs in a southwesterly direction. It is 30 km long and 3-5 km wide. The 24 km long side 'arm' of Masfjorden runs in a northeasterly direction.

The lighthouse Holmengrå can be seen on the starboard side. The lighthouse was built in 1892. It was rebuilt and relocated in 1950 and remained in operation until 1991. The lighthouse is comprised of a building with a 16 m high tower and the beacon has a range of 17 nautical miles. Holmengrå lighthouse had a foghorn, a diaphone, installed in 1954. This was later replaced with a compressed air operated signal. The lighthouse also had a radio beacon that was in operation from 1947 until 1992.

60°50'40"N 4°45'47"E   + 3 hrs 35 min ⑫

The large oil refinery at Mongstad can be seen over on the port side. It is the largest oil refinery in Norway (of medium size by European standards). The refinery is owned by Mongstad Refining – the Norwegian company StatoilHydro and Dutch Shell own 79 % and 21 % of the company respectively.

The oldest of the refineries at Mongstad was built at the start of the 1970s. When the refinery was expanded in 1989 the processing capacity increased from 6.5 to 8

million tonnes of crude oil per annum. The capacity was increased further to 10 million tonnes in 2006. A desulphuring plant for diesel and marine gasoil the same year, and in 1997, a new plant for the production of benzene began operations. In 2003 a new advanced desulphuring plant was completed.

Petroleum is refined from the crude oil (all of which comes from the Norwegian continental shelf and is brought on land via pipelines). This corresponds to approximately one and a half times the Norwegian demand for diesel, aviation fuel and other lighter petroleum products. In addition the plant produces petroleum coke (petcoke) from the heaviest components in the crude oil. This is used in the production of anodes for the Norwegian aluminium industry. Approx. 60 % of production is exported to Europe, North America and Asia.

StatoilHydro also operates a separate crude oil terminal at Mongstad. Six reservoirs built into the mountain have a total storage capacity of 9.4 million barrels of crude oil. Two quays can handle crude oil tankers up to 380 000 tonnes, and a transhipment quay can handle oil tank-

ers up to 440 000 tonnes. The port facility at Mongstad is the largest in Norway, measured in tonnage, and the second largest in Europe after Rotterdam in the Netherlands.

A new heat and power installation is being planned at Mongstad. The construction work will be carried out in 2007-2009 and the installation will be on-line in 2010.

Our voyage continues into **Fedjefjorden**.

ᘓᘔ

Approx. 60°50'N   4°45'E
Fedje municipality passes on the starboard side

Fedje municipality

Municipal coat of arms, significance: Symbolises the hard struggle to survive along the coast of Norway.
Meaning of name: From Norse: *Fedjar*, related to Gothic *fath*, 'fence or wall', meaning here 'chain of islands'.
Municipal seat: Fedje (pop. 452).
Position: 60°46'50"N 4°42'17"E. **Area:** 9 km².
Population: 620. **Pop. density:** 68.9 /km².
Area distribution: Farming 3 %, forestry -%, fresh water 5 %, other area 92 %.
Trade and industry: Fishing, landing stages, fish processing. Fish farming. Fedje Vessel Traffic Services. Metalworking and machining industry. Tourism.
Activities to return to: Sea fishing, lighthouse safari.
Fedje municipality's home page: www.fedje.kommune.no

© JENNIFER DEVINE

ᘓᘔ

60°47'30"N   4°45'E   + 3 t 40 min ⑬

The island of **Fedje** (7.5 km², 42 m above sea level) is passed on the starboard side. It is a conservation area and a nature reserve for seabirds. More than 200 different species have been observed on the island, which has excellent wetland areas.

The pattern of settlement on Fedje has always been connected with fishing and the ocean. Several thousand years ago, Stone Age farmers (p 83) cleared the forests to use the flat island as winter grazing for their livestock. Whaling was the most important commercial activity for

© POLINA ISICHENKO

many years. Around 1900, industrial peat cutting started at Fedje to provide fuel that was in demand in (among other places) Bergen. Peat cutting continued up to 1920. There has also been a fish oil factory on the island based on products from the whaling industry and a fish-canning factory. These are no longer in operation.

© ALEX EDGAR / WWW.FLICKR.COM

Fedje Vessel Traffic Service is located on the north side of the island. The Vessel Traffic Service monitors the north and south-bound ships that sail along the coast of western Norway, to and from the port at Bergen and the ships that sail into and out of Mongstad. The Vessel Traffic Service Centre is situated on the island's highest point and is built upon the foundations of a German radar tower that was built during the Second World War. More than 300 German soldiers were stationed on the island during the war.

Fedje church is a longhouse-style church built of stone, constructed in 1941. The church has seating for 400 persons.

The 87 m long, 2 150 tonne German submarine "U864" was sunk in a battle with the British submarine HMS "Venturer" in February 1945. The battle took place at Fedje, and "U864" was probably the only German submarine to be sunk by another submarine whilst both vessels were below the surface. The submarine had received orders to sail to Japan via Bergen. Its cargo comprised of, among other things, 1 857 containers holding a total of 65 tonnes of mercury that was to be used in the manufacture of weapons by the Japanese, who were German allies. The submarine also carried advanced jet motor components for German Messerschmitt fighters. Hitler's plan was that the components would help the Japanese to attain dominance in the air war in the

Pacific and thus force the USA to redeploy their forces that would otherwise be sent to support the Allied war offensive against Germany.

British code breakers had intercepted messages concerning the submarine's destination and its cargo. HMS "Venturer" was therefore sent to intercept "U864". After a three-hour game of 'cat and mouse', the British submarine fired four torpedoes. Three of them missed their target but the fourth struck "U864" amidships and the submarine broke in two. 73 submariners were killed.

In 2003, the submarine was found at a depth of 152 metres, approximately 2 nautical miles west of Fedje. The wreck is an environmental time bomb. The large cargo of steel bottles containing mercury are slowly rusting and dissolving after more than 60 years in the sea. An area of approx. 150 m around the vessel is polluted and fishing and diving close to the wreck is prohibited. There have been many intense discussions in an attempt to find a solution the problem, at the highest political levels in Norway. The alternatives are; to enclose the submarine and the surrounding area, or to raise the vessel and dispose of the dangerous cargo. The international media has also reported the unresolved issue and the potential for immense environmental problems. As of May 2007, a final decision had still not been taken on the issue of the wreck of "U864".

Hellisøy lighthouse stands on the islet of **Hellisøy** just south of Fedje. The 32 m high iron tower was erected in 1855 and the light has a range of 18.8 nautical miles. It was automated in 1992. The lighthouse received a conservation order in 2000.

In February 2007 the Cypriot cargo vessel M/S "Server" ran aground at Hellisøy lighthouse. The ship carried ballast and sailed in poor weather; there was a near gale in  the area. The crew of 25 was rescued but the ship broke in two, causing some pollution. The ship's fore section was towed into land, the aft section lies on the sea bed close to the lighthouse.

60°44'40"N   4°48'42"E

We cross the boundary between Fedje and Radøy municipalities on the port side

Radøy municipality

Municipal coat of arms, significance: Archaeological finds made in the municipality.
Meaning of name: From Norse: rod, 'moraine'.
Municipal seat: Manger (pop. 829).
Position: 60°39'37"N 4°58'45"E. **Area:** 112 km².
Population: 4 658. **Pop. density:** 41.6 /km².
Area distribution: Farming 24 %, forestry 17 %, fresh water 4 %, other area 55 %.
Trade and industry: Foodstuffs industry. Mechanical engineering Timber industry Manufacture of fishing gear. Agriculture with livestock, cattle, sheep and chickens. Fish farming.
Places to return to: Western Norway Emigration Centre. Borgatunet. War memorial Marøy.
Radøy municipality's home page: www.radoy.kommune.no

The municipality boundary between Fedje and Øygarden municipalities passes on the starboard side

Øygarden municipality

Municipal coat of arms, significance: Symbolises the sea.
Meaning of name: Refers to several smaller islands that form a 'wall' (*gard*) between the sea and land.
Municipal seat: Tjeldstø (pop. -).
Position: 60°33'N 4°53'E. **Area:** 67 km².
Population: 4 134. **Pop. density:** 61.7 /km².
Area distribution: Farmer 5 %, forestry 20 %, fresh water 4 %, other area 71 %.
Trade and industry: Petroleum industry. Fish farming (salmon, cod and shellfish). Agriculture/cattle farming, in combination with other activities.
Activities to return to: Sea fishing.
Øygarden municipality's home page: www.oygarden.kommune.no

60°43'N   4°49'36"E   + 4 hrs 08 min ⑭

The villages of **Rossnes** and **Risnes** are on the northernmost tip of **Radøya** on the port side.

On the starboard side are the small islands of **Nordøyene** and **Hernar** in Øygarden municipality.

60°42'N   4°50'E **+ 4 hrs 12 min**

The voyage continues into **Hjeltefjorden**, past the islands known as **Marøya** and the villages of **Bøvågen** and **Hordabø**, thereafter the islands **Uttorska** and **Toska**.

60°41'18"N   4°51'25"E **+ 4 hrs 17 min (15)**

Sture Terminal in Øygarden municipality can be seen to starboard up ahead. The crude oil terminal receives crude oil and condensate from the Oseberg field, via a 115 km long pipeline that has a diameter of 28 inches (71.1 cm). It also receives crude oil from the Grane field via another 212 km long pipeline. These fields lie west and southwest of Bergen.

Sture Terminal began operations in 1988 and it is one of the most important transhipment ports for crude oil extracted from the Norwegian continental shelf. The installation includes two quays that can handle oil tankers up to 300 000 tonnes. There are 5 mountain reservoirs for storage of crude oil with a total capacity of 10 million barrels, another reservoir for storage of LPG (Liquefied Petroleum Gas) (6 million barrels) and another for storage of ballast water (2 million barrels). The terminal has a separate unit for treatment of VOC (Volatile Organic Compounds, various liquid gases that are emitted during tanking) from tankers.

Approx. 60°38'N   4°55'E

The boundary of Meland municipality passes on the port side

The municipality boundary of Askøy municipality passes on the starboard side

Meland municipality

Municipal coat of arms, significance: Refers to the local production of augers, an important industry.
Meaning of name: From Norse: *Medalland*, 'centrally located farm'.
Municipal seat: Frekhaug (pop. 1 596).
Position: 60°30'34"N 5°14'E. **Area:** 91 km².
Population: 6 016. **Pop. density:** 66.1 /km².
Area distribution: Farming 13 %, forestry 31 %, fresh water 5 %, other area 51 %.
Trade and industry: Mechanical workshops. Timber industry. Agriculture - cattle and sheep. Some horticulture. Many of the population work outside of the municipality.
Places to return to: Holmeknappen.
Meland municipality's home page: www.meland.kommune.no

60°36'30"N   4°56'39"E

Askøy municipality

Municipal coat of arms, significance: Formed from the name of the municipality – a green ash tree on an island against a silver background.
Meaning of name: From the farm Ask north east on Askøy, from the ash tree species.
Municipal seat: Kleppestø (pop. 17 754).
Position: 60°24'13"N 5°13'10"E. **Area:** 100 km².
Population: 23 018. **Pop. density:** 230.2 /km².
Area distribution: Farming 5 %, forestry 18 %, fresh water 6 %, other area 71 %.
Trade and industry: Agriculture - cattle and sheep. Strawberry growing. Fishing. Oil tank installation. Approx. 50 % of the population work outside of the municipality. Chemical and mechanical industries.
Places to return to: Kongsgården at Hop. Herdla. Bird sanctuary on Herdla.
Askøy municipality's home page: www.meland.kommune.no

The ship sails alongside the west side of the island **Holsnøy** (88.8 km², 324 m above sea level) in Meland municipality, on the port side. At the northernmost tip of the island we pass the small islands of **Prestholmen**, **Store Agnøy** and **Lille Agnøy** in Askøy municipality.

Holsnøy, which represents 98 % of the area of Meland municipality, is largely marshland with a slightly hilly landscape. Most of the population lives in the south west. The island has several bridges connecting it to the mainland.

60°35'N   4°59'E **+ 4 hrs 47 min (16)**

Our voyage continues further into **Herdlefjorden**, between Holsnøy on the port side and the eastern side of **Askøy** to starboard. The island **Herdla** (1.6 km², 32 m above sea level) lies at the northernmost tip of Askøy. The flat island is distinct from the other, more rocky islands in the area. Herdla is a terminal moraine (unconsolidated debris deposited at the end of a glacier) with fertile moraine soil formed from earth and gravel masses pushed by the ice that covered the land approx. 10 000 years ago. The fertile soil creates excellent conditions for agriculture. In 1597 Herdla became a breeding station owned by Bergenhus palace. Right up until modern times the largest farm in Hordaland county has been at Herdla.

Archaeological excavations have discovered evidence that people have lived on Herdla for 7-8 000 years. North on the island, traces have been found of a town fort dating from the migration period. Evidence uncovered during excavations shows that there was once a chieftain seat north of the church on Herdla. Remains have been found of a large courtyard and buildings. Stratigraphy has revealed many artefacts and leather products from the Middle Ages have also been found (p 83).

As early as 1146, Herdla church was mentioned in written documents, in a letter from Pope Eugenius III. The church was dedicated to St. Nicolaus of Myra, the patron saint of seafarers. Like the church at Kinn (p 373) the church was constructed of stone without a spire. It was built in a simple romance style. However it was later rebuilt, this time in a gothic style with pointed arches. The church has been owned by several parties, among them Munkeliv monastery and Krist church in Bergen. The castellan of Bergenhus fortifications (p 9) gave the pulpit as a gift to the church in the 1630s. This bore the signature of King Christian IV (1577-1648) from 1631. The old church was destroyed by a storm in 1861, after which it was demolished and the stone was re-used to build the new church. A fire in 1931 destroyed most of the old pulpit, however a copy was constructed from photographs, that now stands in the current church.

During the Second World War (1942), the church spire was demolished. The German forces believed that it could be used as a landmark for Allied aircraft flying on sorties from England. The church roof was taken down and the inventory was stored in various places. The church was given a flat roof and was used as an ammunition store and as horse stables. Russian prisoners of war dug tunnels in several directions, radiating from the church and it was forbidden to bury the dead on the island. A new church was built in 1951.

"Festung Herdla" was the name given to the German installations that were built on Herdla during the war. The local population of approx. 155 persons was forcibly evacuated and parts of the flat landscape were covered with timber and concrete to create a new, larger airfield. Aircraft hangars were constructed along with storage buildings, barracks, quays and tunnels and a number of gun emplacements. The airfield was the most important military installation between Stavanger and Trondheim and was vital in the defence of Bergen submarine base (p 12, p 24). It remained in operation until 1955, when Flesland airport in Bergen was opened.

When the residents of Herdla returned to the island after the war, there was a considerable amount of restoration work to be carried out. Many of the barracks were dismantled and transported to Finnmark, where the need for accommodation was acute due to the destruction caused during the German forces' razing of the county (p 221). The Norwegian Defence Forces overtook control of the defence positions and several new ones were built. These have now been decommissioned. Only ruins remain of the German fortifications.

The sea and wetland areas on Herdla are part of an area that has been granted official status as a nature reserve. The island is rich in bird life and 225 different species have been registered, among them Eider ducks, Velvet Scoters, Common Shelducks, Skylarks and Dunlins.

60°33'23"N 5°00'E   + 4 hrs 54 min

On the starboard side we can see a stone quarry with a shipping quay. The quarry is just north of the village of **Abbedisso** on Askøy.

The island of **Askøy** (89 km²) is the largest island in Askøy municipality, the neighbouring municipality to Bergen. The island was connected to the mainland in 1992, when the Askøy bridge was opened. The bridge is 1 150 m in length and the distance between the 150 m high bridge towers is 850 m. The free height under the bridge is 63 m. Prior to the construction of Storebælt bridge between Denmark and Sweden, Askøy bridge was the longest in Northern Europe.

The bridge connecting the island to the mainland to a considerable increase in the population of Askøy, especially in the southern part of the island.

Over on the port side we sail along Holsnøya municipality, and now we can see that we are finally approaching Bergen. The villages of **Fløksand** and **Holme** pass by. On the island's southern tip is the municipal seat of Frekhaug.

60°32'48"N 5°01'E   + 5 hrs 18 min ⑰

Just inside of **Frekhaug** is Nordhordland bridge that connects the island **Flatøy** and Nordhordland to the mainland and Bergen. The bridge was opened in 1994 and is Norway's second longest, with a length of 1 614 m. A suspension bridge has been built across the sailing channel, the rest of the bridge is a floating construction, 1 243 m in length. This the world's longest floating bridge without side stays. From Flatøy a shorter bridge goes over to Knarvik in Lindås municipality.

60°32'18"N 5°02'40"E

We are now in **Byfjorden**, and pass **Tertnes** and **Eidsvåg** on the port side. Also on the port side are the villages of **Ask**, **Erdal**, **Florvåg** and **Kleppestø** on Askøy.

The panorama of Vågen and Bergen can be seen ahead of the ship. The city with the seven mountains is described on Day 1, p 8.

The ship docks at the quayside in Bergen

Sogn and Fjordane County

County coat-of-arms: Represents the three fjords in the county and indicates the three main areas: Sogn, Sunnfjord and Nordfjord.

Origin of name: From Norse Sogn, from the verb súga, 'suck', referring to the strong currents in the fjord, the actual name of Sognefjord.

Area: 18 623 km². **Population:** 106 650.

Adm. centre: Hermansverk.

Municipalities passed on the southward voyage, in order: Selje, Vågsøy, Bremanger, Flora, Askvoll, Hyllestad, Solund, Gulen.

Topography: The topography of the county has been formed by erosion processes caused by flowing water in fissures and along weak zones in the bedrock, later enlarged by major ice erosion. This is especially obvious in the deep fjords and the U-shaped valleys that continue the head of the fjord. The largest fjords in the county run in an east-west direction, with shorter traversing fjord arms. North of Sognefjorden is the largest glacier in Europe, Jostedalsbreen. The shoreline is largely undeveloped. The tree line falls from maximum 800 metres above sea level in inner areas to 200 metres above sea level at the coast. The county has two national parks (one of these is Jostedalsbreen National Park) as well as several designated protected landscape areas. Nærøyfjorden is included on UNESCO's list of heritage sites as a fjord landscape.

Climate: Most dominant air streams and the mobile low pressure and precipitation fronts come from the west and the south-west. During the winter, the surface winds blow along the fjords and valleys, i.e. from the east. During the summer the wind blows most often from the north-east on the coast. Outer and central areas receive a lot of precipitation, in the range of 1 500-3 000 mm near the coast. Inner areas are sheltered by the mountains. In coastal areas, February is the coldest month with a mean temperature of 1-2 °C. August is the warmest month with a mean temperature of 14 °C. The interior has a typical inland climate. The northernmost part of the county, especially near Stad, has frequent high winds and storms.

Population: Most of the population lives along the fjords and in communities at the heads of fjords. The county is the country's least urbanised. Several municipalities do not have a municipal 'centre' as such.

TRADE AND INDUSTRY

Agriculture and forestry: The county has the greatest proportion of employment within the primary industries in the country. Agriculture and animal husbandry (cattle, sheep, goats). 98 % of all agricultural areas are used for grazing and haymaking. The size of farms is under the national average. Some fruit and berry production in central and interior areas. Vegetable growing.

Forestry is mainly a secondary industry carried out as a supplement to agriculture.

Fishing: Fishing is very important along the coast in the county. Most fish is brought on land in Måløy.

Other industries: Food production and processing industry using local raw materials, dairies, abattoirs, fruit and berry processing, fish processing. Boatyards and repair workshops. Car body panel production. Metalworking industry based on local hydroelectric power, including machining of aluminium. Smelting plant. Textile and clothing industry. Chemical plants. Plastics industry. Ski factory. Furniture production. Oil industry.

Energy: The county has a total of 77 hydroelectric power stations producing more than 1 MW of power.

Tourism: Sogn and Fjordane is an major tourist county. The many fjords and glaciers are popular attractions, as are Flåmsbanen, stave churches, glacier museums, summer ski centres, Stadlandet and Nærøyfjorden.

Transport and communications: Many sea routes due to the deep fjords. Road and tunnel construction has led to a considerable increase in overland transport. Several road connections with the rest of the country that are kept open all year round. The Lærdal tunnel is the world's longest road tunnel (in 2006, 24.5 km in length). The county has four airports: Sogndal, Førde, Florø and Sandane.

Source: Store norske Leksikon.

© J. T. SOLHEIM, WWW.SVANOY.COM

MAPS

City of Bergen

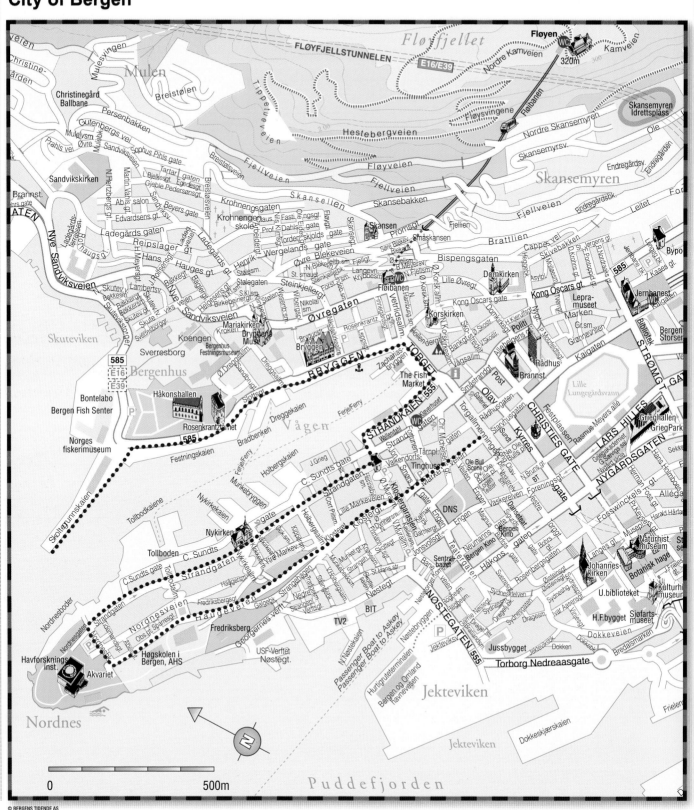

Måløy - Torvik

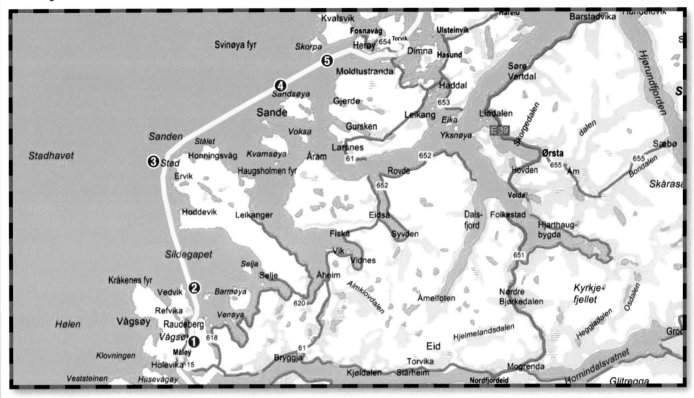

Torvik - Ålesund

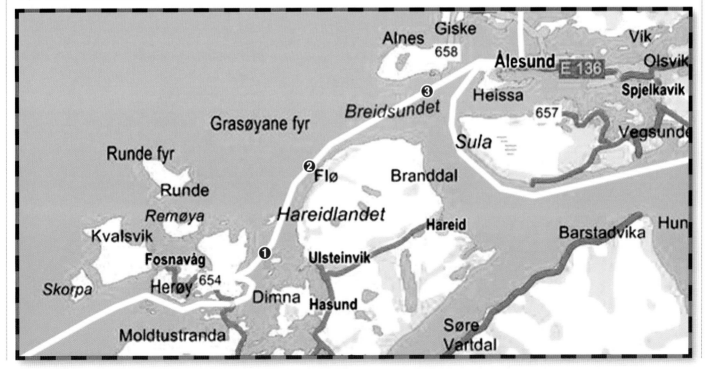

Ålesund - Geiranger - Ålesund

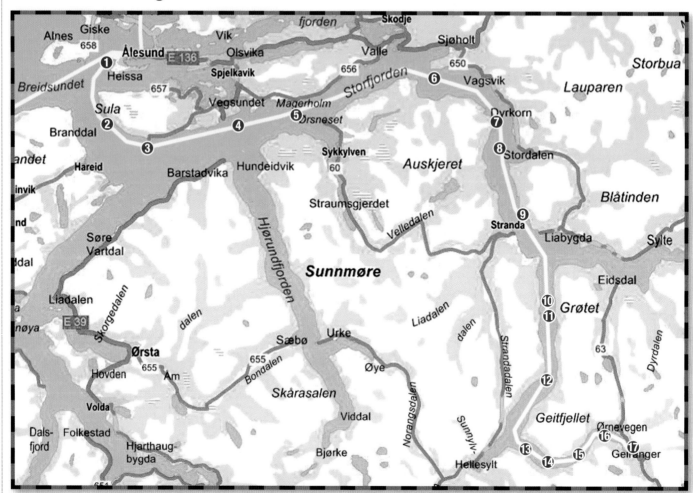

Ålesund - Molde

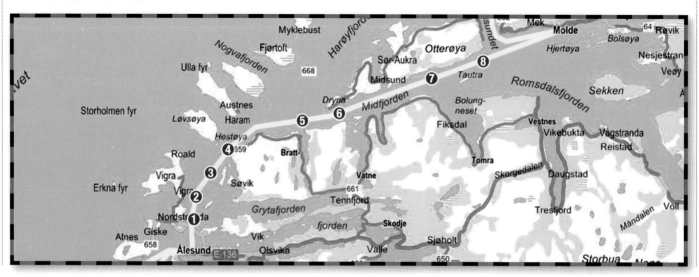

City of Ålesund

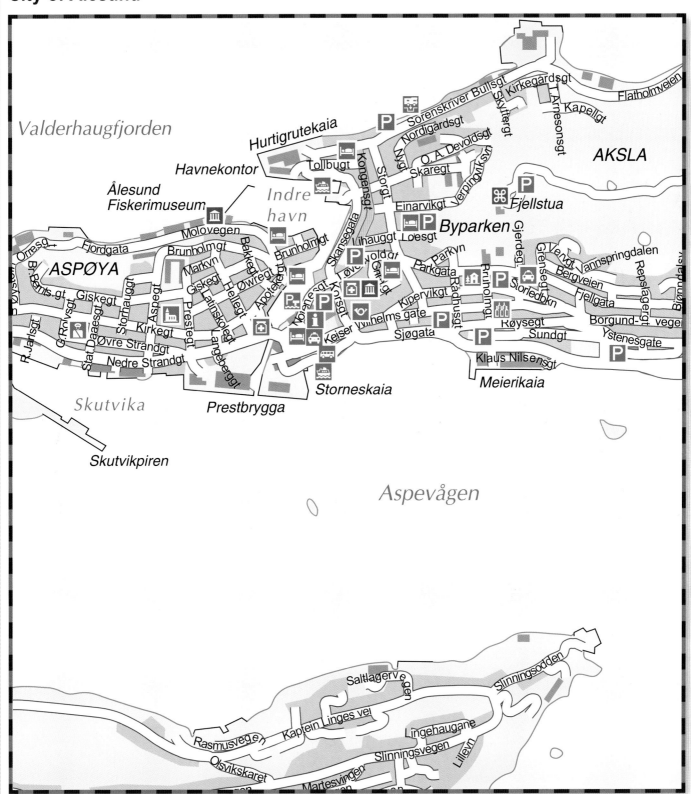

City of Trondheim

Trondheim - Bjugn

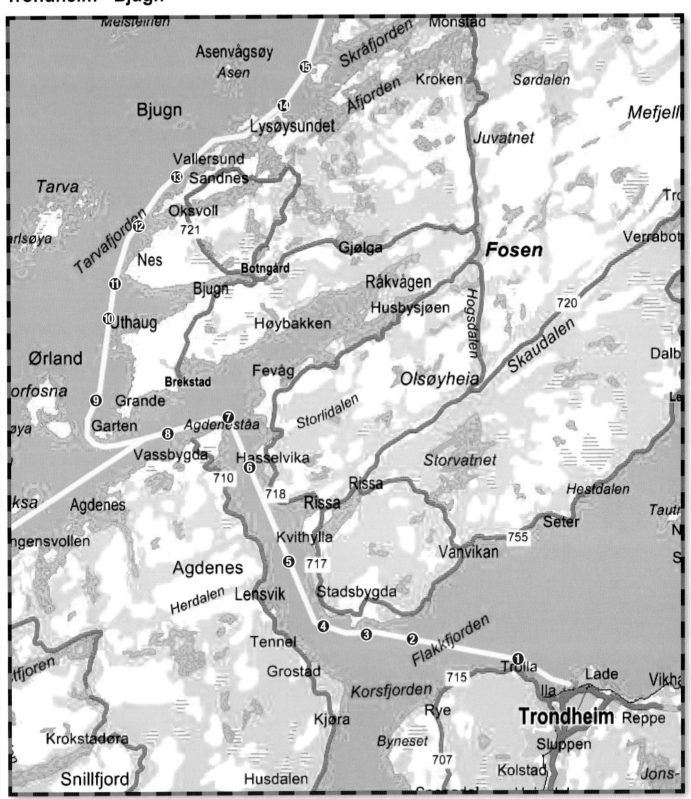

Meisteinen

Asenvågsøy
Asen
⑮
Skråfjorden   Monstad

Bjugn

Afjorden   Kroken   Sørdalen

⑭ Lysøysundet

Juvatnet   Mefjell

Vallersund
⑬ Sandnes

Tarva

Oksvoll
⑫   721

Gjølga   Fosen   Verrabot

Tro

Nes   Botngård

Råkvågen

⑪ Bjugn

Husbysjøen

⑩ Uthaug   Høybakken

Hogsdalen   720

Ørland   Fevåg

Olsøyheia   Skaudalen   Dalb

Brekstad   Storlidalen

orfosna   Le

⑨ Grande   ⑦

Garten   Agdenesståa

Storvatnet

⑧   Hasselvika   Hestdalen   Tautr

Vassbygda   ⑥   Rissa   N

710   718   Rissa   S

øya

iksa   Agdenes   Seter

hgensvollen   Kvithylla   755   Vanvikan

Agdenes   ⑤ 717

Herdalen   Lensvik   Stadsbygda

④   ③   ②   ①

Tennel   Flakkfjorden   Trulla   Lade   Vikh

Grostad   715   Ila

ttfjoren   Korsfjorden   Rye   Trondheim   Reppe

Kjøra   Byneset   Sluppen

Krokstadøra   707   Kolstad   Jons-

Snillfjord   Husdalen

Bjugn - Rørvik I

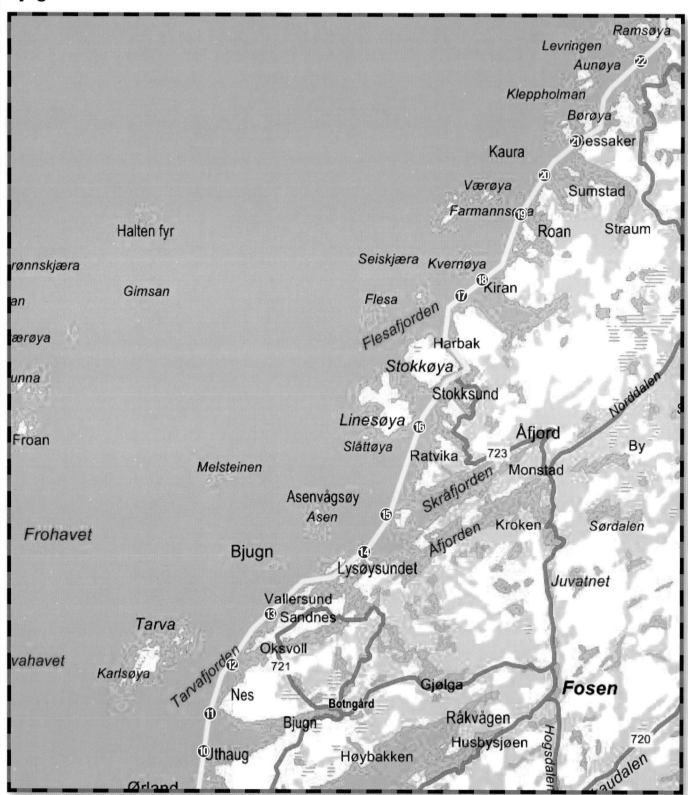

Ramsøya
Levringen
Aunøya ㉒
Kleppholman
Børøya
㉑ essaker
Kaura
Værøya ㉑
Farmannsø ⑲ a   Sumstad
Roan   Straum
Halten fyr
rønnskjæra   Seiskjæra Kvernøya
an   Gimsan   Flesa   ⑱ Kiran
ærøya   ⑰
Flesafjorden
unna   Harbak
Stokkøya
Froan   Stokksund
Linesøya ⑯   Norddalen
Melsteinen   Slåttøya   Åfjord   By
Ratvika   723
Monstad
Frohavet   Asenvågsøy   Skråfjorden   Kroken   Sørdalen
Asen   ⑮   Afjorden
Bjugn   ⑭   Juvatnet
Lysøysundet
Vallersund
Tarva   ⑬ Sandnes
vahavet   Oksvoll
Karlsøya   Tarvafjorden ⑫   721   Gjølga   Fosen
Nes
⑪   Botngård   Råkvågen
Bjugn   Hogsdalen   720
⑩ Uthaug   Husbysjøen
Ørland   Høybakken   audalen

Bjugn - Rørvik II

Fruflesa   Hellesøya

Hunnestad   Vikna   Ofstad   Torstad

Binnerøya   Svinøya   770   Sørå

Skjerværet   Skipperøya   Rørvik

Bondøya   Brønnøyfjorden   Rørvik
                                    lufthavn   Varøya

Nordøyan   Edøya   ㉘

Fiskflesa   Nordøyan

Sørøyråsa   Krokøya   Arnøyfjorden   Torla
                                              768   Falli

            Grinna

Gjeslingene   Abelvær   Folda

Vestbraken   ㉗   Moflesa

            Aldgården   Skogøya   Sals

Nylandskjeret   Hovsodden Dun

                                    777

                     Finnanger

Folda   Bjørøyværet   Utvorda   769

      Ellingen   Skorstad   Elvalande

      Lyngværet   Otterøya

Glaøyværet ㉖   Sitter

Store Grøtholmen   Ledang   Skomsvoll   Ra

㉕   Lauvsnes   Hoddøya   767
Flatanger   766

Lausflesa   Kvaløya   Sundsøya

Hasvågøya   Flatanger   Tøttdal   Skjerpøya   N

      Jøssundfjorden   Hemnafjellet   Selne

Buholmråsa fyr   Eidbyggskardet   Bangsur
㉔

Raudøyan ㉓   Jøssund

Skokkeløyan   Oppland

Ramsøya   Rørvassdalen

Levringen   Sjøåsen

Aunøya ㉒

Kleppholman   Osen   Øyensskavlen   17

Børøya   Årgård

Nesna - Ørnes - Bodø

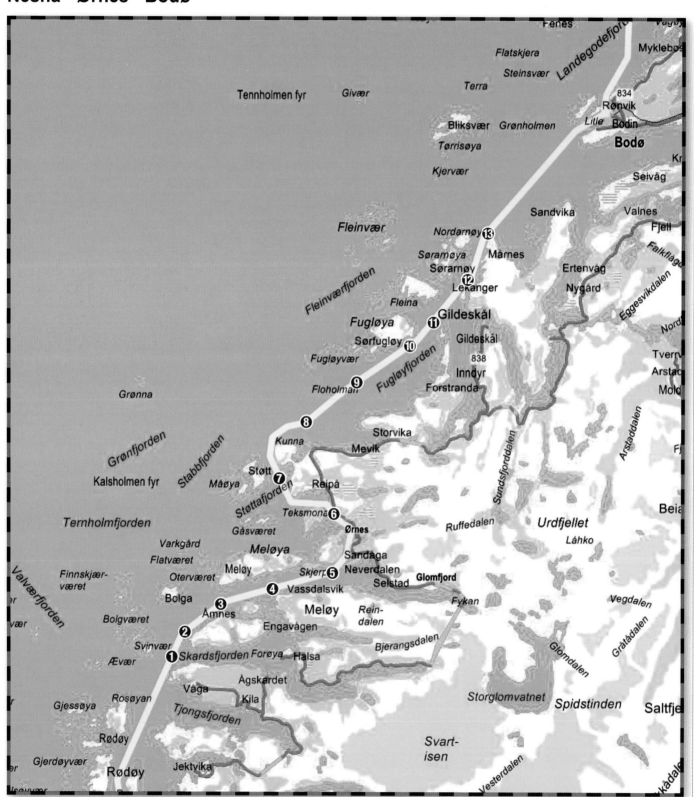

Bodø - Stamsund

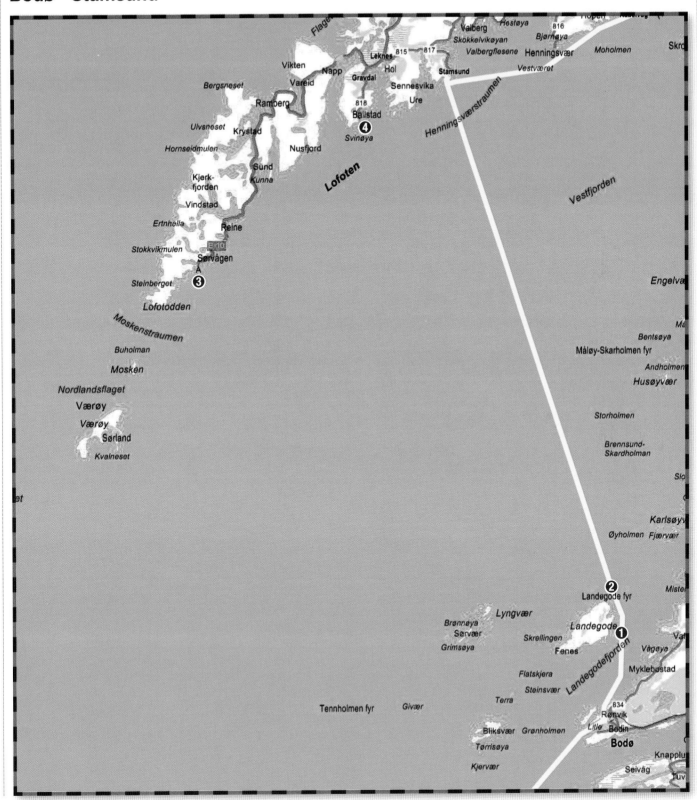

City of Bodø

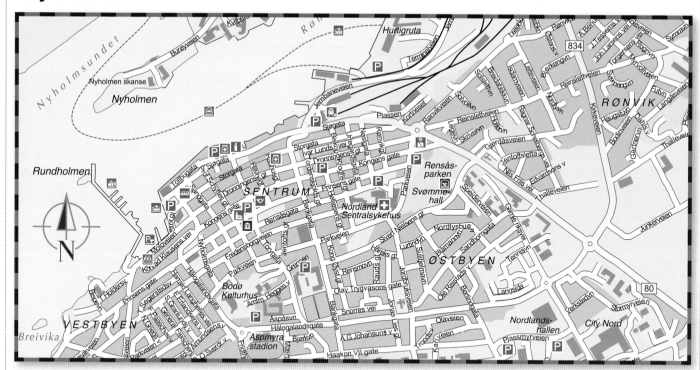

Stamsund - Svolvær

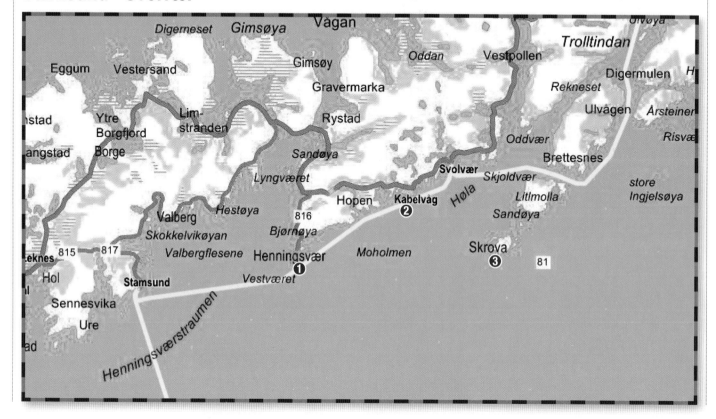

Harstad - Finnsnes

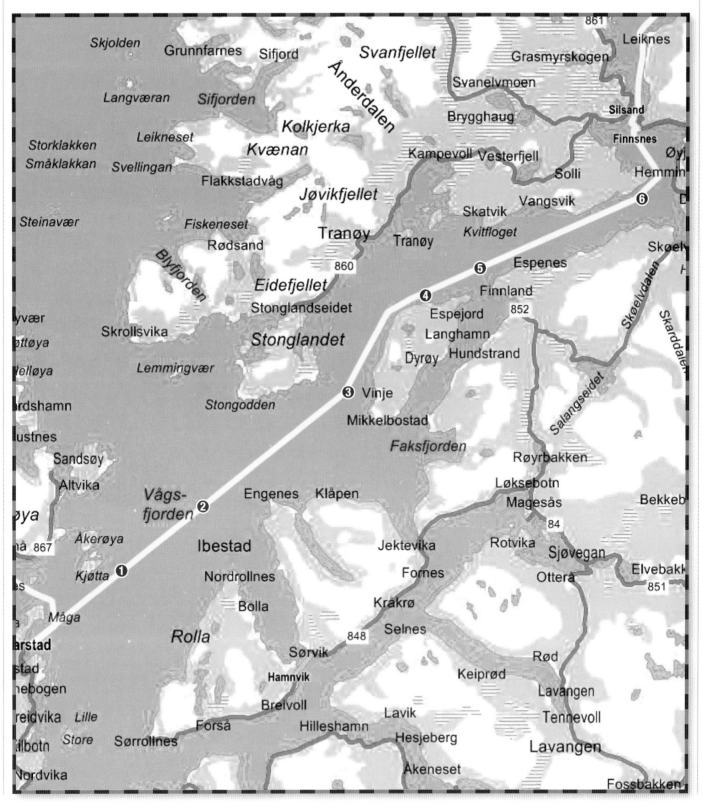

Finnsnes - Tromsø

City of Tromsø

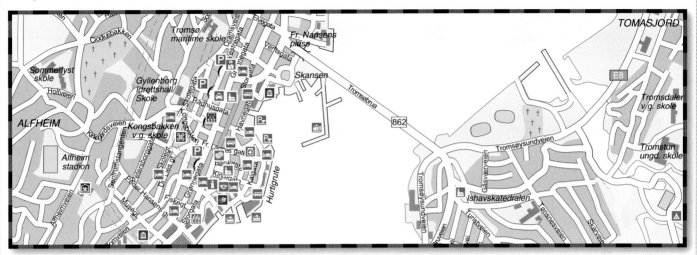

Tromsø - Skjervøy

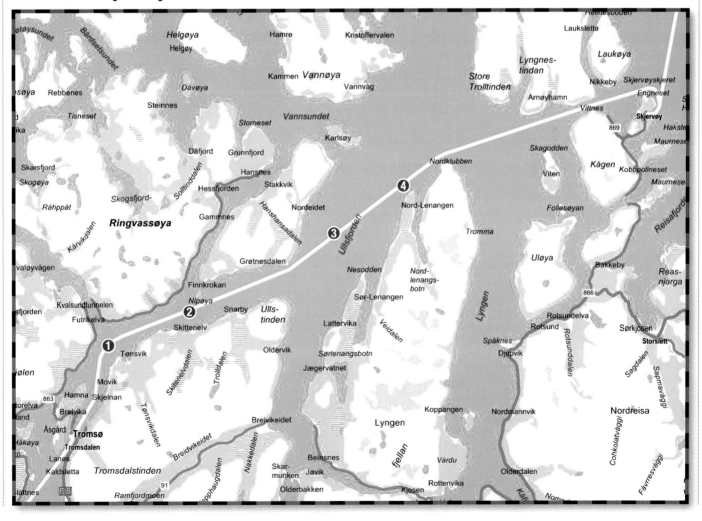

Hammerfest - Havøysund

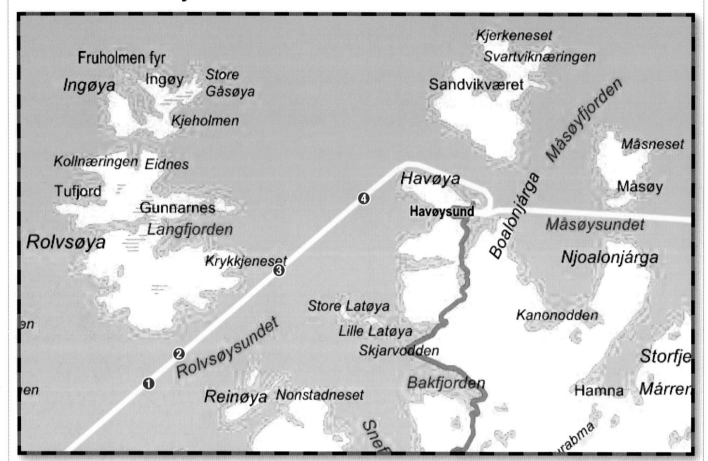

Havøysund - Honningsvåg / Nordkapp

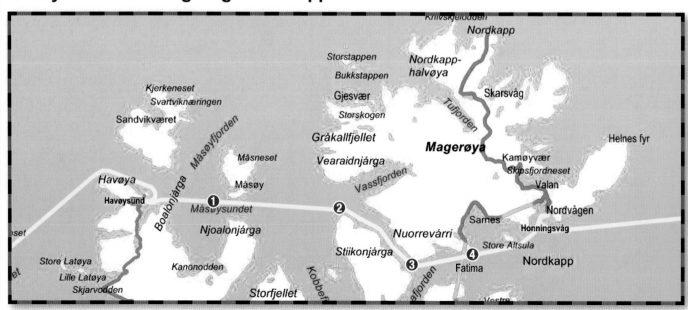

Honningsvåg / Nordkapp - Kjøllefjord

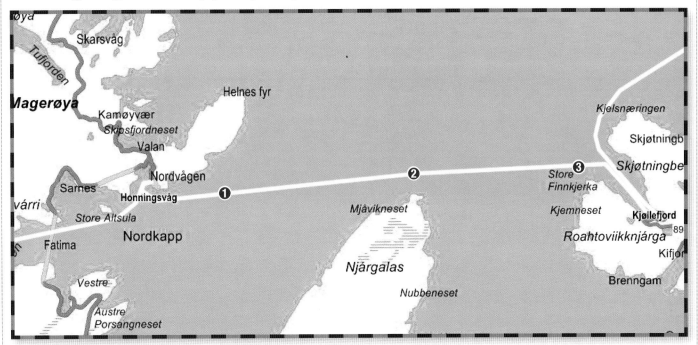

Kjøllefjord - Mehamn - Berlevåg

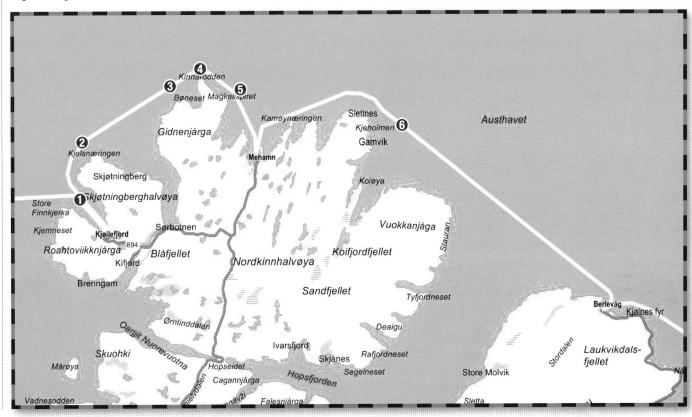

Vadsø - Kirkenes

Kirkenes - Vardø

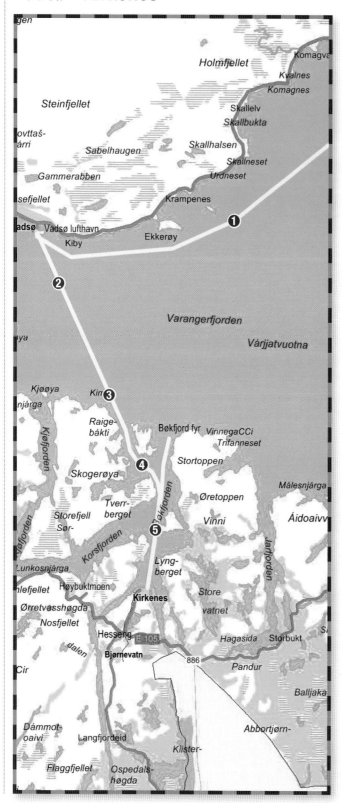

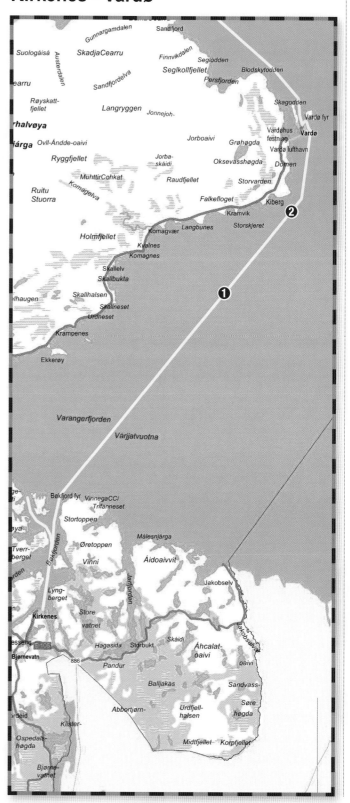

City of Kirkenes

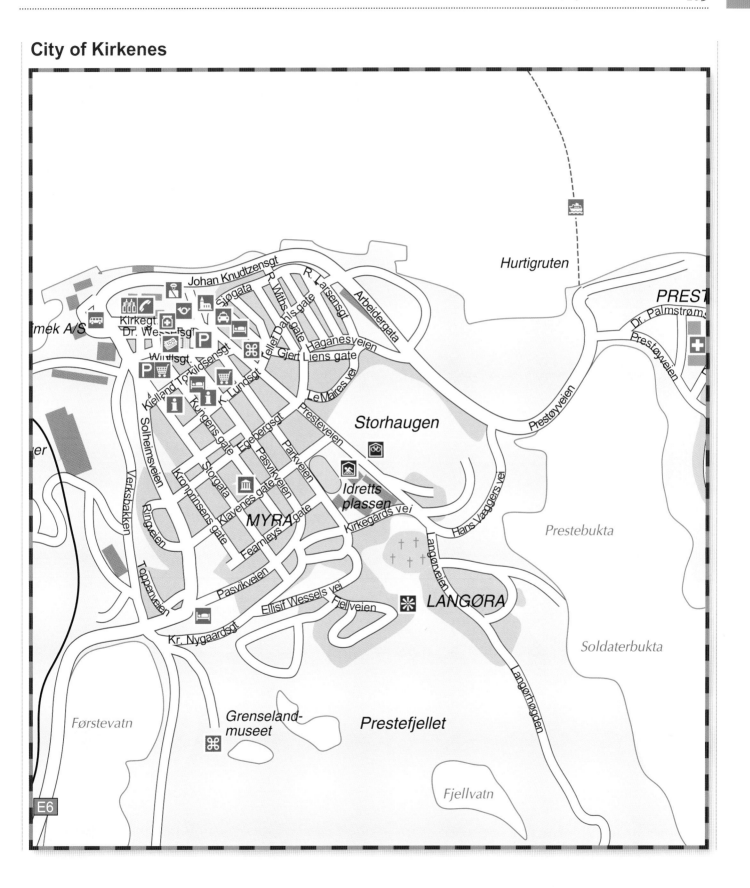

imek A/S

Kirkegt.

Dr. Wessel-sgt

Johan Knudtzensgt

Sjøgata

R. Miths gate

R. Larsensgt

Arbeidergata

Hurtigruten

PREST

Dr. Palmstrøms

Prestøyveien

Wirilsgt.

Hellef Dahls gate

Haganesveien

Gjert Liens gate

Le Maires vei

Kjelland Torkildsensgt

K. Lundsgt

Prestøyveien

Storhaugen

Kungens gate

Egebergsgt

Presteveien

Solheimsveien

Storgata

Parkveien

Idretts plassen

Hans Vaaggers vei

Prestebukta

Verksbakken

Kronprinsens gate

Klavenes gate

Pasvikveien

MYRA

Fearnleys gate

Kirkegards vei

Ringveien

Langønveien

LANGØRA

Soldaterbukta

Toppenveien

Pasvikveien

Ellisif Wessels vei

Fjellveien

Langørnøgden

Førstevatn

Kr. Nygaardsgt

Grenseland-museet

Prestefjellet

Fjellvatn

E6

City of Vardø

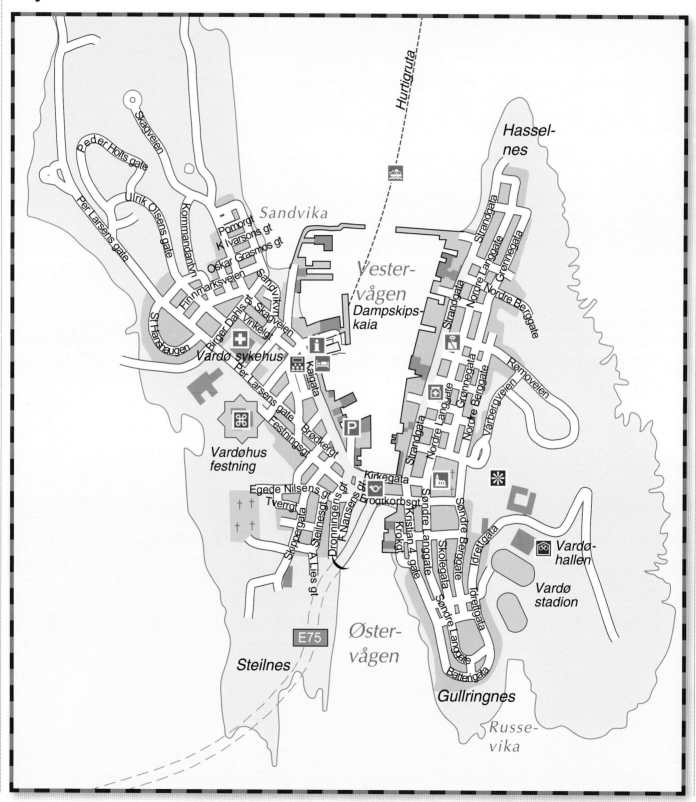

Hurtigruta

Hassel-
nes

Skagveien

Peder Holts gate

Ulrik Olsens gate

Per Larsens gate

Kommandantvn

Sandvika

Pomorgt
K Ivarsons gt
Oskar Grasmos gt

Finnmarksveien

Sandvikveien

Vester-
vågen

Dampskips-
kaia

Strandgata

Nordre Langgate

Grønnegata

Nordre Berggate

St Hanshaugen

Birger Dahls gt
Vinkelgt
Skagveien

Vardø sykehus

Kalgata

Per Larsens gate

Festningsgt

Brødkergt

Strandgata

Grønnegata

Nordre Langate

Nordre Berggate

Rørnoveien

Vårbergveien

Vardøhus
festning

Egede Nilsens gt
Tverrgt
Dronningens gt
F Nansens gt

Kirkegata

Brødtkorbsgt

Nordre Langate

Strandgata

Søndre Berggate

Kristian 4 gate
Krokgt

Søndre Langgate

Skolegata

Søndre Berggate

Idrettgata

Vardø-
hallen

Vardø
stadion

Skippergata
Selnes gt
A Lies gt

Søndre Langgate

Battengata

E75

Øster-
vågen

Steilnes

Gullringnes

Russe-
vika

Vardø - Båtsfjord

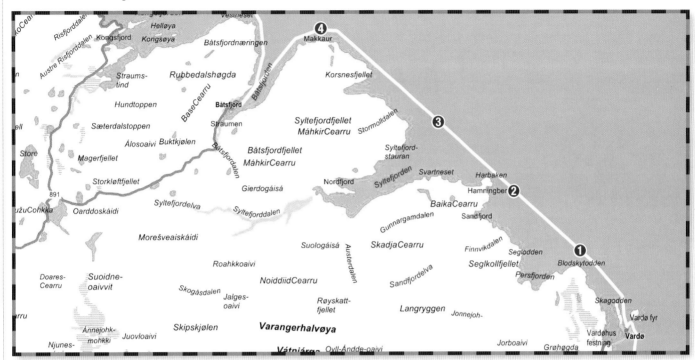

Båtsfjord - Berlevåg

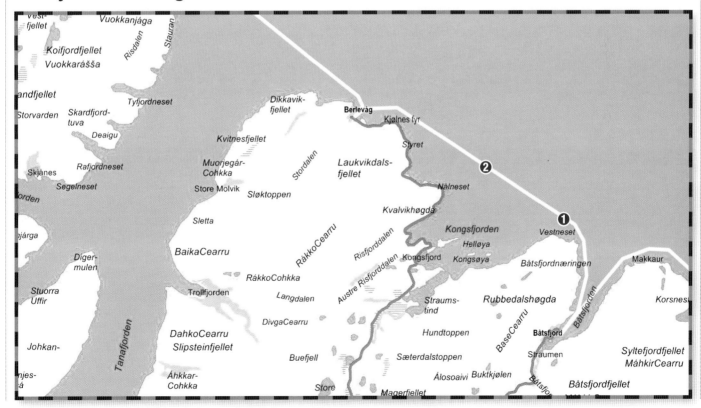

Honningsvåg - Havøysund - Hammerfest

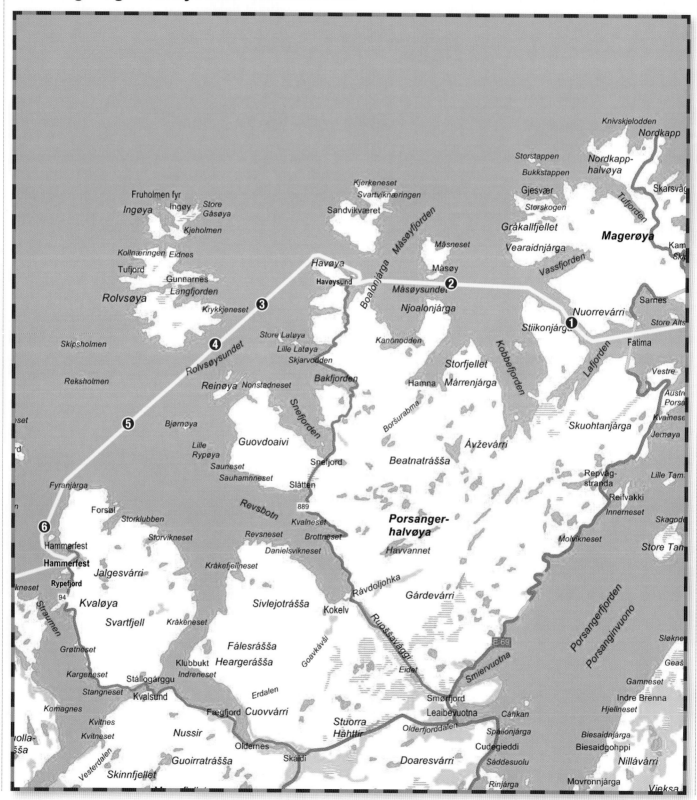

Hammerfest - Øksfjord

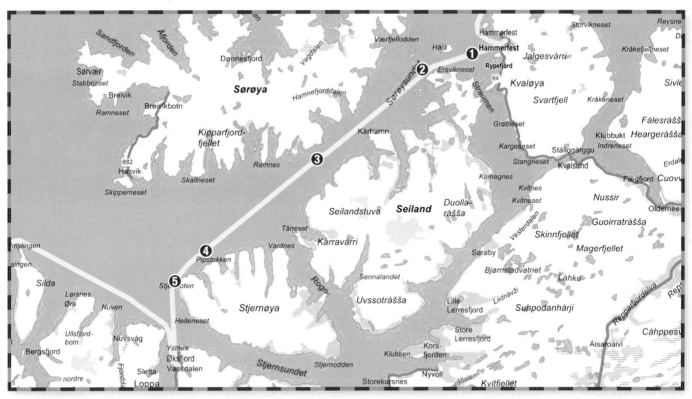

Øksfjord - Skjervøy

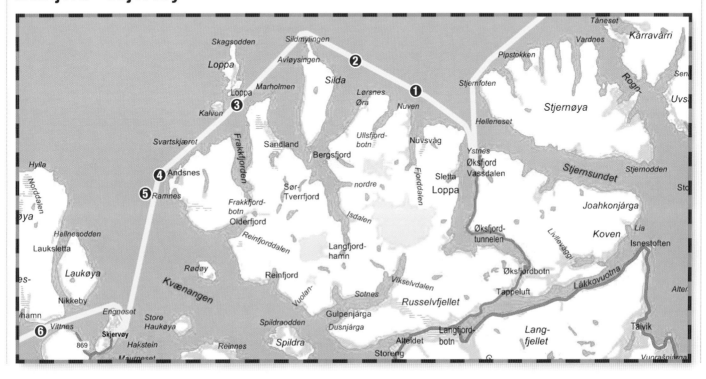

Harstad - Risøyhamn - Sortland

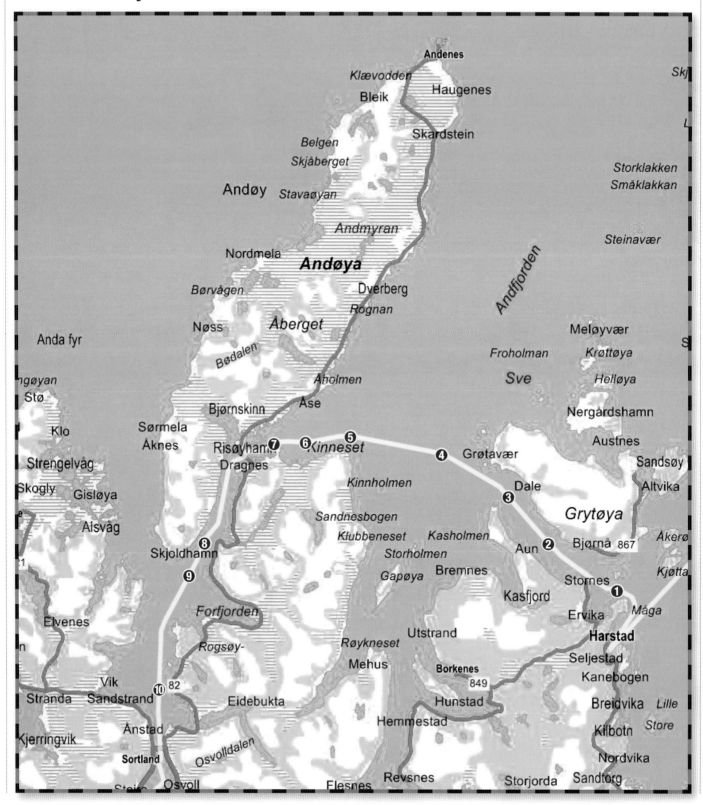

Sortland - Stokmarknes

Stokmarknes - Svolvær

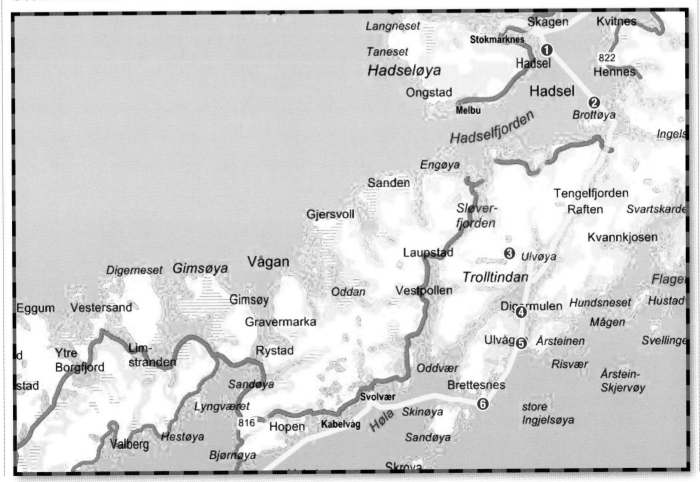

Ørnes - Nesna - Sandnessjøen

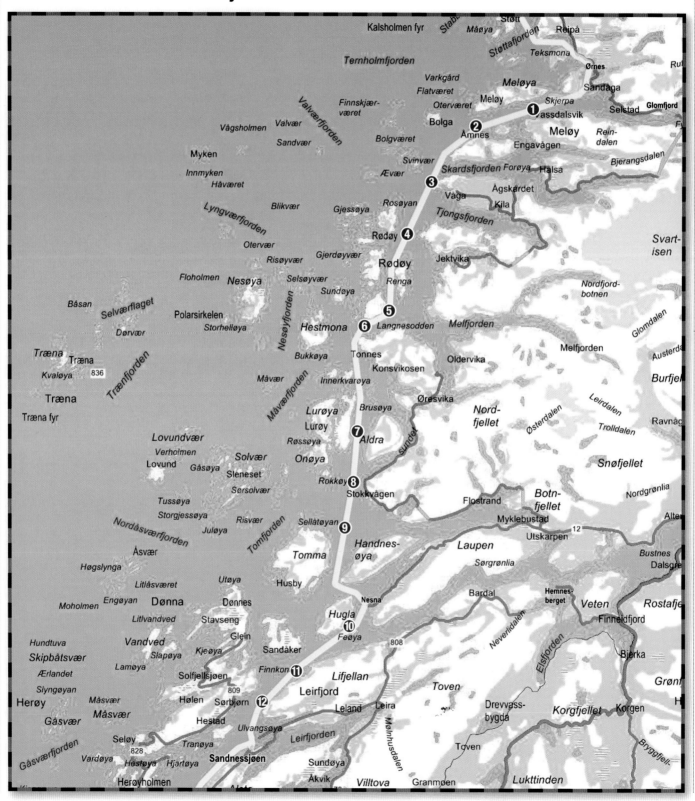

Sandnessjøen - Brønnøysund

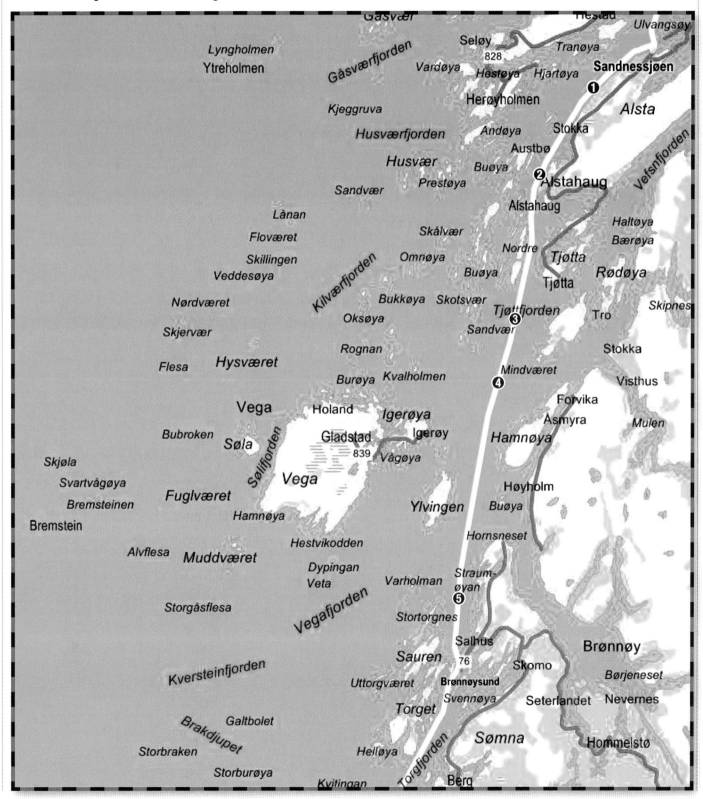

Brønnøysund - Rørvik

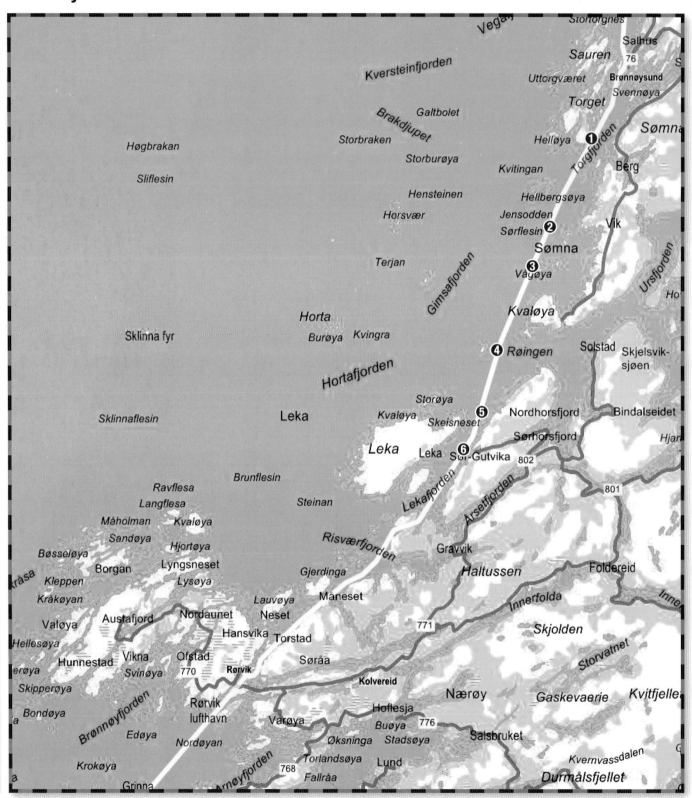

Trondheim - Kristiansund

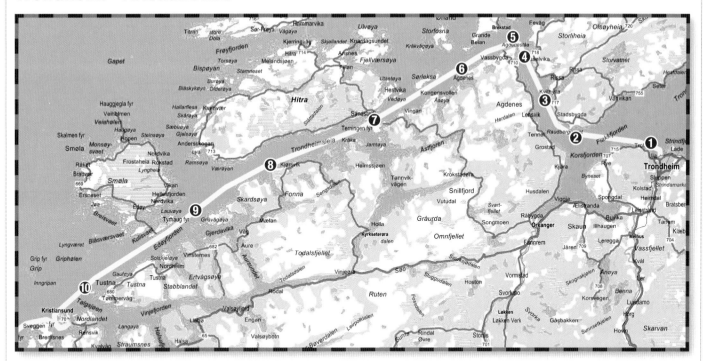

Kristiansund - Molde

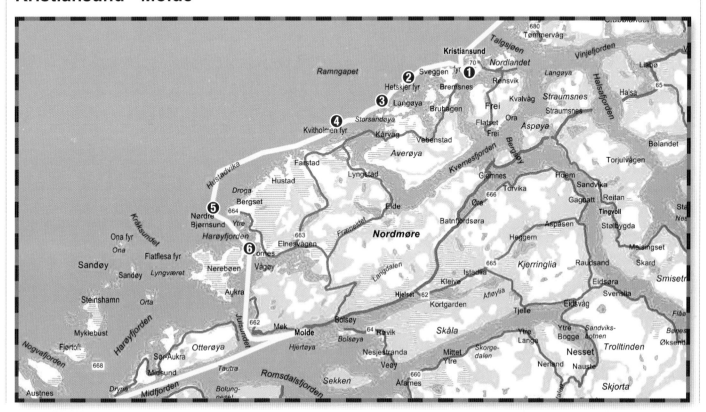

City of Kristiansund

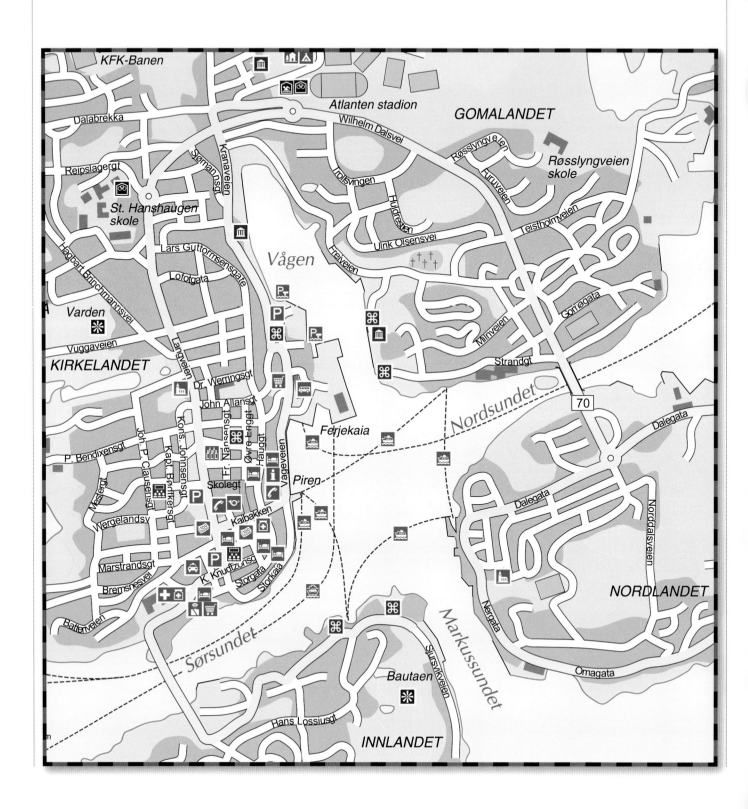

City of Molde

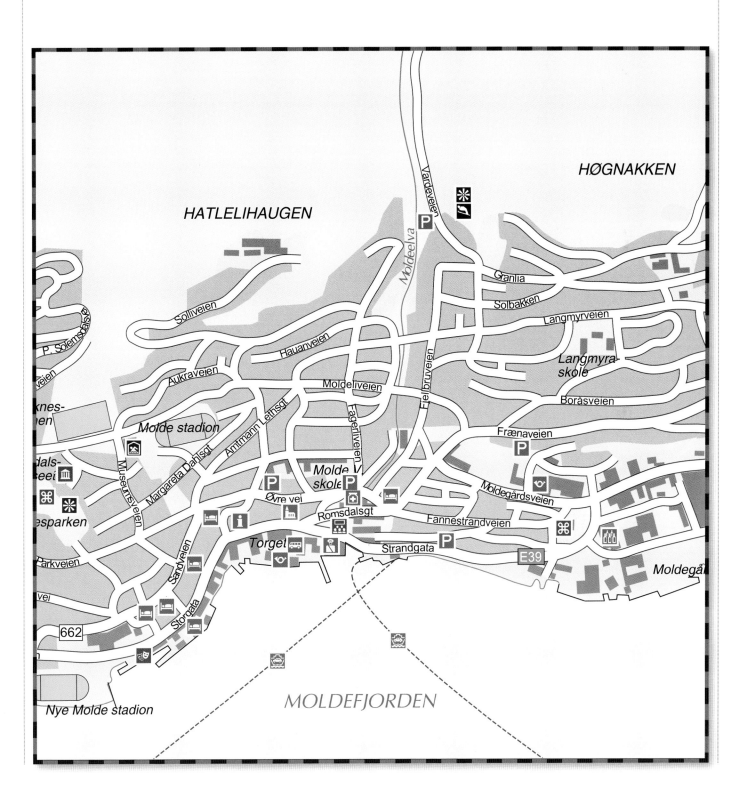

HØGNAKKEN

HATLELIHAUGEN

Vardeveien

Moldeelva

Granlia

Solliveien

Solbakken

Langmyrveien

Hauanveien

Langmyra-
skole

P. Solemsdals...

Aukraveien

Moldeliveien

Borasveien

Fjellbruveien

Fræneveien

knes-
...en

Molde stadion

Amtmann Lethsgt

Fagerliveien

Moldegårdsveien

dals-
...eei

Margareta Dahlsgt

Molde
skole

Museumsveien

Øvre vei

Fannestrandveien

...esparken

Romsdalsgt

Parkveien

Torget

Strandgata

E39

Sandveien

Moldegå

662

Storgata

Nye Molde stadion

MOLDEFJORDEN

Måløy - Florø

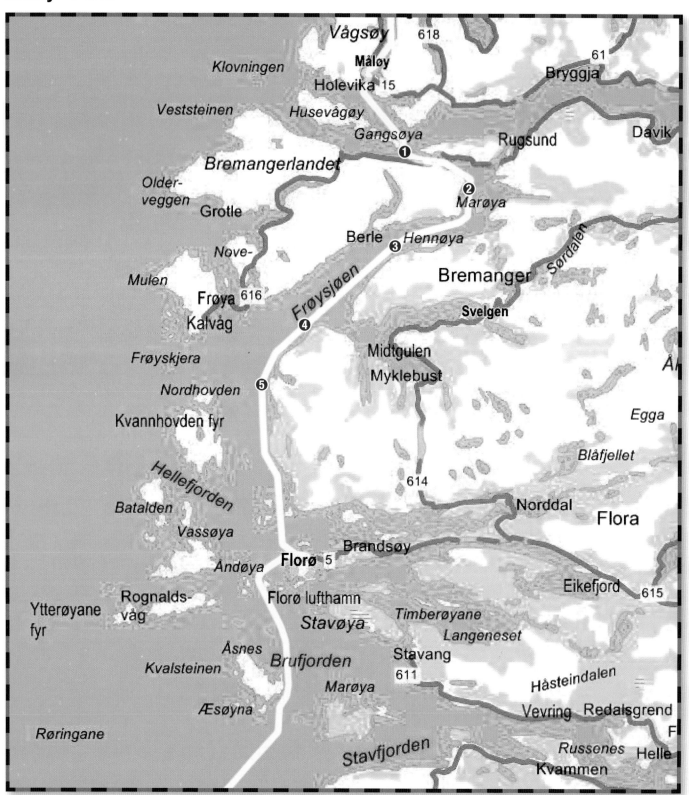

Florø - Bergen I

Florø - Bergen II

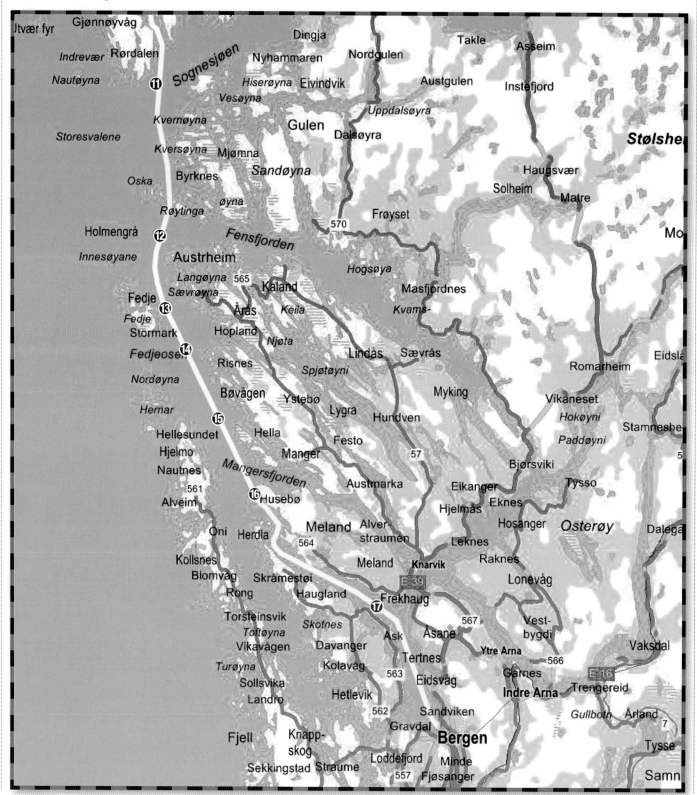

NAVIGATION MARKERS AND SYMBOLS

LATERAL MARKS

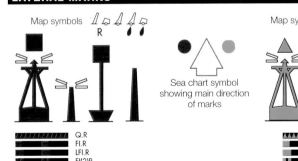

Map symbols   R

Sea chart symbol showing main direction of marks

Q.R
Fl.R
LFl.R
Fl(2)R

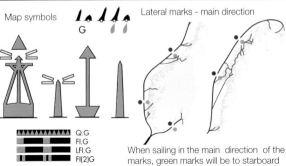

Map symbols   G

Lateral marks - main direction

Q.G
Fl.G
LFl.G
Fl(2)G

When sailing in the main direction of the marks, green marks will be to starboard and red to port

ISOLATED SHALLOWS/ DANGERS

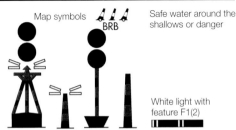

Map symbols   BRB

Safe water around the shallows or danger

White light with feature F1(2)

MID-CHANNEL MARK

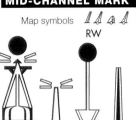

Map symbols   RW

Safe water around the marker. Does not indicate danger. Most often used to mark the centre of a channel or separation zone

White light with feature   Iso
                                  Oc or
                                  LFl 10s

COMPASS MARKS (Cardinal marks)

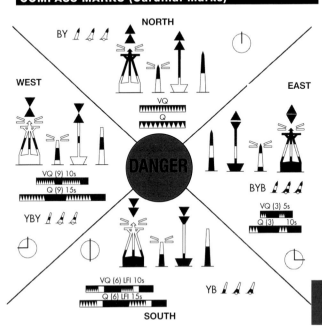

BY

NORTH

WEST

EAST

VQ
Q

DANGER

VQ (9) 10s
Q (9) 15s

BYB

VQ (3) 5s
Q (3)   10s

YBY

VQ (6) LFl 10s
Q (6) LFl 15s

YB

SOUTH

SPECIAL MARKS

Indicates areas that are restricted, e.g. bathing areas or installations. Motorised vessels or sailing vessels (including windsurf boards) are prohibited within these marker buoys and a 5 knot speed limit applies within 50 metres of bathing areas.

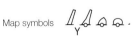

Map symbols   Y

FIXED METAL RODS

Indicates smaller skerries and shallow rocky areas. The indicator points toward safe water. In case of stakes without indicators, examine the chart carefully to see the location of the stake in relation to the hazard.

Map symbols

Q = Approx. 60 flashes per minute
VQ = Approx. 120 flashes per minute
UQ = Approx. 240 flashes per minute

NOTIFY FAULTS IN NAVIGATION MARKS/BEACONS TO:
NATIONAL COORDINATOR FOR NAVIGATION WARNINGS:

Tel.:	22 42 23 31	24 hrs
Telefaks:	22 41 04 91	24 hrs
E-mail:	navco@kystverket.no	

INTERNATIONAL ABBREVIATIONS FOR COLOURS		
R	Red	
G	Green	Example:
W	White	BYB = Black-Yellow-Black
Y	Yellow	
B	Black	

THE HURTIGRUTEN FLEET

Hurtigruten ASA was established in 2006 after the merger of the two former Hurtigruten shipping companies Ofoten og Vesteraalens Dampskibsselskab (OVDS and Troms Fylkes Dampskipsselskap (TFDS). **Hurtigruten**, a passenger and cargo route along the Norwegian coast, has daily sailings. The round trip **Bergen – Kirkenes – Bergen** takes 11 days and has a number of ports of call. There are 11 specially-built ships sailing along the route.

In addition to this route, Hurtigruten ASA also offers cruises to **Greenland** and **Svalbard** in the summer season. In the winter season, the company operates a cruise to **Antarctica**.

Ships in the Hurtigruten sailing plan for the summer season:

Ship	Built, year	Berths	Cabins	Passengers
MS Midnatsol	2003	650	304	1000
MS Finnmarken	2002	643	283	1000
MS Trollfjord	2002	652	304	822
MS Nordnorge	1997	455	214	691
MS Polarlys	1996	479	224	737
MS Nordkapp	1996	464	218	691
MS Nordlys	1994	482	225	691
MS Kong Harald	1993	490	235	691
MS Richard With	1993	466	219	691
MS Vesterålen	1983	314	147	560

Replacement ships in the Hurtigruten sailing plan for the winter season:

Name	Built, year	Berths	Cabins	Passengers
MS Lofoten	1964	155	90	410
MS Nordstjernen	1956	168	75	450

Hurtigruten cruises to Greenland and Svalbard in the summer season:

Ship	Built, year	Berths	Cabins	Passengers
MS Fram (Greenland)	2007	318	136	500
MS Nordstjernen (Svalbard)	1956	168	75	450
MS Polarstar (Svalbard)	1969/88	100	46	

Hurtigruten cruises to Antarctica in the winter season:

Ship	Built, year	Berths	Cabins	Passengers
MS Nordnorge	1997	455	214	691
MS Fram	2006	318	136	500

The experience cruises have their embarkation/disembarkation ports in Chile and Argentina.
The history of the Hurtigruten (p 299).
More information about Hurtigruten ASA can be found at: www.hurtigruten.com

TABLES

OFFICIAL FLAG DAYS IN NORWAY

1ˢᵗ January	New Year's Day
21ˢᵗ January	HRH Princess Ingrid Alexandra's birthday
6ᵗʰ February	Sámi National Day
21ˢᵗ February	HM King Harald V's birthday
23ʳᵈ March	Easter Sunday
1ˢᵗ May	Official holiday
8ᵗʰ May	Liberation Day 1945
17ᵗʰ May	Constitution Day
7ᵗʰ June	Dissolution of the Union 1905
4ᵗʰ July	HRH Queen Sonja's birthday
20ᵗʰ July	HRH Crown Prince Haakon Magnus' birthday
29ᵗʰ July	St. Olaf's Day
19ᵗʰ August	HRH Crown Princess Mette-Marit's birthday
25ᵗʰ December	Christmas Day

CONVERSION TABLE CELSIUS–FAHRENHEIT

Celsius	Fahrenheit
40 °C	104
30 °C	86
20 °C	68
10 °C	50
0 °C	32
- 10 °C	14
- 20 °C	- 4
- 30 °C	- 22
- 40 °C	- 40

From Celsius to Fahrenheit: Multiply degrees Celsius by 9. Divide the result by 5 and add 32.
(Example: 10 °C x 9 = 90 -> 90/5 = 18 -> 18 + 32 = 50 °F)

From Fahrenheit to Celsius: From degrees Fahrenheit, subtract 32. Multiply the result by 5, and then divide by 9.
(Example: 68°F - 32 = 36 -> 36 x 5 = 180 -> 180/9 = 20°C)

RELATIVE TEMPERATURES

			25	20	15	10	5	0	-5	-10	-15	-20	-25
Beaufort	**Knots**	**m/s**	**Experienced temperatures in degrees Celsius:**										
2 Light breeze	5	2.5	25	19	14	9	3	-2	-7	-12	-17	-23	-28
3 Gentle breeze	9	4.5	22	16	10	4	-2	-8	-14	-20	-26	-32	-38
4 Moderate breeze	13	7	21	15	8	2	-4	-11	-18	-25	-32	-38	-45
5 Fresh breeze	19	9.5	21	14	7	0	-7	-14	-21	-29	-36	-43	-50
6 Strong breeze	24	12.5	21	13	5	-2	-9	-17	-24	-32	-39	-47	-54
7 Near gale	30	15.5	20	13	5	-3	-11	-18	-26	-34	-42	-49	-57
8 Fresh gale	37	19	20	12	4	-4	-11	-19	-27	-35	-43	-51	-59
9 Strong gale	44	22.5	20	12	4	-4	-11	-20	-28	-36	-44	-52	-60

The concept of relative temperature – or effective temperature – was developed in 1941 by Paul Siple, an American Antarctic explorer. He wrote a mathematical formula in order to calculate the heat loss experienced by the human body in a combination of wind and cold temperatures. The table has later been revised, as recently as in 2001 and is now based on standard measurements taken 10 metres above ground, converted into wind speed at head height.